EDVARD GRIEG IN ENGLAND

Edvard Grieg in London, 1888 (Photo: Elliott & Fry)

Edvard Grieg in England

Lionel Carley

THE BOYDELL PRESS

First published 2006
The Boydell Press, Woodbridge

ISBN 1 84383 207 0

This book was published with the financial support
of the Royal Norwegian Embassy in London
and of NORLA (Norwegian Literature Abroad)

The Boydell Press is an imprint of Boydell & Brewer Ltd
PO Box 9, Woodbridge, Suffolk IP12 3DF, UK
and of Boydell & Brewer Inc.
668 Mt Hope Avenue, Rochester, NY 14620, USA
web site: www.boydellandbrewer.com

A CIP catalogue record for this book is available
from the British Library

This publication is printed on acid-free paper

Designed and typeset in Bulmer by
The Stingray Office, Chorlton-cum-Hardy, Manchester

Printed in Great Britain by
Biddles Ltd, King's Lynn, Norfolk

CONTENTS

V. Interlude (2)

VI. Final Curtain Calls

VII. Closure

LIST OF ILLUSTRATIONS

Illustrations originate from the author's own collection, the Grieg Archives, Bergen [GA], the Grieg Museum, Troldhaugen [TR], the Delius Trust [DTA], the Foreman Collection, and the Clapham Society. Original concert programmes are in the collections of the Grieg Archives, the Royal College of Music, John Bird, Malcolm Binns, and the Delius Trust.

for Finn and Inge Benestad

Other books by Lionel Carley

Delius: The Paris Years
Delius: A Life in Pictures (with Robert Threlfall)
Delius: A Life in Letters, 1862–1908
Delius: A Life in Letters, 1909–1934
Grieg and Delius: A Chronicle of Their Friendship in Letters
Frederick Delius: Music, Art and Literature

PREFACE

By the time Grieg made his final visit to England, he had accumulated a number of honours from British institutions, the first and most unlikely being his appointment in 1884 as a member of the Council of Welcome to the American People (in conjunction with a large American exhibition proposed to be held in London in 1886). Rather more appropriately, he was elected an honorary member of the Philharmonic Society in 1888. The first of two honorary doctorates was conferred on him by Cambridge University in 1894, and in 1895 he was appointed an honorary member of the Union of Graduates in Music. In 1901 there followed an honorary fellowship of Trinity College of Music. His second doctorate was awarded by Oxford University on the occasion of his final visit to England in 1906, a year in which he was also elected honorary member of the Folk Song Society. One more distinction was to follow: shortly before his death in 1907 he was appointed patron of the Royal Manchester College of Music Club.

This, for a foreign composer, was no ordinary collection of accolades, honours that can be seen as a collective token of the enormous regard and affection in which his music was held in this country. For the concert-going public, and equally for the amateur pianist in homes across the land, by the 1880s Grieg had assumed Mendelssohn's former mantle as the most popular living composer in England, and during the course of his several tours over here his concerts were almost invariably sold out. It is perhaps a little-known fact that in all he spent some six months of his life in England; and had it not been for constantly recurring bouts of ill health he would have spent an even longer time, for more visits had been planned but were cancelled as health problems returned to plague him.

Why 'Edvard Grieg in England', when the composer twice visited Scotland? His first visit north of the border in 1888 was transitory, with Grieg disembarking at Aberdeen and stopping overnight there and then in Edinburgh en route to London. And in 1897 the London agent for his longest tour included in his itinerary a single recital in Edinburgh, once again involving just two nights' stay in Scotland. Allowing a genuflexion to Grieg's Scottish ancestry, it soon becomes clear from all the available evidence that the composer's sights were, right from the outset, set on England – and on London in particular. After some years, with a first London concert very much on Grieg's mind (the Polish violinist Wieniawski urging him already in 1877 to make an appearance in the capital), the really serious plans were being laid by the beginning of 1880. Joseph Joachim and Clara Schumann supplied him with various letters of recommendation, and Edward Dannreuther advised him on the planning and programming of a concert or recital. However, with all seeming to be falling in place for a first appearance in London in the spring of 1880, ill health intervened, and eight years were then to pass before Grieg finally reached the metropolis – a city in which he hoped to achieve much-needed financial as well as artistic success.

Enthusiasm was high when he at last arrived in London in 1888. For some years his albums of *Lyric Pieces*, together with other of the earlier piano pieces, had rapidly been gaining in popularity in homes across the country. London had first heard the Piano Concerto in A minor in 1874, and by the time Grieg arrived to play it here himself it had become established in the concert repertoire. When, for the first time in England, he emerged onto the concert stage from the St James's Hall artists' room he was accorded a rapturous reception by an audience of 2,500 and – utterly taken aback and as yet unaware of the extraordinary scale of his popularity – found himself having to acknowledge the storm of applause for some three minutes before he was at last allowed to move to the piano.

In London, George Augener not only published Grieg's music but welcomed the artist/performer as an honoured guest in his home in Clapham, and whenever Grieg was in the capital he lodged there until Augener's deteriorating domestic circumstances meant that his final stay was with another host in Mayfair in 1906. A happy by-product of work on this book has been the erection by English Heritage in September 2004 of a Blue Plaque at 47 North Side, Clapham Common, to commemorate Grieg's visits to London. Between the first and the last visits, there were further concert appearances in England: later in 1888 (Birmingham), in 1889 (London and Manchester), 1894 (London and Cambridge), and 1897 (London, Liverpool, Birmingham, Manchester, Brighton, Cheltenham – and Edinburgh).

During all this time there were many highlights, such as appearances at Windsor Castle and Buckingham Palace before Queen Victoria and King Edward VII and his Queen Alexandra respectively, Grieg having already established a degree of intimacy with the latter pair when they were Prince and Princess of Wales. Staying in a Unitarian household when performing at the Birmingham Festival in 1888 led him to a more settled religious belief for the rest of his life, as well as to an affectionate and enduring relationship with the Harding family. There were legions of friends in England, some of whom had first been encountered in younger days in Germany, and the admirers of his music were countless, among them youngsters who were to achieve later musical fame and fortune. Prominent figures on the London stage, on getting to know his *Peer Gynt* music, offered him commissions to write incidental music for their own productions, and the Philharmonic Society pressed him to write a second Piano Concerto. Grieg resisted all such requests, well aware of the limitations imposed upon him by his health. Nor did his stays in England allow time for composing, with travelling, concerts and rehearsals taking up so much of his time. The social side could not be entirely neglected, but on the whole he preserved a sober distaste for grander feasting and for the receptions to which he was inevitably invited, much preferring intimate evenings spent among friends, particularly when music might be made.

Until Grieg's music made its breakthrough in England, Norway had remained for most people on these western shores of the North Sea a remote and little-known corner of northern Europe. From it the Vikings had issued a thousand years earlier, long to pervade the cultural consciousness of our islands. There was then a centuries-long gap until early in the nineteenth century, when English and Scottish sportsmen – primarily hunters, anglers, and then climbers – began to discover a romantic and wild land seen as challenging anything that Alpine mountainscapes could offer. The first tourists followed in their wake, and Norway began at last to reveal its magnificent secrets. At this time Norwegian literature meant to the Englishman little more than travel memoirs and collections of fairy stories. The tales collected by Asbjørnsen and Moe in *East of the Sun and West of the Moon* were to find their way into the bedrooms of many an English child, far distant from the magical and at times fearsome stages upon which they were originally played. The violinist Ole Bull meanwhile proved himself to be the outstanding representative of Norwegian music, first appearing on the London concert platform in 1836. A major virtuoso if a minor composer, he was the first musical star in the Norwegian firmament. Otherwise Norwegian music, art and literature remained a closed book for the average Englishman.

With the arrival of the 1870s the picture begins to change. Halfdan Kjerulf is perhaps the first Norwegian composer rather than performer whose songs and piano pieces gradually become known and achieve occasional public performance. Johan Svendsen is the next to break through, furthermore achieving recognition as an outstanding conductor. But there is something different, something quite fresh and new, in Grieg's music, appearing in the concert hall at about the same time as Svendsen's. It is seen as reflecting the composer's homeland landscape of mountain, glacier, forest and fjord, in all its changing seasons. If English audiences from the 1870s on have any doubts as to the source of this music, they are guided by Grieg himself, through many of the titles to his pieces: 'Song on the Mountain', 'Folk Song', 'Norwegian', 'Evening in the Mountains', 'Last Spring', 'Beside the Stream', 'Upon a Grassy Hillside', 'The Pine Tree', 'On the Water', and so many more. This is music that breathes the air of his native country. Grieg takes Norwegian folk-songs and arranges them – and then, suffused with the idiom, he writes his own folk-songs. He rides the wave of National Romanticism and becomes its prime figure in Norway. And audiences in England come to love what he offers them.

Henrik Ibsen is Grieg's contemporary, if somewhat older. His work and his name are unknown in England until in 1871 the young Edmund Gosse visits a bookshop in Trondheim and is served by the equally young Hans Lien Brækstad. He buys Ibsen's collected poems, recommended to him by Brækstad, and is seduced by Ibsen's work, soon telling readers of the *Spectator* about this important new writer from the North. In the 1880s London's cognoscenti are on the trail, and William Archer begins his series of translations of Ibsen's plays. Meanwhile Brækstad has emigrated to England and become a prime mover in the dissemination of Norwegian literature and music in London – electing in his journalistic capacity, moreover, to become Grieg's enthusiastic champion. Other Norwegian writers enjoy a minor vogue – Bjørnstjerne Bjørnson and Jonas Lie, for example – but they do not have Ibsen's staying power, appearing to English readers to be more parochial in their interests and expression when compared to Ibsen. The plastic arts remain relatively unknown. Edvard Munch will enjoy twentieth-century appreciation in England, but that is to come only slowly. Around 1890 the first Englishman to understand his enormous significance and to encourage him in his work is his friend Frederick Delius.

Fridtjof Nansen, explorer and diplomat extraordinary, should not be forgotten in this truncated survey of what Norway meant to England at this period. His exploits in the Arctic are eagerly followed in the London press, and he is to be a frequent lecturer at the Royal Geographical Society. In 1906 he is appointed newly-independent Norway's first envoy to London. For his English contemporaries it may well be said that Nansen comes to represent the archetypal Norwegian, living during his expeditions the kind of rugged existence in extreme conditions that could easily be seen as relating modern Norway to its Viking past.

The two foremost representatives abroad of Norwegian music and literature towards the close of the nineteenth century, then, are Edvard Grieg and Henrik Ibsen, and one of Ibsen's most inventive and distinctive plays calls forth Grieg's *Peer Gynt* music, an enormous favourite with English audiences of the period. For a while Hans Lien Brækstad and George Bernard Shaw get together and begin the difficult work of translation of the play, only to abandon it when Shaw's fertile mind moves elsewhere. Grieg sets to music many of the poems of Norwegian writers, including Ibsen and Bjørnson, and these too become favourites in the concert hall. His wife Nina sings them in England and herself earns the admiration and affection of English audiences.

In this book I have set out to explore the Grieg phenomenon in England. I have restricted it to Grieg's lifetime, whilst acknowledging that his music has continued to be loved by the many up to the present day. There were a few works on the larger scale from Grieg's pen, but for the most part he worked in the now familiar smaller forms, in which he excelled. One of the principal reasons adduced for this is that he suffered such ill health throughout his life – a pulmonary infection in his mid-

teens had left him with just one fully functioning lung – that he never found it easy
to indulge in the shaping of lengthy symphonic structures. (He could happily leave
the field to his English contemporaries where the all-pervasive Victorian stream of
oratorios and sacred cantatas was concerned.) Grieg found his own niche as something much more than just a miniaturist, conjuring up a melodic and harmonic
invention seen in its time as being scarcely rivalled. Here was a counterbalance to
the weight of the Austro-German symphony, the folk idioms of Norway being deployed in subtly shifting forms to make quite new sounds. English composers were
quick to seize on Grieg's sound-world as an inspirational source, just as, of course,
were many other European and American composers. In just a few this might be
said to have led to a perhaps dispiriting pastoralism, but the fault for that does not
lie at Grieg's door. Grieg at his best is sovereign, and our enjoyment of his work
need know no bounds.

The story of Grieg's almost regal progress in England – hitherto uncharted ter-
ritory – is told chronologically. A major source is the letter collection of the Bergen
Public Library: the Grieg Archives are a genuinely rich resource on which much
excellent work has been done during recent years under the expert eye initially
of Karen Falch Johannessen and now of Sirén Steen, to each of whom I am much
indebted. The Archives' web site is a model of its kind, with a proportion of the
collection's most significant letters, programmes and photographs steadily becoming accessible online. Grieg's small notebooks, maintained over many years, in
which he not only kept daily accounts of his spending but, among other things, jotted down the names and addresses of his friends and acquaintances and the dates
and times of various engagements, have proved to be a vade-mecum of incalculable
value in tracing his activities and preoccupations while in England. Without reference to these notebooks (at the time of writing not available online), still little used
by Grieg scholars, it would often have been impossible to establish dates of the
composer's constant comings and goings or even to locate where he stayed in some
of those towns and cities in England that featured in his concert schedules. Often
pencilled in, too, are frequently-changing plans for the music to be played in his
concert programmes. By the time of his last visit to England, Grieg had abandoned
his notebook but instead had resumed, very late in life, a habit of his much younger
days – keeping a diary. As with the notebooks, it is a valuable resource.

For accounts of the concerts themselves, English and Norwegian papers have
been widely trawled – both musical journals and national and local presses,
whether daily, weekly or monthly. The emphasis, however, has been on the British
press, from time to time admitting sidelights cast by its Norwegian counterparts.
Then there has been the Grieg literature. To a number of books I am enormously
indebted, above all to Finn Benestad's magnificent two-volume edition of Grieg's
letters, published in Norwegian in 1998. This carefully chosen selection has subsequently been published in English in an abridged single-volume form in 2000, the
translations by William Halverson. (I should add that most of my own translations

of letters intended for *Edvard Grieg in England* had been completed by the time the Benestad/Halverson edition was published. Any errors in these or indeed in letters from the Danish or German as they appear within the present covers are therefore due to me.) Another exceptional source is a volume containing Grieg's diaries together with collected articles and speeches written by the composer. This appeared in English in 2001 and is again the impressive work of Benestad and Halverson. Again, many of the articles and speeches having been published in Norwegian as long ago as 1957 (and the diaries in 1993 by Benestad), my work of translation from passages required to illustrate the present book had already largely been completed.

For more general purposes the indispensable work of reference has been Finn Benestad and Dag Schjelderup-Ebbe's monumental *Edvard Grieg: The Man and the Artist*, first published in Norwegian in 1980 and in English in 1988. This remains the major Grieg biography, with the 1988 edition helpfully at last establishing (around the time of the appearance of the Collected Edition of Grieg's music) definitive titles in English translation for all of Grieg's works. Among the more important of the many other books consulted are those containing Grieg's letters to the C. F. Peters company (in German), to Frants Beyer (in Norwegian), and to Julius Röntgen (in German). Details of these, as of the principal sources given above, can be found in the Bibliography at the end of this book. The significance of Frederick Delius, Grieg's closest English friend, will I think be clear from the following pages, but Delius is allotted less space than he might otherwise have merited, simply because my own *Grieg and Delius: A Chronicle of Their Friendship in Letters* has already told the tale in considerable detail elsewhere.

The Norwegian language then and now has two versions: the official form as adopted by government, Church, and so on, with its spelling derived from Danish forms, and a second version that has been adapted from the speech of the people – a town Norwegian and a country Norwegian, so to speak. In Grieg's time, progressive writers and poets such as Aa. O. Vinje and Arne Garborg decided that the 'country' form was essentially Norwegian and the 'town' form alien; they therefore set out to write in *nynorsk*, or new Norwegian, a language to which Grieg was naturally attracted and in which he set a number of songs. There has always been a problem in Norwegian orthography, and it took a long time – well into the twentieth century in fact – for the spellings of place-names, for example, to settle down. Norwegian place-names in this book are, except where directly quoted, given in their present form. When in Grieg's day English papers tried to put down in print examples of this rather confused language they did their best, but the composer's Norwegian titles and indeed his own name often defeated them. As *Musical News* put it on 2 June 1906:

> Grieg's recent works have proved pitfalls to many a guileless compositor. Some will not permit him to spell his own name as he likes, but insist that it is Greig, while one credits him with the Christian name of Edoard. 'Bergliot' appears as 'Bergliat' and

'Berglidt'. Mdlle. Dolores is given the masculine name of Antonio, and even Miss
Stockmarr was transformed into Stockman!

In fact the forms Grieg and Greig became thoroughly confused by English
writers (even Augener, his London publisher and friend, on more than one occasion advertised his works as coming from the pen of Edvard Greig), and he was,
moreover, frequently dubbed Edward in the London and provincial press. Where
such misspellings occur in concert notices and the like quoted here they are left
without correction.

⁂

The publication of this book is the end result of an invitation extended some years
ago by Professor Finn Benestad and Professor Arvid Vollsnes to participate in
a project at Oslo's Institute of Advanced Studies, a project that brought together
Grieg experts from around the world. Had I been able to stay as long as the time
for which I was originally invited, this study would have appeared much earlier.
Finn Benestad has followed progress on *Edvard Grieg in England* with unfailing
interest from the outset, has read the work in draft and has been extremely helpful
through his advice and encouragement. I owe him a major debt of gratitude. I have
already mentioned Sirén Steen of the Grieg Archives: she and her helpful staff have
always been ready to respond to my many queries, and she has furthermore made
me at home and allowed me into the deepest recesses of the Bergen Library on my
several visits there. To her and to the Library's director Trine Kolderup Flaten go
my warmest thanks. Equally I must thank Erling Dahl jr, director of the Grieg Museum, Troldhaugen, and his colleagues Eilif Løtveit and Monica Jangaard for their
ever kind and patient assistance and encouragement, as well as for allowing me to
peer into all corners of Grieg's house, a house first opened to me by its late curator
Sigmund Torsteinson thirty years ago.

I have particularly valued the ever-ready and indeed generous assistance of the
Norwegian Embassy in London. Øystein Braathen, when Minister Counsellor,
proved – and has remained – a friend indeed, and the encouragement of his successors Øyvind Stokke and John Petter Opdahl has also been much appreciated.
For Anne Ulset of the Embassy's Press, Information and Cultural Section, no praise
can be too high. Whenever asked for help in one form or another, she has provided
it, and I remain deeply grateful to her and to the other members of the Section who
have over the years been a real resource. To the Norwegian Ambassador goes my
gratitude, as it does to his recent predecessors. I must not omit to thank Marianne
Wimmer of the Ministry of Foreign Affairs in Oslo and to congratulate her on her
patience in maintaining interest during the rather long gestation of this book.

To a number of scholars in Norway, friends all, go my thanks, too – in particular
to Magne Seland and Øyvind Norheim of the National Library, and to Nils and

Kirsti Grinde; also to friends and colleagues at the former Institute of Advanced Studies, Oslo.

I wish furthermore to express my gratitude to the staff of the British Library (in particular Nicolas Bell), the British Library Newspaper Library, the Westminster Music Library, the Barbican Library, the Borough of Lambeth Archives (John Henderson and Nilu York), the National Archives, the Birmingham City Archives (Rachael Nicholls), Cheltenham Library, and The Royal Archives (Pamela Clark). I have been grateful, too, for the co-operation of the Glasgow University Library, the Grainger Library at Melbourne University, the Norwegian Club in London, the Pierpont Morgan Library (Rigbie Turner, the Mary Flagler Curator of Music Manuscripts and Books), the Royal Academy of Music Library (Kathryn Adamson and Bridget Palmer), the Royal College of Music Library (Pamela Thompson and Peter Horton), the Royal Northern College of Music Library, and Edition Peters, Leipzig (Norbert Molkenbur). To Alyson Wilson of the Clapham Society I also owe thanks.

I furthermore wish to express my thanks to Boydell & Brewer — and in particular to Peter Clifford, Bruce Phillips, Caroline Palmer and Vanda Andrews — for having taken on this publication and then for having seen it through the press. I am, too, indebted to The Stingray Office's Jeffrey Dean, in whom a combination of expertise and erudition calls for particularly grateful acknowledgement.

Many individuals have proved to be of assistance in some form or other. I particularly wish to thank Robert Beckhard, John Bergsagel, Malcolm Binns, Anthony Boden, Margaret Bryan, Roger Buckley, Rolf and Angela Christopherson, Oliver Davies, Thom Dibdin, Peter Dickie, Reidar Dittmann, Jeff Driggers, Asbjørn O. Erikson, Lewis Foreman, Beryl Foster, Don Gillespie, Paul Guinery, Stein Grieg Halvorsen, Bo Holten, Lyndon Jenkins, Kees Kramer, Irene Lawford-Hinrichsen, Robert Layton, Stephen Lloyd, Peter Lyons, Robert Matthew-Walker, Barry Ould, Malcolm Rudland, Trygve Sørvaag and Jurjen Vis. I hang my head over any unwitting omissions from this brief list.

SUMMARY OF CONTACTS WITH ENGLAND

1797 Grieg's immigrant Scottish great-grandfather appointed head of British Consulate at Bergen.

1803 Grieg's grandfather appointed head of British Consulate at Bergen.

1843 Edvard Grieg born in Bergen. Scottish godmother.

1844 Grieg's father appointed head of British Consulate at Bergen.

1862 **Summer visit to London, in the company of his parents and brother.**

1870 Grieg's elder brother John appointed head of British Consulate at Bergen.

1875 Grieg's brother resigns from his Consular post.

1879 Edvard Grieg's first concert visit to England organized for the following year, with the help of Clara Schumann, Joseph Joachim and Edward Dannreuther. Cancelled January 1880 owing to ill health.

1883 Invited by Philharmonic Society to London to perform Piano Concerto in spring of 1884. Cancelled early 1884 owing to ill health.

1884 Invited by Philharmonic Society for spring season 1885. Declines because of building of Troldhaugen. Failure of negotiations to appear at Birmingham Festival 1885.

1886 Further invitation to appear in England.

1887 Invitation by Bach Choir to perform Piano Concerto.

1887 Invited by Philharmonic Society to London for spring season 1888 and by Birmingham for 1888 Festival. Beginning of friendship with Delius.

1888 **May: two London concerts, as pianist, conductor, and accompanist. Brief holiday on Isle of Wight. London base (until 1897) in Clapham at home of publisher George Augener.**

1888 Appointed Honorary Member of the Philharmonic Society.

1888 **August: two Birmingham Festival concerts as conductor. Staying with a Unitarian family brings embrace of new religious belief.**

1888 Invitation from Liverpool Philharmonic Society.

1889 **February–March: concerts in London and Manchester. Recital at French Embassy, meeting Prince and Princess of Wales for first time. Invited by Prince and Princess of Wales to Marlborough House and also meets their daughter Maud, future Queen of Norway.**

1890 Invitation to Scotland.

1891 Invited by Philharmonic Society.

1892 Invited by Herbert Beerbohm Tree to write incidental music for London production of *Hamlet*. Invited by Philharmonic Society and by Leeds Triennial Musical Festival. Agrees to conduct at Music Festival in Glasgow 1893.

1893 Accepts invitation from Philharmonic Society, and from Cambridge University to accept honorary doctorate of music; both eventually postponed owing to ill health, as is probably the case with the Glasgow Festival.

1894 **May: Hon. D.Mus. degree conferred at Cambridge. Philharmonic Concert in London.**

1896 Invitation to give February concerts in Manchester and Liverpool. Invitation to write incidental music for London production of D. G. Rossetti's *Sister Helen*. Invitation to undertake March concert tour of England.

1897 **October–December: concert tour of London, Birmingham, Liverpool, Manchester, Edinburgh, Cheltenham, Brighton. Invited to Windsor Castle to perform for Queen Victoria. Brief holiday at St Leonards on Sea.**

1898 Invitation to Cardiff Festival.

1900 Invited by the Philharmonic Society for spring season concert. Invited to make regional tour in England and Scotland. Invited by Chappell to perform at two or three Popular Concerts around end of year.

1901 Invited to undertake a series of chamber concerts and to appear at the London Musical Festival, April–May.

1902 Invitation from Philharmonic Society. Invitation to write Coronation March for Edward VII. Invitation to Bristol Festival in October.

1903 Cancels plans for spring visit to England.

1904 Cancels plans for another spring visit to England.

1905 Invitation to write incidental music for London production of Hall Caine's *The Prodigal Son*. Accepts invitation to London for the following year. Sends telegram to Edward VII asking him to intervene in dispute that threatens war between Norway and Sweden.

1906 **May: stays at Mayfair home of Sir Edgar Speyer. Three concerts in London. Invitation to Buckingham Palace to play before Edward VII and Queen Alexandra. Spends time with new Norwegian envoy to London, Fridtjof Nansen. Hon. Mus. Doc. degree conferred at Oxford. Beginning of friendship with Percy Grainger. Brief visit to St Leonards on Sea to see George Augener.**

1907 Invitation to appear at Leeds Festival in October. Dies shortly after leaving Troldhaugen on first stage of journey to England.

I

PRELUDE

❧ 1 ❧

A BRITISH INHERITANCE

No fewer than four generations of Griegs served as Britain's official representatives in Bergen (see illustration overleaf).[1] Each of these Griegs, from
the immigrant Alexander (1739–1803) on, was titular head of the British
Consulate in Norway's premier port, but only one of them succeeded in being
appointed full Consul (a condition to which each of them in his turn aspired) and
then only after a long and hard-fought campaign to be recognized and paid as
such. Three, at least, of these four generations found themselves actively involved
in the musical life of Bergen. Alexander Grieg's son John (1772–1844) played in the
orchestra of Det dramatiske Selskab (The Dramatic Society) from the Society's establishment in 1794. He furthermore married the daughter of Niels Haslund, who
had been among the founding fathers of Harmonien, Bergen's orchestral society,
and who had run it for some fifteen years. John went on to become a director of
Harmonien – and, like his brother Joachim (who for a brief period also served as
British Vice-Consul), was a member of Harmonien's Club. John's son, the second
Alexander (1806–1875), continued the musical tradition mainly through his wife
Gesine. She was a gifted singer and pianist who performed at many of Harmonien's concerts, and she was also a highly respected piano teacher. She was also said
to have continued her studies in London, 'which she visited repeatedly with her
husband'.[2] Edvard Grieg could scarcely have had a better teacher. Finally we have
Alexander and Gesine's first son, another John (1840–1901, Edvard's brother), who
was a fine cellist and who himself played many times at Harmonien, acting also as
a music critic.

Having emigrated from Scotland around 1770 and taken Norwegian citizenship
in 1779, the elder Alexander Grieg[3] took up the consular post in 1797 following the
death of his good friend John Wallace (who had himself succeeded to the position of British Consul on the death of his father Alexander Wallace). Founder of
Alexander Grieg and Son, a successful fish and lobster export business, the first
of these Norwegian Griegs suffered the disappointment of seeing his post immediately downgraded to that of Vice-Consul, although he could scarcely have

inherited a more demanding position, since the still neutral port of Bergen had become a haven for privateers during the relentless course of the Napoleonic Wars. Prisoners of war, taken from ships captured by both sides, were traded in the town,

---

Alexander Grieg (1739–1803): *Edvard Grieg's great-grandfather*

Unpaid Vice-Consul 1797–8. Is helped for a short time by his brother James Grieg sr. Alexander Grieg continues acting unofficially from 1798 until his death, assisted by his son John.

John Grieg (1772–1844): *Edvard Grieg's grandfather*

Son of Alexander Grieg. Brother of James Grieg jr (1773–1821) and of Joachim Grieg.

Unpaid Vice-Consul 1803–31. Consul 1832–44 at a salary of £200 per annum. Gives up his mercantile work entirely at end of 1826 in order to devote himself full-time to consular business. Is assisted by his son Alexander Grieg.

        Joachim Grieg (1787–1836): *Edvard Grieg's great-uncle*

        Son of Alexander Grieg. Brother of John Grieg and James Grieg jr.

        Unpaid Vice-Consul 1834–6 (during his brother John Grieg's consulship); but he has helped John Grieg since 1832, if not earlier.

Alexander Grieg (1806–1875): *Edvard Grieg's father*

Grandson of the first Alexander Grieg. Son of John Grieg.

'Unpaid Vice-Consul at Bergen, in the Consular District of Christiania, Norway, from May 29, 1844, till February 15, 1870, when he resigned.' [Foreign Office Class List] In fact he has acted as Vice-Consul since his uncle Joachim Grieg's death in 1836.

John Grieg (1840–1901): *Edvard Grieg's brother*

Son of Alexander Grieg.

'Unpaid Vice-Consul at Bergen, in the Consular District of Christiania, from February 28, 1870, till December 6, 1875, when he resigned.' [Foreign Office Class List]

The Griegs and the British Consulate at Bergen

and on various occasions Alexander Grieg found himself responsible for the temporary care and upkeep of hundreds of British sailors until he could organize their repatriation to England or Scotland. The consequence of this and allied problems was that he soon tried to divest himself of his consular work, informing the Foreign Office in London that he could only continue to represent Britain in Bergen if his post were to be upgraded from Vice-Consul to full – and fully paid – Consul. His expenses were horrendous, and his business and worst of all his health were suffering. Alexander Grieg's death in 1803 was undoubtedly hastened by problems that he had found it difficult to surmount and for which he had received little advice or assistance from the Foreign Office.

Nonetheless, John Grieg, his son (Edvard Grieg's grandfather), despite the self-evident drawbacks inherent in the post, willingly accepted the offer to succeed Alexander as Vice-Consul. Like his father, he considered it an honour to serve the British cause as His Majesty's representative in Bergen. And even more than his father, he devoted a great deal of ink and paper over a great many years to pleading with London for the post to be upgraded. The end of the wars saw Norway a much impoverished country, with the Grieg business having joined many others in Norway in steep decline. Towards the end of 1830 John decided that the only way to save both his business and his family's fortunes would be to go to London and lay his case before the Foreign Secretary. He calculated that he had by then expended £9,000 of his own money on his consular duties, and he desperately needed to recoup as much of this outlay as possible. With the support of the British Consul-General, now located in Stockholm rather than in Copenhagen as in his father's time, he travelled to London with the goal of obtaining an appointment as full Consul, paid at an appropriate rate, as well as securing the repayment to himself of the monies he considered the Foreign Office owed him. He had taken with him sufficient funds to enable him to stay in London for just a few weeks, but he suffered a nervous breakdown that was so serious that it kept him in the capital for a year and a half. With doctors' bills to pay, ruin threatened. Fortunately the Grieg firm's London agents stepped in to ensure that he did not want for everyday necessities. Back in Bergen, he at last found himself upgraded to Consul, paid at the rate of £200 p.a. He was also awarded an ex-gratia sum of £500, to which Lord Palmerston himself assented. John Grieg was almost pathetically grateful, but he was never to return to full health, securing the appointment of his brother Joachim as his Vice-Consul in 1834. Sadly, Joachim died only two years later, and John then came to rely almost entirely on his son Alexander to take care of much of the consulate's day-to-day business.

Alexander Grieg, father of Edvard Grieg, stepped willingly into John Grieg's shoes in 1844, only to find the Bergen post downgraded yet again. He pleaded for a return to its former status, but found himself firmly directed by the Foreign Office to serve as unpaid Vice-Consul. All he would receive would be his expenses, and he would have to live off the family export business, the very same business which his father John had been requested to set aside when he became full-time Consul. Like each of these generations of Griegs, Alexander recognized that the post nonetheless carried a certain prestige, and he must reluctantly have accepted

British Vice-Consul Alexander Grieg, father of Edvard Grieg

this renewed downgrading. He continued in the post until 1870 (apparently without having to live through most of the vicissitudes that had befallen his father and grandfather), when, feeling his age, he resigned in favour of his son John – Edvard Grieg's cellist elder brother. John, who duly took over the family business on Alexander's death, had studied like Edvard at the Leipzig Conservatory. He himself resigned the Vice-Consulship in 1875, and with that the Grieg family's hegemony at the British Consulate in Bergen came to an end.

The ties had anyway gradually been loosening. The first of these Alexanders and Johns had shown real devotion to Britain and the British cause, but neither had been well served by the Foreign Office in London. The second Alexander and second John, on the other hand, saw their first loyalty as being to the country of their birth. Edvard Grieg's father, nevertheless, had notably close personal ties to England. As a young man he had been sent to London to complete his education and had made the best of his cultural opportunities whilst living in the capital, with the theatre evidently having been one of his first loves. Of Edvard's brother's consular work we know even less than of his father's, and it can probably be assumed that John did not find it particularly congenial, resigning from his post as he did after just six years. There would appear to be no real evidence of overriding personal ties enjoyed with the old homeland.

As for the the young Edvard Grieg, there seems not to be a shred of evidence that he was ever remotely attracted to what in the end had proved to be for his forefathers a long and costly diversion from the family business. For that, posterity has to be grateful.

THE LEIPZIG STUDENT
AND SOME ENGLISH CONTEMPORARIES

EVEN by the time of the resignation of Edvard Grieg's father, the family business – now run by his son John – was in a state of slow decline. Edvard, John's younger brother and the fourth of five children, was born on 15 June 1843. His godmother was a Scotswoman, Mary Wedderburn Stirling (1814–1893), who lived near the Scottish town of the same name. There is no evidence that as a boy he accompanied his father on any of the latter's frequent business trips across the North Sea. Alexander had a lively interest in all things English, notably in art and literature; his favourite author was Dickens, a taste very much shared by his younger son. There would have been tales told in the Grieg home of Alexander's visits to London. One that must surely have gripped the young Edvard's imagination was his father's recounting of how he had heard Liszt play in the capital in 1824. There would inevitably, too, have been occasional encounters at home with his father's British clients. Bergen, after all, was Norway's largest port, and a substantial part of the international fleet that called there would consist of vessels ferrying back and forth across the North Sea. Nor by this time was the content of these vessels solely of a commercial nature, for a first generation of tourists – drawn almost exclusively from the British upper classes and aristocracy – had begun to arrive to fish, hunt and climb in fjord and fell.

There is little evidence from Edvard's schooldays to suggest that the study of English was taken really seriously by him, for he was never to be as fluent in the language as he was to become – through his Leipzig study years – in German. In fact his written English, according to a school report, ranked among his worst subjects. He wrote English haltingly, as he spoke it at the time, and in later years, when his visits to England became relatively frequent, he would express regret at what he felt to be his poor command of the language. He was, however, being less than generous to himself. His English was to improve, and he would be able to write tolerably fluently in the language of his forbears and, when actually in England, to cope well in conversation. Of his efforts when young, Grieg himself recounted – among the various school embarrassments suffered by a shy youngster – how he had cheerfully offered a translation into English of the Norwegian word for a veal roast, and how his teacher had laughed at him: the British Vice-Consul's son talking of 'beef of veal'? 'Just you go on home and tell your father that you called "kalvesteg" "beef of veal"!' Grieg said he blushed with shame. On the other hand, he also said his Scottish ancestry could serve him well, as on one occasion when his teacher had asked the class which generals had served under Catherine II on the Black Sea. 'Generals Greigh and Elphinstone', was Edvard's eager reply, remembering that his father had told him of how the Greig/Grieg family's coat-of-arms, in which a ship figured prominently, almost certainly indicated that the family had descended from the Scottish Admiral Sir Samuel Greig. The two names had consequently long remained etched on his mind. Inordinately proud at having been able to give the correct reply, Grieg later felt this to have been one of the greatest feats of his schooldays. Otherwise, what he may have owed to his diluted Scottish blood is debatable, even if in later life some discerned something of that bloodline in him. 'Some of his Scots ancestry', wrote Frederick Bridge, 'was perhaps responsible for the snap and go so frequently revealed in himself and in his compositions.'[1]

At the early age of fifteen, having by then demonstrated musical abilities of a high order, Edvard was enrolled on 6 October 1858 at the Leipzig Conservatory, a young institution that had rapidly become a centre of excellence in music study. Louis Plaidy, Ernst Ferdinand Wenzel and Ignaz Moscheles were in succession his piano teachers; in harmony he took instruction from Ernst Friedrich Richter, Robert Papperitz and Moritz Hauptmann; in counterpoint Richter and Hauptmann; and in his final year at the Conservatory he took lessons in composition from Carl Reinecke. Lonely at first, Edvard soon adapted to his environment, delighted now to be able to devote the whole of his time to music, something he had long since decided was to be his life's calling. In due course his brother John, three years older and a promising cellist, joined him as a student at the Conservatory. Friendships established there were interrupted in the spring of 1860 by a serious chest infection. Edvard's mother travelled to Leipzig to care for him, and as soon as he was well enough she took him back to Bergen. He returned to Leipzig in the autumn in his brother's company and resumed his studies, but for the rest of his life he suffered from recurrent breathing difficulties, exacerbated by the loss of function of one lung.

It was in Leipzig that Grieg for the first time came into day-to-day contact with a number of English students of more or less his own age. Arthur Sullivan, just a year older, had also enrolled in the autumn of 1858. They were never to be close, but Grieg remembered him as a particularly bright star:

> Sullivan immediately attracted attention to himself through his talent for composition and the advanced techniques of instrumentation which he had already acquired before his entry to the Conservatory. While he was a student there he composed music to Shakespeare's 'The Tempest', an extract from which he wrote down in my album;

it shows a hand as practised as that of an old master. Although I did not associate much with him, I nevertheless did once have the pleasure of being together with him on an occasion I shall never forget. It was during the final rehearsal of Mendelssohn's 'St Paul'. We sat together and followed the music from the score. But which score? Mendelssohn's own manuscript, which Sullivan had been allowed to borrow for the occasion from the director of the Conservatory, Conrad Schleinitz, who, as is well known, had been an intimate friend of Mendelssohn. With what reverence we turned page after page! How we admired the clear, firm notation, which was so very much in keeping with the concept of the composition.[2]

The impetus to write incidental music to *The Tempest* had derived from a need Sullivan felt to take back to London a work that would show the progress he had made at Leipzig. Mendelssohn had chosen Shakespeare in the case of *A Midsummer Night's Dream*, and Sullivan decided that he too would set out from one of the Bard's plays. He borrowed a copy of Shakespeare from one of his fellow students and selected *The Tempest*. It was to prove his springboard to fame in England, the end of his student days and the beginning of his professional career being marked by the first performance of the work at the Crystal Palace on 5 April 1862 and the critical praise that ensued. Considered a prodigy, Sullivan had studied at the Royal Academy of Music in London, where he had been supported by the Mendelssohn Scholarship for two years. The Scholarship Committee had elected to extend his scholarship for a third year so that he could undertake more advanced studies, and its chairman Sir George Smart had written a strong letter of recommendation to Ignaz Moscheles. It served its purpose well, as is shown in Sullivan's letter home to Smart some months later:

> I cannot tell you how [kind] Mr and Mrs Moscheles are to me. From the first day I came here they have treated me more as a son than a stranger. I am sure I shall always love and respect them. I have nothing to do with money matters. Mr Moscheles pays everything for me and whenever I want some money I go to him.[3]

In a letter dated 27 May 1860, Moscheles sent a letter to his friend Herbert Oakeley, an English organist and composer who had studied at Leipzig, enclosing a programme of the latest Conservatory concert. 'Sullivan's Overture', he wrote, 'is full of poetic feeling and spirited effects. He was warmly applauded and twice recalled.'[4]

Sullivan inevitably shared some of the same teachers as Grieg. But one of his own teachers at Leipzig was the Dutch violinist Engelbert Röntgen, whose son Julius would in later years become one of Grieg's most intimate friends and – as pianist and conductor in Amsterdam – one of his leading champions. Among Sullivan's several student friendships formed in Leipzig was one with another Londoner, John Francis Barnett (1837–1916), a promising pianist who had, like him, studied at the Royal Academy of Music. He was at Leipzig from 1857 to 1860. Three of his cousins, Rosamond, Clara and Domenico Barnett, were fellow-

Arthur Sullivan, student at Leipzig; and an autograph for Grieg

Leipzig contemporaries:
John Francis Barnett, Franklin Taylor, Walter Bache, Edward Dannreuther

students, chaperoned by their mother (John's aunt), whose temporary Leipzig home was a popular meeting-place for English students there. Grieg greatly admired Barnett:

> The Englishman J. F. Barnett, a sworn follower of Plaidy, could boast of the finest technique of all the students. Industrious and energetic, he brought this quality to a performance of Beethoven, which in the simple way it delineated the great contours of the work commanded our highest respect. One particular recollection I just cannot keep to myself: It was a dark winter evening, when Barnett was for the first time to play Beethoven's E-flat major Concerto at the Gewandhaus. A rare honour for a Conservatory student. Just before 6 (the concert was to begin at 7 o'clock) I had gone to the Conservatory — at that time of day there was generally nobody about — to retrieve some music I had forgotten. To my astonishment, I heard from a staff room the sound of music being played as if by a complete novice. One note would be sounded, slowly followed by another. A moment later I realized that it was one of the passages from the allegro movement of Beethoven's E-flat major Concerto played not adagio, but even more slowly still! I opened the door slightly. It was Barnett. He had the courage to carry through this [Plaidy] method to extremes, and, what is more, only just before he was to appear in public. And I did not begrudge this amiable and modest artist the results of his tenacity. A couple of hours later, the allegro passages sparkled with the loveliest clarity. He had a brilliant success. Here again, as so often, Goethe had a word for it: 'Eines schickt' sich nicht für Alle' [What's good for one isn't good for another].[5]

Despite Grieg's clear admiration for Barnett and his talents, a sidelight is cast — by Barnett, writing many years later — on the shy young Norwegian student's own impact on him at the time, and perhaps on other of his fellows. The Englishman, having already made a name for himself as a composer and pianist by the time Grieg first came to London in 1888, decided to call on the now-celebrated Grieg in the artists' room at St James's Hall following Grieg's performance of the A-minor Concerto. He introduced himself — as he thought — for the first time, only to be reminded by Grieg that they had been fellow-students at the Conservatory. Barnett had simply forgotten.[6]

Another Englishman at Leipzig, who was not to forget Grieg, was the pianist Franklin Taylor (1843–1919), just a few months older than the young Norwegian. He was to become a long-serving professor at the Royal College of Music and to become known throughout the length and breadth of England as a fine concert pianist. An interesting Leipzig connection lies in his later arrangement for piano four hands of Sullivan's music for *The Tempest*. He understandably felt close to this work, for it was he who at Leipzig had lent his own copy of Shakespeare's play to Sullivan.[7] He was able to help Sullivan elsewhere, too, after his friend had completed *The Prodigal Son*, an oratorio first performed at the Worcester Three Choirs Festival in 1869. The published vocal score credits 'the orchestral accompaniments arranged for the piano by Franklin Taylor'. Taylor studied at Leipzig from 1859 to

1861, so was there for the whole of the time that Grieg was a student, and later in life he was to seek out Grieg when the Norwegian came to London.

Another fellow student was another pianist, Walter Bache (1842–1888), who was at Leipzig from 1858 to 1861. Grieg knew him quite well, but they were not close. Walter's life, though short, was longer than that of his elder brother, the composer and pianist Francis Edward Bache, who had preceded him at the Conservatory in 1853 but whose own studies had been cut short by illness. One of the earliest letters Walter Bache wrote home from Leipzig told of an Englishman with whom he was to establish a warm friendship: 'There is a new pupil here from the Royal Academy, named Sullivan, whom I like very much. He cannot play well, but he has written some things which I think show great talent.'[8]

Bache already knew Franklin Taylor when the latter arrived at Leipzig in July 1859, duly to settle down in the same house there. He envied the younger man's prowess: 'I cannot help telling you', he wrote home to his family,

> because I feel it so much, how Taylor's coming has discouraged me; he is half a year younger, and about three-quarters of a year further on than I am. I believe that, when I have had the same chance as he had, I shall be able to do as much, but he has had two years under a first-rate piano master, and I only eleven months.[9]

Another side of Taylor's talents was recounted by Bache in the following year:

> Taylor is really a very clever fellow; last night he gave us an entertainment at Mrs Barnett's, which he called 'Professor Taylor's Two Hours of Magic', consisting of juggling tricks. He has been practising them for a long time, and he has brought his sleight of hand to such a point that he might pass for a professional man in the art.[10]

Bache was to emerge as a very fine pianist – becoming, too, Liszt's prime advocate in England – but at times he was as self-depreciatory as we know Grieg to have been, the evidence showing in his comments at the time on the playing of Clara and Rosamond Barnett: 'The two girls really play very well, and have great talent; in fact they discourage me more than anyone else in Leipzig.' Bache was an ever welcome visitor at the Barnetts in Leipzig, who kept open house on Sundays and who organized many a musical evening at their home. 'Sullivan and I', he wrote home, 'went and had tea at the Barnetts'! I have been there a good deal lately: they are such kind people, and you can do what you like there.'[11]

Among the concerts that Bache attended in 1860 was a performance of Mendelssohn's second Piano Concerto at the Gewandhaus by John Francis Barnett. The soloist, he reported, 'had great success, being called forward at the end'. Later, on 23 April, he was at a students' concert where 'Frau Rosamunde Barnett aus Cheltenham' and 'Fräulein Clara Barnett aus Cheltenham' played movements from concertos by Beethoven and Chopin respectively, the former also singing some Rossini. Another performer at this particular concert was 'Herr Carl Rose aus Hamburg', now less remembered for his skills as a violinist than for his founding and directing of the Carl Rosa Opera Company, long to flourish in England.

One interesting, if indirect link between Grieg and the Bache family was the fact that Walter's father, the Reverend Samuel Bache, was a leading Unitarian minister in Birmingham. It would be in 1888, when Grieg first travelled to that city, that he himself came into first real contact with the Unitarians and ever afterwards felt their beliefs to be close to his own. By then, however, both the Bache brothers had died, and the rest of the family had become widely dispersed. Grieg characterized one of the first of his English friends in a few succinct words: Walter Bache had been a gifted musician and a tireless proponent of Liszt's music in England and was 'too soon taken from us'.[12]

In his reminiscences, Grieg admitted to having been almost awestruck by these English fellow-students, above those of all other nationalities at the Conservatory. So many colleagues, it seemed to him, were making great strides at Leipzig, whilst at the same time he felt himself being left behind. He singled them out, those bright English stars, 'who, partly through their tireless application and partly through the ease they demonstrated in acquiring their knowledge, accomplished things in the face of which I keenly felt my own distressing limitations.'[13] Younger, smaller, and shyer than his fellows, he appears not to have left much of an impression on most of the English group, and yet he was ultimately to outshine them all.

What is particularly notable is how almost all of Grieg's young English friends were pianists. Another friendship he would come to value in later years was with the Strasbourg-born Edward George Dannreuther (1844–1905), whose pianistic abilities were of a high order and who was ultimately to settle in England. At the age of five Dannreuther had been taken by his parents to Cincinnati. There his younger brother Gustav, later a distinguished violinist and teacher, was born in 1853. Edward was sent to the Leipzig Conservatory in 1858, remaining there for five years before moving to London in 1863. He was, as Grieg described him, 'one of the first to take up the cudgels for Wagner in England . . . a notably intelligent and masterly pianist.'[14] It was only *after* Dannreuther had given the first performance of Grieg's Piano Concerto in England in 1874 that Grieg was to learn of the event. Dannreuther's teaching of, and consequent friendship with, Hubert Parry meant that he himself was to play a part in the English musical renaissance that was gathering pace during the second half of the nineteenth century.

Nearly forty years after Grieg had left Leipzig at the end of his student years there, he was asked by a German journalist to recount the history of his first attempts at composition. His response was reported in London's *Musical Standard*:

> My first attempts in composition belong, all of them, to my school-boy days, and were given to the flames long ago. Then followed the apprenticehood in the Leipzig Conservatoire. But I left this celebrated institution, so far as concerns skill in composition, just as ignorant as I entered. The fault may have been mine; but, unfortunately, it is the truth. What I wrote there has likewise, with a few exceptions, been burned up. Among the latter was a string quartet which escaped burning, through a chance which I deplore. It happened thus: a schoolmate, in his enthusiasm for Schumann,

had laboriously made a score of the latter's piano concerto, which had not yet been published, by copying the orchestral parts. When he noticed my great pleasure in it he said: 'It shall be yours on one condition: you shall make me a present of your string quartet.'

So it happened that my manuscript, of which I had but one copy, passed into his possession, and I think yet with horror on the possibility that it may still be in existence.[15]

Grieg returned to Bergen in the spring of 1862, where the 19-year-old soon arranged to give his first public performance in his homeland. In the summer, his father and mother took him and his brother John abroad, their main ports of call being London and Paris. Shortly before this, Grieg had applied – addressing his letter, as was the custom, to the King – for a state stipend to enable him to continue to pursue his music studies abroad, mentioning the fact that his father, 'British Vice-Consul Grieg in this town', was not in a position financially to support him in such studies. His request was not granted.

Precious little is known of this first visit to England of Edvard Grieg. It seems to have left no musical memories, whereas shortly afterwards in Paris there was at least to be the unexpected excitement of the two brothers coming across Rossini in the street. A letter of 18 May 1888 in Bergen's Grieg Archives tells us little, but it is almost all there is. It is signed 'M. A. Shillito', is dated from 3 Geraldine Villas, East Sheen (a south-west London suburb), and begins:

> Dear Mr Grieg –
> How long it is since our families have met – the last time was in August 1862 – when your Father and Mother, Brother John and yourself, came to Earlswood Cottage . . .

There is a reference, too, to Grieg's eldest sister: 'Maren wrote a sad account of her own health in Decr. last – I wrote to her at Christmas.' Shillito was probably a business acquaintance or colleague of Grieg's father (see Chapter 5 below), but of this there is no clue in the letter.

One further piece of evidence does remain in respect of that 1862 visit to London, and it is in the form of a pocket sketchbook with pencil-holder, bought in a shop in the Strand in July. It had cost the princely sum of 1s. 3d., and the pencil it once contained was put by Edvard to good use, as he made four sketches whilst in the city, and his brother sketched Edvard himself, dated 'London Aug. 62'. The first of Edvard's efforts depicts his mother and father seated; it was almost certainly sketched in the Norfolk Street lodgings, just off the Strand, where they were staying. The second drawing is of a table and two chairs; a pipe (Edvard's?) lies on the table, and a dog is seated on one of the chairs. Next comes John's pencil portrait of his younger brother. On the fourth page Edvard attempted to sketch the houses on the opposite side of the street, but then scribbled across his drawing. To the right of this swiftly-dismissed piece of work, though, he drew a cup and saucer with the

Edvard and John Grieg in the early 1860s

caption (in Norwegian): 'My tea-cup / in London / 1862'. The last of these London sketches is entitled 'View from / my lodgings in London. / 1862 / Norfolk Street 18, 2 floor / Strand.' It looks down the short and almost deserted street to the river Thames just a short distance away, and to its busy traffic, with small boats under sail and steam. Across the river stands the murky industrial landscape of Southwark, whose warehouses and factory chimneys are only roughly delineated.

It must of course be assumed that Alexander and Gesine Grieg took their sons to see some of the sights of the city, a metropolis that would have dwarfed anything the youngsters had yet seen. Edvard left no record to indicate whether he might have looked up any of his fellow-students, one or another of whom could well have been in London at the time. Might that self-acknowledged hero-worship of his English acquaintances and his own self-depreciation have played their part in

Portrait sketch by John Grieg of his brother Edvard, London, August 1862

'View from my lodgings in London', 1862, sketched by Edvard Grieg

preventing him from making the effort? At all events, the London musical season was over, and there is no reference to any concert-going during the course of the visit. There would very likely have been an excursion or two outside London. And Alexander Grieg himself would surely have entertained or been entertained by friends or business partners. The Shillitos of East Sheen bear silent witness to the likelihood of such meetings.

We are, then, reduced to a few pencil sketches as the only other witness to the young Grieg's first encounter with London. It would take another 26 years for him to shed his youthful anonymity where London was concerned and to return as a conquering hero.

Another Norwegian visitor to England at this same period was the poet (and lawyer) Aasmund O. Vinje. Arriving early in 1862, he remained much longer than did Grieg. Staying at first in London, he 'spent weeks' at the Great Exhibition and travelled quite widely before leaving for Scotland. 'I got tired of London, its bustle and its din; and in order to make the change as complete as possible, I betook myself to the far-off valley of Glencoe.' In 1863, having lived for some months in Edinburgh, he published a book of his experiences, giving it the title *A Norseman's Views of Britain and the British*. It took the form of a series of letters home – these having been written in Edinburgh between 2 February and 27 May 1863 – and it was published in Edinburgh by William P. Nimmo later that same year. Vinje's subjects ranged widely: parliament and politics, literature, law, religion, as well as the social divide: 'I feel hurt . . . at seeing such contrasts of wealth and poverty in this lovely land.' A moralist, he showed a distaste both for the aristocracy and for the lower classes, marked as he saw them by 'debauch' on the one side and by 'want' on the other. But he hugely admired the middle classes in Britain, noting how money really mattered in his temporarily adopted country; and he found much to admire too in what he saw as the vitality and humour of the British. The tone Vinje adopts is on the whole drily philosophical, and his book is far from vital and humorous in itself, but it is unusual in that it presents to us (almost uniquely) the views of a Norwegian travelling in Britain at a time when travelogues telling of British adventures in Norway were beginning to be common. Music does not figure in Vinje's book apart from a brief and rather odd reference to a choral piece to words by Tennyson that he heard at the Crystal Palace: 'It sounded in my ears like the dirge of deceased poverty and starvation.' On the other hand, Grieg was some years later to find singular inspiration in Vinje's poems, exemplified in the twelve songs of his Opus 33 – some of the finest in his canon.

In 1863 Grieg left Bergen for Copenhagen, where, apart from relatives who lived there, he could enjoy the company of the composer Emil Horneman, whose friendship he had gained at the Leipzig Conservatory. He had begun to take a wider interest in Scandinavian culture generally – something that Leipzig alone could not have given to him – and also in the music of Danes like Niels Gade and J. P. E. Hartmann, two composers whose work particularly attracted him. He joined a circle of promising younger musicians and settled down as far as he could to the business of composing, turning gradually away from the language of German Romanticism and developing a more personal form of expression. The summer of 1864 was devoted to Bergen and his immediate family, and it was not until the summer of 1865 that he again left for Germany and afterwards Italy. In the meantime, at the end of 1864 he had become engaged to his Danish-born cousin Nina Hagerup.

There is little if any evidence that Grieg had either time or inclination from now on to think very much about England or his erstwhile English companions at Leipzig. His new friends were Danish and Norwegian, and he had after all become engaged (though both sets of parents had set themselves against the liaison). Furthermore, he was now composing and indeed performing. In December 1865 came a complete change of milieu. He travelled to Rome, where he immediately hired a piano, and he remained in Italy for the next four months. He soon located the quarters of Rome's lively Scandinavian Society, making the acquaintance of fellow Norwegians like the writers Andreas Munch and Henrik Ibsen, together with a range of other Scandinavian artists and musicians. He kept a diary during the period of his stay, which does make brief mention here and there of newer English acquaintances and confirms his lasting interest in the works of Dickens. 'Read "David Copperfield" by Charles Dickens', he noted in his entry dated 18–19 January 1866; 'Marvellous book'. A few months later he recorded a visit in Berlin to the Opera: 'Saw "A Midsummer Night's Dream" by Shakespeare with Mendelssohn's lovely music.'[16]

One of his English acquaintances in Rome was a certain Dr Renton, who joined a small cosmopolitan group at Grieg's rooms on 14 February to rehearse a choral piece by Grieg's late lamented friend and countryman Rikard Nordraak. Renton's professional expertise was put to good use later in the month, as is shown by a short diary entry dated 24–8 February: 'Confined to bed with an attack of fever and stomach-ache. Dr Renton visited me twice daily. Very weak and exhausted after this illness in spite of its brief duration.' On the evening of 15 March, the local consul responsible for Danish, Norwegian and Swedish affairs gave a party for fellow Scandinavians in a Rome café. There were many toasts, including one, as Grieg noted, 'for Renton, as representative of the English nation'. On 20 March Grieg presented his English doctor with a paperweight 'as a token of gratitude for his many visits during my illness'. A final reference to Renton occurs in the entry for the following day, when he, Grieg and two friends came together in the evening for dinner and a 'jolly whist party'.

There is just one further English reference in Grieg's Rome diary. On the afternoon preceding the whist evening, he had been present at a recital given in the rooms of an Italian violinist acquaintance, following which he was introduced to 'an Englishman, Kennedy, one of those really inimitable youths of the type Heine mentions in his poems. He is wild about music, organizes 8-hand performances of Liszt's Dante Symphony in his home, to which he invites a small, select company.'

Kennedy had recently listened with enthusiasm to Grieg's *Humoresques*, played at another private party, and had wanted to invite their composer to one such rarefied event at his home. Ill on the actual date, the youngster recorded his relief at having missed 'this comedy'.

Grieg left Italy in April 1866, returning by gentle stages to Copenhagen, where he was to stay for some months. One of the first things he did on arriving back in Norway in September was to advertise in a Christiania newspaper for piano pupils.

'WIENIAWSKI HAS URGED ME
TO GO TO LONDON'

A SNAPSHOT of just one musical journal published in London in the early 1870s reveals the progress made back home in England by some of Grieg's former Leipzig friends and colleagues. John Francis Barnett's oratorio *Paradise and the Peri*, composed for and first given at the 1870 Birmingham Musical Festival, had its first London performance in February 1871, conducted by the composer, and was reviewed favourably in *The Monthly Musical Record*.[1] A few weeks later it was given at a Crystal Palace Saturday Concert. Two years later Barnett had another large-scale work ready for performance: a three-hour-long oratorio, *The Raising of Lazarus*, which was first given at a New Philharmonic Society concert at St James's Hall and was 'received with every mark of approbation by a very numerous and appreciative audience'.[2] *The Monthly Musical Record*'s September 1873 issue accorded the publication (by Novello) of *The Raising of Lazarus* a long, detailed and highly complimentary review, with an occasional reservation about particular numbers.[3] Shortly after this, however, a second performance of Barnett's overture to *A Winter's Tale*, given at another Crystal Palace Concert, failed to make much of an impression.[4]

Franklin Taylor was in the process of making a considerable mark on the London concert scene as a pianist. On 6 March 1871 he took part in a Monday Popular Concert, playing Beethoven's 'Les Adieux' Sonata among other works and joining no less a duo than Joachim and Piatti in Schubert's Trio in B-flat major. He was judged 'undoubtedly one of the very best of the rising generation of players'.[5] Less than a year later Taylor gave a 'most admirable performance' at the Crystal Palace of Beethoven's Piano Concerto no. 5 in E-flat major. At this same concert, on 20 January 1872, Barnett's 'clever' *Ouverture symphonique* received a second hearing, its first having already occurred (on 11 May 1868) at a Philharmonic Society Concert.[6] The following year found Taylor engaged on Beethoven's Piano Concerto no. 4 in G major at yet another Crystal Palace Concert, giving an 'admirable rendering'.[7]

Walter Bache gave a concert in the Hanover Square Rooms on 26 May 1871 and drew appropriate compliments: 'Mr. Bache is a pupil of Liszt, and is not only a pianist of very high attainments, but an ardent disciple of the "music of the future".'[8] For a while Bache's concerts, predominantly devoted to the music of Liszt, would remain an exemplary feature of the London concert scene and would attract consistently enthusiastic reviews. Both Taylor and Bache were associated with the foundation of the new 'School for the Higher Development of Piano Playing', which opened in London on 1 October 1873. Its director was Oscar Beringer, who was 'assisted by' Taylor, Bache, Frits Hartvigson, C. Guenther and Ebenezer Prout.

Sullivan's name was already a draw, with his music for *The Tempest* particularly popular. The fourth Crystal Palace Concert of the autumn season of 1872 contained 'a selection' from the suite of incidental music. 'It is Mr. Sullivan's first work, and was first heard at the Crystal Palace in 1862; it still sounds delightfully fresh, and better bears repeating than any he has subsequently produced.'[9] (Among other works that Sullivan had produced later in the 1860s were the *Irish Symphony*, a Cello Concerto and the light opera *Cox and Box*, together with the inevitable oratorios which English audiences continued to demand of their composers. In 1871 he met William Schwenk Gilbert, and *Trial by Jury*, the first of their many collaborative works, followed soon afterwards.)

Edward Dannreuther, too, was beginning to attract reviews as a pianist. As for Norwegians – or Scandinavians generally – who featured in the columns of *The Monthly Musical Record* during this period, there is not a great deal to say. The March and May issues of 1871 recorded that works by Svendsen had been played at the Gewandhaus in Leipzig. Of these, 'a new symphony by a young Norwegian, Johann [*sic*] Svendsen' earned a favourable, if brief report, while 'a new violoncello concerto by Svendsen' was received less enthusiastically.[10] Otherwise the elder statesman of Scandinavian music, Niels Gade, had the field virtually to himself. Several of his works were reviewed in 1871 and 1872 subsequent to their publication, and at a Crystal Palace concert in January 1873 his overture *Im Hochland* was welcomed as 'the work of a composer of whom both Mendelssohn and Schumann expressed the highest opinion, but who in England has not yet met with the recognition he deserves'. Much more recognition would accrue to him following his appearance at the Birmingham Festival in 1876, when he conducted his *Zion*. When visiting Copenhagen in 1874, the young Edmund Gosse paid a call on him and noted Gade's admiration for the English musical scene:

> Gade was full of interest and curiosity about the festivals at Birmingham, and the Cathedral-Week at Worcester, Gloucester and Hereford. He was pleased to be very attentive while I described what little I could remember of the performances of Bach's Passion-music in St. Paul's and Westminster Abbey. He spoke with great appreciation of the generosity and enthusiasm of English connoisseurs, and of the rare opportunities offered to foreign masters by the Philharmonic and by the Crystal Palace. He said that the temptation of England to a foreign musician was sometimes more than

could be resisted, and he mentioned his own gifted pupils, the Hartvigsons, Fritz, and Anton, who had left Denmark and had settled for good in England.[11]

Gade's link with Grieg was a significant one for the younger composer, who admired both the man and his works. One other link dating from 1872 that is illuminated as a kind of sidelight for us in the pages of these earliest issues of *The Monthly Musical Record* was that with Julius Röntgen, who first came across the music of Grieg around 1872 and some years later would become one of his closest and most treasured friends. In that same year the journal's Leipzig correspondent filed a critique of one of his early works:

> The sonata for pianoforte and violoncello by Julius Roentgen is the work of a youth of seventeen years. The young man is the son of our second Concertmeister, Engelbert Roentgen. The work has pleased us very much, not because it produced ideas of great importance – and who would expect such from so young a man? – but because it shows in style, construction and drawing a very considerable artistic ripeness. In this we find a very promising forecast of the future of this youth, who, without particular purpose, without endeavouring to put himself on an unnatural pedestal, which would not be suitable for him, truly and naturally brings into correct form and shape what he feels. So we find, too, in the first works of our great masters by no means the high flight of ideas which they have taken later.[12]

The 1870s were years of industry for Grieg, as he gradually became established in his native country as a composer, pianist, and conductor. Times were hard, for the family too (there were tales from his father of business difficulties, for example: spoiled cargoes of lobsters destined for England, and so on), and Edvard had to make his own way in life. Fortunately, a friendship established in Leipzig with Dr Max Abraham, director of the publishing firm of C. F. Peters, was to mean that he would never lack a publisher dedicated wholeheartedly to his music. In Abraham he had found someone who would become both a close friend and a generous benefactor, the result being that most of Grieg's compositions were to be issued under the Peters imprint.

Grieg spent long periods in Bergen, Christiania and Copenhagen, but Christiania was essentially to be Grieg's home until 1877. The music began to flow, early landmarks having been the first book of *Lyric Pieces* in 1867 and the Piano Concerto a year later. Grieg married his fiancée Nina Hagerup in Copenhagen on 11 June 1867, and the Concerto was a fruit of their first happy year, a period that culminated in the birth of their daughter Alexandra on 10 April 1868. Little more than a year later, the idyll came to a premature end with the child's death in May 1869. There were to be no more children. The previous month had seen the first performance of the Concerto, with Edmund Neupert as soloist, in Copenhagen on 3 April 1869. At the beginning of this same year Grieg had tried once more to obtain state support for further studies abroad, his letter to the King again mentioning the fact that his father was British Vice-Consul in Bergen. This time his application was successful.

Edvard Grieg's fame gradually spread beyond Scandinavia and Germany. England began to discover him in the 1870s, a period that saw the composition of the incidental music to *Peer Gynt* (1874–5) and, among other works, a whole range of songs and piano pieces. In March 1874 a Danish pianist friend who had established himself in England gave him news of how certain of his works were making their way across the North Sea. Anton Hartvigson had played the piano at a New Philharmonic Society concert that had included Grieg's first Violin Sonata. It had been 'very successful'. He had also played it with the celebrated violinist Henry Holmes, who had been 'very taken' with the work. Hartvigson had furthermore recommended the *Humoresques* to various leading teachers, who were now, he told Grieg, using these pieces with their piano pupils. And he claimed to have shown the Piano Concerto – published in Leipzig just two years earlier – to most of the capital's outstanding musicians. All had expressed warm approval of the work, and Hartvigson was hoping that he himself might manage to find the opportunity to play it in London.[13] Might Edward Dannreuther, now permanently settled in England, have been one of the 'outstanding musicians' to whom Hartvigson had expressed his enthusiasm? For without Grieg knowing of it, Dannreuther had been able to programme his fellow-student's Concerto at one of the prestigious Crystal Palace concerts in London on 18 April 1874. *The Monthly Musical Record* (published by Augener, C. F. Peters's London representative) for May reported on the performance and included some clearly necessary, if not entirely accurate, background information on the little-known composer.

Of no less than thirty-one works heard here for the first time, during the series of twenty-five concerts now brought to a close, by no means the least important was a concerto in A minor, for pianoforte and orchestra (Op. 16), by Edvard Grieg, for the first hearing of which in England we are indebted to Mr. E. Dannreuther. Edvard Grieg, whose name was probably now brought before an English public for the first time, was born at Bergen, in Norway, in 1843. At an early age he evinced great natural musical talent, and was sent to Leipzig, where he studied at the Conservatorium for four years. On leaving the Conservatorium, he took himself off to Copenhagen, attracted by Gade's presence there. Here he remained during four years, drinking in to the full the characteristics of Danish, Swedish, and Norwegian people's songs and dances. At present he resides in Christiania, fulfilling the duties of conductor and professor, and, we hope, also those of composer. Judging from those few of his works which are familiar to us – viz., the concerto in question, his 'Humoresken' (Op. 6), and his pianoforte sonata in E minor (Op. 7) – a singularly pleasing and strikingly original work – we should say that it has been stated with truth that his compositions bear the stamp of a particular nationality more clearly than any man's, except perhaps Chopin's. This concerto, which follows the form of those by Mendelssohn and Schumann, is as remarkable for the originality arising from the quaintness and melodious charm of its leading themes, and its striking harmonic combinations, as for the brilliant and effective manner in which it is laid out, both for the principal solo instrument and the orchestra. Its importance demands a notice in itself in our review columns. We defer, therefore, saying more about it at present; it should be added, however, that it was played with the greatest effect by Mr. Dannreuther, and seemed so thoroughly to please the audience that no doubt he will be called upon to play it again and again.[14]

The Musical Times, too, found that the month's concerts at the Crystal Palace had been 'highly interesting', singling out both Reinecke's 'clever' Overture in D major and the Grieg Concerto, the latter 'excellently played' by Dannreuther. It was 'a work of much originality, the young Norwegian composer having evidently dared to think for himself, instead of imitating the style of those who have preceded him'. The reviewer added that it had been received 'with the warmest applause'.[15] Some time, however, seems to have passed before Grieg received the news of the introduction of his Concerto in England. He wrote to Dannreuther on 7 June:

> I was of course very happy to receive the surprising news that you have played my Piano Concerto in London. There is no need for me to find out from the newspapers that you have done an outstanding job. When the author of the programme notes (is it you?) surmises that Liszt and Wagner have not been of importance to me, he is profoundly mistaken . . . It is with pleasure that I have read of your fine efforts in London, and it is really not at all too soon that the modern school in the English capital has managed to acquire as warm and gifted an exponent as you.

There can be little doubt that this and other performances – and publications – of Grieg's music around this time now stood to the composer's long-term advantage, for when his application for financial support was discussed in the Norwegian parliament on 1 June 1874, one of the speakers drew attention to the fact that English and American papers currently showed how highly his music was regarded. The recommendation that both Grieg and Svendsen should receive an annual composers' stipend was carried by 61 votes to 44.

In July, Dannreuther gave the Concerto its second English performance, in the context of an adventurous and well-attended concert of Scandinavian music given at the Crystal Palace. It was, wrote *The Monthly Musical Record*,

> one of the most original and effective works of this class which have been produced in our day. Mr. Dannreuther was again called upon to interpret it, and this he did in a most masterly manner. In theatrical parlance, he may be said to have 'created' it, at least so far as England is concerned, but that he will have it all to himself cannot for a moment be expected, for other pianists are sure to take it up. That he will be asked to play it again and again there can be little doubt; that he should not have been invited to play it by either of the Philharmonic Societies would seem surprising, but for the fact that our Metropolitan institutions seem to have been designed more for the benefit of foreign visitors than for resident artists, however excellent.[16]

A performance of the Concerto, for which Charles Hallé's orchestra had been engaged, was, according to *The Musical Times* for February 1876 (p. 363), scheduled for the Edinburgh Orchestral Festival due to take place on 11, 12, and 14 February of that year. However, no mention of the work appeared in the journal's report of the festival a month later.

Further evidence of the steady progress of Grieg's music towards public acceptance in England comes when, about this time, Hallé gave a series of eight piano recitals in London. At one of them he accompanied the violinist Wilhelmina Norman-Neruda (later his wife) in a performance of Grieg's second Violin Sonata. At the same time, English acquaintances from Leipzig days were making even more notable progress, among them John Francis Barnett. A review of the year's music for 1874, while noting that 'the Norwegian composers, Svendsen and Grieg, have also been represented in our concert programmes', makes mention of 'a very clever and pleasing orchestral work, "The Lay of the Last Minstrel," by Mr. J. F. Barnett', which had been given at the Liverpool Festival.[17] In fact the Barnetts were by now well established on the English musical scene: 'Among the works by English composers have been Mr. J. F. Barnett's pianoforte concerto, played by his sister and very promising pupil, Miss Emma Barnett.' Two years later his Concerto was again to be given by Emma, who introduced it at one of the Crystal Palace Concerts. Barnett himself had been the soloist in Sterndale Bennett's Piano Concerto no. 4 in one of the Royal Albert Hall Concerts. Franklin Taylor, too, continued to gain recognition. At a Monday Popular Concert in February 1874, he played Beethoven's Sonata in E-flat major, Op. 27, no. 1, and 'barring the fact that (as it seemed to us) he might have made more of the adagio, he played in a thoroughly artistic manner and with admirable spirit'.[18]

Grieg's first Violin Sonata made its appearance at one of the Popular Concerts in London early in 1875; it was performed by the fine French violinist Prosper Sainton and the celebrated German pianist (and conductor) Hans von Bülow. Sainton, who had studied at the Paris Conservatoire, had thirty years earlier accepted a teaching appointment at the Royal Academy of Music and had remained in England ever since. *The Monthly Musical Record* was enthusiastic:

> Grieg's sonata, which is as charming as it is remarkable for its originality, met with so warm a reception, that we cannot but think that Mr. Chappell will do well to lose no time in following it up by the same composer's sonata in G, introduced by Mr. Hallé at one of his 'recitals' of last year.[19]

Grieg's published music was meanwhile beginning to attract wider attention, and a prophetic notice relating to several of his works was offered to the readers of *The Monthly Musical Record* of 1 May 1875:

> For the first introduction in England of a work by this interesting young composer we are indebted to Mr. E. Dannreuther, who, it will be remembered, came forward at the Crystal Palace with his concerto, for piano and orchestra, in A minor, Op. 16, in April, 1874. Recalling the favourable impression it then made, and the opinion very generally expressed at the time that no more original or more effective work of the

kind had appeared since Schumann's concerto in the same key, one cannot but feel surprised that it should not have been heard again. We happen to know, however, that many of our resident pianists, taking example from Mr. Dannreuther, have set to work to study it. That it will eventually take its place as a stock piece among the best pianoforte concertos there can be little doubt. Of Grieg's other works which have come to a public hearing in London, we can only recall, but with the highest satisfaction, his two sonatas for pianoforte and violin, which have been heard at the Monday Popular Concerts and at Mr. C. Hallé's Recitals. A no less interesting work than these is his pianoforte sonata, in E minor, Op. 7 ... The list of pieces with which we have headed this notice are among the smallest of his compositions, but they have an importance seldom to be met with in works of so restricted a compass. The 'Poetische Tonbilder' and 'Lyrische Stückchen' consist, the one of six, the other of eight, short pieces from a page to two pages in length. They are replete with charm and fancy; being refined in character they will not bear rough handling, but at the same time offer no great difficulties to the practised amateur of taste. The 'Humoresken', of which there are four, are of a more extended scope, and all of a lively character. 'Aus dem Volksleben' consists of three longer and more important pieces, entitled: 1, 'Auf den Bergen'; 2, 'Norwegischer Brautzug im Vorüberziehen'; and 3, 'Aus dem Carneval'. The music of each, which is highly characteristic of its title, is brilliant and effective. So fresh and original, so remarkable for their quaint but pleasing turns of melody, harmony, and rhythm, are all these pieces of Grieg's, that they cannot prove otherwise than in the highest degree welcome to both professional musicians and cultivated amateurs.[20]

Slow to catch on it may have been, but the final movement of the Grieg Concerto was included in the Annual Prize Concert of the Royal Academy of Music, given on 21 July 1875 at St James's Hall. The Academy's orchestra was directed by its conductor Walter Macfarren, brother of the institution's principal George Alexander Macfarren. Lindsay Deas, who one may guess had heard the work given by Dannreuther the previous year, had chosen to play the piece.[21]

Another London publication by Augener in 1875 was of the *Marche funèbre pour le Piano* (presumably the *Funeral March for Rikard Nordraak*, first published in Copenhagen in 1866), characterized by *The Monthly Musical Record* as a product out of other celebrated dead marches, 'but with the super-addition of an immense amount of originality of matter, harmonisation, and general treatment'.[22] In the same number of the journal, Franklin Taylor's progress was documented: the twelfth Crystal Palace Concert of the season had fallen on the 99th anniversary of Weber's birthday, 18 December, and the whole of the programme had in consequence been devoted to the composer. Taylor had played the 'Invitation à la Valse' and the Second Concerto for piano and orchestra. Credit was due to him, wrote the reviewer, 'for his spirit in undertaking so capital a work as the concerto in E flat, which, on account of its difficulty, has so seldom been brought to a hearing, but which well repays the trouble of studying'.[23] Taylor was now president of the National Academy for the Higher Development of Piano Playing, and at the institution's second concert was no doubt responsible for programming Grieg's Violin Sonata no. 1.[24]

In August 1876, thanks to Max Abraham (who was delighted at the levels of sales of Grieg's compositions), Grieg was at Bayreuth. He sent a series of articles on the *Ring* cycle back to the Bergen daily *Bergensposten*. In one of these he referred to the cosmopolitan make-up of the visitors he saw both in the Festspielhaus and in the town itself:

> This place is so swarming with composers, authors, painters from every corner of the world that one stumbles over them, so to speak, wherever one goes. The biggest names in Europe are all gathered here – indeed, there are many who have flocked here even from America.[25]

The England contingent included Dannreuther, Parry and Stanford, but Grieg does not record meeting or talking with them, any more than he does in respect of the luminaries from other countries who were present.

There can be no doubt that Grieg's progress in England, as elsewhere, was facilitated by the new series of the Peters Edition, which brought out at cheap prices a great deal of music new and old, and which was to be very much to the forefront in presenting Grieg to a new public. The company being based in Leipzig, C. F. Peters's London agent was George Augener of Augener & Co., and much the larger part of the composer's work was, during his lifetime at least, published in English editions by Augener. Advertisements for Peters's 'New Cheap Editions' began to appear in the musical press, and they included a two-volume album of Grieg's songs. *The Monthly Musical Record* felt that 'his remarkable individuality as a composer is strikingly apparent' in these.[26] The American soprano Antoinette Sterling, possibly owing to this publication, was to take up Grieg, singing his 'Sunset' – qualified by the *Record* as a 'thoroughly beautiful' song – at a Popular Concert in London in November 1877.[27]

Grieg's *Ballade* was soon added to Peters' series:

> After his pianoforte concerto (Op. 16) it is one of the most advanced of his works that we have made acquaintance with. Abounding, almost to excess, with all the characteristic traits, especially of harmonisation, which we are accustomed to associate with Grieg, it is at once strikingly original, artistically clever, and highly dramatic; and in the hands of a practised player – for it is by no means easy to execute well – would, doubtless, prove most effective. That Grieg has by no means stood still, though it is some time since we have received a work of importance from his pen, it seems to afford a welcome proof.[28]

A month later, *The Monthly Musical Record* reviewed another Grieg publication, this time *Zwei symphonische Stücke*, Op. 14, by Eduard [*sic*] Grieg, these being the two middle movements of Grieg's Symphony in C minor, arranged for piano.

> Though we cannot but think that there is internal evidence in certain passages that they were originally designed for orchestra rather than for pianoforte, and though

they are not so strongly marked with Grieg's remarkable individuality as are several of the works which bear both a higher and a lower opus number, they offer much to admire both in point of melody and harmony. The one is as smoothly tuneful and impassioned as the other is vigorous and spirited. If they had been brought before us as pianoforte arrangements of orchestral works, we should have no hesitation in pronouncing them to have been very cleverly made. As pianoforte pieces, we are inclined to regard their intrinsic material as superior to the manner of its presentation. Regarding the reproduction of orchestral effects upon the pianoforte, especially in duets, as perfectly justifiable, we hail these two symphonic movements as a valuable addition to our library of pianoforte music for four hands.[29]

The major event of 1877 in London, where Grieg was concerned, did not take the form of a publication but rather of yet another professional performance of the Piano Concerto. Little more than a year earlier, on 6 January 1876, Charles Hallé had been the soloist when the work was given for the first time in Manchester. The critic of *The Manchester Guardian* had been impressed by Hallé's performance and felt the work had 'sufficient originality to justify the belief that from this composer we have the right to expect much more in the future'.[30] Now, on 22 February at the opening concert of the 65th season of the Philharmonic Society's concerts, the Concerto was once again played by Dannreuther, this time under the baton of William Cusins. The performance brought forth curiously mixed reviews in two of the major musical journals of the land. *The Monthly Musical Record* was entirely positive:

[The concert's] most satisfactory feature was certainly the engagement of Mr. E. Dannreuther, who, though he has been resident among us for the last twelve years, and though with justice his claims as a pianist of the first rank, as a conductor, and as a writer and lecturer upon musical subjects have been widely recognised, strange to say, had never before been invited to play at one of this society's concerts. Having at length broken through a rule, which of late years has been too strictly observed by this society, of ignoring the merit of resident pianists, it may be hoped that a similar compliment will be paid to others who have attained to high eminence. Mr. Dannreuther came forward with Edvard Grieg's concerto in A minor (Op. 16), which was now heard for the first time at these concerts. Recalling the warm reception accorded to it on two occasions of Mr. Dannreuther's playing it at the Crystal Palace in 1874, and regarding it as the most strikingly original, and at the same time the most pleasingly attractive of pianoforte concertos of a classical form which has appeared since that by Schumann in the same key – not, however, forgetting that by P. Tschaikowski, for a single hearing of which, in March last, at the Crystal Palace, we have also to thank Mr. Dannreuther – we cannot but feel surprise that it should not ere this have been more frequently heard. It was played by Mr. Dannreuther in a thoroughly masterly manner, and with much power and feeling.[31]

The Musical Times thought otherwise, deeming that Dannreuther had played the Concerto with an earnestness and artistic finish which indicated that he estimated the work at a higher value than did the majority of his auditors. We cannot certainly say that definite themes are wanting in the Concerto, but many of them are uncouth – the first, especially, with the ascent of two augmented fourths in consecutive bars – and they appear thrown together, as if the composer had resolved to use up all the melodies he had jotted down at various times in his sketch-book. Occasionally we have some excellent writing, and the orchestration is exceedingly effective in many parts; but the composition left a sense of weariness upon the audience which somewhat checked the well-merited applause which the executant received at the conclusion of his difficult task.[32]

Grieg's sights on a professional and personal appearance in London seem first to have been set in 1877. He was staying in the hamlet of Børve – where, high above the Sørfjord, he was at work on his great String Quartet – when he penned in August that year a letter to a Danish friend, telling of how he had received encouragement from one of the greatest violinists of the day:

> I didn't get the grant I applied for and without which I dare not go abroad with my better half. This development is all the more annoying in that Wieniawski, with whom I performed in Christiania a couple of months ago, has urged me to go to London this winter, where he will arrange opportunities for the two of us to perform sonatas together. But – now that's all gone up in smoke.[33]

1878 seems merely to have been a year of marking time in England. The publication of Grieg's *Twenty-five Norwegian Folk Songs and Dances*, Op. 17, erratically attributed to 'Eduard' Grieg, was cautiously received by *The Monthly Musical Record*:

> Both in his original compositions and in his arrangements of his country's tunes national characteristics and individuality predominate far more strongly than in like essays by Gade. Though often sombre in tone, and somewhat restricted in their scope, this new series of Northern Dances and Songs will be welcome alike both to pianoforte players and collectors of national tunes.[34]

Later in the year, *Album Leaves*, Op. 28, and *Improvisations on Two Norwegian Folk Songs*, Op. 29, brought forth a more enthusiastic response:

> The name of the composer of these two sets of pianoforte pieces is growing into familiarity among those who take notice of rising merit. The few examples of his works already given to the world have impressed musicians most favourably with an idea of his great ability in writing, as well as with a belief in the high degree to which he may aspire as an inventor. The 'Albumblätter' now before us, which consist of four short pieces, no one of which is of more than moderate difficulty, yet are very effective, novel in their harmonies, and sweetly original in their melodies; and whether used for teaching pieces, or as brief means for the exhibition of tasteful execution on the part of those called upon 'to play something', will bring with them the pleasure which must arise from the exhibition of refined ideas, or of ideas charming in their simplicity, and losing no point by being displayed in a refined style.

The 'Improvisata', two pieces of greater length and less moderate pretensions, have all the power and spontaneity which might be expected as the expression of the mind of one who has much to say, and the power to say it well. The ingenious way in which the leading idea is presented in varied *tempi*, with a slight change of harmony and of accompanying figure in the first piece, in A minor, will commend itself to all who can appreciate the value of husbanding a good theme; and the dashing impetus of the second, in F major, springing forward like the earnest outcome of an enthusiastic soul, is not unlikely to find the greatest favour among those who can sympathise with true artistic efforts. Each of these new pianoforte works will add to the reputation of the composer, and tend considerably to create an interest in his greater works.[35]

It was while he was spending some time in Leipzig in the spring of 1879 that Grieg got to know yet another English student at the Conservatory. Ethel Smyth, who was also taking private lessons with Heinrich von Herzogenberg, remembered the occasion well:

> My first meeting with Grieg, whom I afterwards came to know so well, I remember chiefly because of a well-deserved smack in the face it brought me. Grieg, whose tastes were catholic, greatly admired the works of Liszt. Now it was the fashion in my world to despise Liszt as composer. But what had to be borne as coming from mature musicians may well have been intolerable as a student, and some remark of mine causing Grieg's fury to boil over, he suddenly enquired what the devil a two-penny halfpenny whipper-snapper like me meant by talking thus of my betters? Next day at cockcrow the dear man came stumping up my stairs to apologise, and this incident laid the foundation of a very warm feeling between me and the Griegs which came to fruition later on.[36]

Smyth sent Grieg a piano work that she had composed in 1878 (*Variations on an Original Theme*), and asked him to comment on it. He complimented her on having been so charming as to have sent the piece. 'The one thing that is not charming is . . . the legions upon legions of mistakes in the MS! There are moments when I feel as if I were playing the riot-scene in the "Meistersinger"! Your permission to correct these mistakes "according to taste" is all very fine, but . . . !'[37] Much later Ethel was to find herself in Leipzig again while Grieg, too, was there, and the friendship would be renewed with greater warmth.

In August 1879 the Delius family from Bradford found themselves in Filey, a Yorkshire seaside resort to which they travelled each year for a six weeks' summer holiday. The Spark family from Leeds also happened to be in Filey at the same time. Best known of the latter was William (1823–1897), organist, composer, and writer, although it is unclear whether he was among those in Filey on this particular occasion. His younger brother Frederick was editor and publisher of the Leeds *Express*, and in 1877, after some twenty years' connection with the Leeds Festival, he had become the festival's honorary secretary. During the course of an informal concert given by the members of these two families in Filey on 19 August (an extant programme being handwritten on a single sheet of paper), the 17-year-old Fritz Delius played one of Grieg's first two violin sonatas – the programme indicating just 'Violin Solo' – and Frederick Spark sang a song by Théodor Marzials. It may well be that Delius performed just one movement of the Grieg sonata, following immediately on from the only other item he played, the popular *Cavatina* of Raff, but we are unlikely ever to know the full story.

It was, curiously, around this time that Grieg at last began seriously to explore avenues of opportunity for himself in England. The boy Delius could never have guessed that he would become Grieg's most treasured English friend. Nor could Fred Spark, who during his final year as secretary of the Leeds Festival was to secure Grieg's agreement to conduct at the 1907 festival, have guessed that he would see Leeds deprived of that event's greatest attraction by the composer's untimely death.

⊰ 4 ⊱

'IT IS MY INTENTION TO VISIT ENGLAND'

O N 1 July 1879, *The Monthly Musical Record* published the first instalment of a study by Frederick Niecks of Grieg's music.[1] Continued in the journal's August issue and concluded in September, it was unquestionably the first real attempt to examine and to explain Grieg's music to an English public. Niecks was yet another musician from continental Europe who had come to Britain – in his case establishing himself in Scotland, playing viola in the Edinburgh Quartet and becoming a professor at Edinburgh University. He was a busy writer, who published essays on many aspects of music – in *The Monthly Musical Record* in particular – over a good many years. It was quite possibly after having become aware of Niecks's writings on him that Grieg raised the question once again of a visit in a professional capacity to England. The evidence comes in a letter written by George Augener on 4 November 1879 and addressed to Max Abraham, head of C. F. Peters in Leipzig. Augener is enthusiastic, but advises that the timing of a visit is all-important.

> However delighted I am to hear that Grieg wants to come over here, I cannot really think that the present time is suitable. The real Season is during the parliamentary session and begins around February. Nevertheless, Grieg comes with a fine reputation and can scarcely fail to succeed.

Augener recommended that the Peters company should get in touch with Narciso Vert, concert agent for most of the more important visiting artists, for his advice. He further recommended that Grieg himself should write to August Manns, conductor of the Crystal Palace Concerts, where some of his works had already been played.

George Augener was to become a key figure in Grieg's personal and musical life. Born in Fechenheim, Hesse, in 1830, he was one of the multitude of gifted Germans who established themselves in England in the Victorian era and who contributed so richly to the musical life of their adopted country. He had founded his music-publishing business, Augener & Co., in 1853 at 86 Newgate Street, initially to import foreign music into Britain, later establishing two branch warehouses in the West End, and later still moving his headquarters to Regent Street. In 1873 he became sole agent for the British Isles of C. F. Peters. Only two years earlier he had founded *The Monthly Musical Record* – a journal that continued until 1960 – with Ebenezer Prout as its first editor. In 1878 he established his own printing works, which he placed under the direction of his son William, then in his early twenties. Augener published virtually all of Grieg's music that appeared in England. He retired in 1910, five years after the death of his son, and he himself died in 1915.

A few days after this letter from Augener, Grieg heard from Max Abraham on the subject. In view of Grieg's seemingly imminent concert tour in England, he regretted that the composer had not permitted him to print English texts in a third volume of songs that he had just published. 'In spite of this, I do hope that your stay in England will be accompanied by great success.' Usefully, he had recently dispatched piano albums in large numbers to England – specifically, Op. 6, Op. 12, and Op. 19.[2] Abraham took further advice and towards the end of November recommended that Grieg should write letters to August Manns (echoing Augener's suggestion) and to Edward Dannreuther in England, to Joseph Joachim in Berlin, and to Clara Schumann in Frankfurt, in order to gain further advice as to the best way forward. Grieg should ask Manns if he might play the Piano Concerto at the Crystal Palace and seek advice from him too as to how to go about organizing a longer stay and about what kind of arrangements Chappell's, the concert agents, might be able to make. He should ask the same of Dannreuther, and through Joachim and Clara Schumann he should seek suitable introductions. Should Grieg still be uncertain after receiving replies, he should send all of the responses to Abraham himself, who would debate with their mutual friend, the composer Heinrich von Herzogenberg, what the next step should be.

> You are quite right to be careful, as in the metropolis that is London everything depends on the right approach. In England you have a very good &, if I am not mistaken, a greater name than in Germany. If you had asked me earlier if you should come to give concerts in Germany, I would have said: 'No, it's still too soon'; but ask me if you should go to London, and my reply is: 'Yes, but set about it in the right way.' As soon as you have decided to put your plan into operation, I shall be delighted to recommend you to Augener, something which will hopefully be of use to you.[3]

Grieg immediately got down to writing his letters, each of them in German, and – apart from that to Dannreuther – each in a notably formal style. The first went to Manns and others followed immediately on to Dannreuther, Joachim and Clara Schumann. Grieg must surely have felt that his plea to Manns held the key to unlock England's door.

> Dear Director
>   As it is my intention to come to England in the spring of 1880 in order to introduce my compositions, I humbly take the liberty herewith to ask whether there will be an

opportunity to participate in a Crystal Palace Orchestral Concert with the performance of my Piano Concerto (A minor, op. 16). (I last played it on the 30th November at
a Gewandhaus Concert in Leipzig.) If circumstances should permit the performance
of the said work it would very much interest me to conduct at the same concert a work
for solo voices, women's chorus and orchestra '*at the cloister-gate*' (op. 20.). However,
the Piano Concerto is the main thing for me.

Unknown in London as I am, you will not take it amiss from me if I take the liberty
of applying to you direct with this request for advice. I wish to find as many engagements as possible during the Season, given a stay for some time in England, NB, *only*
with my own compositions, among which chiefly *chamber music* and songs. Does
Chappell engage artists for the whole Season, or does he only arrange chamber music
concerts? Since I do not, for pecuniary reasons, wish to make the journey just on the
off-chance, you would be doing me a very special favour by letting me have an absolutely frank reply to this equally frank letter of mine, for which I shall hopefully have
the pleasure of thanking you personally in London.

With the greatest respect,
Edvard Grieg
Norwegian Composer[4]

Some twenty years earlier, when he was a 15-year-old student at Leipzig, Grieg had
heard Clara Schumann play her late husband's Piano Concerto ('magically', as he
remembered), but now he was writing to her as a stranger, stressing that it was on
von Herzogenberg's recommendation that he was approaching her.

I intend to go to England in the spring to perform some of my own compositions
(a piano concerto, chamber music works, and songs). Might you be so extremely kind
as to prepare the way for me with some recommendations? To whom? You yourself
will certainly know best! Herr von Herzogenberg, who will write in more detail to
you about the matter, has told me that you know something about me; had that not
been the case, it would have been difficult for me to dare to address myself directly
to you.

You will hopefully excuse my request and my poor German. Honoured lady, it
pains me to burden you with such things, indeed, I can honestly say that I am embar-
rassed even as I write these lines – all the more so inasmuch as I myself am always
annoyed by all forms of recommendations and therefore in this sort of thing am acting most inconsistently. London, however, is a city where every artist is more or less
inconsistent when he – in order to make progress in certain matters – must, so to
speak, forget his principles.

Finally, begging you once again not take my request amiss, I sign myself with deep
respect
Edvard Grieg
Norwegian musician[5]

To Joachim he also pointed out that he was completely unknown in London and
that a few lines from the great violinist would be likely to ease his path 'in a thousand ways'. Whatever introductions he needed, Joachim would know best, for

Grieg himself knew no-one in London. The only person he had so far written to was Manns, and that, he said, had been about the Piano Concerto. These letters soon bore fruit. Clara Schumann sent him at the beginning of the year letters of recommendation to personal friends in London – Mrs Wattenbach, Miss Horsley, and Arthur Burnand – and visiting cards to be presented to Henry Broadwood and Arthur Chappell. 'I think', she told Grieg, 'it would be good if you went to London as soon as possible, as the Populars, Chappell's chamber music concerts, offer you the best opportunity.'[6] On her card to Chappell, she wrote, in English, 'Dear Mr. Chappell! This is Mr. Grieg, whom I wrote you about, and I beg you kindly to receive him'. Meanwhile Joachim sent a letter of recommendation to be presented to William Cusins, conductor at the Philharmonic Society.

Grieg had already corresponded with Dannreuther and had of course known him since their student days, and his letter seeking advice is accordingly more informal than the others.

Since it is my intention to come to England next spring, you will probably easily guess why you are getting a letter from me today. This is the situation: A word of advice from you would mean very, very much to me as you, based on collegial feelings, would give me the right advice. I have written to Manns about playing my Piano Concerto in the Crystal Palace. I have been told that this is where one must begin. What advice would you give me regarding a longer stay? Next season I would like to play as much as possible in London (England) so as to introduce my compositions. I would mainly like to perform my chamber works and arrange for my songs to be sung – and, if possible, also to conduct my little choral work, 'Before a Southern Convent'. But I just don't know to whom I should turn. I wouldn't want to fall into the wrong hands and thus waste my opportunity – and it is altogether too easy to do that in London!

I have heard of *Chappell*! Does he engage artists for the entire season? Or does he only arrange chamber music concerts? My economic circumstances unfortunately do not permit me to come to London just on the off-chance; I must have definite assurances – preferably a full programme of engagements. But for one thing I have a fear of simply approaching the first and best 'entrepreneur', and for another I need to have a so-called 'name'.

And so to a question strictly between ourselves: Do you think my art has any chance of success in London – artistically and materially? A naïve question! Kindly give me an equally naive answer! Kindly think of me as a little child and write:

1. You must do this and that!
2. " – " so and so!
3. " – " etc. etc.

When ought I to be in London in order really to get anywhere?
With warmest greetings to you and your wife, I remain
Yours very sincerely,
Edvard Grieg

Dannreuther's reply was extraordinarily helpful. 'Come in Easter-week – or *earlier*' was his advice. Just as Augener had done, he recommended Vert as agent. Grieg should immediately write to the directors of the (old) Philharmonic Society and to Dr Wylde, the director of the 'new' Philharmonic; to Arthur Chappell, too, particularly with regard to the matter of chamber recitals. Chappell's larger enterprise was the series of Monday Popular Concerts (the season ending at Easter), and Joseph Joachim had overriding influence in choosing the works to be programmed as well as the performers to play them. Should Grieg already be on good terms with Joachim, he should write direct to him. Grieg's *Before a Southern Convent* could well be suitable for Manns, but Dannreuther was unable to see any other opening for the work. The outlay needed for a choral and orchestral concert of one's own works would be in the region of £200, with the income falling far short of covering that sum. Better to have a recital of chamber works, where an outlay of £60 might well bring in £50.

Financial matters apart, Dannreuther had no doubt as to the artistic success Grieg would enjoy in London. 'Your piano works are well known and are *much* played. You would find your gifts appreciated everywhere, together with genuine interest in any new works that you might bring with you.' Again, he warned that any artist emerging financially unscathed from a first visit to England should consider himself fortunate. His own advice, he wrote, coincided nicely with that of Iago: 'Put money in thy purse!'[7]

Preparations gathered pace. Grieg decided that he would stay on at the 'King of Denmark' Hotel in Copenhagen for some time after Christmas and then hopefully take himself off to London. So far, he told a friend, nothing was decided though. He started to study English for two hours a day, using the Ollendorff method, which was designed to aid speed-learning. By 10 December he had already reached Lesson 42. 'After 100 lessons', he cheerfully affirmed, 'I'll be able to get by in the language.'[8] Meanwhile Dannreuther had given Grieg the green light to approach Arthur Chappell, who sent an encouraging letter as soon as he had received Grieg's own: 'I . . . shall be only too happy to arrange to give you one or two Concerts of my series *if possible*'. He would write to Grieg again shortly, as soon as he heard from Frau Schumann 'as to whether she will come to London this winter for her Farewell Concerts.'[9] A month – rather than the promised week to ten days – later, Chappell wrote to confirm that in all probability he could offer two Monday Popular Concerts, reminding Grieg that the final concert of his season was on 22 March.

Some days later there came word from Dannreuther, mainly in answer to further questions Grieg had put to him. Grieg, he suggested, might play the Concerto at one or both of the Philharmonic societies' concerts after playing it at the Crystal Palace. Each had their own particular audiences. The New Philharmonic was, he told Grieg, connected to 'a kind of *conservatory*', giving evening concerts, as in Leipzig, 'only worse'. Unlike the old Philharmonic it also gave chamber concerts. It would be best to leave the matter of fees to Chappell or to the Philharmonic so-

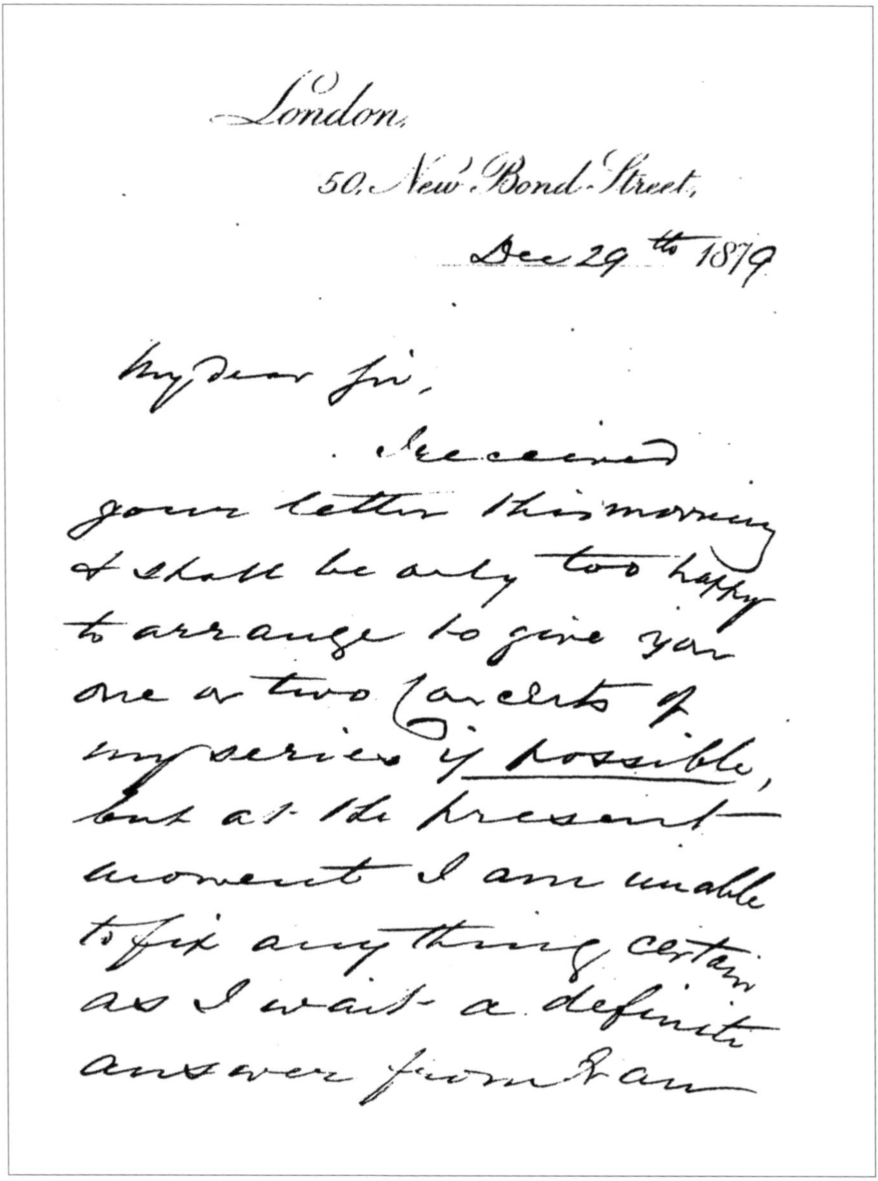

London,

50. New Bond Street,

Dec 29th 1879

My dear Sir,

Received your letter this morning & shall be only too happy to arrange to give you one or two concerts of my series _if possible_, but at the present moment I am unable to fix anything certain as I want a definite answer from & am

Arthur Chappell hopes to offer London engagements in 1880

cieties, but Grieg was not to accept an honorarium that was less than ten guineas – rather would it be better to appear _gratis_. There was a final exhortation: 'the earlier you come, the better' – and absolutely not later than Easter.[10]

Grieg now plucked up courage to write on 4 January 1880 to the management of the Philharmonic Society, almost certainly on further advice received from one or other of his initial contacts.

> As it is my intention to visit England this winter in order to introduce my compositions, I take the liberty to enquire of the management of the old Philharmonic Society if they might find it appropriate to engage me for one of their concerts; – the work that I should like to play is my own Piano Concerto (op. 16, A minor). However, as I do not intend to travel to England without firm engagements, I would be very grateful to the management for an early reply with information regarding terms.
>
> As to my qualifications, I beg leave to refer to a letter from Joseph *Joachim* to Mr *Cusins* the conductor.
>
> In conclusion I beg your indulgence in respect of my deficient knowledge of English, which is why I make use of German, a language with which I am more familiar.
>
> Yours faithfully
> Edvard Grieg
> Norwegian composer[11]

Henry Hersee, the Philharmonic Society's Secretary, sent a reply on 13 January. It would be another week before the directors of the Society would meet, so a firm response would have to wait. But the Society's 30 June date was, so far as he could see, still free, and he felt sure that the directors would be highly honoured by a visit from Grieg and that suitable terms could duly be agreed. Grieg replied immediately. He had originally aimed at staying in England from the middle of February until the end of April, but as playing at the Philharmonic Society meant so much to him he would be happy to prolong his stay until the end of June provided that he could be offered further engagements – in the provinces, for example, as well as in London. But he was still decidedly uncertain as to how to go about the matter. How was he to secure such engagements? He had by now written to Charles Hallé too, but altogether too late for anything to be put in train for the forthcoming season. What then was to be done about staying on? At all events, a Philharmonic engagement would be worth altering his travel plans for; and if the Society were able to offer him a chamber concert in which he could perform some of his smaller-scale works, the way ahead would clearly be eased.

All this, however, was to be of no avail. It had begun just after Christmas: first a cold and a sore throat, followed by insomnia. By 27 January 1880, when he next wrote to his friend Johan Budtz Christie, all was lost: 'I had intended to go to London, but must now change my plans.' He had become subject to an increasing weakness, particularly in his limbs; he had headaches, and his eyesight was affected. His doctor had diagnosed nervous debility, and that was that. Grieg himself had no idea how all this had come about, since he could not see how he could have come to overstrain himself, at least to any real extent. He had, he remarked, always been proud of his nerves, which until now had never let him down. At all events he had been made aware of what his health meant to him and felt that he had been given a useful warning.

Dear Sir:

In answer to your letter I beg to inform you that it was formerly my intention, to stop in London from february till the end of April, and as it would be of particular interest for me to play at the "Philhm Soci. Concerts" I would prolong my sojourn till the end of June, presuming that in the mean time other engagements in the provinces or elsewhere would turn up.

But as I am unacquainted with the english customs you would greatly oblige me by letting me know the ways hope to proceed in order to obtain such engagem[ents]

To Mr. Ch Hallé I have unfortunately written too late this year, if I gat an engagements enough to prolong my stay in England It will be an honour to me to alter my plans in ordre to play in the Phme Soc Concert —

the Philms soc. Does the Ph Sc, proforme Chambermusic, if so woud it be possible that I play then some of my Chambermusic. Grieg

Grieg's draft (January 1880) of an offer to play the A-minor Concerto
at the Philharmonic Society

To Carl Warmuth, his music-publisher friend, he wrote on 30 January that he was under doctor's orders and it was for that reason that he had had to give up the planned London tour. His programme for the immediate future needed to be restricted: he was arranging instead to travel to Christiania for most of March and April, giving four recitals, and would then spend the summer months in his beloved Lofthus, alongside the Sørfjord, where a full recovery could be hoped for. In fact he left Copenhagen at the beginning of March, feeling rather better but still without having regained his full strength. Following his two-month stay in the Norwegian capital he hurried off to the countryside in order to restore himself to full health. Once in the mountains in June he found time to reflect on a lost opportunity: 'You can well imagine how annoyed I was: all those preparations for the London trip, and in the end all for nothing.' On the other hand, he felt in writing to Max Abraham that some good may have emerged from the situation. 'Now that I'm beginning to feel better, I often think that I might not have achieved anything in England. The one thing that still distresses me is that I gave you and others a lot of trouble for nothing.'[12] Progress had been good, if slow, and he was once more composing again. A wonderful Norwegian summer among the mountains had evidently done the trick.

Serious thoughts of making a concert tour in England were now to be put aside for some years, but English interest in his music was only to increase in the meantime. Abraham told him at the end of the year that he had had an enquiry from England as to whether – and indeed where – the full score and orchestral parts of the *Peer Gynt* incidental music had been published. The work's first stage performance in conjunction with Ibsen's play had taken place in 1876 in Christiania, but word of its success had travelled quite widely. The two suites, both in orchestral and piano guise, were several years into the future, and in full score the Copenhagen firm of C. C. Lose had published only part of the incidental music that same year. England would have to wait yet a while for *Peer Gynt*.

If Dannreuther had been, so far at least, the most eminent pianist to have taken up Grieg's cause in the British Isles, others had also come into the picture. Dannreuther himself sent Grieg a programme detailing some of his fortnightly concerts given early in 1880 at 12 Orme Square. One of the works played had been Grieg's second Violin Sonata, performed on 15 January. Little more than a year later, Grieg's String Quartet was to find itself on an Orme Square programme. Other notable performances at Dannreuther's were to be of the Cello Sonata on 29 November 1883 and the third Violin Sonata on 19 January 1888, each given soon after publication.[13] Then there was Helen Hopekirk, born in Edinburgh in 1856, who was including Grieg in her recitals by the beginning of 1880, notably 'the rattling and musically grotesque "Humoresken"' in Dunfermline;[14] and in London on 20 July she included a work (or works) by the composer in a morning concert given in the home of Mrs Morrell Mackenzie (who maintained a noted salon) at 19 Harley Street, in the course of which 'in all her efforts [she] showed herself to be the possessor of high intelligence and skill.'[15] In November 1883 more Grieg followed in the course of a piano recital at the Edinburgh Literary Institute. Shortly after this Hopekirk left for an extended American tour, no less than 2,500 people attending a concert in which she participated in Boston on 10 December. Early in 1884 she included works by Grieg in a programme in Brooklyn, and towards the end of the year *The Monthly Musical Record* was able to report:

> Miss Helen Hopekirk is becoming quite a popular pianist in the United States of America, and will remain there for a few seasons. Edward Grieg has re-scored the orchestral part of his concerto, and Mme. Hopekirk has been engaged to introduce it to America in its new form in New York in October.[16]

Hopekirk had studied for two years at Leipzig and had made her début there with the Gewandhaus Orchestra on 28 November 1878. At that time Grieg too was in Leipzig, where he was to spend some five months, and it is quite possible that she had made the acquaintance of her future idol during this period – something that would inevitably have given impetus to her playing of his works. Hopekirk was to enjoy a successful career in England and Scotland for some years, but after her marriage to William Wilson, a Scottish businessman, she made her home in America in 1883. Touring widely in Europe as well as in the USA and Canada between 1887 and 1897, she also composed with some success, her many works including a piano concerto and a *Konzertstück* for piano and orchestra. While in Europe in 1887 she played the Grieg Concerto in Leipzig in January under the baton of Hans Sitt, and enjoyed 'a great success by her brilliant performance' of the work.[17] By the turn of the century she had become a distinguished teacher at the New England Conservatory in Boston and would play and teach widely in America in the succeeding years, many of Grieg's works no doubt remaining in her repertoire.

Towards the end of 1880 contact was renewed with the violinist Andreas Pettersson (1841–98), a Swedish fellow-student from the Leipzig days who was now settled in England. Pettersson's acquaintance with Grieg had led Ernst Pauer (or perhaps Pauer's publisher) to get in touch with him in order to seek out factual information about Grieg for a book on modern piano music and its composers on which Pauer was engaged. Pettersson told Grieg that he regularly looked for Grieg's name in a monthly musical journal (which one was left unspecified), but in vain, with the consequence that he himself knew nothing later than Grieg's Op. 29 (*Improvisations on Two Norwegian Folk Songs*). If only Grieg could write a violin concerto, Pettersson would be delighted to play it. 'I shall never forget that time when in Leipzig we played your Sonata in F for Piano & Violin.'[18] In fact this had been the first performance of Grieg's very first Sonata.

At the beginning of 1883 Pettersson wrote again in answer to Grieg's questioning about his life since their student days together. He had left Leipzig in 1866 to take up a teaching job in Liverpool. It had been 'awful', and he had put up with it for little more than a year before gratefully accepting a post at Rugby School. The relative lack of good music in the locality was compensated for by an evidently happy home and working life: he had married a Swedish girl, and they now had two young children, a girl and a boy, 'sweet, pretty and musical little angels who gladden my life'. If rather poor, he was 'happier than a rich man'. Pettersson had long adored Grieg's music and felt that he understood and appreciated it more than anyone else could possibly do. He assured Grieg that the String Quartet was considered in London to be the finest of its genre ever written, and that that had been his own opinion when he himself had first played it. Again he pressed Grieg to write more violin works. He still received 'the music paper' from London each month and had been delighted to see his friend's fourth book of songs reviewed. Always happy to sing, he had had a visit from a pianist friend living in Birmingham a few days earlier and had sung through almost all of Grieg's songs. He had worked too at the Piano Concerto ('almost ruining my fingers'), just as he had done with the *Ballade*. He hoped Grieg would come to England, if possible visiting – or staying with – him and his family in Rugby: 'England is a grand country and the people are splendid.' The English would take him to their hearts, just as they had taken Gade to their hearts at the Birmingham Festival. He ended by enclosing a photograph of himself, 'so that you may see whether 18 years have made me unrecognizable.'[19]

Pettersson laid plans to visit Norway and Sweden for a month during that coming summer of 1883. 'As you cannot now come over here, I have decided to come to Bergen together with a good friend who is a genuine Griegian, besides being a rather good pianist'. The friend was a certain Perkins, who was also an 'excellent' organist and who must indeed have been that same friend from Birmingham who had so recently visited Pettersson: Charles William Perkins (1855–?) was to become organist at Birmingham's Town Hall in June 1888, the year in which he was also appointed organist at the Birmingham Festivals. Pettersson and Perkins proposed to stay for up to a week in Bergen around the beginning of August, but only if Grieg were to be at home, he being the real reason for their visit. But Grieg had to be in Germany by the latter part of July and would not return to Bergen for the best part of a year. A mountain tour together was therefore not to be.[20]

Throughout the early 1880s, notable performances of Grieg's works are recorded from time to time in the pages of English musical journals. The German musician Max Laistner (1853–1917), who settled in London and wrote a number of choral works, gave his 'Annual Pianoforte Recital' at the Royal Academy of Music, airing on 16 June 1880 Grieg's *Ballade* 'in the presence of a distinguished and numerous audience'.[21] Later, in 1883, he was reported to have performed the Grieg Piano Concerto 'not over well' at a concert given by the London Musical Society.[22] The Swedish soprano Louise Pyk (1849–1929), giving 'great pleasure by the dramatic and expressive style with which she sang her songs', included 'Margaret's Cradle Song' and 'I Love But Thee' in her programme at a Crystal Palace Concert on 4 December 1880.[23] And at a Monday Popular Concert on 17 January 1881 the German soprano Thekla Friedländer sang 'A Swan'.[24] Friedländer sang frequently in England – having made her début in London at a New Philharmonic Concert – for a decade or more from 1875, and graced many of the Popular Concerts during that period before returning on a permanent basis to Germany. In January 1882, Hallé included 'Solveig's Song', sung by Mrs Hutchinson, in one of his Manchester concerts, following shortly on from a concert which had included Edward Hecht's *Eric the Dane* – yet another token of the continuing interest shown by the musical world in Scandinavian subjects.

Meanwhile, the demand for more scores gradually increased. Throughout 1881 Augener advertised proudly their 'list of music used at Harrow Music School', a list that by then included various piano solos by Grieg as well as the first Violin Sonata. In 1882 came two requests from minor London publishers, one for a piano sonata to be included in a series of works 'by the principal composers of the present day'. How much, asked Henry W. Carte, of Rudall, Carte, & Co. of 23 Berners Street, would Grieg require for it?[25] The project, which was to include nine other piano sonatas by, among others, Gade, Reinecke, Dvořák and Barnett, came to naught. Then there was the firm of Monttie & Son of 55 Baker Street, asking a little later for a few short pieces for piano, 'altogether 6 or 8 pages . . . similar to your Norwegian Dances', and asking Grieg to name his terms.[26]

The pianist Frederick Dawson (1868–1940) would much later (in November 1897) be engaged to play the Grieg Concerto at a Philharmonic Society Concert in London. But many years before this, in 1883, as a 14-year-old from Leeds he had made an early mark in Bradford, playing Gade and Grieg at a concert presented by George Haddock, who was at the time director of Bradford's School of Music. 'Master Fred. Dawson', wrote *The Monthly Musical Record*, 'obtained much applause for his pianoforte playing. He took part in Gade's Noveletten for Piano, Violin, and Violoncello, and Grieg's Sonata for Piano and Violin (Op. 8).'[27] Dawson was to study under Hallé, Dannreuther, Klindworth and Rubinstein, and performed widely in England in the 1890s, playing at the Inaugural Concert of the Queen's Hall on 2 December 1893. He introduced the two Brahms concertos to England and also played in Germany and Austria. Grieg was to find his technique good, but at the same time found his interpretation of the A-minor Concerto to be lacking in poetry. Nonetheless, Dawson would come to be highly regarded by his peers – Busoni, for example (who also grew to admire the pianism of yet another excellent Grieg interpreter, Leonard Borwick).[28]

Although the popular picture long to be entertained by the public was of a Grieg contentedly locked into a happy marriage, the true picture over a considerable period of years was rather different. There had been friction between himself and Nina quite early on, both of them being notably strong-willed individuals, and as the 1870s had progressed the distance between them had grown. In 1883, leaving Nina behind, Grieg simply quit Norway for several months, intending to meet in Paris Elise ('Leis') Schjelderup, a young painter whom he had earlier met in Bergen and to whom he was greatly attracted. Many years later, Percy Grainger noted down something the widowed Nina had said to him: 'Edvard and I lived like cat and dog. We were both so unfaithful and both so jealous.' He had felt this to be a rather 'jokey' overstatement, but had not of course known the Griegs during their earlier years together. Grainger saw Grieg as a man of 'flawless' taste, at the same time detecting what he felt were flaws in Nina's personality. He considered that, nonetheless, in the light of the later, more settled years of the marriage, Grieg's taste had led him from the outset to make the right choice of partner.[29]

In the summer of 1883 came the first serious direct invitation from the Philhar-monic Society. Henry Hersee wrote to Grieg on 3 August from St James's Hall to tell him that at the last meeting of the directors it had been unanimously resolved 'that Herr Edvard Grieg be invited to produce an Orchestral Selection or Piano-forte Concerto during the Society's Seventy-second Season (1884).' Would Grieg be prepared either to conduct such a concert or to play his Concerto? Grieg's reply elicited, on 12 October (after a meeting of the Society's directors), a choice of dates on which 'to play a Pianoforte Concerto, and a separate Solo' and the offer of a fee of 15 guineas, 'terms being the same as those paid to other eminent pianists who have performed at the Society's Concerts'. Two further letters from Hersee, on 1 and 14 December, demonstrate a mounting anxiety at a lack of any reply from Grieg. The plain fact was that Grieg was angered about what he saw as a 'paltry' fee (which he had anyway misconstrued as meaning £15, a still slimmer sum). He was now aware of his own value. 'I think', he wrote from Leipzig to his friend Frants Beyer on 1 December,

> the fee is reason enough for me to reply no thank you. I don't know what I must be made of, as I hear that everyone else would jump at the invitation, even at a loss. There must be something wrong with me, but I don't care a jot about the so-called honour. I suppose I can now say this more easily than many others can, as I now have a considerable reputation in both England and Germany.

Grieg's final decision to turn down the Philharmonic Society's invitation, and in-deed to cancel a planned performance in Paris beforehand, mirrored much more the situation that had obtained at the beginning of 1880. A month-long concert tour of Germany and Holland, with the Piano Concerto at the centre of his per-forming repertoire, had by Christmas left Grieg yet again physically and emotion-ally drained. Recuperating at Julius Röntgen's home in Amsterdam, he wrote to a friend on 28 December: 'I have only just sent my excuses to Paris and London, where I was invited to appear.' Instead he and Nina, at least partially reconciled, would travel to Italy in order to help him recover his health.[30] Later letters on the subject curiously make no mention of turning London down on account of the low fee. Rather was it the fact that on arriving in Amsterdam it was because he had felt so totally overstrained 'that I had to send messages of cancellation to both Paris and London, where I was engaged to appear.'[31] Later, in May 1884, he remembered how, when in Amsterdam he had come to the end of his tour, he was completely done in, couldn't stand music and couldn't play for more than 5 minutes at a time. So I made a rapid decision, and, think what it cost, sent a message of cancellation to Colonne in Paris, who had engaged me for the 6th January at a Chatelet concert, and to London, where I should have appeared at the Philharmonic Society. To date I haven't regretted this.[32]

Grieg returned from Italy to spend the summer of 1884 at Lofthus, leaving for Bergen at the end of October. Meanwhile a couple of performances of note had occurred in London. There was a recital at St James's Hall on 12 March by Oscar Beringer (1844–1922), when the German-born pianist played Grieg's Sonata in E minor.[33] Beringer had studied at Leipzig from 1864 to 1866 and could well have met Grieg there towards the end of 1865, when the young composer had spent a month or so in the town. He subsequently spent most of his life in England, became a noted pedagogue, and in 1873 founded in London the Academy for the Higher Development of Piano Playing. In 1885 he was appointed Professor of Pianoforte at the Royal Academy of Music. Yet another distinguished pianist of German extraction, though born in London, was Max Pauer (1866–1945). Most of his life from 1887 on was spent in Germany as a noted teacher in various major musical institutions. In fact he was to be appointed director of the Leipzig Conservatory in 1924, a post he retained until 1932. On 29 May 1884 Pauer gave an afternoon recital at the Prince's Hall in Piccadilly, in which he included what the reviewer called Grieg's 'characteristic tone-picture', 'Bridal Procession'.

Yet another approach was to emanate from London in the summer of 1884, the year in which Francesco Berger, who had begun his association with the Philharmonic Society in 1859, was appointed Secretary to the Society. This time, however, the invitation came at an inauspicious moment, for Grieg was now involved in the planning, design, and not least the financing of his new house, 'Troldhaugen', a little outside Bergen. He and Nina were to move in in April 1885. So it was that on 4 August he wrote, during a short visit to Bergen, a reply in English to this latest overture from the Philharmonic Society.

> Dear Sir!
>   As I intend to stay at home the next season, I shall not be able to visit London the time you have mentioned. But I hope, I shall have the honour to appear in your concerts another year.
>   I am, dear Sir.
>   Your[s] faithfully
>   Edvard Grieg.

It would probably be fair to say that with this third attempt to provide a London platform for Grieg, the directors of the Philharmonic Society may have begun to become a little disenchanted at their lack of success. Maybe Grieg, too, was a little disenchanted with England. In the summer, in response to a request from an English journal, he had sent the manuscript of a short piano piece for publication, having received the promise of a relatively high fee. Some three months later he had still not received a word in return. 'That's the way with people – I mean the English', he had written to Max Abraham late in October. He may also have found further reason to mistrust the English musical establishment. Charles Harding, vice-president of the prestigious Birmingham Musical Festival, had been on holiday in Norway with his wife in the summer and had met the musician and writer Didrik Grønvold while staying at a hotel on the Nordfjord. Grønvold subsequently introduced Harding to Grieg's brother John in Bergen, and John told Edvard of the meeting and of Birmingham's interest in him. Harding had unfortunately found himself in Bergen whilst Grieg and Nina were at Lofthus, but he plucked up the courage there and then to write, proposing that Grieg compose a work for the triennial festival, which was to take place the following year. Grieg was clearly interested. He had been 'overworked', as he put it in response to Harding, by playing too much and too frequently in Germany and Holland recently, so he proposed conducting his Piano Concerto with a pianist such as d'Albert playing the solo part. If the festival should want one or other of his choral works, he suggested *Before a Southern Convent* or *Land-sighting*. However, he needed first to know what the financial arrangement was likely to be. 'Is it an engagement or a matter of honor? I am obliged to know this.' He added that he did not expect to have any newer choral work ready for the following year, 'being for the time occupied with other compositions'.[34] However, when Harding returned home he found that arrangements for 1885 were already so far advanced that Grieg's participation would not be possible. He wrote again to convey this contradictory news to Grieg, who must by now have been finding English behaviour a little odd and off-hand.

Despite such rebuffs, Grieg agreed towards the end of 1884 to his name being added to the 'Council of Welcome to the American People' in respect of a major American Exhibition to be held in London in 1886. A letter inviting his acceptance as a patron had been sent from London on 22 November by John Robinson Whitley, Director-General and Executive Commissioner, The American Exhibition. Quite why Grieg should have been asked is something of a mystery, and one can only guess that his ready acceptance may have been due to the notion that being associated with such an event might be another way of keeping his name before the public in areas of Anglo-Saxon culture on both sides of the Atlantic. Wimbledon High School for Girls, too, kept the Grieg flag determinedly flying when Miss Emma Mundella gave an adventurous Grieg recital on Saturday 18 October 1884; she sent the composer a copy of the programme together with a letter asking whether he might be able to resolve a problem relating to tempi in 'Bridal Procession'.[35] The school enjoyed a high musical reputation, and the gifted Emma Mundella ensured that this would remain the case for a number of years. The next year was to pass with comparatively little seeming to happen on the English front. Grieg himself, now with landed property of his own, travelled relatively little, staying in Norway until November 1885 before electing to spend the winter in Copenhagen.

Late in 1885 *Warmuth's Collection of Norwegian Music* was reviewed in the pages of *The Monthly Musical Record*, a song by 'Edward' Grieg supplying some 'food for our admiration'.[36] In London in December Gertrude Griswold, an American composer and singer, sang a song (or songs) by Grieg at the last of four Brinsmead Symphony Concerts.[37] More significant was a performance of the String Quartet on 15 December at the Prince's Hall, 'introduced' by the Heckmann Quartet.[38] *The Musical Times* thought the work 'very characteristic of the Norwegian composer, especially in the middle movements, which are charming'.[39] Robert Heckmann (1848–1891) was a Cologne violinist to whom Grieg, after composing his Quartet in 1877–8, had turned for advice on technical matters relating specifically to the string writing; Heckmann had responded readily, being rewarded by Grieg with the dedication of the piece. Heckmann's quartet had given the work its first perform-ance in Cologne on 29 October 1878. Their first appearance in England had come at the Prince's Hall in the spring of 1885, and English audiences had been quick to respond to the extraordinary quality of their ensemble playing. Heckmann, incidentally, was yet another Leipzig product, having studied at the Conservatory from 1865 to 1867.

London would continue to remain on the back burner in 1886. In March it was reported in Norway that Grieg's compositions were now regularly being per-formed in Germany and France, and 'sometimes too in England'. It was further-more noted that the Cello Sonata was beginning to make headway abroad.[40] So this was perhaps the right time for his Dutch friend, the composer and pianist Julius Röntgen, to remind him of the usefulness, not to say the necessity, of making personal appearances. Röntgen himself had played in London in March, a work of his own being performed at the same chamber concert. Now there was a promise of more work in London in November, when he would be returning to play in several concerts, a prospect that delighted him. He reported to Grieg:

> London has made a quite enormous impression on me . . . Do go over there soon. In London it's particularly necessary that one present one's works oneself to the people there. You can see this again in the case of Dvořák, who has been there several times and in consequence is now the most popular of all composers. There's a real Dvořák-fever in London, there's more of his done than e.g. Brahms! He [i.e. Brahms], of course, has never been there.[41]

Abraham, meanwhile, was urging Grieg to press on with the composition of a second piano concerto and then to take it in person to Europe's musical centres – including London – during the autumn and winter seasons of 1886/7.[42] But Grieg was unable to offer any reassurance to his publisher; a new work for the autumn was unlikely, and he anyway intended to spend the winter at Troldhaugen. He had apparently received renewed invitations from London and from Hamburg, but had declined. The peace and quiet that Troldhaugen could now offer him was better for his health.[43] Nina Grieg said as much in a letter to her old friend Hanchen Alme on 15 November. 'He has continual requests from Paris and London to come there and play and conduct, but as yet he has not felt himself strong enough to do so.'

Two years earlier, the completion of a new work had been signalled – if in singular terms – in England: 'A suite entitled "Holbergiana" has lately been composed by Grieg: the music illustrates some of the composer's best paintings.'[44] First published in 1885, Grieg's *Holberg Suite* appears to have had its first two London performances in November 1886, when the Cheltenham-born pianist Fanny Frickenhaus (née Evans) (1849–1913), played its first, fourth, and fifth movements on 15 November at a Monday Popular Concert, and a Miss Jenkins, at a College Concert under the auspices of the Royal College of Music, received a 'favourable mention' for her playing of the whole of Grieg's 'quaint suite'.[45] *The Musical Times* felt that the work ought to be given in its entirety:

> This suggestion was carried out [at a Popular Concert on 14 Feb. 1887], Mr. Max Pauer being the executant. The work made a lively impression, thanks to the skilful manner in which the composer has imitated the early eighteenth century style, introducing, however, various little figures and progressions indicating a Scandinavian origin; and also to the admirable playing of Mr. Pauer, who is rapidly advancing in his art.[46]

This judgement was counterbalanced, however, by what was – in contrast to the prevailing attitude to Grieg's music demonstrated in *The Monthly Musical Record* – an unusually negative review.

> Raff, Bargiel and others, knew how to infuse the freshness of modern ideas into this form of composition: Grieg presents the dry bones of ages gone by. The choice of so tedious a work is therefore difficult to comprehend, more especially having regard to the inexhaustible stock of the genuine article bequeathed to us by the wigged-and-powdered pianoforte writers. The clever performer gave as an encore one of those charming specimens of the real Grieg with increased effect.[47]

Having spent the larger part of the year at Troldhaugen – a year during which a young piano student from the Royal Academy of Music, Stanley Hawley, had paid Grieg a visit – the Griegs set off in September for Leipzig, pausing for a while at Carlsbad, where Grieg took a curative break. Once established in Leipzig in mid-October, they were to stay there until the following April, when plans were once more to be laid for a visit to London. Soon after arriving in Leipzig, Grieg heard again from Charles Harding in Birmingham. Harding told him that he had once more been in Bergen in July and had again spent some time with their mutual friend Didrik Grønvold. He had discussed with Grønvold the possibility of persuading Grieg to participate in the 1888 Birmingham Musical Festival. Oddly, he had once again missed an opportunity to speak to the composer. Harding had been at the railway station in Bergen together with Grønvold, and they had spotted Grieg deep in conversation with a friend. Whether out of shyness or perhaps embarrassment over the matter of having let Grieg down in respect of the previous Birmingham Festival, Harding had not introduced himself. At all events, the Festival Committee had suggested that Grieg might wish to write a new orchestral work (preferably a symphony!) and come to conduct it himself in the autumn of 1888. The Birmingham Festival had become something of a Mecca for the leading musical talents in Britain, and Harding mentioned the names of various composers, including Mendelssohn, Hiller, Sullivan, Gade and Max Bruch, who had taken part in the past. No fee was touched upon; just the fact that travelling expenses, accommodation and the costs of copying manuscript and parts would be covered by the Committee. Grieg was invited to stay at the comfortable Edgbaston home of the Hardings, where Gade had already stayed twice.[48] Grønvold wrote to Grieg about the matter, and Grieg replied that he was never happy at writing 'on command' and that he was, too, continually worried about his health. Nevertheless he would do his best to fulfil the proposed engagement.[49] He offered to conduct his newly-orchestrated *In Autumn*, originally written in 1866 for piano four hands, but now dubbed a 'Concert Overture'. It seemed, then, that Birmingham would be the first city in England at last to welcome Grieg. But London was not going to give up quite so easily.

In November came a renewed invitation from the Philharmonic Society. Henry Hersee had served as Honorary Secretary to the Society from 1880 to 1884, and Grieg's initial correspondence with the Society had been conducted through him. On 14 June 1884 Hersee had tendered his resignation at a General Meeting of the Society, and two weeks later his successor, Francesco Berger, a man of many astonishing parts, had been elected Hon. Sec. 'pro. tem.' Born in London in 1834, he could boast a father who was a merchant from Trieste and a mother from Bavaria. He was fluent in several languages and had studied music in Munich, Trieste and Vienna, taking piano lessons from Louis Plaidy. He composed songs and piano pieces, taught at the Royal Academy of Music and elsewhere, accompanied singers, and organized concerts. Becoming an Associate of the Society in 1859, he had been elected a full member in 1871. He held the office of Secretary until 1911 and died in 1932 at the ripe old age of 98, having, among other writings, published two books of memoirs in 1913 and 1931. 'Berger's genius', Cyril Ehrlich has written, 'lay in seeking out new possibilities and exploiting them on behalf of the Society, with minute attention to detail, at a time when the map of concert life was being redrawn and to do nothing was to invite oblivion.' Berger later remembered how one of the directors of the Society had reacted when he first recommended that Grieg be invited to London: 'Greg, Grig – how do you spell it? and who the deuce is *he*?'[50] Berger certainly loved dealing with the great musicians of his day. He cajoled, flattered and fussed around them to a point that was ultimately to irritate Grieg. In consequence their particular relationship was to remain cool and correct, each often finding fault with the other, even if on the whole they disguised the fact whenever they met. But Berger cannot lightly be dismissed on just this account, certainly where Grieg's relations with London were concerned, for he was, after all, central to procuring for the Norwegian composer over a long period of time a series of genuinely high-profile engagements. Ehrlich has summed up Berger's achievements succinctly:

> Such were his talents as organizer and enabler that he was one of a handful of men who transformed London's music for a generation; and without his rare combination of skills and unique energy, the Philharmonic would not have survived into the twentieth century.[51]

Grieg appears by this time at last to have accepted as inevitable the fact that to gain a much-desired personal footing in England he would – in the first instance at least – have to sell himself cheaply. If he were indeed to come to England in the spring of 1888, he told Berger, he would wish to be assured either that his travelling expenses would be repaid or that any fee offered would be sufficient to cover such expenses. The package that he himself offered was attractive: ideally a full concert that would include a suitable selection of his works and allow him to appear in the three guises of composer, pianist and conductor. Berger's approach had been cautious. Earlier plans had, after all, come to grief on account of Grieg's poor health. He had simply asked if Grieg might recommend a short orchestral work that the Society might give at one of its concerts and then, almost as a rider to this query,

Letter from Francesco Berger to Grieg, 12 November 1887

Francesco Berger

had enquired as to whether Grieg might himself be likely to come to England and so play 'one of your Concertos'. Berger had written in English and Grieg in his reply had apologized for writing in German on the grounds of his poor knowledge of English. Their correspondence was to be conducted randomly in German or English.

There were further reasons for settling at last on a London engagement, with all the impetus that such an engagement would be sure to give to sales and performances generally of Grieg's works in England, all hopefully leading to more lucrative offers in the future. The building of his new home had put a considerable strain on his finances, and he needed the money. With his health largely restored, personal appearances in the larger cities of Europe, and particularly in England, were clearly the way forward. In the meantime there were, in the short term, sacrifices to be made. At a Gewandhaus concert on 10 December he had agreed to play his new Violin Sonata no. 3 with Adolf Brodsky, without fee. Plans to appear in Vienna had fallen through, and a proposed spring holiday in Rome would have to be given up for the sake of London. Berger offered a range of dates between 8 March and 16 June 1888 for an all-Grieg concert, offering a fee of 400 Marks, the sum that the Society had paid recently to both Moszkowski and Dvořák. Grieg would further-more have to guarantee that the Philharmonic engagement would constititute his very first London appearance. There had in point of fact been another approach from London, the Bach Choir inviting him to participate in a concert (more spe-cifically to play his Concerto) to be given on 1 March. The Philharmonic directors, alarmed at hearing this news and anxious that Grieg should not appear elsewhere beforehand, aware too that their first offer would by no stretch of the imagination cover Grieg's travelling expenses, raised their proposed fee to 600 Marks, with the concert to take place on 22 March. Grieg sent a letter of acceptance on 21 Decem-ber. The concert would include the Piano Concerto, an orchestral work and some songs. 'Agreed', replied Berger on Christmas Day.

Meanwhile, Birmingham returned to the picture. The Committee hoped for a specially-composed symphony from Grieg, to be given its first performance at the festival. Should this not be possible, they would accept 'An Orchestral Fantasy, Autumn Songs' (i.e. *In Autumn*) and the *Holberg Suite*, provided Grieg were present to conduct both works. The Committee would pay for any reason-able costs incurred in the copying of parts, and there would be an honorarium of fifty guineas. So long as neither of the two works had yet been performed in their orchestral form, 'they must not be given before our festival'. The Leipzig journal *Musikalisches Wochenblatt* was quick to report, presumably based on information supplied through Abraham by the composer himself, that Grieg had been asked to compose an orchestral piece for Birmingham, a fact noted immediately in the December issue of Christiania's *Nordisk Musik-Tidende*.

Yet another leading German musician who had settled in London was the con-ductor George Henschel (1850–1924), a man of many talents: he was a fine baritone singer, pianist and composer, who had studied at the Leipzig Conservatory from 1867 to 1870. After some three years as conductor of the Boston Symphony Or-chestra, he had come in the mid-1880s to London, where he was appointed profes-sor of singing at the Royal Academy of Music in 1886, the year in which he founded the London Symphony Concerts, conducting them until the series finally ended in 1897. Now, in November 1887, a year after the inaugural concert, he conducted Grieg's *Two Elegiac Melodies* for string orchestra, the only novelty in this particular concert.[52] *The Musical Times* felt that Grieg had written 'nothing more charming ... In their present form they are remarkably attractive, full of Norwegian character, and deserve to be heard again.'[53]

Grieg's own contacts with English musicians were actually widening in 1887. Eaton Faning (1850–1927), professor (and former Mendelssohn Scholar and Silver Medallist) at the Royal Academy of Music and since 1885 director of music at Harrow School, met him on a Bergen steamer in the summer of that year. 'We both remember our pleasant day on the Fjord in the summertime', wrote Faning's wife the following March. Faning had then promised to send some of his compositions to the Norwegian master. Grieg had talked of his British fellow-students at Leipzig – Arthur Sullivan, Walter Bache and Franklin Taylor – and Faning promised to pass on to them Grieg's 'kind messages'. Grieg had evidently, too, spoken of his hopes to come over to England, and Faning indicated that he and his wife would be pleased to welcome him whenever that happened.[54]

Then Ethel Smyth returned to Leipzig, re-establishing contact with the Griegs in the process. In her memoirs she remembered the time affectionately:

> Throughout the greater part of the winter of 1887–88 the Griegs were in Leipzig and it is then that my real friendship with them began. When Grieg appeared on a platform, whether alone or accompanying his wife's superb rendering of his songs, the audience went mad, but there was a simplicity and purity of spirit about them that success could not tarnish. Out of action, these two tiny people looked like wooden figures from a Noah's Ark, the transfiguration which ensued when they got to work being all the more astonishing. Frau Grieg sang in Norwegian of course and one often had only a vague idea as to the meaning of the words, but her performance was, as Vernon Lee once said about someone else's singing, 'explosive literature', and one wept, laughed, and thrilled with excitement or horror without knowing why. The

Eaton Faning

song over, she again became Noah's wife. Grieg is one of the very few composers I have met from whose lips you might hear as frank a confession as he once made concerning one of his later works. I had been so enthusiastic, and he was always so keen to get at honest impressions, that I ventured to say the coda of one of the movements seemed not quite up to the level of the rest. 'Ah yes!' he said, shrugging his shoulders, 'at that point inspiration gave out and I had to finish without!' – I remember too on a certain occasion his being invited for a huge sum to conduct not only his own work but the whole programme, and refusing on the ground that he was too bad a conductor. 'But the public won't mind that', pleaded the manager, 'they'll come to *see* you conduct: besides which, as you conduct your own music you surely can get along with other people's well enough for all purposes?' At this remark Grieg shook his pale yellow mane angrily: 'My own music?' he snapped, 'any fool can conduct his own music but that's no reason for murdering other people's' – and the manager had to drop the subject.[55]

A little later, the young Norwegian composer Christian Sinding attended a private performance in Leipzig of Smyth's *Hohelied* (*The Song of Love*, Op. 8, based on the biblical Song of Songs). He felt there was much good about the work, but that it was rather too Christian in tone. He admitted that that was how she had seen the original poem, but thought Solomon's song had 'damned little' to do with Christianity and would work better if some 'oriental dance music' were thrown into the mix. Meanwhile, like many another innocent, he had fallen foul of Smyth's famous temperament. 'I've had the misfortune to injure her most sacred feelings. It's really serious. Yet again I've given offence over some petty thing or other, and I have to confess that I find it enormously satisfying. She is, to put it bluntly, just too full of herself.'[56]

Much the most significant meeting of 1887, at least in connection with England, occurred in Leipzig some three weeks or so before the end of the year. This was with the 25-year-old Fritz Delius, then in his second year at the Conservatory. Two other aspiring composers in particular were also studying at Leipzig: Christian Sinding and Johan Halvorsen. Halvorsen recalled the time in glowing terms:

> I was together daily with the Griegs, Sinding and Delius. We took lunch at the 'Panorama' and this was always followed by a game of whist. This card party has been immortalized in a photograph and is of interest because both Sinding and Delius have since become world-famous. – There were many good sides to Delius. One of them was that he often invited us to his place – of course I include the Griegs in 'us' – and treated us to the most wonderful things. Furthermore he was kind in lending us money. We were constantly in financial straits, and we often had to go without a midday meal. But all the same that was a glorious time. Particularly while we had the Griegs down there. We admired and loved him and were very proud of being able to number ourselves among his friends.[57]

Sinding and Delius had by this stage of Delius's first term established a warm friendship. Just how early in the term that friendship started we do not know; but

A card party in Leipzig:
Nina and Edvard Grieg, Johan Halvorsen, Fritz Delius, Christian Sinding

we can make a fairly good guess when Delius' first meeting with Grieg took place. For many years of his life Grieg kept meticulous accounts of his everyday expenses in small notebooks, most of which have survived. Turning over these little pocket-books and restarting from his fresh first page, he would jot down names, addresses, and various odd notes and *aides-mémoire*, sometimes sketching out routes and timetables for his concert tours as well as noting down possible programmes and running orders for one of his forthcoming concerts. So if one ever wanted to know how much he paid for his and Nina's lunch, for coffees and a packet of cigarettes, or for a game of bowls with his young Norwegian colleagues in Leipzig and then a cab home, one usually need only take a look at the day's notebook entries for an answer. Should we want confirmation, for example, that Grieg wrote from Leipzig on 8 December 1887 both to the Philharmonic Society and to the Bach Choir, we should find the addressees of his letters recorded, together with the fact that he paid 20 Pfennigs for each of the appropriate postage stamps that day. Sinding and Delius used to lunch together at Leipzig's well-known Panorama restaurant. The two friends were on their way to lunch one day when Sinding, who already knew the Griegs, spotted them and introduced Delius. All four then continued to the restaurant to have their midday meal together. The likelihood is that this was on

7 December, when Grieg, as he noted, paid for coffee and liqueurs after lunch —
a suitable celebratory moment after all, probably marking for Grieg this first meeting with the young man who would become his most intimate English friend.

Another Conservatory student who enjoyed a brief acquaintance with Grieg at
this period was the Canadian Wesley Octavius Forsyth, who lived almost opposite
at the time. Some years later he painted a pen-picture of the composer in the context of a short piece on Grieg's music that he wrote for the American journal *The
Musician.*

> He is a hard worker, and composes almost entirely at the piano . . . from my window
> occasionally I could see him in his room. Many a time have I gone up the stairs lead-
> ing to his apartments, and listened to him as he improvised his weird harmonies and
> enchanting melodies, stopping now and then to write them down. Not long after
> I was introduced to him, and was invited to visit him on a certain morning in his own
> room. I accordingly availed myself of the opportunity, and passed an hour on that oc-
> casion in the happiest manner. I remember it well. Manuscripts and music were lying
> on the piano, and scattered around on the table and floor were a few books and sheets
> of music paper. Grieg had been composing.[58]

The order in which Grieg jotted down current Leipzig addresses in his notebook offers at least an approximate indication of the order in which he met certain
of his friends there. Sinding comes first, followed by Halvorsen, Adolf Brodsky and
Ethel Smyth; then, for the first time, the address appears of the London concert
agent Narciso Vert. The meeting and the subsequent warm friendship that was to
develop with Brodsky was particularly significant, for Brodsky and his wife Anna
were to settle in England some years later when Adolf — in due course anglicized
to Adolph — was appointed principal of the Royal Manchester College of Music
and so became Grieg's main point of contact in the north of England. Last in the
roster of friends comes Fr. Delius, shown as living at 'Harkortstr. 5. IV Tr.' On 10
December Delius went for the first time to hear Grieg play at a public concert. His
Norwegian idol was accompanying Brodsky in a performance of the third Violin
Sonata at the Gewandhaus:

> It was a beautiful performance and I was very enthusiastic, and after the concert
> I wrote Grieg an enthusiastic letter with my impressions, enclosing in the letter
> a sprig of heather which I had gathered on the Hardanger Vidde. Next day I was very
> much moved to see what a deep impression this had made upon him.[59]

The Griegs, Sinding, Delius and Halvorsen became almost inseparable companions until all went their separate ways in the spring of 1888, but by then the
respective friendships had become firmly established and were to endure until
the end of Grieg's life. At the age of 43, Grieg had already become accustomed to
enjoying the company and support of many of his contemporaries and elders. The
six months that he and Nina spent in Leipzig had, however, been marked out for
much of the time by the regular company of the 23-year-old Halvorsen, the 25-year-

Mr. Eaton Faning.
Meadowside,
   Harrow on the Hill
(London.)

Mrs. Wodehouse
56, Chester Square, S.W.
(Musical friend of Miss Smyth)

Mr. Fritz Delius
Claremont
   Bradford (England)

C. C. Macrae, № 6
Cambridge Terrace, Regents
Park, London.
(Thorvald Beyers Ven, musikelsker,
Sportsman, laksefisker, besynget
med Genin af Ill. London News.

Chr. Sinding
Peters Steinweg 24, 3. Leipzig

A. Pettersson.
19, Warwick Street.
(England)   Rugby,

P. Tschaikowsky
Conservatoire de Musique
   Moskau.

G. Augener Esq. X)
Newgate Street 86
   London E.C.

Jonas Lie.
7. Avenue de la grande-Armée,
   Paris

Francesco Berger
6, York Street, Portman Square
   London

Fru Wilma Norman - Neruda
20 Linden Gardens
   Bayswater.
   London, W.

Anton Hartvigson
18, Fulham Place
   Maida Hill W.
   London

X) 5 The Cedars, Clapham Common,
   London, S.W.

Some addresses in Grieg's 1888 pocket-book

old Delius and the 31-year-old Sinding, and one cannot help but feel that Grieg was rejuvenated by these companionships.

The first issue of Christiania's *Nordisk Musik-Tidende* for 1888 announced Grieg's forthcoming visit to England to the composer's compatriots. 'Edvard Grieg will be undertaking at the end of March a trip to London, where at the Philharmonic Society he will be appearing before an English public for the first time, both as composer, conductor and pianist.'[60] The journal also noted that Wilhelmina Norman-Neruda had recently played Grieg's Violin Sonata no. 1 with great success at one of the Popular Concerts in London.

At the same time, the composer's notebook begins for the first time to take on an English flavour. Eaton Faning's name is one of the first to figure, Grieg carefully – if not quite accurately – noting '(London.)' after the Harrow address. Adela Wodehouse, of 56 Chester Square, is defined as a 'musical friend of Miss Smyth'. Mr Fritz Delius has evidently gone home from Leipzig to Claremont, Bradford. C. C. Macrae lives at 6 Cambridge Terrace, Regents Park, Grieg noting that he is a friend of Thorvald Beyer and that he is a music-lover, sportsman and salmon-fisher who is related by marriage to the proprietor of the *Illustrated London News*. The A. Pettersson of 19 Warwick Street, Rugby, is of course Grieg's Leipzig fellow-student Andreas Pettersson, now permanently domiciled and teaching music in England. P. Tschaïkowsky, Grieg's note tells us, can be reached at the Conservatoire de Musique, Moskau. The two composers had met for the first time at a New Year's party at the Brodskys' in Leipzig, at which Brahms had also been present, and each had taken an instant liking to the other. Significant names and addresses follow on in rapid succession: George Augener, whose business and private addresses are separately recorded, Francesco Berger, Norman-Neruda, Narciso Vert, Frederic Cowen, Dannreuther, Carlotta Elliott and Charles Hallé. Then there are two Danes, the pianist Anton Hartvigson (1841–1919), a teacher at the Normal College in London, and the soprano Otta Brønnum (1869–1949), living at 58 Harley Street; she sang frequently in England for several years from the late 1880s and performed in 1888 at the opening of a large Danish-English exhibition at the Albert Hall. Shortly after this, she sang at the Norwegian Club in London, where 'her beautiful rendering of Grieg, including "Solveig's Song" and "Min tankes tanke" . . . evoked strong emotions of nostalgia'.[61] When he travels by public transport to Steinway's in Lower Seymour Street, Grieg notes that he needs to get off at Orchard Street in Oxford Street. We are then left with Charles G. Rotter, of Ivy House, The Burroughs, Hendon, identifiable only through a letter his wife wrote to Nina Grieg in May. In it she refers to her sister Marie (who evidently knew the Griegs well) and expresses a wish to get to know the Griegs while they are in London.[62] Born in Germany, Clara and Charles Rotter were of independent means and were now British citizens, but it seems that they were not to reappear in the Grieg story. Then 'Hermann' is named in Grieg's notebook; he can, temporarily at least, be reached at 10 Lexington Street, Golden Square. This was in fact G. L. Theodor Herrmann, Max Abraham's right-hand man, responsible for the financial side of the Peters business in Leipzig and consequently paymaster of Grieg's generous honoraria from the company. Delius earns a second entry in Grieg's notebook in May, himself writing down for the older composer the address of his uncle Theodor Delius in Paris, an address to which Delius was very shortly to travel.

The first note of alarm of the year came with Joachim's advice that Grieg should bring forward his London visit by a week or two so as to avoid the Easter period. It would be no good trying to give any further concerts at this particular time of year, and Joachim himself would be leaving London then. Grieg would see from this that he would miss the opportunity of setting up a chamber concert at which they both might play. The composer consequently put the case to Berger, asking if an earlier date might be possible. Berger's reply, dated 4 January 1887 [*sic*], was terse and to the point. There *was* only one Philharmonic Society date earlier than 22 March in the forthcoming season, and that was 15 March, when Clara Schumann had already been engaged to play. Grieg had accepted the engagement for the 22nd and Berger felt obliged to remind him of the fact. Joachim, he said, had been mistaken in suggesting that the short Easter break should have any serious effect on the concert season. Grieg should not say yes on one occasion and no on the next, but should keep to his word.

Berger was not being entirely transparent in his reference to the London Season. Little more than two years earlier, a perceptive French commentator had told his readers that Easter was ill-suited to concert-giving (and by extension to concert-going):

> Easter is not the signal for pleasures, rather the contrary, it is the signal for defec-tions; everyone leaves, on the pretext of holidaying, to take the country or the seaside air for a week, indeed sometimes two or three. May is the month of the trumpet call . . . Generally speaking, the Prince of Wales's Ball, which takes place on the Queen's birthday, is akin to the three blows that usher in the rise of the curtain . . . All this lasts until the middle of July.[63]

Irritated by Berger's rather peremptory tone, Grieg replied to him from Leipzig on 9 January:

> Your letter of 4th January has both alarmed and pained me. I did not write to you that I did not wish to fulfil my responsibilities, but only asked in a polite way if it might be possible to bring forward my 22nd March appearance at 'The Philharmonic Society' to an earlier date. In the meantime you reply in a manner that is the opposite of polite, and I suspect that you have either written in a moment of irritation, something for which there was absolutely no reason, or that you have misunderstood my letter.
>   I look forward to your elucidation of the matter and sign myself
>   with respect
>   Edvard Grieg

The problem was, in the event, quickly settled, Berger regretting that an unfor-tunate way of expressing himself should have caused offence. He might well, he explained, have misunderstood one particular phrase in Grieg's letter, and this had probably contributed to the misunderstanding. To demonstrate the Society's good faith, it would be a pleasure for them to try to arrange an engagement at the Crystal Palace Concerts for Grieg, to follow the Philharmonic's own concert. For his own part Berger offered, too, to consult with local agents and so try to obtain for Grieg further engagements in the provinces.

Grieg was mollified and, writing from Leipzig on 15 January, happily explored the way forward, while at the same time declining on health grounds the offer of provincial engagements. He saw the proposed Crystal Palace concert as a means of bringing forward two of his choral works, *Land-sighting* and *Before a Southern Convent*. In the end it was, however, left to August Manns, conductor at the Crystal Palace, to point out that he had no vacant date available, all of his programmes for the season already having been decided before Christmas. Otherwise one of Grieg's thoughts had been to give a recital or two soon after the main concert. Berger told him that there was only one really good agent in London and that was

Vert, but because Grieg did not – in England at least – as yet have any reputation as a virtuoso pianist, Vert would almost certainly not agree to arrange a recital or recitals except at Grieg's own cost.

While all this was going on, the Birmingham Festival engagement for later in the summer was finally confirmed. Grieg had agreed to conduct the first performance of his *In Autumn*. He also agreed to do his best to ensure that his *Holberg Suite* would not be given a second performance in England before then. Life in Leipzig meanwhile continued to be convivial, as letters to friends make clear. There was one particular theatre visit in the company of Sinding, Halvorsen and Delius, at which all enjoyed the evening so much that they sat up until two in the morning enjoying Grieg's favourite delicacy, oysters, washed down with good wine. All the same, there was in Grieg a constant undertow of worry about London, a state of mind confirmed in a letter to Frants Beyer that would persist until the first concert was safely past.

> In March it's off to London. But the £ you talk about are rather going to have to be laid out rather than gathered in, as what I'll be earning is so infinitesimally small compared to the high costs of the stay there. But – it has to be done once.[64]

Expressions of reluctance in respect of the impending visit abound, particularly in subsequent letters to Beyer, Grieg's closest friend and neighbour, but Grieg also acknowledged that, like it or not, he had now to 'get on with the job'. Twenty-five minutes a day devoted to gymnastics, as he proudly reported, meant that his health was holding up well; and to that greater sense of well-being one could no doubt count in the contribution made by the company of his new, younger friends and the admiration and affection that they showed for him. Yet the forebodings continued. 'I'm really sorry for you where the trip to London is concerned,' wrote Beyer on 7 April, 'knowing well that you would prefer to be elsewhere . . . How I'd love to pop over to Hull and London to be with you.'[65] Beyer was to continue to encourage Grieg right up to the time of his concert: 'You're now over there in London and the concert is approaching', he would write on 25 April. 'May you only stay fit and well, and the rest will take care of itself . . . Just think of Norway and home and the spring, and you'll knock the English sideways with your playing'.[66]

The publicity machine was at work by now, with the *Nordisk Musik-Tidende* again drawing attention to Grieg's engagement in London and adding, slightly misleadingly, 'after which he will attend the great Music Festival in Birmingham'. The journal also referred to a quite lengthy article on Grieg appearing in the current issue of *The Musical Times* and to the fact that Miss Hermine Kopp had recently appeared at one of the Popular Concerts and sung some Grieg songs. She had made 'a very favourable impression on the large audience'.[67] *The Musical Times* piece, unsigned and entitled simply 'Edvard Grieg', begins on an odd note. How could Englishmen begin to understand the artistic character and work of someone like Grieg? We, the masters of a great empire, could hardly be expected fully to comprehend the intense national feelings of poor countries, and we even grow irritated and impatient with the Scots, Welsh and Irish and with manifestations of their own 'local' spirit.

> The Norwegian has a poor country, counting for little in the world's estimation of physical and moral forces, and overshadowed as a State by its greater and wealthier neighbour, Sweden. But he loves his motherland with a passionate devotion; he is proud of her traditions and history – the history of an unconquerable few; his affection for her valleys and mountains is a commanding passion; he answers as no other can to the spirit of her literature and art, and is far more proud of all she is, and hopeful of all she may be, than the dwellers in mighty lands can conceive. This intense sentiment finds many outlets, but we are concerned here only with its influence upon the art of music.
>
> More than most northern races, the Norwegians are lovers of music, to the instinct of which everything in the physical features and the history of their country makes appeal . . . music entwines itself with every form of the life of this interesting people.

Coming down at last from the heights of his introductory remarks, the writer went on to refer to an article by Otto Goldschmidt, written long before for *Macmillan's Magazine*. Goldschmidt had never heard the people sing during his long walks through the streets, lanes, high-roads and woods of south-east England. On the other hand, in the Norwegian countryside he had listened to a girl singing folksongs to the accompaniment of the *langeleik* and had been transported into another world reaching back to a fabled past. Seen in retrospect, what Goldschmidt had not done, of course, was to have sought out (with the later passion of a Cecil Sharp, Percy Grainger or Vaughan Williams) the living folk-song that was always there in the English countryside. He had not (like Grainger – or like Grainger's idol Evald Tang Kristensen in Denmark) invited himself into the homes of the poor or into the grey workhouses where the old still remembered in song the words and melodies passed on to them by preceding generations. He had simply strolled in the open air and had been surprised that he had not heard people sing.

Endorsing Goldschmidt's words, *The Musical Times* went on to refer to current trends in musical naturalism, although it was a long way from the truth, stated as an inalienable fact, that Scandinavian composers 'almost entirely limit themselves to the musical dialect of their own land'. Nonetheless, as Chopin was to Poland and Dvořák was to Bohemia, so was Grieg to Norway. They were all 'patriots in music, embodiments of the musical instincts of their people.' At this period, relatively little was known in England about Grieg's background, and his life is described as having been 'singularly uneventful'. His Leipzig career is outlined briefly. Apart from this we learn that he was believed to have lived entirely in Norway. There is no reference to the Grieg family's British, or more particularly Scottish, connections; only that Grieg's father 'represented some foreign country as consul' in Bergen.

Nonetheless, when the baggage of ignorance has been discarded and Grieg's music is reviewed, the air becomes clearer and the writer more positive. The stress is laid upon the short piano pieces (there is not, for example, a single mention of the Piano Concerto), the reviewer leaning heavily on the albums published by Novello, Ewer & Co. He remarks on melodies that are 'strongly marked by Norwegian characteristics . . . artless and charming'. Two albums of *Lyric Pieces*, Op. 38 and Op. 43, are also at the writer's hand: there is hardly a piece that is 'altogether free from local colouring'. Also touched on are the *Two Elegiac Melodies*, with a reference to their recent airing at the London Symphony Concerts. Here Grieg is seen as 'carrying the sentiment and character of his country's art into compositions of a larger form and higher class'. And if the two Violin Sonatas, Op. 8 and Op. 13, together with the Cello Sonata, Op. 36, show the more cosmopolitan side of Grieg, they are still infused 'more or less of the national dialect and feeling', particularly in respect of the opening of the first Sonata. The writer sums up:

> Foreigners cannot be expected to share all the sympathy which a Norwegian must feel for what is national in Grieg's art, but we can enjoy, and be thankful for an opportunity of enjoying, its freshness and beauty. The conventional language of music is so far exhausted that only a man of genius can hope to command attention in using it. The man with no genius is confined to platitudes, and his hearers are consequently driven to weariness. The remedy for this is – and musicians are beginning to find it out – a closer alliance with that which is distinctly national, which means resort to the original sources of music as they lie, a living power, deep down in the hearts of the people. There, as Grieg proves, may strength and variety be found, and there may the secret be learned which enables a musician to emulate the fabled deeds of Orpheus, who 'made trees, And the mountain tops that freeze, Bow themselves when he did sing'. In music, as in other arts, we must now and then go back to nature. The painter who composes landscapes in his studio soon becomes stilted, artificial, conventional, and so does the musician in an analogous case. There is no doing without the breezy hill-side, the quiet sun-lit lake, the magnificent ocean, the peaceful valley, the calm summer-day, the roaring winter-storm. One of Edvard Grieg's claims to honour and regard is that he has shown the way to nature and the advantage of her company.[68]

A further puff for Grieg's visit appeared a few pages on in the same issue of *The Musical Times*:

> The article on Edvard Grieg, which appears in another part of our present issue, will be read with none the less interest because the Norwegian composer is expected to visit England in connection with the performance of one of his works at a Philharmonic Concert, and also to be present at the forthcoming Birmingham Festival. Our notice of Grieg may help to invest him with an added personal interest, but, in any case, a cordial welcome awaits the musician from the North. England has not always been pleased to see the 'hardy Norseman', but times have changed. He comes now with the music of the song-bird, not the hoarse croak of the raven.[69]

Dannreuther meanwhile was busily programming Grieg in his series of Chamber Concerts, *The Monthly Musical Record* noting that 'high-class Lieder by Brahms, Grieg, &c., [are] *en vogue* at these concerts'.[70] A month later, under the identical

heading of 'Edvard [*sic*] Dannreuther's Chamber Concerts', the journal reported
that

> Some important novelties were again brought forward at the second and third con-
> cert of the series, viz: a violin sonata, Op. 45, by Grieg, but which, except in the re-
> markably bright and fascinating Finale in Northern dance rhythm, proved inferior to
> his magnificent violoncello sonata, Op. 36 (published also for the piano and violin),
> from which indeed whole passages are bodily transferred into the new work.[71]

The Musical Times had other ideas about the Violin Sonata, played on 19 January at one of 'Mr. Dannreuther's Musical Evenings', deeming it as music to be 'far
superior' to Navrátil's Piano Quintet in C minor, which had also featured on the
same programme.

> Here we have music full of character and energy, a little vague perhaps in matters
> of detail, but never dull. The last movement is in the Scandinavian composer's best
> manner, and the whole Sonata should be brought forward at some of our leading
> Concerts.[72]

National character as expressed in music was of growing interest to the journals
of the day. Reviewing the 20-year-old Hamish MacCunn's 'ballad for orchestra'
The Ship o' the Fiend, premiered in March, and noting that it was a 'powerful piece
of tone painting', *The Monthly Musical Record* hazarded: 'Whether Mr. Hamish
McCunn will develop into a Scotch Grieg, Dvořák, or Tschaïkowsky, time must
show.'[73]

Aware that Joachim would be absent from London at the time of his visit and
with his mind turned to the problem of securing a second engagement, Grieg
decided to approach Wilhelmina Norman-Neruda, a major name in the musical
world and by some distance the leading woman violinist of the day. Born in Bohemia in 1838, she had married the Swedish composer Ludvig Norman, but later
separated from him. In great demand throughout Europe, she settled in London in
1869. Her second marriage, on 26 July 1888, some three years after Norman's death
in Stockholm, was to be to Sir Charles Hallé. Grieg had got to know her when he
accompanied her in a performance of his first Violin Sonata at the first concert he
gave in Christiania in 1866. He now wrote to her, care of Francesco Berger, from
Leipzig on 6 February reminding her that some years had passed since they were
last together in Copenhagen, an occasion on which he had asked her if he might at
some time again have the pleasure of playing together with her. She had been care-
less enough, he told her, to reply 'Yes, if you come to London'. Well, now he *was*
coming in mid-March, and he would be unhappy if she were to escape him.

Neruda penned her reply from the Adelphi Hotel in Liverpool on 19 February, her absence from London having been the reason for Grieg's letter only just
having reached her. She agreed, with pleasure, but just as Joachim had done, she
warned him about the problems posed by the Easter holiday, a 'highly unfavour-
able' time for concert-going, as Society people (who would be expected to make up

a significant part of the audience) then took themselves off to the country. Luckily, events had taken — even before she wrote — an unexpected turn, with Berger conceding that Grieg would be more likely to secure the extra engagement he was seeking once the inconvenience of an Easter timing were removed. In consequence, the Philharmonic Society would do their best to help him by rescheduling the date of their Grieg concert to 3 May. London, he told Grieg, would be much busier in May than in March, with better results for Grieg's affairs. Grieg annotated Berger's letter in English: 'Accept 3rd May insted [*sic*] of 22nd March', and the deed was finally done. He informed Neruda, telling her that he and Nina now intended to spend the whole of May in London, that he had composed two more violin sonatas since they last had played together, and that he was enclosing them for her to read through. He was still very unsure as to how to go about actually arranging recitals in London and asked for her advice as well as for her terms. To Berger, who had been hoping for a larger work than the *Two Elegiac Melodies* — which had been given so recently in London — Grieg wrote that he was anxious to keep them on the programme. After all, they had not, in London, actually been conducted by the composer, had they?

A few days earlier he had taken a long afternoon walk in fine spring-like weather in Leipzig with Sinding and Delius and had penned on his return to his lodgings a letter to Frants Beyer.

> Since February 1st I've been a Conservatory student in the mornings, that's to say that I practise the piano for several hours so that I won't completely disgrace myself in London. I horribly regret promising to play my Piano Concerto, but it's done now, and I can't go back on it.[74]

Meanwhile, he set about keeping Tchaikovsky informed of his London arrangements. 'My first concert in London takes place on 3rd May. Where will you be then?' asked Grieg on 27 February. Tchaikovsky had already accepted an invitation from the Philharmonic Society to conduct his own music in London. He replied on 2 March,

> From Prague I sent a telegram to Francesco Berger telling him that I would like to perform with *my friend Grieg* on 22nd March. But he replied that this was impossible, since you would not be playing until 3rd May. I will, however, conduct my *Serenade* and *Suite* on 22nd March. It's very sad that we will not see each other in London.

Once the new date had been settled, Grieg informed George Augener that he and Nina intended to arrive in London around 23 April. Augener's address, 5 The Cedars, Clapham Common, was to be Grieg's first in England since the rooms off the Strand that he, his brother and his parents had occupied more than a quarter of a century earlier. Augener was more than happy with the change of date: March could after all be 'quite raw'. He and his wife would do all they could to make the Griegs feel at home, promising them peace and quiet. Furthermore Grieg could choose a room with piano on either the first, second or third floor; it would be ideal for work, as it looked out over 'a mile-long heath'. Augener's invitation to stay had in fact come as a considerable relief to Grieg, who estimated that the Philharmonic's fee would do no more than cover the travel costs for himself and Nina.

> If I can get to give a couple of these so-called 'Recitals' with Nina and the help of one or two prominent string players, then we'll get by, but only then. It's the best time, May is really the high season. We'll soon see – I have so little experience in this sort of thing.[75]

Grieg busily alerted various of his friends to the change of date. The news from Tchaikovsky that their dates were not to coincide had of course disappointed him. To Julius Röntgen in Amsterdam Grieg wrote on 3 March: he and Nina would be leaving for London towards the end of April. 'But sadly, because of our seasickness, I'll have to travel there by way of Calais and Dover instead of Holland.'

With the possibility of a Crystal Palace Concert having disappeared (Berger had approached Manns on Grieg's behalf, but, as he told Grieg, 'with his usual lack of courtesy he has simply not replied to me'), and with Berger's further advice that an agent like Vert would be expensive in respect of setting up any further recitals, Grieg decided to wait until he was in London before proceeding any further. The expense could clearly be kept down by having Nina and himself as performers, and the only other performing fee would need to go to Neruda. Should his Philharmonic Concert prove to be the success that he hoped for, then he ought, after all, to be able to get a good audience for a second engagement in London.

Grieg's constant anxieties about his forthcoming trip were aired in letters to his closest friend. There was still a month to go before his departure when he wrote to tell Beyer:

> If only I had this damned England-tour behind me, because there's nothing to be gained from it, but a goodly portion of my health to lose. I can't give of my best by travelling around and playing to people, something I feel more and more, nor will it happen again. It's not a problem with chamber music and small things, but when it's a matter of my having to use a sledgehammer on the piano, I can't manage to produce the effect I'm aiming at but simply finish up as a wreck.
>
> The time for departure is now rapidly approaching. We're off in the middle of April and hope to have the company of the Hardangervidda man [Grieg's affectionate nickname for Delius, who had been on long walking tours of this mountain/moorland region of Norway].[76]

Just three days later, in a further letter to Beyer, Grieg intimated that he was fortunate to be under the generous, even paternal wing of a publisher of the calibre of Max Abraham, adding:

> You see that the gold-mine is in Leipzig and hardly in London. All that business of high life and paid invitations to make music in their society circles until well past midnight isn't my sort of thing either. I'm not only unpractical, but too proud for it too and anyway in the end my health says no thank you.

I'm determined to spend as little time as possible in London.[77]

Invitations were beginning to come in. The Fanings hoped that Grieg might actually come to spend a few days with them. 'I think you would like Harrow and its surroundings', wrote Carrie Faning, '& should Mrs. Grieg be coming with you I need not say how pleased we shall be to make her acquaintance and will do our best to make you both comfortable.'[78] Had Grieg kept to his original dates he might well have taken up the Fanings' invitation to attend the Harrow School concert on 24 March.

From an artistic and pecuniary view, a perhaps more attractive offer came from W. J. Leaver in south-east London. Charles Stephens, honorary treasurer of the Philharmonic Society and therefore a close associate of Berger, had told him of Grieg's forthcoming visit to London, and Leaver asked if he would like to give a piano recital at Blackheath and what his terms would be.[79] Grieg evidently – and understandably – expressed interest, and it seems that he ultimately met Leaver in London on 9 May and agreed terms. A letter finally settling the date for the recital – Friday 18 May at The Rink, Blackheath – and asking if Nina Grieg might sing was dispatched by Leaver on Saturday 12 May, with the writer proposing to meet the composer in town the following morning to help arrange the programme. But something went wrong, and on 16 May a dispirited Leaver was to send the last of his four letters to Grieg, full of regret that the composer's 'indisposition' would prevent his appearance.

One Leipzig fellow-student who was not to see Grieg in London was Walter Bache. His sudden demise on 26 March, from complications that developed following a chill, was widely reported in the press. His death, felt *The Musical Times*, 'will be counted as a great loss to the musical profession'.[80] Among the many mourners at his funeral in Hampstead on 31 March were the new principal of the Royal Academy of Music, Alexander Mackenzie, John Francis Barnett, Franklin Taylor, Eaton Faning, and one of the Hartvigson brothers.[81]

Meanwhile, Tchaikovsky's London concert had come and gone. His appearance at the Philharmonic, when he had conducted his Serenade for strings and the 'Tema con Variazioni' from his Suite no. 3 for orchestra had been a great success. The rest of the items in the concert – which included the first London performance of Svendsen's *Norwegian Rhapsody* no. 2 – was directed by the Society's regular conductor Frederic Cowen. That Tchaikovsky shared elements of Grieg's temperament is shown in a letter he wrote to his publisher at the end of a long tour that had begun in Leipzig at the beginning of January – where the foundations of that firm friendship with his fellow-composer from Norway had been laid – and had finished in London.

I have expended a great deal of money and, even more, health and energy. In return
I have gained some celebrity, but every hour I ask myself – why? Is it worthwhile?
And I come to the conclusion that it is far better to live quietly, without fame.[82]

Brodsky had told Grieg that Tchaikovsky was back at home, so Grieg wrote to his Russian friend on 12 April: he and Nina were off to London at the end of the following week 'and for my part, alas, I have to say that I'm not looking forward to it. I'm very anxious to hear what your impression was.' Tchaikovsky's reply indicated that letters he had sent both to Grieg and to Brodsky seemed to have gone astray. At all events he did not comment on his own experiences but suspected that all would by then have gone well for Grieg in London: 'You are highly regarded and popular in London, which you are anyway everywhere.'[83]

Grieg also wrote to Beyer on the 12th, a long, long letter only completed on the following day:

> We are going to travel on the 22nd, so will be in London on the afternoon of the 23rd. I'm not looking forward to the trip, that's for sure, and have a sort of dark premonition that something unpleasant may happen. All my feelings pull me towards home and absolutely not to England, for the damned '£-feeling' is no real feeling at all. I've mused on doing some stupid thing or other so as to be quit of the whole business, but I've already reported sick once before, so that won't work, and I don't know any other way out.[84]

Delius, he told Beyer, had suggested that he excuse himself by saying that an old aunt of his had died. 'That's just like him!' A few days earlier, he and Nina had accompanied their young English friend to the station at Leipzig to wave him off to England. Their 'little colony' had finally disbanded. 'I already miss you all very much', wrote Delius after arriving home:

> If you should feel like spending a day or two here in Bradford I should be very pleased to make you & your wife welcome, but if not I hope we will meet at least once in London before my departure for Paris.[85]

During all this time the Birmingham Festival arrangements were continuing to tick over. Charles Harding had written on 23 February asking when Grieg would be coming to London, 'as I am hoping you will be able to come to my house for a day or two or at any rate that we may meet'. Grieg had somehow failed to register the exact date of the Birmingham event and, nonchalantly scanning a Leipzig paper, had been given a jolt to learn that the festival was to take place in the final week of August. He knew that he was expected to be there at least a week beforehand. All this meant that plans he had gradually been formulating to make a tour with Frants Beyer in the Jotunheim mountains at the time would have to be abandoned. He reassured his friend that a 'Jotun-tour' meant much more to him than ten Birmingham Festivals and that, if the timing were right, he would quit the rostrum like a shot after conducting his own pieces and come straight back for a joint holiday at the tail end of the Norwegian summer. The rest of the festival could go hang. At all events he was to meet Harding in London soon and would find out exactly where the arrangements for his participation in the festival stood.

The gradual accretion of new names and new contacts in his notebook gave

Grieg yet further cause for alarm. Beyer's cousin Thorvald, a Bergen bookseller, had recommended a visit to his friend Macrae. Grieg told Beyer, 'between ourselves', that he would have quite enough to do, given the little free time he expected to have at his disposal (and given, too, the constant worries about his health and strength), rather than to make visits that in the circumstances would not strictly be necessary.

Fan-letters from England, perhaps slow to come in during the preceding years, were beginning to arrive and would become a regular feature in Grieg's life both during and after his first visit to London. A certain T. T. Rowe of Nottingham, for example, no doubt intending to be at the Philharmonic Concert, wrote to tell the composer that he was giving in Nottingham a concert that would include music by Grieg and that moreover he was hoping at some stage during the next winter season to give an entire Grieg concert.[86] Meanwhile, various artists were including works by Grieg in their programmes. Winifred Robinson, accompanied by Fanny Davies, concluded her concert on 17 April at the Prince's Hall by playing the first Violin Sonata. Two days later Helen Trust sang 'Solveig's Song' in Birmingham at a concert that included the *Two Elegiac Melodies* for strings. The 'new' Violin Sonata, no. 3, was given by a Mr Bernhardt at the Prince's Hall on 9 May, accompanied by Madame de Llana (a pianist, *The Musical Times* noted much later in the year, 'of whose antecedents we are entirely ignorant'). The distinguished cellist W. E. Whitehouse featured the Cello Sonata in a concert at the same venue on 22 May, with Joseph Ludwig, better known as a violinist, at the piano. Also on the programme, the soprano Bertha Moore gave a 'tasteful rendering of songs', including one or more by Grieg, a process she repeated with 'Solveig's Song' at the Marlborough Rooms on 6 June.[87] *The Musical Times* carried advertisements from Novello, Ewer & Co. in its March, April, and May issues for several Grieg piano albums as well as for an album of 24 of the composer's songs. 'Grieg-fever', in other words, was beginning to affect musical England.

II

FIRST SUCCESSES IN ENGLAND

'A HEARTY WELCOME TO THESE SHORES
TO EDVARD GRIEG'

GRIEG's destination – 5, The Cedars, Clapham Common – was to be the London base for most of his concert tours in England. Situated on the north side of the Common, a huge expanse of green and open land that can scarcely have changed from then until today, George Augener's house was an imposing edifice at the western end of a terrace incorporating five tall houses that fronted the Common. The portico entrance to number 5 was actually round the corner in Cedars Road, running due north from the Common. Immediately across this road to the west and also facing the Common was a similar terrace, erected at the same time in the mid-1860s. The site had originally been occupied by a large mansion, 'The Cedars', built in 1718 for the nephew of Samuel Pepys, the diarist; this was demolished in 1864, and the architect J. T. Knowles jr had erected the terraces, which still stand today. When first built, they had been quickly bought up, being considered by the more prosperous inhabitants of what was then a fairly genteel suburb to be the most desirable residences in the neighbourhood. At some point during the 1890s there was a change of name, and Grieg's letters home in 1897 bear the address 47, North Side, Clapham Common. But this was still the same house, and it remained the London home of the Augener family. Over half a century later a local historian recorded that 'on the ridge over the main entrance in Cedars Road may still be seen the flagpole from which he [George Augener] flew the Norwegian flag when Edward Grieg stayed with him during his visit to England to give pianoforte recitals at St. James's Hall'.[1] The flagpole, however, no longer exists today.

The Griegs left Leipzig as planned on Monday 23 April 1888, travelling by train via Cologne and taking the Calais–Dover ferry to arrive in London at five in the afternoon of the following day. Grieg's notebook indicates that their luggage had been heavily overweight and that there had been extra to pay at Leipzig station. The Channel crossing, as Nina was to tell Delius, had been 'appalling'. One of Grieg's final actions before departure had been politely to decline the

Philharmonic Society's proposal, out of the blue, that he stay on in London and conduct the Society's concerts of 31 May and 16 June, its final concerts of the season. Frederic Cowen had some time earlier accepted a lucrative Australian engagement as musical director of the Melbourne Centennial Exhibition and so would have to miss these concerts. Grieg had by no means been the first to be invited to step into Cowen's shoes, Von Bülow having been a prime target of the Society – and there had been others. In the end it was nonetheless to be a Norwegian who would accept the engagement, Johan Svendsen opening the 31 May programme with his own Symphony in D major.

It is clear that there had been some confusion in Grieg's and Svendsen's minds over the Philharmonic Society's invitation, a letter from Svendsen on 27 April showing concern that both had been invited at the same time to conduct the final concerts. He charitably accepted that the Society needed swiftly to be assured of a conductor and so had written to several possible substitutes at the same time, adding, 'It would be nice to hear how you are getting on in London. I feel sure that you will derive much pleasure from your stay there.'[2] Grieg's excuse to Berger for declining the commission was that he was committed to a Nordic Music Festival that was to be held in Copenhagen at the beginning of June. In point of fact he could probably have taken on both of the London concerts as well as the Copenhagen festival, since the latter was scheduled for 3–10 June. No doubt, however, he found all the extra travelling, as well perhaps as delayed or last-minute rehearsals, to be altogether too daunting a prospect. In a letter to Beyer on 20 April he described his decision simply as an 'extravagant' one, an extra £50 having gone to the devil.

George Augener had written to Max Abraham in Leipzig ten days before his guests were due to arrive. The Griegs would be staying at his home, and they should – in case it were not possible for someone to meet them at Victoria Station – take a cab (a 'four wheeler') for the 25-minute drive to Clapham. He even took pains to enclose a number of address-labels for his guests' various items of luggage. Grieg duly engaged a cab at the station, and they were soon settled in at 5 The Cedars. The first full day was spent fairly quietly, with Grieg certainly needing time to recover from the long journey. But the pressure was already on, and letters and invitations arrived daily. One of the earliest to be sent had come from the wife of his fellow-student from the early Leipzig years, Franklin Taylor, now living in Bayswater. Written on 23 April, it had been sent to Andreas Pettersson in Rugby, with a request for it to be forwarded. Pettersson had duly complied, including a letter of his own at the same time. He had not known that Grieg would be coming to London so soon, but assured the composer that if he were to pay a visit to the Taylors he would be warmly received there. He himself had been asked to come too.[3] Mrs Taylor herself had not met Grieg, but she reminded him how he and Taylor had been friends 'in the old days' and how they would 'greatly like to make you welcome at our house one day during your stay in London'. Her husband was away at

London in Grieg's time

the time, the reason for her writing this letter. But once he was back they would get together old friends like Mr and Mrs Petterssen [*sic*] of Rugby, through whom she was sending her letter. They were friends too with the Fanings, Mrs Taylor supposing that the Griegs would be going to stay with them in Harrow. Meanwhile, she would be coming to Grieg's Philharmonic Concert on 3 May.

Another friend who quickly got in touch was the Danish pianist Anton Hartvigson, of Maida Hill in west London. Hartvigson had already written in February suggesting that Grieg give a recital in London with Nina, something that he assured Grieg would be a guaranteed success. Now that Grieg had actually arrived in town, he proposed a meeting: 'there are a few things I'd like to discuss with you'.[4] He evidently called on Grieg in Clapham, but the composer was not at home at the time, so the subject that Hartvigson had wanted to air in person had instead to be detailed in a long letter. It largely took the form of a detailed description of the background and activities of The Royal Normal College and Academy of Music for the Blind, at which institution in Upper Norwood Anton and his brother Frits – both long since settled in London – taught piano, Anton for five years now and Frits for twelve:

> It was founded by Dr. Campbell, who is American, 12 years ago and now has 170 pupils; Dr. Campbell is blind himself and is a capable musician; perhaps you have already heard of him; two years ago he was in Norway and travelled through much of the country by velocipede with his eldest son and his wife.

The college, which lay close by the Crystal Palace, boasted a distinguished teaching staff, and among the musicians who had come to perform could be numbered Bülow, Pachmann, Manns and Sophie Menter. Hans Richter had paid the college a visit, describing his afternoon there as one of the most interesting he had ever spent. Hartvigson came to the point:

> I will only say that your name is held in honour and the highest esteem by all of the pupils and your compositions are constantly played there, and I want now to ask you if, finally, you can come out there to pay a visit; when the students heard that you were coming [to London], they all said, aah, if only he would come out here, it would be marvellous to *see* (they all talk as if they were sighted) and hear Grieg.

Before he closed, Hartvigson, not for the first time, suggested that should Grieg give a recital in London and should he want some help with any of his four-hand works, he might care to think of Hartvigson himself. He followed this proposal with a characteristic quirky 'ha! ha!'[5] Whether Grieg was able in the end to visit the college is doubtful, as the correspondence closes at this point.

It is possible, in some measure at least, to reconstruct a good number of Grieg's engagements during this, his first full month to be spent in England, by recourse either to his notebook relating to the period, to his correspondence, to press reports, or to the memoirs or other memoranda left by those he met. His notebooks rarely give precise dates, just odd jottings of days, perhaps, and times for which particular meetings or engagements are scheduled. Berger had immediately been in touch: he had, he wrote, much of importance to impart to Grieg, and he suggested times when they might meet at his Portman Square office. However, all was not going well, as Nina reported to Delius on the 26th:

> Grieg has such a frightful lot to do that he simply has no time at present for letter-

writing. I am afraid that he is not in a very good mood, he gets annoyed about every-one and everything and keeps wishing he had never come to London. I hope things will be better after the concert. The weather is atrocious, windy and cold almost like in winter, I can't tell you how frozen we are, and we long for our lovely Leipzig days again.[6]

A few days later Grieg wrote to Svendsen, whose reply makes clear how dissatisfied Grieg was during the period leading up to his first concert. 'I am sorry to learn from your letter that you do not feel particularly agreeably affected by the conditions in London, but it is only the beginning, and I shall hope that you will end up by enjoying your stay there.'[7]

Grieg went into town for the first time that Thursday. In his pocket-book he notes a railway fare on the 26th, seemingly pinpointing it as the day on which he travelled in by train from Clapham to be met at Waterloo by a young pianist, Stanley Hawley (1867–1916). Such at least is the claim of the composer Eric Coates, who recorded

> the lovely story of the time when he [Hawley] was a student at the Academy and was sent to meet Edvard Grieg at Waterloo Station when this great musician came over to England to play his concerto at a Royal Philharmonic Society Concert at Queen's Hall. Grieg had promised to come to the Academy in Tenterden Street, where he had signified his intention of hearing Stanley Hawley play his concerto with Mackenzie and the Academy Orchestra. Could Hawley get Grieg across Waterloo Bridge? He refused to budge, standing there in his tweed cape, mushroom hat and leggings, fascinated by the shipping down towards Tower Bridge; talking, gesticulating, pointing, anything rather than bother about such trivial things as pianoforte concertos in A minor. After a good deal of persuasion, Grieg consented to continue the walk to the Academy, and, judging by the way Hawley said he stopped and looked at everything *en route*, it must have taken literally hours. At any rate, Tenterden Street was reached at last and the concerto, as played by Stanley Hawley, made such a deep impression on the composer that he said it was quite absurd for him to be playing the work himself at the Queen's Hall the next day. As Hawley played it so much better than he – Stanley Hawley must certainly take his place; he insisted on it and would not hear another word. However, when it was pointed out to him that he was under contract to the Royal Philharmonic Society and also how disappointed the audience would be at having to hear an Academy student instead of the great maestro himself, the enthusiastic little Norwegian smiled and saw reason.[8]

Perhaps young Hawley (who had entered the Academy in January 1884 at the age of 16) did at some stage take a walk in London with Grieg, although it would not, when he was a student, have been to Queen's Hall, which was not opened until 1893. Nor was the Philharmonic Society yet 'Royal'. Furthermore the Royal Academy of Music has no record of an Academy concert in 1888 that includes the Grieg Concerto; nor in its Minute Books is there any indexed entry for Grieg – something that certainly would have been recorded had he visited Tenterden Street for an Academy event. If we add to this the fact that the Academy's principal concerts during the 1880s were held at St James's Hall, it will be seen that Coates's memory – in this instance at least – was notably fallible.[9]

That said, Stanley Hawley had indeed featured the Allegro molto moderato from Grieg's Concerto at an Academy concert nearly two years earlier, in July 1886, as the 11th of 14 items. He was to gain a fair reputation as a composer and pianist – particularly as an accompanist – and for the last two or three years of his life he was Secretary to the Royal Philharmonic Society. (Berger, who retired in 1911, was briefly succeeded by William Wallace, from whom Hawley took up the reins in 1913.) Hawley's admiration for Grieg's music was genuine and lasting: he was, for example, later to edit albums of Grieg piano solos for the London publisher Alfred Lengnick. Nevertheless, the two letters that are preserved from Hawley to Grieg make no mention of the supposed Academy performance. The first, written from Winchmore Hill, north London, on Wednesday 25 April 1888, asks Grieg if Hawley might see him for a short time 'anytime tomorrow? Thursday or on Saturday afternoon. . . . You may not remember my name but you will remember me when I say I am that enthusiastic (young student) admirer of yours who managed to see you in Bergen last year.' Three days later, Hawley asked Grieg if he might be 'disengaged' on Monday or Tuesday afternoon, as he would dearly love to see him again before the concert.[10]

'Lunch with Herman' (Theodor Herrmann) on Friday 27 April was preceded by a meeting with Frederic Cowen and followed by another with Francesco Berger. Grieg notes a payment, too, on that same day of 2 s. 6 d. to 'Steinway's people'. This first meeting with Cowen might well have taken place much earlier, had Cowen had any luck in the later 1870s when he had performed in Norway while touring in Scandinavia. 'I was very desirous of meeting Grieg while I was in Bergen, but unluckily he was away from home, so I did not have the pleasure of making his acquaintance until he came to London some ten years later.'[11] Cowen had also written to greet the visitor on his arrival in London. He invited Grieg to visit his home on the evening of 2 April (there was to be a first rehearsal that morning for the Philharmonic Society Concert), 'so that you can give me the opportunity to introduce my family, as well as a few musical friends, to you'.[12] Cowen was yet another Leipzig alumnus, having studied at the Conservatory (where he was apparently its youngest student) from 1865 to 1868, and where his friendship with an older fellow-student, Johan Svendsen, had begun. Most of Grieg's first weekend was probably spent at home in Clapham, though a visit to the barber's is noted on Saturday the 28th. There is, for example, no indication that he went to hear Eaton Faning's choral work *The Vikings* (a work that for some time remained popular with choral societies), which was given at a Popular Musical Union concert in the Grosvenor Hotel later that day.[13] The month of April closed with a call on Steinway's on Monday the 30th and a message from Alfred Mapleson, the Philharmonic's music librarian. 'I will send to your house *tomorrow (Tuesday)* for all your music for the

Philharmonic Concert – please kindly *have it left out for me* and oblige.' Record-ing this in his notebook, Grieg also noted that the Concerto – presumably the full score – needed to be sent direct to Cowen.

Delius meanwhile had written from Bradford offering all the help possible until he had to depart for Paris on 6 May. He would arrive in London on 30 April and would be staying at the Metropole Hotel, 'where I shall be constantly at your dis-posal'. He offered to be the Griegs' guide to the sights of London for the first few days in May and invited them to join him for supper at his hotel on the 4th. In the event, Edvard and Nina spent quite some time with their young friend before his departure, with Grieg recording lunches with Delius, and with Delius himself at-tending Grieg's final rehearsal as well as the concert on the 3rd. All duly converged on the Metropole on the evening of the 4th to meet and to dine with Delius's father and mother, who had also come down to London.

Another English musician to get in touch with Grieg was the 23-year-old pianist Ernest Kiver, who around this time was appointed organist at the Brompton Ora-tory. He had embarked on a series of annual chamber concerts at the Prince's Hall in 1885, playing Grieg's Piano Sonata in E minor, a work which he had already given at the Royal Academy of Music, where he had been a student since 1880. At his forthcoming concert in the series, which he hoped Grieg might be able to at-tend on 4 May, he would be accompanying Grieg's latest Violin Sonata (the third, which had only been published in the previous year) and would also be playing the *Ballade. The Musical Times* found the concert 'chiefly interesting on account of the items by Grieg, who is at present one of the "lions" of the musical season'. The *Bal-lade*, it decided, 'is somewhat laboured, though clever, and cannot be numbered among the Scandinavian composer's best utterances. The Sonata, on the other hand, is a very piquant and characteristic work, the *Finale* being especially charm-ing.' Kiver himself was viewed as 'an exceedingly promising young pianist'.[14]

There were still more invitations. One was from Mrs Nina Gould, sister of the music publisher Emile Hatzfeld. Hatzfeld had published Grieg's *Reminiscences from Mountain and Fjord*, and his sister had translated the six Drachmann poems that made up this collection (Grieg's Op. 44). Mrs Gould wrote on 31 [*sic*] April, apologizing for the mistakes in her Norwegian (the language of her letter) and tell-ing Grieg that she had once lived in Christiania, where she had been a member of that city's Philharmonic Society and had studied piano with Agathe Backer Grøn-dahl. She was a friend of Carlotta Elliot, who was to sing at the Grieg concert, and she hoped that Grieg might care to come to lunch at her Blandford Square home, joining Miss Elliot and Hatzfeld himself at the same time.

Grieg's notebook filled with ever more names and addresses: the Swedish-Nor-wegian envoy, [Count Edward] Piper, who can be reached at 47 Charles Street, Berkeley Square; Elliot[t] & Fry, photographers, of 55–56 Baker Street; Sir Lau-rence Alma-Tadema, the celebrated painter, available on Monday afternoon at 17 Grove End Road, an address which Grieg carefully notes can be reached via (the

Nina and Edvard Grieg in London (Photo: Elliott & Fry)

long since closed) Marlborough Road station. The singer Thekla Friedländer lives at 40 Roland Gardens, South Kensington, the pianist Arthur O'Leary (under whom Arthur Sullivan had in 1856 studied piano at the Royal Academy of Music) at 9 Notting Hill Square; publishers Pitt & Hatzfeld are at 62 Berners Street, W. (off Oxford Str); W. J. Leaver, trying to organize his Grieg concert at The Rink, lives at 6 Hervey Road, Blackheath; there is Augener's business address at 86 Newgate Street, London E.C., as well as his home address; and Berger is at 6 York Street, Portman Square; Wilhelmina Norman-Neruda's home is at 20 Linden Gardens, Bayswater; 'Mr. Vert, Agent' is to be found at 6 Cork Street, Burlington Gardens, and F. H. Cowen at 73 Hamilton Terrace, St Johns Wood Road; Dannreuther is at 12 Orme Square, Bayswater; Carlotta Elliot at 43 Blandford Square and Mrs Gould at 29 Blandford Square; Charles Hallé Esq. is at 1 South Villas, Campden Hill Road, Kensington W. – he can evidently be seen between 12 and 2, but no precise date is given; 'Hermann', Max Abraham's chief accountant, is at 10 Lexington Street, Golden Square, close to Regent Street; and Romeike & Curtice's Press Information Agency is at 12–14 Catherine Street, Strand W.C. English addresses are also given for others already mentioned: Pettersson, Delius, Mrs Wodehouse, Faning, Macrae, Hartvigson, Rotter, Steinway, Harding and Brønnum; and a number of other names are simply – and homelessly – jotted down, among them [Clotilde] Kleeberg, [George] Grove, and [Arthur] Chappell.

On Tuesday 1 and Wednesday 2 May Grieg lunched with Delius. He seems to have been content, even enthusiastic, to travel into town by omnibus on most days and then, business over, to take a cab back to Clapham. And he would have noticed how the musical press was generating further interest in his visit, in particular by Niecks in a somewhat rambling lead article in the May issue of *The Monthly Musical Record*, discussing the 'Norwegianness' of Grieg and of various of his better-known compatriots (whether musical, artistic or literary) and listing many of Grieg's compositions: 'we cannot but regard this artistic outcome of a life which began in 1843 as quantitatively highly respectable. And when we examine it qualitatively our respect is not only raised many degrees but also reinforced by admiration and affection.' Niecks ended his piece resoundingly:

> The time has not yet come when an exact measure of Grieg can be taken. But this much can be said already with certainty: He is a true poet, and has added another string to our lyre. And now let me express the chief purpose of my writing on the present occasion —
> A HEARTY WELCOME TO THESE SHORES TO EDVARD GRIEG.
> Though only speaking in my own name, I am sure I am speaking in the spirit of all music-loving people.[15]

Towards the end of this same issue, Augener advertised, in a long column, 'Edvard Grieg's Complete Works',[16] an advertisement that also ran in the June and July issues. Perhaps more importantly, the journal gave a first intimation that there was to be a second appearance:

> Musicians and lovers of music generally in and near London, who, no doubt, are all anxious to hear and see as much as possible of Grieg, will be glad to learn that, about a week after his appearance at the Philharmonic Concert of May 3rd, he will give a recital, which, if we are rightly informed, is to consist entirely of his own compositions. At any rate, Grieg will play a number of his pianoforte solos, and with a violinist one of his sonatas; and his wife will sing some of his songs. The bill of fare is inviting, and cannot fail to bring together a large company. This, moreover, is as it should be, for Grieg is one of the most interesting artistic individualities of our time.[17]

There was a rehearsal on the morning of 2 May at St James's Hall, and there were separate rehearsals with soprano Carlotta Elliot. Friends, including Delius, attended one or other of the rehearsals. Adela Wodehouse, the 'musical friend of Miss Smyth' as recorded in Grieg's notebook, charmed at having met the Griegs, wrote to say that she wished to attend. And the composer sent visiting cards to Dannreuther and his wife in case they should have any difficulty in getting into the hall, complaining at the same time to his pianist friend about the difficulty of getting to meet August Manns. He and Nina had already paid one fruitless visit to the conductor's home, from which — in London — Grieg felt he lived so far away that he could not see the way clear to finding the time for a second try. Dannreuther, unable to be at the actual concert, attended the rehearsal. A few days earlier Grieg had called at Orme Square, only to find that his old friend was out. Nevertheless,

Dannreuther was not going to miss the opportunity of hearing 'one of my favourite works since 1872' played by the composer himself – so the rehearsal it had to be. As soon as he received a report on the concert, he was to write to congratulate Grieg on 'yesterday's triumph'.[18]

The morning of the Philharmonic Society's concert dawned, prompting the *Pall Mall Gazette* that day to devote three paragraphs to the composer, under the title 'The Music of Norway: Notes on Edvard Grieg'. Some biographical background on the composer was offered; there was a reminder that 'his music has frequently been heard in England'; and a list of his best-known pieces was printed. Meanwhile, Grieg was expecting Max Abraham to arrive from Leipzig later in the day. Abraham had written to ask him to arrange for a ticket for the concert to be waiting for him at the Grand Hotel, where he would be staying. Charles Harding, Grieg's Birmingham contact, unable at the last minute to come, sent a telegram to request a meeting with the composer in London on the following Saturday morning. The first half of the concert itself was made up of music by Bizet and Grieg, with the second half allotted to Mozart, Massenet and Mendelssohn. The Concerto in A minor, with Grieg as soloist ('His first appearance in England' ran the concert's listing), followed Bizet's *Jeux d'enfants* suite, and was itself followed by the two songs, 'The First Meeting' and 'Farewell to Tvindehaugen', in which Grieg accompanied Carlotta Elliot; and finally the *Two Elegiac Melodies* ('First time at these concerts') were conducted by the composer. The chief conductor was Frederic Cowen, who later recalled his initial impressions of Grieg and his wife:

> He was not a great pianist, but he could play his own music with much effect. The popularity of his compositions, too, made everyone curious to see him in *propria persona*, and added not a little to the success he achieved. He and his wife (who was a very capable singer) were an interesting couple. They were both quite short, with bright intellectual faces and rough grizzly hair, and looked more like brother and sister than husband and wife. They had simple, unaffected natures, and seemed as much attached to each other as they were to the art they both followed.[19]

St James's Hall, with entrances from the Regent Street Quadrant and Piccadilly, was at this time London's premier concert hall and would remain so until the Queen's Hall was inaugurated at the end of 1893. A large proportion of the capital for the building had been subscribed by the music business of Chappell's. Opened in 1858, with a seating capacity of some 2,500, it was first to become the home of the Monday Popular Concerts and then a few years later of the Saturday Popular Concerts. The Philharmonic Society started to use it for its own concert series in 1869, and ten years later the conductor Hans Richter inaugurated a further series of concerts there that would bear his own name. Sir George Henschel in turn began his seasons of London Symphony Concerts at the hall in 1886. Renowned in its time for its excellent acoustics, St James's Hall had rapidly become the principal port of call for visiting virtuosi, among them Liszt and Paderewski. Demolished

SEVENTY-SIXTH   SEASON, 1888.

PHILHARMONIC SOCIETY

UNDER THE IMMEDIATE PATRONAGE OF

Her Most Gracious Majesty the Queen,

THEIR ROYAL HIGHNESSES THE PRINCE AND PRINCESS OF WALES,
THEIR ROYAL HIGHNESSES THE DUKE AND DUCHESS OF EDINBURGH,
THEIR ROYAL HIGHNESSES THE DUKE AND DUCHESS OF CONNAUGHT,
THEIR ROYAL HIGHNESSES THE PRINCE AND PRINCESS CHRISTIAN,
HER ROYAL HIGHNESS THE PRINCESS LOUISE (MARCHIONESS OF LORNE),
HER ROYAL HIGHNESS PRINCESS MARY ADELAIDE (DUCHESS OF TECK),
HIS ROYAL HIGHNESS THE DUKE OF CAMBRIDGE,
HIS SERENE HIGHNESS THE DUKE OF TECK.

FOURTH CONCERT, Thursday, May 3, 1888.
ST. JAMES'S HALL.

Doors open at Half-past Seven o'clock.   To commence at Eight o'clock precisely.

✧ *Programme.* ✧
PART I.

PETITE SUITE, "Jeux d'Enfants"...   *Bizet.*
(First time in England.)

CONCERTO in A minor, Pianoforte and Orchestra ...   *Grieg.*
Mr. EDVARD GRIEG.
(His first appearance in England.)

LIEDER { *a.* "Erstes Begegnen" }
{ *b.* "Farewell to Tvindehougen" } ...   *Grieg.*
Miss CARLOTTA ELLIOT.

TWO ELEGIAC MELODIES for Stringed Orchestra ...   *Grieg.*
(First time at these Concerts. Conducted by the COMPOSER.)

PART II.

SYMPHONY in C (No. 6)   *Mozart.*
AIR, "Il est doux" (Hérodiade) ...   *Massenet.*
Miss CARLOTTA ELLIOT.
OVERTURE, "Ruy Blas" ...   *Mendelssohn.*

CONDUCTOR   ..   ..   MR. FREDERIC H. COWEN.

Programme of Grieg's first concert in England

in 1905 to make way for the Piccadilly Hotel, it was remembered with affection by concert-goers for a long time afterwards.

The Grieg concert was given to a packed and enthusiastic house. Under the rubric 'London', *The Daily News* recorded the fact that 'Edvard Grieg, the most renowned musician of Scandinavia, received an enthusiastic welcome last evening from a Philharmonic audience on his first appearance in England.' A further rubric, 'Music', underscored Grieg's achievement that evening:

St James's Hall; sketch by Howard Fenton

The first appearance in England last night of Edvard Grieg, the most renowned musician of Scandinavia, is likely to be the principal event of the present season of the Philharmonic Society. An enormous audience assembled to bid welcome to the distinguished composer, and his reception was as enthusiastic as even less modest a man could possibly desire. Grieg is forty-five, and were it not from his sufferings from a pulmonary complaint, he would now be a man in the prime of life. From 1858 till 1862 he was a member of that famous class at the Leipsic Conservatoire which included Sir Arthur Sullivan, Walter Bache, Carl Rosa, J-F. Barnett, Franklin Taylor, and other musicians, who in various branches of the art have since gained eminence. Moscheles was his teacher for pianoforte playing, and the influence of that master was abundantly observable in Grieg's performance last evening of his own concerto in A minor, which, so far as his orchestral compositions are concerned, may fairly be considered his most representative work. Grieg's beautiful touch, so velvety, and yet so firm, recalling to a striking degree the touch of Liszt when he last appeared here in England, quite charmed the Philharmonic audience - that is to say, perhaps the largest assemblage of professional pianists in this country. In mere physical power he may be more or less deficient, but the defect – if defect it be – in these days of performers who are happily described across the Atlantic as 'pianists of the John L. Sullivan school,' is not likely to be placed to his disadvantage. The concerto itself need not again be described. It was played first at the Crystal Palace in 1874 by Grieg's constant friend and champion, Mr. Dannreuther, who three years later performed it at the Philharmonic, since when it has been heard in the hands of Miss Helen Hopekirk, Mr. Rummel, Miss Kuhé, and others. As amateurs are aware, the national characteristics of the Scandinavian style are an important feature of the concerto, and perhaps even still more of the 'Elegiac Melodies' for strings, which Mr. Henschel had already introduced to London, but which were last night conducted by the composer in person. The second of the two 'Melodies' was encored, a compliment which, with less reason, was paid to the second of two of Grieg's songs sung by Miss Carlotta Elliott.[20]

The Standard was similarly impressed by the distinguished character of Grieg's audience:

that the occasion was generally considered one of unusual moment was sufficiently attested by the presence of as brilliant a gathering of musicians and connoisseurs at St. James's Hall last night as has been seen of late years in these precincts to welcome, in the new-comer, one who was indeed an old friend . . . The reception awarded to the composer was flattering in the extreme, and he was obviously touched by the heartiness and unanimity of the acclamations which greeted him, both on his first appearance on the platform and after each section of the Concerto. He won all sympathies at once, and the applause increased in vehemence, until it culminated, after the end of the work, in an enthusiastic double recall for the distinguished visitor . . . Mr. Grieg proved himself as clever with the *bâton* as in his other provinces of musical art and in the second of the Elegiac pieces obtained so pure a *pianissimo* from the orchestra – one of the rarest things to be heard nowadays – that a repetition of the melody was insisted upon. After this the artist was called back again and again to the platform, and must have finally retired in the full assurance of the friendliness of his English hearers and fellow musicians.[21]

The Queen, among the weeklies, reported that Grieg had played 'with great delicacy of touch, much technical proficiency, and with genuine artistic perception, the beautiful Adagio being very keenly enjoyed by the audience, who at the conclusion of the work recalled the composer again and again'. Interestingly, the writer felt that Grieg was known among his English public 'chiefly perhaps by his songs', rather than by his piano pieces. Nevertheless, the journal's conclusion was reassuring: 'Herr Grieg's reception throughout was of the most cordial character, and he has every reason to be satisfied with the result of his initial appearance among us.'[22]

The concert was widely reviewed by further major dailies, *The Times* in particular declaring the composer's performance of his Concerto to have been perfect, both in a technical and intellectual sense. If Dannreuther had invested it with real 'poetic charm' in his performances several years earlier, Grieg's own rendering of what was now a familiar work was 'a revelation'. The two songs that had been programmed were 'charming melodies', but lacked the lyrical depths of some of Grieg's other songs. Under Grieg's direction, the Philharmonic Society's orchestra had played the *Two Elegiac Melodies* 'admirably'. 'Once more the enthusiasm of the audience rose to the highest pitch at the end of the performance and Grieg at least will have no reason to complain of the impassive attitude towards modern music generally attributed to English, and more especially, Philharmonic audiences.' *The Daily Telegraph*, though unable to find 'virtuosity' in Grieg's execution of his Concerto, nonetheless recognized a good performance – clear, full of expression and intelligent – and lavished praise on Grieg for his magical conducting of the *Elegiac Melodies* and for the superb ensemble playing that he had drawn from the orchestra.

Of the monthly journals, *The Musical Times*, although a little disappointed that Grieg had not brought a new work to display, and noting briefly 'the couple of songs delightfully sung by Miss Carlotta Elliot', accepted that the chief interest of the evening lay in Grieg as a pianist and conductor:

> The Norwegian shone in both capacities. He cannot be called a piano virtuoso, but in the exhibition of his Concerto he exhibited qualities far higher and more precious than those necessary for mechanical display. Nothing could be more neat, clear, and intelligent than his rendering of the solo. In it the artist predominated over the mere executant, and the audience were held closely observant by what seemed to be, in Grieg's hands, a new work. The success gained was immense, while its causes were the most legitimate conceivable. Grieg, as a conductor, gave equal satisfaction. The little pieces styled 'Elegiac Melodies' acquired a significance under his direction such as had not been suspected previously, and the performance – a triumph of delicacy and refinement – left absolutely nothing to desire. Of the applause showered upon the Norwegian musician it would be vain to speak in attempt at description. Grieg, though personally a stranger, seemed intimately known to the audience, and ap-

peared to have all their sympathy. This was no doubt due to the charm of the songs and pianoforte pieces which long since made his name a household word. It is now to be hoped that the greatest musical representative of 'old Norway' will come amongst us every year.[23]

Musical Opinion's reviewer 'J.B.K.' also acknowledged Grieg to be 'a pianist of the first rank, gifted with the power of fascinating the listener to an unusual degree' and added that he was, too, a perfect accompanist in respect of his songs. Under his 'masterly conductorship', the two beautiful *Elegiac Melodies* had been rendered 'in magnificent style', with the second piece 'rapturously encored'.[24] *The Monthly Musical Record* echoed other reviews, Grieg's performance of the 'magnificent' Concerto being judged 'a combination of poetic feeling, exquisite delicacy and grace, irresistible élan, and remarkable crispness of touch, that electric effect which is the gift of the chosen few'. As elsewhere, the 'extraordinary enthusiasm' of the ovation that had greeted Grieg was particularly remarked upon, rightly accorded to 'one of the most gifted and "individual" composers of the day'.[25]

Even the *Lady's Pictorial* was moved by the occasion, which had been 'far more interesting than the débuts of Tschaikowsky and Widor . . . Connoisseurs went justly into ecstacies [*sic*] over his delicious velvety touch and the mingled poetry and passion which he infused into his fine pianoforte concerto in A minor.'[26]

Grieg's own elated reaction to the concert is best conveyed in the news he sent to Frants Beyer the following day. Anxious that his friend should hear immediately how the evening had gone, he telegraphed: 'Yesterday glorious. Jubilant, unending reception. Colossal success. "Spring" was encored.' The letter that followed added the necessary detail:

> To be frank, it's really difficult for me to tell you about yesterday evening. You just can't imagine how it went.
>
> When I was conducting 'Spring', and it sounded as if the whole of Nature back home wanted to embrace me, well, then it made me proud and glad to be Norwegian. I really believe that the appreciation of the English for my art must come from their appreciation for Norway, for I can't explain yesterday's ovation in any other way. It reminded me of when in the old days Ole Bull with his fiddle appeared before the people of Bergen. Except that it lasted much longer here. When I showed myself at the door opening onto the orchestra, the applause that broke out in the huge hall (St. James's Hall), filled to the last seat, was so intense and interminable – I think for more than 3 minutes – that I didn't know what to do. I went on bowing in all directions, but it just wouldn't stop. Isn't that astonishing? In a foreign country.
>
> Yes, art is indeed a mystery! "More did I receive than I deserved" [a quotation from Vinje's poem 'Last Spring'], and that's certainly the truth. But then – in my dear homeland, I've more than once received *less*. So it is that everything evens itself out in this world.
>
> You may well think that it's not much like me to talk so much of all these super-ficialities instead of getting down to the real business of the performance. But the impression that that reception made on me was all too overwhelming, in that it was

so unexpected. I was perfectly aware of the fact that I was well known, but not that my art was held in such high regard here. I played on a superb Steinway grand, and the Concerto went well enough as far as I was concerned; of course my performance doesn't come close to satisfying me, but even so it was passable. The best thing was that I improved as I went along.

The conductor, Cowen (the one who wrote the so-called Scandinavian Symphony), was a *blockhead*, so the orchestra in the Concerto left a lot to be desired.

But believe me, I made up for that when I myself conducted the string orchestra. And what an orchestra. Nearly 60 strings, and all of them of absolutely top quality! I've never heard such a sound in Germany. If only you could have heard 'The Wounded Heart' and 'Last Spring'! How I thought of you. There were things that I could have wept over, such was the sound. I had rehearsed it in the minutest detail and they all vied with one another to give of their best, so that the effect was absolutely captivating. There were *ff*s and *pp*s, touches of accentuation and passages that soared, it was all like a song whose harmonies reach those ethereal heights that you know we music folk like to aspire to – but so seldom achieve.

An English singer, Miss Elliot, sang 'The First Meeting' in German, and then – well, believe it or not: 'Farewell to Tvindehaugen' in English! And she sang well! Just how I felt when I heard the word 'Tvindehaugen' – that's something you alone will understand! When she was called back she sang one encore, 'Good Morning' (in German).

How long we shall stay here and whether I shall be giving a concert (with Nina and Madame Norman-Neruda) I still don't know. I'll write again soon.

After a few days, Grieg's criticism had become rather more muted when he wrote to tell Brodsky on 10 May that he was simply 'not very satisfied' with the orchestral accompaniment to the Concerto. Furthermore, it is interesting to note that when he had conducted the *Two Elegiac Melodies* in Leipzig in October 1883, he had written to Beyer in remarkably similar terms about the quality of the playing there.

Grieg's strictures in respect of Cowen's conducting seem not to have been echoed in the principal reviews. Frederic Hymen Cowen (1852–1935) was both a competent composer and a gifted conductor. He had not been the Philharmonic Society's first choice to succeed Arthur Sullivan in 1888, but ambitious approaches to Richter, von Bülow, Rubinstein and Joachim were each in their turn rejected, and Cowen, a comparatively home-grown product (though born, exotically, in Jamaica), was finally offered the post. He had already conducted at the Society's concerts, and his third symphony, the 'Scandinavian', had had its first performance at St James's Hall in 1880 and had gone on to establish itself for a decade or so as one of the most popular symphonic works in the repertoire. In 1890 his opera *Thorgrim*, with its action taking place in Norway, was given in London.

Cowen's inaugural concert as chief conductor had taken place less than two months before the Grieg concert, and during what were to be his two periods in charge (1888–92 and 1900–1907) the distinctly conservative repertoire of the Philharmonic was to be appreciably widened and his own reputation assured, to the extent that Joseph Bennett, one of the country's leading critics, would describe him at the turn of the century as 'now to be reckoned with as among the comparatively few masters of a difficult art'. The *Scandinavian* Symphony was written after Cowen had returned from Norway in 1879. The composer made three trips to Scandinavia between 1876 and 1879, mainly as piano accompanist to the soprano Zelia Trebelli, and he had been particularly struck by the magnificent Norwegian landscapes:

> The grandeur of the inland fjords, the sombre mountains, the glaciers reaching down almost to the water's edge, the alternate gloom and sunshine, the old traditions which make Norway so unique among European countries, all created a deep impression on my mind – an impression that found utterance not long afterwards in my third symphony . . . had I never written the symphony, my slight reputation might have been slighter still.[27]

Cowen's new symphony was rapidly taken up. Hubert Parry noted on 19 May 1881 after attending a Richter Concert that he himself 'was as much pleased as ever with

Frederic Cowen (Photo: John Collier)

the slow movement and the scherzo, the latter is quite astonishing'.[28] And later that year Richter again conducted the work, this time at a Vienna Philharmonic Concert.

One other notable 'Scandinavian' symphony was written about this time by a British composer. This was Frederick Cliffe's Symphony no. 1, first performed in 1889 and given often both at home and abroad over the next decade or so. As a later review noted,

> The Symphony was suggested and thought out by its writer during a summer holiday spent first in Norway and then at Ems. The picturesqueness of the northern land, with its towering mountains, gigantic cliffs, vast fiords, and lofty waterfalls, has left its impressive effect on Mr. Cliffe's music.[29]

Scandinavian journals were not slow to pick up on Grieg's remarkable London début, the Christiania daily *Morgenbladet* receiving a correspondent's report on the concert and the reaction to it in the British press. 'All of the papers speak of our compatriot with high praise', and even the conservative *Standard* had referred to his reception as 'flattering in the extreme'. The comparison in *The Daily News* of Grieg's playing to Liszt's was also recorded. The audience, noted *Morgenbladet*'s reporter, was both numerous and fashionable and numbered among it a good many Scandinavians, who 'could only have felt themselves flattered by the success that the great Nordic composer achieved with the English public'. These various reviews were subsequently considered in a wider context by *Nordisk Musik-Tidende*, which remarked that the *Kölnische Zeitung* had received a report from its London correspondent to the effect that not since Dvořák and Liszt had a foreign composer been the recipient of such an ovation in London; his readers were reminded that the English had long since taken to Grieg as one of their best loved composers for the piano. In Copenhagen, *Musikbladet* noted the reviews in *The Times* and the *The Daily News*, mentioning how the latter paper had referred to the presence in the audience of perhaps the largest gathering yet in the country of professional pianists and writing of the whole as having been a complete and glittering triumph for the composer. And *Stockholms Dagblad*'s reporter had also signalled the 'great success' of the concert to his newspaper.[30]

Nordisk Musik-Tidende returned to the subject in its next number under the headline 'Edvard Grieg in London'. 'In connection with Edvard Grieg's concerts in London we take it that our readers will be interested to see how unanimous the principal papers of the great capital city are in their appreciation or rather admiration of the genius who is our countryman.' After an extended quotation from *The Daily News*, the entire *Daily Telegraph* report was reproduced, much of it discussing Grieg and his music in a Norwegian historical context. *The Daily News* reviewer's comparison between Grieg and Liszt was noted – whereas the *Telegraph*'s man had been rather more realistically prepared to accept Grieg as a composer than as a virtuoso pianist.[31]

The Philharmonic Society itself was no less delighted. Its orchestra was by now acknowledged to be of the highest quality, and at a dinner held a little later and presided over by one of its directors, W. H. Cummings, members were told that no less a quartet than Widor, Tchaikovsky, Grieg and Svendsen 'had unanimously stated that the Society's band was the finest they had ever heard'.[32] Berger hoped that Grieg was content with his 'extraordinary success' and passed on to the composer a request from the leading London photographers Elliott & Fry for Grieg to grant them a sitting. Grieg duly jotted down in his notebook the firm's address.

Norwegian friends, too, were elated to learn of Grieg's success. 'That must have been a great moment', wrote Christian Sinding; 'what fun it would have been to be present'. He and an English fellow-student, Charles Braun, were still in Leipzig, and he had learnt from Braun of the lyrical reviews in the English press. They had even considered making the journey to London to be there, but Sinding, short of cash as ever, had demurred, even though Braun would have covered his expenses.[33] In a postcard written just a little earlier that same day, Sinding had congratulated Grieg on his success and sent his greetings, too, to Nina and to Delius. Johan Svendsen wrote a week later:

> First and foremost my heartiest congratulations in connection with the glittering reception you had on your first appearance in London. All the papers over here have longer or shorter articles about it, but a particularly good one, I feel, in the Norwegian *Aftenposten*. — Now to business! I told you in one of my earlier letters that I had decided to come to London. Well, some time after that I received a renewed offer and moreover one that was put in such a form that I decided to say yes. That was why I sent a telegram to you, and as soon as I had your agreement I informed H^r Berger that I would come.[34]

As so often with Grieg, elation was accompanied by exhaustion. He was to turn down most invitations for the weekend, but one engagement he was determined to keep was with Delius and his parents on the evening of Friday 4 May at the Metropole Hotel. The dinner will have been hosted by Julius Delius, as no payments for meals are recorded in Grieg's notebook for that day as they are on so many other days. More important than any conversation about the previous evening's concert was the support that Grieg would voice to Julius Delius relating to a musical career for his young friend. Delius's father had been in two minds about the matter, but the firm encouragement now coming, face to face, from a figure as respected and as celebrated as Grieg was sufficient for him to agree to continue supporting his son's musical aspirations. Delius junior left London the following day for Paris. In effect, he was leaving England for good to establish a home – and to inaugurate a lifetime of composition – in France. Without Grieg's intervention, it is highly doubtful that this might ever have come about. 'We all had dinner together at the Metropole', Delius later recorded, 'and Grieg persuaded my father to let me continue my musical studies.' Julius Delius's cautious final acceptance that he should continue to make an allowance that would ultimately enable his son to settle down to the life of a composer was of course a momentous one, and Delius was to remain ever grateful to Grieg and his powers of persuasion that evening.

Another young composer was hoping to meet the Norwegian idol in London. Moir Clark had originally written to Grieg earlier in April, expressing a wish to study with him in Bergen in the summer. Born in Aberdeen, he was 25 years old and had been a student at the Royal Academy of Music. However, he had left after two years of study, explaining that the late Sir George Macfarren had not permitted his compositions to be played at any of the Students' Concerts 'because of their modern harmony'. He sent three of his works in the hope that Grieg would pass judgement on them. If he should approve of them, Clark would send him manuscripts of his 'larger and better' compositions.[35] Clark tried again on 8 May. He hoped that Grieg had received his pieces, together with a letter of recommendation that he had enclosed with them, and proposed to pay a visit to the composer 'on Tuesday afternoon at four o'clock'. Should this be inconvenient, he would like to learn of another time when he might speak with Grieg at leisure. Maybe Grieg did find time to see him; he could scarcely have been willing, however, to spare the time at this juncture to read through Clark's works in any detail. It is equally possible that he simply decided to send the aspirant composer a note to say that he would

Four Norwegian composers:
Grieg, Svendsen, Sinding and Iver Holter

have more time to look at them when back home in Bergen. Whatever the case, Moir Clark was in Bergen in July. 'Since you promised me to read through my compositions, I venture to ask you to give me a time when I may lay them before you.'[36] The story must remain without resolution, as the correspondence ends here. But Clark went on to enjoy modest success as a composer, writing among other things a *Scotch Suite* for orchestra and a Piano Quintet that is said to have become quite popular.

Grieg spent the weekend fairly quietly, probably seeing Harding as requested on Saturday to discuss the August engagement in Birmingham, but otherwise avoiding party invitations as well as some London sightseeing proposed by Dannreuther; 'a little trip out into the countryside' was all he proposed to allow himself on Sunday. Such an excursion would seem to have ruled out Grieg's acceptance of yet another invitation for that day: the French pianist Clotilde Kleeberg, to whom he had earlier written, had invited him to lunch at her Chandos Street residence on Sunday. She congratulated him on the success of his concert, thanking him for the 'artistic pleasure' she had experienced. 'I was present at your triumph, and I congratulate you on it, all the more so in that I have rarely seen the English public so enthusiastic.'[37] Although Dannreuther would not be seeing Grieg at the weekend, they would have the opportunity to get together again before long: 'I will be here for some time' Grieg wrote to him, 'so as to give a concert.'[38] Chappell had by now evidently agreed to undertake the arrangements for this second concert. Wilma Norman-Neruda would play, and Nina had been persuaded to sing, the latter fact explaining an entry in Grieg's accounts – a new pair of gloves bought on Monday 7th for three shillings. A meeting – probably a private rehearsal – at 11 o'clock with Norman-Neruda is recorded on the following day, as is a further lunch with Theodor Herrmann and a rehearsal at 3 o'clock at St James's Hall a day later, a day when telegrams were dispatched to various friends. Bus and cab fares are recorded on Thursday the 10th and Friday the 11th, but the nature of the Griegs' engagements on these two occasions is not. Might he and Nina have visited the O'Learys? The song composer Rosetta O'Leary (wife of Arthur) of Notting Hill Square wrote in a letter dated 6 May that she would be happy if Grieg and his wife could spare the time to visit them one afternoon, even if only for an hour.

London was a 'monster', Grieg had told Andreas Pettersson, who replied in heartfelt agreement, inviting his friend to come to Rugby, which he described as a 'very healthy' town, for three or four days of rest and recuperation. This would be after the concert on the 16th, and Nina must of course come too. Pettersson promised a grand piano, with all of Grieg's sonatas to hand, and it is clear that he dearly hoped the Griegs would take up the invitation. One can imagine, too, that the thought of playing again with his old friend, this time quite informally rather than on a Leipzig platform, must have thrilled him. Pettersson hoped to be able to come to Grieg's second concert appearance in London, but only if he could manage to get away from Rugby for the occasion.[39] However, we know that the Griegs themselves were unable to escape to Rugby (accepting instead the delights of the Isle of Wight in the company of Max Abraham), and no further record remains to tell us whether or not there was a reunion at St James's Hall on 16 May.

It would seem unlikely that Grieg would have been aware of the activities of the Madrigal Society and still less of the person of J. Edward Street, its honorary secretary, who wrote to him on 3 May from Caterham, inviting him to the society's festival on 10 May. The Madrigal Society claimed to be the oldest musical association in the country, founded in 1741 (although the Three Choirs meetings had started some years earlier) and boasting a long line of distinguished presidents, among them Otto Goldschmidt, Arthur Sullivan and Frederick Bridge. Street himself, secretary since 1871, was to succeed Bridge as president in 1904. The current musical director was Bridge, appointed in 1887, and one of the assistant conductors was Eaton Faning, which probably gives an indication as to how this particular invitation to Grieg may have come about. There is, however, nothing in the Grieg correspondence to show that he took the matter any further. He had more than enough on his plate already, after all, and madrigals were not known to be a particular dish of his choice.

There were to be further invitations of this nature while Grieg was in London. Apart from Leaver and the abortive Blackheath recital, a certain Ed. Rawlings wrote on 11 May from Richmond House, Wimbledon Common, asking if the Griegs might pay a visit for an hour on the afternoon of Saturday 2 June. What might Grieg's terms be? To add weight to his request, Rawlings added that he was 'a Knight Commander of the Order of St Olaf of Norway'. Three days later, having received no reply, the imperious Rawlings sent a messenger to Clapham Common 'to fetch an answer to my letter of the 11th instant'. The reply – if one was given – would have been a fairly sharp one. Grieg was neither for private hire nor would he be in England in June. Nor could a letter of 14 May from one Anna M. Ditt of Bayswater have had any better effect, asking for a slot for her to sing at Grieg's forthcoming concert just two days later. More innocuous, but probably not over-welcome, were the more straightforward fan letters. One such, dispatched some days after Grieg's departure, was from Brooke Silk, of Granville Place, Portman Square, who sent a poem and asked Grieg for the favour of saying whether it was 'suitable for music'.

On the other hand, Sir George Grove wrote from the Royal College of Music (of which he was director) on 14 May, regretting that he had missed seeing the Griegs when he had called at their Clapham address the previous day. Grove knew the area well, having been born nearby in 1820. He had spent most of his boyhood in Clapham, and his first school had been at Clapham Common; from there he had gone on to Clapham Grammar School at Stockwell, leaving at the age of 15. Grove had already met Nina at the home of Adela Wodehouse. Might Grieg, 'a composer whose music I so greatly admire', pay a visit to the College, he asked, and perhaps, too, play to the pupils and professors, even for just half an hour? Barnett and Taylor would be among those present. Grieg replied immediately, despite his response having to be in the negative. He simply could not see a way through his crowded diary. 'London is a true predator', he had remarked in a letter to Brodsky a few days earlier. 'It devours days and weeks as other cities devour minutes and hours.' Nonetheless, Grove's own immediate and courteous response of 15 May intimated that he looked forward to making the acquaintance of the Griegs when they next visited England.

One of the most intriguing letters received by Grieg on this first concert visit to England has been referred to in Chapter 1. It came from 3 Geraldine Villas, East Sheen, S.W., and was written on Thursday 10 May. And it poses to 'Dear Mr. Grieg' a number of questions.

> How long is it since our families have met – the last time was in August 1862 – when your Father and Mother, Brother John and yourself, came to Earlswood Cottage – our relatives on *both* sides have diminished greatly – a sister and myself being the only ones left in *our* household – Maren wrote a sad account of her own health in Decr last – I wrote to her at Christmas –
> We have taken advantage of hearing and seeing you in public at St. James' Hall on Wednesday last – and were delighted with the music and songs – of course your time is much occupied – but if you and your wife could spare us a few hours we should be so glad to renew acquaintance – Could you come and lunch with us – getting here about one o'clock being a fine day and we could take a drive to Hampton Court or Richmond Park – any day but Monday, next week would suit us – an early answer would be agreeable. – From Clapham Junction to *Mortlake* Station the trains are very frequent 12.32 arriving 12.47 – would do nicely – we could meet you – a few minut[e]s walk would bring you
> With hopes of seeing you
> I remain
> Yours truly
> M. A. Shillito

The Shillito family's initial contact with the Griegs went back to 1821, when a London merchant, James Shillito, who conducted his business from 145 Upper Thames Street, while in Bergen got in touch with Edvard's grandfather John Grieg at the British Consulate and asked for his help in collecting moneys owed to him. In 1830, John wrote to Shillito asking him to write to the Foreign Office mentioning the 'vigilance and interest' displayed in his cause by the then Vice-Consul. Such intervention might at last bring the Office properly to recognize the strength of John's case in respect of the consulship and the financial elements pertaining thereto. James Shillito immediately obliged: 'I cannot omit to name the kind Attention & hospitality shown to Englishmen while I was at Bergen and I feel afraid no one can better deserve the appointment of Consul in that Country.' These lines and those of others around this time went a long way finally to securing the full consulship for John Grieg, and the Grieg and Shillito families clearly kept in touch for many years afterwards. The Maren mentioned in the letter must be Grieg's eldest sister, whose name happens to have been jotted down in Grieg's notebook, apparently while he was in London, as living at Räcknitzstrasse 9,III, Dresden.

Why did M. A. Shillito leave it so long after the concert of 3 May to get in touch? Was any effort made to see Grieg personally at the concert hall, or did the crowds – or any other circumstance – act as a deterrent? Did the Griegs actually take up the invitation? There is no evidence to show that they did in the limited time available to them or indeed on any future occasion when they visited London. We must assume that the old ties had by this time virtually ended.

Wilhelmina Norman-Neruda had happily agreed to be Grieg's violinist at his chamber concert at St James's Hall on Wednesday 16 May. Meetings or rehearsals with her were recorded in Grieg's notebook on 8, 9 and 13 May, and in this same notebook Grieg drafted in English a short letter, presumably to Chappell: 'May I take the liberty to come to morrow morning at 10 o'clock and study an hour or two in your hall?' The firm invited him instead to be at St James's Hall at 3 o'clock on 9 May, when they would arrange for a piano to be there: 'our men will wait till you have quite finished; to bring the Piano away'.[40] Complimentary tickets had to be arranged for Dannreuther, Hartvigson, Kleeberg, the Rotters, 'Modern Truth', Steinway and Sarasate. Other reminders were jotted down: flowers, a carriage for Neruda, someone to turn the pages, proofs, settle with Augener. And further names were added to the list of those to receive complimentary tickets: Grove, Pauer, and (in parentheses) Miss Davies, among others. Grieg appeared to be leaving nothing to chance. He had first played with Neruda in Christiania some 22 years earlier. Reunited with her, he could write to Brodsky after the first rehearsals:

> She plays very beautifully, and moreover there are certain things where the 'ewig weibliche' really carries me away. There's a verve and animation in her playing, but it's a feminine verve. The big, masculine sort can't of course be there. She has been very charming ... The concert is being arranged by Chappell. He is to have *half* of the net income. Fine conditions indeed! But in Rome one must do as the Romans do.[41]

The day of the chamber concert dawned. According to the critic J. A. Fuller-Maitland (who had studied piano with Dannreuther), Nina had not originally intended to appear in public in England but had been persuaded to do so by friends who had heard her sing in private earlier in the month. Earlier in the day there had been time to make a shopping excursion to buy more new clothes for her for the evening. But Fuller-Maitland nonetheless relates how 'the expedients adopted by some English ladies to turn one of her gowns at a few hours' notice into something resembling the conventional evening dress of the period were amusing', noting how necessary such niceties were in the 1880s, 'as if any human being in our own day [he was writing some forty years later] would care a straw how so delightful a singer was attired'.[42]

There was a final rehearsal at 4 o'clock, and the concert was billed to start at 8.30

Wilhelmina Norman-Neruda

in the evening. Grieg was to play throughout, either as soloist or as accompanist to Neruda and to Nina. The programme opened with the first Violin Sonata, after which Nina sang three songs: 'Two Brown Eyes', 'I Love But Thee', and 'Moonlit Forest' (or 'Wood Wandering'). The first half ended with two piano solos: 'In the Mountains' and 'Bridal Procession'. To open the second part, Neruda played the Romance and Finale from the third Violin Sonata; Nina then sang three further songs: 'To Springtime My Song I'm Singing', 'I Walked One Balmy Summer Eve' and 'Good Morning!'; finally Grieg played the Alla Menuetto from Op. 7, 'from' *Humoresques*, Op. 6, and three Norwegian folk songs and dances from Op. 17. The critics were entranced, none more so than the representative of *The Monthly Musical Record*:

> Edvard Grieg, who had already excited extraordinary enthusiasm at a Philharmonic Concert as composer, conductor, and performer of his remarkable pianoforte concerto, renewed the same well-nigh phenomenal success as the executant of some of his own chamber compositions; and no wonder, for as a pianist his finger-tips seem charged with electricity, rousing the emotions to an unusual degree. The selection

included his Sonata, Op. 8, in F, and the last two movements from the new sister work, Op. 45, for pianoforte and violin, with the co-operation of that perfect artist, Frau Norman-Néruda, and a rich selection from his compositions for pianoforte alone. These pieces were played as they certainly have never been played in this country before; indeed, the performance must have proved an absolute revelation to many. To dwell upon their musical charm is superfluous, since they are included among the special favourites of every amateur able to appreciate true poetry in music. The apparently inexhaustible stock of strikingly original yet perfectly natural harmony alone would, apart from the rare melodic charm, suffice to place Edvard Grieg in the front rank of modern composers, whilst as a nationalist, in the best sense, he is unique. The same applies to a number of his songs, which are as beautiful as they are varied in character. The specimens presented at this concert were rendered by the composer's gifted wife, Madame Nina Grieg, with a degree of alternate grace and intensity of expression which it would be impossible to surpass, and her reception was deservedly of the warmest description. It is to be hoped that the distinguished Norwegian's remembrance of his first (and surely not his last?) London season will be as gratifying to himself as to those of his numerous admirers who had the good fortune to attend on those two memorable occasions.[43]

Frederick Bridge was later to sum up the critical reaction to one aspect of this particular concert:

surely the rare charm of that evening was the singing by Madame Grieg of some of her husband's songs to his accompaniment – songs which led several of the critics to proclaim a new range of emotion found in subtlety of rhythm and curiously arresting turns of expression.[44]

The dailies also had their say. The concert, according to *The Standard*, had been 'a distinct success', Grieg and Neruda having been 'applauded to the echo'. As for Nina,

Madame Grieg has a pleasant soprano voice and an emotional style, which occasionally leads her to break through the conventionalities of a London concert-room; her singing, however, was so truly impassioned that all other considerations were abandoned in the general admiration of the fervour and spirit of her manner. That flattering encomiums were passed on M. and Madame Grieg will be readily understood.[45]

The Daily News declared that it was 'a genuine treat to hear so refined a pianist as Herr Grieg play some of the national dances (with truly awful names), bridal and other "folk-songs" of his native land . . . The composer's wife, Madame Nina Grieg, also sang charmingly half-a-dozen of her husband's songs.' Also placed on record was 'an amusing little hitch' in the course of the performance,

when the composer declared something had gone wrong with the piano, and ten minutes' grace was publicly asked while search was made for some tuners. But when the experts arrived, they had nothing further to do than – in the language of the British workman – to 'cast their eye over the job,' as the piano, without any other operation than being looked at, was found to be in perfect order.'[46]

Nina Grieg

Successive issues of *Nordisk Musik-Tidende* brought the good news home, with translations of concert reviews taken from *The Standard*, *The Times*, *The Daily News* and *The Daily Telegraph*. Attention had been drawn to Nina's warm and attractive voice; in these Grieg songs she was simply 'unsurpassable'. *Morgenbladet* too had recorded the storm of applause, while at the same time observing that Nina's voice – light, after all – was hard put to carry in the huge hall. Again many Scandinavians had been present in the 'numerous and fashionable audience'.[47] In their letters to friends, too, the Griegs continued to marvel over their reception in London. On the day following the concert Max Abraham had taken them to the Queen's Hotel at Ventnor on the Isle of Wight for a short break, and it was from here that Grieg wrote to Frants Beyer: the concert had gone splendidly and Nina had had an unbelievable success, singing encores of several songs, while Grieg himself had played 'Bridal Procession' as an encore. There had been tremendous applause, 'masses' of curtain-calls, and Neruda had played superbly. Similar reflections went to a Danish friend, the banker Martin Henriques: Nina had fortunately been in good voice for the occasion, had sung beautifully and had had a 'quite enormous' success, with Neruda, too, having had a wonderful reception.

Nina herself was almost overwhelmed by it all, writing, on her return to London from Ventnor, to her friend Hanchen Alme:

> You simply cannot imagine the ovations of which he has been the object. We have never experienced anything like it before. To me they were remarkably kind too, when I sang 6 of Edvard's songs at his concert on Wednesday in St. James's Hall. They called me back time after time and I had to sing again 'I Love But Thee', 'Wood Wandering' and 'Good Morning'. Strange – but of course it comes from their knowing the songs and liking them so much. Afterwards we were invited to go down to the Isle of Wight, which is beautiful beyond all description, and came back yesterday evening.[48]

Grieg's own description of the Isle of Wight to Martin Henriques was even more complimentary, if more than a little surprising. Have you been here? he asked. 'If not, I'll just say that it is the easiest way to happen upon Italy. Sorrento – Amalfi – Salerno have nothing more beautiful to show.'[49] Grieg admitted to Beyer that he had been exhausted on arriving at Ventnor. 'But here, beside the roar of the sea, I'm reviving.' This resemblance of the Isle of Wight to Italy is perhaps not so easily noticeable today as it appears to have been to Grieg in the late spring of 1888. But the island was a popular and fashionable resort, the favoured home of Queen Victoria and of Lord Tennyson, and its undoubted charms were evidently endorsed by composers: some 15 years after Grieg's visit, Richard Strauss 'spent a long holiday' at Sandown, where he apparently did some work on his new *Sinfonia domestica*.[50]

Returning to London on the 20th might even have reinforced Grieg's mood of contentment. Edward Chappell informed him that Neruda had returned his (Grieg's) cheque, 'saying she had no intention of being paid & was only too happy to play for you for "auld lang syne"'. And Francesco Berger invited him to come back to London and present a new work at the opening of the Philharmonic's season the following March. Grieg demurred at the idea of writing a new piano concerto, but felt that when he did return to London – as indeed he hoped to do in 1889 – he would find it a great pleasure to bring a new work with him for such an outstanding orchestra.

Meanwhile Grieg had told Frants Beyer that Svendsen had been engaged to conduct the Philharmonic Society concert due to take place in a few days' time and that, although he himself had originally been asked, he had declined. It would simply have been too much for him. Grieg, by now longing for home, was wondering if he would be able to get any further north than Copenhagen, where he was to be much involved at the beginning of June in a pioneering Festival of Nordic Music. Since he had agreed to participate in the Birmingham Festival in August, he felt that it was likely that he would have to stay in Copenhagen until then. But the much-desired goal of Bergen and Troldhaugen was after all to be attained, if for a shorter time than Grieg would have liked. On Tuesday 22 May, he and Nina left on the Dover–Calais boat-train from Victoria, travelling to Denmark by way of Hamburg. They both had to miss a landmark performance later that day in the Prince's Hall of the Cello Sonata, in which William Edward Whitehouse, the leading cellist of the younger generation, was accompanied by Alma Haas. The occasion was the opening concert of a series of four chamber music concerts given jointly by Whitehouse and the violinist Josef Ludwig. The work had earlier been given at one of Dannreuther's semi-private musical evenings, but this was claimed to be its first public performance in England. The *Monthly Musical Record* and *Musical Opinion* reported that

> among numerous items of interest Madame Haas and Mr. Whitehouse may claim the credit of a first, and at the same time excellent, public performance of E. Grieg's beautiful but equally difficult Sonata for Pianoforte and Violoncello . . . The remarkable purity of intonation and lightness of bow on the part of the 'cellist was especially noteworthy.[51]

Bertha Moore also sang one or more of Grieg's songs in this same concert.

Once settled in Denmark, Grieg wasted little time before reporting to Tchaikovsky:

> My stay in London gave me more pleasure than I had ever dared to hope for. In addition to my appearing at The Philharmonic Society I also gave a concert of my own works in St. James's Hall, where the English – obviously to their great pleasure – were served up with some of my smaller pieces. My wife sang (fortunately she was in very good voice), and madame Norman-Neruda charmed the audience with her beautiful violin-playing . . . Is there anything in the rumour that you may be coming to Birmingham in August? That really would be something![52]

Grieg's publishers were delighted with the outcome of the two London concerts and with the personal impact that he and his wife had made upon the capital and its musical circles. One concrete result of the composer's first visit as a performer was, according to *The Musical World* many years later, to take the form of 'a rush for reprints of the piano pieces, and the issue of song translations by several English publishers'.[53] Max Abraham, back in Leipzig, thanked Grieg for the way he and Nina had made the journey such an enjoyable one for him. 'The reception, your recital & Ventnor are the three highlights of my whole trip, which I shall certainly never forget.' Grieg, he wrote, could now be sure of a glittering reception if he appeared again in England, whether in London or in Birmingham, and in the metropolis he could be confident, too, of real material success in the future. Sinding met Abraham in Leipzig and told Grieg: 'He beamed like sunshine when he spoke of your success in London. He couldn't have looked more proud if the whole thing had been about himself, and it was plain to see that in a way he felt himself part and parcel of your success.'[54] George Augener also wrote of how much he and his family had enjoyed the Griegs' visit. If they honoured Grieg as a great artist, they now also treasured both him and his wife as friends and as guests who would always be welcome in their home. Even if they were at some distance from the centre of the city, their rooms would always be made comfortable for them.

Rather nearer to home, Grieg's impact on London was described by the Danish pianist Henrik Knudsen:

> Just think where Grieg has got to now. Nina Grieg told me that when they went to London for the first time, there were many minutes of applause before a single note was heard. Why? Here was no English Miss, playing 'Erotik' and 'An den Frühling' or singing his songs. Here were Grieg and Nina themselves as brilliant performers of his own things, Norway had become the fashion, and they looked as if they had only just emerged from the fells. Everything was set fair for Grieg's success.[55]

Finally, two of the leading London musical journals were to sum up the Philharmonic Society's season and to place Grieg at the top of the class:

> The season was made memorable by the appearance of Edvard Grieg, who brought some of his own clever and original orchestral works to a hearing, and demonstrated conclusively an unusual amount of skill, tact, and sympathy in conducting the orchestra.[56]

> Many new works were introduced and three famous foreign composers – Edvard Grieg, P. Tchaikowsky, and Ch. M. Widor – were engaged to conduct their own works. Amongst these, the first-named in particular was received with extraordinary enthusiasm in the triple capacity of composer, conductor and pianist; and a masterly performance of his chamber works at a special concert at St. James's Hall was one of the most memorable features of the musical year.[57]

⊰ 6 ⊱

THE BIRMINGHAM MUSICAL FESTIVAL

IT was Johan Svendsen's turn to take centre stage on 31 May and 16 June at the Philharmonic Society's last two concerts of the 1888 season. Cowen had, as usual, been in charge of the fifth concert when Grieg had made his first London appearance, but his departure for Australia meant that his place needed temporarily to be taken by another conductor. Svendsen featured his own Symphony in D major in his first concert. *The Monthly Musical Record* conceded that he was a very welcome guest, even if either as composer or conductor he was not quite 'on a par with his countryman Edvard Grieg, whose appearance at a previous concert had created such almost unprecedented enthusiasm'. The Symphony was deemed not to be a happy choice, the reviewer finding that Svendsen's scoring seemed 'tentative and ineffective' and wondering why a juvenile work should have been preferred to one of the composer's Norwegian Rhapsodies. Much more attractive and pleasing, it seemed, had been the *Pastoral Suite* by Grieg's fellow-student John Francis Barnett. It was 'spontaneously melodious, picturesque, and excellently-scored'.[1]

Among the first letters Grieg was to receive from England after his visit was one from the Leeds violinist Edgar Haddock, whose father George, a violinist of some distinction and founder of the Leeds College of Music, had given violin lessons to the young Delius. Edgar Haddock wrote from Newlay Hall, some five miles from the centre of Leeds, regretting that Grieg appeared not to have received an earlier letter from him and informing the composer that he intended to present an entire Grieg evening at one of his next series of recitals. It was to consist of the first two sonatas, which Haddock had already played 'repeatedly' at his recitals, two groups of songs, and some piano solos. 'To enable me to carry out my great wish I wrote you to ask if you would kindly transcribe one of your lovely Northern melodies for Violin solo with piano accompaniment as I understand you have not yet written anything for *Violin Solo*.'[2] One wonders whether Grieg responded, as only one other letter from Haddock is preserved in the Bergen Library's Grieg Archives, and that dates from ten years later.

There were letters too from George Augener, relating to payments in respect of Grieg's recent chamber concert and giving news from home. The family hoped that the Griegs would visit them again soon, perhaps when they came over for the Birmingham Festival. They would then prove to be better hosts, having given notice to their 'bad' domestic servants and having installed in their place 'decent and capable' ones instead. In the meantime they were missing some of the family games that had been played in the garden when the Griegs had stayed. Augener later found that he and his wife would have to be away in August, but, provided Grieg did not find Clapham too far from the venue for his London orchestral rehearsals, their son William would be able to take good care of him and Nina for the few days he would need to be in town.[3] In the event, Grieg and Frants Beyer, who had agreed to accompany his friend, decided to stay at the Langham Hotel, close by St George's Hall where the London rehearsals were to be held. Julius Röntgen wrote from Germany to tell Grieg that he had heard a great deal about his London triumphs. In London, he again reminded his friend, it was particularly important to make personal appearances as Grieg had now done, even if one were already celebrated as a composer.[4] More news came from Berger. At a General Meeting of the Philharmonic Society, Grieg had been appointed an Honorary Member. The directors were anxious that he should come back to London in the spring with a new work for their next season; it could be a symphony, an overture or another concerto – whichever Grieg preferred. Perhaps Grieg might like to conduct his new Suite, due to be published in October? A cautionary note followed: 'What are your terms & demands. We hope that you will remember that we are an *Artists'* Society, not business people, & that you will not require too high a fee.'[5]

Charles Harding, meanwhile, had earlier established the parameters of Grieg's participation in the forthcoming Birmingham Festival:

> I have mentioned the subject of our conversation, and now write to say that it is decided to limit your works to be given at the Festival to the two for which we have already arranged, as so many others have been accepted. The days of performance are the 28th – 29 – 30 & 31 August and your works will be given at the Evening Concerts on the 2nd & 3rd days.
>
> The rehearsals will take place in London on the 20th Aug & three following days, and if you will let me know some time beforehand on which of these days you would find it most convenient to be there, I could probably arrange that your rehearsals shall take place when it suits you.
>
> I shall not be in London for your Concert on the 16th, but my brother in law Mr. Peyton will be there with his wife, & you may see him. Mr. Peyton until recently had the great part of the musical arrangements for our Festival in his hands & managed them most successfully.
>
> You will let me know whether you decide to return to Copenhagen & Bergen before August – in case I go to Bergen I may see you.[6]

Richard Peyton, like his brother-in-law a Unitarian, was president of the Birmingham Festival Choral Society, with Harding, George Hope Johnstone and Phipson Beale figuring among the vice-presidents. The Society's conductor was William Cole Stockley. Peyton would endow the Chair of Music at Birmingham University in 1904, nominating Elgar as its first incumbent. Elgar, who disliked teaching, was none too keen. After much persuasion from various corners, it was to be Harding who applied the final touch by taking the great man to meet Peyton and at last securing his agreement to the professorship.

Ada Harding had written to Nina Grieg on the same day as her husband had to Edvard, hoping that she too would come to Birmingham and stay at the Hardings' home.

> I feel sure that if you can come, he will enjoy it more & also I shall be able to make him more comfortable as you can tell me what he likes and dislikes! He shall be as quiet as he wishes & shall have a sitting room where he can always be alone if he wants to rest.[7]

And Didrik Grønvold reassured Grieg as to the particularly amiable character of his hosts-to-be:

> Mr Harding is evidently extremely proud and happy with regard to the celebrated guest for whom he is to have the honour of providing a home. As far as I know the family, they possess . . . the most warm and friendly qualities and will do everything to make your stay as interesting and untroubled as possible.[8]

Birmingham, the second largest city in England, was at the time of Grieg's first visit the home of what has been described as the most famous festival in all of England, an event considered to be rivalled in Europe only by the Lower Rhine Festival. The first Birmingham Musical Festival, intimately bound up with the foundation some years later of the Birmingham General Hospital, had run from the 7th to the 9th of September 1768. Devoted to Handel oratorios, its profits, like those of all subsequent festivals, went to the hospital fund. The second festival followed ten years later, again according pride of place to Handel but nonetheless including music by other composers. After a further six years the third festival took place. However, the fourth in the line of festivals, in 1784, was effectively the inaugural meeting of the Birmingham Triennial Festivals, to be given (apart from in 1793) every three years until the final event of 1912. The festival was held until 1834 in relatively modest venues, but the opening that year of Birmingham's new and 'giant' (as Mendelssohn described it) Town Hall ushered in an era of great expansion and growing renown for the festival, with regular visits by internationally celebrated composers and performers and a corresponding increase in the size of audiences. The Birmingham industrialist Joseph Moore, closely involved in the festival since the beginning of the nineteenth century, had been one of the foremost promoters of the building of the Town Hall and would remain a leading light of the festival itself for almost fifty years. A visit to Mendelssohn in Berlin by Moore procured for Birmingham the first performance of *Elijah*, which was conducted by the composer himself at the 1846 festival. Ignaz Moscheles, Mendelssohn's close friend and colleague at Leipzig, had first appeared at the festival in 1834, and Mendelssohn's own first personal appearance there had come three years later as conductor, when he also played his own organ works. In 1840 he again came to the city with a new work, *Lobgesang* (Symphony no. 2, *Hymn of Praise*), whose first performance he conducted at the Town Hall during the festival. Moscheles came that year too, and they both stayed at the home of Joseph Moore for the duration of the festival. *Elijah* was to remain, like *Messiah*, a staple of the festival during the lifetime of the series, but by mid-century Beethoven, Mozart, Spohr, Rossini, Neukomm and many others were frequently programmed. Beethoven's music retreated and Bach's remained virtually invisible during the tenure of the festival's first 'star' conductor, Michael Costa, who directed the series between 1849 and 1882, bringing in a number of contemporary British composers as he went along. One finds, for example, Sullivan and Barnett contributing important works to the series in the 1860s. 'Since 1834 – the period of reorganisation –', ran a management statement in 1870, 'the Festivals have obtained a European celebrity, and have frequently been distinguished by the production of new works of the highest rank.'[9] Thousands of pounds were accruing annually to the benefit of the General Hospital, and composers at home and abroad were queuing up to offer new works – Niels Gade, for example, writing his *Zion* expressly for performance at the 1876 festival.

The era of celebrity visitors coming to conduct or to play their own works was well under way. In 1882 Gounod came to conduct his *Redemption*, and in 1885 Dvořák arrived to conduct *The Spectre's Bride*. By then, following Costa's death in 1884, the directors had pulled off a major coup in engaging Hans Richter – widely acknowledged to be Europe's finest conductor – as chief conductor for the festivals, and it was during his period in charge that the Triennial Festival achieved its greatest measure of fame. A considerably widened repertoire, bringing of course Wagner and others more fully into the fold as well as giving further encouragement to native talent, was the immediate result, composers such as Stanford, Mackenzie, Cowen and Prout, for example, featuring in Richter's first festival in 1885. Earlier in the year Oxford University had conferred on him the degree of Doctor of Music. The only previous occasion on which the university had conferred the honour on a foreigner had been as long ago as 1791, when a doctorate had gone to Haydn. Richter had tellingly noted in his diary at the time of the 1885 festival: 'Chorus splendid, orchestra likewise. The soloists mainly excellent. After and *along with* Bayreuth, the finest thing I have experienced.'[10] He was already tolerably well acquainted with Grieg's music, having conducted the first Viennese performance of the Piano Concerto in 1882. A member of the festival's chorus who sang under him in the 1890s described how Birmingham saw him:

> Richter was burly in form, heavily bearded, and slow in movement. His manner decisive, brusque, and at times harsh. He was always handicapped through his lack of

Hans Richter

knowledge of the English language, and his struggle to express his wishes was often apparent. As to his ability as a conductor, there could be no doubt whatever. Was there a fault, he saw it; and he was not satisfied until it had been corrected.[11]

Back at last at Troldhaugen, Grieg turned his mind to preparations for Birmingham and its festival. He wrote on the subject to Charles Harding on 7 July, giving specific instructions as to how the two works of his that were to be performed – *In Autumn* and the *Holberg Suite* – were to be styled in the programme. For a third time, Grieg's and Harding's paths had failed to cross in Bergen. Harding, together with his wife Ada, had stopped over in the town just two days earlier, on their return from a journey by coastal steamer to the North Cape. He had left a card at the home of Grieg's brother John, who unfortunately was out at the time, and then, on trying again by calling at John's office, had been told that Edvard Grieg was in Copenhagen.

The Hardings were looking forward to entertaining both Grieg and Nina, and were disappointed when they learned that Nina would not be accompanying her husband to Birmingham. They would do their best, however, to find a room in their house for Frants Beyer, Grieg having intimated that 'a musical friend' of his would be accompanying him: 'I should be very happy if you could manage to procure him a room, near your house, for the festival days.' Harding reminded Grieg that the orchestral rehearsals were to take place in London from the 20th to the 23rd of August.

> I am trying to get the Committee to take the Rehearsals of *your works* on the 23rd so that you may leave home as late as possible ... Will you come straight to London, or to my house and rest a little before the London Rehearsal? we shall be glad to see you at any time and for as long as you like ...[12]

To Grieg's earlier postscript ('I hope you will find my music better than my English!') Harding responded, 'Your English needs no apology. I call it excellent.' It is perhaps worth mentioning that all but one of Grieg's extant letters to Harding are in a valiant English, the exception being one written in German in December 1887. How much easier, of course, it was for Grieg to correspond with someone like Francesco Berger, as fluent in German as he was himself.

Grieg was unable to make up his mind about the time of his departure for England. He had written to Abraham on 21 July reminding him to ensure that orchestral parts were ready and saying that he intended to sail from Bergen to Newcastle on 18 August, so as to be in London on the 20th when rehearsals began. But a week later, having learned that his first rehearsal was not to be until the 22nd, indecision reigned. He was for a start anxious to hear from Harding whether his own works were to be given an equal number of rehearsals as other works on the programme. Harding set out to reassure him: 'You may have an hour on the 23rd and the Orchestra is so clever in reading music at sight that I think this would be all you would require'. Should Grieg feel that he needed more time, Harding would do his best to help, but that could well prove difficult as there were a considerable number of works to be rehearsed. Harding clearly hoped that Grieg would want no more than just the one hour in London, something that must have dismayed the Norwegian, who was used to much more rehearsal time both in his own homeland as well as in Denmark and Germany. English orchestral musicians, whether *par excellence* or *faute de mieux*, were then as now the musical world's eternal and indefatigable sightreaders. Nonetheless, appended to Harding's address in his notebook at this time is what must have been the draft of a telegram to Harding: 'Must obtain 2 rehearsals London. Grieg' ('obtain' having been written above a deleted 'have').

Securing at least two rehearsals had, however, not been a problem — nor was it to be one on future occasions — with the Philharmonic Society. Some years later Berger wrote a sharp rejoinder to a criticism that he had read in *Musical Opinion*: 'Foreign conductors', it ran, 'cannot understand how one day's rehearsal is considered sufficient for the concerts of our leading musical society, — the Philharmonic.' Berger's response was emphatic. 'For *many* years past each concert has been preceded by two rehearsals; and the directors have never allowed the question of expense (though a heavy one) to stand in the way of granting a *third* rehearsal whenever their appointed conductor has seen fit to ask for one.'[13]

Travelling arrangements had still not been made by 4 August, when Grieg wrote to tell Max Abraham that he did not know whether he would leave on the 11th or the 18th; it all depended on the London rehearsal dates, which he expected to have confirmed by telegram at any time. 'What a shame', he added, 'that you are not coming to Birmingham.' By 9 August it was all change again, a letter to Delius making it clear. 'I am going by steamer from here to Aberdeen and am not really looking forward to the whole business.'

In the event Grieg and Beyer arrived in Aberdeen on 15 August, Grieg having been wretchedly seasick en route ('I shall never forget that night of horrors – never!' he later told a Scottish acquaintance), and they stayed overnight at the Palace Hotel. He had not realized before how common the name Greig was in Scotland, something he discovered while perusing the hotel register. In a later letter to Johan Halvorsen, Grieg remembered this brief visit.

> Just think, I was in Aberdeen last summer together with Frants Beyer. We stayed at the Palace Hotel and spent the evening – in The Park, or whatever it's called. A brass band was playing some wretched music and all of Aberdeen's youth and beauty was out for a stroll – among them many delightful creatures – indeed, if from among them all you can't find for yourself a Miss Greig or some Miss So-and-So or other, well then I really don't know what sort of stuff you're made of. In your place, I'd have been done for a long time ago.[14]

'When you were in Aberdeen you will certainly have seen Halvorsen', wrote Delius. 'How is he getting on?' Halvorsen had earlier been appointed leader of Aberdeen's orchestra and in March had travelled to Aberdeen direct from Leipzig, from where he had been seen off at the station by the Griegs and by Delius. Grieg's notebook gives his Aberdeen address in the summer as 1 Afflecks Street (the entry immediately after this showing Sir Charle Hallé's address as 'Greenheys', Manchester), but when he first arrived Halvorsen had lodged at a house in Langstane Place, from whence he had written to Grieg with mixed views on his new environment. The air was fine, the natural surroundings beautiful, and the people had many similarities to the Norwegians. But this latter fact was not all to the good, for just like Norwegians every single Aberdonian went to church on Sunday, and if one dared venture forth on a Sunday without hymn-book in hand, one's good name and reputation were at great risk. 'Aberdeen has 115,000 inhabitants and 80 churches. Comical in the extreme!' Musical conditions were awful, and were he not so well paid he would not stay a moment longer.[15] Also active in Aberdeen as a teacher of the violin, Halvorsen made his Scottish début as soloist at the final concert of the Aberdeen Philharmonic Society's season on 3 April and had rapidly endeared himself to the town's concert-going public; there is furthermore some evidence of his helping to lift the town orchestra's standards. It was, however, unfortunate for Grieg and Beyer that he spent the summer of 1888 in Norway, where he had engagements in Christiania and in Drammen; in point of fact he was very shortly due back in Aberdeen for the new season. He left Scotland finally in June 1889 to take up an appointment in Helsinki.

On the 16th Grieg and Beyer left Aberdeen by train for Edinburgh, spending their second night in Scotland at the Balmoral Hotel in that city. 'I admire Edinburgh — Princes Street, the Gardens, the old town. Ah! they are beautiful', Grieg was to remark some years later. On the following day they travelled by train to London, taking in a lunch in York en route. In London they booked into the Langham Hotel, where they stayed from 17 to 23 August. (Some four decades later, Delius would put up at this same hotel on his final visit to London, when a six-day festival was devoted to his music.) The journey had not been without its travails, as is clear from two separate notes drafted, under the address 'Perth Railway Station', in Grieg's notebook. One or other of the pair had left a blue topcoat, 'lost by changing carriages', on the train. 'Please send to London, Langham Hotel'. A helpful Mr William Paton of the Lost Property Office at Waverley Station, Edinburgh, duly — and smartly — obliged by having it sent on to King's Cross. 'Please call there', he wrote, '& I shall be glad if you will let me know if it is the one wanted.' No

Johan Halvorsen, as portrayed in *The Northern Figaro* [Aberdeen] (1 June 1889)

The Langham Hotel

doubt it was – Grieg recorded on 21 August the cost of the postage of his letter of acknowledgement to Mr Paton. Following this note is a draft for a telegram to Nina: 'Hurra! Frants, Edvard'.

It is difficult to disentangle from the available evidence exactly how Grieg and his best friend spent their week in London. Orchestral parts for the two works of his to be rehearsed were delivered to the Langham Hotel, and two rehearsals in St George's Hall were, in the event, granted to the distinguished visitor. 'Aften [evening], Scott', recorded in Grieg's notebook on the evening of their arrival, is a sure indication of the composer having quickly found where he could partake of his favourite dish, for Scott's in Coventry Street was famous for its oysters. On the following morning, the 18th, letters were posted to their respective wives and, somewhat incongruously, a pincenez was bought by Grieg for Beyer. Lunch that day appears to have been taken in Oxford Street, and a visit to the barber's (as always, an almost daily item of expenditure) is also itemized. There was a trip to the Crystal Palace, Grieg recording the payment of three shillings for a ticket. Might he have attended a 'Festival of Co-operative Societies' on the 18th, at which he would have been able to hear a concert given by 4,000 singers drawn mainly, according to *The Musical Times*, 'from the humbler ranks of society'? If so, the main attraction for him would doubtless have been the first performance of *The Triumph of Labour* by his old friend John Francis Barnett, an 'Ode' composed specially for the occasion to a poem by Lewis Morris.

The subject is no doubt important, but it is almost too prosaic to receive serious musical treatment, and Mr. Morris's lines are mainly an exhortation to the masses to band together for the purpose of enforcing a fair division of profits with 'the bloated capitalist.' We can well believe that Mr. Barnett felt puzzled how to deal with such a theme, and if his music is not so worthy of him as could be desired, there is small cause for wonder. Its character is sedate and almost church-like, and the choral portions are in unison, with the exception of one bar. There is a part for soprano solo, which was fairly well rendered by Mdlle. Ernestine Ponti.[16]

Grieg's sympathies undoubtedly lay with the working man. He came, after all, from a country where all aristocratic titles and privileges had been abolished by Act of Parliament in 1821 and where, as one English writer has perceptively put it: 'It is not a paradox that in a country without aristocrats the Norwegian farmer's boy can meet the English salmon-fishing lord on equal terms and get along famously with him. They have in common a completely natural sense of their own worth.'[17] The condition of Norwegian society in Grieg's time is succinctly summed up in a perceptive book, *In Viking Land*, published in 1908:

> The feudal system, with its serfdom, never got a foothold in the north. The people have always been small land-holders which has developed among them an independence of character not found in countries where the mass of the inhabitants have no direct property interests. There is no class in Norway corresponding to the country gentlemen of England or to the grand seigneurs and provincial noblemen of the continent. The wealthiest landlord is only a peasant.... Bjørnson is probably correct when he asserts that 'no other country possesses so many men in official positions – doctors, clergymen, engineers, teachers, and merchants – who are peasant-born, often from the tenant and working classes; and that in no other country have so many eminent poets, artists, men of science, and statesmen risen directly from the peasantry'.[18]

With this kind of background, Grieg, a democratic Norwegian through and through, would have been well aware of the social divides in Victorian England. Nevertheless, if he had heard and attempted to digest *The Triumph of Labour*, he would surely have come away from the Crystal Palace wondering at the apparently lost – or at least aberrant – musical promise of his formerly so much admired friend from Leipzig days. In any case, another of the wonders of south London was especially memorable: Grieg commented nearly four years later on the celebrations surrounding his silver wedding, 'I dare say that if I except the exhibition in the Crystal Palace at Sydenham, I have never seen so many flowers.'[19]

The most expensive item in Grieg's account book at this period (apart from the settling of his bill at the Langham) is enigmatically recorded as 'Havelock £1.11.6'. Lunch or dinner guests in London are not recorded, although Grieg's notebook hints at dining at the Guildhall Tavern, a City restaurant in Gresham Street. Another lunch was taken at the German Club – presumably the German Athenaeum in Mortimer Street, frequented by Hans Richter whenever he was in town (and

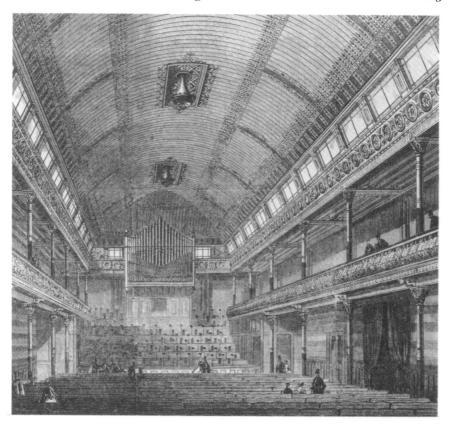

Interior of St George's Hall

seemingly by Anton Hartvigson). The address of the Scandinavian Club at 80 Strand is also jotted down, almost certainly indicating a meeting or meetings with Hans Lien Brækstad.

Under the headline 'Birmingham Musical Festival: The Band Rehearsals', the correspondent of *The Birmingham Daily Post* recorded on Tuesday 21 August how members of the festival committee had gathered in London in order to be present at rehearsals. The mayor of Birmingham was among them, as was one of his predecessors, together with George Peyton and the Festival vice-presidents Harding, Beale and Johnstone. On Monday the paper had recorded how

the dingy little building in Langham Place [St George's Hall] which does duty for the nonce as the Temple of the Muses re-echoes with unaccustomed strains of song and symphony by some of the most eminent vocal and instrumental artists of the day. For the long and laborious preparations for the Musical Festival which takes place in Birmingham next week, have now reached that advanced stage at which it is deemed desirable to call in the assistance of the band and leading vocal artists, whose co-operation is needed to complete and perfect the work of the chorus, upon which the musical reputation of the town chiefly rests.

Dr Richter had, it seems, been 'early at his post' for the first of the four days of rehearsals that were scheduled in the capital. On Tuesday 21st Grieg and Beyer probably lunched as guests of Charles Harding, who called at the Langham soon after 10 that morning and offered to accompany them if they wished to attend the rehearsal of Sullivan's *The Golden Legend*. That Grieg, at least, did so is clear from an item in one of the Birmingham newspapers the following day:

> The Norwegian composer, M. Edvard Grieg, who contributes two orchestral examples to the Festival programme, was present during the greater part of the morning and evening; consequently the musical people of Birmingham will have occasion to rejoice in the presence of at least one great modern continental master.[20]

The Birmingham Daily Post noted that some of Grieg's music was expected to be rehearsed that day, and its correspondent drew particular attention to the fact that Grieg's 'strongly marked personality soon attracted the attention of the other musicians present and the Festival authorities, who hastened to welcome the distinguished stranger'. It proved to be a long day, and there was no time for Grieg's pieces, Richter rigorously attending to other works requiring rehearsal. Finally, 'when at length the master was satisfied, and the signal of dismissal given, the band dispersed as gleefully as a pack of schoolboys on holiday thoughts intent.'[21] Grieg came into his own on the afternoon of Wednesday 22 August, the day being devoted to the composer-conductors of the festival, with Richter absent and presumably engaged on other pursuits. The morning rehearsal was given over to Parry's *Judith*.

> After the luncheon interval the Norwegian composer Grieg, who met with a cordial reception, took his place at the conductor's desk for the purpose of rehearsing his concert overture 'In Autumn'. Before starting the rehearsal he expressed in broken English his pleasure at meeting the band, and gave a few preliminary hints as to the reading of his work. He is a little man, of a very blonde type and intensely nervous temperament, with quick grey eyes, and a shock of frizzled flaxen hair that surrounds his head like a mediaeval nimbus. Owing partly to defects in the band parts and partly to the composer's imperfect acquaintance with our language, the rehearsal was a trying and protracted one, though Herr Grieg's vehement and eloquent gesticulation in conducting ought to have rendered the use of words almost superfluous. Of the work I must speak at present, of course, with all reserve, and shall only say that it is a picturesque and brilliantly scored arrangement of well-contrasted themes, the principal one a hunting song, in which the horns are freely and effectively used. A more important work of the same composer, an orchestral suite in the old style, will be rehearsed to-day.[22]

The rest of the day was devoted to rehearsing Frederick Bridge's cantata *Callirhoë*. At the close of proceedings, George Johnstone came forward to draw attention to the timings of the following morning's rehearsals and to announce arrangements 'for the conveyance of the members of the band to Birmingham'. George Grove was among those present at Grieg's first London rehearsal, and he had observed the conductor intently. Under the heading 'Beethoven', he noted in his pocket-book:

> Such men cannot be judged by the standard of ordinary men – of Englishmen particularly. They are free from conventions which bind us, they are all nerves, they indulge in strange gestures and utter odd noises and say strange words, and make everyone laugh till we find that the gestures and looks and words are the absolute expression of their inmost feeling, and that the inmost feeling is inherent in the music and must be expressed in the performance. And they get what they want. Those who have seen Grieg conduct will know what I am attempting to describe.[23]

The *Holberg Suite* was rehearsed on Thursday 23rd, the *Post* recording that 'the little Norseman' had taken the podium after the morning rehearsal of the Berlioz *Messe des Morts*, having until then 'occupied a seat in the artists' box during the latter part of the Requiem'. The newspaper's correspondent then gave a general description of the work, noting how the 'Musette' was opened by the second violins 'with characteristic drone effect' and how 'the quaint and tuneful manner of this movement to-day evoked general applause'. At the close, 'hearty and prolonged applause greeted the conclusion of this refined and dainty work, after which Dr. Richter resumed his place at the desk'. Friday was to be a free day, and on Saturday 25th the band was expected 'to muster for the purpose of the first grand rehearsal of combined vocal and instrumental sections in Birmingham Town Hall'.[24]

Grieg's fellow composer-conductor Frederick Bridge recalled how

> Grieg was rather a terror to the orchestra at the London rehearsals. Extremely fastidious, and demanding the most minute attention to the nuances in his music, he kept the band hard at it for a very long time, when he had finished appearing a complete wreck from his exertions. He was a very fragile-looking man.[25]

Grieg had not been well, as recorded by a doctor's bill of a guinea prior to his departure for Birmingham. A letter from J. G. James, of 30 Harley Street, dated 23 August, apologizes for the fact that Grieg had left the Langham before his prescription could reach him. It was now enclosed, together with a word of advice: 'Pay particular attention to your diet & always avoid articles of diet that give rise to these troubles.' Unusually, Grieg lists in his notebook the food eaten during his meals between 18 and 23 August. This could simply be the act of a careful man intending to check his hotel bill at departure time; but it is probably more likely to be a record of his intake that might be informative to his doctor. Perhaps this setback in health may indicate that friends Edvard and Frants had been living a little too well in the world of some of London's choicest restaurants.

A second missive, also dated 23 August but sent just too late to reach Grieg in London, came from Arthur Chappell, suggesting a meeting some time on the following day in order to discuss the possibility of Grieg's paying another visit to London to play at the Saturday and Monday Popular Concerts. A concert tour in 1889 was already beckoning.

From the evidence of Grieg's notebook, it would seem that he and Beyer took a cab to Euston Station later in the day on 23 August, after the *Holberg Suite* rehearsal, and then travelled by train to Birmingham. They were both to be the guests of Charles Harding and his wife at their home at 16 Augustus Road in the pleasant residential suburb of Edgbaston. Another visitor staying with the Hardings was the family friend Didrik Grønvold, like his host a Unitarian. Two other guests were Wentworth and Honor Brooke, son and daughter of one of the most celebrated proponents of the Unitarian cause in England, the Reverend Stopford Brooke. Then there was an American, Edward Cummings, a Harvard philosophy graduate in 1883 who had gone on to study at Oxford; he was subsequently to teach at Harvard and to become a Unitarian minister preaching in Boston and Cambridge, Massachusetts. He crowned his career as executive head of the World Peace Foundation, but his fame was to be overshadowed by that of his son, the poet E. E. Cummings. A celebrated contemporary photograph of the company also includes – beyond the members of the Harding family – Agatha Lawrence. It is likely that this was the same Miss Lawrence to whom many years later Stopford Brooke addressed his personal thanks in respect of an illuminated address signed by the great and the good, which congratulated him on his 80th birthday.[26]

Grieg's own notes and accounts during the course of the festival reveal little about his movements or his expenditure in Birmingham. The lone entry for a cab is firm enough evidence that his host must have had him driven to rehearsals and back, assuredly in the company throughout of Frants Beyer.

The London rehearsals had been for the orchestra and the principal singers, with Hans Richter conducting most of the festival's featured works. In Birmingham, the chorus came into its own, and much of the rehearsal time was taken up by the principal choral works on offer: Sullivan's *The Golden Legend*, which had been composed for the Leeds Festival two years earlier, Dvořák's *Stabat mater* and a new work receiving its first performance, Frederick Bridge's *Callirhoë*, specially commissioned for the festival. Handel's *Messiah*, also on the festival programme, was of course unlikely to have demanded as much rehearsal time as these less familiar items. Saint-Saëns, the star of the 1879 festival, had in his own time reflected on the quality of the choral singing at Birmingham:

> I should like all those who have been speaking about the unmusicality of the English to hear the Birmingham choir. They have everything: intonation, perfect rhythm, fine shading of dynamics and a lovely sound. If people like this are unmusical, they nevertheless perform as if they were the best musicians in the world.[27]

According to *The Birmingham Daily Mail* on Saturday 25 August, among the principal visitors to the first rehearsal in Birmingham could be numbered Grieg,

House party in Birmingham, August 1888
Back row: Frants Beyer, Charles Harding, Edward Cummings, Emily Harding,
Edvard Grieg, Wentworth Brooke, Didrik Grønvold.
Front row: Ethel Fiedler (née Harding), Agatha Lawrence, Copeley Harding,
Ada Harding, Honor Brooke. (Photo: H. J. Whitlock)

Sir John Stainer, Sedley Taylor, Frederick Bridge and the Mayor of Birmingham. Taylor would reappear in the Grieg story some years later, as would Austen Leigh, who a few days later was reported as having been present on the final day of the festival. The *Post*, with a later deadline, went into rather more detail in respect of those who had chosen to be present at the outset of rehearsals, and wrote too of Grieg's rehearsing his two works on that first day:

> as the day wore on a good number of composers, artists and critics found their way into the building, and at the evening rehearsal the ranks of the visitors were swollen by a sprinkling of choral supernumeraries, whose services were in abeyance during the performance of the Berlioz Requiem. Among the musical notabilities present were the composers of the novelties – Herr. Grieg, Dr. Hubert Parry, and Dr. Bridge; several of the principal artists . . . musicians like Sir John Stainer, Professor Sedley Taylor . . . whilst musical literature was represented by Mr. Joseph Bennett, Dr. Franz Hueffer, Mr. Sutherland Edwards, and other well-known Metropolitan critics . . . The Norwegian composer, though still necessarily handicapped by his imperfect knowledge of English, appeared to be in better *rapport* with the band than at the London rehearsals, and, though several corrections were made and repeats called for,

both in the overture and the Holberg suite, the final rendering of both works left little to be desired. The blithe hunting song in the overture, with its attractive colouring for horns, evoked general admiration, and the audience were greatly impressed also by the quaint and characteristic melodies which are so daintily enshrined and embellished in the suite.[28]

Grieg in Birmingham, August 1888 (Postcard photograph: H. J. Whitlock)

On the following Monday Grieg, now freed from further rehearsing, was present at the Town Hall for a part, at least, of the final group of rehearsals, no doubt renewing acquaintance with Arthur Sullivan, who had now joined the company. Another old Leipzig friend due to be in Birmingham at festival time was John Francis Barnett, billed, according to the *Post*, to 'play an Offertoire of his own composition on the organ'.[29]

'The Musical Festival Opening Today' ran a heading in the *The Birmingham Daily Mail*'s edition of Tuesday 28 August. The first concert had taken place that morning. Outside the Town Hall, it was a tale of grey skies and steady rain that 'made everything look sombre and dull'. Even so, 'quite a large crowd of curious people gathered around the barriers that surround the hall and the approaches to it'. Although the paper made no mention of Grieg's presence, he must surely have been there, taking up an invitation from the Mayor of Birmingham to 'Mr. Grieg & Friend' to luncheon at the Council House 'during the twenty minutes interval on the morning of Tuesday, the 28th August, 1888'. Grieg's sense of humour must surely have been tickled by the idea of squeezing a lunch into the space of twenty minutes. His less easily pleased digestive powers – well, rather less so.

The festival's Norwegian visitor made the first of his two appearances as conductor of his own works at the evening concert on 29 August. The other items on the programme, all conducted by Richter, were Sullivan's *The Golden Legend*, Beethoven's 'Invocation to Hope' from *Fidelio* (soloist: Anna Williams), and Wagner's overture to *Die Meistersinger*, which concluded the evening. Grieg's *In Autumn* opened the second half of the programme. This was the first performance of the piece in its orchestral form. Readers of *The Monthly Musical Record* had been reminded in the journal's August issue that it was available, published by Augener in London, as a piano duet:

> Since Grieg has been heard and seen, admired and *fêté* in London, his compositions have obtained an additional interest. Still further interest is added to the composition which we here recall to the reader's mind, by the fact that the master has scored it for the orchestra for performance at this year's Birmingham Music Festival. The Fantaisie ['pour Piano à quatre mains'], Op. 11, however did not stand in need of such additional interests in order to make it appreciated. It is indeed a strong work, grandly conceived and powerfully executed. Norwegian nationality and Grieg individuality have put their clear impress on it.[30]

Grieg and *In Autumn* received a good press. *The Musical Times* thought that it would in all likelihood become 'a favourite in concert-rooms', even if it was 'in no sense a great work' – perhaps the only negative comment to be found in any of the papers. Its two main themes had been 'worked out with considerable ingenuity and very pleasing results.'[31] The same reviewer thought that Sullivan's *Golden Legend*, the work that he felt had been responsible for attracting 'the largest and most distinguished' audience of the entire week, had had a rather disappointing performance. Elsewhere it was reported that *In Autumn* was 'rapturously received', mention being made of its 'exquisite instrumentation . . . having a perfect orchestra at his command, Grieg was enabled to present his overture under exceptional circumstances'.[32] *The Monthly Musical Record*'s critic found the piece in its orchestral garb to be 'a delightfully picturesque and charming work, full of national colouring, and its performance was such as to warm the audience to unwonted demonstrations of delight, the composer being recalled again and again'.[33] *Musical Opinion* called it 'a charming little work, full of national colour and delightfully scored', otherwise simply recording that the audience had received it 'with enthusiasm'.[34] *The Birmingham Weekly Post* thought that

Grieg in Birmingham, August 1888 (Photo: H. J. Whitlock)

The ideas represented would appear to be the pleasures of the chase and the rejoic-
ings over the ingathered harvest. The national spirit is evident throughout, in marked
contrasts of light and shade, in alternations of joyous and sad expression. The scoring
is exceedingly effective, and the variety of colouring remarkable. The composer was
received with enthusiasm; and after a magnificent performance of the overture under
his direction, the applause and cheering gave testimony to the delight his music had
afforded the audience.[35]

Much the most interesting and perhaps revealing account was one, however,
that was destined for a Norwegian audience back at home. Didrik Grønvold duly
reported on events for the readers of *Dagbladet.*

I was together with the composer in Birmingham during the whole of the Musical
Festival in 1888. This was after his first appearance in London earlier that same year
so he was already known to the wider public, but not yet at the height of his English
fame. We stayed with an English family, the Hardings, Mr Harding being a solicitor
who had long been a warm admirer of Nordic music and from whom the invitation
for Grieg to appear had been received.

When he showed himself for the first time at rehearsals – this was on the morning
of Saturday 25th August – there was already great excitement in the hall, and all eyes
were fixed on him. When he mounted the conductor's rostrum he was greeted with
hearty applause by the orchestra and by the audience of artists, journalists and those
who had been specially invited to be present.

Grieg did not attend the first concerts on Tuesday morning and evening. The
morning concert was given over to the oratorio 'Elijah' which had attracted a house
that was packed to the rafters. In the evening the German conductor celebrated some
marvellous triumphs. This was a musical treat scarcely capable of description. The
effect was of perfect grandeur. The Jupiter symphony glittered with Olympian majesty. The horns in the Oberon overture sounded as smooth and pure as one's most
romantic dreams could have wished them. Madame Albani's glorious, luminous soprano filled the hall, as much as in Dvořák's *Stabat mater* as in an aria from the opera
'Esmeralda', with sounds as mellifluous as though from a fairy-tale.

Then came the evening concert. The electric light streamed from innumerable
lamps out over the formally dressed audience, out over the orchestra and the choir
in which the rows of ladies stood out like a gaily coloured ribbon against the dark
masses of the gentlemen. It was a full house. There in the circle was the Duke of Norfolk, England's premier duke, who presided, together with a large number of the vice-
presidents and their ladies, all people of high social standing. In the programme book
they were ranged according to rank. After three dukes came the Catholic primate,
after that ten earls and then viscounts, baronets, bishops, knights and finally public
officials, members of parliament and the landed gentry. Masses of people had flocked
in to the concert from town and country. There was an endless stream of carriages.

After Arthur Sullivan's 'The Golden Legend' there followed an interval of ten
minutes. Then Grieg appeared on the stage. He was received with the warmest of
applause from the hall and from the 150-strong orchestra. Once he had climbed onto
the rostrum he was again hailed by the audience.

Just then, our English host later told us, a curious fellow-countryman had whispered to him:

'*Is that Wagner?*'

He was duly rewarded with the required information and settled down to listen, together with the rest of the huge auditorium, to what was about to come.

Which was the concert overture 'In Autumn'.

And so it was that the spirit of the autumn storm roared through the hall. This was something quite new. A breath of nature, living, great and true, penetrated into the farthest corners of the hall. In its arrangement for orchestra the four-handed piece had won an uncommon victory. Nothing could have better depicted the roaring power of the autumn storm than did the richly instrumented orchestra. The themes stand in opposition to each other, clear and plastic, the principal theme in the strings, the subordinate one in the wind. The sweep and flow with which the autumn's wild, melancholy and changing moods rush by, expressed in sound, creates an illusion for us all.

As a brisk conclusion Grieg has added a well-known folk tune which chases the burden of autumn away and gives new hope, like the blue of heaven glimpsed between the riven skies. The conclusion is exceedingly effective.

I shall never forget the applause that followed. In the artists' room the great Hans Richter embraced the composer and called him 'Meister Grieg'.

The next evening Grieg performed the Holberg Suite which had an equally great success. Each movement was followed by warm applause. At the end Grieg was called forward and received a tremendous ovation.

They were great days.[36]

Noting in the first instance the receipt of a telegram that had reported Grieg's 'great success', *Nordisk Musik-Tidende* also carried a report, probably also originating from Grønvold:

A numerous, smartly-dressed audience had filled the Town Hall. A large portion of the county's aristocracy filled the centre of the gallery, and above the frock-coated gentlemen and the ladies with their ball dresses, above the ranks of the orchestra and the choir, whose ladies stood in a band of flowery colour, there played the electric light from innumerable lamps.

After the performance of Sir Arthur Sullivan's Cantata (the golden Legend) there was an interval of ten minutes. There then appeared before us on the platform a well-known figure, and immediately there broke out from the audience as well as from the all the ranks of the musicians, right up to the very top, a storm of applause. Grieg bowed, climbed onto his conductor's rostrum, and the storm broke out again. It was followed by Grieg's own storm for orchestra. This will be known from the song in the Grieg-Album called Efteraarsstormen [Autumn Storm], and from the four-handed piece 'I høst' [In Autumn] which came out some years ago as Op. 11. But this splendid piece of music was now clad in the richer colours of the orchestra, and the 150 instruments, played by excellent forces, made the performance unforgettable. No 'tone-painting', it is very much the living spirit of the autumn storm that rages in the theme, introduced by storm fanfares, of the first part of the overture. The artist's intention is developed further through a more gentle second theme, full of melancholy, and each individual part is disposed so as to form a characteristic whole. After the autumn themes have been played once more there follows, to end the piece, a well-known, cheerful folk-tune, which with its lively rhythm and its freshness chases all oppressiveness away and sets up an impressive, splendid and fully instrumented close to the work.

After the last note had died away, an even more powerful storm of applause broke out and amid renewed enthusiasm from the entire hall Grieg was obliged to appear once more to receive homage.[37]

The following day saw Grieg conduct his *Holberg Suite*, billed as 'Suite in Old Style'. Bridge's now-forgotten *Callirhoë* (the Festival commission) dominated the newspaper reviews, but Grieg was again the object of popular attention, even if in some of the reviews his suite was only mentioned in passing. *The Birmingham Daily Gazette*, however, found much to admire in the work; it was 'one of the most charming things of its kind we have ever listened to', and was 'admirably dealt with and evidently gave great delight'. The composer 'was received with acclamations and twice re-called, the reception being an earnest of the manner in which another visit to Birmingham will be welcomed'.[38] *The Midland Counties Herald*, too, liked the work, taking a naïve pleasure in finding it 'free from those eccentric and sometimes discordant touches which are found in this composer's very original though sometimes peculiar works'.[39] Otherwise the *Herald*'s critic seemed as much concerned to discuss problems relating to the festival's organization as to discourse on the musical offerings, with Grieg's first visit to Birmingham receiving scant coverage in the paper. Stephen S. Stratton, *The Birmingham Daily Post*'s regular critic, reported on the festival for *The Monthly Musical Record*. 'This very fanciful and pleasing work was given to perfection, and Mr. Grieg retired from the orchestra almost overwhelmed with plaudits.' And elsewhere in the same edition of the journal another correspondent informed his readers that 'the eminent Norwegian composer . . . had a most enthusiastic reception'.[40] The *Post* itself recorded how

> The Norwegian composer Edvard Grieg then came forward amid applause from band and audience to conduct his sonata in the old style . . . Owing to the smallness of his stature he was accommodated with a raised box, which enabled him to control the band as he wished . . . The playing of these various movements under the composer's direction last night was distinguished by wonderful delicacy, precision, and expressiveness, which admirably brought out the tuneful and dainty nature of the work. On the conclusion of the performance there was loud and long continued applause, and the Norwegian composer was honoured with two recalls.[41]

Apart from Bridge's cantata, which was conducted by its composer, the rest of the programme, given under Richter's baton, consisted of the Schumann Piano Concerto with Fanny Davies as soloist, Brahms's *Academic Festival Overture*, the Prelude to Act III of *Die Meistersinger*, and songs from Emma Albani ('Softly sighs') and Edward Lloyd (the 'Preislied'). Grieg's conducting technique elicited some interesting reactions. George Grove had been present at the performance of *In Autumn* and for a second time recorded his impressions of the Norwegian and his style:

> A very interesting thing was Grieg's overture last night and his conducting of it. How he managed to inspire the band as he did and get such nervous thrilling bursts and such charming sentiment out of them I don't know. He looks very like Beethoven in face, I thought, and though he is not so extravagant in his ways of conducting yet it is not unlike.[42]

Hubert Parry, also at the festival to present his newly-composed oratorio *Judith*, had been at the original Bayreuth Festival in August 1876 at the same time as Grieg, although there appears to be no record of their having met there. Richter himself had, in Grieg's own words, been 'the conductor of genius' at that first festival. Since the early 1880s Parry been an enthusiastic frequenter of the concerts at Dannreuther's, at the St James's Hall 'Pops', and at the Crystal Palace – listening intently to newly introduced works by Grieg, Dvořák and Sgambati, and finding himself best pleased by Grieg in his 'strongly flavoured national vein'.[43] Now able to study his slightly older Norwegian contemporary at close quarters, Parry, too, commented on Grieg's conducting style:

> Grieg turned up to conduct his Suite – a most characteristic little object, with about the sweetest expression I ever saw on a man's face. And he is altogether of a piece with his own music – on a tiny scale, so tiny that a big stool had to be brought in for him to stand on. His conducting is very funny to look at, but it is very good all the same.[44]

Barnett, too, was impressed to see his Leipzig contemporary on the podium. 'It was a wonderful specimen of conducting to which Grieg treated us when he directed the performance of his "Holberg Suite". . . . One could never have divined that such novel effects could have been produced out of these instruments unaided by the wind.'[45] In the closing pages of his autobiography, Barnett was to recall how, when he was young, 'no one would have thought it possible to weave such ingenious and novel effects of harmony as are to be found in Grieg and other modern composers of the advanced school.'[46]

Grieg was a great admirer of Dvořák, and he noted how popular the Czech composer's music had become in England – more popular, he felt, than in any other country. He had been delighted to find the *Stabat mater*, 'one of Dvořák's most beautiful works for chorus, soloists and orchestra', on the programme for Birmingham, subsequently commenting on how Richter's enthusiasm for the work had communicated itself to performers and audience alike. Grieg was right about Dvořák's popularity, which compared closely with his own. There were many points of similarity in both composers' engagement with England. Dvořák made nine visits between 1884 and 1896, taking in both the Birmingham and Leeds Festivals (death was to prevent Grieg's participation in Leeds in 1907) and the Worcester Three Choirs Festival in 1884 (Grieg's fewer choral works were

Grieg conducts 'In the Hall of the Mountain King'; caricature by Moritz Kaland

little known, and he was never commissioned or invited by the Three Choirs). Dvořák was first asked to England by the Philharmonic Society (of which, like Grieg, he was elected an Honorary Member), was awarded an honorary doctorate by Cambridge, and furthermore mostly stayed at the London home – south of the river at Sydenham – of his publisher Henry Littleton, of Novello, Ewer & Co. The earnings from his first London concerts went some way towards financing the construction of his country house, 'Rusalka', into which he moved in the autumn of 1884.

Much later, Grieg was to meet Dvořák; and on the latter's death in 1904 he penned a eulogy of his fellow-composer for a leading Christiania newspaper, recognizing in him another 'truly national composer' and pointing out that it was in England that Dvořák had acquired his largest and most faithful following.[47] Shortly after the end of this 1888 festival, the *Post* printed a charming extract from a letter that Dvořák had sent to a Birmingham friend, in which he had asked for news – and newspapers – about the festival to be sent to him:

Three years passed away, and your Music Festival has come again, much music is to
be heard, all the people are delighted, and I am not present! How pity is it! ... once
more the happy time may come when I shall be standing on the desk and conducting
a great work of myself, I promised you![48]

As for his own contribution, Grieg summed his feelings up in a letter to Delius,
who had sent him a telegram as well as a letter wishing him well in Birmingham:
'The overture "In Autumn" sounded quite superb, and its performance gave me
great pleasure.'[49]

Grieg and Beyer left Birmingham for London on 1 September, dining once more
in the West End at Scott's oyster house and staying overnight at the Grosvenor
Hotel, adjacent to Victoria Station, from whence they were to leave for Brussels
on the following morning. Emma Albani, the distinguished soprano who had been
a fellow executant at the festival, had advised Grieg well, as he was later to report to
Harding: 'Please tell Mrs. Harding that I used 3 of the powders from Mad. Albani
and was not seasick at all!'[50] The Festival Committee was convened on 1 September, a round-up meeting being reported on later that day in *The Birmingham Daily
Mail*, with the Chairman moving the acknowledgements of the Committee to Parry,
Bridge and Grieg for their contributions to the Festival. A later report noted that

> it was also resolved, on the proposition of the PRESIDENT [the Duke of Norfolk],
> seconded by Mr. A. KEEN, 'That the committee desire to express the great pleasure
> it has given them to welcome Herr Grieg, and the pleasure with which they have
> listened to the remarkable works he has conducted'.[51]

Another, more singular, legacy of Birmingham was the firm link that Grieg had
now forged with members of the Unitarian movement. Christian dogma had, over
the years, found Grieg at odds with the Church; and the more simple faith, largely
divested of dogma, as expressed by nonconformist and nonsectarian believers
attracted him powerfully. Born in 1839, Charles Harding was a committed Unitarian, like his father and grandfather before him. A solicitor by profession, he gave
much time and effort to charitable work, whether connected to the church and
denomination to which he belonged, to the General Hospital (on whose management committee he served), to Birmingham University – of which he became a life
governor and where he personally funded a number of scholarships – or to various
musical institutions. He remained a steward at the Birmingham Festival until his
death in 1904 and was a vice-president of the Festival Choral Society. He furthermore helped to raise funds for scholarships at the National Training School for
Music. He had two daughters and a son, Charles Copeley Harding, the latter being
engaged in 1907 as secretary of the newly founded, if short-lived, Musical League,
an appointment that brought him into contact with some of the leading composers
of the day, including the League's president Edward Elgar and its vice-president
Frederick Delius.

Also a Unitarian was another leading member of the Birmingham Festival Committee, George Hope Johnstone, whom Grieg had first met at the London rehearsals. Johnstone had a large and splendid house, 'Headingly', at Hamstead Hill, well to the north of Birmingham, where he would entertain some of the festival's leading visitors. The pianist Adelina de Lara remembered him as 'a great man and a good man . . . He taught me about Swedenborg and we used to attend the New Church'.[52] There seems to be no record of any discussion on religious subjects that Grieg may have had with Harding, Johnstone or others while he was in Birmingham, but before his death he was to write to a Swiss theologian friend: 'During a visit to England in 1888 I was impressed by the "Unitarian" views, and in the nineteen years that have passed since then I have held to them.'[53] Some two years earlier he had acknowledged to another friend, the English-born but Norway-settled clergyman Thomas Ball Barratt, that he was very close to the Unitarians, 'among whom I – especially in England – have met some of the noblest people that I know'.[54] Another pointer at about this time to this new preoccupation of Grieg's is to be found in a leaflet loosely inserted into his notebook for 1888/89. Headed 'THE THEISTIC CHURCH, / SWALLOW STREET, PICCADILLY, LONDON', it sets out the main objectives of the Theistic Church, which had been founded in 1880, and explains in general terms the leading principles of Theism. How Grieg came by this little leaflet or whether he actually attended a service in Swallow Street is not known. But the church was literally just around the corner from St James's Hall, and he could perfectly well have called in during the course of either of his London visits of 1888 or indeed when he returned to the city in the spring of 1889. Nina too involved herself in Unitarian affairs. After Grieg's death, she was to spend much of her time in her native Denmark, where she became a member of the Danish *Unitarsamfund*. As late as 1927, when a fine new Unitarian church was built in Copenhagen, she helped by participating in concerts that were given in the building to fund the purchase of an organ, an instrument which is still in use today.

Among the people Grieg met for the first time at the Hardings' home was a Liverpool stockbroker, Henry Edward Rensburg, whose further occupations included the chairmanship of the Liverpool Philharmonic Orchestra. It would appear that while in Birmingham he invited Grieg to come to Liverpool to conduct one or other of his works, for on 16 September, from his home at 2 Grove Park in that city, he put the request in writing. He had discussed the subject with his friend, the President of the Liverpool Philharmonic Society, and the Society's committee had proposed that Grieg come to conduct *In Autumn* or even other works on one of four dates offered in January or February 1889. What might Grieg's terms be? Rensburg would be happy to mediate for him, and would be happy too if Grieg would care to stay at his home when he came to Liverpool. However, there were difficulties from the start concerning both programming and dates, as well as apparently with Grieg's terms. Rensburg returned to the matter by suggesting that Grieg conduct just one work at the city's Philharmonic Society (whose conductor from 1880 to 1883 had been Max Bruch), and then give a recital at the Liverpool Arts Society and possibly, too, a further concert in St George's Hall, all of which would certainly make a visit to Liverpool a financial success for the composer.[55] In his reply Grieg indicated unequivocally that ill health would preclude his undertaking more in Liverpool than just the one concert that had originally been suggested.[56] There, it would seem, the whole matter petered out, at least so far as the immediate future was concerned.

The Harding family's hospitality in Birmingham was to be long remembered by Grieg. In a subsequent letter to his host he wrote of how much of his heart he had left in their home, sending at the same time gifts of silver brooches for Harding's wife and daughters. Learning, some years on, that Grieg was expected in England in 1893, Harding invited him to stay — this time together with Nina — with the family once again. Grieg responded, adding an apology for his 'bad English' by saying how great a pleasure that would be. 'If possible, I should wish to have Frants Beyer in my pick-pocket. Then he is, what the Germans say: "Mein guter Geist" — my good spirit. Please, do invite him to come with us! How he should enjoy it!'[57] And ten years further on Grieg was to assure Harding: 'I never forget the happy days in the autumn 1888, and I shall always feel thankful for your kindness and hospitality'.[58]

Harding himself expressed the pleasure that he had derived from Grieg's visit in emphatic terms:

> I am sending a Photograph of the group of friends who were at our house during the Festival week and who formed so happy a party, it is a time I shall *never* forget, we seemed all to harmonize so completely that it was a time of perfect enjoyment or would have been if only we could have numbered Mrs. Grieg & Mrs. Beyer amongst us . . . I see you contemplate going to Paris presently and being in London for the early part of the spring season — if you do go there, try and come to us for a few days and give us the opportunity of showing you some of the pretty country round and Stratford on Avon where Shakespeare was born & if you can, induce Mr. Beyer to come also, he also will have such a welcome!!!
>
> Good bye (may I say) dear friend . . .[59]

There were to be further expressions of affection. They would all be thinking of Grieg, Harding told him, when the toast to absent friends was proposed at the family's Christmas dinner at the end of the year. And later letters from Grieg himself were, unusually for him, to conclude with 'My love to all' or 'my best love to you all'. The photograph to which Harding had referred (reproduced on p. 117 above) was, it appears, an idea of Grieg's. 'It is owing to your thoughtfulness and generosity', wrote Ada Harding, 'that we have this exceedingly pleasant remembrance of the happy Festival week.'[60]

All the evidence for Grieg's stay with the Hardings calls into question the pianist Adelina de Lara's muddled account of how she remembered Grieg staying at this time at 'Headingly', George Johnstone's palatial home.[61] Her memoirs were published in 1955, when she was in her eighties, and in them she remembers Grieg's 'sweet little wife' being there with him for the week of his stay. 'Sometimes', she writes, 'his wife would join us and I sat enchanted as she sang to his accompaniment'. Nor was she too accurate in other matters, asserting that Grieg arranged his orchestral *Holberg Suite* 'for the piano just for me', when in fact the suite had been composed for piano in 1884 and orchestrated the following year. If Grieg was expecting to stay at the Johnstones', why, one wonders, should he have asked Harding, some six weeks before the festival, to procure a room for Beyer 'near your house, for the festival days'. 'Headingly' was considerably further away from the city centre than was the Harding home in Edgbaston, and it was a considerable distance too from Edgbaston itself. One can only assume that de Lara misremembered a visit by Grieg (with or without Nina) to Headingly while she was there.

Sadly, the Hardings' home has not survived, most of the houses on Augustus Road having by now given way to more modest residences. But the two houses that still stand immediately to the west of 16 Augustus Road – including the neighbouring no. 18 – give a fair idea of how grand a locality the road once was, each being an imposing mansion of many rooms. It would certainly have been no problem for Charles Harding to entertain a sizeable group of friends during the festival week. Thirteen years later, after the family had moved not very far away to Knutsford Lodge in Somerset Road, they were shown in the 1901 census to have no fewer than five domestic servants: a cook and a kitchenmaid, a housemaid, a sewing maid and a waitress. A later resident of no. 16, incidentally, was the distinguished Birmingham engineer William Edward Hipkins, who would be numbered among the firstclass passengers who met their death on the maiden voyage of the *Titanic*.

Looking back on the festival, *The Birmingham Daily Post* regretted that fewer new works than usual – or had been hoped for – had been given on this occasion. Gounod had been asked to contribute a new oratorio, but had 'felt himself compelled to decline the invitation'; Sullivan had been unable to offer a new work; Dvořák had originally accepted a commission, but 'unexpectedly withdrew from it'; and Alexander Mackenzie, because of ill health, 'was obliged to relinquish his engagement'. However, by coming to the festival and conducting two of his own works 'Mr. Grieg, the Norwegian composer, has added in a marked degree to the reputation he had previously acquired in this country'.[62] The Birmingham Musical Festival of 1888 had come to an end, and the music-loving denizens of the city could turn their attentions to matters of lesser import for the next three years. The end of the week had anyway seen another subject come to the forefront in the city's newspapers. 'Horrible Murder in London: Another Whitechapel Mystery', ran the headlines. The ongoing story of the crimes of the man soon to be dubbed 'Jack the Ripper' would now provide more gripping fare, not just for London and Birmingham but for the country as a whole.

⚜ 7 ⚜

A MUSICAL LION IN LONDON AND MANCHESTER

THE 1888 musical year had been made extra special for the Philharmonic Society by its visitors from abroad, representing a 'new departure' for the Society. Grieg, Tchaikovsky and Widor had come and conquered, and it had been Grieg who had made the greatest impact.

In a letter to Berger on 10 August 1888, Grieg had accepted the offer of honorary membership of the Society, at the same time suggesting a fee of £50 for his next appearance at one of the Society's concerts. He sought to pave the way for Agathe Backer Grøndahl to play his Concerto, telling Berger that she was not only a phenomenal pianist, but also was pre-eminent in the genre in Norway. Berger replied with a list of conditions that must have irritated Grieg, but at least it was clear that the Society was keen to have him back, with possible dates in March and April 1889 being suggested. One of the irritants lay in the fact that the Society had declined Grieg's suggestion of a performance of *Before a Southern Convent*, on account of the first British airing of the work having been already promised to August Manns for a Crystal Palace Concert in October. Berger and his directors wanted to parade first London performances of Grieg's works and were little disposed to negotiate. Meanwhile Grieg updated Delius on his English adventures, both past and prospective:

> The overture 'In Autumn' sounded quite superb and its performance gave me great pleasure. After Christmas my wife and I will probably go to England again for a couple of months. I have been invited to conduct the suite from 'Peer Gynt' at the Philharmonic Society and to perform some of my chamber music at the Monday Popular Concerts. I shall try it once but I hope never again. I would much rather stay at home, but 'Troldhaugen' implores me most urgently to provide a few £ sterling![1]

In October Berger proposed a date for the *Peer Gynt Suite* – the first of the two that Grieg arranged from the incidental music to Ibsen's play. Could Grieg conduct it at the Philharmonic Society's concert on 14 March? Once he had secured Grieg's agreement, he suggested that Nina sing some of her husband's songs in the

August Manns

second part of the concert, ideally with Grieg at the piano. Grieg demurred; latterly Nina had not been too well and he could not make any promises concerning her participation. Meanwhile Arthur Chappell confirmed that he had fixed three dates – 23 and 25 February and 9 March – for Grieg to appear at the Popular Concerts. And by the end of the year Agathe Backer Grøndahl wrote to the composer agreeing to play the Concerto (a work Grieg understood she had not yet played) under his baton in London. It seemed that the much-needed pounds sterling were comfortably guaranteed. There remained the invitation from Liverpool to conduct *In Autumn* at the beginning of February. It appears that Grieg had an eye, too, on a further Birmingham Festival appearance. 'I am really pleased that you are composing a choral piece', wrote Abraham on 15 October. 'If however it is intended for Birmingham 1891, I do hope that in the meantime I shall receive from you a goodly number of other works'. Included in Abraham's (as in so many others') dreams was the 'so long and so greatly desired' second piano concerto.

Manns gave two works by Grieg at his Crystal Palace Saturday Concert on 27 October, a concert that included Barnett's *Offertoire* for organ, given its first performance by the composer himself. (The recently expected Birmingham Festival performance of this work must have fallen by the wayside.) *In Autumn* was duly accorded its second British performance, *The Athenaeum* describing it in its original form as

> a most interesting and characteristic work, though the brilliant and often piquant orchestration of Grieg undoubtedly adds much to its effectiveness . . . the piece, considered simply as music is full of charm, and being excellently rendered under Mr. Manns's *bâton* it obtained a decided success.[2]

The Musical Times was less impressed; the work was 'full of charming snatches of melody and quaint surprises, but as a whole fails to impress the hearer to anything like the same extent as his songs and less ambitious instrumental music. It is scrappy and wanting in continuity.'[3] *Before a Southern Convent*, performed in Edmund Gosse's translation, elicited more interest from the two journals (the piece has traversed a range of English titles, and was at this time known as *At the Cloister Gate*). *The Musical Times* found it

> a sombre but interesting work, somewhat marred by a conventional Finale, indifferently rendered by the chorus, and overweighted by the organ. The bulk of the declamation fell to Miss Anna Williams, who entered thoroughly into the spirit of the situation, and was in all respects admirable. The interlocutor was Miss Marie Curran, for whom the contralto part proved too low.

According to *The Athenaeum*'s reviewer,

> The whole scene, though its first part appears somewhat lacking in contrast, is most dramatic, and full of the wild Northern tone which is the special characteristic of most of Grieg's music. Its thorough originality evidently impressed the Crystal Palace audience, the applause at the close being loud and prolonged.

As might have been expected, *The Monthly Musical Record* was more indulgent to one of its favourite composers, referring to 'the charm of this fascinating work' in the case of *In Autumn*, and to 'the peculiarly weird and impressive orchestral portion' of *Before a Southern Convent*, at the same time praising the concluding chorus as 'a piece of well-defined and exquisite melodic beauty, with a remarkable progression of powerful musical accents to a triumphant close.'[4] Back in Norway, the London reviews were reported to have been 'full of praise'.[5]

Another feature of London's autumn season was the first British performance of the first *Peer Gynt Suite*; it was given on 20 November at the opening concert of George Henschel's third season of London Symphony Concerts. The suite 'was received with marked favour by the fairly numerous audience, Herr Henschel resisting (according to his commendable practice), with considerable difficulty, an encore of the two middle movements'.[6] Another journal also noted Henschel's forbearance. 'The Suite met with unusual fervour, and encores were with difficulty (but wisely) resisted by the conductor.'[7] Interestingly, *The Musical Times* had been critical of the standard of performance of other works in Henschel's programme, noting, however, that 'by far the best performance' was that of the *Peer Gynt Suite*.

This little work was first written for the pianoforte, and in its new form it is almost certain to become popular. It is in four brief movements, all of them full of the composer's individuality, while the orchestration is remarkable for its daintiness and piquancy. The light and delicate handling of this music by the band proved that the material at Mr. Henschel's disposal is capable of excellent results, and the rest lies with himself.[8]

Recitals including songs by Grieg were also in evidence in London in November, particularly one given by William Nicholl, who featured the song cycle *Reminiscences from Mountain and Fjord* at the Prince's Hall on the first day of the month. And Bertha Moore included more Grieg in a selection of works that she sang at a Saturday Popular Concert at St James's Hall on the 24th.

There was some discussion with Abraham around this time concerning faults in Frederick Corder's translations of some of Grieg's songs. Corder (1852–1932) was a composer and teacher who had written an opera, *Nordisa*, first produced in Liverpool in 1887, in which he used Norwegian folk-tunes including a cradle song and 'Halling' in the first act and the heroine's cattle-call in the second. Grieg was particularly unhappy about Corder's English versions of 'I Love But Thee', 'The Princess' (where he thought the final verse had been completely misunderstood), 'I Walked One Balmy Summer Eve', and 'A Swan' (which he also felt had been misinterpreted). He asked Abraham to have these texts attended to. A number of the songs were to be sung by Nina. 'Just imagine,' she wrote to her friend Hanchen Alme,

I am engaged to sing at all 4 of the concerts in London in which Edvard will be appearing, isn't that extraordinary? However, it probably won't come to anything, as I am much too much up and down, have recently had another gruesome attack of gallstones too, and that sets me back for long periods.[9]

Unusually, the Griegs spent a fairly relaxed autumn at Troldhaugen before leaving for Berlin at the beginning of the new year. There was consequently more time for correspondence, exchanges with Delius being particularly in evidence. To his English friend, who had recently advised him: 'Please take care this winter & do not exert yourself too much for the sake of Pounds stirling [*sic*]', he replied:

As far as sterling is concerned, it's all very well for you to talk, dear friend! It's precisely because of this that I *must* make every effort. I most certainly don't do so for pleasure. It is ridiculous that I should have to play, for I have no talent for playing in public. However, the Pounds sterling don't come in from conducting. – Your idea that we meet again in Paris this winter has no hope of being fulfilled, of this I'm quite sure, for I'm fully engaged during the winter months. At the end of January I'm conducting at a Bülow Concert in Berlin, and from there it's straight on to Liverpool and London.[10]

Delius in turn counselled his mentor: 'do your gymnastics thoroughly & take care in London. I hope that the Pounds stirling will flow in.'[11] Meanwhile, the

Augeners were looking forward to Grieg's forthcoming visit. At the same time as he had sent some pieces of silver jewellery for Charles Harding's wife Ada and their daughters Ethel and Emily, he had sent similar gifts to the Augener ladies. Augener thanked him on 22 December, sending in return at Christmas a carefully-packed English porcelain figurine as a token of their friendship. Grieg would see from the clipping from *The Athenaeum* that he enclosed how respected and admired he was in England. And he would be particularly amused to hear how one of Augener's representatives, newly returned from Scotland, had been assured there that Grieg was a Scotsman, or at least (and more accurately) was of Scottish descent.

Yet another concert proposal came in from England after Christmas, with Grieg advising Abraham: 'I have today received an offer of an engagement from Manchester (Hallé) for 28th February. However, as it's a question of the Piano Concerto I shall now telegraph, just as you would have done anyway: Sorry, impossible! Grieg.'[12] The date however was free, and the problem was to be resolved by Grieg's agreeing to conduct the work at the Free Trade Hall with Hallé himself as the soloist, the mooted Liverpool concert having fallen by the wayside.

Leaving Bergen on 2 January 1889 by the sea route to Christiania and continuing to Berlin via Copenhagen, Grieg next performed in the German capital before continuing to Leipzig, where he and Nina spent the first half of February. *Nordisk Musik-Tidende* announced his programme in London: there were to be four concerts, the first on 23 February and the last on 14 March, when the *Peer Gynt Suite* and the Piano Concerto would be conducted by the composer, 'who had succeeded in persuading the Concert Management to engage Fru Grøndahl to play the piano part'.[13] The journal also noted that she was to play the Concerto in Christiania on 2 March –a useful rehearsal for the Philharmonic Society's concert. In fact Grieg, once all had fallen into place, was to take part in six concerts in London and two in Manchester. On 19 January *The Musical Standard*, under the rubric 'Philharmonic Society', made an error-strewn announcement to its readers: 'EDUARD GRIEG, the distinguished Norwegian composer – but semi-English by birth – whose playing last season created so much interest, will appear at the first concert'.[14] The *Standard* was a fine journal, which usefully tended to include small news items and reviews of concerts both in and around the capital and in the provinces that its principal sister publications often failed to record. At the same time, it was rather more prone than its competitors to gaffes – well exemplified here.

The Leeds violinist Edgar Haddock had a penchant for music from Scandinavia, and one of the first reported Grieg performances of 1889 took place on 14 January when, accompanied by Miss Kate Haddock, he played Grieg's third Violin Sonata in his native city. In March he would devote a whole evening to works for violin and piano by Niels Gade.[15]

Birmingham was still hoping for a return visit, with William Stockley suggesting that Grieg might be willing to conduct (at the next concert he was giving on 7 February) a further performance of *In Autumn*. He could, however, only offer a fee of ten guineas, a sum – he pointed out – that Dvořák had accepted on an earlier occasion.[16] Stockley had been a central figure in the musical life of Birmingham since 1845, when he had been offered the conductorship of the Festival Choral Society. A year later he formed an orchestra, intended at the beginning to accompany the chorus in its usual fare of oratorios. In due course he set to improving the quality of his orchestra and in 1874 inaugurated his first season of orchestral concerts. Looking through the list of works that he performed over the years, Grieg could have noted adjacent to them the names of many people he knew: composers like Gade (a Birmingham favourite, represented by *The Crusaders*, *Psyché*, and the 4th and 5th Symphonies), Svendsen (the Cello Concerto), Sullivan, Barnett, and Cowen; pianists such as Franklin Taylor, Leonard Borwick, Walter Bache and Agathe Backer Grøndahl; violinists of the distinction of Johannes Wolff; and a whole range of distinguished singers. Niels Gade, in Birmingham in 1883, told Stockley and his chorus that Stockley knew *Psyché* better than he did himself. And Arthur Sullivan summed up the impact of Stockley's efforts by declaring, 'When I first knew Birmingham it reminded me, in musical matters, of a huge boa constrictor that took an enormous gorge once in three years and fasted in the interim!' In the late 1870s the unknown Edward Elgar played among Stockley's first violins and was rewarded by seeing his *Intermezzo Mauresque* included in one of the concerts. Stockley reaped his own reward, with Elgar dedicating *Sevillana* to him, a work duly played at a later concert. Stockley stayed with the Festival Choral Society until 1895, resigning exactly fifty years after founding it; and two years later he retired from the orchestral society that he had founded and that had borne his name. Grieg did not take up his offer to conduct at one of his concerts, but his name was not to be absent from Stockley's programmes, with *In Autumn*, the *Two Elegiac Melodies*, one at least of the two *Peer Gynt* suites, and music from *Sigurd Jorsalfar* having been offered to the Birmingham public by 1895.

Charles Harding kept the Birmingham flag flying, writing to Grieg later in the month and addressing letters simultaneously to Augener in London and to Peters in Leipzig. He wanted to know 'when we may look forward to the pleasure of seeing you and Mrs. Grieg to whom I much desire to be introduced'. He had heard from his colleagues Rensburg and Stockley that Grieg was unlikely to be at 'the Liverpool or Birmingham Concerts', but encouraged Grieg to come for a week, once his London concerts were over, and enjoy the peace and quiet of the countryside, a break that would enable him to see 'something of Warwickshire, and our special attraction to foreigners, Shakespeare's birthplace and home'. He had furthermore received 'a charming letter from Mr. Beyer, how beautifully he expresses himself and in a foreign language too!!'[17] His letter to Leipzig of the same date expands a little on his invitation:

> I want to know when we are to have the pleasure of seeing you and Mrs. Grieg for a few days or a week at our house to renew the very agreeable intimacy of last year. Mrs Harding and I are both anxious to have the pleasure of an introduction to Mrs. Grieg.

Probably a little after your London Concerts will be pleasant for you and we shall be able to show you something of the beauties of Warwickshire scenery, though we cannot boast of your rugged mountains & grand waterfalls, still we have a special interest in the birthplace and home of Shakespeare, who I learn from Mr. Beyer you reverence as we do. I shall be glad to know the dates of your London Concerts as Mrs. Harding & I hope to go up to one of them for I hear from Mr. Rensburg and Mr. Stockley that you have given up the idea of appearing in Birmingham and Liverpool.[18]

In the event, Grieg's programme for the several weeks he was now to spend in England was to be far too heavy to allow of a second visit to the Hardings, however pleasurable the prospect. Indeed, he was very soon obliged to turn down what in better days he might have seen as a particularly attractive proposition, for reasons which he himself supplied. It was Berger who made the offer, suggesting that in view of Cowen's now being unable to be back in London from his Australian engagements in time to conduct the Philharmonic Society's concert of 14 March, Grieg might care to accept the conductorship of the entire concert. For this he would receive a fee of sixty guineas. Would Grieg care to be the Society's 'good angel' and take over responsibility for the remaining works on the programme, as well as his own? 'Should you agree, you would be doing the Society a great favour, & it may interest you to continue the sequence of famous conductors (Mendelssohn, Spohr, Wagner, etc.) who have collaborated with us.' Beethoven's Symphony no. 4 would have to stay on the programme, but Grieg would be free to substitute other works of his choice should he feel disinclined to conduct the two further works earmarked for the concert, Sterndale Bennett's overture *Parisina* and the *Danse macabre* of Saint-Saëns.[19] But Grieg had to decline the tempting prospect of perhaps having the opportunity to introduce works by other of his fellow countrymen:

> It grieves me, but because of my poor health it is impossible for me to accept your honourable offer. If I were to take over the conductorship of the whole concert, it would – with my present state of health – be the last concert of my life! Believe me, I would dearly have loved to give both you and myself the pleasure, had I only been capable of taking on the concert. Beethoven's B-flat Symphony is one of my favourite compositions. How very much I would have liked to have conducted it! But there can be no question of it. I should quite simply not be able to get through with it.
>
> In the hope that it is not your wish that I should, on the 14th of March, co-operate with 'The Philharmonic Society' for the last time in my life, I sign myself with all respect
> Yours
> Edvard Grieg[20]

Grieg was now resting in Leipzig after conducting two successful concerts in Berlin. 'Just imagine,' he wrote to Delius,

> the rush to attend the last concert was so great that *hundreds* were turned away. The critics were abusive, but it was a success nevertheless, and a very considerable one.

And I have become so blasé that the approval of an unbiased audience is worth more
to me than all the critics put together, whether they rage or praise.[21]

The problem that Grieg had with German critics was never going to go away. It
was a problem from which he suffered far less when in England, although there was
always the odd reviewer prepared to take a pot-shot at him. George Bernard Shaw
found Grieg hard to take, among other reasons simply because his music didn't
sound like Wagner's. The consequence has been that the book of music history in
England has become slightly distorted in Grieg's case, since it is Shaw's collected
and frequently reprinted criticisms that are most often quoted. It is nevertheless
perfectly clear that English critics on the whole remained well-disposed to Grieg's
music. And at the same time, just as in Germany and elsewhere, audiences loved
it and always came back for more. As for the forthcoming trip, there remained the
question of Nina's health. In Berlin a doctor had decided that there was less to
worry about than had at first seemed likely; it was, it seemed, quite probable that
gallstones did not lie at the root of her condition. 'May God grant that London
doesn't become a source of grief for her and so for us both', Grieg told Beyer. 'Just
like last time, I'll be going there with a heavy heart, but this time for a different
reason.'

A significant figure, the Reverend Stopford Brooke, staunch ally of the Unitarian
movement, was coming for the first time into Grieg's life, as Grieg also told Beyer:

> Apropos London: Just think, I had a letter from Miss Brooke, a charming letter with
> a greeting from her father, saying that we must visit them when we come to London.
> I think I shall try to find some time for this, simply so that I'll be able tell you a little
> about it. This father of hers must really be a remarkable man. He has recently read
> something of Ibsen's in an English translation which has affected him deeply. What
> can it have been? Only a little of Ibsen has been translated – but latterly, according to
> what I have been informed, 'Emperor and Galilean'. And that's perhaps just the thing
> for him, this renegade priest.[22]

The letter in question had been written on 30 December 1888 from the Brookes'
London home at 1 Manchester Square. Honor Brooke had had news of Grieg's
likely visit and wanted to know if it were true that he was returning to England:

> I hope you will let me know if it is so – for it would be such a pleasure – if you would
> allow us to do so – to welcome you amongst us – Father asks me to say from him how
> glad he would be to see you – if you could & would come & dine or lunch with us
> any day you liked to give . . . Father & I have lately been reading a translation of some
> of Ibsen's works & he is greatly struck by their strength & powerful individuality –
> Do you think any more of his works will be shortly translated, for the sake of some of
> us Englishmen who know not your language? I hope it may be so.

Shortly before leaving Leipzig, Grieg wrote to Hallé. With London dates having
largely fallen into place, he could see that a further concert was now a possibility.
He was glad to be able to tell Hallé that his health had taken a distinct turn for the

better; he had a 'renewed enthusiasm for life' and could, he felt, now travel up to Manchester between his London engagements. He offered to play the Piano Concerto and perhaps conduct his *Two Elegiac Melodies*. 'I do not wish for any fee, just reimbursement of travelling expenses and hotel for me and my wife'. His offer may have come late, he wrote, but it would be an honour to collaborate with Hallé.[23] The offer was eagerly accepted, but the two men were subsequently to come to an agreement to reverse their performing roles in the case of the Concerto.

It is appropriate to take a snapshot of London musical life as Grieg found it at the end of the 1880s, for he was to come into contact with many of the institutions that helped to make it up. He had for a long time been in touch with the Philharmonic Society and had, of course, made his first appearance in England at the fourth concert of the Society's 1888 season. The season, generally of seven concerts, lasted from March until June each year, and the concerts were usually given on Thursday evenings in St James's Hall, Piccadilly. Then there were the Monday and Saturday Popular Concerts, under the direction of the firm of S. Arthur Chappell; these were also held at St James's Hall during a season that lasted from October to March. So by arranging to spend the second half of February and the whole of March 1889 in England, Grieg was ultimately able to secure engagements at no less than four Popular Concerts as well as two Philharmonic Society Concerts. The weekly Crystal Palace Concerts, under the veteran August Manns, were held on Saturday afternoons at the Crystal Palace in Sydenham, south London, throughout the winter; a 'summer' season began in February and continued until the first week of June. Another important element in the concert calendar was the annual season, established in 1879, of Richter Concerts in St James's Hall from May to July. Hans Richter was a frequent visitor to England and would move to Manchester when he ultimately took charge of the Hallé Concerts in 1900. Then there was Henschel's London Symphony Concerts season, which lasted from November to February, during which period Charles Hallé would also come to London to give his own concert series. Large-scale choral works could find welcoming homes both at the Crystal Palace and at the Royal Albert Hall. At the latter venue the Royal Choral Society would hold a series of concerts from January to April each year. Lighter fare was provided by the London Ballad Concerts, under the aegis of John Boosey, which were given weekly from November to March at St James's Hall.

There was much more: concerts by the schools of music, pre-eminent being those given at St James's Hall by the Royal Academy of Music between February and July; recital series offered by first-class instrumentalists and singers; and private concerts galore organized in the grand houses of London society and also in the rather less grand homes of those who sought to emulate the social elite. The musical possibilities of London, in other words, were endless, probably helping to account for the extraordinary rate of immigration of musicians from continental Europe, musicians who because of political or economic circumstances at home had for decades come to seek their fortune in the world's greatest metropolis, often subsequently fanning out to and settling in the English provinces, where they might be more easily able to make a living as performers or teachers. A 'land without music'? London's concert life was second to none.

Early on the morning of 16 February the Griegs left Leipzig by rail for London, travelling by way of Cologne and Brussels and making the crossing from Calais to Dover. The journey had been a good one; they had had a rail compartment to themselves for almost the whole of the way, the Channel crossing had been quite splendid, and England had greeted them with fine spring weather. George Augener's son William met them at Victoria Station on the 17th and accompanied them to Clapham, where they were again to stay with the Augener family. On the 18th Grieg boarded an omnibus into the West End to see 'Steinway's people' and bought an expensive bouquet of flowers for Augener's wife. His Cello Sonata was one of the items on the programme of the Saturday Popular Concert of 23 February, and it was arranged that the composer should have a rehearsal with the legendary Alfredo Piatti on the 19th. He had been forewarned by Neruda, however, that the elderly cellist was past his best and was advised not too place his hopes too high. With Nina by now engaged to sing at all but one of the London and Manchester concerts (the exception being the second of the two Philharmonic Society Concerts, which was now scheduled for 28 March), there were further rehearsals, most of them being held at home at the Augeners'. Both Hallé and Neruda, married the previous year, insisted – 'with indefatigable energy', according to Grieg – on Nina singing in Manchester, and a busy correspondence was conducted with Hallé for the whole of the first week in London. 'As my wife is well now,' wrote Grieg to Abraham, 'it would be a pity after all to engage another singer for my songs.'[24]

At the same time, the composer's worst fears were confirmed when he first opened the album of 60 of his songs just published by Peters and Augener. 'The songs have now come out *with all the old mistakes* in the English translation that I referred to!! Why?' he asked Abraham. Nothing had been done about the faulty versions – a not unfamiliar failing in the publishing business. Just one letter from Frederick Corder to Grieg survives. It was written from Corder's home in Brighton some three weeks later, on 14 March, Corder sending a presumably revised translation of the last verse of 'The Rosebud'. He told Grieg that he would 'try again' at his translation of 'The Swan', which Grieg had found to be unsatisfactory, and he pointed the composer in the direction of 'Mr. Peters', who held at the time the only copy of his translation of *Bergliot*, something that Grieg had asked him for.[25] Nonetheless, this particular 'Grieg Album' was brought out at just the moment to maximize its sales, featuring prominently, 'As Sung at the Monday Popular Concerts', for some months in the advertisement columns of *The Monthly Musical Record*.[26] Grieg was not alone in complaining of Corder's work, Frederick Delius some thirty years later simply describing song-translations of Corder's with which he was acquainted as 'bad' – quite possibly of course referring to versions of some of these Grieg originals. It may well be that Corder was piqued at Grieg's criticism of his work, for some years later he wrote an article for *The Musical Standard* entitled 'On the Study of Scores', in which he picked holes in Grieg's scoring, comparing him unfavourably with his contemporaries Tchaikovsky and Dvořák:

> Grieg's scoring appears to me to be forced and laboured; its undoubted originality is mechanical, not musical. No musician who could really hear what he was writing would commit such absurdities as may be found in 'Bergliot' and the 'Holberg Suite,' pieces obviously written for the piano in the first instance. Grieg's music is so simple in structure that it affords no scope for the ordinary devices of instrumentation, and this has forced him to invent these organ-like duplications of string parts in the octave above and below, which are his specialty.[27]

It is perhaps worth remembering that both of the works to which Corder refers date from before the winter of 1887–8, a period Grieg spent in Leipzig specifically to study and update himself in the techniques of orchestration. Moreover, while praising Tchaikovsky and Dvořák, Corder goes on to propose that they were 'apt, however, to lay the colour on with a trowel'.

In his notebook Grieg records his expenditure on a number of bus trips over the first few days and on a cab just once, on 20 February, which seems to have been a particularly busy day. Letters are sent to Charles Harding, Max Laistner, Helen Hopekirk, Richard Gompertz,[28] the Hagerup family – and to Frederick Corder. On Friday 22 February there was a trip to Maida Hill, where Piatti lived at 15 Northwick Terrace. Grieg was expected at 12.30, presumably for lunch, and then there was to be a final rehearsal with the venerable cellist.

The day of Grieg's first public appearance – a Saturday Popular Concert at St James's Hall – dawned. The dispatch of the concerto parts to Hallé in Manchester had first to be attended to. 'Drops' – or boiled sweets – had been bought two days earlier, no doubt for Nina, who had a sore throat; and now 'ammonia' too – 5 d. worth, presumably in the form of smelling-salts – was purchased on the morning of the concert, 1½ d. subsequently being spent at the barber's. The bus or tram as a means of transport was temporarily abandoned, with cabs the order of the day. Two string quartets were on the programme: Spohr's Quartet in A major, Op. 93, and Haydn's Quartet in C major, Op. 33, no. 3. But it was Grieg who was the principal draw, playing the Cello Sonata with Piatti, accompanying Nina in six of his songs, and playing two pieces from *Pictures from Folk Life*, Op. 19. As an encore he played from the *Improvisations on Two Norwegian Folk Songs*, Op. 29. Grieg's reappearance in London was deemed by *The Monthly Musical Record* to be 'the great event of the season',[29] and the journal's subsequent issue included a review of the concert, under the heading 'Monday and Saturday Popular Concerts', by 'J.B.K.', a review that was repeated almost verbatim (apart from the interesting deletion of 'exceptionally' in relation to Grieg's 'fascinating qualities as a pianist') in *Musical Opinion*:

> Two important events have distinguished the current series of these concerts. The

Alfredo Piatti

first in order [the second being the appearance of Joachim shortly afterwards] was Edvard Grieg's reappearance, whose music – a rare blending of true poetry and exemplary skill with the popular (i.e. Scandinavian) national element – has instantly become a favourite wherever (France included) the name of Grieg has become known. The most important work from his pen brought forward was the Sonata for Pianoforte and Violoncello, Op. 36, in A minor, played by the composer with Signor Piatti, which – for originality, spontaneity, melodic and rhythmical wealth and charm, variety and piquancy of harmony (quite apart from the Northern local colour), nervous force, stirring passion and *entrain* – is hard to match in modern chamber music. And if the working out of the first *allegro* consists chiefly in repetitions in different keys, let us have such repetitions – so novel and striking in the change of tonality – by all means; whilst in the *finale* (of Schubertian length, but without a bar to spare) the truly organic development of the beautiful subject-matter, which rises at time to a lofty height, would do credit even to Brahms. No wonder that the sonata was chosen by Liszt for performance at one of the famous Weimar festivals! The reception bestowed upon the hero of the day – whose exceptionally fascinating qualities as a pianist were again exemplified in the performance of the above-named work . . . and of some of his exquisite little pianoforte pieces – was, like last year, of a most enthusiastic description, in which Madame Grieg, as the sympathetic exponent of her husband's delightful *lieder*, took her share.[30]

There were favourable reviews in *The Illustrated London News*, which informed its readership that Grieg's music 'has a distinctive character of Northern romanticism, and his playing is that of an intellectual artist',[31] as well as in *The Globe and Traveller*, which wrote of St James's Hall 'attracting more visitors than could be accommodated, Herr Edward Grieg being announced to make his first appearance this season', adding that the composer and his wife 'won hearty and abundant applause'.[32] *The Musical Standard* was disappointed that Grieg had not offered a third solo piano piece and found the 'Bridal Procession' to be 'of peculiarly "decomposed" rhythm' – whatever that might have meant. Its reviewer noted how well Nina and the songs were received, adverse criticism being reserved for the Cello Sonata. 'We do not greatly esteem Herr Greig's duet sonata in A minor. The "working out" chiefly consists of repetitions in other keys, an old device of Rossini in some of his overtures.'[33] 'The public came literally in strong force', reported *The Musical Times*. 'The cause of this unwonted excitement was the announcement that Herr and Madame Grieg would appear for the first time at these Concerts.' The Cello Sonata was deemed to be 'very winning and attractive', and the 'fresh and unconventional *Finale*' was particularly remarked upon. There had been no need for the apology made beforehand on behalf of Nina, who was suffering from a sore throat, as she was heard 'to much advantage' in the songs that she sang.[34] Nina had sung each of her husband's songs in the original Norwegian, a fact that seemed to be of no special hindrance to the audience's appreciation. And a leading woman's journal remarked that 'although the indulgence of the audience was solicited on behalf of the singer, who was suffering from sore throat, there appeared little necessity for the apology, for each song was delivered with much expressive power and great refinement of style'. As for Grieg's solos, they had been played 'with remarkable delicacy of touch and great technical mastery'.[35] At each of Grieg's piano recitals in England, a regular feature was the focus on the make-up of his audiences, with their preponderance of young women with whom the *Lyric Pieces* were great favourites – by now a matter of staple fare in so far as the home entertainment of the middle classes was concerned. Shaw could scarcely conceal his disdain:

> As to Mr. Grieg, at the Popular Concerts, I tried to get in on Saturday, but found the room filled with young ladies, who, loving his sweet stuff, were eager to see and adore the confectioner. So on Monday I forebore St James's Hall altogether, lest my occupying a seat should be the means of turning away even one enthusiastic worshipper.[36]

Later in the month, Shaw was slightly more circumspect when writing for a Norwegian readership, as the *Pall Mall Gazette* reported:

> Those of our young ladies who count among the admirers of Herr Grieg will be interested to hear what Mr. Bernard Shaw says of them in an article on the Norwegian composer and his wife, which he contributes to a recent number of Dagblad. He

says: 'It is especially our young ladies who are quite delighted with Grieg's melodious shorter compositions and their beautiful variations. When they hear Grieg play they say, "How very Northern this is! How natural for the one who was born in the country of the fjords and of the midnight sun! How true his local colours are." '[37]

Despite the evident warmth of his reception, Grieg's report in a letter to Delius dispatched the following day was sober, to say the least:

> I had my first Popular Concert yesterday. Played my Cello Sonata with Piatti, as famous as he is boring (between you and me). It was absolute torture for me. The hall was crowded and the enthusiasm great. My poor wife was not well but nevertheless had to sing, as well as she could in the circumstances. But it is so very cold inside the houses here that any singer is bound to catch cold. Tomorrow I have my 2nd Popular Concert, I am playing with Mad. Neruda. Thank goodness there is fire and vitality there.[38]

When finished with 'the damned piano playing', he added, 'I'll be as happy as a sandboy.' Later that day there was another trip into town, no doubt in order to rehearse for the following day's concert. Still with an eye on his purse, Grieg took the bus one way, but from the 26th on – until he returned from Manchester a few days later – he evidently decided that cab travel would be more convenient, whatever the cost. The Grieg programme on the 25th was to be shared with Dvořák's Quartet in E-flat major, Op. 51, with Neruda (henceforth Lady Hallé) as leader, and Beethoven's Trio in G major, Op. 9, no. 2. Grieg was to play a selection of six of his *Lyric Pieces*, Nina to sing five songs, and the centrepiece was to be the first Violin Sonata, with Grieg accompanying Lady Hallé. Meanwhile, more 'drops' were purchased for the suffering Nina. Their effectiveness appeared to have been more than sufficient, with the Norwegian daily *Dagbladet* reporting that, like Grieg's playing, Nina's singing had been received with great applause.[39] *The Musical Times* almost reluctantly accepted that Chappell had secured for his Concerts a 'musical lion' in Edvard Grieg, whose appearance 'had the effect of crowding St. James's Hall in all parts', but the journal added a condescending note in declaring that the 'trifling pieces' that he played were 'not very interesting'. The 'delightful' Violin Sonata, however, was a 'welcome item', and Nina's rendering of five of her husband's songs was 'equally appreciated'.[40] *The Court Circular* was equally dismissive of the piano solos, the choice of which it did not find 'felicitous'. It nonetheless proclaimed 'A gala week this at the "Popular Concerts" in honour of Herr Grieg, the Norwegian composer and pianiste', and its reviewer was more complimentary in respect of the Violin Sonata and Nina's singing of her husband's songs.[41] Grieg's audience, however, welcomed the piano pieces with open arms. 'He was recalled to the platform again and again after the performance, but declined to play a supplementary piece, and contented himself with bowing his acknowledgements'.[42] *Musical Opinion*, too, was perfectly happy with Grieg's choice of piano solos, and was delighted with the 'lovely' Violin Sonata. Finding, on the other hand, the

Dvořák quartet to be 'as barren of interest as can be', the journal's reviewer felt that the latter work 'might have made way for Grieg's remarkably original and fanciful work of this kind, both on its own merits and as a graceful compliment to the illustrious visitor'.[43]

The Musical Standard offered a lively, if quirky review:

Herr Edvard Grieg again attracted a large audience, and the shilling seats were filled to the last. The hall was very badly lighted. On the Norwegian musician's appearance to play his solos, salvos of applause burst forth. The 'Improvisata' in A minor, is a characteristic effusion with 'snaps,' by way of impressing a national character. The 'Album-leaf,' in F major, sounds decidedly Chopinesque, a thoroughly sentimental ditty in the tenderest vein of the somewhat effeminate Polish pianist. The 'Stabbe-lat' in C, a Norwegian dance, has a very captivating theme, quite what Weber has styled an 'Invitation to the Dance'; the time is 2-4; here we have rhythmical and graceful music. The wretched 'insatiables' demanded an *encore*, but Herr Grieg declined the honour, after two tiresome 'calls.' A Steinway pianoforte was used as on the previous Saturday. The sonata for pianoforte and violin in F, heard on former occasions, is interesting throughout the three movements. The first allegro, a little too protracted, reminds one of Rubinstein's style. The allegretto in A minor continues the charm, and the finale, in the rondo form, is all dash and *entrain*. Exquisite was the *finesse* of Mme. Néruda's execution, and the composer, as a matter of course, took good care of his own part. This sonata would be perfect if Herr Grieg knew at what point to stop. So people sometimes say that an excellent sermon is spoiled because the preacher, at a good climax, *will* go on with a 'sixthly, my brethren.' . . . Mme. Grieg again pleased the public, and one of her songs, 'A Fair Vision,' won a *bis*. The English words have been criticized, but we cannot believe that Mr. F. Corder is responsible for the word 'pourtray' (portray). The Norwegian vernacular sounds sufficiently uncouth; *ex gra*: 'men burte *og* burte *og* burte;' 'Og Andlidets Drag,' 'Med Elskovs Leg og Lyst,' 'Eg ser Lena best när eg blundar,' &c.[44]

It was left to *The Graphic* usefully to sum up Grieg's two opening concerts:

This eminent Norwegian composer and pianist has made his re-appearance at the Popular Concerts, where his poetical and fanciful music, in which the Norwegian national element plays so important a part, has formed an agreeable change from the ordinary classical repertory. For his solos Grieg selected some of his most characteristic works, including a Norwegian dance, entitled 'Stabbe Lat,' from his *Norwegian Folk-Songs*, and two of his 'Scenes from Norwegian national life,' viz:– *On the Mountains*, and the scene in which *The Norwegian Bridal Procession* gradually approaches, and as gradually dies away in the distance. Far better from a musical point of view were his two duet sonatas, one the early work in F, played on Monday, with Lady Hallé, and the other the beautiful sonata in A minor, in which the composer was, on Saturday, associated with Signor Piatti. No less remarkable was the singing of the composer's wife, Madame Grieg, of eleven of her husband's Norwegian songs.[45]

The Saturday Review, too, bundled both of the Popular Concerts into one review, remarking on the 'immense audiences' attracted by the Griegs, but allowing a degree of ambiguity to creep into its recording of the performances. In respect of the two Norwegian executants, it was

impossible to judge whether their powers are of wide extent. The probability is that they are not; but within the limits to which they are confined no more perfect nor interesting performances have been heard. Without possessing much power, Mme. Grieg charmed the audience by the singularly unconventional style of her singing. Her voice is not remarkable for tone or quality, and it is no longer in its first freshness; but her singing is so delightful that it captivates the ear and disarms criticism. Herr Grieg's playing has many of the same qualities as his wife's singing. Both in their own way are perfect, and the pianist shows that he is an executant of high merit, while at the same time his playing is remarkable for the total absence of the least degree of affectation or eccentricity. It is full of poetic charm and expression, and, like his music, has a character of its own which it is impossible to explain otherwise than as an echo of the artist's nationality.[46]

Yet another journal which presented to its readers an overall view of the two concerts was the *Lady's Pictorial*. On each occasion, it reported, St James's Hall was 'crammed to excess'.

We had proof last year of the wonderful hold Grieg's music has obtained over English amateurs, and also of the wonderful degree in which that music gains when rendered by himself or his talented wife ... Grieg has been aptly described as the 'Scandinavian Chopin,' and he deserves the name, not only as regards the tender poetic sentiment and ineffable grace of his compositions, but for the perfection of touch and technique that he brings to bear on their interpretation. Enough, then, that he was applauded with enthusiasm, and recalled to the platform again and again ... Madame Nina Grieg has not a particularly fine voice, and is not a great singer in the accepted sense of the term. But she knows how to sing her husband's songs as no one else does, and therein affords a pleasure in its way unsurpassable. It is manifest that she has caught his inspiration in every tiny *nuance*, in the highest gradation of tone and feeling. On Saturday Mdme. Grieg was complaining of a sore throat; on Monday, when I heard her, her high notes were still slightly affected by the same cause. The composer, of course, accompanied her, coming forward to do so before he played his solo pieces; and I could not help noticing the sweet modesty of the wife in purposely standing aside for a moment at the top of the platform steps, so that the audience might bestow a greeting of welcome upon her illustrious spouse. Her first two songs were 'The Princess' and 'Wood Wanderings,' the latter being encored after much persuasion. The second group comprised 'The first primrose,' 'Spring,' and 'O fair Vision'. To hear these songs sung and accompanied in such ideal fashion was an unalloyed treat.[47]

With these first two concerts of the tour having successfully been completed, it was time on the 27th to travel to Manchester. But not before Grieg had written to Francesco Berger to try to finalize arrangements for the second of his two forthcoming Philharmonic Society concerts on 28 March. Although he was prepared to conduct the Piano Concerto, he expressed the wish also to conduct a further piece, feeling that he could not appear 'with the Concerto alone'. His wife was feeling much better and could now sing at the first concert on the 20th, with Grieg's proviso that no other singer should be engaged to sing on the same occasion. His fee for this concert would be £30, and that of his wife £20.[48] All was beginning to fall into place, although the Philharmonic Society was unable to accede to his request to conduct a second work on the 28th. He generously agreed to waive his own fee for the concert in favour of Agathe Backer Grøndahl, should agreement be reached that she be engaged to play his Concerto. 'For my splendid "lady compatriot" I am prepared to do everything within my power.'[49] It seems extraordinary that at this late stage Backer Grøndahl had still not formally been engaged for such an important concert, and Grieg four days later asked Berger to let him know her response. The indefatigable Berger was also programming one of Grieg's works elsewhere while the composer was in England, a report in *The Queen* under the heading 'Musical Doings' providing evidence of his activity. 'Herr Francesco Berger has

Charles Hallé

commenced at 6, York Street, Portman-square, the twentieth year of his Après-Midi Instrumentales, which have as their object the affording to musical amateurs opportunity of practising concerted music of standard composers with instrumentalists of acknowledged reputation.' Berger usually played the piano himself on these occasions, and on 1 March his next 'afternoon' was to include Grieg's first Violin Sonata.[50] (In the same issue of the journal, a query from a reader asking in respect of Grieg's fellow Norwegian Halfdan Kjerulf (1815–1868), 'Is this composer living, and of what country is he a native?', elicited the response 'He is living, and was born either in Sweden or Norway. – ED.')

Taking the midday train from King's Cross on 27 February, the Griegs arrived at 4.20 in Manchester, where they were booked in for the nights of 27 and 28 February at the Queen's Hotel, not far from the city's London Road Station. (It should perhaps be noted that Hallé had programmed on 3 January an anticipatory first *Peer Gynt Suite*.) Grieg's notebook contains the cryptic entry: 'Steinway, Pianof in Queens Hotel, Manc. Wednesday'. The only important extra-musical task on the day of the concert – Thursday the 28th – was to buy a new pair of gloves for Nina. In the evening 'Sir Charles Hallé's Grand Concert', with an orchestra of 'upwards of one hundred performers', was to take place (as the programme informed its readers) as 'the last concert but one of the season'. Of the English song-translations printed in the programme below the original Norwegian texts, all but one were by Corder, the exception being 'I Love But Thee' in a version by Ethel Smyth. The concert began with Weber's overture to *Oberon*, which was followed by Grieg's Concerto, played by Hallé under the composer's baton. Three songs were then sung by Nina, accompanied at the piano by Grieg: 'Two Brown Eyes', 'I Love But Thee', and 'Moonlit Forest'; and the first part of the evening was concluded with a performance of Schubert's 'Unfinished' Symphony. After the interval Grieg conducted his *Two Elegiac Melodies*, following which he accompanied Lady Hallé in a performance of his first Violin Sonata. Nina next sang a further three songs, her husband again accompanying her at the piano: 'To Springtime My Song I'm Singing', 'Margaret's Cradle Song', and 'Good Morning!' Lady Hallé then played Beethoven's Romanza in F major, and the concert came to an end with Wagner's *Tannhäuser* overture. On this, their first appearance in Manchester, Grieg and Nina received a genuinely warm welcome. Carl Fuchs, who was to play the cello in Grieg's String Quartet around the time when the composer returned to Manchester in 1897, was in the audience, and he particularly remembered how Nina sang the songs 'in a truly artistic manner'.[51] *The Musical Times* wrote:

> Herr Grieg was especially fortunate with his executants, for Sir Charles Hallé undertook his Pianoforte Concerto (Op. 16), and Lady Hallé so thoroughly co-operated with the composer in Op. 8 as to secure a perfect realisation of the pleasing duet. Madame Grieg, with modest powers as a vocalist, gave probably the most sympathetic interpretation possible of the little *Lieder*, which so happily display her husband's fertility in bright, sketchy fancies, rather than gift of bold and sustained flight.

By insisting upon an absolutely *pianissimo* rendering of portions of his brief poems for strings, and by the general shading of their delicate effects, Herr Grieg has taught our orchestra a welcome and important lesson.[52]

The Manchester press, as might have been expected, on the whole accorded good coverage to the concert, with the *Manchester Evening News* showing itself in a reflective mode:

A certain halo of romance seems to be inseparably associated with everything Scandinavian, and the mere mention of Norse music conjures up visions of the weird and mysterious . . . As a composer [Grieg] is invariably delightful. He does not affect grandeur, and while a German training has enabled him successfully to grapple with the composition of a sonata, we feel that it is in his smaller pieces for orchestra, pianoforte, or voice that he is so entirely charming. Although as a conductor he lacks that commanding presence which we are accustomed to look for, he never fails to infuse into his subordinates some of his own spirit and animation. As a pianist he is an admirable interpreter of the lighter and more graceful side of musical literature, albeit at times he shows ample evidence of power and self-repression . . . There are many greater vocalists before the world than Mdme. Grieg, but it can safely be said that there is not one who could render the songs she gave last night in the same exquisitely perfect manner.[53]

The concert was reported in London, too:

The presence of Edvard Grieg, the now well-known Norwegian composer, at the concert last evening gave the performance a special and peculiar interest. The occasions on which it is given to us to hear concertos and sonatas played either by or under the direction of the composer are few and far between . . . There is something in the personality of the creative artist which is independent of mere executive skill. But when this is associated with original genius, as in the case of Grieg, our interest in the artist is doubled. What would some of us not give, were it possible, to hear Mendelssohn play the G minor concerto? . . . No wonder, then, that such an audience assembled last evening as rarely is seen at Sir Charles Hallé's orchestral concerts . . . the Norwegian songs were, we think, appreciated even more highly than Grieg's larger works. They may be supposed to breathe the very spirit of Scandinavian melody, and we can hardly imagine their being more perfectly sung than they were by Madame Grieg. Indeed, though her voice is not either very powerful or of great range, we doubt whether we have ever heard *lieder* sung more chastely or more attractively than on this occasion. In all of them Madame Grieg had the advantage of her husband's pianoforte accompaniment, and we are but expressing a general feeling when we say that no more enjoyable vocal performances have been heard in Manchester . . . Last evening's concert will long live in the recollection of those present; and whenever Herr and Madame Grieg visit us again they will meet with an enthusiastic reception.[54]

The comments of another paper on the Concerto, however, might raise the eyebrows of readers today:

This week's concert, the last but one of Sir Charles Hallé's series, was made memorable by the presence of Herr and Madame Grieg, and, as was to be expected, there was an unusually large audience . . . [The concerto] was played by Sir Charles Hallé and conducted by the composer, who received a most cordial greeting when he appeared at the desk. The concerto was listened to with the greatest interest, not only on account of its own merits, but also because of the brilliant playing of Sir Charles Hallé, and the artistic feeling which made itself recognised even in the time beating of the gifted composer. Still it is questionable whether Herr Grieg's style effectively vindicates itself in works of this importance and extent; for although the concerto is brimful of originality and has passages of great beauty for both orchestra and piano, it is imaginable that with playing any less skilful than that of last evening, its length, its prevalent sombreness of tone, and its occasional vagueness of rhythm might make against its general acceptability.[55]

Grieg's own subsequent adverse comments on Hallé's performance make it clear that any blame for an apparently substandard airing of the Concerto should more probably have been laid at the pianist's door. *The Manchester Examiner*'s critic, who was responsible for the above passage, was clearly in Hallé's thrall and unwilling to censure a local hero. At all events, Hallé would again play Grieg's Concerto at one of his Manchester concerts on 8 November 1894.

Another of Grieg's English friends from the time spent together in Leipzig early in 1888 might in other circumstances have made the short journey from Liverpool to Manchester to hear Hallé's concert and so meet the Norwegian composer once again. Only a few days later, on 5 March, the young Charles Braun, a native of Liverpool, was present at the premiere of his cantata *Ritter Olaf* in that city's Philharmonic Hall, a performance given by the People's Orchestral Society and the Liverpool Musical Association and conducted by the accomplished Alfred Rodewald. 'The orchestration', wrote *The Musical Times*, 'is never wearisome, but undoubtedly clever and ingenious, and often, particularly towards the close, decidedly impressive.' The composer had received 'a most flattering ovation' at the end of the performance.[56] In fact Sinding had alerted Grieg just a few months earlier to the work in progress:

> He's working on a large score for soli, chorus and orchestra which is going to be performed in Liverpool, I believe, some time next year. Damn it, if I could only get up there with Delius when it happens! Will just have to see if business prospers this winter.[57]

The Musical Standard had announced the concert in its issue of 2 March, noting that also on the programme would be Grieg's *In Autumn*. However, Braun apparently now lived near Norwich and would appear to have travelled up to Liverpool unaware of the near-coincidence of his and Grieg's concert dates and of the temporary geographical proximity of his Leipzig friend. The evidence comes in the only letter he wrote to Grieg that survives. It is dated 30 January 1890 and was sent from The Lodge, Bixley, nr. Norwich. Braun had, as he somewhat confusingly explained, looked for Grieg the whole time the Norwegian composer had been in England, but had not succeeded in finding him. He had very much hoped that Grieg and Nina might, at an earlier date, have been able to come to his wedding. Now his wife had just given birth to a son. 'You were so kind and friendly to me when I was in Leipzig that I think you will be pleased to hear this.' *Ritter Olaf* had had a successful performance in Liverpool, and Braun was therefore enclosing a piano score of the work in the hope that Grieg might like it. *In Autumn* had indeed been given at the same concert, and although Grieg had sadly not been there to conduct it, it had nonetheless 'gone splendidly'. Braun explained that he was now at work on a large-scale composition, *Sigurd*, the text being taken from an old Norwegian saga, and he was hoping that it would be performed in the autumn of 1890. (It was certainly published by Novello.) At the same time, six songs of his had been engraved. He closed these lines to Grieg with a request for Sinding's address. Charles Braun enjoyed success of a sort. *The Musical Times* accorded a brief, if complimentary review to his operetta *The Snow Queen*, for children's voices, on its publication in 1897 by Novello.[58] And many of his songs found publishers in the early 1900s. However, he appears to have sunk into musical obscurity thereafter, and there is no record of any subsequent reunion, either with Grieg or other Leipzig friends such as Sinding and Delius.

On returning to Clapham there were a number of letters to write, none better detailing Grieg's concert experience in Manchester than that sent to Max Abraham on 2 March:

> Since I have been here, I, no *we*, my wife & I, have nothing but 'enormous successes' to record. Both of the Popular Concerts went off extremely well, and Chappell is rubbing his hands, for the hall was sold out.
>
> On Thursday (the day before yesterday) we were in Manchester and played with Hallé! There too the hall was sold out (just imagine, over 4,000 people), and I have to admit that the hackneyed old charmer has done just a little too well out of us. In gratitude to his wife I offered, as you know, to co-operate with him by conducting the Concerto and the elegiac Melodies. Then he asked that I play op. 8 with his wife into the bargain, something I could not refuse, (she played it, by the way, really divinely) and then he pestered my wife for so long that in the end she had to sing twice. Well, in her place I would not have done so, but it was an enormous success. It goes without saying that the Concerto had a very mediocre performance, there was nothing else, after all, to be expected of the old man, but – the Elegiac Melodies! They were really wonderfully played by this large orchestra.
>
> On the 9th I am playing op. 13 with Joachim, then probably on the 30th op. 45 with Mad. Neruda, and then Chappell wants absolutely to arrange a recital, for which he offers me £80. I still don't know what to do. My wife has become such a favourite of the public that I'm quite jealous!
>
> The mistakes in the Songs are only the poor translations in 'The Swan' and 'The Rosebud'. In 'The Swan' there is a horrifying B-natural in the 4th bar which must be got rid of! And in Song no. 36: 'My Mind is Like a Mountain Steep', 4 bars are miss-

ing, namely on page 30 after the 29th bar of the song. On the enclosed sheet I have written in the bars concerned using the Danish edition.

With kind regards

Yours

Edvard Grieg

My wife sends many greetings, The doctor in Berlin did wonders, I feel. I am rather thinking of going to Paris in April, am however not yet decided. Delius, to whom I spoke recently, very much advises me to do so.

THE MAN ON THE CLAPHAM OMNIBUS

Hans Lien Brækstad (1845–1915) was a major Norwegian presence in London. A political activist, writer, critic, translator and lecturer, he had settled in the city in 1877 and soon became well known in Anglo-Norwegian circles. A member of London's Scandinavian Club, he was also a leading and somewhat controversial member of the Norwegian Club, a club that was founded by statute in 1888 and still prospers today. Until his country achieved independence from Sweden in 1905 (soon after which he was appointed Norwegian Vice-Consul) he enjoyed a reputation as Norway's unofficial – and of course unpaid – ambassador in London. George Bernard Shaw described his activities briefly:

> in a quiet but effective way [Brækstad] is a kind of private Consul General for Norway in London, is frequently involved in various official undertakings, and has initiated ties between Norway and Norwegians, being the one who first persuaded Mr Edmund Gosse to write about Ibsen.[1]

Brækstad, serving in the family bookshop in Trondheim, had met Gosse when the young Englishman came in during his first visit to Norway in 1871. Gosse later recalled the occasion. He was there, he told William Archer, 'as a common tourist'.

> I strolled into the principal book-shop to buy a Tauchnitz. The foreman (Brækstad), who was unfastening a huge parcel, talked to me in English, and I asked him if there were any Norwegian poets. He said, with indignation, yes, indeed! And added that the parcel before him, just arrived from Copenhagen, contained the last new book of the greatest Norwegian poet, Ibsen. I bought it. It was the *Digte* of 1870; I sent for other books, and finally in the autumn, I reviewed the *Digte* (very ignorantly, in the *Spectator*). That was the first time Ibsen's name was printed in any English publication.[2]

In March 1890 Brækstad was to give a lecture at the Norwegian Club on current relations between Norway and Sweden. (Another Grieg was briefly chairman of the club at the time. This was Alexander Birger Grieg (1866–1947), who also served as club secretary for most of the time between 1889 and 1891. He subsequently

Hans Lien Brækstad

returned to Bergen to run a shipbroking business, later being appointed Brazil-
ian Vice-Consul there.) Brækstad's radical views – 'full equality with Sweden, or
Norway out of the union' – which he frequently promoted in the British press, infuriated a number of the older, more conservative members, with the result that for
some years afterwards the club considered it prudent not to host talks of an overtly
political nature. Indeed, those very members, both of the Scandinavian Club and
the Norwegian Club, whom he himself characterized as unprogressive and 'half-
baked patriots', in turn called Brækstad a 'political agitator' and a 'fiery radical'.[3]

However, Brækstad's views were on the whole dear to Grieg's heart, and like
many other visiting Norwegians he quickly fell within the circle of Brækstad's
acquaintance, and the two became good friends. Some years later Bokken Lasson, Norway's best-known cabaret singer, when in London, found Brækstad to
be 'a man who knew everyone in the world, always on the go, had countless business dealings and commissions and yet always found time to help others'. He
rapidly found an engagement for her at the Empire, Leicester Square.[4] Among
Brækstad's published writings are volumes of translations of Nordic fairy tales,
among them works by Hans Christian Andersen, Peter Christen Asbjørnsen and

others; of Hjalmar Johansen's memoir *With Nansen in the North*; and of works by Bjørnstjerne Bjørnson and Jonas Lie. Finally there was a small book, published in London in 1905 and entitled *The Constitution of the Kingdom of Norway: An Historical and Political Survey*. Written during the fraught period immediately before Norway's achievement of full independence, when a possible war between Norway and Sweden threatened, this was an attempt to mobilize the diplomacy of the British government and those in these islands sympathetic to the Norwegian cause. Brækstad was also a friend of William Archer, the translator of Ibsen's plays, and acted as a kind of unofficial literary agent for him.

Braekstad's name appears in Grieg's pocket-book around this time, his address in town being given as '80, Strand (2nd Floor) / Skand. Klub' and his home address as 138, Loughborough Park, London S.W. He invited the Griegs to join him one evening, having sent them some newspapers containing concert reviews – one of them, *The Graphic* of 2 March, including a portrait of the composer that Grieg thought 'quite good'. Grieg replied that although in principle he and Nina did not go out in the evenings, they would be more than willing to make an exception in Brækstad's case. This would, however, need to be after a short trip to Paris that their intended host was about to make. 'Manchester was a great pleasure', Grieg told him. 'We made Norwegian music for over 4,000 people. And there was real enthusiasm. But I didn't earn a penny! Yes, we artists really are something else.'[5]

With a break of a week before the next concert, due to take place on 9 March, there were everyday tasks to be carried out, the writing of a host of letters among them. One letter was to Oluf Svendsen, Engineer, perhaps the son of the flautist Oluf Svendsen, who until his death in London on 15 May the previous year was probably the best-known and best-loved Norwegian musician working in England – among other things playing first flute in Richter's orchestra. It is scarcely likely that Grieg had met him in London in the earliest days of that first visit, less than a year earlier, for Svendsen was by then quite ill and had not played for some time.

Among the addressees of other letters were Charles Harding, Berger, Joachim,[6] Chappell, Elliott & Fry, Johannes Wolff, Max Abraham, and – again – Brækstad. Grieg chronicles the purchase of a packet of cigarettes, which cost him 6 *d.* on 4 March, just as he lists his barbering expenses, which were to double to 3 *d.* on 7 March. Nina's health evidently still gives cause for some worry, as she has medical treatment at a fee of 12 *s.* 6 *d.* and is prescribed medicine that costs a further 3 *s.* 6 *d.*, again on 7 March. Grieg had written two days earlier to arrange an appointment for her with Dr Felix Semon, a German throat specialist with a Wimpole Street practice, who diagnosed a catarrhal condition that would, however, be unlikely to prevent her from singing. (Perhaps Grieg might have been a little more helpful to his wife by giving up cigarettes for the duration.) At all events, and no doubt well advised, he had gone to the very top for Nina's consultation. Felix Semon (1849–1921), born and later graduating in Berlin, was yet another of those distinguished Germans who had settled in London (in his case in 1874), studying

Oluf Svendsen, Norwegian flautist

with the eminent English physician Sir Morrell Mackenzie. Probably the most celebrated laryngologist of his day, Semon was to be knighted by Queen Victoria in 1897 and four years later was appointed Physician Extraordinary to her son Edward VII. Musically talented, he frequently acted as accompanist to his wife, who was a fine singer.

A day after her consultation there came the consolation of a new pair of shoes for Nina. A fresh item of clothing bought a day or two before a concert in which she was to sing had become something of a tradition. And Nina's voice was again to be protected by a further purchase of boiled sweets on the day of performance. There were, too, almost daily bus trips during the first week of March, one of which was made into town to buy two Norwegian books in English translation: Alexander Kielland's novel *Garman and Worse* and Bjørnstjerne Bjørnson's *Synnøve Solbakken*. A letter to Sigurd Hals, of the Christiania music firm Brødrene Hals, summarizes the programme for the rest of the month and gives some idea of how concert arrangements were frequently made on the hoof in England at this period:

I send you my likeness from 'The Graphic', so that you can see how the debauches of London have affected me. We are beginning to be lion and lioness here now, so it's time to get away while we still haven't quite forgotten who we really are. I'm not sending any reviews, as once you've read one of them, you've read them all. Tomorrow I play the G-Major Sonata with Joachim, you can well imagine how it sounds once he gets going. Then on the 14th I have the Philharm. Society, (the 'Peer Gynt Suite') and on the 20th I give my own recital. On the 28th I hope I shall be conducting for Agathe Grøndahl (though I don't yet know whether she is coming) and on the 30th we play and sing for the last time at a popular Concert. Just where we go from there, I don't know for sure.[7]

A copy of *The Graphic* was also dispatched to Max Abraham: 'My hair has grown rather grey after the London triumphs' was Grieg's comment on the paper's portrait of him.

✦

Grieg, Nina and Joachim were the stellar attractions of Saturday afternoon's Popular Concert at St James's Hall on 9 March. The non-Grieg items on the programme were Mozart's Quintet in D major, which opened the concert, and the Andante and Scherzo from Mendelssohn's unfinished Quartet, which closed it. The first music of Grieg's was two songs sung by Nina, with her husband at the piano: 'I Walked One Balmy Summer Eve' and 'Hope'. Then followed the *Holberg Suite* in its two-hand version, played by the composer, followed by the second Violin Sonata, in which Grieg partnered Joachim. Nina finally sang three more songs: 'To Springtime My Song I'm Singing', 'A Swan', and 'Good Morning!' The *Pall Mall Gazette* wrote of the event's drawing power:

> Saturday afternoon's concert at St. James's Hall for once fully deserved the generic title which the Messrs. Chappell have for thirty years given to their Saturday and Monday musical entertainments. From early in the forenoon an eager crowd had blockaded the entrances to the cheaper parts of the hall, and before the performance began Mr. Basil Tree was turning away money from the stalls. The reason for the popular support on Saturday was the appearance of Dr. Joachim and Herr Grieg as instrumentalists and of Mdme. Grieg as vocalist.[8]

'The hall was full to overflowing', confirmed another journal,[9] while a further weekly wrote of 'one of the largest crowds ever seen at a Popular Concert. It was the first occasion on which these eminent musicians [Grieg and Joachim] had been associated in a London concert-room, and amateurs did not underrate the significance of the event.'[10] *The Musical Times* remarked that 'every seat in the St. James's Hall could have been sold twice over. Every square foot of standing room had its occupant and the room presented a remarkable appearance.' It continued,

> To musicians the most interesting item in the programme was the Sonata in G minor [*sic*] (Op. 13), for pianoforte and violin, which was given for the first time at these

Grieg as depicted in *The Graphic* (2 March 1889)

Concerts. The work, like its companions, is in three movements, all of nearly equal merit and full of Scandinavian character, though rather unsatisfactory as regards development. Each movement is a series of themes, rather than a homogeneous structure. The charm of the melodies themselves, however, affords compensation for this defect, and the Sonata, as played by the composer and Dr. Joachim, excited much enthusiasm. Mr. Grieg also played his clever Suite 'Aus Holberg's Zeit,' and Madame Grieg was heard in five of the songs, which, as usual, she rendered to perfection.[11]

The Sonata in fact attracted divergent views from the critics. In contrast with the first, Grieg's second Sonata, in the view of one journal,

scarcely conveys the same impression of spontaneity and freshness; it is more elaborate in treatment and development and presents greater executional difficulties. Nevertheless the sonata is piquant and interesting, while the rendering it received on Saturday is only to be expressed by the word perfection.[12]

The pages of *The Saturday Review* were less than complimentary:

Though there is much in it of interest, it is never likely to be as popular as the composer's earlier Sonata for the same instruments, which was played by Herr Grieg and Mme. Neruda a few weeks ago. The themes of both works are strongly Scandinavian in colouring, but in the second Sonata the composer seems to have been more trammelled by the classical form of the composition, and the result is a certain deficiency in spontaneity, without which any music which, like Herr Grieg's, depends for its principal charm upon local colouring, becomes at once tedious and unsatisfactory.[13]

The Times, too, was not particularly assured of the Sonata's qualities, even if its reviewer's opinion was obliquely expressed. 'That the great violinist played with all possible charm and perfection of style goes without saying, though the work is hardly broad enough to afford scope for his noblest effects, which are only fully attained in compositions of more strictly classical structure.' The paper deemed the *Holberg Suite*, however, to be 'one of the most satisfactory of his pianoforte works', adding, with a conservative sideswipe, 'he has succeeded in freeing himself from certain mannerisms which are too constantly prominent in his other compositions, as for instance in some of the songs sung by Madame Grieg.'[14] Much more enthu-

Joseph Joachim

siastic was *The Globe*, pointing out that the concert 'attracted many more visitors than could be admitted; Joachim, Grieg and Mdme. Grieg forming a powerfully attractive combination'. Grieg had played the *Holberg Suite* 'with brilliant success', and the Sonata's performers had been 'heard at their best, and were rewarded with vigorous and prolonged applause'. The songs 'were sung with admirable taste and power of expression by Mdme. Grieg, who is equally successful in pathetic and lively strains, and was aided by the skill and sympathy with which the pianoforte accompaniments were played by the gifted composer'.[15] *The Graphic* concurred in the matter of Nina's singing. 'Madame Grieg in five of her husband's songs appeared to her very best advantage'.[16] Even *The Saturday Review*'s correspondent, again in two minds in respect of Nina Grieg, acknowledged that her contribution was accompanied by 'all the charm of manner which atones for the deficiencies of her voice'.[17] 'The Norwegian songs pleased as before', was the sole (and laconic) note made in respect of Nina's contribution by *The Musical Standard*, which remarked that 'Herr Grieg attracted a very large audience, and once more rebuked the vulgar "insatiables," by declining an *encore*.' The *Holberg Suite* was 'rather dull' and the Violin Sonata 'hardly equal to Herr Joachim's capacity'.[18]

Dagbladet's London correspondent informed his newspaper's readers that Nina had been called back three times after her first two songs (The *Lady's Pictorial* had found that she sang these 'with wonderful fervour and impulse'), and that Grieg's performance of the *Holberg Suite* had been greeted with 'unceasing applause' and had brought forth no fewer than five curtain-calls. The composer and his wife were called back twice more after the second group of songs.[19] Grieg reported to Abraham that he was called back three times both after the Suite and the Sonata. 'Joachim played famously', he added.[20]

Not reported by most of the critics was the behaviour of the audience, attracted to the concert above all by the presence of Grieg. The Mendelssohn item that rounded off the programme was clearly deemed by many to be rather an anticlimax to the proceedings. 'The rude and selfish behaviour of some scores of persons who quitted the hall before the last-named selection concluded interfered sadly with the enjoyment of the better-behaved majority of the audience.'[21] This was not to be the only time this happened when Grieg appeared in London.

There now followed a break of five days leading up to the first of Grieg's two Philharmonic Society Concerts. As before, there was a succession of letters to write, among others to Haddock in Leeds, Honor Brooke, Frederick Corder, Lady Hallé, Chappell, and the contralto Augusta Mary Wakefield. (Wakefield's posthumous reputation is largely based on the thriving biennial music festival in Kendal, in the Lake District, which she founded. She had originally met Grieg in Italy and had spent 'many hours' singing his songs there, accompanied by the composer.[22]) A telegram is sent to Nina on the 13th at the same time as one is sent to 'Bennet' (presumably Joseph Bennett). Newspapers are bought, as are more 'drops' for Nina, and a particularly generous 8 *d.* is spent at the barber's on the 13th. In respect of Nina, no less than 5s. is spent on 'various' items on the 13th, probably for fresh clothing accessories to wear at the following evening's concert. And once again, cab travel is abandoned in favour of public transport.

The non-Grieg items at St James's Hall on 14 March were to be conducted by Alexander Mackenzie, 'as Mr. F. H. Cowen is picking up golden opinions and golden guineas in Australia beyond the anticipated time'.[23] The visiting Norwegian composer was to conduct his *Peer Gynt Suite* and to accompany Nina in five of his songs. It had been only a few weeks earlier that August Manns had conducted the *Peer Gynt Suite* at a Saturday Crystal Palace Concert. In reply to a letter from Berger, Grieg once again could scarcely conceal his irritation, this time at what he considered to be unnecessary demands:

> I did not think that it would be necessary for *me personally* to write programme notes for the suite. This was not required of me last year. Nevertheless I would be willing to do so if desired. I will obviously conduct the whole suite. (It certainly lasts no more than 20 minutes.)
>
> If there is already a Broadwood grand on the podium, I will of course lay no claim to another instrument, even if personally I prefer a Steinway. So I will accompany on the Broadwood.
>
> Kindly let me know when the rehearsals are to take place.[24]

Grieg, 'desired' to produce a programme note, duly sent a text in the post on the following day. Although the programme as printed credits the whole of the concert's analytical notes to Joseph Bennett, there can be no doubt that the piece was squarely based on what Grieg had supplied and is more than likely almost entirely Grieg's own work. As such, it is well worth reproducing:

> The dramatic poem of 'Peer Gynt' is one of the most important creations of the Norwegian dramatist, Henrik Ibsen. The character of Peer Gynt is taken from one of the Norwegian Folk legends. He is a Norwegian Faust, whose superabundance of imagination will bring him to destruction if he is not saved by a woman. Peer Gynt is a peasant lad, whose parents were once well-to-do people, but the father is now dead, and the widow and son are living in great poverty. The lad is full of great ideas and has many wonderful plans for the future. These he confides to his mother, who, notwithstanding his wild ways and fantastic ideas, believes in him. His youthful arrogance knows no bounds. He goes to a wedding and carries off the bride to the mountains, where he afterwards deserts her. During the night he wanders about and meets with some frolicsome dairy-maids. He harbours at last in the hall of the King of the Dovre mountains, where he falls in love with the King's daughter, but is finally turned out of doors. He returns home, where he finds his mother, Aase, on her deathbed. After her death he sails for foreign climes, and lands, after the lapse of many years, a rich man, on the coast of Morocco. In one of the Arabian deserts he meets Anitra, the daughter of a Bedouin chief. She only succeeds in captivating him temporarily and leaves him. Peer Gynt dreams about Solvejg, the love of his youth, who faithfully has been waiting for him, and to whose arms he at last returns old and grey.
>
> The Suite for Orchestra contains fragments of the voluminous music composed

for the production of the drama on the stage. No. 1, 'Daybreak,' is of a general pastoral character. No. 2, 'The Death of Aase,' is one of the most touching scenes in the drama. Peer Gynt's mother is in the pangs of death, while he, in ignorance of this, and sitting on her bedside, relates one of his wild, fantastic tales, during which his mother dies. No. 3, 'Anitra's Dance,' is taken from one of the scenes on his Eastern travels. No. 4, 'In the halls of the King of the Dovre Mountains,' describes the moment in the subterranean kingdom, when the imps, on the rising of the curtain, are wildly chasing and tormenting Peer Gynt.

Alexander Mackenzie, who would have been present when Grieg rehearsed the *Peer Gynt Suite*, remembered how at this, his first meeting with Grieg, 'an extremely nervous disposition, partly owing to delicate health, was apparent enough . . . Extremely particular regarding the smallest details when rehearsing, none could fail to appreciate the Scandinavian composer's artistic sensitiveness.' And in referring to 'the different temperamental peculiarities exhibited at the conductor's desk by our composer-guests', he singled out Grieg's 'nervous anxiety over trifles'.[25] Grieg's 'nervous anxiety', it must be said, must have been exacerbated by what was described as a 'deplorable' first rehearsal of his work on the morning of Wednesday the 13th, when it seems that a number of the members of the orchestra were either missing or not prepared to take much trouble with their parts. As so often happens, however, the orchestra responded readily to Grieg's demands on the evening of the concert itself, their playing surprising the conductor no less than it overwhelmed the critics, who duly recorded another Grieg triumph:

> The presence of the Princess of Wales and her daughter at the first concert of the season of the Philharmonic Society at St. James's Hall last night gave an added interest to an important programme . . . Mdme. Grieg was very well received during her singing of her husband's characteristic songs – especially 'Good Morning!' – but the Scandinavian composer was at his best when he conducted his inimitable suite for orchestra 'Peer Gynt' (op. 46). It is marvellous music, running up and down the gamut of human emotions . . . The enthusiastic audience redemanded, successfully, [the final] movement.[26]

The Times, together with other papers, reported that both the Prince and Princess of Wales (the future King Edward VII and his Queen), together with Prince Albert Victor and Princess Victoria, were in the audience. Their late arrival, just after the opening of Sterndale Bennett's *Parisina* overture, scarcely contributed to the appreciation of the work, as 'half the audience, on jumping to their feet, disturbed the progress of the music'.[27] An under-par performance, then, of *Parisina* was followed by a poor rendering of the Schumann Piano Concerto by Carolina Geisler-Schubert, a great-niece of Franz Schubert and pupil of Clara Schumann. Grieg and his wife would inevitably do much better, and it was *Peer Gynt* that provided the high point of the evening. Grieg's conducting ability was much admired:

> The composer has the power of imparting to his orchestra that kind of influence that can only be called magnetic; it was difficult to believe that the players were the same

sober London artists who had shortly before given a somewhat ordinary performance of Schumann's pianoforte concerto.[28]

The conductor himself appeared to have been genuinely surprised by the sounds that emerged from the orchestra:

> We have it on authority that Grieg was simply amazed by the Philharmonic band in his 'Peer Gynt' suite. Never had he heard before such a *pianissimo*, such *nuances* of colour, such transitions from light to shade! Well, that astonishment was fully shared by the audience, which had the additional delight of realising for the first time the true significance of these poetic, exquisitely-scored movements . . . To know the exact source of Grieg's inspiration was to enjoy his music the more . . . The concert was an unqualified triumph for the Norwegian composer and his wife, who made her Philharmonic début and sang in her usual quaint, impulsive manner, holding the while a simple nosegay of pink flowers.[29]

It was left to *The Globe* once again to record a further example of uncharacteristic behaviour on the part of the audience. 'Considerable annoyance was caused last night by persons who persisted in quitting the hall during the performance of the final selection [Mackenzie's own *Scotch Rhapsody* no. 2, 'Burns'], disregarding the example of the Royal visitors, who remained in their seats until the last note had been played.' Nevertheless, the journal, like its confrères, reported that in the *Peer Gynt* music Grieg had been able 'to procure the most delightful effects; the pianissimo passages being no less remarkable than the amazing crescendo of the final movement'.[30] *Musical Opinion*, again sharing its reviewer with *The Monthly Musical Record* (insignificant discrepancies again appearing), was equally enthusiastic:

> The Philharmonic Society, which has the credit of Edvard Grieg's first introduction to a British audience last year, again conferred special distinction upon its first concert this season by the reappearance of the Norwegian master, whose exceptional gifts as orchestral conductor were again illustrated by a truly marvellous performance of his suite, 'Peer Gynt' (Op. 46). Although familiarized by other performances, it acquired new charm and significance under the composer's electrifying *bâton*, notably in the second number, 'The Death of Aase' gaining in impressive solemnity by a slower *tempo* and some almost unique *pianissimos*, and by a quicker speed and more marked accentuation in the fourth number, with the additional important explanation given in the programme 'The imps are chasing Peer Gynt'. The result was an enthusiastic reception of the whole work and an irresistible encore for the fourth number.[31]

The 'irresistible encore' of 'In the Hall of the Mountain King' would remain a staple of the English musical scene for many years. Some ten years on, a performance of the suite by Henry Wood and his Queen's Hall Orchestra was received with such cheering that the last piece had, 'as usual', to be repeated.[32]

The Musical Times recorded 'a remarkably good beginning' to the Society's 77th season, with 'the public attending in number sufficient to exhaust the capacity of St. James's Hall':

The hero of the evening was unquestionably Mr. Grieg, the heroine being Mr. Grieg's wife, who sang, in her own unique and most artistic fashion, a selection from her husband's songs, he accompanying with such delicacy and poetic feeling as drew almost an unfair measure of attention to the pianoforte. The Norwegian master further conducted a performance of his Suite in four movements, made up from incidental music to Rosen's [*sic*] 'Peer Gynt,' and called by the name of that drama. Amateurs will have it in mind that this Suite was introduced at the London Symphony Concerts last November, but then heard under the disadvantage of no key to the meaning of the music and apart from the composer's supervision. Under Mr. Grieg's direction, helped by general knowledge of the dramatic significance of the various numbers, the work appeared at its best, making a genuine 'sensation.' The performance was most masterly, the splendid Philharmonic orchestra seconding the Composer-conductor to a marvel. No more striking and picturesque effects have been produced in our concert-rooms for a long time.[33]

The response to *Peer Gynt* under the composer's baton appears to have been near-unanimous. It was 'the success of the evening', according to *The Graphic*, Grieg having conducted 'with such amazing spirit, that the audience tried to encore two movements, and after four recalls succeeded in having the dance of imps repeated'.[34] *The Queen* described the suite as 'the chief feature of the evening . . . its full import can hardly be said to have been realised until it was given under the composer's own direction on Thursday'.[35] This too was the opinion of *The Saturday Review*, which remarked on the effectiveness of the composer's direction. 'The colouring he produces from the orchestra by insisting upon the most delicate gradations of light and shade is quite extraordinary, and roused the audience to a pitch of enthusiasm.'[36] 'T.L.S' in *The Musical Standard* began by noting the differences between the respective interpretations of Manns and Grieg:

> The No. 2, 'The Death of Aase,' was taken much slower, and the extraordinary scene, no. 4, 'In the Halls of the King of the Douvre [*sic*] Mountains,' much faster than Mr. Manns led them . . . All these movements are really simple in character, but so wonderful is the harmonic colouring, and so exquisitely are they scored, that the most weird effects are produced, surprising the ear by their novelty. Indeed it would puzzle the most gifted and trained ears to analyse and determine the mysterious coloured chords and the instrumental tone combinations employed. The conductor and composer of this remarkable work had his orchestra most completely under control, and produced *pianissimos*, gradations of tone, and emphasizing of points such as are rarely to be heard.[37]

The reviewer was equally enchanted by 'the singular charm and pathos' of Nina's vocal offerings. 'For once, one cared nothing about the little-known language she sang in. From her expression and style, it was easy to guess the art-meaning of her songs; rarely is so perfect and expressive a singer heard.'

Shaw wrote of Grieg's reception in London ('You Norwegians cannot accuse us of a lack of appreciation for your composers!') and reviewed the concert in a piece published on 18 March in Christiania's *Dagbladet*. He had attended the rehearsal, where he had met both Grieg and Brækstad at 10 in the morning of the 13th, and had found it poor, but was distinctly pleased with the performance itself on the evening of the 14th and acknowledged that Grieg was 'more than ever now the public's favourite'. In addition, there might, he felt, have been many voices that were 'better, fresher, and more flexible' than Nina Grieg's, but the way in which she interpreted every nuance in her husband's songs was 'incomparable', and her 'precise articulation' delighted the writer. Shaw's London review of the concert appeared on 16 March. It opened unpromisingly: 'Hitherto I have not been a great admirer of Edvard Grieg'. Why was this? Shaw was not particularly fond of the Norwegian composer's 'sweet but very cosmopolitan modulations' and the odd 'pretty snatch of melody' that he found here and there in Grieg's works. His attitude softened, however, and he went on to acknowledge that there was rather more to Grieg's music than he had so far suggested. He also noted that physically there was 'a certain quaintness about the pair', and described Grieg as 'a small, swift, busy, earnest man', in whose hair and complexion he saw 'the ashen tint that marks a certain type of modern Norseman'. As for Nina Grieg, he remarked: 'she holds herself oddly and sings with unrestrained expression. The voice, unluckily, does not help her much.' The *Peer Gynt* music was, for him, no match for Ibsen's play, which was 'a masterpiece of Norwegian literature, as Faust is a masterpiece of German literature'. Grieg's four movements were trivial, if 'gracefully and fancifully expressive'. There was a final, grudging observance of the fact that 'they pleased the Philharmonic audience more and more as they went on' and that Grieg was recalled to repeat the final movement.[38] Despite his strictures, two days after the concert Shaw sat uncomplainingly at the piano and played duets – 'Grieg's *Peer Gynt* music' – with a friend.

Shaw, great (if often verbose) playwright that he was, knew only too well how to achieve an effect, no less on the printed page than on the stage, and in his musical criticism he can probably be seen as an Irish-English version of Debussy's Monsieur Croche – a leavening of malice, verbal audacity, and, it must be said, *amour-propre* distinguishing the work of both writers. Grieg's work in performance was to suffer under the pens of both Corno di Bassetto and Monsieur Croche.

In fact Shaw had a particular interest in *Peer Gynt*: in October 1888 he had started work with Brækstad on a translation of the play. The parameters of their collaboration were set out in his diary entry for 28 August that year. He noted how he had gone to an address in Fleet Street that day, only to find that Brækstad had left,

> so I went after him to the Scandinavian Club ... We discussed a project for translating Ibsen's Peer Gynt. The idea is that I should go down to the club, and that he should read out the play to me, giving me the meaning in English, and that I should put it into shape.

They 'set about translating' Ibsen's play on 9 October – 'did five pages of *Peer Gynt* at the Club' – and the work continued sporadically, whenever the two men were able to meet, until March 1889, when it appears that the project was dropped.

The leading article in the April edition of *Nordisk Musik-Tidende*, far more typical than Shaw of contemporary critical reactions to Grieg, carried the rubric 'Edvard Grieg in London', with the subheading: 'From a Letter to "Morgenbladet" of the 15th March 1889'. For an artist, the paper's correspondent – surely Brækstad again – declared, it was important to be understood by one's contemporaries, and moreover it mattered a lot to be able to take London by storm. 'Over here one has the opportunity to hear the best that Europe can produce in the domain of art.' If ever a pair of artists had succeeded in raising people in London to a state of genuine, unalloyed enthusiasm, that was what Grieg and his wife had done on the previous day. It was difficult to describe the impact they had made with the first of the songs, and when Nina sang 'Good Morning!',

> one forgot that one was in St. James's Hall with its numerous gas-jets and its rich gilt decorations, one forgot the fine dresses and all of the fashionable and distinguished company – Edvard Grieg had us see and feel how 'over the glowing fells / the King of Light's soldiers pitch their tents'!

As for the *Peer Gynt Suite*, *Morgenbladet*'s reviewer went on to describe Grieg's conducting:

> From the place where I was sitting I was so lucky to be able to witness the genius with which Grieg conducted the foreign orchestra; economical in his gestures, everything proceeds so calmly, but so precisely, that it all seems to be the easiest thing in the world. At the same time a flush of enthusiasm comes now and again to the composer's fine, pale countenance. I do not know if the orchestra felt it, but they were working absolutely hand in hand, and, as I said, the effect was magnificent. . . . For people like me, who have been away from home for so long a time, [two of the songs] were like a breath of air from home. . . . Grieg carried people away with him, and never has Norwegian music celebrated a more handsome triumph.[39]

One of those present, ready to congratulate the composer/conductor at the close of the concert, was young Fritz Delius, again in England. A pencilled note, in English, on Grieg's visiting card, dated 14/3/89, has 'Mr. F. Delius and Compagnon is admitted to the *artist-room* this evening.' Grieg's own delighted reaction to the concert is clearly seen in a letter he sent to Frants Beyer:

> Well, you can just imagine the enthusiasm the day before yesterday! Each movement of the Suite brought forth enormous applause, but I just let them clap and then got on with it. After it had finished the noise was like the howling of animals! You'll understand me, I'm sure: something inarticulate which only finds expression in moments of high excitement. I was called back three times and so I had to repeat the Troll business. But the performance itself was quite brilliant. Nina was also on excellent form and made a great hit. She was called back three times. One of the songs she sang was 'Spring', when I had to sit and play the whole postlude with the audience applauding loudly.

Taken altogether our appearances here have been exceptionally successful. May that continue! On Wednesday I give a concert (which Chappell has 'bought' from me for £80!) in which I will play my last Violin Sonata with Johannes Wolff. We had a rehearsal today. He is absolutely brilliant. On the 28th I conduct the Piano Concerto with Agathe Grøndahl. On the 31st [*sic*] I play the 3rd Sonata again with Mad. Neruda . . .

It is late in the evening and I am so tired, so tired. I feel that I shall be good for nothing unless I get some sleep.[40]

Johannes Wolff, Grieg's favourite violinist, was born in The Hague in 1863. He studied in Dresden and Paris and toured widely in Europe and America. He first came to England in 1889, playing at a Manns concert at the Crystal Palace. Before long he established himself in London, finding a home in Chelsea and joining the staff of the Guildhall School of Music. Shaw was much taken by him, 'the most goodnatured-looking violinist I ever saw: a man whom no one would have the heart to criticize adversely', as he wrote in *The Star* on 16 March. Much later he was to be similarly characterized elsewhere: 'Besides being in the top rank of violinists, he is in private life one of the most popular of men and *persona grata* in all cultured circles'.[41] Wolff was certainly frequently asked to play to members of the royal family – to Victoria herself at Balmoral in the first year that he came to England and again subsequently at Windsor and then Osborne. But it would be with Edvard and Nina Grieg that he would share a royal command performance at Windsor in 1897; and he continued to be Grieg's violinist of choice whenever the composer-performer was in England.

Grieg also told Beyer that he and Nina had had a visit from Charles Harding and his wife. 'They were as amiable as before and asked that we greet you most warmly from them. They love you!' This particular letter to Beyer also records another significant moment in Grieg's life. It had occurred on the afternoon of Friday 15 March, just a day earlier, and Grieg had waited until that moment had been well savoured before describing it to his friend. He and Nina had paid a visit to the home of Honor Brooke and her father. Honor had earlier proposed lunch or dinner to Grieg, but if this were not to be possible had suggested a visit of just 'an hour or two, if nothing more'.[42]

It was yesterday afternoon that we strolled over to No. 1 Manchester Square. A quiet, stately square, with equally stately, aristocratic buildings. We were led up a stairway, after which the door was opened and the estimable Miss Honor B. welcomed us in person. She looked radiant and noble and I thought almost more handsome than before. She took us into the big living-room, where a number of ladies were gathered. I didn't like this and remained standing somewhat hesitantly by the door, until Miss Brooke made the introductions: 'My sisters!' I stumbled backwards a step: 'What do you say? All these your sisters? Impossible.' – 'Yes, indeed, they are all my sisters!' I clapped my hands. General delight.

That set the tone, and I don't need to tell you that we found ourselves among a group of noble, amiable, pretty and cheerful young women. Their father, who has a bad foot, could not come down. So after a while we went up the 3 flights of stairs to his study. He received us outside the door – just like an old acquaintance. What a man!, Nina said, and it is true: How much in him reminds one of Bjørnson! A big, splendid, sparkling personality, full of fire and power. We talked of this and that: about Unitarianism, Socialism, about Ibsen and Bjørnson and also a little about politics (the Parnell business) and I would say that he felt just as I do. Only once did we disagree: He maintained that art and science had nothing to do with each other and that a person who cultivated both of them could never accomplish anything. And that after all, for a Unitarian, is to be pretty illiberal. But I think that here too we would have come to an understanding if I had been able to express myself in English in the way I wished. He must be a splendid public speaker. I may go over to hear him tomorrow morning.

Nothing in this world is without its disappointments. So also here: There was no feeling for music. I can with certainty draw this conclusion from the fact that no-one in the whole family has heard a single note of ours, in spite of all the times we have performed here. I had looked forward in particular to hearing what they thought of the *Peer Gynt Suite*, which I had conducted the previous evening, and I had even written from Berlin to tell them the date, as I thought that Miss Brooke with her interest in Ibsen and in us would have wanted to hear it. Indeed, it was something that I more or less assumed. But not a word either about it or about music in general. Well, so much for that. This much is certain, I left happy and enriched in spirit as never before here in London! But that's not saying anything special here. For God knows, the talk over here is about everything but ideals. If only you knew how I long for ideal air!!! –[43]

Stopford Augustus Brooke (1832–1916) was born in Ireland. He was an outstanding preacher and was for a time chaplain to Queen Victoria at the Chapel Royal at Windsor. But in 1880, unable to believe in miracles, he seceded from the established church and, attracted to Unitarian ideas, afterwards preached from his own proprietary church, Bedford Chapel in Bloomsbury. He had come by this to feel time that the Church was on the side of the rich, whereas he himself stood squarely on the side of the poor. Devotees from near and far were drawn by the power of his oratory and came to hear his sermons. His first biographer wrote of the range of these sermons:

He would preach on public events, and national policy; strikes, riots, wars, trades unions, temperance, housing, women's work: he would give lectures on the poets and the painters; and again he would find suggestions in his own moods as they chased one another like lights and shadows in a landscape. He set human nature to music.[44]

Brooke's home at 1 Manchester Square was a treasure-house of fine books, paintings and etchings, with works by Turner, Blake, Gainsborough and Burne-Jones among those of many other artists to be found along passages and stairways as well as in the various rooms of this large and comfortable family home, with much of its décor and furniture in the William Morris style. Brooke also loved the great outdoors and, like Grieg, revelled in elemental landscapes, in his younger years finding himself at ease in mountain country, walking or climbing with the wind in his hair and (as he himself would have asserted) joy in his soul. By the time Grieg met him it was said that there was no name in the religious world of London better known than that of Stopford Brooke. A liberal when he was young, he admired socialism, although emphatically not Marxism, and much of his religious life was devoted to the cause of the poor and the underprivileged. Although Brooke sometimes called himself a Unitarian – a name he in fact disliked – he never actually defined himself as a member of that body, nor did he seek to ally himself with any other religious sect. However, it was in Unitarian churches and to Unitarian

Stopford Brooke

associations that he most frequently preached, and his son was to become a Unitarian minister in America.

Grieg's experience at Manchester Square, where Stopford Brooke kept virtually open house, was an experience shared by many visitors from all walks of life and from many parts of the world. Brooke's study was perched, as he himself expressed it, 'like an eagle's nest' at the top of the house, and he welcomed visitors there at almost any time of day, never stinting of the time he devoted to this hospitable practice. He had studied German privately in the 1860s, and by the time he met Grieg he could certainly read the language easily. That he spoke it fluently, however, seems unlikely; English had to be their lingua franca in March 1889. Grieg remarked in his letter to Beyer on Honor Brooke's interest in Ibsen. It must certainly have been for her that he had bought the volumes of Jonas Lie and Bjørnson a few days earlier. This is borne out by an entry in his pocket-book accounts: 'Bookpost', followed by the 1 Manchester Square address. It would have been of considerable interest to have had a record of Grieg's conversation on Ibsen with her father, since Brooke later recorded his distaste for Ibsen's plays, and in particular in respect of the characters in them whom, as he wrote, he would have hated to meet. 'Who would touch', he queried in his diary in 1901, 'even with a fishing-rod, ten yards long, the woman in a "Doll's House", or the Doctor, or the husband? Or any folk in the "Wild Duck" or "Hedda Gabler" or "The Master-Builder", or any of them anywhere?... They are humanity with rickets and scrofula'. Three weeks after this Brooke reread Shaw's *The Quintessence of Ibsenism*, but remained unimpressed.

There remains Grieg's disappointment at the lack of any mention of music, and in particular of his own. But in point of fact there seems to be little if any indication that Brooke had any more than the slightest interest in the subject, even though one of his closest friends by this time was George Henschel. So if Grieg regretted that the talk had not been of his music, he had, nonetheless, met a great man that day, and the encounter would long live in his memory. Like Stopford Brooke himself, he seems never actually to have defined himself as a Unitarian, but he had spent time together with the one man who embodied all that he could possibly seek in religious terms, and had left Manchester Square with an extraordinary sense of elation that he had never quite experienced before. It was enough.

⊰ 9 ⊱

'THE GRIEG FEVER IS STILL RAGING'

In the days between Grieg's London concerts there were many more letters to write, not only to various correspondents at English addresses but also to friends and associates in Norway and Denmark. There are one or two people whose identities remain unclear, such as Miss Pollak, Mundahl and Morley – the latter somehow connected, it seems, with 'Lille Håkon'. Other letters went to Chappell, Corder, Herrmann, Elliott & Fry, Wieniawski, and Charles Stephens of the Philharmonic Society. Further correspondence was addressed to the concert agent Waldemar Norman-Neruda, son of Lady Hallé, to the wife of the French Ambassador, and to Agathe Backer Grøndahl, who went to stay at the home of a Miss Dick of 5 Blackheath Avenue when she arrived in London.

Grieg sent unspecified 'texts' to Chappell on 17 March 1889 and to the Wardour Street printing firm of A. S Mallett, Allen & Co. on 19 March. Newspapers were bought on the day following the concert of the 14th, and on the 18th and 19th a number of complimentary tickets for the next concert were dispatched. Several pairs went to Brækstad, Norman, Ernst Pauer, Johannes Wolff and Agathe Backer Grøndahl, and others to Dannreuther, Augener and Herrmann. An appointment was made at Elliott & Fry's, and it seems that on one Monday, presumably 18 March, lunch was actually taken at the home of Clarence Fry. That Grieg had become friendly with Fry is evident from the fact that the latter's home address at Gloucester Terrace in South Kensington is written in his notebook and that Grieg dealt with him direct, rather than the firm in general, in the matter of ordering extra cabinet photographs (at 12 *s.* a dozen) and 'panel' photographs (at 6 *s.* each). Nina's throat was still giving cause for some concern, medicine and barley-sugar having been purchased for her on that same day. Expenses mounted towards the date of the concert on the 20th: more cabs needed to be taken, 'things for Nina's gown' had to be bought, and Johannes Wolff was (expensively) entertained to lunch. Delius returned to Paris around the middle of the month. Grieg noted down his room number at the Charing Cross Hotel; they must have met again shortly before the younger man's departure for the Continent.

For the first time during the course of this particular concert tour, the recital at St James's Hall on Wednesday 20 March was to consist exclusively of Grieg's own music, with Edvard and Nina being joined by Johannes Wolff, who was billed to perform with the composer the third Violin Sonata. Grieg himself played the *Holberg Suite* and a number of piano pieces, and Nina sang a selection of songs. The novelty of the occasion was provided by Nina joining her husband for a piano duet performance of the *Norwegian Dances*, Op. 35, the first time she was to be heard in this country in the role of pianist. 'The Hall will be crowded', Grieg had told Abraham three days earlier, in an uncharacteristic burst of English. In fact for once Grieg did not attract a sell-out audience, the reason for which was supplied by George Bernard Shaw in a piece he wrote for *The Star* on 30 March: 'it paid Messrs Chappell the other day, at Grieg's recital, to turn away the shilling frequenters of the orchestra – their most faithful patrons – by charging three shillings instead of one'. Shaw maintained that the result was 'more than half' of these particular seats remaining empty.

'Herr and Mdme. Grieg, now quite the rage, held a recital at St. James's Hall on Wednesday afternoon', announced *The Court Circular* to its classy readership.[1] *Dagbladet*'s correspondent (again presumably Hans Lien Brækstad) detailed the order of the programme for his readers back in Norway. Beginning at 3 o'clock, it had started with the *Holberg Suite*, which was followed by Nina singing 'Ragna' and 'Hope'. Then came the *Norwegian Dances*, in a performance which was rewarded with 'spirited applause and recalls'. The next work on the programme was the third Violin Sonata, in which Wolff's brilliant playing now brought 'tumultuous' applause, the two artists being recalled to the platform no less than four times. Nina then sang 'With a Water Lily', 'Margaret's Cradle Song' and 'The Rosebud', followed as an encore by 'Good Morning!' Grieg closed the proceedings with his 'Cradle Song', one of the *Humoresques* and 'Bridal Procession'.[2]

'The Grieg fever is still raging', reported the *Pall Mall Gazette* on the following day, noting how a 'large and distinguished audience' had enjoyed an 'excellent' programme and remarking on the fact that Nina had appeared 'armed with a large and beautiful bouquet in place of the small posey which she usually carries'. The mainstays of the musical press likewise continued to be highly complimentary. It was no surprise that Grieg's latest London appearance would prove to be another triumph – the verdict of *The Monthly Musical Record* – since his music

> appeals to all – cognoscenti and the unlearned – gifted with ears to hear and hearts to feel. Grieg, moreover, writes no 'potboilers.' Hence his smallest sketch embodies an inspiration, and is worked out, even to the marks of expression, with the finish of a finely-cut diamond.

The songs on the programme were performed by Nina 'with intense feeling', and she also proved herself a competent pianist in the *Norwegian Dances*, 'which for striking novelty and beauty of harmony, besides their attractive themes, are remarkable even for Grieg'. In the view of the *Record*, the chief success of the afternoon was, however, the 'magnificent' third Sonata. Wolff's realization of the work called forth 'demonstrations of applause from the gratified composer at the conclusion of the first movement. The entire concert was an artistic no less than a popular success of the rarest kind. Recalls and encores too numerous to mention.' The reviewer ended with a plea for performances of some of Grieg's less familiar, or indeed unknown, works, ideally on the occasion of an early return to London by the composer – such works as the String Quartet, *Land-sighting*, *The Mountain Thrall* and *Bergliot* being cited in particular.[3] *The Musical Times* echoed its sister journal's plaudits, mildly critical only of the first movement of the Sonata: 'the themes have scarcely as much spontaneity as is usual with Grieg'. Again Wolff was highly praised, 'the pure refined style of the violinist being exactly suited to the music'. Nina's vocal and pianistic contributions were also applauded.[4] As for Shaw, in *The Star*, there was this time – and uncharacteristically – no evidence at all of point-scoring. The concert had been an event 'which the musical world of London may look back upon with considerable pleasure and satisfaction.' Shaw praised the *Holberg Suite*, both in its conception and in its performance. Nina's execution of her husband's songs, as well as her piano-playing, was much admired. 'The more we hear Mrs Grieg the more we are convinced that no one else can sing these songs so feelingly, and do such justice to them, as she.' However, 'the event of the day' was the performance of the third Violin Sonata, in parts of which Shaw compared Wolff's playing to that of Ole Bull. As for the pianist, 'no virtuoso on the violin can desire a better accompanist than Mr Grieg'.[5]

In the evening, Grieg wrote to Max Abraham:

> Just home from the recital. Everything tip-top. Recalled 3 times after the 3rd Violin Sonata. But the violinist Johannes Wolff played (between ourselves) even better than Joachim and Neruda rolled into one. It was frankly wonderful. What a piece of luck it was for me that Joachim and Neruda were both prevented by other engagements from participating. And what do you think? My wife and I then together played op. 35, the Norwegian Dances, with great success. Twice recalled. And the songs proved so appealing that both times an extra number was given . . . In Pall Mall Gazette on the 20th a long interview with me was printed which contained a lot of nonsense, (e.g. that I never had any success in Germany, something I never said). I'll send it to you, it's just too silly for words.[6]

Grieg's assessment of Wolff's playing and his contrasting of it with that of Joachim went deeper than at first appears. Years later when close to the end of his own life, on hearing of Joachim's death Grieg reflected on their brief professional relationship. 'I felt very clearly when I played with him in London that he did not really take to me. Or rather not *me*, but my art.'[7] Grieg felt that he had had the bad luck only to have known only the cool academic side of Joachim, although he was fully prepared to acknowledge his greatness as a violinist. So despite the public acclaim, this was not an artistic relationship made in heaven. That accolade, where

Grieg's music was concerned, went to Johannes Wolff. As for the matter of his latest interview, Grieg turned to Brækstad for advice:

> I'm furious with 'Pall-Mall Gazette'. I thought they would have known better, otherwise I would never have run the risk of such treatment. At their request I even sent a song in manuscript to the editor, for which he hasn't even thanked me, but on the contrary had his critic say unpleasant things about my Concerto, which is one of my best works. How can I set this to rights? Talk with him personally?[8]

He asked Brækstad whether he would be in town for the concert on the following evening, so that they might discuss the matter. In the event Grieg sent to Brækstad a draft response to the editor (in his 'impossible English'), which he asked Brækstad to correct and return to him. And on the 25th, with Grieg first of all entertaining Brækstad to lunch in town, a fair copy was sent to the *Pall Mall Gazette*.

The original interview had appeared under the heading 'The Chopin of the North' and had started innocuously enough:

> Away from the tumult of the town, high up on Clapham-common, where the March wind rushes through the old elms in front of their windows, Mr. Grieg, the famous Norwegian composer, and his wife have taken up their temporary abode, where they live in peaceful retirement between the intervals of their triumphs at the St. James's Hall. A day or two ago Mr. Grieg was good enough to receive one of our representatives, who gives the following account of the visit:–
>
> One thing which struck me at once as I sat waiting in the large dining-room for Mr. Grieg was that almost the same flowers ornamented this room which, a few days before, I admired in Dr. Joachim's bright little sanctum. The perfume of lilies of the valley seems, indeed a fit atmosphere for one who is so passionately fond as Mr. Grieg, of the nature of his home in the North, where every spring time millions of the white 'maiblomster' send clouds of sweet incense through the great pines and firs overhead. In pots and vases they stood about near both of the pianos. On the sideboard the roses bloomed, and in the window overlooking the common a tall azalea tree was covered with a wealth of tender pink blossoms. Plainly, music and flowers still belong together, even in our prosaic days. Presently Herr Grieg came in, a tiny flower in his button hole, which had evidently been suffocated by the thick overcoat which was now carelessly thrown down on the sofa. Herr Grieg, like Dr. Joachim, was of opinion that there was not much to tell concerning himself which would be of interest to the public:–
>
> 'But if you will question me,' he said, 'I dare say one question will lead to another, and thus you will perhaps get what you wish to know.'

However, when the conversation turned to 'the sympathetic chord between Norseman and Briton', as a subheading had it, Grieg ran into trouble:

> 'Now, Mr. Grieg, I am anxious to know what is your opinion of your English admirers, or perhaps I should say audiences, though it amounts to the same thing?'
> – 'I have the very highest opinion of them, and as far as I am concerned I am far more in sympathy with an English than with a German audience. They do not make many

words, but what they do say is sincere; it comes from the heart and goes straight to the heart. To judge from my own experience they are far more broad-minded than the Germans, who are so enamoured of their own music that they cannot appreciate what is good in composers of other countries. Their patriotism makes them narrow and jealous, and the foreigner has not a fair chance with them. Their criticisms are often venomous in the extreme, and altogether my experience with Germans has not been fortunate. But in England I was welcomed very warmly when first I came over. I saw they knew and they understood me, and this year this is the case in a far greater degree than during my first stay. I don't know how it is, perhaps it is the relationship dating from the times of the Vikings, which accounts for the sympathies between the Britons and the Scandinavians.'

And with that came the interviewer's *envoi*:

My time was up, and as the regions of Clapham Common are fresh fields and pastures new to me, I asked Mr. Grieg whether a cab was within the pale of possibilities in the vicinity of his abode. 'No,' said the Chopin of the North, 'not near here; but I tell you what I do. I walk down the road, and go by tram to Westminster Bridge.'

Grieg's response, 'Mr. Grieg and the Germans', was printed in the *Gazette*'s issue of 29 March, with Grieg regretting that his 'bad English' had been the cause of his being misunderstood in respect of his experiences in Germany:

What I meant to express was that the great traditions of German music often make German musicians and critics one-sided in their judgment of the works of foreign composers. And I would here like to add that I, for my part, am not surprised at this, as no music has gone to my heart like the German. With regard to what your interviewer reports me as having said about the foreigner not having a fair chance in Germany, I am sorry to say that your interviewer has entirely misrepresented me. My own experience in Germany, the way in which Norwegian music generally, and my own especially, has been received there, is a proof of the contrary being the case; and it would be more than ungrateful of me to forget this, and all the sympathy I have met with at the hands of the German public, as well as of German musicians, especially as it is through Germany that my music has reached England.

This was not the end of the story, however, for Grieg's worst fears were realized when German newspapers reprinted the interview, with musical journals in that country adding their own glosses on it. 'A Berlin friend', he told Brækstad on 12 April, 'has written to tell me that people are furious and that I must defend myself. It's shameful that they haven't taken up my reply, but the fact is that the article has fallen into the hands of my enemies.' He begged Brækstad to send to the *Berliner Tageblatt* a copy of his letter of complaint to the editor of the *Gazette*.

There was a break of eight days between the concert of 20 March and the penultimate London concert of Grieg's 1889 tour. Again there were letters to write, trips to be taken into the West End and a short, unscheduled recital to be given on Friday 22 March. One letter was penned to the pianist Dora Bright, who was to give a recital – the last in a series of three – at the Prince's Hall on the 27th. Included in her programme was Grieg's *Ballade* and the 'Irlandaise' from Francesco Berger's Suite in G major. It is not recorded whether Grieg was present. Other artists programming Grieg around this period were 'those clever juvenile instrumentalists', the young Harold Bauer and his sister Ethel, whose musical afternoon at the Prince's Hall on 26 March included the performance of 'several works by Herr Grieg'.[9] In fact a 'capital interpretation' of the third Violin Sonata was reported, but Ethel Bauer's pianistic qualities were apparently not good enough to do full justice to the *Ballade*. And on the evening before the Griegs left London, the Clapham-born pianist and teacher Tobias Matthay, who lived at 40 Manor Street, was to hold the annual concert given by his pupils at the Clapham Assembly Rooms in Gauden Road. Matthay was music master at Dr Pritchard's Grammar School in Clapham, where George Grove had studied as a boy, and he was later to have his own pianoforte school in Oxford Street. Among his students' offerings were three of the *Lyric Pieces*; and Grieg's Violin Sonata no. 3 was 'splendidly executed' by Miss Emily Johnson, violin, and Miss Dora Matthay, piano.[10] The apparent vogue for Norwegian music generally is further evidenced by a brief report in the *Pall Mall Gazette* of the Monday Popular Concert of 25 March, when Miss Margaret Hall, accompanied by Fanny Davies, 'sang a "Spring Song" and "On the Ling, ho!" by the latest "rage" Herr Kjerulf, with considerable effect'.[11]

The Court Journal (as well as *The Court Circular*) recorded a royal presence at the reception at the French Ambassador's late on 22 March: 'The Prince and Princess of Wales, accompanied by Prince Albert Victor and the Princesses Louise and Victoria, were present at an evening party given by the French Ambassador and Madame Waddington on Friday evening at the French Embassy.'[12] It was left to *The Court Circular* additionally to inform its readers of the presence of a suitable number of courtiers – the Countess of Morton, Major-General Ellis and Captain Holford being in attendance. Grieg had earlier written to Max Abraham to tell him of the invitation that he and Nina had received to this musical evening, informing him at the same time that the Ambassador's wife had written to Mme Carnot, wife of the French President, to tell her of their forthcoming visit to Paris. In this way, wrote Grieg, 'I should straightway reach the *so-called* élite'.[13] Hans Lien Brækstad meanwhile was becoming progressively more involved with Grieg's English affairs, procuring for him copies of newspapers and journals from home and himself continuing to send reports to Norwegian papers of Grieg's activities in London. *Nordisk Musik-Tidende*'s report of the evening at the Waddingtons will certainly have come from his pen.

> Last Friday, the French Ambassador's wife, Madame Waddington, invited Grieg and his wife to a Soirée musicale at the Embassy's splendid premises close by Hyde Park 'to meet the Prince and Princess of Wales', as the invitation had it. It was towards 11 o'clock that the Prince and Princess arrived with two of their daughters, and later in the evening came Prince Albert Victor. Grieg and the violinist Johannes Wolff played

first of all the 2nd movement of Grieg's Sonata in C minor for violin and piano and then the 2nd part of the finale from his Sonata in F Major. Fru Grieg, in her usual expressive and fetching fashion, sang 'Min Tankes Tanke' and two more of her husband's songs, and finally Grieg played two of his compositions for piano solo ('The Bridal Procession' etc.). The salon was full of the crème de la crème of London Society, and all seemed enchanted by the rare treat accorded to them by the artist pair. Fru Grieg's singing seemed especially to have taken their hearts by storm. Apart from the Prince and Princess of Wales, there were assuredly not many present who had heard Grieg and his wife before. During the Soirée the Prince and Princess and many other of the distinguished guests chatted with Grieg and his wife, both of whom understand English very well and converse quite excellently in this language. The Princess of Wales expressed her great delight in hearing Grieg's music again and invited him and his wife to visit her at Marlborough House. Lord Salisbury was present for about half an hour and stood in one of the adjoining rooms, deep in admiration of Fru Grieg's singing. He looked melancholy and depressed. It is not comfortable to be Lord Salisbury just now, and it was no doubt a great solace for him to escape for a moment from the day's political tumult and let his troubled soul benefit from the relief that music can bestow, but he had, as already mentioned, little time for repose and soon left. Among the guests were furthermore to be seen, in addition to the German, the Russian, the Spanish, the Turkish and the Norwegian-Swedish Ambassadors, Lord Lathom, Lord and Lady Wimborne, Lord Alcester, the Duchesses of Bedford, Leeds and Marlborough, Lady Dufferin, Lady Bath, Lady Cadogan, Lady Randolph Churchill, Sir Frederick Leighton (President of the Royal Academy) and many other celebrities. At 1 o'clock an elegant supper was served, and towards 3 o'clock the party broke up.

Yesterday, in response to their invitation, Grieg and his wife paid a visit to Marlborough House. The Princess of Wales and her three daughters were present and received them with great kindness and courtesy. The Princess of Wales is a great admirer of Grieg's music, and it was plain to see, from the many of his works which lay about on the piano, that they were often in use. The Princess honoured Grieg with a diamond breast-pin and Fru Grieg with a diamond brooch.[14]

In fact the Embassy reception had not entirely met with Grieg's approval. Like nearly all such affairs, it was expected that music would be made. Performers could and would, after all, earn a considerable portion of their income by accepting engagements for such events. But these were not the musical soirées held by the Dannreuthers of this world, where music and society found a natural union, the making of music being the prime reason for coming together. The upper reaches of society tended to hold musicians in lesser – if not actually low – regard, and conversation came first, no matter what was being played or sung or by whom. Only those musicians of the highest reputation – the Mendelssohns and the Joachims – might expect to command a respectful silence, and even then Royal patrons in particular might just feel free to break the rules. Such had been the case at the French reception. *The Musical Standard* much later quoted a report that referred to the event.

Madame Waddington . . . tells how when he was playing at a reception she had given,

one of the Royalties present, after sitting in silence until near the end of the performance, made some remarks to a neighbour. Grieg heard the voice, and was only persuaded by the united efforts of Johannes Wolff and Madame Waddington to finish the
piece. Wolff himself, whom the French ambassadress introduced to London – a debt
for which she can never be repaid – suffered continuously from the thoughtlessness
of Society folk, and his experiences largely influenced Madame Waddington in limit-
ing her really musical parties to people whom she knew understood and appreciated
music – a method by which she avoided insulting the artists and her own tastes.[15]

Which it was of the royals present is not recorded, but it is quite possible that the
offender was the Prince of Wales. He was, after all, to irritate Grieg similarly some
17 years later when the composer was invited to Buckingham Palace.

One of the guests at the Waddingtons had been the legation secretary and
sometime Swedish-Norwegian chargé d'affaires Baron Fredrik Wedel Jarlsberg,
meeting the Griegs for the first time and commenting on how 'this remarkable little pair played and sang themselves into the hearts of the English public'.[16] A little
over four years later, as Minister in Madrid, Wedel Jarlsberg was to write to Grieg
to tell him that HRH the Infanta Isabella had asked him if he could procure for her
a signed portrait of the composer. Would Grieg be so kind as to send one and to
pack it particularly carefully? He hoped Grieg would excuse his request, reminding him of the pleasurable time they had spent together in London.[17] In 1898
Wedel Jarlsberg was to buy the Palsgaard estate in east Jutland (bringing over, at
a high cost, British gardeners to re-landscape the grounds), where he was to host
negotiations that were to play an important part in finally bringing Prince Carl of
Denmark to the restored Norwegian throne in 1905. Grieg had performed nearby
in the towns of Aarhus, Horsens and Vejle, but there is no record of his visiting
Palsgaard (whereas Delius was to be a welcome visitor there some years later, after
the Schou family, who were great music lovers, had taken over the property).

Playing themselves into people's hearts the Griegs may well have been doing,
but the additional royal and diplomatic engagements were making inroads into
the composer's purse. There was, inevitably, extra expenditure on cab journeys;
and – as ever – various new items of clothing (even a special bag in which to carry
a change of clothes) needed to be bought, including a fresh pair of gloves for Nina
and a necktie for Grieg himself. And on the 26th Agathe Backer Grøndahl was duti-
fully entertained to lunch by her admiring compatriot.

The visit to Marlborough House took place on the 27th and was duly (and
briefly) recorded by *The Court Journal*. 'M. and Madame Grieg had the honour
of singing and playing before the Prince and Princess of Wales and the Princesses
Louise, Victoria, and Maud at Marlborough House on Wednesday'.[18] Of the informal programme there appears to be no record. However, Grieg reported on the
event to Max Abraham. They had enjoyed it much more than what Grieg had felt
to be the 'tedious' evening they had spent at the Waddingtons.

The day before yesterday we were invited at 3 in the afternoon to Marlborough

House to meet the Princess of Wales, who together with her 3 daughters received us *very* charmingly. We played 2 & 4 handed, sang and wrote in X albums, were given at the end a diamond breast-pin for myself and a brooch for Nina, and very much enjoyed the unaffected simplicity of it all.

As we were on our way out we met the Prince of Wales, who first of all expressed his appreciation of the P.G. Suite and then spoke of the Norwegians as 'too radical', whereupon I replied: 'Indeed, we are radical, I admit it frankly; we are also proud of it.' And then he laughed heartily.[19]

Serious music could not perhaps be numbered among the major predilections of Albert Edward, Prince of Wales. He was, however, acknowledged as a welcome patron of music, an example of his activity in this field being the decisive role that he played in the foundation of the Royal College of Music. Where his wife was concerned, it was quite another matter. 'Fond of all the arts,' reported *The Queen* on 27 April,

> she is particularly devoted to music. She seldom fails to attend the best classical concerts, and when St. James's Hall rings with applause of Mme. Schumann, Dr. Joachim, Sir Charles Hallé, and Herr Grieg, the presence of Her Royal Highness generally gives the crowning grace to the ovation.

Added to this, Princess Alexandra was of Danish birth, her father being King Christian ix of Denmark, and she and the Griegs would inevitably have been able to converse with ease in Danish. Her fifth child, Maud, born in 1869, would in time marry Prince Carl of Denmark. With his accession — taking the title of Haakon vii

Marlborough House from the Park; sketch by Howard Fenton

— to the new Norwegian throne, Maud would become Queen of Norway. She and her husband were then next to meet the Griegs in the Royal Palace in Christiania.

Alexandra, Princess of Wales, in her robes as Doctor of Music

For the Philharmonic Society's second concert of the season at St James's Hall on 28 March, Grieg had proposed his countrywoman, then quite unknown in England, Agathe Backer Grøndahl as soloist in his Piano Concerto, with himself conducting. Besides Grieg, a second guest conductor was also to take the rostrum: this was Charles Villiers Stanford, directing the first London performance of his Violin Suite in D major, Joachim being the soloist. A rousing reception was accorded to Frederic Cowen, recently returned from his long sojourn in Australia and himself on 22 March the subject of an interview in the *Pall Mall Gazette*. (On 30 March, the *Gazette*'s subject would be Johannes Wolff. Perhaps pointedly, it would include no reference to Grieg.) Cowen was to conduct the bulk of the programme, which consisted of Schubert's Unfinished Symphony, arias from Mozart's *Don Giovanni* and Rossini's *William Tell* (the soloist being Antoinette Trebelli), and excerpts from Mendelssohn's incidental music to *A Midsummer Night's Dream. Punch*, the weekly magazine noted for its political satire rather than for its rare musical coverage, accorded Cowen the honour of a piece of doggerel entitled 'Back Again':

> ONE note of music sound we, *inter alia*,
> A note of joyful welcome to
> Composer FREDERICK COWEN, who
> Returns, a conquering hero, from Australia.[20]

In the event Backer Grøndahl was little short of a sensation, with *The Times* acknowledging that it had been present at 'the *début* of a pianist of very great merit'. She had played the concerto 'with extraordinary brilliancy and artistic feeling, winning the hearty admiration of the audience'.[21] The newspaper's critic was in fact as new to his readers as Backer Grøndahl was to her audience, *The Court Journal* of 23 March recording his engagement and providing an intriguing insight into its financial terms:

> The new musical critic of the *Times* is Mr. J. A. Fuller Maitland, who will at once enter upon his duties. Mr. Fuller Maitland, who is only about 32, has won his spurs by his *Biography of Schumann*. His salary is £450 a-year, and an allowance of seven shillings and sixpence for every concert he attends.

In a much later volume of memoirs, Fuller-Maitland tells an anecdote — surely apocryphal — about one or other of the Griegs' earlier visits to London, guessing that it may have related to 1888:

> I am not sure whether it was at this or another visit that I had the honour of meeting them at luncheon, but I remember the consternation some of the guests felt when the hostess went up to Mme. Grieg, after a song, with 'Oh, do tell me what that dear old thing is; I know it so well,' and it turned out that Grieg had thrown it off fresh that morning.[22]

Returning to March 1889, *The Globe* felt that Backer Grøndahl had 'proved herself a pianist of the highest rank, equally successful in brilliant bravura playing

Agathe Backer Grøndahl

and in sentimental expression.' Grieg had shared with her 'the honours of a great success, composer and pianist being recalled no less than five times, and enthusiastically applauded'.[23] *Musical Opinion* remarked upon the soloist's 'extraordinary success', to which had been contributed 'poetic perception, lightness of touch, airy grace, and impulsive energy, combined with an irreproachable *technique*', all qualities necessary, it felt, for an adequate interpretation of the Concerto. The reviewer proposed that she should be heard again in other music. Grieg's conductorship, at the same time, was described as 'inspiriting'.[24] *The Musical Times* was no less forthright:

A thorough legitimate success was gained by the rendering of Grieg's Concerto in A minor by Madame Backer-Gröndahl, a Norwegian pianist of remarkable powers. We learn from a somewhat effusive essay concerning her career that she has passed most of her life in comparative retirement in Christiania, refusing brilliant offers to undertake tours in Europe and in America. We can well believe that such offers have been made, for Madame Backer-Gröndahl showed herself a superb executant, the warm, pure tone, deep expression, and exquisite phrasing showing the true artist. Grieg himself conducted, and as on a former occasion had the orchestra under such perfect control that the performance was exceptionally fine, and presented the work in quite a novel light.[25]

According to *The Queen*, Backer Grøndahl

proved to be an instrumentalist of exceptional powers. She plays with great manipulative proficiency, phrases admirably, and is equally effective either in passages calling for brilliancy and finish of execution or in the interpretation of tender and expressive sentiment. She achieved a thorough and complete success.[26]

The Saturday Review decided that, of all the evening's offerings,

the best orchestral performance was that of Herr Grieg's Concerto; the Norwegian composer is a far better conductor than he is a pianist, and the laborious exactness with which he insists on the due observance of every shade of *piano* and *forte* resulted in an admirable rendering of his interesting work. The pianoforte part was played by Mme. Backer-Grøndahl, an artist whose reputation has hardly travelled beyond her native country, though her extremely fine and artistic playing, in which the beauty and delicacy of her touch were especially noticeable, will cause her future appearances to be looked for with interest. That so mature an artist should come before the English public without being heralded by any previous report is a rare phenomenon nowadays.[27]

The Musical Standard added its own approving voice to the encomiums passed on Backer Grøndahl, her exemplary pianistic qualities having contributed to 'a most excellent performance':

To this issue the admirable rendering of the picturesque orchestral parts under the composer's *baton* materially contributed. Mr. Grieg has the gift of thoroughly commanding and securing the confidence and sympathy of his band, and so with the splendid material placed under his direction at the Philharmonic concerts, he attains perfection in the setting forth of his idea. The lady played on a sweet-toned but weak Steinway piano, hardly fit for concert-room use when a large band is employed as a balance against it.[28]

It was left to an irritable *Pall Mall Gazette* to supply a dissenting voice, although it did accept that Backer-Gröndhal [*sic*] was 'a consummate artist': 'her technique is phenomenal, and she richly deserved the enthusiastic recall which she accepted hand in hand with Grieg'. However, it had found the concert as a whole 'a little disappointing', and pointed out that although the hall ought to have been 'crammed', it was only 'fairly full' – for which it was prepared to offer an explanation. 'The fact is that London is already full, and there is a great deal coming on, and music goes to the wall vis-a-vis dinners and receptions.' On the subject of Grieg himself it admitted, in syntactically questionable mode, that 'just now this master man to the English public is the fashion', but preferred his songs and smaller-scale piano compositions, declaring him to be 'the Heine of the concert room. His larger compositions exhibit that rabid and restless impatience with all the usual close and normal combinations and intervals which seems to be the malady of the latest school.'[29] Had the *Gazette*'s reviewer perhaps imbibed a post-concert brandy too far? *Nordisk Musik-Tidende* unveiled the writer to its readers as 'the well-known London priest and authority on music Mr. H. R. Haweis', quoting only his enthusiastic comments on the playing of Backer Grøndahl. The Reverend Hugh R. Haweis (1838–1901), who had conducted the fateful interview with Grieg, was in fact a busy writer, amateur violinist, and traveller, with books on the violin and, among others, musical and travel memoirs to his credit. His *Pall Mall Gazette* interviews might almost be said to be an English counterpart to those so expertly conducted by the painter Christian Krohg a few years later in the pages of the Christiania daily *Verdens Gang*. *Nordisk Musik-Tidende* meanwhile conveyed the good news relating to Agathe Backer Grøndahl's conquest of the London musical public to its readers in Norway, quoting from reviews in *The Times*, *Pall Mall Gazette*, *The Globe*, and – extensively – from *Lady's Pictorial*.

Various entries in Grieg's accounts during this particular week bear witness to regular contact with Brækstad, either by meeting or through correspondence; 'Newspapers, Brækstad' was entered on the 28th and 'Tea with Brækstad', at the cost of 2s., on the 30th. So there can be little doubt that the principal musical journal in Norway was being regularly supplied with news of Grieg's progress by the home country's unofficial man in London. 'Fru Backer Grøndahl's playing', he wrote, 'is so well known to your readers that I will not go into any details concerning it, but will only state that all the newspapers today are talking about her in the most appreciative way.'[30] As for Grieg himself, as his letter to Abraham written on the day after the concert bears witness, the pressure of London events was catching up on him: 'I'm very tired after yesterday evening and am so fed up with this continual "glorification" and more "glorification" that I more than ever long for some peace and quiet.' He added, 'My countrywoman Madame Backer Grøndahl had a colossal success with my Concerto yesterday evening at the Philharmonic. We had to come back 4 times.' On the following afternoon at 3 o'clock he would make his final appearance on this particular tour, and then 'I'll be as free as a bird and, curiously, don't know where I'll be going.'[31] This last comment related to the falling-through of concert plans for Paris, although he and Nina still intended to travel to that city and would spend just over a week there.

First, though, came the Saturday Popular Concert at St James's Hall on 30 March. Grieg bought another new necktie for his last appearance in London – perhaps over-conscious of the fact that the Princess of Wales was again to be present? The concert opened with Dvořák's Quartet in E-flat major, Op. 51, and closed with Schubert's *Allegro assai* in C minor (the *Quartettsatz*, D 703). In between came Grieg's third Violin Sonata, in which the composer was joined by Lady Hallé, surrounded by five songs sung by Nina and the third set of *Lyric Pieces*, Op. 43, as the composer's solo contribution. All in all this proved to be a splendid farewell to London; *The Queen* summed up its impact:

There was an immense audience at the Popular Concert at St. James's Hall on Saturday, the Princess of Wales and her daughters being among the number, when Herr Edvard Grieg, the Norwegian composer and pianist, and Mme. Grieg, his wife, made their last appearance this season. Herr Grieg introduced on this occasion one of his

---

SATURDAY POPULAR CONCERTS.

SATURDAY AFTERNOON, MARCH 30, 1889.

PROGRAMME.

QUARTET in E flat, Op. 51, for two Violins, Viola, and
Violoncello ....*Dvorak.*

Madame NERUDA,
MM. L. RIES, STRAUS, and PIATTI.

SONGS { "A mother's grief" } ....*Grieg.*
      { "Autumn storms" }

Madame GRIEG.

LYRIC PIECES, Op. 43, for Pianoforte alone................*Grieg.*
Herr EDVARD GRIEG.

Schmetterling
Einsamer Wanderer
In der Heimath
Vöglein
Erotique
An den Frühling.

SONATA in C minor, Op. 45, for Violin and Pianoforte......*Grieg.*

Madame NERUDA and Herr EDVARD GRIEG.

SONGS { "With a water-lily" }
      { "Margaret's cradle song" } ....*Grieg.*
      { "The rosebud" }

Madame GRIEG.

ALLEGRO ASSAI in C minor for two Violins, Viola, and
Violoncello...*Schubert.*

Madame NERUDA, MM. L. RIES, STRAUS, and PIATTI.

Concert programme, London, 30 March 1889:
Grieg spells out the individual *Lyric Pieces* he is to perform

later compositions in his 'Lyric Pieces,' Opus 43, for pianoforte alone, a delightful set of half a dozen pieces, each of which, save the last, which is more amply developed, consisting of a single theme, the character of the respective numbers being indicated by the titles prefixed to them, namely, 'Papillon,' 'Voyageur Solitaire,' 'Dans mon Pays,' 'Oisillon,' 'Poème Erotique,' and 'Au Printemps.' The whole six pieces are most daintily and charmingly written, and they were played by the composer with exquisite grace and delicacy, Herr Grieg being compelled to return to the platform no fewer than four times to acknowledge the persistent applause with which his efforts were rewarded. The pieces were followed by his Sonata in C minor, Opus 45, for violin and pianoforte, another of his later compositions, but one which, although it was heard on Saturday for the first time at these concerts, had already been heard in the same building at one of Herr Grieg's own recitals. It was admirably played by Lady Hallé and the composer, the beautiful Romance which constitutes the second movement being specially enjoyed. In the course of the afternoon Mme. Grieg sang five of her husband's characteristic songs, Herr Grieg in each instance playing the pianoforte accompaniment, the farewell accorded to the artists being of a very enthusiastic character.[32]

The songs given by Nina were 'A Mother's Grief', 'Autumn Storms', 'With a Water Lily', 'Margaret's Cradle Song' and 'The Rosebud'. They had 'delighted the audience as usual', and the Princess of Wales 'would naturally appreciate the Scandinavian poetry, such as it is, in spite of the harsh words, almost as bad as the Sclavonic [sic]'.[33] The Musical Times, meanwhile, had found the programme 'in every respect interesting', acknowledging what Grieg's appearance for the last time had meant to his London public: 'of course . . . many hundreds of people could not gain admission'. The Violin Sonata, it felt, was superior to its two predecessors, with the first movement especially gaining on a second hearing, and the second and third being 'gems of beauty and poetic fancy'. As for the theme of the Allegretto, 'no lovelier melody ever came from the brain of a gifted composer'. The Lyric Pieces, if not 'of any very great value', were nonetheless 'pleasing and characteristic of the composer, perhaps the best being No. 5, "Poème Erotique"'. Nina, meanwhile, had sung 'with her customary charm'. The review ended on an optimistic, if ultimately inaccurate note. 'It will be welcome news to the frequenters of these Concerts that the Norwegian composer is delighted with his reception in this country, and will repeat his visit next season.'[34] Curiously, The Monthly Musical Record found this particular set of Lyric Pieces to be 'less characteristic of himself' and so 'somewhat inferior' to his previous works in this genre. The Sonata, however, was deemed 'magnificent'. 'To expect of Grieg (as has been done) that he should also play other composers' music is absurd, since he does not "tour" as a pianoforte virtuoso, but happily visits us as an almost inimitable exponent of his own works.'[35] The Graphic briefly remarked on the concert: the Lyric Pieces had been 'pretty, though not very pretentious', and Lady Hallé and the composer had given 'a remarkably fine performance' of the Violin Sonata.[36]

The organist and composer Myles Birket Foster, son of the distinguished artist of the same name, wrote an essay on Grieg towards the close of this particular visit, in which he referred briefly to Lady Hallé's performance of the 'latest' Sonata. He opened by praising the composer:

> Edvard Grieg, the Norwegian musician, whose visit to these shores is just now attracting the interest and attention of musical professors and amateurs alike, owes much of the honour which is being paid him, and the sympathy which is everywhere extended towards his work, to the fact that in every note he writes he really communicates to the players and listeners the patriotic enthusiasm which prompts him to write; and in every piece, however small, he admits us into his own heart, and compels us to admire nature as he admires her, and to gaze with him upon the wonders and the beauties of his beloved country. It is evident that he has lived and walked amongst scenes of the sternest grandeur, with eyes and heart receptive, and that mountain, fjord, and waterfall alike have spoken to him and have been hearkened to by responsive ears.

There followed some biographical facts and figures, brief notes on just a few of the works, and finally a reference to the links the writer discerned between Grieg and his compatriots and the English:

> May he be spared in health to double the present number of his works – works towards which our evidently strong sympathy is extended. This may be attributed, in part at least, to the affinity in race between our people and his, the Vikings of old and the East Anglians.
>
> A strong, hardy, straightforwardness is the tie between us, the common ground upon which we meet and fraternise, and upon which rests our manliness and strength . . .
>
> Skaal to Gamle Norge, and her faithful son![37]

A whole raft of letters and telegrams was dispatched during the last few days in London as bags were packed and preparations made for departure. To Elliott & Fry yet again, to Fanny Davies, to Johannes Wolff, to the English composer Robert Orlando Morgan, and to the Amatör [*sic*] Society. A photograph (no doubt a signed one of Grieg himself) was addressed to 'Miss Knollys'. Her address in Grieg's pocketbook – Miss Charlotte Knollys, Marlborough House, Pall Mall S.W. – clearly identifies her as a Lady-in-Waiting to the Princess of Wales. And still further correspondence was dispatched to France, Germany and home to Norway. One of the latter items went to Sigurd Hals on 3 April:

> Give Ole my best wishes and say that I spoke with Cowen and brought the matter up. Cowen informed me that he had already had a letter from Ole on the subject and that he would be interested in it. Agathe B. was very successful. I think things will go well if she stays on here, since she is paying visits to all and sundry.[38]

Ole Olsen, composer and conductor, was brother-in-law to Hals, whose family ran the largest music business in Christiania. It remains unclear what 'the subject' under discussion happened to be.

On 1 April, Grieg had written to Johan Halvorsen telling his younger compatriot

No 4. | April 1889. | 10de Aarg.

Nordisk Musik-Tidende udkommer aarlig med 12 No. (hvert No. med 1 Portræt og 4 Sider Musik-Bilag). Abonnements-pris 3 Kr. for hele Aaret; i Porto for de skandinaviske Lande 30 Øre (ved Bestilling paa resp. Postkontorer), for der øvrige Udland Kr. 1,20. Abonnement kan tegnes hos hver Bog- og Musikhandler i Skandinavien, paa ethvert Postkontot elle ogsaa direkte hos Forlæggeren, Carl Warmuth, i Christiania.
Bekjendtgjørelser betales med 20 Øre for hver Petitlinie. Enkelte No. af Bladet sælges for 40 Øre, enkelte No. af Musik-Bilaget for 25 Øre.

Edvard Grieg i London.

(Af et Brev til »Morgenbladet« af 15de Marts 1889.)

»At blive forstaaet af sin Samtid« er vel alle Kunstneres inderligste Ønske, og at se Verden bringe ham sin Hyldest er sikkert Kunstnerens lykkeligste Drøm. Der hører imidlertid en hel Del til at tage London med Storm. Man har her Leilighed til at høre det bedste, hvad Europa kan produ-cere paa Kunstens Omraade, og selv om man ikke anlægger Englænderens saa vel-bekjendte flegmatiske Ro, saa udfordres der noget ganske ualmindeligt, naar det skal lykkes at faa Folk herover arbeidet op til en virkelig Begeistring.

·Er det nogensinde lykkets for et Kunst-nerpar, saa lykkedes det igaaraftes for Ed-vard Grieg og hans Hustru.

Den første Koncert i det »filharmo-nike Selskab« afholdtes igaaraftes i St.

James Hall. Man er altid vant til at høre ganske fortrinlig Musik ved disse Koncer-ter; men det er længe siden, at man har hørt noget saa originalt og i sin Slags saa fuldendt som ved Koncerten igaaraftes, og Edvard Grieg var Aftenens Helt. Hans Kompositioner udgjorde næsten Halvdelen af Programmet, og at dømme efter den Bi-faldsstorm, der hilsede hvert enkelt Numer, havde det store og elegante Publikum, hvori-blandt jeg bemærkede D. Kgl. Høiheder Prinsen og Prinsessen af Wales med Prins Albert Victor og Prinsesse Victoria, Lyst nok til at høre langt mere end selv det rige Program af den norske Tonekunstners geniale Kompositioner.

Det er vanskeligt nok at beskrive det Indtryk, som Komponisten selv og hans talentfulde Hustru gjorde, da Fru Grieg sang det første Numer: »Jeg elsker dig«. Saaledes maa H. C. Andersen akkurat have tænkt sig Musiken til hans deilige lille Digt. Den første Strofe: »Min Tankes Tanke ene Du er vorden!« sungen, som Fru Grieg synger den, slog strax an hos Folk, det er vel ogsaa vanskeligt nok at tænke sig no-get mere stemningsfuldt end denne glim-rende Komposition.

Grieg's London triumph is reported in Christiania

that he had sent from London just two days earlier a letter to the Church and Education Ministry in Christiania recommending that Halvorsen be granted a state stipendium such as he himself enjoyed. An omnibus trip to the West End and back was taken on the 3rd for some last-minute shopping, including a dictionary, a hat for Nina, yet another necktie, and 'manchettes'. Finally there was a cab to Victoria to catch the 11 o'clock boat-train on the morning of Thursday 4 April, with goodbyes said to the Augeners and tips of 10*s.* each given to the household's four maidservants. The Griegs travelled first class at a joint cost of £6 3*s.* As usual they travelled well overweight, their extra baggage costing them 17*s.* 6*d.* Arriving that evening in Paris, they put up at the Grand Hotel.

Another English adventure was over. Meanwhile the Philharmonic Society prepared itself for the third concert of its season, and on 11 April, 'the foremost Norwegian was succeeded by the first Russian composer, Peter Tschaikowsky. The directors of this ancient institution have from staunch Conservatives obviously turned Communists, and, in respect of art matters, so much the better.'[39]

III

INTERLUDE (1)

⊰ 10 ⊱

STAYING IN TOUCH WITH ENGLAND

I F there was to be no concert-giving in Paris, there would at least be the opportunity to broaden contacts and to see one or two old friends. And there
would be time to write thank-you (and other) letters to London, among them
to the Augeners, Chappell, Wolff and Brækstad. To Brækstad, as to Sigurd Hals
in Christiania, Grieg continued to confide his worries about the disastrous *Pall
Mall Gazette* interview, news of which — as he was shortly to discover — had even
found its way into a Dresden paper. But at least the journal had also carried his
letter of denial. There had clearly been further offers encouraging him to make
a speedy return to London, confirmed by a later letter from Chappell giving the
dates of the first and last of the following season's Popular Concerts and asking
Grieg if it would suit him to come over either before or after Christmas.[1] That this
was unlikely to be possible for Grieg had already been signalled, though, in a letter
to Brækstad. 'If only we could meet in London again next year. But I'm not very
confident. It will most likely be Paris, quite apart from earlier promises to Prague,
Brussels and several other towns.'[2] To Hals he wrote on the 12th asking where he
could have got the idea that Grieg could possibly have forbidden the singing of
his songs in London. 'There is of course nothing to stop Frøken Nordgren [the
Swedish singer Ellen Nordgren] from going there and singing my — or any other
— songs. I would think she should do well with them.'[3]

From a letter that Grieg's notebook records as having been written on 14 April
to 'Th. Delius', it would seem that he had paid a visit to the home of Delius's uncle
Theodor in the rue Cambon, where Delius junior was now staying for a time.
'Please give our regards to your uncle', Grieg wrote from Troldhaugen on 1 June.
Plans were being laid with his younger English friend for a summer stay at Troldhaugen, to be followed by a walking tour together in the Norwegian mountains, in
which they would be joined by other friends.

The Griegs left Paris on 14 April, travelling first to Leipzig, where they spent
most of the rest of the month with Max Abraham, before making their way to Copenhagen (with brief stops in Dresden and Berlin en route), where they arrived

on 1 May, staying for a further week before returning to Bergen. George Augener replied to Grieg's letter of thanks. 'Our only wish was to make you both comfortable in London'. His son William was likely to come to Norway in the summer, but was a little worried, as he was unable to understand the language and wondered too whether he would be able to cope with the mountain terrain. They had had several days of exceptional weather in London, with April temperatures reaching an extraordinary 95° Fahrenheit, but now it was once again cold and rainy.[4] What a contrast to Leipzig, where just five days later Grieg was to complain: 'I'm longing for home more than I can say. Here it's full winter with snowdrifts and night frost.'[5] Complications arose with regard to William Augener's proposed visit to Norway, and it had to be cancelled. Grieg had hoped that William could join the small group expected to make a tour in the mountainous Jotunheim region in the second half of July. In the event he was to be accompanied only by Delius and Sinding, their tour coming to an end on 10 August.[6] Grieg had hoped that Max Abraham might join them too, but Abraham did not feel strong enough to undertake such a trip. Meanwhile Grieg asked him, enigmatically, 'Apropos Delius: What was the outcome of the business about the Conservatorium Hall?' The answer followed: 'In respect of your question as to how the Delius-affair ended, I can reply: Very well for both of us.'[7] This particular 'Delius-affair' remains a mystery.

News of further performances in London of Grieg's works could well have continued to trickle through to the composer. Lena Little included 'Autumn Storms' in her programme when she sang at Steinway Hall on 16 April, and Algernon Lindo played the *Holberg Suite* in a recital presented by Emanuel Aguilar at the Portman Rooms on 2 May.[8] Joseph (sometimes Josef) Ludwig and Alma Haas played the third Violin Sonata, confirming its rapid establishment in the London concert repertoire, in the Prince's Hall in May. Both performers were German-born, Ludwig having studied in Cologne and subsequently with Joachim. He had become a British citizen, teaching at the Royal Academy of Music, after settling in London in 1870. Alma Haas (née Holländer) taught piano in London and Bradford. In July Johannes Wolff was joined by Agathe Backer Grøndahl at the same venue, where they performed the same work. Backer Grøndahl was winning superlative reviews in London, having been invited to return and play Beethoven's fifth Concerto in E-flat major at the Philharmonic Society's concert on 6 June. Shaw, a great admirer, interviewed her at some length in the Blandford Square apartment where she was now staying, finding there 'the invaluable, the ubiquitous H. L. Brækstad, who explains our errand to our hostess, and at intervals corrects my propensity to neglect my business and talk eloquently about myself'. Corno di Bassetto professed himself 'infuriated' by her admiration and respect for Grieg, than whom, he declared, she was 'a thousand times a finer player'.[9] The reviews of her Beethoven in *The Times*, *Daily Telegraph*, *Daily News* and *Sunday Times*, all glowing, were quoted fully by *Nordisk Musik-Tidende*.[10] In June, at one of 'Sir Charles Hallé's Concerts of Chamber Music', London was able to hear Lady Hallé again in Grieg's third Violin Sonata, this time accompanied not by the composer but by her husband, the event eliciting a brief if scarcely weighty comment from *The Musical Standard*: 'Grieg's sonata is a fine composition, original and interesting, with an agreeable Scandinavian flavour. The first movement sounds like a cooing of apposite turtle-doves, and so appeared to be very apposite after a recent marriage of affection.'[11] The same journal had somewhat earlier reported yet another mark of royal approval: 'The King of Denmark has conferred the Danebrog order on ... the Norwegian composer Edward Grieg.'[12]

Then there was a Boosey Ballad Concert in November, in which Mary Davies and Alice Gomes respectively sang 'Solveig's Song' and 'I Love But Thee', *The Musical Times* pointing out the superiority of these songs over the usual run of ballads. Eaton Faning's 'small, but well-trained choir' also happened to feature in this concert.[13] Towards the end of the year *Land-sighting* was performed, for the first time in England, at a Crystal Palace Saturday Concert. *Musical Opinion* thought that it had 'very little to say', finding 'the all but complete absence of local colour in a work on a Scandinavian subject by this essentially nationalist composer being also worthy of remark.'[14] One unusual reference to Grieg, filed under 'Musical Notes' in *The Monthly Musical Record*, carried with it its own denial: 'According to a report, subsequently contradicted, Grieg is busy writing an opera, the libretto of which is based on Glucksmann's poem "Alexandria" (the bombardment of the town by the English).'[15] One would be hard put to think of a subject (and even more, in Grieg's case, a musical genre) less likely to engage the Norwegian composer than that of an English (or British) force, whether treated as heroes or villains, engaged in the bombardment of Alexandria.

In Norway, Grieg's principal autumn success was gained in the first performance of his *Three Scenes from Olav Trygvason*, an opera far more likely to have been written but in the event never completed. Even all his London successes 'paled', Grieg felt, in comparison with the reception of this work in Christiania, conducted by the composer on 19 October. Performances were duly scheduled for Copenhagen and Leipzig. Shortly before the end of the month, Grieg wrote to Brækstad about the *Three Scenes*.

> My publisher yesterday sent me an English translation (no doubt by Corder, the Wagner translator) which seems fine to me. This gave me a lot of pleasure, because I think this work will be something for England. If I didn't find the Philh. Society's Secretary, Mr. Berger, of sorry memory, so utterly unbearable, I would get in touch with the Society, but, never mind, an opportunity will occur. I'm unlikely to come to England for this season. However, if anything should change, I shall let you know.[16]

Quite what had happened to drive the wedge between Grieg and Berger, it is difficult to know. Berger was ever a fusser, but his impact on the fortunes of the Philharmonic Society had been enormous. Almost single-handedly he had re-energized and modernized a Society that at one stage had appeared to be terminally ill and near to expiring. He successfully cajoled distinguished international musicians to come to London for relatively modest fees, taking pains to impress on them the honour and glory of their being invited to appear under the aegis of the august and venerable institution that had, after all, commissioned from Beethoven his Ninth Symphony. But Grieg had been pestered at almost the last minute to write his own programme notes for *Peer Gynt* and had at the same time forgone his own conductor's fee so that, just a few days later, Agathe Backer Grøndahl could be paid for performing his Concerto. Berger had pleaded the Society's poverty, but this had perhaps been a plea too far. There are, however, always two sides to any falling-out, and Berger, who in his memoirs seems to have had a cheerful word for just about every musician he ever met, struck quite a different chord when recalling Grieg:

> My personal reminiscence of him is not particularly happy. I found his conceit amounted almost to snobbishness, his want of courtesy almost to rudeness. Whatever small services I rendered him (and felt proud to render), he received quite as 'a matter of course' and seemed unwilling to say 'thank you' for. This does not detract from my admiration of his talent, nor from the high esteem in which I hold his Music.[17]

As for Frederick Corder's latest translation, some corrections had evidently needed to be made, according to a letter from Abraham on 4 November. Grieg replied a week later from Copenhagen, saying that he had not yet found anyone competent enough to judge the quality of the English translation of another work, *Bergliot*. 'I have brought Corder's work with me and will send it to you right away as soon as you require it.'[18] *The Musical Times*, finding that the local colour was 'laid on with an unsparing hand' in *Bergliot*, found cause for mirth in Corder's translation, quoting four of the lines from the drama.

> Trudfang's Hlorrida, Bilskirnir's fire-flame,
> Thou of the strength-belt and hammer
> * * * *
> Horn-bearing Heimdall, Ull in Ydaler,
> Nyörd, mighty North-dweller – Hear us!

A rueful postscript carried the recommendation: 'The publishers should really add a glossary – and a dentist.'[19]

Unwell in Paris in mid December, Grieg again reverted to the subject of Berger, telling Brækstad,

> Between the Phil. Soc and me, nothing has happened since we were last in touch. I will have nothing to do with the Secretary. Mr. Chappell has made various proposals to me, which unfortunately I haven't been able to accept. I have decided not to go to England this coming year.[20]

Brækstad was obviously disappointed and sought the reasons for Grieg's decision. Grieg replied by giving him the latest news about Paris engagements and adding a postscript: 'Why do you want to know all about my relations with the "Phil. Society"?'[21]

The end of the year approached. Grieg jotted down in his pocketbook a draft telegram to Charles Harding: 'Merry Christmas! Love to all / Grieg'. He noted, too, Delius's new address, just outside Paris in Croissy-sur-Seine. The December edition of *The Musical Times* had in the meantime advised its readers of another figure emerging on the musical scene. 'A new Norwegian composer is announced – Christian Sinding by name. He has written a Pianoforte Concerto of which report speaks highly. Is the sceptre of musical art passing to the North?'[22] Some six months later the journal, in its 'Foreign Notes' appeared to suffer a memory lapse, reporting, accurately enough, that a new symphony which was 'said to be a remarkable work and full of promise' had been given by the Philharmonic Society of Christiania. Its composer had been a pupil at the Leizig Conservatorium and his name, *The Musical Times* told its readers, was 'Othon' Sinding.[23] One of Sinding's finest works was his Piano Quintet in E minor, which had a muted reception when given at a Saturday Popular Concert on 30 March 1895. It would take the arrival of 'Rustle of Spring', published in the Peters Edition in the following year, for his name to become truly well known to a British public.

Grieg's reception in Paris was as warm as that he had enjoyed in London, even if, on his first professional appearance there, he restricted himself on health grounds to giving just one recital at the Salle Pleyel on 4 January 1890. He acknowledged to Abraham that the applause he had received in England had been quite unique, but here in Paris, too, both he and Nina had had a rapturous reception, with admiring crowds coming out to see and hear them.[24] The Griegs left Paris late in the month for Leipzig (travelling via Stuttgart, where the composer conducted a single concert of his works), and they were back at Troldhaugen in April. Meanwhile, notable events in London in February and March were a concert by Hallé and his orchestra and concerts by Agathe Backer Grøndahl. Hallé and his 'celebrated Manchester Band' played Grieg's *Last Spring* for strings and, curiously, just the last three movements of the *Peer Gynt Suite*.[25] Shaw's review concentrated on the ineptness, as he saw it, of Hallé's conducting. Grieg had done 'nothing more pathetic and natural' than 'Aase's Death', and yet 'the way in which Sir Charles Hallé contrived to make us feel before the end of the first bar that all this was a blank to him was quite wonderful'.[26] Meanwhile Backer Grøndahl had been engaged to appear at a Crystal Palace Saturday Concert on 1 March and to play the Grieg Concerto. She did so, wrote *The Monthly Musical Record* and *Musical Opinion*, 'in a manner which could scarcely have been surpassed by the composer himself – the highest praise possible'.[27] And 'her success on this occasion', felt *The Musical Times*, 'was unquestionable'.[28] Shaw, typically perhaps, thought that she was wasting herself on Grieg's 'scrappy' Concerto.[29] Because of the demand, extra rows of stalls had to be moved into the Steinway Hall for a recital that she also gave. Grieg was represented by 'To Spring', 'Erotikon' and 'Bridal Procession', and furthermore Ole Olsen was represented on the programme by his 'wild and furious national dance movement ['Fanitullen'] of striking originality'. Some short pieces of her own were given by the pianist, and a number of her songs were sung. At least two of London's musical journals, however, found Grieg's two-piano arrangement of Mozart's Fantasia in C minor, K475, in which Backer Grøndahl was joined by Alma Haas, to be 'of doubtful expediency'.[30] *The Musical Times* went further:

> Unfortunately, it is impossible to complete a record of the Recital without some words of censure for a piece of vandalism more than usually atrocious. Some evil spirit has tempted Grieg to write a part for a second pianoforte to Mozart's well-known Fantasia in C, full of discord and extravagance and utterly alien to the spirit of the original music. Madame Haas assisted in the performance of this monstrosity, and the thoughtless audience applauded.[31]

By an odd coincidence Anton Hartvigson had given a recital at the Prince's Hall on that same afternoon and had included a second of Grieg's Mozart arrangements 'with a freely composed second piano part', this time of the Sonata in F major, K533. *The Musical Times* again castigated Grieg as 'the offender', complaining of yet another 'outrage on good taste'.[32] Shaw positively spluttered with anger at what he too described as an outrage perpetrated by the composer; he furthermore hoped that Backer Grøndahl might soon be given the chance to demonstrate her prowess in works that were more profound than those that had taken up most of the concert.[33]

With just these exceptions – and Shaw notwithstanding – Grieg's music would continue to attract positive reviews in London for a long time to come, and there were regular requests for him to return. Chappell, who had already invited him without success to appear during the 1889–90 season, now asked if he would care to come over and play at the Popular Concerts during November 1890. Concerts and recitals could readily be arranged.[34]

Nonetheless, the Philharmonic Society's developing practice of inviting foreign composers to come to London and conduct their works, with Berger having brought over such figures as Widor, Dvořák and Moszkowsky during the 1890 season – a practice that was saluted by most music-lovers – was still criticized by a vocal minority. *The Monthly Musical Record* and *Musical Opinion*, however, applauded the Society:

> Fault has been found by some ultra-fervid patriots with the production of so much modern foreign music. But facts are stubborn things, and even they will hardly venture to deny that the present success of the once moribund Philharmonic Society is mainly due to the interest excited by the works of Grieg, Dvořák, Tchaikowsky, Moszkowsky, &c. It is to be hoped that the directors will persist in the same open minded policy next season.[35]

An operatic premiere that was much remarked upon in the spring of 1890 was of Cowen's *Thorgrim*, which had been commissioned by Carl Rosa. *The Musical Times* was hugely taken with the work, its reviewer celebrating the music, the staging and not least the libretto. 'So much interest has been taken of late in

Scandinavian music and literature that Mr. Bennett cannot be accused of rashness in selecting a subject from the fierce, stern epoch of the Vikings.' It had pleased the audience too on that evening of Tuesday, 22 April. 'The composer, who conducted, was enthusiastically cheered at the conclusion of the performance, and in this auspicious fashion was "Thorgrim" launched on what can scarcely fail to be a successful career.'[36] Sad to say, Cowen's opera – like so much British music of his period – has long since vanished from public view.

In May came an invitation from Edinburgh. R. Roy Paterson, of 27 George Street, a concert agent and prominent dealer in musical instruments, hoped that Grieg might agree to write a new work to be played at his concert series. What might the composer's terms be? And might he himself come over to conduct such a work in Edinburgh – again, on what terms?[37] Grieg must have told Paterson that he was unable to write anything for him, but this did not deter the enquirer from returning to offer Grieg and Nina £175 for five recitals to be given in Scotland in either October or November 1890.[38] Paterson may well have taken a particular interest in visiting artists from Scandinavia, for some ten years on we find the company managing the Norwegian mezzo-soprano Theodora Salicath, who included Grieg in a recital that she gave in Dundee in November 1900, this being the second occasion that she had performed in that city.[39] Highly regarded, she would sing before Grieg on his last visit to London in 1906. Like Paterson, Joshua D. Horwood, an organist from Hull, would find himself up another musical cul-de-sac, having written on 30 April to ask Grieg if he had composed any music for organ. Would Grieg tell him, if such music there should be, where it might be bought in London?

Then there was the matter of visitors from across the North Sea, for the Griegs at Troldhaugen were again hoping to see Delius sometime in the summer; but for once the Englishman decided to holiday in Jersey and then subsequently in Normandy. 'I must definitely come next summer', he told Grieg on 14 September. Meanwhile he instead sent manuscripts of a number of newly-minted songs that he had dedicated to Nina. Nonetheless, two distinguished musicologists, Ebenezer Prout and George Grove, *had* set their respective sights on seeing Grieg at Troldhaugen in the summer of 1890, even though both were in the event to be disappointed. Prout knew Norway extremely well and had visited Bergen the previous summer, only to be saddened at not finding Grieg at home. This time round he had written from London in Norwegian to the composer on 20 July to say that he would be arriving in Bergen on the following Sunday and would love to come out and visit him. In response Grieg sent a welcoming postcard to Prout's Bergen hotel, but it arrived too late after Prout had left to continue his journey to Trondheim, and the chance to meet was missed once again. On his return to Bergen a month later to catch the boat back to Newcastle and discovering Grieg's postcard still waiting for him, Prout was mortified to find that he had left insufficient time to make his way out to Troldhaugen before his embarkation for England. He promised to write in good time before he came over to Norway again the following year.[40] (It is interesting to note that no fewer than eight of Prout's books on music theory would eventually be found in Grieg's library.) Incidentally, Prout wrote from Smeby's Hotel, which had only three years earlier housed no fewer than 559 visitors from England and Scotland during a three-month summer period – almost four times as many as the rest of its guests during that same period from Norway and other countries.[41] Here was a clear indication of the pull exerted by Norway on British travellers in the later years of the nineteenth century. 'Norway is becoming more "the rage" every year', wrote Violet Crompton-Roberts in a novel published in 1888.[42]

Like Prout, George Grove, writing from the same hotel on 6 September, apologized that in the end he had found his time in Bergen cut too short to allow of his coming out to Troldhaugen. Johannes Wolff had told Grove that Grieg was hoping to write something for him (Wolff). 'Bravo! Pray let it be a Concerto! there are so few of them for the poor players!' was Grove's response, as he signed himself 'always your devoted though humble admirer'. The Norwegian coastal route presumably taken by Prout and Grove was already a popular one with British visitors to Norway. Grieg had received a letter the previous year from an Englishman who claimed to have met him briefly and who simply wanted advice from him on how to get to Trondheim from Bergen.[43]

George Johnstone, vice-president of the Birmingham Festival, was yet another English visitor to Bergen in the summer of 1890 and seems actually to have attained Troldhaugen. He sent a short letter to Grieg towards the end of August, in which he thanked the composer for having sent him a vocal score of his 'new work' (*Olav Trygvason?*), continuing: 'Please remember me very kindly to Madame Grieg

Ebenezer Prout

'Sir George Grove writing a long note', *Punch* (15 Dec. 1888)

& also to Madame & Mr Beyer. I hope to have the pleasure of seeing you again some day in your delightful house when time is not so pressing'.[44] Another visitor to Troldhaugen before the summer was out was the son of Grieg's Scottish godmother (see Chapter 14 below).

A whole series of Grieg's works was published by Augener in the second half of the year – evidently with an eye to current demand as in the case of 'Bridal Procession':

> Grieg's *Norwegian Bridal Procession* is one of his most popular pieces, nay, absolutely his most popular one. It is heard oftener than any other piece of his, and not only in the drawing-room, but also in the concert-room. Although we ourselves do not number it with his most substantial and valuable compositions, we are not deaf to its interesting, piquant characteristics. Indeed the *vox populi*, if not always the *vox Dei*, has generally something divine about it, enunciating, if not the whole, at least a particle of truth. A separate issue of the piece (No. 2 of Op. 19) seems to us to supply a want.[45]

A considerably more detailed review was accorded rather later to a range of new Peters publications, listed as: *Six Lieder*, Op. 48; *Six Lieder*, Op. 49; *Songs without Words*, Op. 52, Books I and II; *Romance with variations for two pianos*, Op. 51; *Album für Männergesang*, Op. 30; and *Alone (Der Einsame)*, for baritone solo, stringed orchestra and two horns, Op. 32. Where the two sets of songs were concerned, 'the present edition gives, instead of the original words, a French and an English translation, respectively by Victor Wilder and Frederick Corder, than

whom better qualified men could not have been selected for the work.' Similarly
with *Der Einsame* [i.e. *The Mountain Thrall*], 'formerly known as *Der Bergent-
rückte*, we now have before us the full score with English and French words'.[46]

All the time, Grieg continued to be performed widely in England. One might
perhaps single out four more performances of interest between April and the end
of the year, the first of them particularly notable for its distinguished audience, and
the second for the curiosity value of another component of the concert:

> On Thursday, July 24, Mr. Gerald Walenn and Mr. Stanley Hawley, students of the
> Royal Academy of Music, had the honour of playing before Her Majesty the Queen
> at Osborne . . . Mr. Stanley Hawley, a pupil of Mr. Arthur O'Leary, played an 'Album-
> blatt' for the pianoforte, by Grieg.[47]

Soon after this Grieg's music made a first appearance at the Three Choirs Festival
when his *Peer Gynt Suite* no. 1 was given in Worcester on 10 September 1890, the
Festival Orchestra being conducted by Charles Lee Williams. At this same concert
Edward Elgar, then unknown beyond the confines of his native Worcestershire,
was launched on an unsuspecting world when he conducted his overture *Froissart*,
a work that, according to the Annals of the Three Choirs, 'created a very favourable impression'. Then there was a performance of *In Autumn* at a Crystal Palace
Saturday Concert in November.[48] And one of the violin sonatas was given by Lady
Hallé and Alma Haas at a Monday Popular Concert on 15 December.[49]

Edvard and Nina Grieg spent the winter months in Copenhagen and then the
summer of 1891 – with the exception of another brief trip to Paris – at Troldhaugen. That there were moves in the early part of the year to procure another Philharmonic Society Concert appearance for Grieg is evident from a letter Berger wrote
to him from London on 4 February. Teresa Carreño had already been engaged,
wrote Berger, 'to play *your* lovely Concerto' on 6 June. (The performance would
seem not to have taken place.) 'If we arrange with you we would ask you to conduct
that Work for one price; but it would not be sufficient.' Grieg had evidently suggested other works for performance under his baton, but Berger pointed out that
the Society had already given them all (the *Peer Gynt Suite*, for example, 'several
times'), with the sole exception, that is, of *Bergliot*. And the singer already engaged
for that concert would be quite unsuited to the work. Had Grieg anything '*new*,
quite new' that he could offer, or at least something that had not already been
heard in England? 'If agreeable to you, the date 6 June would suit us, & we agree
to the Honorarium of £100 provided some Work can [be] found in addition to the
Concerto.' In fact Grieg could offer nothing that was really 'new', as he confessed
in a letter to Delius that was written during a short stay in Christiania en route to
Troldhaugen. 'I spent a lazy winter in Copenhagen. Began various things, but finished nothing.'[50] However, he was looking forward to Delius's promised summer
visit to Norway.

In June an unusual request from London reached Troldhaugen. It came on the notepaper of the Haymarket Theatre and took the form of a letter written and signed by Herbert Beerbohm Tree.

London, 1 June 1891

Dear Sir,

I have for some time past been intending to write to you in reference to an undertaking in which I hope you may be inclined to be interested.

I intend giving at this Theatre a production of 'Hamlet', and it has always been in my mind that you would be of all composers the one who would be able to do justice to this great theme, by musical illustration.

– I find that all my friends here – where your music is so widely appreciated – share my views, including Dr. Semour [Felix Semon?] whose opinion I value highly, and Mr. Carl Armbruster, who is my musical conductor, and whom you may have remembered meeting at the time of Ole Bull's death. – I am quite aware, in approaching you on this subject, that the work would be no light one, and that – should the idea appeal to your imagination – you would require some time for its execution. – The interest which could be felt in the result of your work would of course be very great in this country, where Shakespeare's Scandinavian tragedy remains to this day the favorite masterpiece of all times.

– I shall be extremely obliged if you will let me know what your view is on this subject, and also upon what terms, should you entertain it, you would be inclined to undertake the work? – I would suggest that I should have the sole English rights of performing the music in a Theatre for a certain term of years, while of course the publishing rights would be yours, and the music could also be performed at concerts. – What would be required is an overture, as well as some short music at the beginning of each act, – also music throughout the ghost-scenes, and illustrative music for the court and graveyard scenes. –

The production would be on a scale of some grandeur, and I cannot help thinking that should you be willing to cooperate with me, it would of course be of great advantage if a meeting could be arranged. – I do not know whether you are acquainted with our work at the Haymarket Theatre, but any of your London friends would, I think, assure you of the standing which this Theatre holds in public estimation. –

I should indeed be proud that your name should be thus associated with that renown, and I remain, Dear Sir,

Yours faithfully

Herbt. Beerbohm Tree

P.S. I should like the music to be prepared by October. Should you prefer corresponding with me in the German, it will be equally convenient to me.

H.B.T.

Beerbohm Tree (1853–1917) was one of the greatest actors of his age on the English stage, rivalled only by Henry Irving, his senior by some fifteen years. He had taken over in 1887 the Haymarket Theatre, which was to be his base for a decade, and his production of *Hamlet* ultimately opened on 21 January 1892 and ran for 116 performances until 28 May that same year. For Grieg, now back at Troldhaugen and looking forward to visits from various friends in June and July, and then to mountain tours in July and August, *Hamlet* 'by October' was never going to be a possibility. He must, too, have remembered his year-long labours on the incidental music to *Peer Gynt* in 1874–5, consequently finding it a fairly straightforward matter to decline the commission. Tree was to ask George Henschel instead to take up the challenge, a challenge that was duly accepted, and Henschel's incidental music, described as 'exceedingly beautiful', accompanied the production. *The Musical Times* felt that the 'five pieces . . . will, it is highly probable, become popular in the Concert-room'.[51]

Tree's judgement in his choice of Grieg should be seen in the light of Ibsen's assessment of his fellow-countryman as a composer of incidental music. He had

Herbert Beerbohm Tree as Hamlet

been unable to recognize Grieg's 'mighty genius' until he heard the music to *Peer Gynt* for the first time and so could see how Grieg had penetrated completely into the spirit of his work:

> I know of no one who could have interpreted 'Peer Gynt' in music as Grieg did, and I feel certain that if he illustrated Shakespeare or Schiller or Molière or any other non-Norwegian author, he would have written as characteristic a score as he did for me.[52]

Almost needless to say, Shaw felt otherwise. According to him Henschel's preludes 'went deeper' and his incidental music was 'simpler and more effective' than was Grieg's for *Peer Gynt*.[53]

Some years later, Tree was one of the chief guests at the second annual dinner of the Musical Directors' Association, held at the Trocadero Restaurant in London, where he responded to the toast, 'The Incidental Music of the Drama', proposed by one of the leading contemporary composers of the day of light music, Lionel Monckton. There was an increasing public appreciation today, said Monckton, of music's value as an assistant to dramatic effect, and distinguished composers like Sullivan, Parry, Henschel, German and Mackenzie (the latter being another guest present at the dinner) were lending their art to the adornment of the stage. Managers, too, were recognising more than ever the advantage of worthy musical surroundings for their plays. In response Tree confirmed that for four of his most important productions, including *Hamlet*, he had drawn music from distinguished composers. In the French theatres, he declared, how one yearned for 'the music that was not'; *sometimes* perhaps in England one yearned for its absence. But of the music rightly used to enhance the effect of the drama without unduly distracting the spectator's attention, he always approved. After all, some of the greatest masters had not disdained to dignify the drama with their art.[54]

One wonders if Tree might have been among the many who had flocked to the Royalty Theatre on 13 March for the London premiere of Ibsen's *Ghosts*, given in William Archer's translation. The production was accorded a vast amount of publicity, most of it almost inevitably hostile – the *Daily Telegraph*, for example, in a leading article terming the play 'an open drain', 'a dungheap' and more of the like. Somewhat incongruously, perhaps, a nine-piece orchestra played selections from Grieg before the curtain rose . . .[55]

Grieg's summer tours in Norway came and went. The hope had been that Brodsky and his wife would at long last be able make the journey from Leipzig and visit them in Norway, but at a late stage Brodsky wrote to cancel, and the Griegs learned to their great disappointment that their friends were now planning to leave for America in the autumn, with Adolph taking up a post in New York. However, Delius was a guest at Troldhaugen for a week at the end of July, following which he and his fellow Leipzig student Iver Holter holidayed in the Hardanger area, together with the Griegs. They were all reunited in Christiania in the autumn, where Holter conducted at concerts that included works by both of his summer companions. Grieg had written to him from Troldhaugen on 5 September: 'Be sure to let me know of the date of the 1st concert so that if possible I can be present to hear Delius's piece.' The piece in question was Delius's concert overture *Paa Vidderne* (*On the Mountains*), given on 10 October 1891 — a notable date as the first ever public performance of an orchestral work by the composer. At the Christiania Music Society's second concert of the season on 14 November, Grieg conducted the first performance of his recently arranged second suite from *Peer Gynt*, as well as *Before a Southern Convent* and the *Scenes from Olav Trygvason*. The Griegs were back in Bergen for Christmas and would stay at Troldhaugen for much of the following year.

Among the more interesting concerts in England that had included works by Grieg during the course of the year had been a Crystal Palace Concert on 21 March, featuring the bass W. H. Brereton and the contralto Emily Squire in *Scenes from Olav Trygvason*; a Philharmonic Society Concert on 27 June, when Cowen had conducted *In Autumn*; a Richter Concert on 13 July, in which the *Peer Gynt Suite* was given 'for the first time at these concerts'; and then at a Monday Popular Concert on 16 November Leonard Borwick had received critical praise for his performance of the *Ballade* in G minor. Two performances of Grieg's first Violin Sonata, which would have gone unnoticed by the world at large, were recorded in the diary of Alice Elgar on 27 July 1891 and 10 April 1892: an old friend of Elgar's, Hilda Fitton, came to his home and played the Sonata together with Elgar.[56]

As usual, most of Grieg's 'English' correspondence throughout the year had been with Delius. However, on 5 September Grieg recorded in his notebook the dispatch of a letter and photograph to his great admirer Stanley Hawley. As for Delius himself, he was to change his French address yet again towards the end of 1891, settling down for the next few years in a small apartment in the Montparnasse area of Paris and getting on with the business of composition, notably the completion of his first opera, *Irmelin*, based on Scandinavian folk-tales.

'I've chosen complete peace for this winter', Grieg wrote to Brækstad from Troldhaugen on 19 January 1892.

> But it's almost too complete. It's rather desolate up here. But, how beautiful! When shall we meet in England? I recently had an invitation to conduct at a Musical Festival in Glasgow in 1893. It must be then, if not before. I also want to conduct 'Olav Trygvason' in London sooner or later.

Yet a further English avenue opened up in March, with a letter from the secretary of the Leeds Triennial Musical Festival asking Grieg if he would be able to let them have a specially-written orchestral work for the next festival in October 1892 and hoping that he might agree to come and conduct it.[57] Nothing, however, was to come of either the Glasgow or Leeds proposals.

On 3 March Grieg wrote to Richter to recommend a young Norwegian pianist, Martin Knutzen, whom he evidently much admired. 'You will certainly have had quite enough of such recommendations – but I hope you will remember our meeting in Birmingham, and that for my sake you will make an exception!' Grieg thought highly of Knutzen, whose interpretation of Grieg's music was particularly highly regarded in his native country. Some years later confirmation came in a review of an orchestral concert and a recital that he gave in London:

> In any other city than London Herr Martin Knutzen, the Norwegian pianist who gave an orchestral concert on Tuesday of last week and a recital on Tuesday last, would make his mark as a virtuoso of uncommon talent. But more than that is required in London. Herr Knutzen is well equipped in every respect, and in one he is unique – his playing of Grieg.

The reviewer conceded that Knutzen had given satisfactory readings of Beethoven, Schumann and Chopin, but in his playing of the works of these composers 'inspiration' and 'magic' seem to have been missing:

> Yet this pianist played the Grieg Concerto at his orchestral concert with a fire and impetuosity that overwhelmed one. The work has never been so well played in London. Again at his recital the piano part of the Grieg violoncello Sonata was uncommonly well done, and a group of small compositions by the Norwegian composer were played with rare poetic insight. If Herr Knutzen could only see other music as he sees Grieg's he would be much more than the sound, meritorious pianist he now is.[58]

Another young Norwegian Grieg hoped to help in London was Christen Smith, brother of Frants Beyer's wife, who was looking to go into business in England. Hans Lien Brækstad was duly contacted, and Grieg asked for his advice.[59]

The Philharmonic Society, as in most years now, included a Grieg performance in their season, Frederic Cowen conducting on 24 March the '*Scena, "Der Einsame"* (first time), M. Eugene Oudin', as the Society records have it. The work is now known as *The Mountain Thrall*, Op. 32, for baritone, string orchestra, and two horns. Composed in 1877–8, it was first published in 1882.

Among other reminders of England in the spring of 1892 was a letter from George Bainton of Coventry, explaining how proud he was of the musical abilities of his young son:

> I have a little boy, Edgar Leslie Bainton by name, who, though only twelve years of age, has developed remarkable musical power, and gives promise of a useful musical career. He has for you and your compositions an enthusiastic appreciation. You are, indeed, one of the enthusiasms of his life.

The doting father had given to his son an album containing 'a few autograph letters and pieces of manuscript by great musical Composers' and asked if Grieg might be willing to add to it on a scrap of paper. 'I write this the more gladly because in our home your music is as familiar as the most familiar friend, and loved with a very special admiration.'[60] One hopes that Grieg may have obliged, in spite of the fact that this kind of request was an often irritating commonplace for him, for young Edgar Bainton (1880–1956) went on to become a fine composer, from works in smaller forms through to operas. He was to be appointed successively Principal of the Newcastle-on-Tyne Conservatory and of the New South Wales Conservatory in Sydney. Bainton studied piano with Franklin Taylor and then composition with Stanford while at the Royal College of Music.[61]

Edgar Bainton

Grieg, meanwhile, was going through another bout of ill health, telling Brækstad that he was suffering from gout, while Nina wrote to Delius in May to tell him that at one stage her husband was unable to walk 'because of rheumatic pains in both feet'. The damp and cold climate of the region, with the Nordåsvand below the house 'frozen as far as the eye can see', had not been good for him, and in March she had confessed to Delius: 'We don't think we shall be so keen on spending another winter at Troldhaugen for some time. I have the feeling that we have both been really longing to get away from the place, but haven't talked about it.' She could not have known quite how accurately predictive she had been. The winter of 1891/2 was the last complete winter that she and her husband would spend at their home in the Westland.

As the summer approached Grieg grew stronger. There had been occasional reminders of England. Johannes Wolff, engaged for some concerts in Norway, had come to spend the day at the end of March. Delius was expected again in the summer, Grieg writing to ask Iver Holter in May: 'Shall we be seeing you this summer? So far as I know, Delius is coming some time in July. You will both be heartily welcome at our home.' In the event Holter accepted the invitation, but Delius opted to spend the summer in Brittany and Normandy on the coast, a decision that earned him reproaches from both Edvard and Nina. The main event of the summer, however, was the couple's twenty-fifth wedding anniversary, celebrated on 11 June with a house-party at Troldhaugen. In the evening a long, banner-waving procession drawn from various musical societies in Bergen arrived and sang in the garden:

> Several thousand people from Bergen who had accompanied the procession had meanwhile collected, some on the hills overlooking the villa, others in boats on the sea … At 1 a.m. a special train, described as the longest ever seen in those parts, carried back to Bergen the enormous and enthusiastic crowd of well-wishers.[62]

The description of the event (recording the fact that congratulatory telegrams had been sent from all over the world, including England) was supplied, somewhat inaccurately, by *The Musical Times*, giving rise to a curt letter in the following issue from Hildegard Werner of Newcastle-on-Tyne, who advised the editor: 'Edvard Grieg celebrated his wedding on June 11, not on June 12. The grand pianoforte, made by Steinway, was given to him by musical friends in Bergen, not by the maker.'[63]

A further bout of ill health meant that Grieg spent a despondent July and August at Troldhaugen. It was hoped that a move to Christiania, where the air was drier, would see him restored to fitness, and there was even hope, as he wrote to Abraham, that he and his friend and publisher might be reunited in Leipzig in October. He told Abraham at the same time of a curious request. 'The editor of an English newspaper, "the girls own paper", wants a song from me for his paper. If you will allow it, I'll dig out some old, unpublished song from my file'.[64] Meanwhile, Hans Richter had programmed the *Peer Gynt Suite* no. 1 in the fifth of his summer concert series at St James's Hall, and in September the same work received a second airing at the Three Choirs Festival, with Charles Lee Williams, organist of Gloucester Cathedral, conducting the Festival Orchestra at Gloucester.

In late September, the Griegs set out on the long overland journey to Christiania. A month later Nina was able to report to Delius: 'Edvard sends his best wishes, he is enjoying life again and is not homesick for Troldhaugen.'[65] Grieg himself addressed a short and cheerful note to his English friend urging him to join them in Leipzig for Christmas. Meanwhile he had read in *Dagbladet* that Bräkstad had married, and so sent to the newlywed a letter of congratulation, which incidentally conveyed some surprising news: Grieg might be travelling to Chicago the following summer, having received an invitation to conduct four concerts of his own works there. This was, however, another project that would not come to fruition.

As we have seen, earlier in 1892 there had been invitations to conduct at the Philharmonic Society and at the Leeds Festival, and from Glasgow had come an invitation to conduct in that city in 1893. Finally at the end of the year came a proposal from Cambridge. The University asked Grieg if he would be willing to accept the honorary degree of Doctor of Music, with the ceremony to take place in the summer of 1893. Grieg replied to the Vice Chancellor from Leipzig on 22 December:

> I naturally regard it as an exceptional honour to receive the degree of Doctor of Music of the University, and I accept with pleasure your invitation to be there personally in June 1893, in the hope that my unfortunately precarious present state of health will be fully restored by that time.
>
> Your kind letter has, as I see, had to make a long journey, first to Norway and then here. Hence my belated reply.[66]

The impetus to invite Grieg and several other leading composers of the day to accept honorary doctorates had come from the desire of the Cambridge University Musical Society to celebrate in some style in 1893 the fiftieth anniversary of its foundation. Such doctorates had been rare in the musical profession, Cambridge breaking its ground with Joachim in 1877; and until 1893 the only other foreign recipient of the honour had been Dvořák in 1891. Initially it had been proposed that just Brahms and Verdi should be invited, but Brahms was unwilling and Verdi unable to come (an honorary degree could not be conferred if the recipient was unable to receive the degree in person). Gounod was considered, but was unable to travel to England because of personal circumstances. Grieg, the man of the day, would obviously be a catch for Cambridge, but he was not considered to be of the stature of Brahms and Verdi (and he, like they, might possibly decline too), and so – with added weight needed – invitations were also sent to Saint-Saëns, Max Bruch, Arrigo Boito and Tchaikovsky, each of whom accepted. Stanford was to organize a concert in association with the ceremony, and Grieg agreed to conduct his first *Peer Gynt Suite*.[67] A visit to England meant that other opportunities for concert-giving also needed to be explored by Grieg, with the result that he dispatched a letter to Berger:

> If my health shall permit me to do so, I intend to visit London end of May and should be very glad to renew the acquaintance with the excellent Philharmonic Orchestra. I hope to be able to bring you a manuscript orchestral work, not before performed and if you also wish to hear the melodies elegiaques or the newly edited [i.e. published] melodies for stringed instruments op. 53 [*Two Melodies for String Orchestra*, arrangements of the original songs 'The Goal' and 'The First Meeting'], I shall with pleasure be at your service. My terms will be 50 £.[68]

Another renewed collaboration was on the cards too. Grieg had been in touch with Richter, at the time conducting in Vienna, to propose a London performance in June of his *Sigurd Jorsalfar*. 'I can never have too much of Grieg', came the reply, Richter expressing pleasure at once again having the opportunity to study and conduct a new work from the composer's hand.[69] 'I thank you – and the Gods', Grieg replied, delighted to have secured the great man's co-operation. In his present state of health he felt that it would be amost impossible to take upon himself the strain both of rehearsals and conducting.[70]

Now it was time for Nina to write of their hopes and plans to Delius:

> Do you know that Edvard has been made a Doctor at the University of Cambridge? He is to receive this 'new honour' at the beginning of June and so he must go to Cambridge and conduct something there as well. But we shall probably go first to London, where he will perhaps also give some music if he is fit enough to carry it off.[71]

Grieg himself, however, in conveying the news to Charles Harding, set it against the background of his problematic state of health, referring to the troubles he had undergone during the whole of the previous year:

> It is just now a year since the beginning of my sufferings — Rheumatismus in the feet and a very earnest stomach-catarrh. You will understand, it has not been easy to exist under such circumstances. And still I am not at all restituted. But I hope, the spring shall bring me all sound again and in this hope I bring you my and my wife's best thanks for your kind invitation to come and see you and your dear family in Birmingham. It should be for us such a great pleasure, and if my health shall permit me to visit Cambridge in the beginning of June, it should be very delightful to spend a few days in Birmingham afterwards . . . But my dear Mr. Harding! I am afraid, you would not recognize me, because I am grown old. You must take on your spectacles to find me, so thin I am![72]

Before long, the proposed arrangements with the Philharmonic Society were going awry, with the Society declining to pay Grieg's requested fee of £50 and offering instead just 25 guineas. Grieg refused, and letters that crossed early in February show that both sides had decided to pull out completely from any arrangement during the forthcoming season. A letter from the pianist Arthur De Greef to the Society — written at around the same time — cannot have helped the situation. He had heard, he told Berger, from his friend Edvard Grieg that the Philharmonic Society intended to engage the Norwegian composer to conduct an entire programme of his own works. Reminding Berger of a letter he had sent on the subject the previous summer, he wrote that he would be 'most happy' to play the A-minor Concerto at one of the forthcoming Philharmonic Concerts.[73] Despite all this, London and Cambridge remained firmly in Grieg's sights during the early months of 1893. Letters to Beyer, among others, serve to confirm the fact. After a stay by Lake Geneva, it would, Grieg wrote in February, be 'on from there to England'. And in March he suggested that Frants and his wife Majs should join them for a week in England. 'Performance in London of several of my things that you haven't heard before, maybe ditto in Cambridge and then concluding with a short visit to the Hardings.' But in April, the problem of bronchial catarrh once more intervened. 'And the England idea? I rather doubt now whether I shall travel there just for the sake of this Doctor-humbug. It will depend on the state of my health.' A few days later Nina, writing to Delius from Menton, where she was hoping for an improvement in her husband's condition, and probably mindful of the remembered attractions of the Isle of Wight, even seemed to be suggesting that a visit to England might be helpful. 'We intend to stay here for the whole month and then perhaps later on to go to Lake Geneva or even to the south coast of England.'[74] Later in the month, Grieg reiterated to Abraham that the England-trip was 'still undecided', and early in May he conceded, after another setback to his health, that the trip was now unlikely to take place. While at Menton the pair had visited the celebrated gardens of La Mortola, near Ventimiglia, Grieg signalling the fact to Abraham: 'The gardens of Mr. Hanbury are a veritable Eden, surpassing anything of which the imagination is capable.'[75] The gardens were the creation of an Englishman, Sir Thomas Hanbury, who had bought 18 hectares of land there in 1867 and had transformed it with the aid of his brother Daniel into an extravagant subtropical landscape, even attracting a visit by Queen Victoria in 1882. Whether Grieg actually met either of the Hanburys during the course of his own visit is left unsaid.

In England Grieg's music remained in demand. In January, at the Sarasate Concerts in London, the first *Peer Gynt Suite* was accorded

> a most masterly interpretation ... We have never but once heard this attractive composition go so well, and that was when the composer conducted it himself; Mr Cusins kept the band judiciously subdued, and the effect was so good that the audience insisted upon the last two movements being repeated.[76]

And in April the second suite was given at the Crystal Palace Concerts. It had been announced as a first performance in England, but in fact the work had already been premiered by Hallé and his orchestra. One reviewer made special note of the second movement, 'a fanciful Arabian dance in honour of Peer Gynt. This is a remarkable movement, so fresh, characteristic and original that it made a remarkable impression upon the audience.' August Manns's rendering of the suite was characterized as 'splendid' and the work was received 'with enthusiasm'.[77] Meanwhile, fresh Augener publications linked two great friends, their newer works being somewhat cryptically described in *The Times* of 3 March:

> NEW SONGS. — The latest songs of Grieg, published in the Peters Edition (Augener and Co.), contain much that is worthy of the composer's reputation, though there is little that will enhance it. The charming 'Gruss', set to Heine's words, and the sombre 'Dereinst, Gedanke mein,' to the well known words by Geibel, are the most beautiful of Op. 48; in Op. 49, all of which are set to words by Holger Drachmann, the accompaniments will deter most of the incompetent from even essaying them; these more elaborate works are all graceful and interesting. Three books of songs by F. Delius show the strong influence of Grieg; the composer is bent on puzzling even the best readers, as when he writes a passage in A sharp major without using its enharmonic equivalent. The songs are thoughtful and well written.

Three songs by Delius to words by Shelley ('Indian Love Song', 'Love's Philosophy', and 'To the Queen of my Heart') were published by Augener in 1892, and two earlier sets of five and seven songs from the Norwegian had also been published by Augener in 1890 and 1892 respectively. There can be no doubt that the company had taken these on at Grieg's recommendation.

It was probably in anticipation of Grieg's aborted London visit that a lecture entitled 'Grieg's Harmony' had been programmed at the College of Organists for 2 May. It was given by the organist, composer and educator Dr F. J. Sawyer, and it earned the approval of *The Musical Times*, which described it as 'one of the most interesting and exhaustive Lectures recently given' at that institution. Sawyer had described Grieg as

> the Meissonier of music. His compositions were full of delicate harmonic detail and originality. Since the time of Purcell the tendency of composers had been to extend the harmonic limits of the scale, and no man had done more in this direction than Grieg. His works abounded in daring departures from traditional treatment.

The paper contained much technical detail to advance its author's thesis, and the audience was supplied with no less than 50 printed excerpts from Grieg's works, with illustrative examples 'admirably' played and sung by four musicians.[78]

Cambridge meanwhile was girding itself for the great occasion. The Librarian and Concert Secretary of the Cambridge University Music Club wrote to ask if the Griegs would do the University the honour of giving a recital in the Hall of King's College on the afternoon of 8 June.[79] A few days later the Provost of King's College, Augustus Austen Leigh (a great-nephew of Jane Austen), wrote to offer his College's hospitality to Grieg while he was in Cambridge. There would be a concert and a dinner on Monday 12 June, with the degree conferment following on the 13th. However, at the end of the month Leigh was to write and express his disappointment on learning that Grieg would, after all, be unable to come. He hoped, however, that the composer would be able to receive his degree at Cambridge the following year and asked Grieg if he would care in due course to suggest suitable dates.[80] Austen Leigh had in 1891 presented Dvořák with his doctoral robes on behalf of the Cambridge University Musical Society. He had been made President of the Society in May 1883 – a position, Stanford was later to write, that

> is never a sinecure, and was more than usually difficult at the time of his acceptance of it. The Society had reached a high level of excellence, and had come to be regarded, in the words of Sir George Grove, 'as one of the powers of the country'. . . . It was not only in administrative matters that he was so invaluable to the Society; he also took a deep interest in its influence upon music generally, and warmly encouraged its efforts to preserve the highest standard of performance, and to keep in touch with the great world of art outside. Cambridge is not likely to forget what it owes to Augustus Leigh . . .[81]

George Augener was taking the cure at Wiesbaden when Grieg finally made the decision not to come to England. He was desperately sorry that Grieg was unable to travel, the whole family having so much looked forward to seeing both him and Nina again and having them stay at Clapham. Augener himself accordingly decided to prolong his stay at the German spa. His son William, he told Grieg, had meanwhile forwarded a letter from Grieg to Stanford (whose London address

— 50 Holland Street, Kensington, W. — was then recorded in Grieg's notebook).
Augener consoled his Norwegian friend:

> For many reasons the title of Doctor has no attraction for you. There are, especially
> in England, so many Doctors (of Music) who have no ability at all that it would have
> been a shame for you to have fallen among them. Quite apart from this you have
> so high a standing as a composer that the title of Doctor could not elevate you any
> higher. But your promise 'that you will soon get well again' you must keep very soon,
> and then you must once again undertake the promised trip to Clapham, where we
> hope we shall soon have the great pleasure of seeing you and your dear wife both
> cheerful and well![82]

Stanford wrote in consolatory fashion: 'We will perform Peer Gynt in the concert under my direction, and we will make a toast to your health and drink to
your quick recovery!', assuring Grieg at the same time that the conferment of the
doctorate could wait until 1894.[83] Although he could be notably prickly, Stanford
maintained throughout a cordial relationship with Grieg. He had a dry sense of
humour, exemplified several years after Grieg's death in his jocular (and unpublished) settings of a number of Edward Lear's limericks, one of which, 'The Hardy
Norse Woman', mimics *Peer Gynt* and is marked 'Allegro griegoso'.[84]

The Cambridge jubilee was duly celebrated in pomp and splendour. Saint-
Saëns, Tchaikovsky, Boito and Bruch received their degrees and were honoured
guests at the jubilee concert. Behind the choir were the flags of Germany, Italy,
France, and Russia, but the flag of Norway was, according to the *Cambridge Review*, left 'pathetically unfurled'. 'May we soon have Edward Grieg among us!',
declared the *Review* piously. Tchaikovsky conducted the first English performance
of his *Francesca da Rimini*, following which Stanford conducted the *Peer Gynt
Suite* no.1. This, wrote Saint-Saëns, 'created an impression of sadness, due to the
absence of the composer, who had to stay at home because of ill health. Everybody
knows this work by now. Grieg and Tchaikovsky belong to posterity.'[85]

Nina confirmed to Delius that although she and Grieg had entertained well
into the month of May the idea of going to Cambridge, it had in the end simply
proved impossible to maintain the deception any longer, Grieg one day seeming
to be a little better and then the next day worse again. 'We could not dare risk all
the excitement that would go with it, and gave England up. Heavens, in the end it
is easy enough to get by without a doctoral cap, just as it is without the so-called
honour that comes with it.' For the time being they were staying at a spa on the
outskirts of Christiania (where they were visited by Ibsen).[86] They left the capital
for Troldhaugen on 25 June. For Grieg the rest of the summer would be spent in
part at Troldhaugen and in part on a mountain tour. Late in September it was off
to Christiania, and from the beginning of October the pair were to overwinter in
Copenhagen.

At the same time the English musical scene was changing, something that was

Stanford conducting 'In the Hall of the Mountain King';
Sketch by G. K. Jones in *The Daily Graphic* (14 June 1893)

noted by a Norwegian journal. There was, it observed, a new movement towards concert-giving on Sundays, not permitted until now. And a new concert hall was to be opened at the beginning of 1894 (although not named, this was of course the Queen's Hall). Over and above an orchestra and a 250-strong choir, it would have room for an audience of 4,000, enabling it to give concerts at relatively inexpensive prices.[87] At about the same time there came the surprising news from Leipzig that a 'Sterndale-Bennett Verein' had been established there, 'under the patronage of Sir A. Sullivan and other English musicians'. Its objects were 'to promote the encouragement of English music, to procure situations or engagements for English artists in Germany, and to assist English scholars' who were studying in the town.[88] It should be added that while they were in Leipzig earlier in the year, the Griegs had been intrigued to hear of a former Conservatory student who was now enjoying a degree of success in England. 'Have you heard from Miss Smyth', Nina asked Anna Brodsky, 'or read that she has had such a great success in London with her

"Missa solemnis"?'[89] Meanwhile a certain Belgian pianist and Grieg-protagonist continued to press the Philharmonic Society:

> I much wish to have the honour of again playing before the public at the Philharmonic Concerts. – As yet Grieg has not finished his second concerto, but as the one in A minor has not been played often, I should like to perform it in case you should kindly engage me. A line in reply will give me great pleasure.[90]

De Greef was unsuccessful in his bid, for the next pianist to play the Grieg Concerto at the 'Phil' would be Sapellnikov, and that was not to be until 1896. As for a second concerto, which the Philharmonic Society was hoping Grieg might write in time for it to be performed at its 1895 season, George Augener was doubtful. 'I know', he told the Society, 'that he will not write to order and only composes when he feels quite disposed.' Augener was soon proved correct. 'We have had an answer from Mr. Grieg, and he says that his Pegasus is not always saddled, and that he cannot therefore undertake to write the Concerto.'[91]

The year was drawing to a sombre close, with Nina lying ill in a Danish clinic in November when the entirely unexpected news of Tchaikovsky's death arrived. Grieg was deeply saddened. How grateful he was, as he told the Brodskys, for their having enabled him to meet in Leipzig such an outstanding artist and human being. The Brodskys themselves, receiving in New York letters and newspapers from Russia, felt that they had lost a dear friend, and Anna movingly conveyed their sense of loss to Grieg.[92]

Finally, in reviewing the musical events of 1893, *The Monthly Musical Record* congratulated Cambridge warmly on its CUMS jubilee initiative. 'The conferring of honorary degrees at Cambridge on such distinguished foreigners as Saint-Saëns, Max Bruch, Tschaïkowsky, and Boito (to whom Verdi and Grieg were to be added) shows that we are getting rid of the insular prejudices with which our nation used to be reproached.'[93]

⁂ 11 ⁑

'I SHALL BE ACTING IN A COMEDY
IN CAMBRIDGE'

ON 18 January 1894, Sedley Taylor dispatched a letter from Trinity College, Cambridge, to Grieg, who was in Copenhagen. Successor to Augustus Austen Leigh as President of the Cambridge University Musical Society, Taylor, a distinguished physicist, was a Fellow of Trinity College. His book, *Sound and Music* ('An Elementary Treatise on the Physical Constitution of Musical Sounds and Harmony'), first published by Macmillan in 1873 and accorded a second edition in 1883, was a standard work on acoustical theory. Among other works, he published books on Tonic Sol-fa notation and on Handel and Bach. Fluent in German as well as in French, he wrote to Grieg in German. All at the University had been extremely sorry that Grieg had been unable because of ill health to come to Cambridge to accept his doctoral degree during the previous year, but the hope now was that he might be well enough to come over at the beginning of June 1894. In association with the conferment of his degree, a concert would be given by the Society, and it would be an honour, wrote Taylor, if one of Grieg's orchestral works could be performed as part of the programme. Grieg, still uncertain of his dates, told Frants Beyer that he would be conducting in Leipzig on 1 February 'and will be in London, or rather Cambridge, in May. More than that I don't know.' He suggested that Beyer might take some time off and come to England once again with him. 'The trip will be on me.'[1]

Grieg was to reply to Taylor from Leipzig some weeks later. In the meantime he had received an invitation from Austen Leigh, Provost of King's College and Vice-Chancellor of the University, to stay at King's College Lodge. Either Leigh's letter (since lost) had given a different slant to the content of the proposed CUMS concert or Grieg had forgotten — or perhaps misunderstood — what Taylor had written earlier. 'Would it not be possible to arrange for an orchestral concert?', he asked Taylor. He would be happy to conduct a few pieces, but his health would not allow him to do more — 'playing the piano makes me so terribly agitated that I must as far as possible avoid doing so to avoid becoming seriously ill during my brief stay in Cambridge'.² The problem was ultimately to be solved by Grieg simply being present as a non-performer at a recital of his own works. His forthcoming visit was presently announced in the pages of *The Musical Standard*: 'Edvard Grieg will probably visit London in the early summer, and in May he will receive the honorary degree of Mus.Doc. at Cambridge. Last year the state of health of the Norwegian composer would not permit him to undertake the journey to England.'³

George Augener sought further London engagements for Grieg. He had been in touch with Frederic Cowen and George Henschel, only to find that they could offer nothing for the month of May. He had then written to August Manns, but 'this peasant was impolite enough not even to reply, so there was nothing left but the Philharmonic Society'. There were to be rehearsals on 23 May and on the morning of the 24th, and the Society's concert would take place on the evening of the 24th. The directors were anxious that Grieg should conduct a new orchestral work that had not already been given in London, and they had imposed a further condition: on this particular visit he should neither perform nor conduct at any other concert in London before the 24th. Augener recommended that Grieg agree to conduct a new work, for which engagement he would receive a fee of £30. He and his wife were much looking forward again to entertaining Edvard and Nina. 'I only hope that my doctor does not send me to Wiesbaden again at the beginning of May, as I do so want to be at home when you come.'⁴

A concert at the Leipzig Gewandhaus on 1 February saw Grieg conducting the first performance of his Op. 56, *Three Orchestral Pieces from 'Sigurd Jorsalfar'*, published during the previous year, the final number of which, 'Homage March', was to achieve particular note. This orchestral suite would be the offering he would make to the Philharmonic Society for London in May. Five weeks later he was in Munich conducting the Piano Concerto, with a new-found friend and champion, Oscar Meyer, as soloist. 'The concert was a triumph for me and a victory for Norway, the like of which I haven't experienced since in London.'⁵ Grieg was still harbouring a wistful hope that Frants Beyer might this year join him in London, but he recognized that this was an unlikely prospect. He acknowledged too that he would be 'extremely busy' during his visit to England and that the fact that they would need to stay in different homes would make it all the more difficult for them to see much of each other.⁶ The last time they had been in England together was of course at the Birmingham Festival in 1888, when they had been fellow members of the large and notably congenial house-party at Charles Harding's.

Meanwhile, the appearance of the sixth book of *Lyric Pieces* was greeted cordially by *The Musical Times*. It found grace and charm in abundance in the six pieces. 'Of the grotesque, the boisterous, the *bizarre* side of Grieg's wayward music, however, this time nothing is seen . . . We have said enough to ensure Grieg's Op. 57 a welcome amongst all who in music prefer feeling to fireworks.'⁷

The ever-itinerant Griegs' wanderings had taken them from Copenhagen to Leipzig, Munich, Geneva and Menton within the space of three months. Much of April would be spent in Paris, where on the 22nd the final concert of the Colonne season at the Châtelet was assigned to Grieg, with the composer conducting various of his works, including the Piano Concerto (soloist Raoul Pugno) and the *Three Orchestral Pieces from 'Sigurd Jorsalfar'*.

In London in the meantime the Philharmonic Society had opened its season on 28 February with Grieg represented by his *Ballade*, played by Leonard Borwick, who was also the soloist in Beethoven's Piano Concerto no. 5. Borwick had already played the *Ballade* at a Popular Concert on 6 January. According to *The Monthly Musical Record*, it had afforded him 'ample opportunity to display his powers of expression and excellent technical gifts. It is called a ballade, but is really a Norwegian melody with variations. It is a beautiful piece.'[8] Leonard Borwick (1868–1925) had studied in Frankfurt under Clara Schumann, who was later quoted as believing him to be the greatest of her pupils, and he made his début there in 1889. His first appearance in England came the following year when he played the Schumann Concerto at the Philharmonic Society, and he soon toured widely in Europe and later in America and Australia. Joachim had a high opinion of him, and they frequently gave recitals together. Lady Hallé, whose son Waldemar Norman-Neruda married Borwick's sister in 1895, found in him an ideal accompanist, as did the distinguished bass-baritone Harry Plunket Greene. Although he was especially noted for his performances of the classics, Grieg's music featured frequently in his programmes, as later did the music of Debussy and Ravel. He rapidly became a favourite of Swedish audiences, appearing with Lady Hallé in Stockholm in November 1897 and giving further recitals there in January and February of the following year. In November 1899 he joined Grieg in Stockholm to play in two (of a series of four) Grieg concerts attended by the King and various members of the royal family. He gave 'an inimitably clear and brilliant rendering' of the Concerto, 'which roused the audience to an unwonted degree of enthusiasm, and the pianist was recalled several times'. In the second of these concerts he played the *Ballade* 'exquisitely' and gave the 'Rigaudon' from the *Holberg Suite* as an encore.[9] Borwick found a staunch friend and admirer of his gifts in the wealthy financier and patron of music, Edward Speyer, who had first come to know him in 1886 and who ultimately came to feel that he would have had a far better chance of achieving real international fame had he elected to live abroad:

Though Borwick possessed a complete command over his instrument, and could let his expression range from the softest and tenderest moments to veritable outbursts of true passion, he never overstepped the bounds of what he considered to be the just proportion. He was a Greek in that sense. In his attitude towards his own art, and indeed in his outlook on life in general, he was both sensitive and discerning. With such qualities, which tended to become more pronounced as time went on, it was impossible for him to achieve a wide popularity in a country like England. He might have made a great career in Germany, where such art as his was appreciated in far wider circles than here.[10]

In a Glasgow season Manns had conducted, at two separate concerts in January, the *Peer Gynt Suite* no. 2 ('heard here for the first time') and *In Autumn*. George Riseley in Bristol included the former work at a concert he conducted in Bristol on 23 April.[11] Meanwhile some of Grieg's songs had been sung at one of the Crystal Palace Concerts, and on 3 April Ernest Kiver, who had first got in touch with Grieg in 1888, had included the *Holberg Suite* in a piano recital he had given at Elm House, Clapham Common. English music-lovers also had their attention drawn to Grieg as a writer on other musicians, *The Musical Standard* devoting several of its columns to a review of a lengthy essay on Schumann that had been commissioned from Grieg by an American journal, *The Century Monthly Illustrated Magazine*, and published in its January 1894 issue. The *Standard* had found it 'extremely interesting' and expressed the view that it was to be expected that 'the dreamy mind of the German master would appeal to a musician whose work is nothing if not poetical, and so we find that Grieg's review is most appreciative in tone.' Apologizing for having merely given a rough idea of the original, the journal advised lovers of Schumann to read it for themselves, 'for it will well repay the trouble'.[12] Further interest in Grieg prior to his Cambridge visit could be found in the pages of *Musical News*, which published some of the composer's reminiscences about his early days in Copenhagen (as extracted from a recent edition of *Stockholms Dagblad*).[13]

Another item of interest appeared in *The Strand Magazine* about this time. Francis Arthur Jones (whose best-known piece of writing would be his 1907 biography of Thomas Alva Edison) wrote from Torquay to a number of composers to ask them about their compositional processes. Among them were John Francis Barnett, Frederic Cowen, Alexander Mackenzie, Parry, Stanford and Tchaikovsky, each of whom could be numbered among Grieg's acquaintance. Jones published his results in two issues of the magazine, the first of which included Grieg's brief – and hardly penetrating – response:

> I have no particular rule when composing. In my opinion the art of composition is not at all to be learned, and yet *must* be learned; for it is impossible for a composer to write melodies correctly without a complete mastery of his art. Just as hopeless as for an illiterate person lacking the necessary knowledge of language to sit down to write a standard work.

In reply to his interlocutor's question as to his favourite composer, Grieg was non-committal. On his personal favourite among his own compositions, however, he was more forthcoming: 'Of his many compositions, Grieg gives his preference to his famous sonata for the violin, "Op. 13", a few bars of which are here given.'[14]

Writing from Menton at the beginning of April, Grieg told Brækstad that after conducting in Paris, he intended to arrive in London – where he would again stay at Augener's – around 1 May. After Cambridge and the Philharmonic Concert he would be off home as soon as possible to 'old Norway'.

> As for my health, it's poor, I think this will be my last journey of this calibre. Here

we have wonderful summer weather, but it's no good for worn-out stomach nerves. If you can help me to avoid too much aggravation in London, I shall be grateful to you. I hope to find my way to you. Should I not have the strength for this, I shall lay the blame on you.[15]

Oscar Meyer, having played the Concerto under Grieg's baton in Munich on 9 March, had let it be known that he intended to join Grieg in London and 'pop into' Cambridge with him. From Paris Grieg asked Abraham to tell Meyer that he was delighted to learn of this and hoped that Meyer would let him know his London address as soon as possible. The composer was in Paris for his Colonne concert on 22 April, and contact was renewed with Delius, who was invited to join Grieg and Nina for lunch on the 15th. Grieg procured for his English friend tickets for the final rehearsal as well as for the concert, and was anxious to hear Delius's opinion of how the rehearsal went. Pugno played the Piano Concerto, the long programme included *In Autumn, Land-sighting, Three Scenes from 'Sigurd Jorsalfar'*, and the *Holberg Suite*, and the Châtelet hall was packed. The Norwegian composer was 'at the peak of his fame in France'.[16] A further result of this particular Parisian engagement was that, through Delius, Grieg met the poet Julien Leclercq as well as the Franco-Norwegian composer William Molard, in whose bohemian-style home visiting Scandinavians found ready hospitality, with Molard's wife, the Swedish sculptress Ida Ericsson, always supplying a warm welcome. Grieg had been particularly dissatisfied with the translations printed in a French edition of his songs, and these younger friends got together to remedy the situation, with Molard apparently playing the major part in the endeavour. On his first visit to Molard's studio Grieg also met the young Maurice Ravel, another friend of Delius's.

Ever prone to physical problems – this time suffering from an abscess – Grieg saw his departure from Paris delayed for several days. He did however take pleasure

An excerpt from Grieg's 2nd Violin Sonata, as printed in *The Strand Magazine*

from meeting Saint-Saëns, who told him what to expect of the forthcoming Cambridge ceremony. Grieg recounted the story:

> I have a trying time ahead of me. On Thursday (the 10th) I shall be acting in a comedy in Cambridge. Costume: blue and white gown, medieval cap. Scene: festively decorated street. Action: procession through the town!
>
> That's how Saint-Saëns described it to me in Paris. He went through the same thing last year. How you view such things evidently depends on your nationality. When I said to Saint-Saëns, 'Basically you have to look upon it all as a comedy', he replied passionately, 'No, far from it, on the contrary, the whole thing is "serieux" in the highest degree.' In other words, this sort of thing really matters to a Frenchman.[17]

The whole procedure then, with all its attendant flummery, was evidently going to be 'comical'. It would certainly be colourful: although the University Senate had agreed just five years earlier that current holders of the degree of Doctor of Music might wear their old scarlet robes until worn out, new holders of this particular honour were henceforth to be resplendent in a gown and hood of 'damasked cream white silk lined with dark cherry coloured satin', a description rather different from that Saint-Saëns had given to Grieg. A Mus.Doc. would also be entitled to wear the round velvet 'doctor's bonnet' as a headdress.[18] Years later, Edmund Gosse, already replete with honours recognizing his advancement of Scandinavian culture in Britain, had been given a similar perspective on the ceremony. 'We are actually starting, in a couple of hours, for Cambridge, where I am to walk a new-plumaged Doctor, in a strange procession of quasi celebrities . . . Imagine this file of flamingos, in scarlet and rose'.[19]

The Griegs finally arrived in London late in the evening of Saturday 5 May and duly settled in at the Augeners'. The Cambridge date had been fixed for the 10th, following which, as Grieg had written to Frants Beyer,

> I'm conducting on the 24th, resting on the 25th and on the 26th we'll be dashing home just as fast as we can. If only we could risk the sea route! But – I just daren't! The first steamship from Aberdeen doesn't go until the 7th June, and I'm not going to wait as long as that.[20]

On arrival, one of Grieg's first tasks was to write to Augustus Leigh in Cambridge to find out exactly what he was expected to do. Leigh's wife must have replied on her husband's behalf, as two days later, on 8 May, Grieg records in his notebook sending a letter to her. Meanwhile on Monday 7th his spirits were lifted by a trip to Kew Gardens and Richmond Park, which he described as 'splendid!'

Once again the question of song translations was on the composer's mind – this time fresh ones into English. Three new collections – Op. 58, 59 and 60 to texts by John Paulsen and Wilhelm Krag – were a little later in the year to be published simultaneously by Peters in Leipzig, Wilhelm Hansen in Copenhagen, and Augener in London. Grieg was unwilling again to undergo his earlier travails in respect of English versions and asked Oscar Meyer to come over to Clapham on the 8th to help him check the newly translated texts. Later that day it seems that there was a trip into town and a payment made to the 'piano people'.

On 9 May Grieg and Nina set off from Clapham for their journey to Cambridge. Arriving at King's College, they were welcomed by their host Augustus Austen Leigh, now elevated to the rank of University Vice-Chancellor. The morning of the 10th dawned, and after Grieg's almost obligatory visit to a barber it was on to the Senate House for the conferment of the degree. Quoting from a report in *The Daily Chronicle*, the *Cambridge Daily News* had signalled the event locally (and Grieg's name doubly erratically) on the previous day:

> We congratulate the University of Cambridge on its resolve to confer honorary degrees on Dean Stubbs and on Edward Greig, the Norwegian musical composer . . . The interest in music at Cambridge is so genuine that the degree given to Greig is eminently fitting as coming from the University which has already honoured Joachim, and which counted Sterndale Bennett in the past, and claims Villiers Stanford in the present among her teachers of music.[21]

For a summing-up of the actual events of the day itself, one can do no better than turn to the pages of *The Musical Times*:

> The degree which should have been conferred upon Grieg last summer, when the Cambridge University Musical Society celebrated its jubilee, had to be postponed till the 10th of last month, when the chosen representative of Scandinavian music was, if not in the most robust health, sufficiently recovered to journey to Cambridge for the purpose. Grieg's remarkable popularity with all sections of cultivated society – of those whose proclivities are not exceptionally musical as well as of the inner circle of musical enthusiasts – was shown by the warmth of his reception, both in the Senate House and at the Concert in the Guildhall, at which he was afterwards present. Like many great composers before him, Grieg's eminence is not to be measured by his height, and some time was spent in adapting to his stature by means of the domestic pin the doctor's gown lent him for the ceremony, while the saying that 'extremes meet' was amusingly illustrated by the presence on the floor of the Senate House of Dr. Alan Gray, Professor Stanford's successor in the Trinity College organ loft, who, in spite of his innate modesty, must perforce look down upon his professional colleagues. At the Chamber Concert given in the evening by the University Musical Society, Miss Fanny Davies and Mr. Gompertz played Grieg's Pianoforte and Violin Sonata in F (Op. 8), with a finish and unanimity which showed that the composer's presence put them on their mettle. Miss Marie Brema sang three of Grieg's songs with much warmth of expression, and Miss Davies gave a powerful rendering of his Ballade (Op. 24). Our older Universities have been accused of narrow-mindedness, but the proceedings on this 'Grieg Day' indicate that Cambridge at least is ready to do honour to genius – even though not home-made. After conferring degrees on nearly all the chief contemporary English composers, and many of the foreign ones, the field of choice is now somewhat restricted.[22]

The Latin oration was delivered by Dr John Sandys, a distinguished classical scholar and a dedicated music-lover who had made the pilgrimage to Bayreuth. As Public Orator he spoke at many Cambridge degree ceremonies, including those of Dvořák in 1891 and Elgar in 1900. Grieg must understandably have been non-plussed when he read a translation:

> We greatly rejoice that the illustrious priest of the art of music, expected last year, has arrived today safe and sound from the shores of Scandinavia. Indeed, we repeat that he is particularly welcome since the folk-songs of the northern peoples are so well known both to us and everywhere in the world. It is said that Apollo himself, the master of the Muses, willingly visited the mild and gentle Hyperborean people every year. There Pindar bears witness that the Muse is present and that everywhere choirs of girls with the harmony of lyres and pipes sing her praises, and that finally the golden locks of those feasting are crowned with laurel. However, with help of this servant of Apollo we can listen to the sweet variety of songs carried across the region battered by the Boreal winds, across the remote tracts of Scandinavia blocked by snows, and although far away, it is as though we ourselves are present among the chorus of dancers. The influence and instigation of such men, while it inspires our hearts as if by a new warmth, immediately, as if at the approach of Spring, 'has loosen'd Winter's thrall'; 'and frost no more is whitening all the lea'; 'the Graces and the Nymphs, together knit, with rhythmic feet the meadow beat'. Therefore today we deservedly crown the northern servant of Apollo with our laurel.
>
> I present to you EDVARD GRIEG.[23]

As for Marie Brema's rendering of his songs, Grieg some time later, when writing to her from Leipzig in January 1897, made it clear how much he appreciated her particular gifts. He told her then that it had been with great pleasure that he had heard from Julius Röntgen that she would be singing some of Grieg's compositions in Amsterdam the following month, adding that he numbered among his finest memories her superb interpretation of his songs in Cambridge. Unsurprisingly both the ceremony and the concert drew less attention from the press than had the Jubilee celebrations of the previous year, a fact reflected in the columns of *Musical News*:

> A correspondent asks for particulars of the recent conferring of the degree of Mus. Doc. on Grieg at Cambridge. We need only chronicle the fact; small interest is felt as to the wholesale conferring degrees on foreign musicians outside the little coterie of Cambridge. The *Times* curtly dismissed the latter in two lines, and the event was unrecorded in many of the newspapers. All the same, we are glad to see this English distinction conferred on the gifted Scandinavian composer.[24]

William Austen Leigh recorded the day in a lighter vein:

> Next year came M. Grieg, whose health had mended; and he also – with Madame Grieg – stayed at King's Lodge. The Provost was by this time Vice-Chancellor, and had to confer the degree. The composer, who had a spirit *corpore majorem*, had not been provided with a Mus.Doc. gown for the ceremony, and the only available one, which belonged to Dr. Alan Gray, was by no means suited to his stature. This gown

was hastily flounced and pinned up in the background till it assumed a shape calculated to move the muscles even of the uninstructed male portion of the audience. The Vice-Chancellor preserved his gravity as long as he was in the Senate House, but he was much amused when his guest insisted on going straight to the post office to dispatch a telegram. He knew well a (medical) doctor Grieg at Bergen, and he had now become a (musical) doctor himself. The message was, 'Doctor Grieg, Bergen, Norway. Kollega, jeg hilser Dem' ('Colleague, I greet thee'). – Doctor Grieg.'[25]

In fact Grieg would continue to find humour in his new academic status for some time to come, jocularly referring to himself in letters to Max Abraham as 'the Cambridge Dr.' (in wishing his friend a return to health) and later (acknowledging Abraham's own legal doctorate) referring to the two of them as 'both of the Doctors'.[26]

The Griegs stayed at King's Lodge for two nights, leaving generous tips for the servants before taking the London train on the morning of 11 May. Once in town, lunch was taken at Grieg's favourite restaurant, Scott's, before a cab took the pair back to Clapham. Photographs, presumably suitably inscribed, were soon dispatched to Austen Leigh and to John Sandys, and a letter was sent to Elliott & Fry, presumably to order further copies from a rapidly depleting stock. One wonders incidentally if some years later Grieg might have been aware of the visit of a later guest of Austen Leigh's at King's Lodge. This was King Oscar of Sweden and Norway, who in 1900 himself received a Cambridge honorary degree and afterwards took tea at the Lodge.

Despite English reports of Grieg's health being so much better that no hindrance existed to deny him his visit to Cambridge, such was not really the case. The day after returning to Clapham he wrote to tell Delius that he was ill again:

> I could have died of laughter at the Doctoral affair the day before yesterday! But I didn't laugh, as I was already ill, and the first thing I had to do as a Doctor was – go to the doctor's. I can neither sit, nor stand, nor walk, nor lie and just don't know how I can carry on. Now I've sent for the doctor, for things cannot go on like this. He'll have to get to the bottom of it. If it hadn't have been for this business, you would have had a jolly letter from Cambridge.[27]

In fact, as he confessed to Abraham, he had already seen a doctor in Cambridge (Dr Humphrey, according to his notebook, to whom he paid a fee of 10 s.), and by 19 May he had seen two more in London: 'What a cheerful life!' One of the London practitioners was a Dr Field, consulted for a fee of one guinea on 15 May, the first day on which Grieg seems to have left the house since returning from Cambridge. Meals were taken at home for about a week, and Grieg had at least been able to devote some of his time to his correspondence. The letter he wrote to Abraham would seem to indicate that, as promised, Oscar Meyer had joined the Griegs for the ceremony, as 'you will probably have learnt from the Court Pianist [Meyer] all you need to know about the Cambridge affair.'[28] 'The Court Pianist' figures in Grieg's notebook of this period at two addresses: 146 Iverson Road, West Hampstead, and c/o Mr Kirchberger, 47 Christchurch Avenue, London N.W.

Translation matters were once again a priority, and Grieg had just examined the recent translations of his songs that had been made by Lady Macfarren. They were 'not at all bad', and he would discuss them with her on Monday 22nd. In Paris at the same time William Molard and Julien Leclercq, overseen by Delius, were at work on French versions of a number of Grieg's songs. On 18 May Molard wrote a letter dealing with the translations they were making of 'At Rondane', 'A Swan' and 'Solveig's Song'. Grieg responded from London the following day. 'Solveig's Song', he felt, was 'a little masterpiece of translation'. His letter to Abraham of the same date was, however, even more laudatory, speaking of 'absolute masterworks'. His Parisian friends had proposed a fee of 35 francs for each song. Abraham had apparently jibbed at this, finding the sum too high. 'I have simply written', Grieg informed Delius, 'to tell him that he can pay what he likes; I will pay the rest.'[29] All was, however, soon settled, with Abraham agreeing to pay the sum that had originally been proposed.

Among Grieg's letters or telegrams to correspondents in England during the fortnight that followed his Cambridge excursion were, as his notebook reveals, those to Austen Leigh, Wolff, Stanford, Sandys, Lady Macfarren, Mackenzie, 'Robbins' (presumably Elizabeth Robins, actress friend of William Archer) and Stopford Brooke. Other entries, under such headings as ointment, medicine, plasters, and honey, indicated a continuing preoccupation with health matters. Names and addresses offer further clues to Grieg's activities. Johannes Wolff is noted as living at 142 Oakley Street, Chelsey [*sic*], Lady Macfarren at 38 Weymouth Street (to be seen on Monday at 11.30), Lady Hallé is at 19 Holland Park, Dr A. C. Mackenzie at 50 Holland Street, E[sther] Sidner, the Swedish singer, at 27 Belsize Crescent; Augener's office is at 22 Great Pulteney Street, and, intriguingly, 'D. P. O'Connor, Esq. M.P.' can be reached at the House of Commons. The significance of this latter entry no doubt resides in the fact that O'Connor ('T. P.' rather than 'D. P.') was just two years later largely to be responsible in Parliament for the passing of the Musical Copyright Bill. An earlier connection may be postulated from an entry in George Bernard Shaw's diary some six years earlier. Having met Grieg and Brækstad at St James's Hall in the morning, he noted: 'Mrs. T. P. O'Connor was at the Philharmonic rehearsal. She introduced me to Wolff, the violinist.'[30]

One name occurs twice in Grieg's notebook, each time at the same address: Max Lindlar, of the Bechstein company, 40 Wigmore Street. The import of this becomes clear in a letter Grieg later wrote from a spa outside Christiania to Carl Rabe on 5 June. Rabe owned the principal music business in Bergen, and Grieg was using the firm as a forwarding address for a number of items he expected soon to arrive from Paris, Leipzig and London, and which were – in a couple of cases at least – dutiable. The most worrying item was a Bechstein concert grand that would be arriving care of Rabe's address at the end of the month. 'It's a present from Bechstein's, and I have asked that it be played both privately and publicly in London before it is sent, so that it can come into Bergen duty-free.' But Grieg had no room for another piano at Troldhaugen, and he asked Rabe to find a music-lover in the town who might like to give it a home – and by all means play it – at least for the duration of the summer. In the end it fell to Johan Halvorsen to keep it at his Bergen address.

In the same notebook Brækstad's business address is given as 243 Temple Chambers, Temple Avenue, which Grieg notes is 'near Fleet Street'. And it becomes clear that a friendship initiated nearly six years earlier continues, for Stopford Brooke's daughter Honor, of Vallombrosa, 40 Abbey Road, N.W. London, is also listed. Grieg had written to her late in April, on the same day as he had written to Charles Harding's wife Ada. The Unitarian friends were not forgotten.

On 21 May Grieg lunched with Oscar Meyer, and life appeared to have begun at last to take a more normal course, with entries relating to cab and omnibus trips reappearing in the pages of his notebook. And on the following day his lunch companion in town was Johannes Wolff. In the composer's sights now was the Philharmonic Society Concert for which he had been engaged to conduct his *Three Orchestral Pieces from 'Sigurd Jorsalfar'* (translated as 'Sigurd the Crusader'), extracted from the incidental music to the play of the same name by his friend Bjørnstjerne Bjørnson. The first English performance of this particular work was to take place at Queen's Hall on 24 May and this was also to be Grieg's introduction to the new hall as a performer. *The Musical Standard* reviewed his life and career beforehand, referring to Cambridge's recent honouring of the composer:

> It may be said, without much risk of contradiction, that compared with the five composers who were honoured in the same way last year the composer of the North is the most worthy of the honour as he is the most distinguished for originality and real creative power.

Whilst Grieg could not, the *Standard* felt, be counted among the very greatest, his many qualities made him a musician to be reckoned with. In addition to this, in its supplement the journal published a portrait print made of the composer in 1886.[31]

On Wednesday 23 May Grieg took a rehearsal at Queen's Hall between 10 o'clock and midday, just as he was to do on the morning of the concert itself. All the other items on the programme were to be conducted by Alexander Mackenzie, who remembered Grieg's 'nervous disposition' from their first meeting and later recalled how

> his unconcealed irritation at the absence of the percussionists from their seats at the rehearsal of the last movement of his Suite, *Sigurd Jorsalfar*, caused me to leave the hall and personally conduct the delinquents from the street to their places, discipline being yet in the making.[32]

Grieg was presumably satisfied with the result of his rehearsing, as the subsequent concert notices were positively glowing. *The Times* reported that every seat in the hall had been taken and that the *Sigurd Jorsalfar* scenes 'were completely successful', their 'author' being enthusiastically applauded and repeatedly called to the platform. 'He conducted them to perfection, and once more proved, at the opening of the second piece, that he is one of the very few musicians who can coax a real *pianissimo* out of the Philharmonic orchestra.'[33] The programme had been something of a mixed bag, with Mackenzie conducting the other works. The pages of *Musical Opinion* are confirmation enough that, in the context of

---

EIGHTY-SECOND SEASON, 1894.

PHILHARMONIC SOCIETY

UNDER THE IMMEDIATE PATRONAGE OF

Her Most Gracious Majesty the Queen,

THEIR ROYAL HIGHNESSES THE PRINCE AND PRINCESS OF WALES,
THEIR ROYAL HIGHNESSES THE DUKE AND DUCHESS OF YORK,
THEIR ROYAL HIGHNESSES THE DUKE AND DUCHESS OF SAXE-COBURG-GOTHA,
THEIR ROYAL HIGHNESSES THE DUKE AND DUCHESS OF CONNAUGHT
AND STRATHEARNE,
THEIR ROYAL HIGHNESSES THE PRINCE AND PRINCESS CHRISTIAN OF
SCHLESWIG-HOLSTEIN,
HER ROYAL HIGHNESS THE PRINCESS LOUISE, MARCHIONESS OF LORNE,
HIS ROYAL HIGHNESS THE DUKE OF CAMBRIDGE,
HER ROYAL HIGHNESS PRINCESS MARY ADELAIDE, DUCHESS OF TECK,
HIS HIGHNESS THE DUKE OF TECK.

FIFTH CONCERT, THURSDAY, MAY 24, 1894.
AT
THE QUEEN'S HALL.

To commence at Eight o'clock precisely.

⇢ *Programme.* ⇠
PART I.

SYMPHONY, No. 8 (in F)	... *Beethoven.*
ARIA, " O del mio dolce ardor " (*Elena e Paride*)	...*Gluck.*
MDLLE. LANDI.	
FANTAISIE DE CONCERT, for Piano and Orchestra ...	*Tschaïkowsky.*
(First time in England.)	
MADAME SOPHIE MENTER.	

PART II.

THREE PIECES (1, Vorspiel ; 2, Intermezzo ; 3, Huldigungsmarsch)	
from Bjornson's Tragedy " Sigurd Jorsalfar "	... *Grieg.*
(First time in England.)	
(Conducted by the COMPOSER.)	
SONGS { *a.* " Reverie "	...*Saint-Saëns.*
{ *b.* " Melodie, " Si tu veux, Mignonne "	... *Massenet.*
MDLLE. LANDI.	
FANTAISIE, for Piano and Orchestra, " Zigeunerweisen " ...	*Sophie Menter.*
(Orchestrated by TSCHAÏKOWSKY.)	
(First time in England.)	
MADAME SOPHIE MENTER.	
SCHERZO AND WEDDING MARCH from " A Midsummer Night's	
Dream "	*Mendelssohn.*
(First performed in England at a Philharmonic Concert, May 27, 1844.)	
CONDUCTOR	DR. A. C. MACKENZIE.

Programme of Philharmonic Society concert, 24 May 1894

a 'memorable concert', Grieg's star, for English audiences, remained very much in the ascendant:

> The extraordinary enthusiasm which marked the reception of Edvard Grieg – who introduced his vorspiel, intermezzo and Huldigungsmarsch to Björnson's tragedy 'Sigurd Iorsalfar' – at the [Philharmonic Society's] fifth concert, given at the Queen's Hall, was a tribute of acknowledgement justly due to one who, in wealth and charm of poetic inspiration, stands foremost among living composers, one of whose countless songs (only equalled by Schubert and Schumann) is worth tons of academic operas, cantatas, and symphonies. Grieg has been made a Mus.Doc. Cantab.: the distinction is on the side of the university. The 'Doc.' can add no more lustre to the name of Grieg than it could to that of Schumann or Wagner, for it has become a household word. His music has delighted the hearts of untold thousands, and is certain to become increasingly popular as it becomes more fully appreciated. The above mentioned three pieces, played under the composer's direction (which demonstrated what *pp* and dynamic shades the Philharmonic band can produce) are essentially scenic. The intermezzo is deeply impressive; the march is remarkable for contrasts of delicacy and gorgeous orchestral effects.[34]

Grieg's control of the orchestra was remarked upon in many of the reviews of the concert. 'As a conductor,' wrote *The Musical Standard*, 'Dr. Grieg asserted again his extraordinary powers; whether he would interpret works by other composers as well we cannot say. He certainly makes the band play with the most perfect refinement imaginable, and with unusual expressiveness.'[35] Grieg's 'original, delicate, and gorgeously orchestrated' music was, according to *Musical News*, 'splendidly played, and such exquisite velvety *pianissimos* were never before heard from the orchestra.'[36] One wonders if the journal's reviewer could had been present at Grieg's first concert in London when, at the time conducting the *Elegiac Melodies*, the composer had first conjured that hushed sound of silence from the orchestra. Whilst *Sigurd Jorsalfar* had clearly been well-received by an appreciative audience, the reviewers generally acknowledged that the work was not vintage Grieg, but all found many attractive qualities in it. The 'Homage March' has of course lived on as a popular piece in its own right, and it was virtually unanimously praised on this particular occasion. *Musical News* noted how the 'broad theme for the 'celli' was afterwards 'taken up and developed by the full orchestra with a brilliancy and power quite extraordinary'. And *The Monthly Musical Record* wrote of its 'original and striking character'. It had made 'a strong impression, and was in every way worthy of the composer'.[37] For *The Musical Times* it had been 'the most elaborate, and, on the whole, the finest movement'.[38]

In all, however, the greatest attraction had been Grieg himself, now hero-worshipped whenever he came to London. The reviews referred to the actual presence of the great man in various ways. He himself was the 'principal attraction' of the concert. The audience had accorded him 'as hearty a welcome as we can remember being offered to any composer for years'. 'Enormous applause' had greeted him as he came onto the platform. He had had a 'magnificent reception', and at the close 'was recalled again and again'. London had once more taken Grieg to its heart, and for concertgoers it had clearly been far too long since he had last appeared in person in the capital.

Of Grieg's own reaction to the performance and its reception, there is little to be gleaned. He wrote to both Abraham and Delius on the following day. The letter to Abraham does not appear to have survived, and all he found time to tell Delius about the concert was: 'The success yesterday was very great – called 4 times – and the fellows played well. But the hall was bad.'[39] Grieg had preferred the old St James's Hall. The reason for this otherwise commendable brevity is straightforward, for the Griegs were packing up to leave, buying that day their tickets to Copenhagen at a cost of £12 5*s.* 10*d.* A telegram was dispatched to Johannes Wolff, who would be performing the third Violin Sonata with Marie Roger-Miclos at Prince's Hall the following afternoon, by which time the Griegs would already be in Belgium, planning to leave on the 10 o'clock boat train from Victoria. Farewells were duly taken of the Augeners on the 26th, tips were given to the maidservants, and Grieg left London. He was not to return until the autumn of 1897.

As always, the Norwegian master's visit spawned a further number of public performances of his works, given before, during and after his stay in London. Miss Rina Allerton ought, it seems, to have known better than to sing 'Solveig's Song' at a Manns Benefit Concert at the Crystal Palace: it 'does not at all suit her style'. But Louise Nanney, the promising young violinist, 'produces a full round round tone, has a broad style, and considerable executive facility', and these qualities appear to have been well displayed when she played Grieg's first Sonata at Prince's Hall with Waddington Cooke. After Wolff's concert on 26 May came cellist Joseph Hollman and pianist Raoul Pugno, who included Grieg's Cello Sonata in Pugno's recital at Prince's Hall. A Royal Academy of Music students' concert included the String Quartet, played by a youthful and distinguished foursome: Gerald Walenn, W. H. Reed, A. Walenn, and B. P. Parker. It was 'artistically performed . . . with commendable skill', and the concert as a whole displayed the 'steady progress' of the Academy. A concert given by the pianist Harvey Löhr offered evidence that his 'splendid technique' was well displayed in Grieg's *Holberg Suite*. If Miss F. Helena Marks's playing in her piano recital at the Steinway Hall was described as 'amateurish', she at least did 'appreciably better' when accompanying Grieg's Violin Sonata no. 1, with Hans Wessely the 'dexterous and successful violinist'. Accompanied by the Revd E. H. Moberly's String Orchestra, Miss Dale sang 'Solveig's Song' so well at St James's Hall that it was encored. *The Musical Standard* decided that although it was given with some effect, 'we thought there should have been more animation from the word "Ah!" that recurs at the close of each stanza. The spirit of the music seems to require it.' Tobias Matthay gave a piano recital at the small Queen's Hall and included 'Butterfly' in 'a neat and delicate performance'. He had earlier played this same piece at a Trinity College concert on 7 May. These notices, drawn from the major musical periodicals of May, June and July 1894, are sufficient to show that lovers of Grieg's music in London were by now more than well served. They had neither far to go nor long to wait if they wished to hear the Norwegian composer's works in the capital.

The popularity of much of Grieg's music would certainly have been such as to find it being played, sung and whistled in the streets of London. It is more likely, however, that the tastes of a visiting Commander of the National Guard of California were offended by music-making of a considerably lower order, an episode piquantly recorded in the pages of *Musical News*:

> A too forcible objection to street music has unfortunately had a fatal result. On Wednesday evening last, an American gentleman, General John Hewston, while passing along Gray's Inn Road, found fault with the playing of three street minstrels. He asserts that one of them struck him with a banjo; the General retaliated with his umbrella, and prodded the man in the eye. Though he was immediately removed to the hospital, and all possible done for him, death ensued in a short time. The General is in custody.[40]

⽣ 12 ⽣

'YOUR MUSIC IS SO UNIVERSAL A FAVOURITE IN ENGLAND'

ROM London it was on to Christiania and a fortnight or so in June at Grefsen Spa on the outskirts of the capital. At about the same time, Grieg's friends George Augener and Max Abraham, both suffering spells of ill health, had taken themselves off to German recuperative resorts at Wiesbaden and Tölz respectively. Grieg himself, back home later in June, appears to be the first of the three to signal an improvement in health. It was already a 'wonderful' summer, and he was feeling very much better. 'Here at Troldhaugen it's splendid', he told Abraham on 2 July, once more content with the world and its ways. Among the letters waiting for him at home had been one from an enthusiast for his music, the Revd Henry J. Trueman, vicar of St Mary's Church, Southampton. Trueman told the composer that he had sung many of Grieg's songs at a number of recitals in the Chapel of the Good Shepherd, and enclosed some of his programmes. Although he seems to have had little wider claim to fame, Trueman was known as the poet of 'Love's Recall', a ballad composed by Frederick Stevenson that was published in 1894. In another direction altogether, it seems that Grieg's eye may have been caught by modern house-and-garden gadgets in use at Clapham. George Augener's son wrote to give him what one hopes was good news: 'We have taken the liberty of shipping to you this week a "Lawn-mower" and a "Carpet-sweeper".' A later letter, also bearing news of members of the Augener family, is evidence that the lawn-mower at least had arrived at Troldhaugen; it included directions as to how to use the machine, a Ransome's 'Chain Automaton'. 'Gardeners', the leaflet announced, 'should paste these "Directions" on the wall of the Tool House.'[1] One hopes Grieg studied the copious directions closely and did as he was told.

More to the musical point was William's confirmation that the corrected proofs of the new songs had arrived safely. These were published by Augener in the autumn in three albums, *Five Songs*, Op. 58, *Six Elegiac Songs*, Op. 59, and *Five Songs*, Op. 60, all in translations by Lady Macfarren. The welcome given to them by the musical press was generally warm, and Natalia Macfarren's 'skilful and experienced pen' was applauded. *The Monthly Musical Record* unsurprisingly placed Grieg 'among the highest class modern living song-writers', while *The Musical Standard* asserted that 'it is not every day that a composer of Dr. Grieg's genius bursts upon the world with sixteen new songs – especially with compositions of so much art and freshness'. But the *Standard*'s review was not entirely uncritical. Grieg 'does not entirely rise to the summit of possible achievement', was its verdict.[2] There had earlier been an announcement in the September issue of *The Monthly Musical Record* that Grieg had promised to write a violin sonata for the Hungarian violinist Eugen Adorján.[3] Unfortunately, no addition to the earlier three sonatas was ever to materialize.

For the winter and spring of 1895 the Griegs based themselves in Copenhagen. Grieg was hoping to travel to Vienna around the beginning of April, having been invited to perform there by the concert agent Albert Gutmann. 'In the Violin Sonata and String Quartet', he told Gutmann, 'no-one captures the style of my works better than Herr Johannes Wolff in London ... and I would be very pleased if he could be engaged for this occasion.'[4] In the event, Grieg did not go, but it is interesting to see how he now regarded Wolff as the prime exponent of his works for violin. In another letter of the period his divided views of London are evident. Oscar Meyer's fine pianistic talents were unlikely, he feared, to gain the encouragement they merited in London. 'The air there, for an artist blest by God, is not favourable. I would never be able to compose a single note in that city.'[5] And he was right, of course, in so far as London's air applied to himself. There is no evidence that he ever composed 'a single note' in the capital. Nor did he think that most of the English compositions he had heard were of any great worth, explaining to Iver Holter that he was not disposed to write the same kind of large-scale work that was the staple currency of music festivals, as so many English composers mistakenly chose to do. Such festivals brought forth from them 'all their big and boring works for choir and orchestra'.[6]

Writing from Holmedale, Exeter, Daniel Wood, who had been in the audience at Grieg's first London concert in 1888, had cause to thank Grieg in January 1895. His young daughter Dorothy had called on Grieg at some point and asked if he would be willing to hear her play:

> It was so good of you to allow yourself to be troubled with so young a child, whose only excuse for coming was her great love for your music, that I cannot sufficiently express my gratitude. I am sure she will always think with delight of her visit and that the autograph with which you have honoured her will be a continual encouragement to persevere in studying the art she has chosen for her life study.[7]

Might Grieg also have agreed to the request, in February 1895, of the conductor of the Warwickshire Ladies' Orchestra to use his 'honoured name to appear as the president' of their society? His response is not recorded, but a further letter (this time to Nina Grieg) from the same source included a report on the orchestra's performance of the *Holberg Suite* (played from memory), together with an expression of regret on learning of the composer's ill health.[8] Perhaps a greater curiosity in the Edvard Grieg Archives takes the form of a letter from a chemist in Ireland who had read of one of the great man's physical weaknesses and offered to send Grieg a seasickness remedy *gratis* whenever he might need it.[9]

Still in the spring of 1895, yet another English composer approached Grieg. The 37-year-old John Edmund Barkworth, formerly a student at the Royal College of Music but now living in Paris and studying with Richard Mandl (whom he believed Grieg knew), wrote in Norwegian to tell Grieg that he had arranged 'Bridal Procession' for full orchestra. Mandl had been so pleased with his pupil's effort that he proposed to have it performed at a concert in the French capital. Barkworth, who had been an admirer of Grieg's music 'ever since my childhood, when it was not so well known in England as it is now', asked Grieg if he would be kind enough to allow this performance of his arrangement. He added, encouragingly, that he was an old acquaintance of Grieg's friend Andreas Pettersson.[10] Grieg's response is unknown. At the time, the work existed in 2- and 4-hand versions for piano. Later it would be orchestrated by Johan Halvorsen, and it is in his arrangement that 'Bridal Procession' is now familiar on the concert platform. However, Delius had produced a full pencil draft of his own orchestration of the work as early as 1891, although this lay largely unregarded and certainly unplayed during his lifetime. (It was finally edited for publication by Robert Threlfall in time for performance in London at the Royal Festival Hall at the Grieg Sesquicentennial Concert of 1993.) As for Barkworth, all that seems to be remembered of him is the remarkable fact that he set Shakespeare's *Romeo and Juliet* as an opera, apparently adhering faithfully to the original, if slightly condensed text. Even more remarkably, this four-act work actually achieved performance in Middlesbrough in January 1916 and at the Royal College of Music ten years later. (His *Fireflies* was given at the RCM in 1925).

Of Grieg performances in London during 1895, there are a number that are worthy of mention. One of the year's earliest was of the *Ballade*, Leonard Borwick having clearly made something of a showpiece of this particular work. It was given at a Monday Popular Concert, when 'snow was on the ground, and the cold so intense as to scare many suburban visitors *en posse*'. Borwick, 'recalled after an excellent execution . . . nobly refused the encore'.[11] The Hungarian pianist Ilona Eibenschütz, a pupil of Hans Schmitt and Franz Schumann, included what was listed as 'Norwegian Bridal March' (possibly the 'Wedding March' from Op. 17, though more likely the better-known 'Bridal Procession') in a recital she gave at St James's Hall on 8 March. It provided a suitable display, we are told, of her 'fine abilities'.[12] George Henschel and his Scottish Orchestra went to Windsor Castle to play to Queen Victoria early in March and included Grieg's *Last Spring* in their programme.[13] Although at a Queen's Hall concert on 15 June one reviewer noted 'certain peculiarities' in Arthur Nikisch's interpretative style in conducting Beethoven's C-minor Symphony, there was no such criticism apportioned to his

Grieg in the same concert: 'Truth to tell, Mr. Nikisch seemed more completely at home in Grieg's *Peer Gynt* Suite, one movement being encored.'[14] Then there was the 'very successful' concert given by 'Mr Moberly's String Orchestra' at St James's Hall on 17 May, which included the *Holberg Suite*. The orchestra was entirely made up of women: ninety strong, it included 17 cellists and nine double bassists. Moberly's orchestra, drawn from women players in Hampshire and Wiltshire, had been giving an annual concert in London for some years. Katharine Ramsay, furthermore, played the *Ballade* during the course of the proceedings. On 9 July Jules Hollander played the *Holberg Suite* in its original piano form at Queen's Hall – exemplifying the enormous popularity at the time of this particular work. De Greef played *Pictures from Folk Life* at a recital in St James's Hall on 20 July. That this was a favourite work in his portfolio can, for example, be seen from its inclusion in a programme he played at Bristol's Colston Hall on 2 October. *Bergliot* was given on 29 August at the newly-established Promenade Concerts, moving 'J.H.G.' of *The Musical Standard* to tears, so impressed was he with the work. In a long and thoughtful piece for the *Standard* he commended Grieg for having understood how to combine music with a spoken text, something that, for example, Mackenzie had not been able successfully to accomplish with his *Dream of Jubal*. In a separate concert review, presumably by the same critic, Henry Wood was complimented for having conducted 'with much tact'. Lena Ashwell, the reciter, had really needed to express the emotion inherent in the work more strongly and more poignantly, but *Bergliot* had nonetheless 'made a lasting impression'.[15] Outside London, *Sigurd Jorsalfar* was on the menu on 11 September for the Gloucester Three Choirs Festival, as it had been in Birmingham when Hallé had conducted it there in March.

As for publications, Augener had brought out at the beginning of the year the album of *Seven Children's Songs*, Op. 61. The Norwegian texts were once again supplemented by English singing translations made by Natalia Macfarren.

> In these seven songs the melodies are delightfully simple, and what the Germans call *volksthümlich*; in the accompaniments, however, we meet with harmonies of the real 'Grieg' stamp. But the composer nearly always includes the melody notes in the accompaniment, and thus the peculiar harmonies, though they may astonish or delight children, will not lead them astray. The songs form then a pleasing combination of simplicity and skill.[16]

The Morning Post echoed these sentiments. The set of seven was 'perfectly exquisite', the songs being 'simple, fresh, and original' and deserving of becoming popular.[17] *The Musical Times* was similarly delighted, although a little less happy with Lady Macfarren's translation.[18] And *The Musical Standard* too was complimentary over this group of songs with their pared-down and transparent simplicity. It furthermore detected an unexpected musical link in

> the wonderfully spirited conceit, entitled *Fisher's Song*, which has several original touches in rhythm and harmony, though the middle section might have been written

by Brahms. It is a strange thing that the individual Grieg has latterly come under the spell of that composer. We noticed the influence in the previous volumes of song, but it was then very faint. It is more than a suspicion in the present compositions. Brahms has influenced many composers; but Grieg of all others![19]

The Griegs were back at Troldhaugen at the beginning of May 1895, and Grieg was soon at work on his magnificent song-cycle *Haugtussa*. In June Ebenezer Prout wrote in Norwegian to ask him if he would consider accepting honorary membership of the 'Union of Graduates in Music', stressing that it was an honorary title, with no fees to pay or responsibilities to assume. Prout was also hoping to visit Norway in July, 'my thirteenth trip to your country', and expected to arrive in

Ebenezer Prout offers honorary membership of the Union of Graduates in Music, in fluent Norwegian

Bergen on 25 July. Would Grieg be at home at the time, so that he might pay a visit to Troldhaugen?[20] Grieg was certainly at home during July, and one hopes that Prout, 'perhaps the greatest theorist of the 19th century',[21] had better luck than on his earlier visits to Bergen.

From Bergen, it was on to Christiania, Copenhagen, and then Leipzig, where Edvard and Nina, ever the migratory birds, arrived in October to spend the winter. In earlier days Grieg would find his old friend Brodsky there, but Brodsky, back in Europe after three years or so in New York, was now in Manchester, where he had just taken up the post of leader in Sir Charles Hallé's orchestra. Shortly after this Hallé died, and Brodsky was offered his post as Principal of the newly established Royal Manchester College of Music. He accepted it and remained in Manchester, where he re-established his celebrated string quartet, until his death in 1929. Grieg recorded in his notebook his friend's new address, 96 Acomb Street, Manchester, and very soon engaged in a little musical politicking. Hermann Kretzschmar, whose musical gifts Grieg admired (he was a conductor, organist, composer and writer) had expressed to Grieg an interest in the newly vacant conductorship of the Hallé Orchestra. Grieg knew him well in Leipzig, where he was a respected conductor, and enthusiastically recommended him to Brodsky, Kretzschmar being unwilling personally to put himself forward. 'If you can somehow contribute to his securing the position, I beg you to do so.' Kretzschmar would need to know about the terms and responsibilities involved, and Grieg had agreed to act as a go-between. 'Please send me a few lines with the necessary information that I can show to K., and forgive me from burdening you with this. I know that you're always happy to take up a good cause.' Grieg added that he had himself conducted the Manchester orchestra. 'I believe it was in 1889. Who knows, perhaps your presence there may hypnotise me into coming again!' Meanwhile he wondered how his old friend was getting on 'under those yellow-grey sooty skies up there?'[22]

The situation in Manchester, however, was complicated. Hallé himself had founded the concerts 38 years earlier, and they had been essentially a personal undertaking. His family had, as a temporary measure, invited Brodsky to conduct a number of already scheduled concerts, the first of which had taken place in Bradford on the very day of the founding conductor's death. The legatees meanwhile were in discussion with Hans Richter, the idea being that when he was free from his contract in Vienna in some two years' time he might take up the Manchester baton. Richter was likely to be granted whatever remuneration he requested. In the meantime various conductors who possessed the qualifications of being either English or 'celebrated' (among them would be Cowen) would be invited to stand in. So Kretzschmar's prospects were minimal, something that Brodsky, who had a high opinion of him as both man and artist, regretted. G. A. Forsyth, the leading music dealers in Manchester, had taken over the day-to-day running of the orchestra, and Forsyth himself was the first to inform Brodsky that Grieg was expected back in England the following February. 'This being the case,' Brodsky told Grieg,

he would like to have a concert (Hallé Concert) exclusively of your own compositions, with you conducting and your wife singing (how I should love to conduct your
Piano Concerto with you). Write just a couple of lines, dear friend, to let me know if
all this might be possible.[23]

Grieg was grateful for this prompt reply from Brodsky, who now signed himself
Adolph, rather than the Adolf of Leipzig years. He conveyed the bad news to
Kretzschmar, finding it an uncomfortable task. But at least, he told Brodsky, he
could see how the Manchester public must have been pleased at the prospect of
having Richter come to join them:

> I know nothing about being expected in England in February. I have plenty of invita-
> tions, but I have to turn them down. Of course it will please and interest me enor-
> mously to be able one day to conduct in Manchester while you are there. But to come
> to England for the sake of just one concert will not do.
>
> As I am not English, it would be interesting to know what kind of terms are offered
> to 'celebrated' conductors. Do you know? A lot depends on this. I must be honest
> and say that I now find public appearances so wearing that beyond whatever laurels
> may come my way I also require English pounds, indeed quite a few of them. I am
> afraid my wife no longer sings in public, and as far as the Piano Concerto is con-
> cerned, I would be extremely satisfied with the conductor – Brodsky –, but on no
> account with the soloist – Grieg.[24]

Forsyth had informed Brodsky that he could offer Grieg £35 for a Manchester concert, but Brodsky, aware that this would not be sufficient to tempt his friend, suggested an extra concert at which he and Grieg might play all three violin sonatas;
and then, to follow this, a brief foray to Liverpool, where a further concert might be
arranged. With typical generosity he offered to top up Forsyth's offer from his own
pocket. What would Grieg actually be prepared to accept to come to Manchester?
Meanwhile, he and Anna had found contentment in their new home town:

> I can scarcely tell you how much I like Manchester (my wife feels the same). We both
> feel very happy here, have made many friends in the short time we have been here and
> people make us heartily welcome. Audiences are musically intelligent and at the same
> time enthusiastic. And the fact that the people here so much love my own dear Grieg
> makes them even dearer to me.[25]

Grieg pondered the offer and expressed his gratitude for Brodsky's invitation to
Nina and himself to stay at the family home in Acomb Street. However, he was by
now less than willing to put up anywhere else but in hotels, so as not to visit what
he described as his 'wretched' health on friends and their families. At the same time
he was not prepared to conduct for less than £50, being unwilling, he claimed, to
subsidize the lifestyle of Hallé's heirs. He confessed to finding it difficult to believe
that a programme consisting solely of the three violin sonatas would bring in a
Manchester audience, but thought the idea of giving an orchestral concert of his
own works in Liverpool was excellent. As ever, though, there remained the ques-

tion of his health. He just might feel better by February, so would need to know the latest date for a final decision.[26] Brodsky determinedly went ahead with arrangements. A date – 13 February 1896 – was fixed with Forsyth for the main concert, for which the fee would remain £35; but better still, on the preceding day Brodsky and Grieg would play the sonatas at a 'Gentlemen's Concert' in Manchester, for which the composer would receive a fee of 40 guineas. Sapellnikov, already studying the Grieg Concerto for his Philharmonic Society Concert, would also be engaged to play the work under Grieg in Manchester should he be available at the time. A concert or concerts in Liverpool, however, might be more difficult to arrange around these particular dates. 'So far, 42 + 35 = £77!' Brodsky proclaimed, surer now that Grieg would accept these engagements.[27] This particular chapter came to a close on Christmas Day, when Grieg sat down to respond. The money was fine, but he remained unwell and February would be too soon. Had it been a question of April or May, the chances would have been much better:

> Since my answer needs to be given right away, in my present poor condition I absolutely cannot find the courage to say yes . . . The visit *must* indeed some day become a reality, perhaps already [later] next year. In this hope and with warmest greetings from us both, we must bring to a close our abortive Manchester fixture . . .[28]

Grieg's second visit to Manchester, at last to be marked by a reunion with the Brodskys, in fact lay nearly two years into the future.

In October, while briefly in Copenhagen, Grieg had come into contact with Bella Edwards, a British-born pianist whose parents had emigrated to Denmark. She gave concert recitals with her friend Margrethe Petersen, a Danish singer. Grieg met them both and fell completely for Bella's charms. Several passionate letters were dispatched to her from Leipzig, with Grieg clearly hoping to secure from her a long-term commitment. Her own letters (which Grieg subsequently destroyed) were, however, cooler in tone, and by late January 1896 he reluctantly but realistically conceded that there could be no way forward for the affair. Some years later, Edwards was to team up and share a home with a younger English violinist who changed her name from the distinctly unromantic Evangeline Muddock to Eva Mudocci. Mudocci attracted the attention of Edvard Munch, with whom for a time she enjoyed a passionate friendship, and a lithograph by Munch, *The Violin Concert*, depicts the two women together, Edwards seated at the piano and Mudocci standing with violin. It was rumoured that Edwards had lesbian tendencies, a factor that may go a long way towards explaining the unequal relationship with Grieg.

Life in Leipzig went on relatively quietly during the first month or two of 1896. 'Had I been healthier,' Grieg told Halvorsen, 'I would not be sitting here, but conducting in one town and another. A trip to England was more or less fixed, but had to be put off.'[29] To another of the former members of the Norwegian colony in Leipzig, Iver Holter, he wrote on the same date of a visit Delius had paid to Leipzig in the late autumn, bringing with him the manuscript score of his latest opera, *The Magic Fountain*. Grieg felt that it had contained 'some excellent things, indeed brilliant and unique, but with anything less than a superb performance the whole thing will come to nothing'.[30] There were briefly hopes that the opera might be given in Prague, even as early as February if Delius were able to make various revisions to the score in time. Perhaps Grieg himself had suggested some of these revisions to his English friend. Nothing came of Prague, however, and of all Delius's stage works, this one had to wait by far the longest — over a century — for a first performance.

A notable addition to the many honours Grieg received over the years came his way in this first month of 1896, when he was made a member of the Légion d'Honneur. He made an interesting comment on his award. Despite this recognition by France and its effect on the good burghers of Leipzig, who now 'bowed and scraped' when he walked by on the street, he set a higher value on the fact that his work was followed with interest in England, a country for which he had a particular liking.[31] England's continued interest had its downside, however. Just as Grieg had had earlier to decline Beerbohm Tree's request for incidental music to *Hamlet*, he now had to do the same with regard to yet another request for incidental music, this time for a proposed London production of Dante Gabriel Rossetti's *Sister Helen*. The attack was mounted on a broad front, with Hans Lien Brækstad, William Archer and Sir George Grove warmly commending to the composer the instigator of the project, the American actress and writer Elizabeth Robins. Robins herself wrote to Grieg to tell him that Burne-Jones, who was designing the costumes and scenery, would — like herself — be delighted if Grieg felt able to join them in the project.[32] Robins was American by birth, but shortly after the suicide in 1887 of her actor husband she had moved to England, inaugurating a successful career on the London stage and embarking on a long-lasting affair with William Archer. She had told Brækstad that Grieg was 'the *only* person in the world who could accomplish what she wished for'. Brækstad himself knew how busy Grieg was likely to be, but very much hoped that he would be tempted to take up the challenge. Robins, he told Grieg, had taken leading roles in several of Ibsen's plays in London, and her persistence, allied to her enthusiasm for the great man's works, meant that every Norwegian ought to be grateful to her.[33] A shorter letter from Archer himself, also written in Norwegian, seems to be the only one he ever wrote to Grieg:

> Honoured Sir
>
> You will, I am sure, not recall that I once had the honour of meeting you, together with Herr H. L. Brækstad, in the Scandinavian Society in London; but you will most likely know my name in connection with the Ibsen movement in England
>
> For this reason I permit myself to assure you that Miss Elizabeth Robins, who now addresses herself to you, is a serious and pre-eminent artist, and that her project is not just one of genuinely artistic significance but one that will, in all likelihood, have the effect of awakening a lively interest on the part of the educated public.[34]

Finally, George Grove, urging the case of this 'gifted American lady', told Grieg that the object of his writing was to ask him 'to consider Miss Robins's request, and not to dismiss it at once'. He added: 'Your music is so universal a favourite in England, that a new composition of yours is sure to be well received'.[35] In hindsight it is easy for us to see how difficult it would have been for Grieg to have taken upon himself this particular task. 'My health', he wrote to Oscar Meyer, 'forbids all forms of exertion for me, and for this reason I have had to decline all invitations that involve music-making.'[36] By 'music-making' Grieg will have meant first and foremost performing, whether on the podium or at the piano, but there is no doubt that composition too was rather in abeyance for the time being. He was indeed working, probably in fairly desultory fashion, on what was ultimately to become his set of *Symphonic Dances*, a four-movement suite for piano four hands (to be orchestrated in 1898) that he completed later that same year, but little else appeared to be in hand. So far as Grieg was concerned, *Sister Helen*, for all its distinguished promoters, could only be a non-starter.

William Archer deserves a further note, as he had by now taken over from Edmund Gosse the role of Ibsen's principal torchbearer in England. His family had close connections with Norway, for his uncle Colin Archer was the builder of Fridtjof Nansen's celebrated polar exploration ship *Fram*. Archer himself came first as a boy and then for many years afterwards to Larvik on holiday and soon learned to speak Norwegian fluently. It was there that he bought his first Ibsen, rapidly followed by many others, and he finally met Ibsen himself in the Scandinavian Club in Rome in 1881. There followed the publication in England of volume after volume of Ibsen's plays, all translated by Archer, who for many years would involve himself in the London productions of the great man's dramatic works.

Interestingly, there was some concern around the mid-1890s, whether really justified or not, that too few of the piano greats were choosing to play Grieg's music in the concert halls of England. 'Why do our greatest foreign pianists treat Grieg's pianoforte compositions in such an unfriendly spirit?' demanded 'J.H.G.' in *The Musical Standard*. 'Is it because the latter have the musical crime of being simple to the accomplished finger?' The fact that Grieg's piano pieces tended to be left in the hands of the enthusiastic amateur pianist was a great shame:

> Because an unskilful amateur can play the notes as written, that is not equivalent to agreeing that he, therefore, gives you all there is in the composer's pianoforte works. They really need a mature interpretative power; more so than those 'stupendous' fantasias of Liszt's, that open the eyes but stupefy the human brain.

Grieg's music, which had 'the beauty of genius', did not deserve the neglect offered to it by the current crop of keyboard maestros. 'Wait until you hear him play the Beethoven Sonata!' was a perfectly natural thing to say of a performer. To which the writer's riposte was 'Yes, precisely; but, equally so, wait until you hear him play Grieg.'[37] C. Fred Kenyon did, however, propose an answer in a subsequent letter to the Editor. Grieg was played by at least one 'accomplished pianist', Arthur De Greef, who was an 'ideal exponent' of the composer and very often played his works in public. 'At De Greef's next pianoforte recital in Manchester, he is to play no less than five numbers by Edward Grieg.'[38]

Oscar Meyer was to give Grieg's Concerto its first performance in Wales — reportedly a huge success — in Cardiff on 14 February. His piano pupils, he claimed, played only Grieg's music, as a consequence of which their teacher had earned from them the nickname 'Griegmeyer'. Just as Brodsky had so quickly taken to Manchester, so Meyer (in spite of Grieg's strictures) happily adopted London as a base, and he was to live and perform there for a number of years. Grieg, otherwise so admiring of the *standards* of music-making in the capital, nonetheless rather sourly responded to Meyer's confessed enthusiasm for London living by countering that in the course of his own brief visits he had had little opportunity to meet really 'musical people' there, which was why he had found the city 'so strangely unmusical'.[39] Perhaps it was unmusical in comparison with Leipzig, where Grieg had studied and where he was presently living — Leipzig with its Conservatory and its Gewandhaus, Leipzig where Bach, Mendelssohn, Nikisch, Brahms, Mahler and countless others had stayed, composed and made music, where Max Abraham had founded his great publishing company, and where so many young Norwegians had come to study. One suspects that Grieg found the Society element in London's musical life to be relatively alien. Leipzig and its citizens lived and breathed music. Audiences in London, however, were drawn largely from the middle and upper classes, not to say the aristocracy. The Season reigned supreme, and serious or 'classical' music formed little or no part of the everyday lives of the working masses. It was to be a long and gradual process before London would become, in the distant future, acknowledged as the musical capital of Europe.

Yet further temptation was put in Grieg's path by none other than the son of Lady Hallé, Waldemar Norman-Neruda, now established as a concert agent in London. He was anxious to arrange at an early date a tour in England for Grieg and Nina, and his mother would be more than happy to participate in a series of concerts. Might therefore Grieg's health be capable of carrying him through the whole of March, giving no fewer than four concerts weekly? The financial rewards, as he pointed out, would be considerable. 'I am absolutely convinced that you would earn significant sums, as you are so *enormously* popular here.'[40] A negative response was inevitable. The only concert at which Grieg conducted during the whole of the time he was currently based in Leipzig appears to have been one that involved a trip to Vienna. It is surprising that he managed to fulfil the engagement, since in mid-March he was complaining of suffering from rheumatism in his right shoulder. Even worse, though, was the fact that Nina had had to undergo a major breast operation at the same time. He was away from Leipzig for just five days, conducting in the Austrian capital on 24 March a concert of his own music that included the Piano Concerto.[41]

Grieg's music duly returned to the Philharmonic Society Concerts in London on 27 February 1896, when Vassily Sapellnikov played the Concerto under Mackenzie's baton. And at the Crystal Palace on 14 March Grieg's 'imaginative' overture *In Autumn* was 'admirably' performed under the direction of August Manns.[42] Interestingly, the piece by which Halvorsen was to become best known featured at a further Crystal Palace concert, again conducted by Manns, just three weeks later:

> Another partial novelty was *The Triumphal Entry of the Boyards*, by the Norwegian composer Johan Halvorsen. It was performed at the Queen's Hall Promenade concerts last autumn. The music has picturesque qualities and some originality, but is rather heavily scored, a fault by no means uncommon in music from the North.[43]

A concert at the Mozart Society on 21 March threw up another interesting link with Delius, with a report that 'Mrs. Jutta Bell sang two German *lieder* of Grieg and Schumann with much artistic feeling.'[44] Mrs Bell, née Jutta Mordt and born in Norway, had been a near neighbour of Delius's in Florida in the mid-1880s and was, it seems, distantly related to Grieg. On returning to Europe she studied singing with Marchesi and then moved to London, where she was to teach singing and voice production for some years – and indeed to give advice to Delius when he was working on the libretto of his opera *The Magic Fountain* – before finally emigrating to America.

The Griegs left Leipzig on 18 April, having spent six months in the town, breaking their journey for a while in Copenhagen, where Grieg again conducted a performance of his Concerto, this time with Busoni as soloist. They were back at Troldhaugen in May, where they stayed for most of the summer, apart from holiday breaks in the Westland. Delius returned to Norway in June, partly working quietly on his third opera, *Koanga*, and partly walking in the mountains. He had hoped that Grieg would join him once again on a mountain tour, but Nina's convalescence made this impossible:

> The operation which my wife had to undergo was enormous. And it turns out afterwards that the experts could not even agree anyway whether it was 'cancer' or not. We hope and believe now that it was not the case. At any rate, everything 'vulnerable' in the breast has been removed. So you will understand that it is not a matter of mere trivialities.[45]

In October the Griegs left Bergen. They would spend the winter travelling, with stays in Stockholm, Christiania, Vienna, Leipzig, Amsterdam, and finally Copenhagen. In Vienna on 19 December an English visitor, Percival Hedley, met him after a concert conducted by the composer. Grieg spoke to him of how, when writing, he was 'invariably led to think of the old folk-tunes of his country'. But it is the description of his appearance that draws attention:

> Touching the personality of Grieg it is the simplicity and unaffected manner and his

modest and unassuming bearing that makes the most attractive impression. A man of small stature, his appearance is most fascinating. It is the noble countenance with the full forehead, surmounted by rich, grey and curly locks; the characteristic energy

The beginning of Grieg's song 'Ragnhild', *The Strand Musical Magazine*, 4 (July–Dec. 1896)

of the mouth and the serious depths in his blue eyes, those grand blue eyes whose glance seemed always as though directed on high ideals, that indicates a calm exaltation and an extremely pure enthusiasm.[46]

Back in London, Henry Wood conducted on 6 October a performance of the *Two Norwegian [Nordic] Melodies*, Op. 63, for string orchestra, and Harry Plunket Greene, accompanied by Leonard Borwick, included Grieg in a recital at St James's Hall on 30 October. At about this time there is evidence of Grieg planning to visit England in the spring of 1897, for he turned down an invitation to conduct his *Olav Trygvason* music in Vienna because 'so far as I know at present, I shall be busy in England in March'.[47] Once again these plans would be frustrated, however, but autumn 1897 would be quite another story.

The December 1896 edition of *The Monthly Musical Record* included a Christmas bonus for its readers, with the journal proudly claiming that it was 'able to offer its contribution towards the Christmas festivities, in the shape of a most charming "Christmas Song," eminently suitable for that purpose, written by the renowned Scandinavian musician Edvard Grieg'. As an extra it added another piece by Grieg, 'Farmyard Song'; both came from *Children's Songs*, Op. 61.[48] It constitutes a reminder of a secondary area of music publishing at the period, in which *The Strand Musical Magazine* was particularly prominent. A survey of its three-year existence, from 1895 to 1897, shows Grieg's song 'Sunset' as the first musical offering in its first issue and four other songs, 'Solveig's Song', 'Ragnhild', 'I Love Thee', and 'Woodland Wandering', scattered over those following, interspersed with various piano pieces – 'Menuet', Op. 6, no. 2; 'Album Leaf', Op. 12, no. 7; 'Folk Song', Op. 12, no. 5; 'Valse Humoreske', Op. 6, no. 1; and no. 5 of *Poetic Tone Pictures*, Op. 3 – and an abbreviated 'Anitra's Dance' for four hands. All the pieces published by the magazine were subscribed 'May be played [sung] without fee or license'. Interest in Norwegian music beyond that of Grieg's is amply demonstrated by the magazine's inclusion of Agathe Backer Grøndahl's 'Danse norvégienne (Huldreslaat)' and 'Sérénade', Op. 15, no. 1, for piano, as well as four songs and the piano solo 'Chanson de printemps', Op. 28, no. 5, by Halfdan Kjerulf. And at one further remove we even find 'A Norwegian Song', with words by Clifton Bingham and music by Henri Logé.

IV

GRAND TOUR

❧ 13 ❧

'ONE WHO HAS EXHAUSTED THE JOYS OF FAME AND BEING ADORED'

Towards the end of January 1897, the Helsinki conductor Robert Kajanus proposed that Grieg should come to Finland in October or November of that year. But Grieg informed a Finnish friend, 'I shall be engaged in England',[1] although it is unclear what arrangements he actually had in mind at just this time. In March Berger asked him if he had made any definite plans for the autumn, as there was a conducting slot at the Philharmonic available either in October or November.[2] Grieg's reply was inconclusive, so Berger carefully set out the position:

In reply to your letter stating that you are not certain whether you shall or not visit England this year, will you permit me to say that the Directors have no intention of asking you to conduct some of your music without being prepared to offer you an Honorarium. –

We would be very happy if you could undertake to come to us on the 18 November or 4 November or 2 December to conduct *3 pieces* in one concert, viz: your Pianoforte Concerto, something vocal, and one orchestral number –

We place at your disposal the sum of one hundred Pounds, only making the reservation that you do *not* appear any where else in London than at *our* Concerts.

If Madame Grieg will undertake the vocal music we shall be happy to include her services in the sum named. If she does not wish to sing, we will find some other Vocalist.

We will find the Soloist for your Concerto, – unless you have a new one, and in that case perhaps you will name the Soloist you would prefer.[3]

Although Grieg was still unsure of being able to come, he was scarcely likely to accept Berger's restrictions on further engagements:

My coming to England in the autumn is not yet quite fixed. But if I shall come, I am obliged to appear in London and other cities in England and so you see, I cannot accept your reservation not to appear anywhere else in London than at your concert. I can promise not to appear *before*, but not *after* your concert.[4]

Following concerts in Stockholm, Christiania and Vienna in the latter part of 1896, the year had started with a further concert in Vienna, after which the Griegs had travelled to Leipzig and then on to Amsterdam in February. Here they had stayed with Julius Röntgen, Grieg giving further concerts in both Amsterdam and The Hague. The final port of call before returning to Norway was Copenhagen. *The Monthly Musical Record* remarked on Grieg's extraordinarily peripatetic lifestyle and, perhaps uncharacteristically, reproved him for leading it:

> Herr Grieg, who seems almost to have abandoned the career of a composer for that of a travelling virtuoso, has been touring in Holland with the success which never fails to attend him; but a very large number of his admirers look back with regret to the days when he stayed at home and wrote songs and lyrical pieces, and the music to *Peer Gynt*, and *Bergliot*, and his piano and violin sonatas, and how many other beautiful works.[5]

If an element of truth lay in this criticism, it was not the whole truth, for Grieg had been working during the autumn on his path-breaking set of *Nineteen Norwegian Folk Songs* for piano, Op. 66, completing it in Leipzig on 28 January 1897. Published in the spring, it had earned from 'Augener's paper', as Grieg informed Max Abraham, 'a very sympathetic review which has pleased me inordinately'. However, there hadn't been a single word, as far as he knew, in the Scandinavian press about it, something that he felt only revealed the pettiness of local conditions.[6]

The review in 'Augener's paper', without acknowledging the contradiction implicit in the fact that it followed immediately on from the criticism of Grieg expressed in its previous number, praised the composer's bold treatment of the folk tunes:

> The harmonization of national melodies is a matter of no little difficulty. Most of them were originally sung without accompaniment of any kind; some with only a few notes or chords from guitar, mandoline, or violin. To make use, in writing accompaniments, of all the resources of modern harmony seems incongruous, and yet this is what Grieg has done, and with triumphant success.[7]

Finally settled in at Troldhaugen in mid-May, Grieg could begin to think again about the proposed England trip, confirming to Berger that he was prepared to accept the conducting engagement offered for 4 November and promising not to appear anywhere in England before that date. He would send proposals in respect of the programme as soon as possible.[8] Grieg, on good form again, felt the peace and calm of Troldhaugen to be almost voluptuous after the vagaries of the winter. But Nina was still recovering from her various ills, having had to have a minor operation on her arm in Copenhagen. In June there came the surprising news that Max Abraham had been given to understand that the Griegs would be staying with Oscar Meyer when in London. Grieg had heard nothing about this. 'I would much prefer to stay, as before, at Augener's, where I can relax completely and where I and

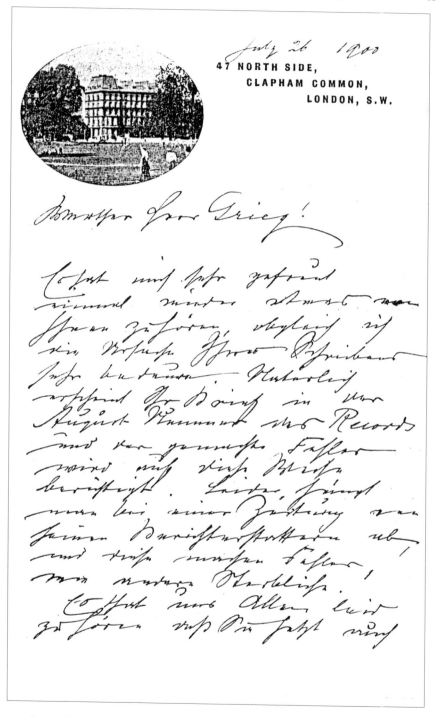

From a letter to Grieg from George Augener, with a vignette of 47 North Side

my wife have always met with such extraordinary kindness. They have very kindly invited us this time too.'[9]

Meanwhile there were one or two Grieg performances of particular note in England during the summer. In the context of a 'Musical May Festival', the Birmingham Kyrle Society performed *Olav Tryvason* on 5 May at the city's Town Hall.[10] And the end-of-term concert at the Royal College of Music featured 'Grieg's cheery and melodious second *Peer Gynt Suite*', conducted by Stanford.[11]

The London agent Narciso Vert was in charge of Grieg's overall autumn engagements, and in July Grieg registered alarm with Berger in respect of what had apparently been arranged in respect of the Philharmonic Society concert. 'I regret very much, that Mr. Vert, without first asking me, has arranged with you my appearing *as pianist* in the philh. soc., as I am sorry to say, that my health does not more permit me to play my piano concert[o].' Grieg would happily conduct, as agreed, and hoped to hear that this would suit Berger.[12] Berger was disappointed, but proposed that Grieg offer for the November engagement an overture, the Piano Concerto, for which a soloist remained to be nominated, and a suite for orchestra. Topping up what was evidently at this stage envisaged as an all-Grieg concert, he proposed to find a female vocalist to sing 'a couple' of Grieg's songs. Meanwhile, if Grieg should have 'something quite new' up his sleeve, the Society would be glad to have it. To Berger's evident consternation, Vert had evidently been doing the kind of job an agent was supposed to do. 'We are paying Mr. Vert the largest fee we have ever paid for one Artist', he told the composer.[13] Grieg professed himself content with Berger's proposals, suggesting *In Autumn*, *Before a Southern Convent*, and three songs ('From Monte Pincio', 'Solveig's Cradle Song' and 'A Swan') as possible company for the Concerto. He would be happy to accompany the songs at the piano, but particularly recommended them in their orchestral accompaniments. The Norwegian soprano Elisa Wiborg or the Dutch bass-baritone Anton Sistermans would both sing his songs well. The Belgian pianist Arthur De Greef would be his first choice as Concerto soloist, but if he had already given the work at the Society then Oscar Meyer, 'a fine, poetic pianist' could be strongly recommended.[14] No mention was made of Ilona Eibenschütz, who played Grieg's music quite often and who had given an 'admirable' performance of the Concerto at a Henschel Concert in London on 14 January.

Grieg's exasperation on receiving Berger's response to his suggestions a fortnight later can only be imagined. *Before a Southern Convent* would, it appeared, have to go, as the Society had no men's chorus at its disposal. *In Autumn* was not even mentioned. Marcella Pregi, from Paris, had already been engaged to sing the three songs, with orchestral accompaniment. And it was hoped that Grieg would agree to the *Peer Gynt Suite* no. 1 being given again, 'as it is much loved here'. As for the Concerto, the young English pianist Frederick Dawson had already been engaged. He intended to travel to Bergen in order to prepare the work with its composer.[15] One wonders why Grieg had been asked at all for his advice, since it would seem obvious that Berger and his directors had had little if any intention of following it. Meanwhile, the Philharmonic Society had issued its prospectus for the three concerts of the autumn season, concerts which were no longer held in the old St James's Hall but now in the Queen's Hall. The prospectus announced that Grieg would be conducting some of his works at the first concert, whilst Moszkowski was to conduct at the second and Humperdinck at the third. Grieg was taking life quietly at Troldhaugen at about the time this notice was issued. It was a matter, as he wrote to a friend, of gathering his strength for the 'autumn campaign' in England.[16] To Berger he wrote on returning home in mid-August from a mountain tour. He was saddened that the soloists he had recommended had not been engaged, 'as the interpretation of my works is a speciality, and the artists you name are completely unknown to me'. He would nevertheless welcome a visit from Frederick Dawson.[17]

Dawson, now 31, had been something of an infant prodigy. Dannreuther and Hallé had been among his teachers, and he had introduced both of the Brahms concertos to the English public. He had a particular facility for committing pieces rapidly to memory – memorizing, for example, Grieg's 'Bridal Procession' in just fifteen minutes.[18] He must have arrived in Bergen by the end of August, and he later recounted something of his visit. He had found Grieg to be extremely kind and courteous and had nothing but pleasant recollections of this episode in his life:

> Grieg has a most charming personality. He lives in a beautiful house on the shore of a typical Norwegian fjord. He himself superintended the building of it, the laying out of the grounds, etc., and the consequence is that it is an almost ideal spot for a composer. He has a little house built away from everyone in his grounds where he composes. It is fitted up with everything that he loves best: the scores of Wagner, a little piano, his favourite books, etc., etc. I think that Grieg's music expresses in a wonderful degree the spirit of Norway. He seems to have caught the very soul of his country, and to have in some magic way turned it into music. I remember that driving through the country we chanced to meet him. We stopped, and I remarked how pretty the scenery that lay about us was. 'Ah! yes!' he replied. 'It is "smiling" here, but farther on it is "earnest," and still farther on it becomes "grandiose" in its awe-inspiring beauty.' And this is so with his music. At times it is 'smiling' but it quickly changes to 'earnest' and 'grandiose.'[19]

Now there came an invitation to appear for the first time in Wales – one that like so many others would not be taken up. Frederic Cowen, appointed director of a music festival to take place in Cardiff in September 1898, asked if Grieg might be prepared to write a new orchestral suite expressly for the festival, and indeed whether he might even come to Cardiff to conduct this work himself. Cowen would, he wrote, greatly enjoy seeing Grieg again, so many years having passed since they last had met. In a postscript to his letter, he made a slip that would have been unlikely to be excused by the Cardiff elders, had their Welsh eyes have happened upon it: 'Should you be unable to compose a work expressly for us, perhaps you have something handy for which we could give the *first* performance in England.'[20]

If Cowen's invitation to Cardiff could be refused, around the beginning of September there came one from the Brodskys that brought forth a quite different reaction. *The London Musical Courier* had given notice in its editorial on 2 September that Grieg's forthcoming tour was not just to include London concerts but also engagements in the provinces:

> Among the tours which Mr. Vert has arranged for the autumn are those of Dr. Richter, with his orchestra, the Meister Glee Singers, Mme. Albani, and the composer Edward Grieg. The latter will also play at one or two 'Pops.,' and give some recitals at St. James's Hall in addition to his appearances before the Philharmonic Society. Mr. Vert has also arranged for some concerts in the provinces for him during his stay in England.[21]

Musical Answers was less informative, announcing baldly: 'In connection with the Philharmonic Society, Edward Grieg will conduct several of his works on November 4th.'[22] One of the provincial concerts had been arranged for Manchester, and

Frederick Dawson

Adolph Brodsky, having learnt of this, wrote to ask Grieg and Nina to come and stay. But Nina had not been intending to accompany her husband on this particular tour, having decided to spend the time in Copenhagen instead. Brodsky's letter changed all this, and Grieg's original plans were rapidly unscrambled. Nina would come to England too, and they both immediately wrote to the Brodskys. Grieg confessed to Adolph that he was delighted that their friends so much wanted his wife to come to Manchester with him. They would be leaving for London at the end of October and, so far as he knew, the Manchester concert was scheduled for 9 November. 'My goodness, how happy I am that we are to meet again! How greatly things have changed since we were last together! Tchaikovsky and Brahms have begun the long journey and neither need any longer be annoyed by the other's works!' Grieg added a final wish: 'During our stay in Manchester you'll have to give that damned fog its marching orders! After all, as I understand it you have a job in which you are accustomed to giving orders! So: please do so!'[23] Nina's accompanying letter to Anna Brodsky told of how delighted she was to be seeing the old friends again; outwardly, she reminded them, she and Edvard might have changed, but inwardly they were just the same.

In England, younger champions of Grieg's music were to provide evidence of their enthusiasm in September, Granville Bantock conducting a wind-band arrangement of the first *Peer Gynt Suite* at New Brighton in Cheshire, and Henry Wood giving the same work in its original form at a Promenade Concert in London. 'On September 4th, Grieg's *Peer Gynt* suite no. 1 was a prominent attraction at Queen's Hall. It was superbly played, the picturesque "Gnome Dance" being rendered with brilliant effect. It was so rapturously encored that the conductor allowed it to be repeated.'[24] It should also be added that in September at Hereford the Piano Concerto received its first airing at a Three Choirs Festival. Oscar Meyer was the soloist in this 'chief feature' of the programme, and George Sinclair conducted the Festival Orchestra. The Shire Hall, according to the Annals of the Three Choirs, 'was filled to its utmost capacity'.

The summer at Troldhaugen had seen Grieg rejuvenated and Nina apparently restored to health. No-one could remember such glorious weather, from the month of May right through to the beginning of September. Grieg could even – especially since receiving the news from Brodsky – look forward to his tour in a way he had never done before. 'I feel, thank God, so well,' he wrote to Abraham, 'that it will be with some pleasure that I shall set out on my English trip.' Lacking a copy of the recently published eighth book of *Lyric Pieces*, including the newly composed 'Wedding Day at Troldhaugen', which he 'of course' wanted to play in England, he asked Abraham to send one. Grieg promised not to let it out of his hands before the beginning of October, when they would be leaving.[25] It seems, then, that the first public performance in England of this exuberant piece was to take place at the hands of the composer. Grieg hoped that Abraham might join them in London, but Abraham, at the time taking a cure at Wiesbaden, was not well enough:

I would love to accompany you on your tour in England, or at least visit you in London, but I am afraid this is impossible & so I only wish that you do not travel around too much over there & do not overstrain yourself. You will have a sensation with 'Wedding Day at Troldhaugen'; I advise you to play this piece as a last number & to put 'latest composition' or 'noveltie' or some similar wording on the programme.[26]

Grieg, beginning to practise piano specially for his England concerts, as before grew pessimistic. Every time he wrote to a friend of a departure date, that date would vary. So that on 20 September he told Albert Gutmann in Vienna that he would be leaving in the middle of October, adding bleakly, 'I'll be happy if I return from England alive.' Within a few days, however, Nina was back in bed 'with her old kidney problem', as Grieg told Röntgen on Saturday 2 October. She had been unwell for several days, and this had meant an abrupt change of plans, since the 2nd had been fixed upon as their joint departure date. 'Now we hope that we can leave Troldhaugen on Monday and then continue [from Bergen] on Wednesday. The problem is: I have to be off, with or without Nina.' At least there was cheering news from Augener, who was much looking forward to having the Griegs as his guests again, usefully abetted by Max Lindlar, manager of the Bechstein business in England:

> There is no need for me to tell you that you are both heartily welcome here and that it is our wish to make you both comfortable and at home.
>
> We were sorry to hear that you are not fully satisfied with your health. The air in your part of the world ought to have quite restored you to health again. We must hope that the Clapham Common air will do you good.
>
> We are preparing for you the same rooms as you had before and Herr Lindlar will shortly instal a fine Bechstein in the front room for you.[27]

Travelling via Copenhagen, the Griegs arrived in the Danish capital on 16 October. The main thing was for Nina to see a specialist without further delay. So far all had gone reasonably well, but after the appointment Grieg was dispirited. Nina was forbidden to travel further, so he would have to continue to London alone. He told Röntgen of his new itinerary:

> It really is sad! But we must obey. So off the day after tomorrow *alone* Prestissimo to London. Tuesday: Copenhagen–Hamburg. Wednesday: Hamburg–Cologne, Thursday: Cologne–Ostend–Dover–London . . . A great, great disappointment! If only these 6 weeks were safely past!!![28]

So it was that Grieg finally arrived at the Augeners' on the evening of Thursday, 21 October 1897, taking up residence in the rooms on the second floor which had been prepared for Nina and himself. He signalled the fact to Anna Brodsky the following day, having arrived 'Alas, alas: alone!' Nina might have to have an operation in Copenhagen, in which case he would need immediately to return to be at her side. 'You can well imagine how I feel. I haven't experienced such feelings of loneliness and isolation since my childhood.' Grieg nevertheless acknowledged that it was no

The end-of-terrace home of the Augener family in the early 1900s

good complaining and that he had to get on and do his duty – something that was made no easier for him in view of the nervous and agitated condition in which he now found himself. In such circumstances he confessed that he was greatly looking forward to being together with his well-loved friends in Manchester, with whom he hoped to be staying – for two or three days at least – in little more than a fortnight's time.[29] A day or two after his arrival, Grieg paid a visit to the theatre to see one of England's finest actors performing at the Lyceum, an event duly noted by one, at least, of London's musical journals. 'The wonderful interpretation of Hamlet by Mr. Forbes Robertson was enthusiastically appreciated by the Norwegian composer.'[30] That this was an isolated experience – there being little if any evidence of theatre-going by Grieg when he was in England – is perhaps surprising given the record of his father, an avid playgoer when in London as a young man.

A glance at Grieg's notebook gives some idea of the planning that lay behind his forthcoming tour. As ever, he scribbled drafts for a number of programmes, jotting down various ideas under such headings as 'Provinces', 'London St James Hall', 'Pops', and 'Pops 2'. Then there are addresses which would probably be necessary to have at hand. Charles Harding is now shown as living at Knudsford [Knutsford] Lodge, Edgbaston, Birmingham; Johannes Wolff at 30 Wellington Square, Chelsea; Oscar Meyer at 1 Cornwall Terrace, Regent's Park; Professor C. Villiers Stanford at 50 Holland Street, Kensington; 'Sir Mackenzie (Alexander)' at 15 Regent's Park Road; Medora Henson at 62 Wellington Road, St John's Wood; F. Busoni at 9 Duchess Street, Portland Square; and Lady Hallé at 30 Cambridge Street, Hyde Park. There are business addresses too: Lindlar of the Bechstein company can be found at 40 Wigmore Street; Augener at 199 Regent Street; Vert at 6 Cork Street; Berger at 6 York Street, Portman Square; and Chappell at 50 New Bond Street. Dates or times of rehearsals are jotted down: 'Philh. Rehersal 3 & 4 Novbr 10 o'clock'; '2 Novbr Kl 12, Frök. Pregi hos mig' [Miss Pregi at my address]; 'Lady Hallé Sunday 12'; and 'Lindlar, Wednesday 10'. Added to this are Grieg's train-times, outward- and inward-bound, all noted down, often together with the name of the terminus and the line taken. All this information, with its crossings-out and its minuscule additions or postscripts, appears at first glance to be pretty chaotic, but to Grieg's practised eye it was a small treasury of information to which it was easy to refer.

On the 26th a detailed letter went off to Abraham outlining the difficult times that Grieg felt lay ahead for him. If he had a choice, he knew only too well what he would have done:

> But – I've crossed the Rubicon and cannot go back. If only I stay healthy, then the rest doesn't matter, but today I haven't dared to go out, as I've had a shivering influenza-like feeling in my limbs and the old phlegm has come back. A repeat of Vienna would be much worse here in London. My concerts have been fixed as follows:
>
>   Nov 4 London (Evening) (Philharm.)
>   "   6 Liverpool (Afternoon)
>   "   13 Edinburgh (Afternoon)
>   "   16 Manchester (Evening)
>   "   22 London (Afternoon) Pops.
>   "   26 Birmingham (Evening)
>   Dec 4 London (Afternoon)
>   "   9 Cheltenham (Afternoon)
>   "   11 Brighton (Afternoon)
>   "   13 London (Evening.) Pops
>
> Everything would probably have come off perfectly well if they hadn't shown a colossal lack of regard in ignoring my suggestions in respect of soloists and, without my knowledge, engaged others who are unknown to me and who can only be termed thoroughly mediocre. Had I known that legally I had the right, I would protest, but I only made *recommendations*, not *conditions*. And so I shall have to put up with the results of my folly. Mad. Henson, the singer, is utterly insignificant, the pianist for the Piano Concerto likewise and Miss Pregi, who is to sing songs with orchestra at the Phil. Soc., is only showing up on the day of the final rehearsal, without my having any idea of her abilities. Mad. Henson, whose only advantage is that she is here in London, has already twice left me waiting in vain and doesn't even know many of the songs which she is expected to sing.
>
>   If only I had my wife here and in good health! But she has stayed on in Copenhagen because the doctor demanded it. Unfortunately a kidney operation is imminent, but of course only when I am back together with her. I feel very lonely, even though the Augener family is kindness personified. I haven't yet been able to look up the Court Pianist [Meyer]. It's difficult making visits here in London, especially when

one is unwell. Johannes Wolff is a really good friend to me. And how wonderfully he plays my Sonatas! That's a great comfort to me.[31]

Henson had recently programmed two of Grieg's songs at the Shire Hall in Hereford, and Grieg would not have been best pleased had he learned that at the last moment she had substituted songs by Goring Thomas and Jacob Blumenthal (pianist to Queen Victoria) for his own, the substitutions being announced on the platform by George Sinclair. He would, on the other hand, have been delighted to read in just this connection of yet another of those magnificent *faux pas* to which critics are prone – notably when they affect to review performances they have failed to turn up at. The *Hereford Times* man proved a perfect exemplar of the condition:

> Mme. Medora Henson sang with effect a couple of Grieg songs. Why the lieder of our own country should not be considered extensive enough or suitable enough it passeth the wit of man to understand. Possibly the artist was desirous to 'air' her German, but it would have been quite as well had she condescended to sing a song in her own vernacular.[32]

Grieg had already written to Berger and alerted him to the fact that he needed to know as quickly as possible just when and how he was to start rehearsing his songs with Marcella Pregi. Before long, however, none of this would matter, as he was forced to take to his bed with a severe attack of bronchitis. He was not even able to attend the Philharmonic Concert at which his own music was played, and the following four concerts had to be rescheduled by Narciso Vert on later dates. It remains something of a mystery why Grieg, ever highly susceptible to chest complaints, should have chosen autumn for his longest tour to date in England. London's smoke-laden fogs, fuelled by a million and more domestic coal fires and countless factory furnaces, were perhaps less widespread and injurious in the fresher winds of spring than in the chill damp of the capital's autumn evenings. Long before, when writing to his sisters, another composer had declared: 'That smoky place is fated to be now and ever my favourite residence; my heart glows whenever I think of it.' But that was Mendelssohn in his early twenties. A whole catalogue of composers and performers – Weber, Chopin, Wagner, Tchaikovsky, Dvořák, and heaven knows how many more – have left in their writings adequate testimony to the deleterious effects of the capital's 'Clowds of Smoake and Sulphur, so full of Stink and Darknesse' – the diarist John Evelyn's description of London's atmosphere, written long before the Industrial Revolution was to wreak its further havoc.

It would not be for another month that Grieg felt fit enough to perform, only taking up his original autumn schedule at its halfway mark, at Birmingham on 26 November. On 26 October, however, unaware of the bleak month that was to follow, all he could sensibly do was to sit at home and write letters, before making one last valiant excursion later that day 'to hear Richter conduct Dvořák's American

Symphony'. He apologized to Brodsky for what was to prove to be only a first change of dates for the Manchester concert. Looking forward to the opportunity of seeing Busoni again, he told Brodsky how well Busoni had played the A-minor Concerto in Vienna the previous winter and how exceptionally sad he was that he could not have him as soloist in England this time around. Berger was adjured to supply a full quota of strings for the Philharmonic concert items: 'The things are intended for a large string orchestra.' He was also pressed to ensure that Marcella Pregi would come to Grieg around midday on 2 November at the latest to rehearse the songs, and that Frederick Dawson should be available to rehearse the Concerto on both 3 *and* 4 November.[33] And to Oscar Meyer, who had proposed a meeting, there could only be, on the 28th, a plaintive reply:

> My condition has got a lot worse since yesterday. The doctor was here and diagnosed bronchitis, but nevertheless hopes that I shall be sufficiently recovered for the orches-tra rehearsal on 3 November to be able to go to Queen's Hall. Now I must have com-plete rest for the time being and cannot receive any visitors. Thank heavens I haven't any fever, otherwise I couldn't sit at the writing desk. But the nights! Couldn't close my eyes and was almost choked by phlegm! Oh, what a wonderful life is this!
>
> My wife is not here, alas, but in Copenhagen. How I long for her in my present lonely state![34]

With that, Grieg took to his bed for a week. Reading one of the items in the latest issue of Augener's journal could scarcely have been cheering: 'We regret to hear that Herr Hugo Wolf, the well-known song composer, has become insane and has had to be placed in an asylum.' On the other hand, happily, it had a review of the latest set of *Lyric Pieces*, Op. 65 (all of them deemed 'fresh and highly attractive'), no. 6 of which was 'Wedding Day at Troldhaugen', a piece that rapidly became a great favourite wherever it was played. The issue also included a prominent advertisement for the *Seven Children's Songs*, together with lengthy extracts from reviews that dated back to the first appearance of this particular set in England in 1895.[35] Grieg had written at least three times already to Nina, but it was a telegram that was finally to bring her from her own sickbed to London. Performing at the Philharmonic Concert on 4 November was out of the question for her husband, as is evident from a short note – the first he had penned for a week – that he wrote to Meyer on the evening of 4 November:

> Still in bed! My wife is here with me. But it would give me much pleasure to see you. I am allowed a half-hour's visit. So do please come at last. I've had a bad time of it and am still very low. But thank goodness I don't have to listen to the concert this evening!!! However good Mr Dawson may be technically, he cannot remotely match the poetry that you dispose of in your own interpretation.

A note had been attached to the programme book to the effect that the distin-guished Norwegian composer was suffering from bronchitis and was unable to leave his home. Others joined in to express their disappointment that Grieg was

PHILHARMONIC SOCIETY.

AUTUMN SEASON, 1897.

Patron—HER MAJESTY THE QUEEN.
Conductor—SIR A. C. MACKENZIE.
Principal First Violin—Mr. W. FRYE PARKER.

FIRST CONCERT, THURSDAY EVENING next, 4th November,
at Queen's Hall, Eight o'clock.

PART I.
Overture, "Fidelio," Beethoven; Concerto, Pianoforte and Orchestra, Grieg.
FREDERICK DAWSON.
Songs—*a.* Solvejgs Wiegenlied; *b.* Vorn Monte Pincio; *c.* Ein Schwan, Grieg.
MARCELLA PREGI.
Orchestral Suite, "Peer Gynt," Grieg.

PART II.
Symphony in A (The Italian), Mendelssohn.

PHILHARMONIC SOCIETY.—EDVARD GRIEG will conduct
his own Works at FIRST CONCERT, 4th November.

PHILHARMONIC SOCIETY.—Mendelssohn's ITALIAN SYM-
PHONY will be performed at FIRST CONCERT, 4th November, in
commemoration of the 50th anniversary of the Death of its Composer.

PHILHARMONIC SOCIETY.—FREDERICK DAWSON will
Play Grieg's Pianoforte Concerto, at FIRST CONCERT, 4th November.

PHILHARMONIC SOCIETY.—MARCELLA PREGI will SING
Three of Grieg's Songs, at FIRST CONCERT, 4th November.

PHILHARMONIC SOCIETY.—Stalls in area or two front rows
in grand circle, 10s. 6d. (evening dress); other rows in grand circle or
front row in balcony, 7s. 6d.; other rows in balcony, 5s. Unreserved seats:—
Balcony, 2s. 6d.; orchestra and area, 1s.; to be had at Stanley Lucas & Co.
(Limited), 84, New Bond Street, W.; Tree's Ticket Offices, St. James's Hall;
and 304, Regent Street (opposite the Polytechnic); R. Newman's Box Office,
Queen's Hall, Langham Place; and usual Agents.

FRANCESCO BERGER, Hon. Sec.

Advertisement in *Musical News* (30 Oct. 1897); Grieg was too unwell to appear

unable to take part in the concert, owing to what the papers described as his serious illness. 'Dr. Edvard Grieg', reported the *Lady's Pictorial*,

> who is staying with Mr. Augener at his residence on Clapham Common, has been
> suffering from a rather severe attack of his old enemy, bronchitis, which has kept him
> to his bed. Madame Grieg, who was visiting Copenhagen, left for England directly
> she received news of her husband's illness, and arrived in London last week. The
> Norwegian composer's numerous friends and admirers will unite in wishing him
> a speedy recovery.[36]

Nina had in fact been seriously worried when she received the telegram that had
alerted her to her husband's condition, and it was with some relief, after a journey
filled with anxiety, that she found on arrival in Clapham that his situation was
rather less dangerous than she had imagined. 'He was immensely glad that I came
and all things considered I think he needed me, even if perhaps in a more prosaic
way than in days gone by.'[37] *The London Musical Courier* reported that Grieg's
physician thought he would be able to fulfil his other engagements, starting with
a Liverpool date on 20 November, but this looked to be overoptimistic.[38]

As it was, the Queen's Hall was completely sold out, and it would seem that the
orchestra played their hearts out for the indisposed composer. Mackenzie received
much credit for the successful outcome of the concert and in particular for his
conducting of the Grieg works:

In the regrettable absence of the Norwegian composer, Sir Alexander C. Mackenzie conducted the entire concert, and, let us add, with exceptional success. There was a marked and welcome improvement in the performances of the Philharmonic orchestra, which has not played so well for a long time. The scheme included Grieg's Pianoforte Concerto in A minor, the solo portion of which was admirably interpreted by Mr. Frederick Dawson; the 'Peer Gynt' Suite, and three of his songs, expressively rendered by Madame Marcella Pregi. The charmingly delicate manner in which the orchestra played 'Anitra's Dance' from the Suite fully merited the encore which it received, a similar compliment being paid to the characteristic 'Dance of the Imps.'[39]

Grieg's reservations about Dawson seem hardly to have beeen shared by the critics. One wrote of 'the solo portion being played with admirable vigour and brilliancy'.[40] Another expressed the view that 'the young Manchester pianist seems to improve each time he appears in London, and his performance on Thursday was, perhaps, the best thing he has yet done here'.[41] The *Peer Gynt Suite* had benefitted from an 'exquisite rendering', and the 'Death of Aase' (actually 'Anitra's Dance') and 'Dance of the Imps' had each been encored.[42] Pregi received varying reviews, some deeming that she was 'out of voice', others finding her quite impressive. But quite how *The Musical Standard* could have known that Grieg was 'highly pleased with Mr. Dawson's interpretation of his concerto' must be left an open question.

Just six days later it was the turn of St James's Hall to give a platform to the Grieg Concerto. Hamish MacCunn conducted and a 21-year-old Austrian pianist, Ella Pancera, was the soloist, following the Grieg with concertos by Chopin (the E-minor) and Liszt (the A-major). She was adjudged by *Musical News* to have a splendid technique, and her effects were produced 'in an easy natural manner, refreshingly free from affected mannerisms', her reading of the Grieg displaying 'musicianly intelligence'.[43] Ten days later she played Grieg's *Ballade* at a Saturday Popular Concert, and again her performance was considered to be 'full of intelligence'.[44] If the hope had been that Grieg might be present, he was too unwell to attend Pancera's first concert and would not have been able to attend her second, only returning from Birmingham on 27 November, the date of her performance of the *Ballade*. Another promising young musician who played Grieg in London around this time was the cellist May Mukle, who was recorded as performing 'the long and rather tedious Grieg Sonata, Op. 36', in the Small Queen's Hall on 15 November.[45]

Grieg finally left his sickbed, at least for a good part of the day, on Sunday 7 November. He still hoped to be sufficiently recovered to undertake his St James's Hall concert on the 22nd, but nonetheless felt in his heart that this was unlikely. The considerable improvement in his health achieved in the summer had been reversed by this bad attack of bronchitis. However his doctor now suggested a short break from London, with some much-needed fresh air down on the south coast. 'I hope', Grieg told Röntgen on the 8th, 'I can get out and about a little before then. But I just don't have the strength at all to go for a walk. And as for playing! That I just daren't think about.' The extent of his misery revealed itself in a letter he wrote to another friend on the 11th, describing 'the sad life I am at present leading. I am very despondent.' He was scarcely likely, he felt, to regain his strength in London:

> If only someone had told me that the climate here at this time of year is poison for people like me. Right up to the last moment I'd hoped to be able to fulfil about half of my commitments here, but today it's clear to me that my only goal should be to get out of here in one piece.
>
> Yesterday I was out for ½ an hour, but had a bad night after that, and today the fog is so thick that I must stay in my room. Meanwhile the day after tomorrow the doctor wants me to go down to the coastal town of Hastings to hasten my recovery. I really can't see how that will come about, but I'm so depressed now that I don't oppose anything but simply let myself be treated like a child. It's a good thing that I got my wife to come here, because at the beginning the loneliness was just too oppressive. Letters I have masses of, but only from people who want to use me.[46]

Two days before leaving for the 'coastal town' of St Leonards on Sea, next to Hastings, there was a tailors' appointment and the unusual purchase of a nightlight, no doubt to comfort Grieg in his frequent bouts of insomnia. A payment on the following day of £4 9s. 6d. went to Mrs Gray, his nurse, for her two weeks of service. On 13 November Grieg and Nina took the train to St Leonards, where they were accommodated until the 17th at no. 68, Marina, a hotel on the seafront, Grieg figuring among the 'arrivals' in the town recorded in the local newspaper. (The hotel did not survive the Second World War, when, together with the nearby parish church, it was destroyed by bombs jettisoned by homebound Luftwaffe aircraft. Buildings on either side remained standing.) There, it would seem, they relaxed at last, with little evidence of any activity bar a little shopping in Hastings (a minor extravagance on Grieg's part being displayed in the purchase on 15 November of no fewer than four neckties, some Italian perfume for Nina, and 3s. worth of 'port-wine'), and no doubt a few walks to and fro along the promenade, well muffled to protect against the brisk sea breezes coming off the English Channel. It would seem that little correspondence was undertaken: a letter to Brodsky ('We have been here for a few days for the air to hasten a cure'), a postcard to Abraham — and that was probably it. Vert had seen to it that the autumn season's concert dates had by now been reshuffled, and Grieg's letter to Brodsky advised him of this fact: they would have less time together in Manchester due to the changing circumstances. The concert there was fixed for 24 November, and because of Grieg's busy schedule thereafter Edvard and Nina would be able to stay with their friends for only two nights. He begged Brodsky's indulgence in the matter of three very particular requests. '1) I cannot receive visitors. 2) Can I have a piano to myself for an hour on the 25th? 3) May I — *after* the concert — ask for *just* one glass of claret and a little cold chicken?'[47] At least the seaside break was aiding his recovery, and the prospect of arriving at the Brodskys on the 24th and so being able to celebrate Nina's birthday together on that same day was a cheering one.

Grieg was at last ready to take up the reins of his tour, and just two days after their return from St Leonards he and Nina set off by train for his first concert date in Liverpool, checking in on 19 November for an overnight stay at the Adelphi Hotel. Liverpool, as he informed Julius Röntgen, was 'just the beginning'.

> If only I have energy enough, as I'm a long way from being what I was before. I have just 2 things to watch: prudence and to keep my temper!! On the 22nd comes London, 24th Manchester, 26th Birmingham, 30th Edinburgh, 4th Dec. London, 9th Cheltenham, 11th Brighton, 13th London. There you have the whole crazy business! If only I can emerge from it in one piece! Once and never again! . . . Nina is not at all well, sadly, and that makes me even more uneasy and nervous.[48]

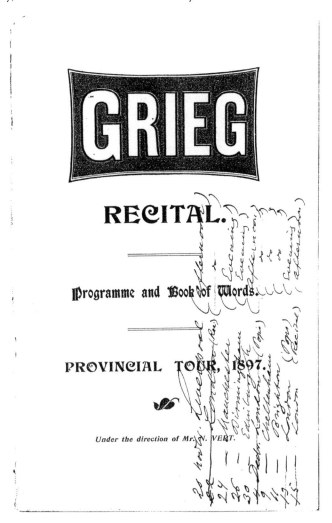

Grieg notes dates and venues of his 1897 provincial tour on the cover
of the *Programme and Book of Words*

In fact Grieg would have two more dates to add to this list: 7 December, to play by invitation at Windsor Castle, and on 15 December a final concert at St James's Hall. Amazingly, the semi-invalid, whose health was day by day to improve, would get through them all.

'Philharmonic Hall: To-day at 3 o'clock. Edvard Grieg, the Great Norwegian Composer, assisted by M. Johannes Wolff and Madame Medora Henson, will give an Instrumental and Vocal Recital at the Philharmonic Hall'. So ran the advertisements for Grieg's first concert on Saturday 20 November. A characteristic of this particular tour was the unusually detailed notice taken by the papers of Grieg's physical appearance and manner. One Liverpool daily noted his 'spare figure' and wrote of him: 'Short of stature and almost fragile in appearance, his extremely nervous temperament at once suggests itself.'[49] Another went into rather more detail:

> There is but little of the accepted physique of the Viking in the Norwegian composer, for he is short of stature, and his figure lacks proportion, but he has a fine head, with flowing hair of a peculiar hue brought about by the intermingling of the silver of age with the gold of youth, and his clear-cut features, well-modelled profile, and luminous eyes sharply separate him from the commonplace. Again, his manner, whether engaged in interpretation or in accepting the plaudits of a crowd, is modesty itself. In brief, the man is a most attractive personality.[50]

Long and enthusiastic reviews were accorded to the afternoon's programme in the following Monday's editions of *The Liverpool Daily Post*, *The Liverpool Courier* and *The Liverpool Mercury*, and the latter journal noted the programme items in detail. It is of interest in that these items would remain the basis – if with occasional variations – of Grieg's concert recitals during November and December:

> Sonata for Violin and Piano in C minor, Op. 45 – Allegro Appassionata, Romanza, Finale;
> songs, 'Outward Bound,' 'The Princess,' 'Thy Warning is Good,' Album (Vol. 1);
> Suite for Pianoforte, in the old style, Op. 40 – Præludium, Sarabande, Gavotte, Air, Rigaudon;
> songs, 'The First Meeting,' 'Wood-wanderings,' 'I Love Thee,' Album (Vol. 2);
> Soli for Violin and Pianoforte, Intermezzo from Op. 56, Alla Menuetto from Op. 8;
> songs, 'The Nightingale,' 'The Way of the World,' 'A Dream,' Op. 48;
> and Soli Pianoforte, from 'Popular Life in Norway,' Op. 17 [*sic*] – 'In the Mountains,' 'Bridal Procession Passing By.'

As ever, the critics were fascinated by Grieg's fastidious piano manner. Mild criticism of his lack of power can perhaps – at least on this occasion – be seen as understandable, with insufficient allowance being made for the depletion through illness of physical strength and stamina:

> Grieg, as the exponent of his own works, made a deep impression, and his powers as a pianist, without being or seeking to be sensational, are exactly suited to the peculiar genius and atmosphere of the music.[51]

The spare figure at the pianoforte at once arrested the attention and won a way to the hearts of all present. He played his music like an artist exhibiting, but with unassuming modesty and deference, the beauties of his pictures.[52]

As a pianist his manner suggests the studio rather than the concert platform; his touch is marvellously delicate and supple and his power of playing softly a thing to treasure up and remember. Under his hands the piano becomes an instrument of exquisite delicacy and sweetness, incapable of a harsh or abrupt sound; yet each note and each chord rings clear and true with the message with which it is laden.[53]

As a pianist Grieg is admirable, his technical attainments being advanced, but his playing is more remarkable for its delicacy and its grace rather than for its force.[54]

Grieg's playing is a counterpart of his inspiration, charmingly delicate and poetic, though lacking somewhat in robustness and breadth.[55]

Wolff received well-merited plaudits, but Medora Henson's contributions were accorded mixed reviews; *The Liverpool Mercury* was unsuspectingly wide of the mark when it reported that she obviously had the confidence of the composer. On the platform, Grieg was evidently a good actor and would of course have seen no advantage in conveying any hint of disapproval of the work of a fellow-artist. Of all the Liverpool critics, the reviewer for *The Musical Standard* proved to be the most enthusiastic of all:

One of the most notable recitals I have perhaps ever attended was the Grieg recital given in the [Philharmonic] Hall. The hall was packed and the enthusiasm of the audience at fever heat. The programme is the same as at the London recital and in every town visited on tour, so that there is no need to give it. Every number was by the Norwegian composer, but no one expected that his interpretation even of his own works would be of such a high order. It is not too much to say that the vast audience was enraptured from the beginning of the programme to the end of it.[56]

The Liverpool audience had come with the desire to make acquaintance, as *The London Musical Courier* put it, 'with the personality of the most popular of living composers', and they had come in droves. As elsewhere, whenever Grieg was to appear in the locality others joined the bandwagon, his music, for example, being included in a recital given in Liverpool's St George's Hall just two days after his own concert – Theodor Lawson, accompanied by H. Steudner Welsing, played the second Violin Sonata. And at a piano and vocal recital in the Claughton Music Hall, Birkenhead, the promising young baritone Frederic Austin sang three of Grieg's songs.[57] An intriguing earlier acquaintance might well have been renewed had Grieg learned earlier that Stopford Brooke would be preaching twice in Liverpool just a day after his concert. As it was, precious little time was spent in the city before he and Nina caught the train back to London on the evening of the 20th, too late to be present (had they wished to be) at that Saturday Popular Concert at which Ella Pancera played the *Ballade*.

'Yesterday', Grieg reported to Brodsky after arriving home at Clapham, 'was the first difficult day. I had to sit for 2 hours at the piano in Liverpool. It went well, thank goodness, even if it called for all my energy.' It had certainly gone well for one grateful member of the audience, one R. T. Bodey, who wrote to Grieg enclosing a poem, 'On a Recital by Grieg', inspired by the 'strong but delicate Northern colouring' of his music:

> The fjord is asleep in the arms of the land,
> > A thousand feet below,
> And the girdling mountains silent stand,
> > Lit up by the Western glow.
>
> Over the fell, far down to the deep,
> > The thund'ring cataract breaks,
> Veiling in silver mist each leap
> > The headlong torrent takes.
>
> And a sad wind moans in the tall grave pines.
> > And down from the gleaming fjeld,
> Where the lingering rose of the sunset shines,
> > In the fresh fallen snowflakes held.
>
> The breath of the North is sad and sweet,
> > Her coast is stern and wild,
> And the soul of the North goes out to greet
> > The music of her child.[58]

There now followed two days of rest and recuperation, the only excursion being to buy postcards, as well as to procure various medicaments at a chemist's shop. Although the date is unspecified, it must have been around this time that a correspondent of *The Musical World* called at the house in Clapham, some years later recalling his brief encounter with the composer and capturing something of the bleak mood of the occasion:

A short, timid-looking man came in from the fog and the frost; his companions chatted and joked, but he made little or no response. He had come from Norway, to conduct a concert or two and give a few recitals; some of his engagements had to be cancelled, for the famous composer was not well, and rest was essential to his recovery. That morning he had been for a walk with his host and a few intimate friends, and he now returned full of lassitude and discontent. He bowed to me wearily as I stood in the hall, took off his heavy fur coat, asked to be excused, and retired to his bedroom. Immediately he had gone, each man ceased to play his part: smiles faded, conversation languished, anxiety and concern were manifest. This was so unlike the Grieg of old that it was feared he was seriously ill. He sent down a message to reassure his host and hostess, but the rest of the day he passed in solitude. In the evening he gave a recital, and the audience was roused to enthusiasm. When I hear the name Grieg, I do not think of the triumphant creator of song, the successful composer of orchestral music; I have a vision of my own – the vision of a tired, sad-faced man, coming in from the cold for comfort and solace.[59]

On 22 November came the first London performance of the tour, in the form of an afternoon concert at St James's Hall with the same performers. There was a slight variation from the Liverpool programme, with Wolff only involved in the last item (another performance of the third Violin Sonata) and Grieg having rather more solo work. He opened the programme, which started at 3 o'clock, by playing three of the four movements of his early Piano Sonata in E minor. The pieces from Op. 19 given elsewhere during the tour were replaced by two 'lyric pieces' from Op. 65, 'Ballad(e)' and 'Wedding Day at Troldhaugen' in what will have been its first performance in England, and an unspecified 'Folk Song' from Op. 66. Grieg gave one encore, 'a charming little *"berceuse"*, one of his earliest pianoforte works'. As always, St James's Hall was packed for the Norwegian composer, with several hundred people having to be turned away from its doors and those inside occupying the gangways as well as filling the seats. *The London Musical Courier* was sorry for all those who had been left outside, 'since they missed something more than the sight of a celebrated musician – they missed an object-lesson on purity and charm in pianoforte playing, which could hardly have failed to do them a world of good'.[60]

The weekly *Brighton Society*, under the rubric 'Talk of Society' and rather more interested in the social make-up of the audience, referred to this concert in its issue of 27 November before going on to announce the composer's forthcoming Brighton engagement to its readers:

> The appearance of Edvard Grieg at St. James's Hall the other night was the occasion of a remarkable scene, the entire Hall being packed to overflowing, and the enthusiasm displayed almost overwhelming. The entire front row of the stalls was occupied by members of the Royal Family and their friends, among the most interested being the Duchess of Connaught, who several times applauded the famous composer-pianist with as much energy as any of the enthusiastic ladies in the balcony. Herr Grieg is coming to give a recital in the Dome on Saturday afternoon, the 11th proximo . . .

Meanwhile, with its focus more on the music, *The Times* found that Grieg played the Piano Sonata and the *Holberg Suite* 'in incomparably beautiful style'.[61] In fact the Sonata was much admired, as much for its content as for its performance on the day, *The Musical Standard* allowing no doubts as to its quality. 'Three movements were heard, including a lovely Andante in C; the execution by the composer may be taken for granted as truly splendid. The entire sonata must be repeated; not a bar is devoid of interest.'[62] It was *The London Musical Courier*'s view

> that the composer does not accentuate his own mannerisms as some of his interpreters think it necessary to do. The harsh harmonies which are so noticeable in some of his pieces became almost sweet under the gentle playing of their inventor, and the fanciful turns and tags which are sometimes rather irritating seemed the acme of grace as they were thrown off with dainty delicacy on Monday. So many amateurs, if they find anything *bizarre* in a composer, proceed to emphasize it. Dr. Grieg is *bizarre* sometimes, but you would not know it if his pianoforte works were played by himself alone.[63]

Again, a general consensus of reviews reveals that the contribution of Wolff to the overall programme was acclaimed whilst that of Henson was debated – 'not in her best form' being one comment.

'Round about me a group of newspaper critics exchanged the childish babble of daily journalism', wrote the novelist Arnold Bennett, in the audience that afternoon, who in a few swift, clear lines painted in his diary of the same date a compelling picture of the composer-pianist:

> Grieg came on in a short jacket of black velvet which serves to decrease still further his short stature. He has a large head with white hair and a bald patch, and the shrewd wrinkled face of a thinker. A restless man, weary and yet the victim of an incurable vivacity. The concussion of his hands on the keys jerked back his head at every loud chord. Between the movements of a sonata he bowed almost imperceptibly and wiped his face every time with the same mechanical movement. He looked like one who has exhausted the joys of fame and of being adored.

Bennett noted disdainfully how the audience was largely made up of 'those idle, well-dressed, supercilious, unintelligent women who inhabit the West End and the more expensive suburbs', and he rounded off his diary entry in positively Shavian fashion: 'As I went out, I thought that in another hour or so a thousand pianos in a thousand suburban homes would echo to the chords of that Grieg Sonata and suite.'[64]

On 23 November it was off to Manchester and the long-awaited reunion with Adolph and Anna Brodsky. This was a late change of plan, Grieg having originally intended to arrive on the day of the concert itself, Wednesday the 24th, and having alerted his hosts to still further special requirements. Arriving at the station at 2.30 so as to have good time to prepare for the concert at 7.30 in the evening, they would, he wrote, then go direct to the Brodsky home at 41 Acomb Street, the address being carefully recorded in Grieg's notebook. Grieg asked if Anna could kindly prepare an 'underdone' beefsteak for him to eat at 4 o'clock. Before a performance he was very careful about how and what he ate: 'It really is absolutely necessary for me.' He would then rest before the concert. Bechstein would be sending to Acomb Street a small piano which he asked to be placed in his room. And finally, he wished to 'get his fingers moving' as soon as he arrived, and accordingly requested that his room be warmed up beforehand. 'You really ought to have let us check in at a hotel'.[65] However, the change of plan rendered much of this unnecessary, and the evening of the Griegs' arrival was no doubt celebrated festively in the Brodsky household.

There had been some judicious pre-publicity, and in *The Manchester Evening Chronicle*'s edition of 19 November, beneath a pen-and-ink portrait of Grieg, 'Staccato' had given a background paragraph on the composer, reminding readers how

> Nine years ago Grieg and his wife visited Manchester, and appeared at 'Hallé's', creating quite a furore. Since then he has been a stranger, so that his concert next Wednesday in the Free Trade Hall should attract a crowd of worshippers, especially from the ranks of his especial devotees, young lady pianists.

Sketch of Grieg in *The Manchester Evening Chronicle* (19 Nov. 1897)

Brodsky himself had been laying the ground, playing the String Quartet (a work oddly described in the December edition of the *Musical Times* as 'wild and patchy') with his regular colleagues in Manchester on the 17th, and indeed in Sheffield a day earlier. Manchester was at this time enjoying some excellent music-making, with Busoni also playing in the city on the 17th, and Eugen d'Albert giving a solo recital only a few hours before the Grieg concert on the 24th and then appearing again at a Hallé Concert the following evening.

Grieg's programme was identical to that given in Liverpool, and it was received equally enthusiastically both by the public and by the press. Perhaps Manchester's *Sunday Chronicle* had given its chief critic a week off, as an enthusiastic – if quirky – short review had Grieg ('the harmonious doctor') as 'the author of "Peter Gynt" and many other suites of a weird and witching character.'[66] Once again, Henson's singing of Grieg's songs proved, on occasion at least, to be the weak point of the afternoon, even if in one newspaper it was was allowed – somewhat contradictorily – that she had been 'in good voice, faithfully interpreting some of the composer's most charming lyrical efforts'. Grieg was recalled five times at the close. 'The applause was long and loud at the end, but Dr. Grieg has learned how to politely repel the persistence of the hungry section of the audience. During his present tour he makes a practice of returning to the platform hat and overcoat in hand.'[67] The following day would seem to have been spent at home with the Brodskys. One recollection of it would come later in a book by Gerald Cumberland, the very personification of what would today be called a gossip columnist, who called at 41 Acomb Street:

Very many years have passed since, one cold winter's afternoon, I met Edvard Grieg on Adolph Brodsky's doorstep. A little figure buried, very deeply buried, in an overcoat at least six inches thick, came down the damp street, paused a minute at the gate, and then, rather hesitatingly, walked up the pathway. He saluted me as he reached the door and we waited together until my summons to those within was answered.

I found him very homely, completely without affectation, childlike, and a little melancholy. He was at that time in indifferent health, and it was at once made evident to me that both Grieg himself and those around him – especially Mrs Brodsky – were very anxious that he should be restored to complete fitness. He said nothing in the least degree noteworthy, but when he did speak he had such a gentle air, a manner so ingratiating and simple, that one found his conversation most unusually pleasant.[68]

It was probably also on this free day in Manchester that the three other members of the Brodsky Quartet came along to 41 Acomb Street (Bauerkeller, who also lived in Acomb Street, having the least distance to travel) and played to Grieg his String Quartet. The cellist Carl Fuchs recalled that Grieg must have been satisfied with the performance, as the composer entered into his autograph book a cello passage from the Quartet, at the same time adding a complimentary remark.[69] Grieg also found time that day to write to Brækstad, who had been at the London concert three days earlier but whom Grieg had not actually met at the time. Brækstad now lived in south-west London, the composer's's notebook showing his address as 33 Hailsham Avenue, Streatham Hill. Grieg hoped they could meet soon, as he needed some advice; he would be in London on Sunday at noon, when he had a rehearsal. He also hoped that Brækstad was keeping the Christiania daily *Verdens Gang* in touch with events and proudly informed him that the ovation he had received in Manchester was much greater than in London: 'In the end I had to do as you do and come in in my overcoat with my hat in my hand.' He was feeling fitter as each day went by, so was hoping for the best, knowing at the same time that he had to be extremely careful.[70]

Bidding farewell to the Brodskys on Friday 26th, Grieg and Nina travelled by train from Manchester to Birmingham. It was to be a flying visit, unlike that first visit in August 1888 when the best part of a week was spent in the city. This time there was just an overnight stay at the Grand Hotel to be paid for, before they both checked out and left Birmingham for London on the following morning. Curiously, there appears to be no record of any meeting with old friends like the Hardings or other members of the Birmingham Festival's committee, but there can be no doubt that many of the people whom Grieg had met eleven years earlier would have come to hear him play on this particular evening. Again, the programme was the same as that presented in both Liverpool and Manchester. A nice point was, of course, the inclusion of the *Holberg Suite* in its piano solo guise, Birmingham having heard the orchestral version conducted by the composer on his former visit to the city.

The Birmingham correspondent of *The Musical Times* described the concert as 'the most notable feature of our busy musical season and one that aroused a great deal of enthusiasm'.[71] 'One of the greatest events of our musical season was the appearance of Dr. Grieg', ran the opening of *The Birmingham Daily Mail*'s review. He was 'one of those pianists who fascinates the listener by his marked individuality, his incomparable touch and sentiment. The peculiar and often bizarre harmonies in some of his compositions fade away under his touch, and we hear only sweet and graceful music.' The third Violin Sonata ('certainly the most beautiful of the three') evoked real admiration. 'No words can adequately describe Dr. Grieg's and Herr Johannes Wolff's rendering of this work ... Indeed, these two artists are well matched, and play, so to speak, to each other.' The Menuetto from the first Violin Sonata was apparently 'a great favourite with local audiences', and it had to be repeated 'in response to an unmistakable desire' to hear it again. Unsurprisingly in view of what had elsewhere gone before, Medora Henson was the only recipient of adverse criticism:

> Nine of his songs ... were given by Madame Medora Henson, to Dr. Grieg's exquisite piano accompaniment. Madame Henson sang most of them in English, some in German, but her enunciation is not clear, and as it is just in these beautiful passionate songs that the words should be understood, this effect somewhat marred her splendid vocal achievements. The 'Waldwanderung' was encored. The hall was completely filled.[72]

However, to maintain the balance, it must be said that a sister paper appearing on the same day had quite other thoughts about Henson's performance. The first group of three songs that she sang showed her to have been 'en rapport with the composer' and earned for her the appreciative applause of 'an especially intelligent audience':

> It is seldom that singers can be induced to give nine songs in a single evening, and no doubt the risk of failing is worthy of consideration. That Mme. Henson should have sustained the ordeal with a success at once so brilliant and so legitimate, is of itself sufficient to demonstrate artistic talent of an uncommon order.[73]

A brief review filed with *The London Musical Courier* was similarly complimentary about the concert as a whole, focusing on the central performer:

> His touch is delightful, though he is not a *powerful* player. So much the better; we've had enough of them ... Grieg is a perfect accompanist in his own songs. He had a cordial reception, and his songs and piano pieces were greatly applauded, and some had to be repeated.[74]

It was back to London on Saturday 27 November, sustained by a 'lunchbasket' bought at Rugby Station for 3*s*. There were to be just two full days at home in Clapham before the Griegs set off again for the composer's only public appearance in the land of his forefathers – Scotland.

⊰ 14 ⊱

A FIRST – AND LAST – APPEARANCE
IN SCOTLAND

GRIEG had received at least two invitations to perform in Scotland, the first from Roy Paterson, who had hoped for some concerts in Edinburgh in 1890, and the second from Glasgow in 1893. Earlier he had briefly become acquainted with Aberdeen and Edinburgh on his way from Bergen to London in 1888. But concert appearances in Scotland seemed never to be at the forefront of his agenda, and when he finally appeared in the Scottish capital it was almost certainly more down to Vert's planning of this 1897 concert tour than to any express wish of his own.

That said, this was of course the homeland of his great-grandfather Alexander, and some contacts still remained. In 1890 a late-summer visitor from Scotland had called to see Grieg at Troldhaugen. He was John Morries Stirling (1851–1912), the son of Grieg's Scottish godmother Mary Wedderburn Stirling, both of Gogar House, Stirling. On his return to Scotland John sent a letter to Grieg in which he promised to send some rhododendron plants over to Troldhaugen.[1] Two letters to Grieg also survive from John's mother, dated 19 September and 28 October 1890. They contain little of consequence, the writer mentioning her son's visit to Grieg, and adding

> I am very glad that you have succeeded so well in your career as a well known composer. Your Mother was a good musician & your father was very fond of music. This year some pieces of your's were performed at a concert in Stirling & they are very much liked.

These three letters from mother and son are all that survive in the Bergen Public Library's Grieg Archives, and there are no pointers to any further meetings. A few years later Grieg would make brief mention of Mrs Stirling, who, he said simply, 'lived near the town of the same name.'[2]

A further point of Scottish reference in that same year of 1890 is to be found in *The Elgin Courant and Courier* of 27 May, which reprints what appears to be the entire text of a knowledgeable lecture entitled 'Songs of the Norseman', given just a few days earlier by the Revd W. A. Gray. The text is subdivided under the headings 'Music During Earliest Ages', 'Folk Songs', 'Characteristics of Norwegian Music', 'The Period of Revival', 'Ole Bull', 'Halfdan Kjerulf', 'Edvard Grieg', and 'The Power and Beauty of Northern Song', and reference is made to musical illustrations played and sung at varying points during Gray's lecture. The author mentions his 'repeated visits' to Norway, as well as his having heard Agathe Backer Grøndahl play a few weeks earlier in London. He also refers to Grieg's Scottish ancestry:

> Knowing, as I do, his relatives in Bergen, I am in possession of facts in regard to his personal history and artistic development which are not yet generally known, and these I shall summarize in a single sentence or two. Grieg comes from an extremely musical family, which hails originally – we cannot, unfortunately, say from Elgin, but from a town as near as may be – Fraserburgh. In the drawing-room of one of his relatives I have seen the tree, with a certain Alexander Greig and Anna Milne, his wife, at the foot of it, who emigrated to Bergen more than a century ago ... Grieg is now in the prime of his life. Though a delicate man, he is a hard and persistent worker. He refuses all invitations, and goes into no society. His Norwegian home Troldhaug, or the 'Witches' Hillock,' lies a few miles from Bergen. It is an ideal artist's residence – a fantastic villa, surrounded by heather knolls and birch plantations, and overhanging a picturesque chain of lakes. Over the entrance to the garden are painted the words, 'Edward Grieg wishes to remain alone till three o'clock.' Interviewers, it is clear, have a poor chance with Grieg. When he is staying in a foreign town, as he often has to do in fulfilment of his professional engagements, he hires a room to work in at some distance from the hotel; and so anxious is he to be left undisturbed that his wife does not know the place, and can thus deal politely with would-be intruders. Grieg's is a picturesque physiognomy, just a trifle weird and uncanny, and one feels that, if the composer of the 'Humoresker' was to perpetrate a joke, it would be of an unconventional and elfish kind. I know only one of his jokes. 'I was at a picnic with Edward Grieg,' writes his cousin to me, 'and he set fire to the heather to boil the coffee.'

A joke, one may think, carried a different connotation in Elgin in 1890 than it does today. And one may be sure that Gray's original text had 'Edvard' for the newspaper's mistakenly corrective 'Edward', just as Grieg is so often misspelled 'Greig' in public prints today. Some years later Gray wrote to Grieg from Elgin, enclosing a copy of a magazine in which he had written about the composer. 'I can only repeat my hope that you will find nothing to object to in my paper, and not set me down as a professional "interviewer!". . . How very nice it would be to meet you again in the fells' – the next best thing, he felt, to seeing Grieg either in London or Edinburgh.[3] A Norwegian speaker, Gray had recently interviewed his hero in Norway as a result of a chance meeting in a hotel where they both happened to be staying:

> Scarcely had I taken my place in the hotel porch, where the tourists assembled after supper for a chat and a smoke in the cool night air, when Grieg stood beside me

alone, and lit his cigar. His figure, even shorter and slighter than I first imagined it to be, was encased in a tight-fitting ulster and gaiters; his thick hair, just turning white, fell down on his collar from beneath a grey felt hat; and ulster, gaiters, and hat alike bore traces of mountain walks and mountain weather, during repeated visits to Jotunheim, the wild Alpine region where Grieg caught his passion for mountain scenery when a boy, and which is still, in his later days, a source of musical inspiration, as well as a favourite health resort. I accosted him, introducing myself briefly, and any doubt I had as to the character of my reception was at once set at rest. Off went the hat, with a courteous Scandinavian sweep; the clear blue eyes, with a light in them like the glint of sunshine through glacier ice, glanced keenly into my face; the attitude was one of frank and friendly attention; it was plain that, at any rate while the cigar lasted, Herr Grieg was at my service.

The conversation turned to Scotland, Gray noting that Grieg spoke fluent English, 'only now and again interjecting a Norsk word':

Of Grieg's ancestral connection with Scotland I already knew something, but I was glad to have the opportunity of discussing it with himself, so when he asked in what part of Scotland I lived, I answered, 'Not very far from the home of your forefathers.' 'Then,' said Herr Grieg, 'you live near Fraserburgh. Alexander Greig, my great-grandfather, who afterwards changed his name into Grieg, emigrated from Fraserburgh last century. There was a Greig, also Scotch, who rose to distinction in the Russian navy, but whether the lines are identical or collateral, one cannot say. See,' he said, displaying the seal at the end of his watch-chain, with the figure of a ship among stormy waves, and the motto, 'At spes in fracta,' 'here is our crest, it is the same as that of the Scotch Greigs. When I passed through Aberdeen some years ago, I was interested to find from the hotel-book that the name is so common.' 'Yes,' he continued, 'I have various ties to Scotland. I have Scotch friends; my godmother was Scotch — Mrs. Stirling; she lived near the town of the same name. I know something of your Scotch writers, too, especially Carlyle. I am fond of reading Carlyle; in what part of Scotland was he born? And I admire Edinburgh — Princes Street, the gardens, the old town, the castle (this with a sweep of the hand, as if dusky Laerdal, with its narrow street and shabby cottages had disappeared, and been replaced for the moment by the noblest city-scene in Europe, the monuments, the greenery, and the skyline of Edinburgh on a sunny day), — Ah, they are beautiful, beautiful!' 'Edinburgh people,' he continued, 'are very kind. They have asked me repeatedly to visit them and to play, and I would do so willingly if it were not for the sea. I am the very worst of sailors. Once, some years ago, I crossed from Bergen to Aberdeen. I shall never forget that night of horrors, never!'

When Grieg and Gray resumed their conversation on the following day there was a brief exchange of views on the subject of 'Scotch music', with Gray advancing the cause of Alexander Mackenzie and Hamish MacCunn. Grieg confessed to being unacquainted with Mackenzie's *Pibroch*, but considered both composers to be 'men of distinction'. MacCunn, he felt, was 'rich in ideas, though he does not yet express them with perfect clearness'.[4]

Arriving in Edinburgh on the evening of Monday 29 November, the Griegs checked in at the (old) Balmoral Hotel on Princes Street for a two-night stay. The Scots had of course been looking forward to seeing him on the platform rather earlier. Under the rubric 'Music in Scotland', *Musical Opinion*'s Edinburgh correspondent had written on 15 November that 'Next to the production of [Hamish MacCunn's opera] "Diarmid," the most notable event of the month so far would have been the visit of Mr. Edward Grieg, the Norwegian composer. Unfortunately, he has been too ill to come.' The journal quoted from Gray's 1894 article, including Grieg's complimentary remarks about Edinburgh and its people, and expressed the wish that it hoped 'to see him in Edinburgh presently, where he will undoubtedly have a warm reception'.[5] *The Illustrated Edinburgh News* of 27 November made a brief mention of Grieg's recent 'grave' illness, but was cheered by the fact that 'although on the platform of St James's Hall, London, on Monday, he looked extremely unwell, he was nevertheless sufficiently recovered to give his long-promised recital of his own music'.

The Scotsman of 29 November carried an advertisement placed by Paterson & Son for the concert. It informed readers that Grieg's instrumental and vocal recital would take place 'tomorrow afternoon at 3', and there was a warning to the effect that there were 'only a few tickets now remaining, for which Early Application is respectfully advised'.

Inevitably, reviewers of the concert – which was given given in the Music Hall, a part of the Assembly Rooms complex, on the afternoon of Tuesday 30 November – were keen to make a particular point of Grieg's Scottish background and to outline his life and career; and two papers even carried portrait sketches of the composer.[6] London's *Musical Standard* devoted the best part of a column to a piece entitled 'Grieg's Scotch Descent', again drawn almost entirely from Gray's article and only adding: 'The composer is only fifty-four, but his bushy white hair and attenuated frame make him look much older.'[7] 'First in point of interest last month', according to the Edinburgh correspondent of *The Musical Times*, 'was the visit of Dr. Grieg to the country whence his name and ancestry were transplanted to his now native Norway. The distinguished composer was greeted by an enthusiastic audience, which severely taxed the capacity of the Music Hall.'[8]

The programme remained the same as before; it was saluted in the 4 December edition of *The Illustrated Edinburgh News* ('His music is well-known in this country, but to hear it from the composer himself is indeed a great treat'), and Wolff and Henson were both praised for their performances. The most detailed review, however, appeared in *The Scotsman* of 1 December, under the heading 'Edvard Grieg in Edinburgh':

A little spare man; with a head somewhat large for his body, adorned with a floating halo of loose hair that was neither silver nor grey, but a sort of rusty white; with a face of somewhat pallid complexion and a weary Carlylean look, brightened only by the light of the keen eyes that peered out under a lofty forehead – such was the figure

Sketches of Grieg in (left) the *Edinburgh Evening News* (1 Dec. 1897)
and *The Weekly Scotsman* (4 Dec. 1897)

that presented itself on the platform of the Music Hall yesterday before an audience that crowded every corner of the building. It was an interesting figure, and those who were present in such numbers were probably as expectant and curious about what they were to see as about what they were to hear. For Grieg is not only one of the most prominent composers in Europe, but he is also one of the most original; and your latter-day public likes nothing better than originality. The originality of his music, too, is racial rather than personal. Personal individuality is apt to be narrow, and to pall. Grieg represents in music the national idiom of the Norwegians. It was Gounod who said that good music belongs to no nationality; its language is universal. But like most truisms, this is true only in a sense. The national element has been a most productive source of originality in music during the latter half of the century now ending. One has only to instance the work of Liszt and Brahms in the Hungarian field, of Smetana and Dvorak in Bohemian, of Glinka and Tschaikowsky in Russian, even of Mackenzie and MacCunn – to come nearer home – in Scottish, in order to realise how vast an enrichment of its materials modern music owes to the reproduction in artistic form of the idioms of the folk-music of different countries. Grieg's music is a sort of poetical echo of the sounds, a musical picturing of the sights of his native felds and fiords and woods and rivers. It is not a mere reproduction of the forms and fashions that are peculiar to the singing and dancing of the Scandinavian peasantry. It is this; but it is something more. If ever musician could be said to 'warble his native wood-notes wild,' it is surely Grieg. Not all the pedantry of a formal course of study at Leipsig Conservatorium could destroy the natural fund of musical material which the youth had gathered into his heart as he had gathered the air of the hills into his lungs.

Gade was before him in trying to reproduce Scandinavian music; but Gade could never escape from the influence of Mendelssohnian melody. Grieg has come much nearer to natural and original melody. He is forced, of course, to work in the main with the same materials and forms as other composers. But he has ears for wayward harmonies, rude but effective rhythms, and a strikingly original chromatic colouring that lends to his music a character all its own. He is not, of course, a very great or very deep composer. His music often suggests the sighing of the wind through the fragrant pines or the tinkling of the sheep bells far adown the valleys, than the complex moral and emotional maunderings which many latter-day musicians try to translate into the language of sounds. It does not move you profoundly; but it charms you; and it is just because of the peculiar charm of Grieg's music that it is played and heard with genuine pleasure wherever music is known. The large audience which greeted Grieg in Edinburgh yesterday was, as we have hinted, not attracted to the Music Hall solely with a view to hearing him play. This was his first appearance in Edinburgh; and as there are no greater hero-worshippers than your musical enthusiasts, the desire to see him must be reckoned as a potent factor in swelling the attendance. What shall be said of his playing? It was not, assuredly, in the grand style. His music, indeed, makes no demand on the grand style. It was amusing to see the palpable effort which almost lifted the pianist-composer off his seat every time he felt compelled to emulate the crashing chord effects on which the great virtuosos of the pianoforte to-day plume themselves. But if Grieg gave his audience nothing in the way of excessive sound and fury, his playing was just as charming in its way as are his compositions. His style of execution has all the limpidity and lucidity with which the late Sir Charles Hallé was wont to delight the older school of concert-goers. Piquancy and daintiness are qualities that were never absent. And occasionally he surprised by an unlooked-for emphasis of stroke which reminded one of nothing more than the sudden stamp or shout of country dancers. To hear him was a liberal education in the art of playing his own music. His reception was enthusiastic in the extreme. On each appearance he was warmly applauded, and at the end of the concert, after he had rendered a Bridal March which everyone knows, he was compelled to play again. His choice fell upon a Berceuse of his own composing. It was a Grieg programme from beginning to end, yet it cannot be said that at any point it was lacking in interest and variety. This may be partly attributed to the presence and assistance of Madame Medora Henson and Mr Johannes Wolff. Madame Henson did not at first seem to sing with quite the necessary sympathy, nor did she speak her words so clearly as might have been desired. But she is unquestionably a grand vocalist, and in her last selections especially she delighted her hearers. Mr Wolff is a violinist who was more frequently heard in Edinburgh four or five years ago than he has been of late. He played with great intensity of feeling, and his duets with the composer-pianist were delightful examples of perfect artistic combination. There have been many greater pianists in Edinburgh in recent years than Grieg; but as a historical musical event his visit is one that will not readily be forgotten by any who were privileged to see and hear him yesterday.

Poor Willy Hess and the distinguished Cologne Gürzenich Quartet, who calamitously had programmed their own concert just a few hours later at the Music Hall. Grieg had been 'so great a draw' that few people bothered to attend their performance – 'but it may be hoped that on another occasion better luck will fall to this quartette of musicians.'[9]

The only Scottish address recorded in Grieg's notebook of this period was that of G. C. Dibdin, at 27 George Street, Edinburgh. Might Grieg mistakenly have written 'G' for 'J'? The local Post Office Directory lists a James C. Dibdin who resided in Edinburgh at this time at 8 Howard Place. The George Street address, however, was that of the music sellers Paterson & Sons, whose proprietor was R. Roy Paterson – that same Paterson who had written to Grieg in May and June 1890 – so Dibdin evidently had some connection with the company.[10] He was doubtless related to the Edinburgh-born Edward Rimbault Vere Dibdin, a long-time friend of William Archer's. George Bernard Shaw first mentions him in his 1885 diary, which shows that Edward Dibdin was then living in London, appeared to be well connected in the capital's Scandinavian circles, knew Hans Lien Brækstad, and was often to be found at William Archer's home. He was to move to Liverpool in 1887 as art critic of *The Liverpool Courier*. That same year Shaw reported that Dibdin's brother came to stay for a while at Archer's, but he does not identify the brother more specifically. Shaw, Archer and Edward Dibdin kept company at Bayreuth in the summer of 1889, so a contemporary family musical connection is certainly indicated. If Grieg did actually meet the Dibdin of his notebook, he seems not to have left any record of the event.

Edvard and Nina returned to London by train on Wednesday 1 December, the day following the concert, with Grieg recording the expenditure of 7 s. 6 d. for 'Lunch, Preston'. 'Edinburgh was brilliant', he wrote to Brækstad that evening. 'And the mountain air or at any rate *the better air* did me good.' After this brief interlude north of the border – an interlude which appears to have received surprisingly little comment in the Scottish press – Grieg's next concert lay just three days ahead.

⇥ 15 ⇤

'THE QUEEN IS *SWEET*'

A s ever, concert promoters ensured that while Grieg was in town his music was unlikely to be in short supply – even out of town, as at the flourishing suburban musical society at Bromley, where on 20 November at the opening concert of the society's 18th season the programme had included the *Sigurd Jorsalfar* suite. Then at the Queen's Hall on 27 November one might have heard the *Peer Gynt Suite* no. 1 under Henry Wood. However, a new star came to town in December, with Richard Strauss (on his first visit to England) conducting a Queen's Hall concert on the 11th that included music by Mozart, Wagner and himself. Earlier in the year, on 24 May, it had fallen to Richter to conduct *Don Juan* in its first London performance.

Edvard and Nina Grieg were once again comfortably ensconced at the Augeners' in Clapham. Grieg had been made to feel even more at home following a gesture by Augener that had delighted him. 'If you come tomorrow Thursday at 12 o'clock,' Grieg advised Brækstad, 'it would give me much pleasure for a special reason. *And you yourself too!* For then you would see the *Norwegian flag* flying on my house. If this doesn't suit you, and you prefer the dark, then come if you can at 5–6 o'clock.'[1] On 3 December, before going downstairs to tea in the ground floor sitting room, Nina wrote to her old friend Hanchen Alme and elaborated on Grieg's surprising recovery:

> He really is bearing up rather well and is coping with all these public appearances far better than I had thought possible. His stomach, which is of course his weakest point, does give him some trouble from time to time, but he has rid himself entirely of the bronchitis and influenza that forced him to take to his sickbed a few days after he arrived here. Touch wood! He has now got through five concerts with flying colours (jubilation and enthusiasm everywhere) and he has five more to go. At the last one, on the 15th, I am singing, Lord have mercy on me. On Monday, too, I am invited to sing for Queen Victoria. If only I can make a good job of it! – but I shall probably be so nervous . . .

The Griegs had indeed been invited to Windsor Castle, thus making renewed contact with the royal family, if for the first time with the monarch herself. But first there was the Popular Concert on Saturday 4 December, bringing a reacquaintance with Frederic Cowen, to whom Grieg had just written. Although the concert was virtually an all-Grieg affair, there was, curiously, an additional item on the programme in the form of three songs by Cowen, in which the composer accompanied the American soprano Esther Palliser. *The Musical Standard* described it as 'a "gala" day at the "Popular"', thanks to the presence of Grieg; *The Musical Times* spoke of it as 'a great event', Grieg being 'extraordinarily popular in this country';[2] and *Musical News* reviewed the afternoon warmly:

> The music of Grieg, and, above all, the presence of Grieg, last Saturday, attracted a large audience. The concert opened with the string quartet, Op. 27, a remarkably fresh and inspiring work, especially as regards its first movement. It was played with hearty appreciation by MM. Wolff, Inwards, Gibson and Paul Ludwig. Grieg's simple and unaffected method of introducing full closes in the middle of his movements proved on several occasions inconvenient, and applause out-of-place was frequent from the musically uneducated, or the inattentive. Grieg, in the capacity of soloist, contributed four of his lyric pieces, to which as an encore he good-naturedly added another of his characteristic productions. His full, pure touch, his unrestrained style, and his absolute simplicity are genuinely restful in these high pressure days. His violin and piano sonata in G was admirably played by himself and M. Wolff, and most of the large audience remained (as an exceptional case) in their seats till the end. Miss Esther Palliser contributed songs by Grieg, and three musicianly lyrics by Cowen, exquisitely accompanied by the composer. The second song, a dainty effusion of both poet and musician – was repeated as an encore.[3]

Ferruccio Busoni had been in the audience, just as he had been at Grieg's St James's Hall concert on 22 November, and he wrote to Grieg on that same evening to apologize for having been unable to stay to the very end of either concert because of other duties to which he had had to respond in London.

There then came a day's rest before the Griegs set off by train for Windsor on Monday 6 December, following an appointment at 1 o'clock at Elliott & Fry's Baker Street premises –presumably to be photographed once more (and perhaps additionally to procure earlier photographs that might be inscribed later in the day). The Queen had long felt constrained to take her pleasures at home, with the result that there was an endless procession of visiting artists and orchestras making their way to Windsor or other royal residences in order to perform for her:

> Her Majesty is precluded from attending the theatres and concert-halls, as she so much delighted in doing before the lamented death of the late Prince Albert; but ample amends are made in the frequent commands to both the musical and dramatic professions for performances before Her Majesty and the Royal circle at Windsor Castle and other residences. On these occasions the Queen's evident enjoyment of the performances, and her solicitude for the comfort of the performers – as her subsequent enquiries and *souvenirs* amply prove – are in themselves real evidences

of the keen interest which our Sovereign takes, and her own capacity to share in the pleasures and amusements of her people.[4]

Together with Johannes Wolff, Edvard and Nina Grieg joined the roster of distinguished visitors who had performed before the Queen, their recital summed up by *The Times* in reproducing the Court Circular issued by Windsor Castle on the day after the recital:

> Mons. and Madame Edvard Grieg and Mons. Johannes Wolff had the honour of performing the following programme before Her Majesty and the Royal Family in the evening before dinner. Some of the Ladies and Gentlemen of the Royal Household had the honour of joining the Royal Circle in the Drawing Room:–
>
> Romance, Violin (from Op. 45)
>> Johannes Wolff and Edvard Grieg.
>
> Songs – (a) 'Woodwandering' - - - - - Andersen
>> (b) 'I Love Thee' - - - - - Andersen
>> (c) 'Good Morning' - - - - - Bjornson
>
> 'Humoresque'
> 'Berceuse'
> 'Norwegian Bridal Procession passing by'
>> Edvard Grieg.
>
> Songs – (a) 'An das Vaterland' - - - - - Paulsen
>> (b) 'Lauf der Welt' - - - - - Uhland
>
> 'Intermezzo' (from Op. 56)
> 'Alla Menuetto' (from Op. 8)
>> Johannes Wolff and Edvard Grieg.[5]

Returning in the evening from the pomp of Windsor Castle to the leafy purlieus of Clapham Common, Grieg immediately wrote to Brækstad to describe the occasion:

> I'm not wild about court affairs, as you well know, but this was something quite different. The Queen is *sweet*, if one can say this about an elderly lady. She was full of enthusiasm. She knew practically everything in the programme, *enjoyed* Nina's singing in Norwegian, and asked for more. I then played the 'Gavotte' from the Holberg Suite. When I was introduced to her, she said: 'I am a warm admirer of your music.' Everything was natural and genuine. She spoke about Peer Gynt and would have liked to have heard 'The Death of Aase' and 'Last Spring' for string orchestra. I declined all offers of a meal and took the next train home.

Brækstad asked for more details and Grieg wrote to him again on the 8th, shortly before leaving for Cheltenham:

> We were received and the concert took place in the Drawing-room. Besides the Queen, just her daughter, Princess Beatrice, and lots of courtiers of both sexes were present. I see that 'Times' has got hold of the programme without mentioning that all

WINDSOR CASTLE,

MONDAY, DECEMBER 6th, 1897.

Romance Violin (from Op. 45) -
JOHANNES WOLFF and EDVARD GRIEG.

Songs—(a) "Woodwandering"   -   ANDERSEN.
    (b) "I Love Thee"   -   -   ANDERSEN.
    (c) "Good Morning"   -   BJORNSON.
      MADAME GRIEG.

(a) "Humoresque"   -   -   -
(b) "Berceuse"   -   -   -   -
(c) "Norwegian Bridal Procession
    passing by"   -   -   -
      EDVARD GRIEG.

Songs—(a) "An das Vaterland" -   PAULSEN.
    (b) "Lauf der Welt"   -   UHLAND.
      MADAME GRIEG.

(a) "Intermezzo" (from Op. 56) -
(b) "Alla Menuetto" (from Op. 8)
    JOHANNES WOLFF and EDVARD GRIEG.

———

"GOD SAVE THE QUEEN."

Programme of Windsor Castle recital, 6 December 1897

the music is by me, on the contrary it almost looks as if Bjørnson, H. C. [Andersen, Uhland] and Paulsen are composers! – Never mind!

Two days on, and still flushed with the memory of the evening, Grieg sent a few lines to Frants Beyer, Max Abraham, and Julius Röntgen:

The other day we visited Queen Victoria at Windsor and made music for over 1 hour. She would have liked to have had even more. It was *very* interesting, compared to other court affairs. She's a *woman*, and one who is interested and interesting to talk with. She speaks German superbly. Nina sang at her best, I played at my ditto – and Johannes Wolff his. She gave me her Jubilee Medal and Nisk received a brooch inscribed with her name.[6]

I don't remember if I told you about Windsor. It was really nice. The Queen is, one might say, charming and surprisingly interested. Now: that *I* find her charming is very natural, because her first words were: (in German) 'I am a great admirer of your com-positions.' We (my wife, Johannes Wolff and I) made music (all by me) for about an hour and she wanted to have still more. I then played the Gavotte from the Holberg Suite, which work incidentally has been taken up here in England with the greatest enthusiasm everywhere. Besides the Sonata Op. 45, I played with Johannes Wolff the first piece from 'Sigurd Jorsalfar'. . .[7]

We played and sang for the Queen at Windsor. It was *very* nice. She is so charming and interested, quite astonishingly so for such an old lady.[8]

Various journals recorded the event, and *Lady's Pictorial* published a pho-tograph of Nina and gave details of the programme in its brief report. 'After the recital', it added, 'Dr. Grieg was presented with the Jubilee medal and Madame

Johannes Wolff and Edvard Grieg:
'These two artists are well matched, and play, so to speak, to each other'

Grieg received a beautiful brooch.'[9] The Queen was of course a great music-lover, and command performances at Windsor were regular events, with world-famous musicians being invited – particular favourites being recalled many times over – to perform before the monarch. Her German cousin the Kaiser was also a great admirer of Grieg's music, so much so that Grieg would be invited to play and to socialize as an honoured guest when the Kaiser's yacht was in Norwegian waters. The King of Sweden and Norway also paid tribute to musicians of distinction. Piquantly it was upon one of Grieg's chosen performers and admired friends, Lady Hallé, that he had just conferred the gold medal of arts, set in diamonds, at a private audience in Stockholm. She had given three recitals in the Swedish capital, and her accompanist had been Leonard Borwick.[10]

Nina Grieg

Although Grieg sought every possible opportunity to rest at Clapham between concerts, especially since after the Windsor visit there were to be concerts on every other day for a week, it seems that there had on the 7th to be a trip into town – to Baker Street again – for repairs to be effected to Nina's dress. On the following day they were off to Cheltenham, checking in at the Plough Hotel on the High Street, just a few doors away from the Assembly Rooms, where the composer was to play. The previous day's issue of *The Cheltenham Examiner*, carried an advertisement for 'The Grieg Concert', to take place 'Tomorrow Thursday after-noon at 3 o'clock', adding 'NOTICE! – All Tickets Sold'. A news item further advised: 'The attendance at the Grieg concert at the Assembly Rooms to-morrow (Thursday) afternoon promises to be a "record" one. Messrs. Dale, Forty, and Co. announce that "all tickets are sold," and request ticket holders to be in their places before a quarter to three o'clock.'

Cheltenham was a fashionable spa town, attracting its fair share of distinguished musical visitors, and both Liszt and Jenny Lind had been among Grieg's forerun-ners in performing in the Assembly Rooms. The venue was demolished in the early 1900s, and the old Plough Hotel, an important coaching inn, followed in its wake in the 1960s. Although many other older High Street buildings have survived, Grieg would have some difficulty in recognizing the area today. Nor would he for a moment have thought of following in the steps of Jenny Lind, who on her visit some four decades earlier had requested the manager of the Plough Hotel to allow all 72 servants of his establishment to be admitted to her concert to hear her sing. 'Mr. Churchill arranged that about half-a-dozen of his establishment should be ad-mitted at a time, and that they should each hear one song, so that their attendance might not interfere with the business of the Hotel.'[11]

Grieg's concert programme was identical to the others of his Vert tour, with Johannes Wolff and Medora Henson again his accompanying artists. Two of the main local papers carried reviews, *The Cheltenham Looker-On* ('A Note-Book of the Sayings and Doings of Social, Political, and Fashionable Life') on 11 December and *The Cheltenham Examiner* on 15 December. *The Looker-On* observed that

> The associations with the name of the famous Norwegian composer are of such a pleasurable kind that it was no matter for surprise that the Assembly Rooms on Thursday was crowded by his admirers, who had come from far and near to do him honour. Grieg is a pianist, but not of the sensational type; his playing is clear and very dainty in style, whilst his phrasing is admirable.

The paper went on to express appreciation of the various items of the programme and to praise the contributions of Wolff and Henson, whilst the *Examiner*'s re-viewer was similarly uncritical:

> That England does much to atone for its lack of musical originality by the hospital-ity and appreciation it extends to foreign masters of the art, has seldom been more strikingly shown than in the reception it is giving to the Norwegian composer, Edvard

Grieg. Following upon the academic honour which Cambridge University conferred upon him in March last [*sic*], the tour he is now making to the principal centres in this country affords remarkable evidence of the hold which his works have obtained upon music lovers everywhere ... Those who trace the broad current of Art are aware how largely of late years the stream has been flowing from the North, that region we associate with truth and tenderness, but also it must be confessed, from the literary standpoint, with a severity alien to the English spirit. From this severity the music of Grieg is free, characterised as it is by a graceful fancy and delicacy such as seems peculiarly suited to the atmosphere of the drawing room. Of its attractiveness in the concert hall, when combined with the personal interest attaching to the presence and performance of the composer himself, last Thursday's recital at the Assembly Rooms was a proof.

'Yesterday at Cheltenham crammed full,' Grieg informed Abraham, 'but only ladies. (More than 40 autographs!)'[12] Grieg, of course, had long been aware of the fact that the larger part of his audiences in England would usually be made up of middle-class young women, a kind of audience even more likely to predominate in genteel Cheltenham than in the great urban sprawls of London, Birmingham and Manchester. He may well have read *John Bull and His Island*, a book that went through many editions in the 1880s and was published in Danish in 1884 under the title of *John Bull og hans Ø*. The book took the form of a humorous look at England and the English and was written by a Frenchman, Léon Paul Blouet (1848–1903), under the pseudonym Max O'Rell. Blouet had taught French at St Paul's School in London from 1876 to 1884 and was well placed to observe the eternal eccentricities, as the French saw them, of the island nation across the English Channel. Only four pages or so of his book were devoted to music, but they were nonetheless perceptive. Blouet admired the quality of the Popular Concerts, as well as the seasons of Richter concerts – both were 'unsurpassable'. Indeed, public concerts in general in London were 'splendid and well attended'. But English singers, even those with good voices, tended to be too stiff and mechanical in their presentation. As for the pianist who happened to be playing at a salon, the first chord would be a signal for general conversation which would only cease when the artist finally stopped playing. And oratorios, of course, ruled the roost, for the Englishman was never happier than when listening to biblical themes set to music. Even if a large number of such works happened to be by the great German masters, it was entirely characteristic that so many were actually composed in England while the one or other foreign composer happened to be resident on John Bull's island. They were the equivalent, decided Blouet, of a Thames fog set to music. A remark often thought to have been coined much later by Delius in referring to Parry concludes Blouet's short chapter on music: 'The English will not be satisfied until the whole Bible is set to music.'

But it is Blouet's opening remarks that characterize amateur piano playing in late-nineteenth-century England:

Even the poorest schoolgirls have a pianoforte in their room. If in London there were the same number of apartments in the house as there are in Paris, then Bedlam, Colney-Hatch and all the other madhouses would not be sufficient to contain all the demented folk that these pianos would dispatch to them. As each family, however, has its own house, so much less the nuisance.

I would say that almost without exception all the women in England play the pianoforte, but apart from at concerts or public soirées I have never heard a lady or a young girl play in a manner such that any serious music-lover could take pleasure from it. They all play without the least feeling. A friend and compatriot of mine, who is an eminent professor and composer, teaches piano playing at one of London's larger educational establishments for girls. He complained to the lady principal one day about the fact that his pupils played without feeling or expression. 'Sir,' replied the lady with a benevolent smile, 'I have not engaged you to teach feelings to my young ladies.'[13]

This was not the only time that Grieg would remark plaintively on the attraction he and his concerts seemed to hold for young ladies in particular, at least in England. And a critic like Shaw inevitably relished the opportunity to score a point or two on just this subject. On the other hand, Grieg could scarcely complain if 'house full' notices were posted at virtually all of the concerts he gave on John Bull's island.

On returning from Cheltenham the composer would have been able to pick up the latest edition of *The London Musical Courier* and to find under the byline 'O.M' a laudatory article about himself and his music, illustrated by a somewhat earlier portrait photograph:

Once more Dr. Edvard Grieg has paid a visit to foggy London, and made himself the hero of our musical autumn season. The London climate in November is not exactly to be recommended for those in delicate health, and as Grieg is none of the strongest, an attack of bronchitis welcomed him immediately on his arrival. A short stay at St. Leonard's, however, has done wonders . . . As a man, he is as amiable as his compositions, his kindness, modesty, and habitual good humour making him a true friend and delightful companion. While being an ardent admirer of Schumann, he never fails to recognize the merits of other composers, both past and present. He enjoys a good joke beyond measure, and has made many a good one himself.[14]

What must surely have pleased Grieg best of all would have been the writer's description of his standing. 'Of all living composers, Grieg is undoubtedly the most popular, but also the most original and poetic' – a reminder of an earlier judgement of him as 'the most popular musician in the home life of England since Mendelssohn'.

Brighton, like Cheltenham long a fashionable resort whose reputation had originally been sealed by royal patronage, looked forward enthusiastically to Grieg's concert on 11 December. True to his word, Grieg had rested on the day before, devoting part of the time to his correspondence. A room or rooms had been booked

Edvard Grieg (Photo: Elliott & Fry)

just for the day at the Old Ship Hotel, to which the Griegs had been conveyed by
cab from Brighton Station following their arrival at 1.30. There was little time to
freshen up and change before a further cab took them on to the Dome, where the
concert was to begin at 3.00. *The Brighton Standard and Fashionable Visitors' List*
of 11 December records them, together with Johannes Wolff and Medora Henson,
as being among the visitors at the Old Ship that day, another guest listed as staying
there at the same time being the singer Clara Butt.

It is perhaps worth mentioning that in his current notebook the composer recorded the rail journeys made by himself and Nina, usually detailing too the cost
of each return journey and the class of ticket. Exceptionally, he recorded paying for
three first-class tickets to and from Brighton, two having been the norm in respect
of the other journeys made during his autumn tour. Who might have been his extra
guest? Either Wolff or Henson, perhaps, as this was the last concert of the Vert tour
and Grieg may have wished to say a thank-you in one form or another. Or perhaps
either Bræstad or Augener might have accompanied the Griegs? From the available correspondence it is not clear. Grieg certainly was not dogmatic in respect of
the class in which he travelled. He had arrived in London from Cologne nearly
eight weeks earlier by first-class train and boat, and he and Nina would ultimately
leave London for Amsterdam travelling in the same class. The joint return journey
to Liverpool had similarly been in first class. To Manchester and then from Manchester to Birmingham had been in first class too, but the final leg back to London
had been in second. However, the costly return journey from London to Edinburgh had evidently given Grieg pause for thought and, aware that the third-class
Edinburgh service offered at least the comparative luxury of padded seats – something that would not have been the case in continental Europe – Grieg prudently
bought third-class tickets for himself and Nina. To Windsor it could of course not
have been anything but first class, but Cheltenham found itself downgraded to
second. The trips to St Leonards and, shortly, to Manchester again – in each case
not for the purpose of concert-giving but for welcome rest and relaxation out of
the public eye – were not made in first class, although Grieg's notebook does not
specify whether they were in second or third. All this is mentioned simply to demonstrate how careful was Grieg's housekeeping. A first-class return to Edinburgh
from London, for example, would have made disproportionate inroads into his
concert fee, whereas shorter journeys would not have had the same effect.

Brighton Society carried in its 4 December (and again in its 11 December) edition
an advertisement informing its readers that tickets ranging in price from 2*s*. 6*d*. to
10*s*. 6*d*. were available for Grieg's forthcoming concert at The Dome. 'Mr Kuhe
begs to announce that Edvard Grieg, the great Norwegian composer, will give an
instrumental and vocal recital of his own compositions, assisted by Madame Medora Henson and Mons. Johannes Wolff (violin)'. Wilhelm Kuhe (1823–1912), yet
another in that long line of musical immigrants who so enriched the cultural life of
so many nineteenth-century English towns and cities, was born in Prague. A pianist

Expenditure accounted for in Grieg's 1897 pocket-book

and composer, he had arrived in England in 1845 and since 1886 had been a professor at the Royal Academy of Music. He was influential in the musical life of Brighton as well as that of London, and although in his autobiography he does not record any meeting with Grieg, whom he only mentions in passing, he had much earlier played in Brighton with Ole Bull at a concert that he himself had organized there.[15]

Unusually, seats were still available on the day, and *Brighton Society* encouraged its readers to go out and buy themselves a place in local history:

Edvard Grieg, fresh from a brilliantly successful appearance before the Queen and court at Windsor, where he played a selection of his delightful compositions, and was presented with the Diamond Jubilee Medal by Her Majesty, will give his eagerly-anticipated Recital at the Dome to-morrow (Saturday) afternoon, assisted by Madame Medora Henson and M. Johannes Wolff. An exceedingly varied and representative programme has been arranged, and we have no doubt that the amateurs of Brighton and Hove will assemble in large numbers to hear so distinguished a musician. The plan of the seats is at Messrs. Potts and Co.'s rooms in North Street and on the King's Road; and places will be obtainable at an improvised box-office inside the corridor of the Dome between half-past two and three o'clock to-morrow.[16]

This same journal would commonly carry comprehensive reviews of Brighton's principal concerts, but it also regularly published a gushing item entitled 'The Ladies' Letter' in its issues of this particular period. In one such letter, the writer looked forward to Grieg's concert and regretted that Nina Grieg would not herself be accompanying her husband. 'I am told that Madame Medora Henson scarcely takes the place of that sweet and refined singer'. Fairly accurate so far, but in the next sentence we learn that it was Grieg himself who had engaged Henson, 'and he ought to know who can sing his songs properly, if anyone does'. The item closed on an implausibly excitable note. 'I am looking forward to hearing her almost as much as I am to hearing (and seeing) Grieg. And then there will be Johannes Wolff, with his violin!'[17] In its later account of the concert, 'The Ladies' Letter' expressed itself even more archly:

DEAR AMY, –
    We went to the Ball on Friday, and enjoyed it immensely – On Saturday afternoon we went to hear Dr. Grieg at the Dome. The big room was not full, but those who were there were very enthusiastic, and the clever little Norwegian gentleman with the long hair and velveteen jacket appeared to enjoy himself very much. I liked his playing greatly. He certainly gets more out of his own music than any other player I have heard. And what characteristic music it is! Quite unlike any other. Herr Wolff was the violinist, and played beautifully; but I was not mightily smitten with Madame Medora Henson's singing. Perhaps the songs did not suit her voice. She certainly did not make so charming an effect as she did when I heard her in a concert in the Pavilion about four years ago. We had to leave the Dome early, as there were three At-Homes on that afternoon! . . .[18]

However, the *Society*'s principal review, of the same date, was considerably more informative. Largely speaking, it echoed other critics around the country who had recorded their own opinions of Vert's tour and its three executants. Grieg had been excellent, as had Wolff, but Henson left much to be desired. And as had sometimes occurred before, physical impressions of the event and of the principal executant occupied as much space as was taken up by the record of music-making:

There was a large audience, although the spacious building was not full, there being one or two notable gaps in the stalls, and the extremities of the Outer Circle being but sparsely populated. Oddly enough, the Balcony was the most crowded part of the room, there being apparently not a vacant seat there. Larger crowds have perhaps been in the Dome, but seldom have we known a concert audience to sit through a somewhat lengthy programme with more obvious contentment. Brightonians are as mad over 'personality' as the amateurs in London or Moscow or even Vienna. They would not have filled a room half the size of the Dome to have heard Saturday's programme discoursed with Grieg himself away. It was Grieg they came to hear on Saturday, and Grieg whom they came to see; Grieg, with his five-feet one inch of wiry humanity, his rugged, sturdy face, his mane of long grey hair through which he would every now and then send a violent hand; and his short velveteen jacket . . . And there they sat from three to five o'clock with opera glasses fixed upon the little grey-headed gentleman, who touched the piano so daintily, and at the end of each piece rose and bowed his acknowledgements of the applause so profoundly; and they went away happy.

The Brighton Standard wrote of 'a large and fashionable audience', without mentioning empty seats, and noted that the Holberg Suite, 'in which the quaint, old-time Scandinavian melodies are most felicitously expressed, met with great favor, and the gifted composer-artist had a double recall'. It noted in the same breath Wolff's 'splendid violin playing' and Henson's 'sweet vocalism', both of which, it rather remarkably considered, made for 'rich musical treats'.[19] Finally, The London Musical Courier spoke of Grieg's 'very hearty reception' by the people of Brighton. It was a real event in one's life to hear him playing his own music: 'one would imagine he were improvising for his own pleasure rather than performing before a crowded audience . . . Grieg was many times recalled at the close of the recital, and good-naturedly played again.' The Courier also included in this issue a short and not particularly original piece by E. Potter Frissell entitled 'Grieg and Norway'.[20]

There remains the unusual matter of the unfilled hall, perhaps in part explained in 'The Ladies' Letter' column, whose writer had mentioned the 'rush' of concerts in Brighton a few weeks earlier, and afterwards had pleaded the need to attend no less than three 'At-Homes' as a somewhat surprising excuse for leaving the Grieg concert early. A Saturday afternoon just a fortnight before Christmas would also seem a less than ideal time to have programmed a provincial concert. Rather would this be a time for shopping and partying – or presumably attending a plethora of 'At-Homes'. One guesses that at just this time of year a weekday evening concert featuring the same artists would probably have sold out with ease.

A seemingly unexpected presence at Brighton was the teenaged daughter of a cousin of Grieg's. Frida Grieg was evidently living there (or at least nearby) at the time. 'You should have seen Joachim Grieg's sweet daughter Frida down at Brighton after the concert', Grieg told Beyer, adding that she had been overjoyed 'to hear Norwegian spoken and played' and that he himself had been 'utterly charmed' by her.[21] Two days later he wrote to his cousin. 'I congratulate you on having such a sweet daughter in Frida. She completely captivated us! A shame we didn't see more of her!'[22]

Back in London that same evening, Grieg could happily reflect on the fact that the core of the Vert tour, with its repetitive programme, was now over. There were just two more concerts to go, still under Vert's auspices, but now they promised variety – and full houses again into the bargain.

⊰ 16 ⊱

'TOMORROW: FINISH! HURRAH!'

12/12/97

Dear Mr. Vert! If it is not too late and if it is not to ask you for too much, I should be very thankfull, if you would be kind enough to send me t[w]o good seats more for the recital the 15th. I am sorry to trouble you so much for tickets, but the circumstances have suddenly made it necessary to make use of your kindness.

    With kind regards
      Yours
        Edvard Grieg

If good seats are not to be had, perhaps it would be possible to place two chairs on the podium?[1]

GRIEG'S enquiry of his agent immediately yielded the two extra tickets that he required for his final concert. Whether Vert had the powers to accede to a further request of a different kind just two days later — evidently deriving from the composer's experience at St James's Hall when he gave his previous concert — is not recorded: 'If you kindly could manage, that the artist-room is warm and if possible, the hall *not* warm, I should be very thankful.[2]

Grieg was to play together with Lady Hallé at what was to be their last concert performance together in England at his recital on Monday 13 December. On Sunday the 12th he took a cab to her home at 30 Cambridge Street, Hyde Park, where they had a rehearsal at midday, and from there on it was a cab to the Café Royal, where they took lunch. Nina would almost certainly have accompanied them. The first part of the Monday Popular Concert was allotted to Grieg's music and the second to Italian songs and Beethoven's String Quartet in E-flat major, Op. 74. Besides Lady Hallé, Grieg was partnered by the mezzo-soprano Isabel MacDougall, who sang three of his songs. In the case of this concert there was no question of empty seats:

> Another manifestation of Dr. Edvard Grieg's popularity took place last night, when the largest Monday night audience of the season assembled to do honour to the Norwegian master, who played four of his 'Humoresken', op. 6, with such charm

and refinement of style that an encore had to be granted. It is curious to see how little change has taken place in the composer's manner of expressing his characteristic
ideas between his earlier and later works – between these fanciful pieces and the last
book of songs. His is one of the cases where artistic maturity was reached early, and
a rare self-criticism has prevented the composer from acquiring the fatal habit of over-
production, so that scarcely a work of Grieg's exists which has not met with lasting
success. He took part with Lady Hallé in an admirable performance of his famous
sonata in F major, op. 8, and three of his songs were sung by Miss Isabel MacDougall
with faultless taste and finished vocal art.[3]

The three songs sung by MacDougall were 'I Walked One Balmy Summer Eve',
'I Love But Thee', and 'Morning Dew', and Grieg's encore was one of the *Lyric
Pieces*. As ever, complimentary comments sprawled across the London press. 'Of
course there was a full house', wrote *The Musical Times* (adding, interestingly, that
of the violin sonatas the first, in F major, was the composer's favourite, although
just three years earlier he had declared for the second),[4] and *The Monthly Musical
Record*, echoing *The Times*, noted in its turn that Grieg had attracted 'the largest audience of the season'.[5] The crowds had come 'in spite of adverse wind and
weather', according to *The Musical Standard*,[6] itself echoed by *Lady's Pictorial*,
which averred that 'in spite of the depressing climatic surroundings, St. James's
Hall was thronged'.[7] Small wonder that Grieg recorded the purchase of a pair of
galoshes on the following day.

The capital's homage to Grieg certainly appeared to have reached its peak at
just this period, his songs being frequently performed at recitals great and small,
as were his piano pieces. On 8 December, for example, the gifted pianist Douglas
Boxall had played 'Butterfly' ('as poetic and fanciful as a butterfly's wing') at the
Queen's Hall. On Tuesday 14 December the Piano Concerto was on the programme of the students' orchestral concert at the Royal College of Music; 'Mr.
Herbert Fryer proved himself the possessor of trustworthy and nimble fingers,
and refined taste, in the solo part'. Cowen's *Scandinavian Symphony* ('too long
left unheard') was on the same programme. And at the students' orchestral concert
given at the Guildhall School of Music on 15 December, the first *Peer Gynt Suite*
(whose first three movements were played 'with much delicacy' and the last 'with
rugged vigour') featured together with the Piano Concerto, performed by Theresa
Haselden: 'with the exception of a little fatigue in the last movement, her playing
was quite remarkable.'[8]

'Tomorrow: Finish! Hurrah!' wrote Grieg to Beyer on Tuesday 14 December.
The end of his tenth public concert within these few weeks would be a wonderful
moment. Curiously, he was still undecided where he and Nina would make for after
the end of their stay in England. 'I still don't know where we'll be for Christmas.'
At least not in England, he hoped – perhaps in Leipzig or Berlin? The problem
was solved on the following day, when just a quarter of an hour before setting off
for his final concert Grieg wrote a short note of condolence to Julius Röntgen,

whose father, he had just learnt by post, had died three days earlier. Röntgen had apparently suggested that the Griegs might like to come to stay with him and his wife in Amsterdam, and Grieg immediately agreed. He could readily understand how in these sad circumstances he and Nina would be a cheering presence in their friends' home. 'We are going to the Brodskys the day after tomorrow for a couple of days and will probably leave London on the 22nd, so will come to you on the 23rd, I expect.'

> Dr. Edvard Grieg will play upon a Bechstein concert grand pianoforte at Dr. Edvard Grieg's recital at St. Jame's-hall to-day.

> Madame Grieg will sing 'Dobbin's Good-night' and 'Come Out, Snowhite Lambkin' from Edv. Grieg's 'Children's Songs,' op. 61, this afternoon, at St. James's Hall (Augener and Co.)

> Madame Grieg will sing 'To the Motherland' (8834a) and 'On the Water' (8834c), by Edv. Grieg, this afternoon, at St. James's Hall. (Augener and Co.).

These successive advertisements in *The Times* of 15 December would seem to have been placed by Augener, perhaps in conjunction with Vert. It was to be an all-Grieg afternoon, featuring Grieg's favourite musical partners in Nina and in Johannes Wolff. *The Monthly Musical Record* wrote of 'an immense demand for seats', and following the concert *The Musical Times* neatly summed up the programme and the performances it comprised:

> Dr. Grieg's second recital, which took place on the 15th ult., at St. James's Hall, was no less largely attended than the first. The personal interest indeed was increased on the latter occasion by Madame Grieg being the vocalist. This lady has arrived at that period in life when experience adds valuable help to the singer, and as she is entirely at one with the spirit of her husband's lyrics, there is much to learn from her interpretation of the dainty songs, which, by their unaffected nature, spontaneity, and pronounced nationality in idiom, have won so many ardent admirers. The programme began with the picturesque and characteristic String Quartet in G minor (Op. 27), which was most effectively interpreted by Messrs. Johannes Wolff, Inwards, Gibson, and Paul Ludwig. The composer himself joined the first-named in the Sonata in C minor (Op. 45), the finest of the three works in this form, for violin and pianoforte, and in the 'Intermezzo' (Op. 56) and the *Alla Menuetto* from the first Sonata in F (Op. 8). Dr. Grieg also rendered some of his small pianoforte pieces with his usual delicacy of touch and refined and piquant style.[9]

The pianist Harold Bauer, who had first met Grieg at the Amsterdam home of their mutual friend Julius Röntgen, was among those present. He later recalled how Grieg (with his 'leonine head') had that evening been 'acclaimed by an enormous audience'. Nina, he wrote, 'sang charmingly with a flutelike voice'. He summed up the 'diminutive' Griegs as two 'simple and delightful people'.[10]

Apart from according quality coverage to concerts, *Lady's Pictorial* remained one of the best sources for deft physical impressions and a conjuring-up of atmosphere associated with the events on which it was reporting:

> St. James's Hall was not large enough to hold all those who desired to be present at the concert given by Dr. Edvard Grieg and his accomplished wife. As early as eleven o'clock knots of musical amateurs took up their stations at the doors, content to wait for four hours ere proceedings commenced, rather than run any risk of being shut out on so interesting an occasion. When the distinguished composer, accompanied by his wife, ascended the steps leading to the platform, applause continually renewed showed plainly the esteem and regard in which the gifted Norwegian artists are held by the English musical public. Madame Grieg had not sung in London for some seven years, and it was not to be expected that her voice would retain all its freshness; but the fire, enthusiasm, and impulse of her singing had fortunately not abated in the slightest degree since she was last heard here, and she threw a tremendous amount of feeling into her interpretation of the seven charming songs from her husband's pen.

After further comment on the programme, the journal advised its readers that

> Dr. and Madame Grieg after visiting Manchester will proceed to Amsterdam and Copenhagen, and later to Germany, returning to their home in Bergen in April. It is hoped that they may elect to pay us another visit in the autumn of next year. That they will receive a cordial welcome goes without saying.[11]

Grieg must have heaved many a sigh of content after the end of this last concert — content that he himself had come through the ordeal of a visit to England that had begun disastrously with a week spent seriously ill in bed; and content that his wife, herself too ill to accompany him to London at the outset, had so far recovered that she was able to join him on his final tour appearance and sing to an enormous circle of devoted admirers. On the day following the concert, Nina bought some presents and Grieg sent signals to four friends: telegrams to Brodsky and to Wolff and letters to Röntgen and to Joachim Grieg. His letter to Röntgen was inevitably full of warmly-expressed sympathy for Julius's loss, but it also told of his delight that the tour had been rounded off so satisfactorily:

> I can't describe to you just how I feel after yesterday completing the 10th and last concert, which went splendidly and successfully. Sold out. Vert has every cause to be in good spirits. Johannes Wolff played the 3rd Violin Sonata and 1st violin in the String Quartet with passion and a glorious tone. Nina sang 9 songs and happily it all went off well. . . . Tomorrow morning we're off to Manchester for a couple of days, and we won't be leaving here until the 23rd, so that we can travel to Holland together with Johannes Wolff. So hopefully we shall be in Amsterdam that same evening.[12]

Pedro Tillett, nephew of Narciso Vert (and his uncle's successor in the agency), recorded an end-of-tour celebration:

> A very interesting evening was meeting Edvard Grieg and his wife. My uncle had engaged them for a limited number of recitals in England, including a London one at

St James's Hall. Their programme consisted of his own compositions for piano and his songs. Madame Grieg's voice was a light one, but her rendering of her husband's songs was most agreeable taking into consideration her age, for they were both past their half century. At the end of the engagement my uncle arranged a little dinner party at the Café Royal for the Griegs, my uncle and myself. It was a pleasant occasion as our guests were very simple and easily pleased. I can remember how they enjoyed a bottle of Veuve Cliquot (the sweeter kind) at the end of the dinner, and their ices. Both being petite, they reminded me of two happy children.[13]

An ongoing preoccupation of Grieg's at this period was an ambitious plan to bring Röntgen's Concertgebouw Orchestra to a pioneering music festival planned for Bergen in the summer of 1898, and a stay with Röntgen would enable the two men to take the matter forward. Cousin Joachim had just been elected as chairman of the festival's committee, and Grieg's letter to him discussed a number of points for the future, including the procuring of publicity in England for the event:

> An announcement from the committee about the holding of the music festival could be published in England without significant expense. I have talked about this with my agent (England's foremost), Mr. Vert, and he has promised to get such an announcement into the papers, as far as possible at negligible expense. As I understood him, it could be done as a news item and not an advertisement. We shall also have a warm friend for our cause in Mr. Bræstad, a Norwegian journalist who lives here and with whom I shall speak. He will be *able to accomplish a great deal* and is a Norwegian to the tips of his fingers at the same time as being an influential man in the press through his acquaintances. – In Germany it's not so good. I don't think we dare expect much from that quarter . . . Not only am I not ashamed, but I'm proud to be able to say that London has been a little Norwegian-crazy of late. The one thing that pains me a little is that the sold-out houses consist of too many 'Schoolgirls'. But – after all they *are* the mothers of the future.

Grieg concluded by sending greetings from Nina, 'who sang yesterday to the delight of both press and public with what remains of her voice but with her never-failing powers of interpretation'.[14] Although there was much controversy in Norway about the decision to import a foreign orchestra to play at this 'Nordic' festival, Grieg always stayed firm on the matter. One of the last things he did while in England at this time was to draft a telegram in English in his notebook: 'Dutchmen only about 4000 Kr. plus travelling lodging. Of Norwegian dearer I propose telegraph Holter this reason why you immediately telegraphic engage Dutchmen'.

On 17 December at midday the Griegs were off to Manchester by train from Euston Station to spend two nights at the Brodskys. The reunion was a happy one, if all too short. Brodsky introduced Grieg to William Dayas, professor of piano at the Royal Manchester College of Music. Christmas presents were bought in town for the Röntgens. And Grieg presented his old friend with an autograph manuscript of the violin part of his third Violin Sonata – a work that had received its premiere in Leipzig on 10 December 1887 by Grieg and Brodsky himself. Grieg inscribed it to Brodsky from 'his friend and colossal admirer' before he and Nina left for London on the morning of the 19th.

Some three years later, Brodsky was interviewed at home for *The Musical Standard* by C. Fred Kenyon on the subject of three of his friends – Tchaikovsky, Brahms and Grieg. Kenyon inspected various framed photographs and portraits in Brodsky's possession and paused when he arrived at one of Grieg and Nina ('a woman with a typically Norwegian face'), which he particularly admired:

> 'Ah, Grieg!' exclaimed Mr. Brodsky, enthusiastically. 'Was there ever a more charming man? And his wife! – was there ever a more womanly woman? But to do her justice it would be necessary to ask Mrs. Brodsky to come in, for she is just as enthusiastic over Grieg's wife, as I am about him. You know what I think of him as a composer? Well, his style is so individual, his sympathies are so keen and so sincere, and his temperament so essentially original, that I place him in a catalogue all by himself, and I label it – well, I haven't found a suitable label yet, so he must be called simply Grieg. There is no other name for him: he is simply himself. But the man, the man – that is where you will find his supreme excellencies, in his tenderness, his manliness, his thoughtfulness, his weakness and his strength. The last time he visited England, he was, for a few days, my guest, but I had met him hundreds of times before in past days in Leipzig. He was by no means in good health when he was in England, but whilst he stayed with us he was pretty cheerful. I remember his trying to persuade us to visit him in Norway for our summer holidays, but in spite of the fact that we have promised to go each year for the last ten years, we have never got there yet. But perhaps next year we shall be able to manage it. But speaking of our promise which we have not kept reminds me of a promise of Grieg's the fulfilment of which he keeps putting off from year to year. He once said he would compose a string quartet for me, but he hasn't done so yet. And for another reason I owe Norway a visit. The only decoration I have ever received comes from that country: it was voted me by Parliament in recognition of my services to Norwegian music in Leipzig. It seems somewhat ungrateful of me to ignore a country that has so honoured me, does it not?'[15]

The final days in London were spent in considerable activity, not least in shopping for presents for the Augeners, for 'Irish plaid', and for Christmas cards. Nine guineas were paid to Dr Field, no doubt representing a fee for attendance on various occasions. And further letters were written and dispatched, among them one to Abraham containing reviews of the final concert. 'As you see, it's all mainly a hymn of praise to my wife, which is very natural, as she was fresh and it was her only appearance'.[16] Grieg suggested that Brækstad come to visit on the evening of either the 20th or the 21st: 'it would give us much pleasure to see you'. On the 22nd, generous tips to Mary, Ada and '2 other maidservants' at the Augeners were recorded in Grieg's notebook. He and Nina bade farewell to England on the 23rd, travelling by way of Flushing to Amsterdam, where they were to stay until the new year.

V

INTERLUDE (2)

❧ 17 ❧

'ALL THESE PEOPLE SO MUCH WANT TO SEE YOU OVER HERE AND AMONG THEM AGAIN!'

I F London's weather had almost turned out to be Grieg's undoing in the autumn of 1897, it proved more than enough for his younger friend and compatriot Christian Sinding in the spring of 1898. Sinding spent some time in London at work on his first Violin Concerto in the early part of the year, a letter to Grieg giving his address as 12, Houghton Place, Hampstead Road. Many years later he would tell an interviewer,

> That was a fine old time. I came to London to look for solitude, and that was where I found it. There isn't a city in the world like London for solitude. Only once, when I was out walking and enjoying the feeling of how splendid it was to be working in this city of millions of inhabitants, did I run into a fellow-countryman. London is an even finer city than Paris for solitude.[1]

However he may have recollected it, in a letter written to Brodsky at the time his mood was distinctly different. He had already spent some time in Manchester with his former mentor, but had decided against making a further visit:

> I can't bear this climate any longer and am leaving. I've dragged around like an idiot for nearly a fortnight without being able to tackle the least thing. And now this snowy weather has finally made me utterly impossible. Quite simply I haven't enough money to go on wasting my time in this way. So I've decided to make a short trip to Paris early tomorrow and after that to Norway. My purpose in staying in London was to complete the violin concert-piece, and in that I've been tolerably successful. The alterations that I shall be making in accordance with your kind advice and for which I am very grateful will have to wait till later. I haven't even been able to get down to that.[2]

Arthur De Greef was in London again at the beginning of the year on the latest of a series of visits that had begun in 1890. He continued to champion Grieg's music at a recital in St James's Hall on 18 January, playing among other works 'a selection of pieces by Grieg with fascinating delicacy and appreciation of their romantic and fantastic character'.[3] In a musical context, Grieg's own contacts with England during the early months of 1898 were dominated by exchanges with Brækstad and Halvorsen. He and Nina had stayed with the Röntgens through Christmas and the New Year before travelling on to Leipzig, where they established themselves until late April. Throughout this period, Grieg's major preoccupation was with the festival to be held in Bergen in the summer. He continued to hope that Brækstad could be a major source of help to him in publicizing the festival in England:

> With regard to your kind offer, I would ask you, by means of notices to as many English (and American) editors as possible, to let it be known that in conjunction with the international fisheries exhibition in Bergen this summer a music festival will be held between the 27th June and 3rd July under my *auspices*, (use only this expression, not leadership or direction) and will be devoted entirely to performances of Norwegian works.[4]

Grieg went on to advise Brækstad to write to Bergen for any further information likely to be of interest to English readers, recommending too that he get into touch with Vert, who had offered to assist in publicizing the festival. Brækstad was as good as his word, and within a fortnight the forthcoming festival was reported on in a dozen or so papers, both national dailies and musical journals. *Musical News*, for example, announced in its 19 February issue that the festival would be given 'under the auspices of Dr. Edvard Grieg'. Brækstad sent Grieg cuttings from *The Times* and *The Daily Chronicle* by way of evidence; he also included a long interview that a correspondent of the latter journal had had with the London impresario Schulz-Curtius about the *Ring* cycle shortly to get under way at Covent Garden. 'The interest in Wagner is rising in England', noted Brækstad. He furthermore sent greetings to Grieg from a mutual friend, Arthur De Greef, who had played a concerto of Saint-Saëns at the Queen's Hall the previous evening and who, on hearing of the festival, had conceived of the idea of taking a holiday in Norway in the summer so that he could be in Bergen at the time. Brækstad had also just met and conferred with Fridjtof Nansen, who was to give his last lecture in England that same evening after having spent several days in the country.[5]

Even where there was no mention of the festival, there might be found still further evidence in the musical press of continued interest in Norway. Edgar Shelton wrote a long essay entitled 'Musical Reminiscences of Norway' that appeared in the 29 January edition of *Musical News*. 'From a musical point of view,' he began,

> a journalist's visit to Norway proves a disappointment, not in the sense that his society is less coveted there than elsewhere, or that his presence is not welcomed at every musical fixture of importance, but from the fact that so little real excitement takes place in Norwegian musical circles, as to leave sparse opportunity for securing the desired "copy," and it becomes a source of irritation to whom to look for information. Little wonder, then, that one's mind, thus left unsatisfied, relapses into other channels of thought, the warlike history of its past, perhaps; anything, in fact, but its present musical doings.

After this unpromising start, the author reflects on historical musical stringed instruments and on the Hardanger fiddle, on the fact that there is always good music to be heard in the country's principal cities, on the efficacy of the capital's many music publishers, on listening to an ill-tuned band at Tromsø, on folk-tunes and dances, and on amateur music-making. By the time he reaches his conclusion, he reflects on how, from the experience of his travels up and down the country, 'striking evidence of their love for music is shown in the fact that every Norwegian now, no matter how inaccessible, boasts of a good piano and a respectable collection of music written for it'. He tells us that a curious fact relative to the Hardanger fiddle is 'that its executants invariably wildly rhapsodize before settling down to a definite purpose. Grieg has caught the spirit of this in the opening of his Sonata in C minor, with its lawless passage which contains so many eccentric intervals.' Shelton did not meet Grieg during his visit, but nevertheless tells the story of the composer's discomfiture at being pursued by tourists like himself:

> Grieg was a frequent visitor at Fleischer's, and many tales, almost laughable for their impertinence, are told there of the ruses that have failed, while trying to make his acquaintance. Some have adopted the bounce dodge, which does not wait for any sign of recognition; the "little" great man has then usually turned his back. A Scotch parson observing Grieg to take a similar stroll each day, discovered on inquiry that the path led to and terminated at a little house, a veritable cul-de-sac. Here the parson dogged his man, and returned with a countenance gleaming with pleasure – 'he had met Mr. Gregg!' The ladies proved a terrible worry in their importunate demands for the composer's autograph; Grieg must have been at his wits end to know how to checkmate the wiles of these enchantresses. One way out was to disappear suddenly from the scene in a stolkaer and never draw rein till he was perhaps 12 miles up the valley, but this was only to be a temporary gain of freedom, for as soon as his flight was discovered, every available carriole would be ordered out, and off would go the party as *merry as a grig*, bent on recapturing their prey . . .[6]

Shelton's essay had warmed to the music of Johan Halvorsen, just as had *The Daily Chronicle*, which a few days earlier had accorded a sympathetic hearing to Halvorsen's suite *Vasantasena*, given under Henry Wood in January. In referring to occasional previous airings of Halvorsen's works in the metropolis, the newspaper felt that more of his music might with profit be offered to the London public.[7] Halvorsen himself hoped that Grieg might – in the very near future at that – help him further to establish himself as both conductor and violinist in London and Paris (where, thanks to a generous Norwegian stipend, he would be travelling in the spring), but Grieg counselled patience. Even Joachim himself, wrote Grieg, could not 'improvise' such short-notice engagements as Halvorsen appeared to be seeking, and he felt that his younger friend was being exceptionally naïve in his approach. Such matters needed six months' – even a year's – notice. Grieg accordingly advised Halvorsen, once he was in London, to get Johannes Wolff to accompany him to Vert's office, with a greeting from Grieg himself, to see what might be arranged. 'Wolff anyway has better contacts than I have and will be able to advise you.'[8]

In a similar way and at about the same time Grieg offered advice to another compatriot, the pianist and composer Signe Lund (1868–1950), sister of the artist Henrik Lund. He was happy to be of service to her, he wrote, and would write to 'the English publisher G. Augener', whose business address he gave her, to see what might be done to assist her.[9] Lund was later to live for some 18 years in America, where she gained a fair reputation as a composer – her work being marked, it is said, by Grieg's influence. She certainly performed her own works in London on one occasion at least. Grieg was far less likely to have been able to assist John Parr, of Sheffield, a bassoonist who had enjoyed playing in various of Grieg's orchestral pieces but who lamented the lack of solo bassoon literature:

> I beg to ask if you can at some time see your way to write a few bassoon solos embracing all the characteristics of the instrument in all its humorous, grotesque, plaintive and even pathetic aspects . . . A romance, elegy, minuet or sonata would be very acceptable to bassoon players, as there are so very few bassoon solos published in England, and I am not aware of any good concerto since Weber's op 75 . . . and as your compositions prove you to possess a thorough knowledge of the Bassoon's capabilities I hope you will kindly grant my request and write and publish a series of solos for the Bassoon. One great feature as you will be aware is not to make them fatigue-ing but to intersperse several rests here and there for breathing purposes.[10]

That Brækstad's publicity machine had been successful is further indicated by Parr's having addressed his letter, if in orthographically challenged fashion, to 'Dr. Edvard Greig / Conductor / Norweigian Musical Festival / at / Bergen / June 26 to July. 3. 1898'. There is no evidence of a reply from Grieg, whose contribution to the repertoire for solo bassoon was to remain what it had always been.

After Leipzig the Griegs had spent some three weeks in Copenhagen on their way back to Bergen, where they finally arrived on 19 May. From then on their time was to be filled with preparations for the festival. The great event duly came and went, as did journalists from England who crossed the North Sea to report on it. Edmund Gosse had written to Grieg to introduce to him one such, W. S. V. Makower, a talented musician and poet who was going to Bergen 'on purpose to give English people an impression of the Fest and of your beautiful music'.[11] Brækstad went too, writing to his friend on 8 July to express his regret at not having met the Griegs after the end of the festival and before he had had to leave Bergen. Describing the festival as 'one of the most important events in our cultural life this century', he had felt immensely happy to have been present.[12] A month later he sent to Grieg an article he had written for one of the English papers – a piece that Grieg felt did justice to Norwegian music, so much so that he recommended that it be translated and sent on to one of the leading Norwegian newspapers. Meanwhile, 'J.S.S.' of *The Monthly Musical Record* had devoted the first two and a half pages of the August issue of that journal to a full and laudatory record of the festival:

In olden times England was invaded by the Northmen; now Norway is invaded by the English, who go there year after year, and in ever increasing numbers, to enjoy the scenery of that land so favoured by nature. Many go a-fishing, and to such, no doubt, the National Fisheries Exhibition at Bergen, which opened in May, will prove an extra attraction. It was not, however, for the sake of fish, fishing tackle, or fishing vessels that I sailed in the good ship *Eldorado* to Bergen, but in order to attend the festival of Norwegian music held there under the auspices of Dr. Edvard Grieg . . . It would be difficult to exaggerate either the interest or the importance of the Bergen Festival, which was not only the first of its kind, but the first musical festival ever held in Norway. The programmes were entirely devoted to Norwegian music; and with the exception of Johan Selmer, who was unable to be present, the various orchestral works were conducted by their various composers. The aim of Grieg was not self-glorification, or his name would have made a greater show on the programmes; it was not to provide an hour or two's amusement for the inhabitants of Bergen or for the visitors from different parts of the globe who came to visit the Exhibition, or merely to pass through that 'entrance to an enchanted land'; but it was to show his and other countries what Norway has done, and what she is still doing, for musical art. The Festival was held in a hall specially erected for the purpose, and capable of holding about three thousand persons . . . Grieg engaged the 'Concertgebouw' orchestra from Amsterdam, and the admirable performances pleased the public, satisfied the various composers who conducted, and fully justified the action of Grieg. A foreign orchestra at first proved a stumbling-block to some patriotic minds, but Grieg was more concerned about the character of the playing than the nationality of the players.

The reviewer commented extensively on the works played during the festival and ended by suggesting that, as it had proved successful, there seemed no reason why other festivals – which might furthermore profitably include the music of non-native composers – should not follow in Norway, 'Why should not Christiania, Bergen, and Trondhjem, each in their turn, institute such a musical gathering?'[13]

Meanwhile, Grieg would have been pleased to learn of an article, 'Grieg's Influence', originally published in *The Musician* in America, which subsequently appeared in London's *The Musical Standard*.[14] It had been written by Henry T. Finck, who some years later was to write the first English-language biography of Grieg, and it sang the composer's unstinted praises, strongly defending Grieg's songs and their roots in Norwegian nature and lauding the composer's 'new and unique' harmonies as well as the modulations ('the most powerful engine of emotion') in his music, which so thrilled the sensitive listener.

Grieg's principal task at Troldhaugen for the remainder of the summer was the correcting of proofs of two major works: the song-cycle *Haugtussa*, and the orchestral version of the *Symphonic Dances*. In the case of the former there was also the correction and reworking of the initial English translation, a cause for some concern, only resolved – as Grieg explained to Abraham's nephew Henri Hinrichsen of the Peters company – through the intercession of two helpers:

The English translations were, I'm afraid to say, atrociously bad. Herr Oscar Meyer in London has been so kind as to effect some significant improvements with them. In the end I had the good fortune to be visited here at Troldhaugen at just the right moment by an Englishman, a poet who at the same time is very familiar with the Norwegian language. He worked together with me for 2 whole days and you now have the result before you; I dare say that it is as good as I could have wished for. Please send one of the first copies of the songs to Herr Oscar Meyer in London.[15]

In fact the initial work of translation had been confided to Natalia Macfarren, who seems simply not to have been up to the job. Grieg sent a heartfelt letter of thanks to Meyer. 'As I studied your translations, I grew more and more astonished at the fabulously supple quality that you, a foreigner, demonstrate in the use of English-language poetry.'[16] In its November issue, *The Monthly Musical Record* signalled the completion of this new 'set of songs' and included a review of the four-hand piano arrangement of the *Symphonic Dances*, described as 'full of characteristic harmonies, wayward rhythms, and quaint melody'. Even in transcription, 'whereby orchestral colouring — one of Grieg's strong points — is lost, [the dances] will give great pleasure. And they are all three [*sic*] good.' The reviewer concluded by giving a thumbnail sketch of each of the four movements.[17] Publication of the full score of the *Symphonic Dances* followed soon after, and Henry Wood conducted England's first performance of the work on 28 January 1899. The critic of *Musical News* enjoyed the new piece, if with minor reservations, and found the orchestration to be 'extremely picturesque, the harmonic treatment bold and striking, and the musical idiom typically Norwegian'.[18] 'J.H.G.B.', reviewing the performance in *The Musical Standard*, was quite overwhelmed: Grieg's Op. 64 was 'full of intensely vital music'. It had 'a keen emotion and a newness that fairly carry one away. There is surprise after surprise in the score.' The work 'triumphally' showed Grieg's genius as a composer:

> The orchestration — if one may be permitted to consider it separately — is very beautiful. The harmonies sound as clear and well-balanced as they would on the most modern pianoforte. That homogeneity of effect is very remarkable; so is the extreme brightness of colouring. But there were instrumental combinations one had not heard before. One would like to study this remarkably brilliant score at leisure. I advise all students to get it at once. One knew that, among other qualities, Grieg was a great 'harmonist,' but one was not equally aware that he could score with such consummate art — not a single effect failing to tell.[19]

Mention of newer publications of Grieg's music is a useful reminder that this remained an ongoing process in London and was a mixture of the familiar and the faintly esoteric. Augener was, of course, to the fore, but there were other firms in the field. Robert Cocks & Co. advertised their publications for 1898 as including 'Greig, Ed. Anitra's Dance, Bridal March, & Poetische Tonbilder', at 3*s.* for the first two and at 4*s.* for the third. Augener offered 'Fisher's Song, arranged for two female voices, with Pianoforte Accompaniment by H. Heale' (also, unusually for them, by 'Greig') for 3 *d.*, and 'Fatherland's Psalm, for 2 or 3 Female Voices', also at 3 *d.*[20]

George Augener's son William had recently married, and Grieg sent a suitably Nordic wedding-present to Clapham. Augener junior and his bride, on honeymoon in Zermatt, heard from home that 'der Pelz' (probably a bearskin rug), which had arrived safely, had aroused much admiration. William thanked the donor warmly and told him that it was destined for the drawing-room, where Grieg would be able to greet it when he next came to London.[21]

Two requests arrived from England while Grieg was still at Troldhaugen. Edgar and George Percy Haddock, co-directors of the Leeds College of Music, asked the composer if he would do them the honour of sending a signed photograph to add to their important College collection. As a sweetener they sent to Grieg a small book of photographs, 'the originals of which were prepared for and sent to H.R.H. the Princess of Wales — the Leeds College of Music being under Her Gracious Patronage'.[22] And Brækstad asked for 'a really good photograph' of Troldhaugen and of the drawing-room, needing them as illustrations for an article he intended to write about Grieg. He had just sent off to the *Illustrated London News* a photograph he had been sent of the group of composers and performers at the centre of the recent festival in Bergen, and this, he wrote, would appear in a few days' time. A little earlier he had sent copies of an article on Grieg in *The Musical Standard* to four different Norwegian dailies.[23]

Grieg's music was evidently proving to be as welcome at the Queen's Hall as it had earlier been at St James's Hall, becoming a regular feature at the Promenade Concerts so recently initiated by Robert Newman and Henry Wood — even if the critic of *The Musical Standard*, describing the concert given on Tuesday 20 September as having been devoted to Grieg and Massenet, had reservations. 'It was perhaps a mistake to give the Norwegian composer's Dances, Op. 35, as scored for orchestra by Hans Sitt, as they are not interesting in their orchestrated version.' The soloist in the Piano Concerto had been Miss Madeline Payne. Again, the *Standard*'s man harboured certain reservations but at least admitted that 'it was a very successful appearance'.[24] It was more than likely the same critic who attended the Grieg Recital given just four weeks later at the Salle Érard, when Hanka Schjelderup played the Piano Sonata and three groups of smaller piano compositions and was furthermore partnered by Carlo Ducci in a two-piano performance of the Concerto. Schjelderup was, the *Standard* felt, 'too powerful a player to do herself justice in so small and resonant a room', but she was nonetheless highly talented, and it was hoped that more of her playing could be heard in the future. However, the programme generally was 'a little too much for one afternoon. A certain stereotyped melodic idiom forces itself on the mind, and one begins to wonder how much Grieg owes to Norwegian folk music and how much to his own originality.'[25] The *Standard* was unduly sour, if *Musical News* is to be believed: 'to all the artist brought feeling, style and glow, as well as technical skill', and Grieg's smaller pieces were 'most fascinating'.[26]

A performance of the Cello Sonata a month later was particularly noticed:

> Mr. Herbert Fryer, a promising student of the Royal Academy of Music [though at
> the time at the Royal College of Music], gave his first pianoforte recital at Steinway
> Hall, on the 17th instant, and was encouraged by a large and enthusiastic audience.
> The first piece was Grieg's Sonata, for pianoforte and 'cello, Op. 36, in which Mr.
> Bertie Withers was associated, and a painstaking presentment was secured.[27]

Fryer remained committed to Grieg, and the following spring would see him performing the Piano Concerto under the baton of Arthur Payne at the Queen's Hall
'with refinement'.[28]

On 12 October Edvard and Nina Grieg left Bergen and set out once more on
their travels. Christiania was simply to be a port of call en route to Copenhagen,
but Grieg was yet again struck down by bronchitis, the result being that ten days
were spent in bed at Odnæs, a village well to the north of the Norwegian capital
where the air was good and so could be expected to aid the composer's recovery. In
a letter written from the hotel to his brother and sister-in-law, Grieg reported on his
reading, mentioning in particular two books by English authors that he had found
especially interesting: *Robert Elsmere*, by Mrs Humphry Ward, and *Darwin's Life
and Letters with Autobiography*, 'which I think has made me a better person'.[29]
The Darwin was in a Norwegian translation, but Grieg does not specify the language in which he read the Ward.[30]

A frequent item in *Musical News* for some years around this period was a column
entitled 'Scandinavian Musical Intelligence', usually supplied from Stockholm by
Hildegard Werner, an Associate of the Royal Academy of Music. Her latest contribution included the news that Grieg had 'just recovered from a slight attack
of inflammation of the lungs', and that he and his wife had taken up residence in
the Hotel 'Konung of Danmark' (as she expressed it) in Copenhagen, where they
intended to spend the winter. She also found time to praise the newly published
Haugtussa.[31]

In November, one of the Leipzig links was finally broken, with the passing of an
old friend being recorded in several journals:

> The death has occurred in Hull of the distinguished violinist, Andreas Pettersson.
> He was a protégé of Jenny Lind, and intimately acquainted with many of the best
> known musicians, and many first rate instrumentalists passed as pupils through his
> hands. He was for twenty-six years music-master at Rugby School, and first violin in
> Hallé's orchestra, and performed in every great European city. His knowledge was
> so comprehensive that he could play almost every instrument, and could speak eight
> languages fluently.[32]

One old colleague and friend of Pettersson was a pianist, organist and composer
who had settled at Port Elizabeth in South Africa and become well known on the
musical scene there. Roger Ascham was anxious to amplify the record on Pettersson, who deserved a longer notice,

for although he was but little known to the general musical public, those musicians who were privileged to know him recognized in him a genius of the highest order, not only as a performer on his particular instrument – the violin – but as a composer. His etude for oboe (or violin) published by Warmuth, and his Scherzo on a Pedal Bass are in my humble opinion unique in musical art, and his 'Ancient and Modern' and 'Scenen auf dem Lande' are specimens of perfect writing; while his Romanze in B major (all for violin and pianoforte) is without exception the most beautiful example of its class with which I am acquainted. A collection of ten pieces for pianoforte are on the eve of publication by Laudy and Co., and these are all gems, and should be known and played by every pianist who desires to add some novelties of the best kind to his repertoire. The monotonous and wearing grind of teaching at Rugby school prohibited my late friend from taking up the position his genius entitled him as a public performer, for undoubtedly had fortune smiled on him he would have made a reputation equal to the greatest of our age.[33]

Continuing to Copenhagen after being repaired at Odnæs, Grieg and Nina over-wintered there. On 4 March his current plans were reported briefly in the columns of *Musical News*: 'Edward Grieg, who has lately suffered from an acute attack of influenza, will shortly leave Copenhagen for Italy, where he and his wife intend to spend some months.'[34] In fact they spent several weeks in Italy, a largely recreational period that on 3 April took in a conducting engagement in Rome that featured the Piano Concerto. Two letters that Grieg wrote from Copenhagen to his publisher friend Sigurd Hals expressed (in the first) the hope that he might shortly see Leonard Borwick again and (in the second) his admiration for the English pianist:

> He really is a first-rate pianist and is inevitably scoring a tremendous success here. This evening he plays for the last time. But what do you think of Hennings, who can't even find the wherewithal to advertise the programme. It really is too bad to offer the public this sort of thing, and I suppose that people will respond by staying away in droves![35]

Borwick continued to champion Grieg, and a Manchester performance that he gave of the *Ballade* in February was commended, even if the reviewer, Arthur Johnstone, was less than enthused by the work itself:

> Mr Borwick played a Ballade by Grieg in the form of fifteen variations on a Norwegian air. The air is plaintive and pretty, and in the harmonization is strongly stamped with the composer's individuality. Some of the variations, too, contain examples of graceful movement, but there is not much more to be said for them. . . . The one really fine work of considerable scope for pianoforte by Grieg is the Concerto. All that was possible, however, to be made of the Ballade was made for it by Mr. Borwick.[36]

Grieg had last met Delius, albeit briefly, in Leipzig in 1896, and for some years after this their correspondence seemed to have drawn to an end. However, it was to be taken up again in 1903, when much of the old warmth returned until Grieg's death was finally to cut the bond between the two men. Grieg had heard, while he

Leonard Borwick, with 'Most sincere thanks for *uniquely* beautiful music!'
(Photo: W. & D. Downey)

Frederick Delius, remembering a summer morning on Haukelid Fjeld (Photo: Histed)

was still recuperating at the Augeners' home in November 1897, of the effect that his English friend's music was just then having on the Norwegian public – Delius's incidental music to Gunnar Heiberg's play *Folkeraadet* [People's Parliament] at the time being performed almost nightly at the Christiania Theatre. Delius had drawn opprobium upon himself by setting the Norwegian national anthem in a minor key, and the hypersensitive Christiania audiences had in consequence found a convenient and not entirely irrational excuse for riotous behaviour. To insult the anthem, written by the intimate friend of Grieg's youth, Rikard Nordraak – who had died tragically young and so had acquired almost an aura of sanctity in the Norwegian collective consciousness – was seen by many as a heinous act in these times of heightened national feeling. Grieg disapproved. 'I am sorry that Delius has deployed his admirable gifts on this work. I do not know the play, but in view of its content it must, I feel, have been under a misapprehension that he took it on.' He definitely failed to see the point of it all. 'The idea of finding an excuse to play it ['Ja vi elsker'] in a minor key very nearly turns my stomach.'[37] But *Folkeraadet* had at last given the still relatively untried Delius the chance to hear, many times over, how his orchestral music sounded, and a year and a half later he was ready to spend a large part of a recent inheritance in mounting a huge concert of his own works at St James's Hall on 30 May 1899. Two movements of the *Folkeraadet* music were included, among a wide range of other works, both vocal and orchestral. The concert provoked a wide range of reviews, one or other of which may well have come to Grieg's attention. *The Monthly Musical Record*, in its record of the musical year, referred to various individual concerts of note:

> We mention also one given by Mr. F. Delius, in which a Symphonic Poem and Fantasia and other short works of his were produced, also a selection from his opera, *Koanga*. The music, very modern in character, and at times peculiar, attracted a good deal of notice, and although opinions differed considerably, the natural gifts of the composer were generally recognised.[38]

If Grieg came to see only one English review of this concert, it must surely have been this one, yet neither he nor Delius communicated with each other on the subject of a landmark event in Delius's musical life.

The summer months of 1899 were spent as usual at Troldhaugen, from where on 1 August Grieg addressed a brief letter to the English press on the subject of concert pitch, a matter of much debate in the musical world at this time. It was printed in a number of journals.

> Since my first visit to England it has always been my opinion that the high English pitch for pianos [$a' = 452$ Hz] was unpractical. You will, then, understand that I am very glad to hear of the intention to take the decided step of a change. I feel convinced that an international uniformity has more and more been longed for by English musicians, and I congratulate all concerned on the approaching settlement of this important question.[39]

At about the same time, Francesco Berger dispatched a characteristically unfortunately worded letter to Grieg, inviting him once more to appear at a Philharmonic Society concert during the spring season of 1900:

> Dear Sir and honoured Master,
>
>   We shall be glad to know if by next year you will have ready some new orchestral Work, or a second Pianoforte Concerto – and if you are disposed to give to our Society the privilege of first performance of such Work under your own direction?
>
>   Our season commences in March & ends in July.
>
>   If it be a Pianoforte Concerto will you play the Solo Part yourself?
>
>   You will, I am sure, bear in mind, that this Society was the *first* in England to introduce you & your music to the British public, and will favour me by corresponding *direct* and *not* through any agent naming the Honorarium.
>
>   With every assurance of profound regard, I remain, dear Sir,
>
>   faithfully yours
>
>   Francesco Berger
>
>   Hon. Sec.
>
>   To the celebrated Maestro
>
>   Edvard Grieg.[40]

Grieg's reply, as might have been expected, was suitably short and to the point. 'Dear Sir! I thank you for the kind invitation, but for several reasons I shall not be able to visit England next spring. Yours faithfully Edvard Grieg.' He would undoubtedly have been irritated by further pressure to write a second concerto, having long since realized that he could never repeat the success of his first and only effort in the genre; and Berger's rather peremptory approach would once again have irked him. And what would he have made of Berger's extravagant *envoi*, 'To the celebrated Maestro'? Nor was there anything obvious that he could offer as a first performance in England, unless it were the *Haugtussa* cycle, with himself at the piano. No, London remained for the time being out of the picture.

Over the years, Grieg's doings at home in Norway or abroad remained a topic of interest in England's musical journals. His refusal to conduct in Paris as a consequence of the Dreyfus case brought down upon him the wrath of the French press as well as that of a considerable section of the French public, but 'after such contempt of justice he felt unwilling to present himself before a French audience'.[41] *Musical News* explained the situation briefly – and with a note of disapproval – to its readers:

> M. Colonne, the Parisian orchestral conductor, recently invited the popular Norwegian composer, Edward Grieg, to conduct some of his own compositions at a concert at the Châtelet. Grieg replied that his indignation at the Rennes verdict would not permit him to visit a country where justice was so prostituted. The letter was published, and it has not pleased the French. Although artists are, of course, at liberty to accept or refuse engagements offered to them, we do not think that this is the sort of

spirit that musicians and artists should cultivate, for the less music or other arts are mixed up with politics the better.[42]

No less a person than the principal of the Guildhall School of Music and Drama, William H. Cummings, was moved to write a letter to the journal's editor in defence of Grieg:

> In your last number you speak of Grieg's refusal to conduct his own music in Paris. Surely he was warranted in declining, having regard to the outraged sense of justice common to our humanity. Politics had nothing to do with his decision, and the publication of his private letter was a gross breach of etiquette.[43]

All this was noted in London, as was a happier event shortly afterwards, when the new National Theatre in Christiania was inagurated in the presence of Ibsen and Bjørnson, the son of the latter having been appointed as the establishment's first director. 'On the third and last day of the three days' inauguration festival, at which King Oscar assisted, Bjoernson's "Sigurd Jorsalfar", with Grieg's beautiful music, was given, both men receiving a triumphant and memorable ovation.'[44] Also reported in London by the musical papers was what promised to be a further collaboration with Bjørnson. 'Grieg has promised to write an oratorio to a libretto by Björnson, the Norwegian novelist and dramatist. The libretto is in praise of peace.'[45] Björnson's *Peace Oratorio* had in fact been completed as long ago as 1891, when he read the work to Delius, who was at the time on a visit to Aulestad, the poet's home. Grieg had pressed him to write it, promising to set the poem to music, but was later to excuse a lack of inspiration on his own part on the grounds of ill health, and the collaboration was never realized.

The Monthly Musical Record signalled the end of 1899 with reviews of the latest album of *Lyric Pieces* (the ninth) and of the early *Humoresques* as arranged for violin and piano by Hans Sitt. It was felt that the 'Humoresken' had been admirably arranged: 'No. 4, in its new dress, is perhaps even more effective than in its original form.'[46]

Once again, the Griegs spent the winter in Copenhagen. Here the composer gave a number of concerts, the first of which comprised the three violin sonatas, in which he was accompanied by Lady Hallé. *The Monthly Musical Record* also manifested an interest in his activities in that city:

> Copenhagen. – Edvard Grieg gave a concert to an audience of small traders and workmen, which the great composer addressed somewhat as follows: 'This evening is a realization of a dream of my youth; for I have always held that art should, as in ancient Greece, extend to all classes of society, just because it is its mission to bring a message from heart to heart. I wish that workmen's concerts like this, which endeavour to fill this object, might prosper and find followers in all countries of the world.'[47]

Soon after the beginning of January 1900 Grieg was approached by Brækstad, who, almost exactly five months after Berger's enquiry, surprisingly returned to the subject of a second concerto and a concert at the Philharmonic during the coming season. Brækstad had made another trip to Christiania in the autumn and on arriving back in London had told his musical and literary friends of the busy artistic life of the Norwegian capital. The first thing he had been asked on his return to England, however, just as soon as he mentioned Grieg by name, was (as he told the composer) 'Well, how is Grieg?', 'When is he coming to England?', 'Has he any new work ready?', and other such questions. Unfortunately, he seemed somehow to have understood from Grieg when they had met in Christiania that another concerto was ready and that it would probably be premiered in Leipzig in the spring. One of his friends who was particularly close to the Philharmonic Society had passed this news on, with the result that Brækstad had been asked if this were indeed true and whether Grieg would like to come over to London in 1900 at a time to suit him and conduct the work at one of the Society's concerts. The composer would be paid £100 and was at liberty to nominate a soloist of his choice.

> Now, it seems to me that this is not a bad offer from the Philharmonic, and there's also a matter on which I lay much weight, and that is (according to what I know from my own experience) that there is a *general wish* among the music-loving public here to see you over here again! – Without the least attempt to want to flatter you, I can honestly tell you that you are now the *best-loved* and *most popular* composer over here! I won't speak of the 'Peer Gynt' suite; – it is played continually at all the larger orchestral concerts and always gets a marvellous reception, and it seems that the public never wearies of it, and anyway your name and works have now become to all intents a '*Household word*' over here among the large section of the public who now take a genuine interest in and love music. – Enough, I won't say another word except what I know is in fact the case! And all these people so much want *to see you over here and among them again!*
>
> And finally I want to say that you will also be doing a great service to our dear fatherland if you come over. The fact is, dear Hr. Grieg, that little Norway must always try to uphold the 'prestige' it has earned over here in art and literature for as long as we have representative men who are willing to do so.[48]

Apart from exerting this particular pressure on Grieg, apparently quite unaware of the outright refusal earlier extended by the composer to Berger, Brækstad pressed his friend to undertake a further tour in conjunction with the proposed Philharmonic Concert – to Edinburgh, Glasgow, Liverpool, Manchester, Birmingham, Newcastle, and even to other cities too. Brækstad himself would undertake the arrangements together with Vert, who would probably offer Grieg £500 for a 'short' tour of this nature. Brækstad was already acquainted with Vert and was aware that he had been Grieg's agent for the last tour. But should Grieg prefer not to deal with Vert, he added, he knew another agent who would be more than willing to take the risk upon himself. Despite Brækstad's urgings, his request to Grieg to revisit England that year fell on deaf ears, just as a further request was to do in June.

'I was asked to conduct 2 concerts in London in July', Grieg told Max Abraham. 'It was very tempting, as the terms were excellent. My health however said a definite no.'[49]

Yet another proposal came from Arthur Chappell at the end of June:

> I have got 7 Concerts to give before Christmas this Season & I should be *very pleased* if you could accept an engagement to play at two or three of them. The terms I could offer you would be £100– pr each Concert & I trust you will be able to accept the engagements.
>
> Hoping you are quite well & with very kindest to Madame Grieg & yourself.[50]

Chappell enclosed a list of dates for the Saturday Popular Concerts for the 1900–1901 season, but again to no result.

An item in the July edition of *The Monthly Musical Record* caused Grieg to put pen to paper in corrective mode. The journal had heard from a Christiania source that 'It is said, and much to the dismay of native musicians, that the National Hymn of Norway, words by B. Björnson, music hitherto supposed to be due to Richard Nordraak, is a "Largo Cantabile" by Joseph Haydn!' This was too much for Grieg who, ever faithful to the memory of the friend of his youth, immediately wrote to the editor:

> I earnestly request you to correct a notice in the last number of THE MONTHLY MUSICAL RECORD to the effect that the music of Rikard Nordråk to the Norwegian National Hymn is taken from a Haydn Quartet.
>
> No one ought to perceive plagiarism in a slight melodic resemblance which, in comparison with the very many points of contact of the great masters, is not worthy of consideration. Then again, the writer out of a few notes of quite different rhythm has made a whole piece of music.
>
> Such an insinuation, as groundless as it is injurious to the posthumous fame of the composer and to his country, ought not to be tolerated. I therefore hope that you will publish the above *démenti* in your esteemed paper.

An editorial note followed: 'The statement referred to was printed as a mere report, but we are glad that the eminent Norwegian musician who signed the above should thus speedily put an end to a fabulous and false report.'[51]

Late in July Julius Röntgen joined Grieg at Troldhaugen, and together they left for a five-day tour in the mountains. While they were away, Nina wrote to Anna Brodsky – not in Manchester at the time but taking a cure in Germany – and reminisced rather touchingly about their late friend Tchaikovsky and his homosexuality:

> Yes, indeed, I've heard a great deal of ill about Tschaikowsky, but prefer not to speak about it, it may be that you can guess what I was thinking of. . . . Unfortunately I knew him so little, but loved him and admired him beyond measure. *If* Nature took the wrong paths with him, who are we that we should judge him? We cannot measure the depths of the great geniuses. For me he will always remain as he was, the great, glori-

ous artist, the quiet, warm friend. What he had to do battle with as a human being, that is *his own* concern, and we have no right to interfere, at all events he himself suffered most from it.[52]

George Augener was another who had taken a cure in Germany. Having just returned from Wiesbaden, he wrote from home to commiserate with Grieg on the composer's recent bout of rheumatism. He too was suffering from the same complaint, which had been the reason for his three weeks' stay in the German resort, but the cure had unfortunately left him no better than before. The family had been hoping to see the Griegs in London again soon, but acknowledged that the composer's return to full health took precedence over other matters.[53]

It is a remarkable fact that during the second half of the nineteenth century a number of pioneering British alpinists made the first ascents of many of Norway's till then unconquered peaks. Many a mountain traverse still carries the name of an English climber, and one man is remembered above all others – William Cecil Slingsby (1849–1929), unquestionably the foremost mountaineering pioneer in Norway. One of his major feats was to have been the first, in 1876, to climb Norway's highest peak of really Alpine quality, the Store Skagastølstind in the western Jotunheim, and he made the ascent of most of the high peaks of southern and western Norway during the 1870s. Thirty years on and well into his fifties, he was still climbing, for there were ever more challenges in the Arctic north. The best known of all the early sportsmen-mountaineers in Norway, Slingsby remains just one of the many Englishmen who stole most of the records before the Norwegians themselves got round to thinking of the matter.

Slingsby greatly admired Grieg's music, but there was no contact until a chance meeting in the mountains in the summer of 1900. It prompted a letter from Slingsby:

> I venture to send to you by this post some re-print copies of papers which I have written on Norway, as you were good enough to express an interest in one which Fröken Bertheau showed to you at Turtegrö.
>
> They are however very light, & wholly unworthy of so great a subject as your glorious old mountains, which I love most sincerely & with an affection which deepens with each successive visit.
>
> Please pardon me for saying that, when I hear or play your music, familiar scenes in your grand old north land are often recalled to my mind, & thus I enjoy a two-fold pleasure. I picture the stern & wild fjeld, the pure snowfields, the pine woods, the fjord, the fos, & the gentle beauties of nature, & I feel very grateful to the composer who has so beautifully & faithfully represented by music his country's especial charms.
>
> Pray excuse me for saying this.
>
> My eldest girl, Katharine, who has been already twice in Norway, hearing that I am writing to you has just said in her impetuous school girl manner 'Do ask Herr Grieg to give me his autograph' & as the Child has a happy way of getting what she wants from her father, I said, I would do so –

> I am writing a book on mountaineering in Norway, but find that it is a much more formidable task than that of climbing the mountains themselves.[54]

Slingsby and Therese Bertheau, Norway's leading lady mountaineer, had met Grieg and Röntgen, who were on their own brief tour, a month earlier at Turtagrø. Slingsby refers to the encounter in his book, an instant and enduring classic, published in Edinburgh in 1904 under the title *Norway: The Northern Playground*:

> Soon after our return [to Turtagrø], I had the great pleasure and honour of a visit from Herr Edvard Grieg, who was staying at the other inn, and I feel sure that much of the delightful music with which he has charmed the civilised world has been inspired by the weird grandeur of the mountains and fjords of his native land, for which he has the most intense love and admiration.

In sending Grieg an inscribed copy of his book, the author referred Grieg to this and to another page in which he paid tribute to the composer: 'No one can possibly love the mountains more than Herr Edvard Grieg, who, fortunately for music lovers all over the world, derives such happy inspirations when wandering over his native mountains, nor can there be found any one the world over who enjoys wild nature more than his friend Franz Beyer.'[55]

The Griegs moved to Voksenkollen Sanatorium, high above Christiania, from October to the beginning of January. It was a well-appointed establishment, and the air did Grieg good. Brækstad was in town early in October, but somehow missed seeing his friend. He had brought with him from London yet another offer of engagements in England that he had hoped to discuss with the composer, but instead found himself having to leave a hurried note with Johan Halvorsen's wife just before he left. She would, he told Grieg, convey the information to him. Whatever was on offer would be worth between £700 and £800 to the composer.[56] This must surely have been a matter of another proposal from Vert – but nothing was decided just then.

Grieg's music continued to be played often in London, of course, and one of the Saturday Popular Concerts at St James's Hall on 1 December is worthy of note, in that Olga Wood (wife of the conductor) made her first appearance in this particular concert series and included Grieg in her programme of songs. She was accompanied by Leonard Borwick. Lady Hallé was also on the platform, leading a performance of the Brahms Sextet in G major.[57] Grieg would have felt very much at home among this particular group of artist friends. Henry Wood himself had conducted, back in May, a concert that had included the *Peer Gynt Suite* in the presence of that devoted admirer of Grieg's music, the Princess of Wales. On 30 October Martin Knutzen had played the Piano Concerto in London with considerable success, and his interpretation of some of Grieg's smaller works at a recital a week later had also won high critical praise. As an interesting contrast, a young pianist, Violet Gordon Woodhouse, had also featured in a St James's Hall recital that had taken place between the two Knutzen concerts. Her solos were Grieg's Sonata in E minor

To Edward Grieg,
a devoted lover of the mountains
of his native Country from which he
has so often derived musical
Inspiration as well as health
& strength, {see pages 13 & 215}
from his sincere friend
& admirer,
Christmas,
—1903— Wm Cecil Slingsby—

NORWAY: THE NORTHERN PLAYGROUND

Inscription by Cecil Slingsby to Grieg

and Schumann's *Papillons*, and they received crushing criticism from *The Musical Standard*, having been played, it considered, with 'eccentric mediocrity'. The paper concluded devastatingly, 'As an amateur she might pass muster with those who do not demand too much.'[58] Fortunately for her later reputation, Gordon Woodhouse found her true métier as a harpsichordist, and she was to become acknowledged as the finest of her generation in England. Many years later Frederick Delius even wrote a *Dance for Harpsichord* for her.

Whatever Grieg may have taken or learnt from England and the English, one thing may surely be said to have been lacking – musical inspiration – with perhaps just one or two curious exceptions. On 17 December 1900, as he turned the pages of the liberal daily *Verdens Gang*, he came upon a first Norwegian translation of an English poem. It had been made by the author and journalist Peter Rosenkrantz Johnsen, and it was of Rudyard Kipling's 'Gentlemen-Rankers'. Much taken with the piece, he immediately wrote to Rosenkrantz Johnsen. The translator's work must have been excellent, he thought, as he felt it appeared to express Kipling's feelings perfectly. He asked if Rosenkrantz Johnsen could send him a copy of the original and asked too if he had translated any more poems from Kipling's cycle (*Barrack Room Ballads*), having understood that the English poet had written a whole series. At all events, he intended to compose a setting of 'Gentlemen-Rankers' right away, and just a day later he wrote to the editor of *Verdens Gang* with the news that he had already set the piece to music. 'I admire and love the deep humanity and the hate of war that lies behind it, not to speak of the hate of chauvinism. And with this he is able to win his countrymen's hearts! That means something!'[59]

Rosenkrantz Johnsen replied immediately. He was delighted that Grieg had been inspired by Kipling's poem and sent translations of several more – with the exception of that of 'Tommy Atkins', of which he happened not to have a copy to hand. He was particularly proud, he wrote, of his version of 'Mandalay'. In the meantime, he hoped that Grieg would send him a copy of his manuscript: 'Kipling will certainly be glad to hear that Europe's most celebrated composer has set to music one of his songs.' He also sent Grieg a copy of *Barrack Room Ballads*, from which his translated poems had been taken; and he promised to mail his version of 'Tommy Atkins' shortly afterwards.[60] 'Gentlemen-Rankers' might well have been published in Grieg's lifetime, rather than waiting until 1989 to be published in the collected edition of his works, had not the composer promptly discovered that Rosenkrantz Johnsen had omitted part of the original in his translation. A few days later he wrote to Frants Beyer:

> Some days ago I saw in 'Verdens Gang' a poem by Rudyard Kipling which was of such a singular hue that I had to find music for it. Since then I've now got hold of the original poem and discover to my sorrow that Rosenkrantz Johnsen has only trans-lated a part of each verse. It is shameful to treat a poet in such a way, and I don't want to become known for letting my music be associated with such vandalism.[61]

Some six months later Rosenkrantz Johnsen was to send Grieg a poem of his own that he thought Grieg might like to set. At the same time he was eager to hear about his 'Kipling-translation'. But 'Gentlemen-Rankers' had evidently been consigned to a drawer at Troldhaugen, and the correspondence lapsed.

Even more oddly, a little earlier in 1900 Grieg had – for the only time – set a poem in English. It was by a Danish poet, Otto Benzon, and was entitled 'To a Devil'. Grieg had met Benzon, a pharmacist by profession, in Denmark quite re-cently, and had been much attracted by some of his poems – so much so that he set ten of them in this same year as his Op. 69 and Op. 70. By late June Grieg had com-pleted these Danish settings and sent the manuscripts of each group of five songs to Hinrichsen in Leipzig: 'The author of the texts, Otto Benzon, is also a great expert in the English language and has written some fine English poems. I will write to him today and ask him if he wishes to translate his poems into English himself.'[62] As with 'Gentlemen-Rankers' – a setting of a Norwegian version of an (abridged) English poem – 'To a Devil', set to a poem written in English by a Dane, was not published in Grieg's lifetime, but was ultimately to appear in the same volume of the Grieg Collected Edition in 1989. Benestad and Schjelderup-Ebbe felt that 'To a Devil' had 'succeeded in capturing the flavour of British folk songs in a merry, rousing melody with fresh and original chord progressions.'[63]

The end of the year was clouded by the passing of Max Abraham.[64] (Another, albeit slimmer, connection with the Leipzig of earlier days had come to an end on 22 November with the death of Arthur Sullivan.) Abraham and Grieg had coinci-dentally exchanged their last letters to each other on 5 December, just three days before Abraham died. Publisher, friend, and benefactor, Max Abraham had also been a father-figure to the composer, and Grieg felt his loss bitterly. Both business and personal correspondence had for some time frequently been undertaken with Henri Hinrichsen, Abraham's nephew, and Hinrichsen was to take the same generous and paternal interest in Grieg as his uncle had done before him. His generosity would furthermore extend to Nina Grieg for many a year after the death of her husband.

⊰ 18 ⊱

'MY HEALTH SAYS NO, AND THAT MUST, AFTER ALL, TAKE PRECEDENCE'

GRIEG'S notebooks for the years 1900–1901 give us a modest idea of what his main preoccupations were so far as England was concerned. There are addresses for Wolff, Vert, Berger, and Robert Newman – the latter, besides being available at Queen's Hall, could also be reached by cable at 'Chord, London'. And a brief pro-forma letter is transferred bodily from the 1900 notebook to its successors in both 1901 and 1902: 'Dear Sir! Will you kindly send me the the photos of me and my wife and where we are together, one dozen each. Yours faithfully E.G. Elliott and Fry, 56, Baker Street'. Grieg is doubtless referring to photographs presumably taken in 1897, when he and Nina stopped off first at Baker Street on their journey to Windsor Castle. Then there are odd jottings relating to a projected 1901 tour – quite probably a consequence of Bræstad's approach the previous October. For London there was to be the Cello Sonata, among other works, and Grieg made notes of works that might be performed in both London and the provinces. Under the headings 'London I' and 'London II', alternative programmes were outlined, and for the Philharmonic Society (of which Eaton Faning had recently been elected a director) he listed four possibilities: *Bergliot*, (the first) *Peer Gynt Suite*, songs with orchestra, and *In Autumn*.

Ill health and the indecision that it entailed were to remain determining factors in Grieg's life during his later years. In January 1901 he and Nina left Voksenkollen for the familiar environs of Copenhagen, where, Grieg told Frants Beyer on 21 January, they were thoroughly enjoying their stay. So much so that Grieg had finally drafted 'a letter to England' specifically to decline the invitation to come over in May for a series of ten concerts – drafted, but not yet sent. May, after all, was a month when the worst of the fog and pollution of England's conurbations would have lifted and so would constitute almost the ideal time of year for him to pay a return visit – in stark contrast to the last time, when the autumn of 1897 and its inclement weather had felled him with an attack of acute bronchitis. 'Quiet work' would suit him best in May, but at the same time he felt that there was 'such a thing as duty to others, so I'd better consider well before sending my refusal'. There was also a rumour already circulating about Copenhagen that Queen Victoria had died on that very morning of 21 January. Should this be true, Grieg reasoned, a trip to England in the spring, if arranged, would quite likely have to be cancelled, presumably on account of the period of mourning.[1] A January event that would certainly not have come to Grieg's notice in Copenhagen was a concert conducted by Edward Elgar in Worcester that included Grieg's *Land-sighting*.

By the end of the month a decision had been made. Urged on by Johannes Wolff, Grieg *would* come to England in May, with Vert acting as his agent for a series of chamber-music concerts. Grieg remembered Berger's earlier request to be informed of any further intended visit to London, and wrote to offer the Philharmonic Society his services once again. He would like to conduct, he told Berger, one of two works that had not yet been given in London – either *In Autumn* or *Bergliot*. Beyond these, he would be happy to conduct either the *Peer Gynt Suite* no. 1, his *Two Elegiac Melodies*, or some songs with orchestra. His fee would be £100 (in other words the sum he had been offered little more than three years earlier).[2]

Before Berger could reply, there arrived from out of the blue yet another tempting offer from London. It was from Robert Newman, lessee and manager of Queen's Hall, who had perhaps already learned of Grieg's proposed tour:

> I should be very pleased if you would conduct one of the Concerts at the London Musical Festival this year. I therefore telegraphed you today asking if you could conduct either on April 29 or May 1. In the event of your being able to accept, Signor Busoni would be the Solo Pianist and the programme would be composed principally of your own compositions & there would be two orchestral rehearsals.
>
> I do not know if you would prefer also to give some recitals in London, if so, may I ask you to kindly let me know what your conditions & terms may be. Perhaps you would like to play a Concerto under the conductorship of Mr Henry J Wood.[3]

All this must have been extraordinarily tempting for Grieg, who could now see that within the space of little more than a month the Vert tour, combined with the Philharmonic and Newman's London Musical Festival, would bring in around £1,000. Letters flew between London and Copenhagen. To Berger's suggestion that he conduct for the Philharmonic his Piano Concerto with Teresa Carreño as soloist, Grieg replied that he had nothing against the idea, but pointed out that he would probably be directing the work with Busoni as soloist on 1 May. Grieg's own view was that it would be of considerable interest both to the public and himself to compare two such eminent soloists in the one work and within such a short space of time. Berger's request for a new orchestral work he was unable to fulfil, but on the other hand he had a number of compositions for string orchestra that would be suitable, provided that the orchestra was sufficiently large. He still hoped that *Bergliot* could be performed, reminding Berger that it required a dramatic actress and not a singer and declaring it to be one of his best works.[4] On top of all this came the offer of an Honorary Fellowship of Trinity College of Music, which Grieg accepted, to the delight of the College Board.[5]

As ever, the Philharmonic Society's conditions caused problems, as did Berger's peremptory tone. 'Bergliot', he declared in a draft letter to Grieg, 'has been repeatedly performed in London & never become a success. So that it is out of the question now.' He continued:

> In your first letter you speak of coming to England to give Chamber music concerts – this cannot mean with orchestra, & we were therefore under the impression that you would *not* conduct an orchestra anywhere in London except at our Society. Now you speak of possibly conducting your Concerto with Busoni at Mr. Newman's.
>
> Mr. Newman's Festival is purely a business speculation, ours is a Society of Artists with no view to profit; and I think you will agree that if we conclude an engagement with you to conduct your Concerto and one other orchestral Work, you will promise not to appear as Conductor at any other Concert in London except for the Concerto.
>
> Please let me have your acceptance of this condition and we can afterwards determine whether the orch. Work shall be Peer Gynt or the Works for Strings you mention.
>
> It will be a great pleasure to see you again . . .[6]

Meanwhile, bronchitis returned, and Grieg, fearful as ever as to how it might develop, came reluctantly to the conclusion that his two forthcoming tours (one of which was to have been to Holland) would probably have to be cancelled. With Queen Victoria's death confirmed, it had seemed to him unlikely that the England tour could come off anyway, and he confessed to Beyer that in fact he was glad this was so. Nonetheless there were regrets:

> The worst thing is that I have accepted invitations to conduct two big concerts in London, which I intended to tie in with the engagement agreed with Vert (the same who arranged everything 3 years ago). Heaven knows what the outcome of it all will be. To conduct a big festival concert with my own works (100-strong orchestra and Busoni as soloist) is something I'd dearly love to do . . .[7]

Indeed, in an earlier letter (of 8 February) to Francesco Berger, Grieg had carefully not mentioned anything about his current state of health, even though he already needed to keep to his hotel room in Copenhagen and not venture out – an indication, perhaps, that he still half hoped that London in May might be a possibility. Without news from the composer, Berger drafted a letter on 22 February:

> Not having been favoured with your reply I conclude you are not willing to accept the cond[ition]s I named in my last letter.
>
> I have now to inform you that the Directors consider your appearance as conductor anywhere else than at the Phil. to be a step which will materially weaken your powers of attraction & they are not disposed to give a higher honorarium than £50 if you do so.

They still offer you the £100 for your exclusive appear[ance] as Conductor of two Works.[8]

Grieg now found himself in a position to treat this offer with the contempt it de-served. He immediately replied with a curt note, regretting that he could not ac-cept Berger's conditions. He had been ill and this was the reason for his delay in replying.[9] In fact, as he explained to Olav Thommessen, to the bronchitis had been added rheumatism and varicose veins:

> In addition to the old afflictions, there have come new ones that completely remove from me both my spirits and my working powers. I'll probably have to give up my intended concert here. The engagements in England in the spring likewise. In other words: the slack season. So forgive me if I am depressed.[10]

By 11 March Grieg was resigned to the wholesale changes that now had to apply to the immediate future. He had stayed indoors for a fortnight and had postponed once again the concert he was scheduled to give in Copenhagen. London, however, still expected him, as is clear from a mid-March entry in *The Musical Standard*:

> Mr. Robert Newman's London Musical Festival next May should prove a singularly interesting affair. The Queen's Hall band will do duty throughout the festival. Ar-rangements are in course of settlement to bring over several eminent conductors. Herr Gustav Mahler, the conductor of the Vienna opera, will, it is hoped, be one, and Herr Weingartner another. If his engagements permit Dr. Edvard Grieg will conduct one concert, and I would suggest that Signor Busoni should then play the Norwegian composer's pianoforte concerto.[11]

Henry Wood was to be the principal conductor at the festival, and it is perhaps worth recalling the impact made by Wood and the Queen's Hall since the build-ing's opening in the mid-nineties — whatever the early criticisms of its acoustics. Orchestral music had at last begun to ease out the oratorio (indeed the 1901 festival attracted criticism precisely because of its lack of choral works), and the Queen's Hall Promenade Concerts had by now come to enjoy enormous popularity. Strauss and Elgar were very much in vogue and drew huge crowds when they conducted their own works in London. Since 1888, when Grieg had first appeared in the capi-tal, London's concert life had been changing with astonishing speed, and since the mid 1890s it was Wood who had very largely been the engine behind the change.

Grieg was to have a further regret regarding his aborted England trip — it ap-peared he would miss meeting Edward MacDowell, who was proposing to come over from America to London and evidently hoped to meet Grieg there. 'I would indeed have enjoyed seeing you in London this spring. But alas! My health does not allow me to undertake such a voyage', Grieg replied.[12] MacDowell was a great admirer of Grieg's music, who dedicated two of his piano sonatas to the Nor-wegian, and Grieg found much to admire in MacDowell. They furthermore had a shared Scottish inheritance: MacDowell's great-grandfather, like Grieg's, was a Scotsman, and it had been his son who had originally emigrated to the United

States. As with Grieg, critics found pointers to his ancestry in the American composer's music. He certainly came to London in 1903, playing his D-minor Piano Concerto at a Philharmonic Society Concert on 14 May that year.

Grieg's forthcoming non-appearance, as it were, was signalled in the press later in March. 'The report that Dr. Grieg will conduct one of his orchestral works at the last Philharmonic Concert is not correct. The composer, however, contemplates paying us a visit in the spring of next year.'[13] Meanwhile, two new sets of songs, Op. 69 and Op. 70, had been published by Peters and had been accorded a somewhat opaque review in *The Monthly Musical Record*:

> We have here two sets of songs by the gifted Norwegian composer which will require much patient study both on the part of singer and accompanist before they can be understood and enjoyed. Grieg indulges in peculiar rhythms and modulations, and until these have become familiar, the meaning of the music might easily be distorted; the phrases require careful study so as to give to each note and chord its proper tone and accent. Their strange effects would at first attract attention, making it almost impossible to feel their relative importance in the phrase or sentence. Then in some cases the very look of the music with its mixture of sharps and flats, and occasionally of rhythms, is certainly bewildering to the eye, while much sounds novel to the ear. With a new composer, one might doubt whether it were worth the time and trouble to familiarize eye and ear with unaccustomed sights and sounds. With Grieg, however, we feel sure that the peculiarities are not there for their own sake, that they are not mere affectations, but the natural way to him of expressing his thoughts and feelings. Patience, therefore, in studying them will be well rewarded. They are remarkable songs; their harmonic interest alone will prove an intellectual delight to musicians.[14]

In March Grieg's String Quartet was given by the Ysaÿe Quartet at one of the Monday Popular Concerts. *Musical News* welcomed the work, 'which it was good to hear again after a somewhat lengthy pause. It was delightfully interpreted'.[15]

Grieg had sufficiently recovered from his ills to be able to play in Copenhagen on 24 March, with Nina singing some of his songs, but his varicose veins continued to trouble him, and for the time being, as Nina told Anna Brodsky, he needed to wear elastic stockings.[16] A month later there was a further concert. Before this, though, Henri Hinrichsen had written to ask if the composer had completed any new works. Grieg summed up the position for him:

> How I would have loved to send you some manuscripts! But I have been ill for more or less the whole of the winter, have had to cancel all my concert invitations for Holland and England, so you will understand that I'm not joking. Of course I'm working on various things. But nothing is ready, unfortunately. However, I hope that it will as usual be possible for me to send you something during the course of the summer.[17]

The Griegs returned in May to Troldhaugen, where they were to remain for the rest of the year, apart from a short stay in Bergen itself. One responsibility that was confided to him by his native town must have given him much pleasure:

At Bergen (Norway) a statue to Ole Bull, the famous violinist, has recently been unveiled. A chorus was sung on the occasion by a choir of 300 voices, Edvard Grieg being composer and conductor. The sculptor was Stephen [*sic*] Sinding, brother to the musician of that name.[18]

In 1885 Hans Lien Brækstad had produced a 15-page illustrated pamphlet intended to promote this monument. Entitled *Ole Bull: Biografisk skitse; Sælges til indtægt for Ole-Bull Monumentet i Bergen*, it was printed in London but published in Bergen.[19] A later list of sponsors of the fund for the statue includes the names of Grieg, his brother John and Johan Svendsen, and both Griegs are shown as members of the fund's executive committee. Christian Sinding's sculptor younger brother Stephan was finally given the commission.

The summer of 1901 was to produce the tenth and final album of *Lyric Pieces*. When Henri Hinrichsen sent proofs in September, Grieg found the English titles of some of the pieces to 'sound much too much as coming straight from the dictionary', recommending that a native English-speaker correct the translation.[20] Another publication of some interest in 1901 was of an album of 20 songs, issued by the London firm of Enoch & Sons of 58 Great Marlborough Street. The 'Publisher's Note', dated London, October 1901, explained why new translations were in order:

Although the songs by the distinguished Norwegian composer, Dr. Edvard Grieg, are fairly well known to musicians in Great and Greater Britain, hitherto only two or three of them have attained general recognition. The reason is not far to seek. Composed as these songs were to poems in the Norwegian language, they are, in their original form, unavailable for the large majority of vocalists, and it seemed to the Publishers that, hitherto, the difficulties of adaptation had hardly been successfully overcome. They therefore decided to publish the songs with a new English version, which has been written by R. H. Elkin, whose reputation for this special class of work is well known.

It has been the aim of the Adapter to adhere as closely as possible to the Norwegian text, and where that was found impracticable, to faithfully reproduce the spirit of the original. Due consideration has been paid to any musical effect allied to some particular idea in the text, and the technique of vocalism has received special attention.

It is the belief of the Publishers that many of the songs in this volume will now attain wide popularity.

Allowing for a degree of hyperbole ('only two or three' of Grieg's songs having so far 'attained general recognition' in England?), Enoch & Sons had put their finger on what was long to remain a major problem with the varying English versions of Grieg's songs. Translations were and continued to be of dubious quality, and perhaps only with the publication of the Collected Edition of Grieg's works towards the end of the twentieth century has this problem approached a resolution. Elkin himself was an industrious translator, later to number among his operatic work versions of *Madame Butterfly*, *The Girl of the Golden West*, and d'Albert's *Tiefland*.

Piquantly, Augener were to publish in 1917 his translations of *Old Dutch Nursery Rhymes*, 'the original tunes harmonized by J. Röntgen'.

It is perhaps worth noting two significant performances of the Piano Concerto in London in 1901. It was the main attraction of a June Philharmonic Concert, when Teresa Carreño was the soloist, and at a Promenade Concert in September it was played by Wilhelm Backhaus. Carreño's performance was much praised. 'It was a remarkable performance, triumphant in the fine tone brought out and the perfect technique exhibited, and in the intellectual grasp of this romantic and original composition.'[21] In October, Berger returned with yet another offer for Grieg to appear at the Philharmonic. He remained optimistic in his hopes for a further concerto, on the subject of which he evidently remained badly misinformed:

> Dear Sir and honoured Master!
>
> Is there any chance of your completing your new Pianoforte Concerto by next Summer, and are you disposed to conduct its first performance in England at a Philharmonic Concert next *June*?
>
> If so we shall hope to be able to arrange it.
>
> May I request the favour of your reply?[22]

Grieg's reply, on a postcard, was succinct. 'I thank you very much for your kind invitation, but I am sorry, I cannot accept it for this season.'[23] His thoughts were elsewhere in any case — earlier in the month his brother John had committed suicide, and Edvard told his friends that he could for the time being think of nothing else. His main task was to console his sister-in-law Marie. If he had intended to spend the winter as usual in Copenhagen, this was now out of the question, as he and Nina needed to give all possible support to Marie and her children for the rest of the year.

After spending the first month of 1902 in Bergen itself, the Griegs moved to Copenhagen in February, taking up residence in one of their favourite hotels, the Phønix. They might shortly have been able to read a favourable review of the tenth volume of *Lyric Pieces* in the pages of the same month's *Monthly Musical Record*. In the middle of the month Grieg received an extraordinary request from the *Record*'s publisher. The date of the coronation of Edward VII had been set for June 1902, and Augener proposed that Grieg should write a coronation march to mark the event. A republican at heart, even though he knew and liked the royal couple, Grieg aired his misgivings in his reply to George Augener:

> I am very happy and grateful to you for thinking of me in connection with the composition of a coronation march. But my view is that I am not the right man for such a task. I have, indeed, written a 'Homage March' for *Sigurd Jorsalfar*. That was in respect of a poetical composition that had inspired me. But to work up any enthusiasm in respect of the coronation festivities for a living royal couple — and a foreign one at that — would, to be frank, be impossible for me. The minimum of energy that my declining health has not yet sapped I would rather use on tasks that are more appealing to me.

However, the English royal couple have treated me so kindly and made such a winning impression that it would hardly have been possible for me to refuse the request had it come from the highest level. But as it comes from you it is a different matter. Our friendly relationship through many years does, I hope, permit me openly to express my views, which lordly folk might have regarded as incomprehensible and insulting.

And one more thing: What would English people – and above all English musicians – say about using a foreigner on a ceremonial occasion such as this? All in all I think that after more careful consideration it would be more appropriate to drop the idea of my involvement in the festivities.

In the hope that you will not take offence at my freely expressed remarks . . .[24]

Did Grieg perhaps recall to himself the time Delius had parodied the Norwegian national anthem in Christiania in 1897? The English composer had drawn upon himself the wrath of a large section of the Norwegian public as a foreigner meddling in purely national concerns. The comparison is of course not a precise one, but parallels might justifiably be drawn. At all events, Augener accepted Grieg's refusal gracefully but then, undaunted, asked Saint-Saëns to step into the gap. This the French composer actually did, producing his *Coronation March*, Op. 117, which was 'performed with great success at Westminster Abbey on Coronation Day' – as *The Monthly Musical Record* was anxious to point out in advertising the work's subsequent publication.[25] A few years later, Norway was to hope for a celebratory work from Grieg's pen for the coronation of Haakon VII. 'I had to smile at your fear that I might perhaps write a coronation cantata', he wrote to a friend then:

No and again no, I would never do anything like that, and I rejected out of hand the request that I do so on this occasion. A few years ago I was offered a commission from England to write a coronation march for the English king, something that I also declined unconditionally.[26]

Early in 1902 Grieg received a new offer from England. It came from the director of the Bristol Musical Festival, George Riseley, who was the conductor of his own chorus, the Riseley Male Voice Choir. Riseley, an organist by training, was an influential figure in the music-making of the west of England and in 1893 had been appointed a professor at the Royal Academy of Music.[27] He was accorded a profile and a portrait in *The Musical Standard*'s issue of 25 Feb. 1899. Riseley had directed the Bristol Festival since 1896 and now wrote to Grieg inviting him to its next incarnation in the autumn of 1902. The hope was that Grieg should conduct works of his own at each of three concerts, but Grieg replied that he would be willing to accept Riseley's invitation only if he could conduct just one work in each of two concerts; to include further works or to have to conduct twice on the same day would be too tiring for him. He pointed out that his fee for each concert when he was last in England had been £100 and that he could not appear at two concerts in Bristol for less than this sum.[28] Riseley agreed to Grieg's terms, and Grieg presently suggested the *Scenes from Olav Trygvason* and *Before a Southern Convent*, each of which required large forces, including a chorus. He appeared by then to be content to conduct both works in one and the same concert and expressed himself willing to conduct orchestral works if required at the second. The overall fee of £100 had been agreed. 'I am looking forward with great pleasure', he wrote, 'to visit Bristol at the Festival October 8–11.'[29] The festival programme, as so often, continued to evolve, and a month or so later *The Musical Standard* announced that 'Mrs. Brown Potter has been engaged to recite in Mendelssohn's "Antigone" and Grieg's "Bergliot" at the Bristol Festival.'[30] Cora Brown Potter was an American 'Actress and Elocutionist' (as Grieg noted in his pocket-book) who had for some time been moderately successful on the London stage.

April saw a visit to Warsaw, where Grieg conducted a performance of his Piano Concerto with Carreño as soloist. Such was his ovation there, he felt able to compare it only with the one he had received on the occasion of his first concert in England in 1888. The Warsaw audience had gone one step further, however, continuing to applaud outside the concert hall. He was proud that he had paced himself carefully on this particular trip and that in consequence his health had held up well.

Back in England, Brækstad learned from the pages of *Verdens Gang* that Grieg was to conduct in Bristol:

> Is this really so? In that case I hope that you will give 2–3 concerts in London. – Mr. Vert would like to secure you. – As you will remember, you had an offer from him

George Riseley

through me a year or two ago. – Shall I get him to take this up again and specify it more closely? I hope you are coming to England in any case. I have masses of inquiries: 'When is Grieg coming to England?' –[31]

Later in May, however, home for the summer at Troldhaugen, Grieg had to report that his health had once more taken a turn for the worse. Things did not look good for Bristol in the autumn. 'October and my bronchitis don't go well together'. All in all, he told Brækstad, it was doubtful whether this proposed further trip to England would come off. He had regretted having to cancel his participation in the London Musical Festival, but if he were to receive an invitation to next year's festival, he would certainly take it up, having absorbed the lessons of his Warsaw visit.[32]

More letters from English admirers arrived at Troldhaugen during the summer. Among them was one from Stepán Esipoff, whose works were published by Augener and who enclosed a piano piece he had inscribed to Grieg – 'accept it, I pray you, from a young composer who greatly reveres & loves your beautiful compositions'.[33] Grieg duly drafted a brief reply complimenting the writer on his music and sending him warm wishes for his artistic success. Things were not, however, quite what they seemed, 'Esipoff' being one of the pen-names of an Englishman, Arthur Bransby Burnand – at 42 years of age no longer exactly a 'young' composer. Burnand had studied with Clara Schumann and at the Leipzig Conservatory, and in the course of his relatively short life (1859–1907) he composed over two hundred piano pieces and songs (also using the pseudonym 'Anton Strelezki') and was also known as a writer on music; Esipoff's piano arrangement of Tchaikovsky's *Nutcracker Suite* is still in print.

Another letter, signed A. Maude, came from an Englishman who a year and a half earlier had been to see Grieg both at Voksenkollen near Christiania and at the Hotel Phønix in Copenhagen. Mr Maude had noticed in his newspaper that the Norwegian composer was due to conduct in Bristol in October and offered hospitality in Oxford to Grieg and his wife ('we have a nice house & can offer you 2 or 3 rooms'). He further offered to arrange concerts in Exeter and Oxford to follow Grieg's Bristol engagement. He and his wife had virtually adopted, following the death of their own son, the young pianist Percival Garratt, who now lived with them and whom Grieg had in fact heard perform at Voksenkollen. Maude asked whether Garratt and a lady violinist of Maude's acquaintance might play one of Grieg's sonatas at one of the concerts, and if he might also play a solo piece of Grieg's; 'and could Mrs. Grieg sing about 8 songs? and would you accompany or would you rather play the whole programme'. The principal impulse behind this friendly letter was the 'wish to give Garratt a chance of playing under your auspices', but Maude was ready to take on all the work behind the endeavour – booking halls, arranging and paying for everything, with the profits going to Grieg himself. 'If Mrs. Grieg does not care to sing I can provide a cousin of mine Gwendolen Lind-Maude a granddaughter of Jenny Lind's & a charming young singer: who has just made a successful début.'[34]

Percival Garratt, born in Oxfordshire in 1877, was a pupil of Louis Rée and Karl Klindworth. Over the course of his career he composed songs and piano, dramatic, violin, and orchestral works, but never achieved more than a modest celebrity. Maude told Grieg that Garratt had already played three times at St James's Hall that very season and had received many successful notices. One of these performances, according to *The Musical Standard*, had taken place on the afternoon of 9 April: 'César Franck's too lengthy Sonata for violin and pianoforte received an intelligent and expressive reading at the hands of Mr. de Sicard and Mr. Percival Garratt. . . . Mr P. Garratt played Chopin's Nocturne, Op. 27, No. 2, in a neat and unpretentious style and the "Etude en forme de Valse" of M. Saint-Saëns.'[35] Among later London performances of his own compositions were, for example, a recital given by Garratt himself at the Bechstein Hall on 20 May 1904, in which he appeared as both executant and composer. And at an annual concert given by Fanny Frickenhaus at the same venue on 21 March 1906, his 'Impromptu-Elegy' and a Mazurka met 'with a deservedly good reception'.[36]

Grieg was scarcely likely to take up Maude's offer, which would have involved more of the kind of travelling and exertion he was now trying to avoid. Less demanding was a fan letter he received from an English student studying at Leipzig but now home for the summer. W. Gray Tisdale wrote to ask for autographs for a friend and himself and sent two photographs for Grieg to sign. He told the composer that he was studying the Piano Concerto and that he hoped to play it at his *Prüfung* at Leipzig the following year.[37] There are many such letters in the Grieg Archives, not only, of course, from England. A number are undated and could have been written at any time between Grieg's first and last visits to London. Mary E. Marriott of Handsworth, Birmingham, sends a photograph of three young ladies (herself one of them) 'who love your music very much and who play it very often'. Bridget M. Keir of Folkestone sends a fan letter and encloses a book that she hopes Grieg will sign. James Watt jr of Streatham tells the composer that he sings his songs 'with delight', and — naïvely — that he would like to sing some to Grieg himself, either at home in Streatham or indeed anywhere in London.[38] Almost certainly later than any of these was a request for help from Annie E. Keeton, who occasionally gave lectures in London on Norwegian and Swedish music, among other things. She asked Grieg for advice on books about Scandinavian music, at the same time oddly asking him for names of 'genuine' Scandinavian composers, and she reminded him, 'You may remember my paper on yourself in Temple Bar for *Jan 1898*.'[39] Keeton's piece in *Temple Bar* was of a fairly general nature, outlining the background to a number of Grieg's more popular works and oddly describing his music as 'representing Scandinavia in general, rather than Norway in particular'. It was nonetheless a mildly useful and instructive piece of work.[40] By October 1900 Keeton had made something of a study of Finnish music too, publishing an article on the subject in *Leisure Hour*.[41]

One can well understand how letters of this nature had for so long proved irksome for Grieg, as he explained in a letter to Frants Beyer in the summer of 1902:

> Since I came home the business of letter-writing has reached its peak. It's now gone so far that either I can't reply or I get a secretary. And yet the latter wouldn't help. Anyone who is able to write a lyric poem palms it off on me. When I came back from Fosheim 4 items lay in wait there, books and single poems. These I dutifully have to send thanks for. Oh well, that doesn't take so much time. But then all the English, French and German letters. Linguistic chump that I am, it's pure Adagio Tempo to reply to these. This explains why the piano hasn't been opened since I got home. But – I don't want to complain. I've become quite another person since coming home. No chimeras of an evening, good sleep, and asthma getting better.[42]

Grieg was later to return to the subject in a letter to Henri Hinrichsen:

> There is quite simply no more shameless a people than the Americans. Today a bicycle factory in Boston sends me a thick package of photographs of myself and they write: 'We *desire* to have your Autograph.' That beats everything. I've just had to send 6 to Genoa (where they've had a Grieg-concert).[43]

Just as demanding as the American bicycle factory was a certain J. H. S. Jackson of Croydon, Surrey, who in 1904 sent a long letter to Grieg requesting 'for his musical library' a sketch of the composer's life and works, a good portrait, and finally an autograph manuscript of a Grieg song; indeed any manuscript fragment would be acceptable. A second letter followed a few weeks later; he had received no reply from Grieg and wished to have one.[44] One can only sympathize with poor Grieg, who does not seem to have bothered to reply to the importunate Jackson. On quite another plane, one Englishman to whom Grieg was grateful at the beginning of August 1902 was an angler called Farrar who had sent up to Troldhaugen from his hotel in Bergen a salmon that he had caught. He told Grieg in an accompanying letter that he was brother-in-law to Cecil Slingsby, who had probably suggested the idea to Farrar in the first place.

Grieg's course was still set for Bristol, but the programme had changed a great deal since the composer had sent to Riseley his original suggestions for the festival, and *Land-sighting* was now on the menu. On 5 July, *The Musical Standard* announced preliminary details. Grieg was to conduct his Piano Concerto on the evening of Wednesday 8 October with Leonard Borwick as soloist, 'and Dr. Grieg will also conduct his Landerkennung ("Recognition of Land").' The Friday morning concert would include *Bergliot*, with Mrs Brown Potter as the reciter. And on Friday evening, 'Dr. Grieg's "In Autumn" will be the introductory number'.[45] So Grieg would after all be conducting two of his pieces on each of two days. But by the end of August the composer's mood was changing, as is clear from a letter he wrote to a German friend. 'It is still very doubtful whether I will be going to England. My health says no, and that must, after all, take precedence.'[46] A few days later, it was the same tale to Beyer:

I still have no idea as to whether the England trip will come off. I'll wait till the middle of the month before deciding. . . . I haven't the heart for a long tour. But the England journey is tempting from an artistic viewpoint, of that one can be quite sure.[47]

What had been worrying Grieg was yet another bout of asthma, although he felt that he was at least beginning to make a good recovery from the attack. But, as he wrote to Sigurd Hals, he had so little energy left that he felt he would simply have to give up the England tour. 'It pains me, because apart from the Piano Concerto with Borwick, I would have got to hear for the first time "Land-sighting" as it is intended: 4–500 singers, 100-man orchestra and grand organ. "Bergliot" as well, with an excellent English actress.' If, nonetheless, he did decide to go to England, he would set off around 20 September, quite probably via Christiania:

I ought of course to take the sea route to Newcastle, but that's no good to me and it's for that reason that I shall no doubt stay at home, for to travel through 6 kingdoms and then get landed with the English fog – no thank you![48]

By the middle of September the decision had, with much reluctance, been made. The autumn trip to England was off.

If I'd been able to put up with the steamer trip, I shouldn't have thought twice about it. But as that particular route is an impossibility for me, I would have had to travel by railway through the 6 kingdoms and then still might have found myself landed with the autumn fogs. That would have meant certain ruin for me. I don't at present have enough energy to cope with a journey of that nature. I would certainly be ill when I arrived and not be in a position to carry out my duties. You are wrong to imagine that it's the concerts, the conducting, that I'm afraid of. All that I can easily manage, and it's fun too. No, it's just the length of the journey and the time it takes. You can imagine that I needed no persuasion, as I was and still am keen. And there's Borwick, whom both Nina and I would have been pleased to meet again. The whole thing is so annoying that I can only say that I don't want to think about it any more.[49]

Grieg sent a telegram to Riseley, who responded with a courteous reply. A short note of explanation followed:

I cabled 'No', as I was obliged to give a definitif answer, and as my health for the present is so very delicate and capricious. Your kind letter has touched me very much, and I beg you bring my best thanks to Mr. and Mrs. Ashley for their kind invitation and to the committee for their good wishes.[50]

The Ashleys had been expecting to host the Griegs at their home, Moodville, Sneyd Park, Bristol, an address that Grieg had entered into his notebook under the name of Sarah W. Ashley. Riseley's address is given in the same book as 3 Priory Road, Tyndalls Park, Bristol, England. A fuller letter was sent to Riseley for publication:

In the Norwegian Highland mountains, where my Dr. sent me for several weeks, I passed a very bad time. I hoped to recover, but instead of this, thanks to the bad summer, unfortunately, I have returned home worse than I went out. As the state of my health continuing is but poorly, I am obliged to tell you that every thought of my taking a long and fatiguing railway journey to England this autumn is now out of the question. Certainly, I should arrive sick at Bristol, and not be able to do my duty. In communicating you this, I feel more sorry of this bad result than I can tell you. For me is only left to thank you for your kind indulgence and your constant efforts to make me come to you.[51]

Though Grieg himself was unable to be in England in the autumn, the music, at least, played on. Katharine Goodson received favourable notices for her rendering of the Piano Concerto at a September Promenade Concert, and Elgar stepped in in Henry Wood's absence to conduct a performance of the same work at Queen's Hall on 22 November. In Bristol George Riseley took the composer's place on the rostrum to conduct the programmed works by Grieg, among them Borwick playing the Concerto and Mrs Brown Potter declaiming *Bergliot*, in which she was judged 'expressive'.[52] And in Manchester we find the young virtuoso Jan Kubelík including the third Violin Sonata in a showpiece recital. His interpretation of the work was deemed by *The Manchester Guardian* to be 'quite adequate', even if in the *Allegretto* movement '– a most tenderly homesick and lovesick little northern Romance – he did not let his violin sing with all the sweetness of which it is capable'.[53]

It is particularly ironic that Grieg had so much wanted this time to take part in Bristol's festival and seemed genuinely to be looking forward to conducting his chosen works there, for he had seldom appeared to anticipate with pleasure the experience of coming to England to perform. For him the prospect of the English Channel was bad enough, but the one experience of the North Sea crossing that he had undergone in 1888 had put him off for life. But for his bad seamanship, England would certainly have been a considerably more attractive proposition for him. A century later, the sophistication and ease of air travel, together with the dissipation of the fog and smoke that ever proved injurious to him, would certainly have seen him much more often in a land in which he would have felt even more at home. The Griegs were in Bergen at the time of Bristol's festival, and left for Voksenkollen and Christiania early in November, overwintering for a change in their home country.

↯ 19 ↯

'HOW GRATEFUL I AM THAT YOU REMEMBERED MY 60TH BIRTHDAY'

Early in March 1903 Edvard and Nina Grieg left Christiania for Copenhagen, where they were to spend a fortnight and where Grieg was to conduct a performance of his Concerto. A little earlier, *Bergliot* had received a rare performance in London, with Henry Wood conducting his Queen's Hall Orchestra. 'J.H.G.B.' defended the work stoutly in *The Musical Standard*:

> Miss Tita Brand recited with striking power in Grieg's 'Bergliot.' It has been said that she was stagey. That is not at all the impression her performance made on me. All I would say is that her power was a trifle wanting in variation, and that, near the conclusion, she became somewhat curiously ineffective. It is true Miss Brand failed in pitch two or three times; but, no doubt, she will see to this in the future. I must confess there were moments when her performance moved me very deeply. One is sorry to see one fervent admirer of Richard Strauss describe the music as commonplace. One hopes he will live to regret having made that grossly wrong statement. Music that is so full of keen, first-hand feeling surely cannot justly be rated 'commonplace.' Think again, my man![1]

One of the Griegs' first engagements in the Danish capital was to attend a recital given on 5 March by Lady Hallé and Leonard Borwick. 'They were both excellent', Grieg told Sigurd Hals. 'Give my greetings to Borwick and tell him that I admired him enormously.' He had hoped to see Borwick in the Artists' Room after the recital, but had found that there was no entrance to it from the main hall.[2]

After Copenhagen, the Griegs once more took to the road, with a two-months' tour taking them successively to Prague, Berlin, Warsaw, Paris, Cologne, Leipzig, Berlin and Copenhagen again, and finally Christiania. Grieg performed on several occasions, mainly conducting, but also recording on 2 and 3 May a number of his piano pieces on single-sided discs in Paris. The recordings, made for the the Compagnie Française du Gramophone, were supervised by an American, Alfred Clark, who was also the Paris representative of the (British) Gramophone Company.

Now was the time when tributes began to appear in the London musical press in anticipation of Grieg's forthcoming sixtieth birthday. *The Globe*, according to *The Musical Standard*, wrote of how Grieg had told an interviewer what he conceived to be his musical mission. Bach and Beethoven had raised temples and churches on the heights. Grieg, on the other hand, had tried, in the words of Ibsen, to build homes for human beings: he had 'noted down the popular music of his country':

> In style . . . I have remained a German 'romantic' of the school of Schumann, but at the same time I have explored the rich treasure of the folk-songs of my fatherland, and from these hitherto unexplored manifestations of the Norwegian genius I have tried to create a national art.[3]

The Monthly Musical Record used almost an entire column of its June issue to advertise various Augener publications of his works and separately offered an editorial tribute to a composer 'who could look back on his art career with pride, and feel that his name will be held in honour and long remembrance':

> The composer is a man of simple tastes and habits, and the celebration will probably be of a quiet, homely character, unless the city of Bergen – of which, by the way, Grieg's father was formerly English Consul – should propose to mark the event by some public demonstration. A fund is being raised, which is to bear the name of Edvard Grieg, and it will be at the free disposal of the composer to dispose of in whatever way he deems suitable. Grieg's many admirers in Great Britain will be glad to know that contributions can be forwarded to John Grieg's Verlag, Bergen, Norway, up to June 5th; also to the firm of C. F. Peters, Leipzig. The list of names of the committee includes those of C. Berner (President of the Norwegian Parliament), Otto Blehr (Prime Minister), consuls of many European cities, and eminent Norwegians in art, literature, and commerce.[4]

As the Griegs returned to Bergen at the end of May, it was time to prepare for the birthday celebrations, which were to be the very antithesis of the 'quiet, homely character' predicted by *The Monthly Musical Record*. There can be little doubt that Grieg had originally made plans to visit England this year too. He had written to the Russian pianist Alexander Siloti the previous summer to say that he was committed to appearing in Warsaw on 14 April and that that date could not be changed, 'as I am going directly from Warsaw to England'.[5] As already mentioned, the principal destination in the spring of 1903 was changed to Paris, where the Griegs were briefly joined by Johannes Wolff. Wolff had just arrived from London, where, as he told Grieg, he had played Johan Halvorsen's *Air norvégien* for violin and piano (which Halvorsen had actually dedicated to Wolff) at a concert only the previous day.

Grieg's sixtieth-birthday celebrations were of an extraordinary nature. The whole of Norway honoured him in festivities that lasted for three days. Johan Halvorsen brought his entire National Theatre orchestra from Christiania to Bergen for the occasion. On the birthday itself, 15 June, there was a reception on a large scale at Troldhaugen, and this was followed by a banquet at the Grand Hotel in

Bergen, at which Bjørnstjerne Bjørnson made the principal speech. Grieg's own speech took Bjørnson as its subject, and it opened with the indication that Grieg had cancelled a trip to England solely in order to be at home for Bjørnson's visit on this notable occasion. He permitted himself some pardonable exaggeration:

> Well, Ladies and Gentlemen!
>   Many strange things happen in this world. Man proposes, but – Bjørnson disposes. I had imagined this sixtieth birthday of mine to have been quite different. Let me tell you why. I had been invited to England on just these days to participate in various concerts. And then the thought occurred to me: What if I, on the 15th of June, were a cosmopolitan giving a big concert in Albert Hall, which holds 10,000 people! That would have irritated our cosy chauvinists here at home – and I am so bad a fellow that I enjoy nothing more than annoying the chauvinists, these mountain trolls whom I hate like the plague. No, they aren't even proper mountain trolls, just poor copies.
>   Well, I began to prepare for my trip to England. But suddenly the word went out in such a way that it was heard all over Norway, and indeed throughout Europe too: 'I shall be coming to Bergen on the 15th of June.' That made me change my tune. Such a beautiful, friendly thought by Bjørnson I could not resist. I got terribly busy. I wrote to east and west and managed to head off the whole England trip.[6]

The Brodskys sent a telegram of congratulation, just one of some five hundred letters and telegrams that arrived from all quarters at Troldhaugen – and which Grieg at least said he intended to acknowledge. He had hoped that Brodsky and his wife might have been able to come over for the celebrations. Johannes Wolff had accepted but had had to call off his visit at the last minute, and the result was that the festivities remained very much a Norwegian affair, with only Julius Röntgen attending from abroad. Delius had not realized that it was Grieg's sixtieth, but had read of it and sent a late congratulation from Grez-sur-Loing, the village, not far from Fontainebleau, in which he had now settled down:

> It is such a long time since we have heard anything from each other which is certainly my fault, but my wishes & greetings for this day are none the less heartfelt. I still think with pleasure of the lovely times we have had together & I hope that life will bring us together again.[7]

After this high point had been reached, almost inevitably there had to come a low. Responding to Delius at the beginning of September, Grieg apologized for his tardiness in acknowledging his younger friend's good wishes:

> But I am afraid that I have only too good an excuse. Since the end of June I have been seriously ill and am not really allowed to write letters yet. The festival (a whole week) with concerts and banquets was beyond my strength. I was allright as long as the affair lasted, but afterwards came the reaction.[8]

Charles Harding, too, had sent a telegram of congratulation. Grieg was genuinely touched:

Since I got your telegram, I have been very, very ill. (Bronchitis and Asthma.) Still I am not permitted to write letters. But I must send you some lines, that you and your dear family may feel how grateful I am that you remembered my 60th birthday. I beg you to be assured, that if writing or not, I will ever keep the same friendly feelings for you all. I never forget the happy days in the autumn 1888, and I shall always feel thankful for your kindness and hospitality.

We have a very bad summer and then we are without our dearest friends Beyers, who are obliged to stay at Christiania from July to October. We intend to leave Bergen in the middle of September and hope to meet with Beyers in Christiania.

I am so sorry, that it is for me out of the question to visit England. My health should not at all permit it. If it was possible to cross the sea by railway, then I would surely come, but to travel through six kingdoms before reaching England, that is too much for me.

And now, dear Mr. Harding, my best love to you all and the kindest greetings from my wife!

Thankfully Yours,
    Edvard Grieg

P.S. I beg you kindly excuse my very bad English!![9]

In the musical press the tributes continued to flow. Percival M. F. Hedley published an appreciation in *The Musical Standard* of 28 July, in which he wrote of the inspiration that Grieg drew from the natural surroundings of his native country, assuring his readers that 'it is impossible thoroughly to understand the great master without this background of a peculiarly grand and manifold character'.[10] This issue of the journal included a portrait of the composer. A month later, the *Standard*'s supplement furthermore presented its readers with 'a facsimile portion of the MS. of Edvard Grieg's "Peer Gynt" music, together with the composer's autograph'. On another page, it quoted from an article written by Henry T. Finck for the New York *Evening Post*, in which the writer had waxed indignant over the ever-growing reputation of Richard Strauss. Grieg was 'infinitely more original and fertile as a melodist than Strauss; yet the myopic critics treat Strauss as the greater man of the two, simply because his works are bigger. Jumboism in music, and always Jumboism!' The *Standard* editorially disclaimed the argument. Grieg was 'admitted to be a genius, but it is a miniature and unexpansive sort of genius. And let the word "genius" apply also to the music of Richard Strauss.'[11] At all events, Grieg was satisfactorily saluted in London on 22 August on the occasion of the opening concert of the Promenade season, with the *Peer Gynt Suite* being included in a programme of popular works by various composers and hundreds having to be turned away from the doors. Incidentally, among the new works announced for first performance at the 1903 Proms was a symphonic poem, *Pompilia*, by the same Edgar L. Bainton whose father had written to Grieg over a decade earlier.[12]

Soon after the middle of September the Griegs arrived in Christiania. Edvard's health remained poor, and on 18 December Nina wrote to Anna Brodsky from Voksenkollen Sanatorium, where her husband, still suffering from bronchitis, asthma and insomnia, had been bedridden for some time. The doctors seemed unable to help, and Nina professed to have little faith in them. Although he was now feeling slightly better and had taken a few steps outside his room, Grieg's spirits remained low. It was hoped he would be well enough to take up a long-standing invitation from the Bjørnsons to spend Christmas with them at Aulestad – their home in the valley of Gudbrandsdal north of Lillehammer. The invitation had taken on an added piquancy, as Bjørnson had just been awarded the Nobel Prize for Literature. Meanwhile, the Brodskys had moved to the Manchester suburb of Bowdon. Nina was pleased for them, though she remembered their previous home – with a little nostalgia – as 'so very nice and comfortable'.

On 1 December *The Monthly Musical Record* published a short review of a new album, *Norwegische Bauerntänze (Norwegian Peasant Dances)*, also known as *Slåtter* (Op. 72). The reviewer gives little indication of the sheer inventiveness and audacity of Grieg's treatment of these peasant dances:

> In a brief but interesting preface he speaks of the originality and the 'untamed wildness as regards melody, and more particularly rhythm,' of the dance tunes, and he also tells us the object which he had in view in arranging them for the piano, viz. 'to raise these works of the people to an artistic level'. . . . It is neither necessary to add that the volume is one of special interest, the importance of folk music being now so fully recognized; nor to emphasize the fact that among folk melodies those of Norway are peculiarly fresh and fascinating.[13]

Among the London musical fraternity, it was left to Percy Grainger first to discover this extraordinary collection. He accepted the challenge with gratitude and was soon to play them – together with some of his similarly-favoured pieces from Op. 66 – whenever he had the opportunity. On the other hand, early Grieg continued to attract London's musical public, with Teresa Carreño again playing the Concerto, under Wood's direction, on 12 December. According to one critic, she used the work 'as a medium for displaying her dazzling technique. Whether Grieg himself would have approved of her treatment of his work, which is the embodiment of dreamy and romantic tenderness, is open to doubt, but the audience seemed to like it.'[14]

The year of 1903 came to a close with seasonal greetings from such English friends as Delius, the Hardings and Cecil Slingsby, who sent Grieg an inscribed copy of his newly published book, *Norway: The Northern Playground*, which would come to be acknowledged as a classic.

In the event, the Griegs joined the Bjørnsons at Aulestad a little after Christmas and stayed for some three weeks. Nina told Anna Brodsky that the two men had spent their time talking together on every subject under the sun, though more particularly about the increasingly fraught political situation between Norway and Sweden. Edvard had had a setback, however, brought about by too much rich food and champagne, and was unwell for the last week of their stay. Bjørnson too had

Bjørnson and Grieg at Troldhaugen:
Grieg sends a greeting from them both to Delius, 23 August 1904

had an attack of bronchitis and had needed to take to his bed towards the end of the Griegs' visit. However, his was a strong constitution, and he was bearing up well. Grieg's fresh troubles meant that forthcoming concerts in Russia and Finland had to be cancelled. But if he were to be well enough at the time, he still hoped to make spring tours to Warsaw and London.[15] As it happened, the entire year of 1904 would be spent, highly unusually, in Norway, with the sole exception of an excursion in March to Stockholm, where Grieg had several concerts. Once again, plans for a trip to London were not to be realized. But as before, the music played on, and there were echoes of old Leipzig friendships when Emma Barnett included Grieg's Piano Sonata, Op. 7, in a recital at Queen's Hall on 24 June that also offered a new work by her brother, John Francis Barnett: a suite of ten numbers entitled *Musical Landscapes*. Almost a year later she would reprise the latter work in the course of a recital in Broadwood's Concert Room at which she played more of her brother's works.[16]

Most of 1904 was spent in Christiania, but three summer months were devoted to Troldhaugen. This period included two memorable days in July, when Wilhelm II's yacht *Hohenzollern* anchored at Bergen. Grieg was invited to breakfast at the home of his friend Conrad Mohr, German Consul in Bergen, and the guest of honour was the Kaiser, who had expressed a strong wish to meet the composer whom he so much admired. They talked together for an hour, after which the accompanying 40-strong ship's orchestra played a selection of Grieg pieces. Grieg was then invited to dinner on the *Hohenzollern* on the following evening. The harbour was crowded with hundreds of small boats, their occupants all eager to catch a glimpse of the Kaiser; and while the orchestra played on the deck, Grieg and the music-loving Kaiser sat together. 'He treated me like a patient, put his cloak round me and fetched a blanket with which he carefully covered me.'[17] Grieg's host had made an enormous impression on him. He had been 'a human being and not a Kaiser'.

Just as in 1903, England appeared to be a long way away, and Grieg's correspondence reflects this; there was, it seems, relatively little contact with his English friends in 1904. He reported, however, to Sigurd Hals that he was looking forward to a visit from Johannes Wolff at the end of July, and that Wolff was bringing two items of interest with him: an Englishman and a pianola. 'That will certainly be an experience', Grieg thought.[18] It proved in fact to be an experience with historic consequences, as later documented by the Englishman of whom Grieg spoke, George W. F. Reed, a director of the Aeolian Company:

> Having taken a personal introduction to Grieg, I went to Bergen, taking with me one of the latest Pianolas, equipped with the Metrostyle. After a little difficulty I succeeded in persuading him to listen to it, at the same time explaining the function of the Metrostyle, and how by its means his own interpretations of his compositions could be marked on the music rolls, and thus enable thousands of music-lovers, and possible future Pianola owners, all over the world in the years to come, to play these compositions according to his exact interpretation.

The thought that his own ideas could thus be preserved for posterity appealed to him, as it has to many other composers who at the beginning were equally prejudiced against the Pianola, and he agreed to assist me in making the following rolls . . . I remained in Bergen for a week, working with Grieg several hours each day, until the marking was complete, and the line on each roll was to his absolute satisfaction. As the work progressed, and he commenced to realise what the invention of the Pianola really meant to the music lover, he became very enthusiastic, so much so that during the few remaining years of his life, Grieg was numbered amongst the staunchest supporters of the instrument.[19]

Reed remembered how, surrounded by family and friends, Grieg played 'piece after piece' and told his guests of some of the sources of their inspiration. Grieg and Wolff would then play movements from the violin sonatas, following which, 'after a simple Norwegian supper, we sat in the music room with the wonderful glow of the Norwegian twilight coming in through the windows, while Madame Grieg sang a number of her husband's songs'. The harvest from the week was 16 piano pieces recorded on 14 rolls.

The year was a tragic one for George Augener, who on 19 June lost his son William, the third of three children of his to die in as many years, the others having been Ella and Charlie. William was just 48; his illness was hereditary, Augener describing it as 'a hyena raging in my family'. Another daughter, Millie, now living in a house that her father had bought for her in St Leonards on Sea, was unwell too when her father wrote to Grieg in December 1904. It had been expected that William would take over the family's music publishing business. His father had bought him a fine house with a large garden on the other side of Clapham Common, and William had gradually assumed charge of the company as George Augener's own health slowly declined. In search of a cure, William had spent his final winters successively in Davos, Menton and St Leonards, but all had been in vain. Now there was no-one in the family to take over, so Augener had formed a limited company in order to secure the future of the business he had founded. With his wife usually spending the winter with Millie in St Leonards, Augener's only company at 47 North Side at this time of year – apart from the remaining servants – was his daughter Elise. 'In this large house . . . we often feel very lonely.'[20] At the end of 1904 it was painfully clear that the Griegs' home-from-home in London was effectively no more.

In Birmingham, too, the final day of the year signalled another painful change, with the death of Charles Harding at the age of 65 (just ten days after that of another English friend, Arthur Chappell). The obituaries recorded the fact that he was, like his father and grandfather, a Unitarian and a lifelong member of the Old Meeting Church. A sermon preached at a memorial service in that church on 8 January 1905 gives some idea of the respect in which he was held in the city. Harding was praised as having been a leader of men to whom any could and did go to seek help and sympathy. 'In temperament, as well as by circumstance, he was one of the happiest of men. He had a hearty enjoyment of life, . . . the gifts of hopefulness and cheerfulness, and a certain brightness of disposition which made sunshine in many a shady place.' Particular emphasis was laid on his thoughtfulness for others and on his absolute integrity and generosity. This warm generosity — both public and private — was especially noted: 'being simple in all his personal tastes [he] had the more to give.'[21]

Birmingham's loss was, of course, Grieg's too.

⁂ 20 ⁂

'I IMPLORE YOUR MAJESTY . . . TO PREVENT THE SHAME AND DISASTER'

It is curious to watch the musical barometer of artists and public alike. A few years ago the compositions of Edvard Grieg held sway in this country, but he now seems to be receding before his colossal contemporaries Brahms and Tschaikowsky. This may be due to a better understanding and appreciation of the former and of the seductive colouring of the latter. Be this as it may, there is a national atmosphere surrounding the music of Grieg, and an individuality only equalled by that of Chopin, which will always delight the hearts of those whose imagination can be stimulated by Norse romance and legend. Appreciating this fact, we owe thanks to Mr. Wilhelm Backhaus for reintroducing the Piano Concerto in A minor. Grieg in one respect resembles Schumann in intellect, Grieg being essentially lyrical. The form or design of the Concerto in A minor is comparatively simple. Running throughout the work is a background of novel harmonic colouring peculiar to Grieg, though his incessant use of short rhythms produces a monotonous impression. The Solo Piano is most brilliantly written for, and Mr. Backhaus gave it an artistic yet reserved interpretation.[1]

THUS *The Musical World*, reviewing a Hallé Concert given in Manchester on 19 January 1905. The reviewer was far more taken by Richard Strauss's *Burlesque* for piano and orchestra, in which the 20-year-old Backhaus had clearly excelled himself. The new school, it appeared, was taking over from the old. Brodsky had appointed Backhaus professor of piano at the Royal Manchester College of Music from 1 January 1905, but the young prodigy – who had first performed with the Hallé under Richter in the 1901–2 season – with his concert commitments growing ever more demanding, was only to stay for a year. The 're-introducing' of the Concerto should not, however, be taken too seriously, referring only to the local circumstance of Manchester rather than to the country as a whole. The work had never gone out of fashion. Backhaus was before long to record the Concerto in abridged form; listed in the HMV *Catalogue of New Gramophone Records, December 1909*, the two two-sided 12-inch (30-cm) discs had Landon Ronald conducting the New Symphony Orchestra, and the result is claimed as the first ever recording of a concerto.

At the very end of 1904 the Griegs had left Christiania for Copenhagen, where they were to stay for nearly five months at the Hotel Phønix. For most of the first two months Edvard, in wretched health, was handed from doctor to doctor, and then Nina herself fell victim to influenza in March. Another who was a prey to ill health in his last years, Edward Dannreuther, died in London on 12 February 1905. A true pioneer of Grieg's music in England, he was just 51. London was changing fast. Just one day earlier St James's Hall had seen its last concert before closing down, a source of considerable regret to the capital's musicians and music-lovers.

Grieg began to worry about money, with his health preventing him from undertaking any concert engagements in Copenhagen. What can he have thought when asked from London to write the incidental music to a dramatization of Hall Caine's *The Prodigal Son*? The invitation came from an international agency whose London office was just off Leicester Square and whose representative there was Reginald Golding Bright. It was, a little surprisingly, written in a reasonably fluent Norwegian and was from Reginald's wife M. C. Golding Bright. Born Mary Chavelita Dunne, she had had a colourful life that included an elopement to Norway with a previous lover, a subsequent short-lived marriage to a Canadian novelist, and then an infatuation with Knut Hamsun, whose novel *Hunger* she translated. *The Prodigal Son* was destined for the Drury Lane Theatre in September. It was to be in four acts, three of them exotically located in Iceland and one in Monte Carlo, and music was required for a wedding scene, a cradle song, an Icelandic dance, and more. Mrs Golding Bright pointed out that Hall Caine was at the time the most popular writer in England and that Mascagni had provided music for his play *The Eternal City*. She hoped that Grieg would agree to this commission and asked what his terms might be.[2] There is no indication of any response from the composer.

Grieg's ill health persisted into April, a blood disorder adding itself to the catalogue of woes, together with hallucinations at night. In the middle of the month he underwent a massage cure and also had some dental treatment. By then, however, he was at least beginning to feel a little better and hoped, as he told Brodsky, to leave the city at the beginning of May and to return to Troldhaugen. He encouraged the Brodskys to visit, saying that he and Nina expected to be at home for virtually all of the summer. Otherwise he registered the sad truth that sickness and productivity were each 'deadly enemies' to the other.[3]

The Brodskys' letters at this time are full of alarm at the war with Japan and the abortive revolution in Russia, the country of their birth, just as Grieg's letters express similar alarm over the continuously deteriorating situation as Norway tried to rid itself of the last vestiges of its ties to Sweden:

> It is a grave time for my beloved homeland. But we stand united as *one* person, and as *one* will. We have an excellent government and are full of optimism. We are actually prepared for an attack, so anything criminal is scarcely likely to occur! Public opinion in both Norway and Sweden is opposed to any such thing. Just think: in

From a first letter to Grieg from Percy Grainger

reality the king cannot form a new ministry to achieve his purpose, since little more than a quite small minority support him. He dares to turn against a whole people, and that will soon cost him the throne. The main questions will have to be answered within the next few days. Yesterday evening I spoke with the head of the government, Mr. Michelsen. It was a real pleasure to observe his composure, straightforwardness and clarity.[4]

Grieg continued to press Brodsky to come to Troldhaugen, but the college principal was caught between term-time dates and performing engagements in August, and all efforts came to nothing. Better luck was to come a year later.

The Griegs at last left Copenhagen for Christiania, spending about a fortnight in the capital before leaving for Troldhaugen on 5 June. Before their departure from Denmark, however, there had been an initial brief exchange of correspondence with the youthful prodigy Percy Grainger, Australian-born but living and performing in London. Herman Sandby, a young Danish cellist and Grainger's closest friend, had shown Grainger's first publications to Grieg and in so doing had opened a path to a new friendship, the last and most affectionate that Grieg would form in the course of his final two years. Grainger and Sandby had recently given a concert at the Bechstein Hall in London, where they had played *La Scandinavie* – Grainger's arrangements of Scandinavian folk-music – and Grainger at the piano had been joined by Ada Crossley, who sang a number of songs including Delius's 'Irmelin Rose'.[5]

And another invitation to appear in London had arrived. It came in the form of a letter from Edgar Speyer, the London-based financier and music-lover without whose moral and monetary support as chairman of the board of directors the Queen's Hall Orchestra would probably have had to close down. Speyer's wife was the American-born violinist Leonora von Stosch, who had studied at the Brussels Conservatory and in Paris with Marsick, but who now found herself at the centre of London's social and musical life. The invitation was for Grieg to perform at the Queen's Hall the following summer and to stay with the Speyers at their opulent Mayfair home. Grieg replied that he would, health permitting, be delighted to accept such a kind invitation, ideally at the beginning of May, and that his concert fee was £100. Johanne Stockmarr would play the Concerto, and an actress of the first rank would be needed to perform *Bergliot*, just as a similarly gifted singer would be needed for his songs. These matters would need to be sorted out in good time. Grieg closed by apologizing for his poor English.[6]

The orchestra's manager Robert Newman duly laid out the terms of two London engagements:

> On behalf of the Directors I beg to offer you an engagement for two Concerts at Queens Hall at a fee of one hundred guineas per Concert, the first Concert to be on Thursday afternoon May 17th at 3 pm, with rehearsal same morning at 10 am for you to Conduct the Queens Hall Orchestra, and the Second Concert to be on Thursday afternoon, May 24th at 3 pm for a Chamber Concert.
>
> The above engagements are offered upon the understanding that they are your only appearances in London during the Spring of 1906.
>
> I am desired to ask if it would be possible for Madme Grieg to sing at the Chamber Concert on May 24th but if that is not possible to suggest that Madme Emma Holmstrand of Paris should be the vocalist on that occasion.
>
> Awaiting the favour of your kind reply
> Believe me
> Yours faithfully
> R H Newman – Manager[7]

Curiously, Grieg did not at first connect Newman's letter with that from Speyer and consequently drafted a reply on the back of Newman's letter: 'Having already accepted an engagement in London at the time mentioned in your letter, I regret very much not to be able to follow your kind invitation.' The true situation, how-

QUEEN'S HALL ORCHESTRA, LTD.

TELEGRAMS: "ACCOMPANY, LONDON."
TELEPHONE: No. 551 PADDINGTON.

Manager—
ROBERT NEWMAN.

Directors {
EDGAR SPEYER, ESQ., *Chairman.*
THE EARL HOWE, G.C.V.O.
LT.-COL. ARTHUR COLLINS, C.B.
H. EGAN HILL, ESQ.
HENRY J. WOOD, ESQ.

Secretary - F. POPE.

Offices:

320 Regent Street, W.

19 June 1905

Dr Edward Grieg Munde
Copenhagen
Dear Sir

In behalf of the Directors I beg to offer you an engagement for two concerts at Queens Hall at a fee of one hundred guineas per concert, the first concert to be on Thursday afternoon May 17th at 3pm, with rehearsal same morning at 10 am for you to conduct the Queens Hall Orchestra, and the second concert to be on Thursday afternoon May 24th at 3pm for a Chamber concert.

The above engagements are offered upon the understanding that they are your only appearances in London during the Spring of 1906.

I am desired to ask if it would be possible for Madme Grieg to sing at the Chamber concert on May 24th but if that is not possible to suggest that Madme Emma Holmstrand of Paris should be the vocalist on that occasion. Awaiting the favour of your kind reply

Believe me
Yours faithfully
R H Newman - Manager

Robert Newman offers engagements at Queen's Hall

ever, soon became clear, and Newman was able on 28 July to confirm both engagements.

Meanwhile, Grieg had appeared in print in the July issue of *The Contemporary Review*, with a translation of his autobiographical essay 'My First Success'. One London reviewer called it 'a very charming article . . . frank and chatty', and recounted two of the author's anecdotes from Leipzig days about Louis Plaidy and Ignaz Moscheles while ignoring references to Grieg's English fellow students.[8] *The*

Musical Standard offered even longer excerpts from Grieg's essay but again failed to mention any English connections.[9] It was left to *The Monthly Musical Record*, in its lead article in September (let down only by its title, 'Edward Grieg'), at least to mention Barnett, adding: 'As in his music, so in his writing, Grieg reveals both charm and humour.'[10]

Apart from having had to take himself to bed with a heavy cold almost immediately after arriving back at Troldhaugen, Grieg had a good summer and was able to ponder his plans for winter and spring. The winter would be spent in Christiania — if necessary in one or other of the sanatoriums above the city, so as to be in the best condition for the spring travels. He had promised to conduct in Warsaw in April and in London in May, but was worried that revolution in Poland might make the Warsaw concert impossible. Furthermore, he had accepted invitations to give concerts in Berlin and Amsterdam too (in the event Prague would also be added to this impressive roster). To Bjørnstjerne Bjørnson's daughter Dagny, holidaying with her two children on the south coast of England, he wrote of these plans, noting that he was due to conduct in London on 17 May, Norway's national day, and hoping that they might meet somewhere during the course of their travels. He envied Dagny's sunning herself 'down there on the glorious English south coast. I was there once in the month of May. It was just like the Riviera, only fresher and healthier.'[11] In spite of these plans, Grieg was quoted in London as having expressed the view 'that he does not think his health will allow him to visit England any more'.[12] No doubt his spirits would scarcely have been lifted by the news that Augener's Regent Street premises had been destroyed by fire in August, presumably with the loss of some stocks of his published music. Rebuilding work was soon put in hand, and the establishment was reopened early the following year.[13]

The larger cloud over the summer was the tense political situation in Norway. Military preparations were under way in case of an attack from Sweden, the new Michelsen government in Christiania with considerable political skill effectively having declared the country's independence from its neighbour on 7 June. Many Swedes were outraged, construing this action as an affront to the old king, Oscar II, but the more liberal-minded among them, encouraged by the Socialist leader Hjalmar Branting, had long been in sympathy with Norway's aspirations. Tensions were high when negotiations between the two countries were opened at Karlstad on 31 August. Troops were mobilized on the border, while neutral zones and the demolition of border fortresses on the Norwegian side were being discussed.

Norway always looked to its leading personalities in such times, and considerable attention would inevitably be paid to the views of patriotic figures of international standing, such as Ibsen, Bjørnson and Grieg. With the negotiations still in progress, Grieg decided on a radical and decidedly unilateral course of action. On the evening of 13 September he found himself playing cards at the home of a distinguished Bergen physician, Gerhard Henrik Armauer Hansen. Also present was Grieg's personal doctor (and the host's brother, despite the different spelling)

Klaus Hanssen. The telephone kept interrupting their game, one of the callers being prime minister Michelsen himself. In due course the players gave up and instead sat and talked about the desperate situation. Grieg's view was that it was time for those whose names bore any weight abroad to speak out, and Klaus Hanssen noted mentally that Grieg had clearly been thinking about what he himself might do. The following day, Grieg called on Hanssen. He had drafted telegrams to King Edward VII and the Kaiser – with both of whom he was of course personally acquainted. In fact the Kaiser had taken the trouble to send him a telegram as recently as the spring following his recovery from his latest bout of bronchitis. Hanssen advised him not to send the two telegrams as they stood but to revise them, removing references to bringing influence to bear on Sweden alone and thus making them more neutral in tone, and furthermore counselling Grieg not to send them 'in the name of Norway'. They should be sent as from Grieg himself. The final wording to both King and Kaiser ran, 'I implore Your Majesty through arbitration to prevent the shame and disaster of a war between Norway and Sweden.'

There could be no doubt that in any case Great Britain and Germany were taking the greatest interest and concern in what was happening to their northern neighbours, and Brækstad's timely 1905 book on the Norwegian constitution would no doubt have been consulted in Foreign Office circles. Downing Street had already intimated that, unless negotiations were speeded up, Britain might officially recognize Norway without waiting for Stockholm. Whatever the effect of Grieg's intervention, with outside pressures building up, not least from Britain, the negotiations between the two countries were beginning to bear fruit, and just ten days later the Karlstad Agreement was signed. The Norwegian Parliament, followed shortly afterwards by its Swedish counterpart, ratified the document on 9 October, and the Act of Union was repealed on 16 October. On 27 October Oscar II formally abdicated the Norwegian throne.

Voices had long been raised in Norway in support of a republic once the longed-for separation from Sweden had been achieved. Grieg, though a republican at heart, was prepared to accept the decision of the majority and was realist enough to accept, too, that the European powers were by and large not in favour of a republic. 'Those of our neighbours of a friendly disposition, above all England, a country we probably – something we're not sure about yet – have to thank for the peace, on no account want a republic.'[14] In the event a plebiscite ensured that by a decisive majority Prince Carl of Denmark was elected King of Norway. On 27 November Carl, taking the name Haakon VII, took his oath to the Constitution, giving his young son Alexander the old Norwegian name of Olav, and of course bringing his wife Maud, daughter of Edward VII, with him as his Queen.

The following day, Tuesday 28 November, was memorable in more than one respect. Grieg attended a gala performance at the National Theatre in honour of the royal pair, following which he closed a diary entry with: 'I felt this first meeting with free Norway's first King and Queen to be something beautiful and meaningful, and therefore I choose this day to start my long-intended diary.' He had not kept a diary since the one he had started when living in Copenhagen at the age of 23, his final entry having been dated 28 August 1866. The nearest later approximation to a diary had been all those pocket-books, covering many years, which contained not only his accounts but also odd jottings and addresses relating to particular periods of his life. By the time he returned to England for the last time in May 1906, these little notebooks had finally been abandoned, with the newly-resumed diary now taking its place as the primary record of his day-to-day activities.

Bjørnson's play *Sigurd Jorsalfar*, for which Grieg had written the incidental music, was the principal fare of the gala evening, and Grieg told in his diary of his meeting with the King and Queen:

> After the 2nd act, Bjørnson and I were fetched by Lord Chamberlain Rustad from our seats in the 1st row of the stalls up to the royal box. The King and Queen received us with the greatest kindness. If they really are the unpretentious and straightforward people they appeared to us to be, then we may dare to hope for a popular monarchy.
>
> The Queen reminded me of the time when Nina and I visited her mother in London in 1887 [*sic*; actually 1889], when she and her teenage sisters came with their albums to get our autographs. She, like the King, spoke in positive terms about my music and said that they were looking forward to the Musikforening Concert at which I have been asked to conduct.

Curiously, Grieg fails to mention in his diary the supper party at Michelsen's that followed the performance, when he, his wife, and Bjørnson were seated almost opposite the royal pair. This he mentioned in a letter to Frants Beyer dated 12 December, in which he also included anecdotes illustrating the character of the new King.

With the rapid unfolding of the disturbing events of the summer of 1905, music had temporarily ceded ground to politics. News came from England in October, however, that the first biography of Grieg to be published in English would shortly be out. It was signalled by a gifted English writer on musical matters, Rosa Newmarch, who had been engaged to edit the book and who felt it to be an honour to have been asked to do so. She had loved Grieg's music since her early schooldays 'and still console myself with it, when a busy life gives me an opportunity of spending an evening at the piano'. She wrote a second letter early in November:

> I have just been through the last proofs of Mr Finck's book. It has been somewhat delayed, on account of waiting for the photographs from Bergen of Bergen. But now they have come, and I feel it was wise to wait, for we now have the ideal frontispiece.
>
> In order to get the book published before Christmas I gave directions to prepare the binding. Although I am a great believer in nationality in art, I do not quite care for the idea of a flag outside the covers of the series. Therefore to keep your volume in harmony with the other, I had a monogram designed for the cover. I think you will be pleased with the book when you see it; especially if you will remember that it is

being published at the popular price of 2/6, so that everyone who loves your music can buy this book.

Newmarch had just edited an English version of *The Life and Letters of Peter Ilich Tchaikovsky*, which, she pointed out, contained 'several graceful and interesting references' to Grieg, and she would have a copy sent to him in Norway. She asked Grieg to consider writing an article on the Russian composer, something the editor of *The Contemporary Review* had promised her he would be pleased to accept. Furthermore, she had spoken to her publisher, John Lane, who had agreed that if Grieg wished to publish any of his essays in book form he would be 'very happy to publish them in England and America'.[15] However much Grieg might have wished to write an essay on Tchaikovsky, let alone assemble his various essays for publication in English, his increasingly precarious state of health would doubtless no longer allow him to consider such tasks as priorities. He was growing ever more conscious of his own mortality and regularly complained of old age, as Nina told the Brodskys towards the end of August. Nonetheless, she herself felt that on the whole he showed little sign of ageing, either outwardly or inwardly.

Henry Theophilus Finck's biography of Grieg came out in December as one of a series of biographies ('Living Masters of Music') edited by Newmarch. Finck, an American, was a skilful writer and critic with a thoroughly-grounded musical education at Harvard, which had been continued in Berlin, Heidelberg and Vienna. He lectured on music history at the National Conservatory of Music in New York and was a critic for the city's *Evening Post*. If Grieg's first impression was that the book was 'fragmentary', he nonetheless professed himself particularly pleased with the chapter entitled 'Norwegian Folk-Music – Grieg's Originality': 'It is exceptionally well-written and finally makes amends in a way for the unjust and obtuse criticism to which I have been subjected by a number of German and English-American critics.'[16] The book was well received, with *The Musical Standard* deeming that 'it would be impossible to imagine a more enthusiastic presentation of the Norwegian composer's life and work'[17] and *The London Musical Courier* finding it 'very near to being an ideal volume where a still living composer is concerned'.[18] *The Musical World* considered its publication to be 'opportune' (and therefore welcome) in view of the expected visit of Grieg to London in the spring. Despite minor reservations it was able to reassure its readers that 'Mr. Finck has given us an interesting and eminently readable little book, that will find its way into the hands of Grieg-lovers in this country'.[19]

Around the same time as the publication of Finck's book there came the publication of Grieg's final piano album, *Moods*, Op. 73, consisting of seven pieces written between 1901 and 1905. 'In every one', wrote *The Monthly Musical Record* in the course of a short review, 'will be found rhythms and harmonies strongly characteristic of the composer.' Of the final number, 'The Mountaineer's Song', evolved from a folk melody, the reviewer delighted in 'the section with canonic imitations of it over double pedals', a section that 'wanders from one key to another with delightful freedom'.[20]

The reviews of Finck's book in the musical press were, naturally enough, not to appear until the early months of 1906, too late to cheer Grieg up before yet another hospital stay for a week or so over the Christmas period in Christiania. Not for the first time, stomach and dietary problems were the cause. However, the new year saw his spirits revived, and he returned to the subject of the biography in a letter to Frants Beyer. 'I hope the book will become as widely known as it deserves to be. It's quite true that the author has praised me too highly. For this I've reproached him. But he won't have any of it.'[21]

⚜ 21 ⚜

'GRIEG IS TO PAY US A VISIT'

> Edvard Grieg has accepted an engagement offered by the directors of the Queen's Hall Orchestra. On May 17 he will conduct an orchestral concert of his own compositions, the Queen's Hall band being under his control, and on May 24 he will take part as pianist in a chamber concert devoted to his compositions. Either concert will take place at the Queen's Hall. During their visit to London Dr. and Mrs. Grieg will be the guests of Mr. and Mrs. Edgar Speyer in Grosvenor Street.

S o ran the report in *The Musical Standard* on 6 January 1906 (expanding slightly on an announcement in *The Times* three days earlier), and other journals took up the refrain. It was confirmed: Grieg would be in town again. The *Standard* had already signalled some three weeks earlier the likelihood of a return visit. 'It is declared that Grieg is to pay us a visit next year, and that he will appear at a concert to be given by the Queen's Hall Orchestra.'[1] Now, though, the dates had been set. All that Grieg himself felt that he needed to worry about, apart from the concerts themselves, were the rehearsals, the social calls, the long journeys involved, and – in effect – whether his ever-precarious health would hold up throughout. The Brodskys had picked up the news. 'We read in the papers that you will be coming to London for two concerts. Then you must both come to us so that you can relax a little after the tumult of London. Wouldn't that be wonderful? *Don't* say no!'[2] This seemed an excellent idea to Grieg:

> It's altogether too sweet and kind of you to invite us. We shall love to come. If only I knew how everything will turn out. It's *possible* that after the concerts in London I'll have to return home prestissimo because of the Coronation in Trondheim in June. But fortunately that isn't *likely*, as I've declined to write a cantata for the occasion and can therefore assume that people will have been sufficiently offended to leave me in peace. In which case nothing will prevent me from going to Manchester as soon as I'm done in London. I suppose that that will be at the end of May, i.e. if I'm still in the land of the living then! . . . In the evenings Nina is reading from Tchaikovsky's life and letters. You can't imagine how greatly I recognize myself in him. It's appalling – that melancholy temperament, those most intimate states of

mental tension, everything. He was absolutely not a happy man. And there again I recognize myself.[3]

Newmarch had been as good as her word; Grieg had already told Frants Beyer, 'During the evenings I'm working my way through an English book: *Tchaikovsky's Life and Letters*. It grips me to the depths of my soul.'[4] A few days earlier he had noted in his diary,

> Have spent a lot of time reading from Peter Tchaikowsky's Life and Letters by Modest Tchaikowsky. English edition. What a noble and true personality! And what a melancholy joy to continue in this way the personal acquaintance made in Leipzig in 1888! It's as if a friend were speaking to me.

The spectre of ill health again raised its head in February. Grieg was obliged to rest for much of the time and was sharply reminded of what had happened shortly after he had last arrived in London. 'I couldn't manage anything other than my work, didn't go anywhere and didn't receive anyone.' Now things, he felt, were ten times worse; he was foolish to have taken taken so much on. In writing to Hinrichsen and giving details of his proposed programme for the second of the two London concerts, Grieg asked rhetorically whether he would, when the time came,

Adolph and Anna Brodsky at Bowdon:
'I sent you at Christmas our old pictures taken a year ago while it was still summer,
Adolph now looks quite different without a moustache.'
(Anna Brodsky to Grieg, 6 January 1905 [actually 1906]; Bowdon)

be in any position to carry it all through. Determinedly, he himself proposed the answer. ' "It must be!" Or rather "It *shall* be!" '⁵

Two letters from English writers arrived before February was out. 'I mustn't forget to tell you', Grieg wrote to Beyer on the 19th, 'that I had a letter today from an English lady in Dresden who was enthusiastic about the "Slåtter". She immediately got the autograph she requested!' The *Slåtter* or *Peasant Dances* are the Hardanger-fiddle dance-tunes daringly harmonized for piano, Op. 72, published in 1903, which were leading the French to talk of 'le nouveau Grieg' but were being conspicuously ignored by Norwegian pianists. Op. 72 had also been discovered by Percy Grainger, who for some years had been playing in England pieces from the *Nineteen Norwegian Folk Songs*, Op. 66, published six years earlier, of which he had included two in his solo London recital on 15 November 1905.

The second letter was a bid to have a young girl of 16 play Grieg's Concerto under the baton of the composer when he came to London:

> Through the medium of the Press I have read of your proposed visit to England. I venture to bring to your notice a fact which I trust may be of interest. I have a daughter, a student at the Royal Academy of Music, aged just sixteen years, who is considered to possess exceptional talent as a pianist. She is under the special care of Sir Alexander Mackenzie, who is taking a great interest in her welfare. She, herself, has a great interest in your compositions & has played with great success your Concerto in A minor with the London Symphony Orchestra, conducted by Sir A. Mackenzie, & also with the Royal Academy Orchestra at the Queen's Hall, London. It has occurred to me to submit to you the suggestion that on your visit to London she should play the Concerto under your direction with the Orchestra. She is well-known in London & I shall be pleased to refer you to Sir Alexander Mackenzie for all particulars.⁶

F. S. Hess enclosed a photograph of his daughter, whose 'exceptional talent' was indeed to become universally recognized in later years. Myra Hess was at the time studying piano at the Academy under Tobias Matthay, and her performance of the Concerto under Mackenzie was deemed to have been 'brilliantly undertaken. Her rendering of the octave passages was especially good and the rhythmic effects in the final allegro marcato were excellently shown'.⁷ She kept the Grieg Concerto in her repertoire, later playing it, for example, with the New York Philharmonic under Mengelberg and also recording the solo part on a Duo-Art roll. Grieg is likely to have replied to Frederick Hess, but he will have had to decline this particular offer.

Early in March the decision was taken to make a move to the Holmenkollen Sanatorium above Christiania. 'I need to strengthen my nerves, which really need it.'⁸ Edvard and Nina stayed there for a fortnight, but to little avail, breathing difficulties and insomnia once again being among the composer's main troubles. 'The great mountain in the form of concert tour to Prague, Amsterdam, London lies before me', Grieg noted in his diary on 19 March, 'and obscures my view of that wonderful, quiet time that I dream of. Might this journey be my last? And will my life come to its close out there?' He avowed, however, that there would be no complaints: 'I shall depart this life with gratitude, wherever this may come to pass'. Nonetheless, it was now being reported in Norway that he would conduct an orchestral concert of his works at the Queen's Hall on 17 May and participate in a corresponding chamber concert, joined by the cellist Hugo Becker, on 24 May.[9]

All this time, Robert Newman was busily involved in making arrangements for the two concerts. He informed Grieg that the orchestra had been engaged for two rehearsals on the mornings of 15 and 16 May. 'Mr Wood desires me to say that the Orchestra is quite familiar with all the items in the programme and the Directors therefore hope that you will consider 2 rehearsals of 3 hours each sufficient under the circumstances.' Grieg had sent a suggested programme for both concerts to Edgar Speyer, chairman of the Queen's Hall Concert Board, and this had been forwarded to Newman, who replied to the composer in respect of the second concert. 'I have advised Professor Hugo Becker and Mons Johannes Wolff. I have also written Mme Holmstrand for the titles of her songs as desired.'[10] The Swedish soprano Emma Holmstrand was at the time living in Paris; she duly sent a selection of Grieg titles to Newman for the composer's approval. For the orchestral concert, the vocalist was to be Antonia Dolores, daughter, as Newman informed Grieg, of Madame [Zelia] Trebelli.[11] Grieg was determined to avoid the social round in London, as is clear from a letter he wrote to John Lane: he could not manage to write a projected article on Tchaikovsky owing to having been unwell for some time now; and as for invitations, including that sent to him by Lane and his wife, he quite simply and politely begged to be excused.[12] Grieg was to write in a similar vein from Amsterdam to Beyer with a warning that for once Frants would be receiving only postcards from London, where Grieg would either be making music or resting; there would be no letter-writing.

On 5 April Edvard and Nina left Norway for Prague by way of Gothenburg, Copenhagen, Berlin and Leipzig. They arrived in the Czech capital on the 12th, and Grieg conducted an all-Grieg concert there on the 16th. It was then on via Leipzig and Berlin to Amsterdam, where they arrived on the 20th. On the 26th came another all-Grieg concert at the Concertgebouw, with the A-minor Concerto being played by Fridtjof Grøndahl, son of Agathe Backer Grøndahl, who had achieved such success with the work in London in 1889. On 2 May there followed a chamber concert, in the course of which the Cello Sonata was played by the young Pablo Casals with Grieg at the piano. Both of the Amsterdam concerts proved to be great successes. Edvard and Nina had stayed with the Röntgens, and the warmth with which he was welcomed by old friends acted as a mental as well as physical stimulus, so that early in May they could inform the Brodskys by letter that Edvard was in 'unbelievably' good health. Nina also told Anna Brodsky that Grieg would prefer it if she and Adolph could come to the first of the London concerts, rather than the second.

London, in the meantime, was preparing for what would prove to be Grieg's last visit to the city – and indeed his last visit to England. Miss Tita Brand, announced *The Musical Standard* on 28 April, 'has been engaged to recite "Bergliot" which will be given with Grieg's music, at the orchestral concert to be conducted by the Norwegian composer at Queen's Hall on May 17. She has, of course, already recited "Bergliot" at the same hall; and very thrillingly, too.'[13] Tita Brand was the daughter of mezzo-soprano Marie Brema, who had herself narrated *Bergliot* (most recently at the first of the two Amsterdam concerts), though not entirely to Grieg's satisfaction. The names Brand and Brema sounded suitably foreign, but the women were English. Brema was born Minny Fehrmann in Liverpool and, having studied with George Henschel, had made her début on the operatic stage in London in 1891. Her daughter Tita, a Shakespearean actress, was to marry the Belgian author Emile Cammaerts. Tita Brand was well-known on the English stage and had already narrated *Bergliot* at the Harrogate Festival of 1905, *The Musical World* reporting that 'A recitation given by her of a dramatic scene dealing with the death of the Norse hero, Einar Tamberskelver, to the accompaniment of incidental music written by Grieg, was an impressive and moving experience.'[14]

Elsewhere the press carried announcements about Grieg's forthcoming visit; there were sundry advertisements for the two concerts; *The Monthly Musical Record* devoted a whole page to advertising the Grieg works available in the Peters Edition; and *The Musical Standard* reproduced an account of a visit recently paid to Troldhaugen by a correspondent of the *Daily Mail*:

Edward Grieg lives a long way over the mountains from Bergen, in Norway, the country that he loves too well to leave. Three times the driver lost his way ... in getting me there, and on the worst part of the road a Berlin artist friend, whose easel was set up near the highway, had said: 'It is only eleven o'clock; you had better turn back; Grieg never receives anyone until four in the afternoon.'

'But I am not supposed to know that,' I answered.

At last we got to the place, shining white between the silver-green of the birches.

'Mr. Grieg is not in; he has walked down toward Bergen,' was the greeting we got from the maid.

Going back, I found the driver mending the carriage with a piece of wire that Grieg's cook had given him. While he went on with his work I viewed the place: the spring violets, the silvery birches and the sombre pine trees, a lake showing white between them – the Norway that Grieg puts into his music.

As I turned toward the half patched-up vehicle, a little man, with piercing, dark eyes, flowing white hair and gnomelike figure, dressed all in grey, with a grey, broad-brimmed hat, came out from under the trees, holding my card in his hand. It was Grieg.

'Don't you know,' he began irritably – 'don't you know that I never see any one in the morning? How could I work if I did? Didn't your driver see the sign on my gate-post?'

'He saw nothing, not even the road,' I answered. 'Look at the carriage!' The driver, bright purple in the face, was still struggling with it.

'Norway doesn't seem to welcome me, does it?'

'It does,' he said taking my hand, his face suddenly breaking into a smile. 'Come in.' And I spent one of the most interesting hours in my life.[15]

On Thursday 10 May the Griegs were seen off from Amsterdam by the Röntgens. They rendezvoused at Flushing with Johannes Wolff, who was to travel with them for the rest of the way. Wolff had made all the onboard arrangements for his friends, renting a cabin on the deck and ordering beefsteak and champagne for lunch. 'At first', wrote Grieg in his diary, 'the sea's whitecaps were unpleasant, but it soon got better and we had a marvellous, fine crossing.' He described the crossing more lyrically to Julius Röntgen:

> The sea was a little Max Reger at first, but that didn't last long. Johannes Wolff had reserved for us a wonderful cabin, where he filled us so full of beefsteak, veal cutlet, red wine and champagne that we at last sank into slumber, during which the sea became much calmer until finally there was no more Reger but just Beethoven. I only now see that during those last few days with you I wasn't at all myself simply because of my nervousness about the coming sea journey. I was tedious and 'difficult'. Forgive me! Another time and I'll go via Calais–Dover.[16]

On the party's arrival at Victoria Station, Edgar Speyer was there to meet them.

VI

FINAL CURTAIN CALLS

⊰ 22 ⊱

'SO MANY CURTAIN CALLS THAT I LOST COUNT'

There is a touch of sadness in the welcome we extend to Edvard Grieg. It is known that we are again to have the great privilege of greeting him in the flesh only to say goodbye. Upon the occasion of a former visit he was honoured with the degree of Doctor of Music from the University of Cambridge; but to-day this academic distinction seems a cold form of courtesy from a country which rather prides itself upon making much of musical genius. Ever since the days of Handel foreign musicians have found a cordial greeting upon these hospitable if unmusical shores; and, if fortune favours, the present occasion should serve for offering a really popular welcome to Edvard Grieg. He has many claims to recognition. First of all, though a foreigner, there are associations of ancestry to which we can point with pride; and then, again, to no other living foreign composer . . . do the piano-playing and concert-going English public owe such a debt of gratitude as they do to the foremost musical personality in Norway.

The thought that Edvard Grieg comes to this country to say farewell must be forgotten in the expression of great gratitude. This country's debt had not, perhaps, fully matured upon the occasion of the composer's visits in the last decade; and . . . in 1897, his indifferent health caused many engagements to be cancelled. Then, he gave one the impression of being a tired, sad-faced man; but at sixty-three years of age, as he will be on the 15th of June, he is apparently younger than he was at fifty-three. At any rate, his health has improved. So has the appreciation of our insular musical public; for in the intervening ten years the early pianoforte works of Grieg have been freely reprinted as copyrights expired, and, moreover, the marked increase in the number of orchestral concerts may almost be said to date from the popularisation of 'Peer Gynt.'[1]

BORN in New York in 1862, educated in Frankfurt, and now domiciled in England, the Griegs' host Edgar Speyer had taken British nationality in 1892. He had earlier become a partner at the age of 22 in his father's three associated companies in Frankfurt, London and New York and had come to London in 1887 as director of Speyer Brothers, active in the field of international finance. He married the widowed Leonora von Stosch in 1902, and their shared musical interests led him to become chairman of the Queen's Hall Concert Board and generously to subsidize the Promenade Concerts. Leonora was a highly regarded professional violinist, who had played in her native America in the early 1890s, in particular winning plaudits at the Seidl Concerts in New York in 1893.[2] She remained active musically, performing in a concert given at the Aeolian Hall on 1 May 1906 by Wood and the Queen's Hall Orchestra: 'The programme will include the Chaconne for violin solo, played by Mrs. Edgar Speyer.'[3] In the year of Grieg's final visit to the capital, Speyer became chairman of the Underground Electric Railways Company of London, having joined the board three years earlier, and in July he was created a baronet. The Speyers' house in Grosvenor Street was home to many a concert and acted as a haven for visiting musicians such as Richard Strauss and Claude Debussy. London's musical community owed a very considerable debt to Speyer for his contributions to the city's cultural life.

So it was that for his last visit to the capital Grieg exchanged the hospitality of George Augener for that of Edgar Speyer, who happened to live just a short walk from Queen's Hall. For the first and only time, Grieg's recently resumed diary is the principal source of information about a visit of his to England. The pocket notebooks have been discontinued, and no longer is there just the purely factual recording of times, dates, addresses and expenditure. A richer field is presented by the diarist's spontaneous reactions to the day's events and by his more interest-

Leonora Speyer and daughters (Photo: Speaight)

ingly subjective views and comments on people in general and music-making in particular. And, as ever, there are letters that throw a complementary light on what he sees about him. This final visit to London, therefore, is here recorded wherever possible in Grieg's own words.

On arrival, the Griegs were surprised to be driven to Claridge's, where they spent the first three nights of their stay in London. 'Hr. Edgar Speyer, 46 Grosvenor Street, has put us up here for the time being, as – rather oddly – he had not expected us to arrive so early.'[4] Grieg had a large pile of letters waiting for him 'with all kinds of requests', something that he confessed made him feel nervous. He also mentioned this in the letter he sent to Julius Röntgen:

> Yesterday evening on our arrival there must have been 50 letters lying in wait with invitations and requests of all kinds, which made me so nervous that it didn't do my sleep any good . . . The hotel where we are staying is so elegant that we're really quite unworthy of setting foot in it. Apart from sitting room and bedroom we have also a servant's room and bathroom. Tomorrow afternoon however we move to the Speyers, 46 Grosvenor Street.[5]

Such grandeur wasn't really for the Griegs, and Edvard already looked back with something approaching nostalgia to their stay with the Röntgens, suffused as it had been with the warmth of mutual friendship and the homeliness of the house in Amsterdam.

Furthermore, Grieg was worried about the time he needed to spend rehearsing with three different soloists. He was, too, 'dead tired', as he told Hinrichsen, after the journey. Nor did he particularly take to Speyer on first acquaintance, however kindly the manner in which his host had received him. 'Well, well, that can all change. It's my health on which everything now depends. This evening what I'd most like to do would be quite stealthily to disappear from London.'[6] However, the fact that he and Nina had been provided with everything – and more – that they required was (as he confided to his diary) a welcome consolation. By the end of the month, he and Nina would leave London as warm and appreciative friends of the Speyers.

In spite of Grieg's decision to avoid all social gatherings (a decision that was rapidly to be reversed), he accepted an invitation to lunch at the Speyers' on his first full day, there to find that Charles Villiers Stanford was a fellow guest. In the evening Johannes Wolff was the Griegs' guest at dinner at the Café Royal. On the following day, the composer lunched with Wolff and in the afternoon called on an old friend, Fridtjof Nansen, independent Norway's first envoy to Britain. Other old acquaintances were in the news, too, with Dr Eaton Faning's appointment as Grand Organist of the Grand Lodge of Freemasons, of all things, being reported on 12 May.[7] On the morning of the 13th the Griegs moved from Claridge's to the Speyers' house, just a minute's walk away, and settled into a comfortable suite of rooms, a suite that was, as Henry Wood tells us, 'always placed at the disposal of his [Speyer's] distinguished visitors. Grieg especially enjoyed the charming English garden.' The Griegs were greatly impressed: 'I really believe we live in finer style than any king or emperor. We wade through masterpieces of old art.' At the same time their feelings towards their host and hostess had begun to warm. In the afternoon, they were Leonora Speyer's guests at a 'Sullivan Memorial' concert at Queen's Hall. *The Daily News*, reporting on the Griegs' arrival in London, told its readers of Grieg's presence at the concert. 'It will be remembered that Sullivan and Grieg were fellow-students at Leipsic, where they became friends. The Norwegian composer has written a delightful record of that period, when, as he quaintly puts it, he felt "like a parcel stuffed with dreams".'[8] Mendelssohn's 'Scottish' Symphony in A minor was fittingly enough on the menu, and the conductor was Henry Wood, whom Grieg declared to be excellent. 'He is at one and the same time both lively and infinitely sensitive. Rare for an Englishman. Later in the evening at the Speyers' I got to know him personally as a charming and natural human being.' Wood had, incidentally, given the first London performance of Grieg's *Lyric Suite* on 20 February.

Much later, Wood himself related how the Speyers would customarily hold a dinner party on the evening of a guest's arrival in their home, Edgar Speyer being 'always anxious for his famous guests to meet the right people'. Of the dinner for Grieg he wrote,

> We were all so taken with this shy, refined, delicate little man whose wife spoke such excellent English. After dinner we went into the library for some music. Speyer was very fond of tiger-skin rugs and possessed some fine specimens, one of which, unfortunately, was the cause of a minor but quite unpleasant accident to Grieg himself. Madame Grieg had been asked to sing some of her husband's songs. Grieg, going over to the piano, tripped over the head of one of those rugs and fell. We were all very much distressed and our host immediately got him some brandy. He was too shaken to play though there were no serious consequences. I played for Madame Grieg but was sorry not to have heard them together for, although her voice was not great, there was a beautiful understanding between these two which was evident to us all.[9]

Wood's memory of the occasion, over thirty years later, may have mixed up this with another occasion, for Grieg, who says nothing about a fall, recorded in his diary:

> First I played various things, then they persuaded Nina to sing, something that moved Mr. Speyer to tears. (!) *That* none of us could have imagined. Then I played the G-major Sonata with his wife, after which she played Bach's Chaconne. To be sure, one sees now and then evidence of amateurism, but otherwise nothing but respect. Fresh, rhythmic, energetic and musical. It turned out that we had been together 9 years ago with Nikisch in Leipzig and played that same sonata there. How small the world is at times!

In his autobiography Wood mentioned that the songs in which he had accom-

Henry Wood (Photo: Histed)

panied Nina were 'A Swan', 'From Monte Pincio', and 'A Dream'. According to Wood, Grieg told Speyer he regretted not having scored the latter two songs for orchestra as he had done with 'A Swan' and wondered whether he dared ask his new-found conductor friend to orchestrate them. Wood jumped at the chance to do so, in due course sending his scores out to Bergen. But in this case it must have been Grieg's memory that was at fault. He *had* written an orchestral accompaniment for 'From Monte Pincio' some ten years earlier. This was something, however, that Wood would never know.

Nina felt a little uncomfortable in these high-flown levels of London society, astonished that her hostess could in just a couple of days undertake seven changes of dress, 'each one the more splendid than the last'.

> But oh, how glad I'll be to turn my back on all these niceties and worldly superficiali-ties in which we live at the moment. It so absolutely doesn't suit us simple Norwegian creatures. . . . I thought I had made myself so fine and elegant, but – es war ein Traum!

— We have servants at the end of each finger, huf! and we are driven around non-stop in a motor car. It's fun.[10]

The social round continued on the following day, in spite of all Grieg's earlier promises to himself and others. At least it was only a question of a lunch, which was taken with the distinguished son of his much-loved teacher Ignaz Moscheles. 'Lunch at the home of Felix Moscheles, who looks very much like his father, my dear old teacher. I think his portraits are excellent, in spite of the fact that he is not recognized as a painter of any great significance. He and his wife showed us and Wolff the greatest kindness.' They also chatted about Felix's niece Jelka, whom Delius had married in 1903 and about whom (as Grieg would later tell Delius) they heard 'some very nice things'. Two days later Grieg met Moscheles again, probably at the final rehearsal for his first concert, inscribing for 'the son of my much esteemed teacher' a few bars of the *Ballade*, 'in friendly memory of our brief meeting in London'. The initial rehearsal on 15 may had gone well. 'First orchestra rehearsal in Queen's Hall. Warm welcome from the orchestra. It was excellent and so receptive that it made my task much easier. Miss Stockmarr surprised me with her energy.'

The Griegs spent the evening at home among a few congenial guests, and music was duly made. The fine German tenor Raimund von Zur Mühlen sang Schumann 'magnificently'. Olga Wood was accompanied at the piano by her conductor husband and sang some songs by Richard Strauss; 'I did not enjoy them,' wrote Grieg, 'much as I wanted to.' Jeanne Raunay, the French operatic singer, sang Grieg's 'A Dream' in French, Grieg noting that she was 'pretty to look at and has a nice

An autograph for Felix Moscheles, London, 16 May 1906

voice'. And Nina sang too and was 'well received'. Henry Wood's presence again proved particularly welcome:

> Mr. Wood is the first English artist (musician) who has treated me with warmth and understanding. How strange human beings are: Their sensibilities tell them *immediately* whether or not they like one another. I was captivated by Wood from the moment we met, and I saw immediately that the feeling was mutual. How touchingly helpful he was during the orchestra rehearsals, like a friend.

Curiously, Grieg does not mention in his diary the presence that evening of Percy Grainger. The Speyers had asked their guest of honour if there was anyone in London whom they might invite to meet him, and Grieg remembered seeing some of Grainger's music a year earlier. He decided that he would like to meet this young composer who had shown such a deep interest in folk music, and Grainger duly came to dinner. It was the beginning of a mutually treasured friendship, with Grieg, astonished to find that Grainger was a brilliant pianist as well as a composer, arranging that they should soon meet again. The opportunity presented itself almost immediately, thanks to an invitation from Fridtjof Nansen. Nansen offered Grieg the chance to meet some English politicians, and in a letter dated 14 May thanking Grieg for the tickets he had just received for the concert, he offered a choice of dates for lunch. He hoped the Speyers would be able to come and wondered if Grieg would like to have anyone else invited. In repect of invitations to politicians the guest unsurprisingly demurred, preferring in a social situation to find himself in 'a little Norway' – even if there might be exceptions:

> Whether there are any Norwegians here interested in *art*, I do not know. But if you wish to do something to please me, do invite a *brilliant* young musician from Australia, Mr. Percy Grainger (14, Upper Cheyne Row, Chelsea S.W.) whom I got to know yesterday. He is crazy about Norway, *speaks* Norwegian (Danish!) and knows everything, the Sagas, Faroese literature, Bjørnson, Ibsen etc. He will be happy to shake your hand. . . . We hope then to see you on the 19th, shall we say at 1.30?[11]

Writing to his Danish girl-friend Karen Holten, Grainger left his own impression of his first meeting with the Griegs:

> And the dear Griegs. As soon as he came he asked Mrs Speyer (who I was together with in Northampton by the way; he – Speyer – owns the Queen's Hall orchestra) to invite me, and I went last Tuesday.
>
> Have you seen Grieg and his wife? Can you think of anything more triumphant than the impression of these 2 small people? They are so completely happy together and both so 'loveable' and kind. And she sang for us; and what jubilation and uplift in her and his song and the 2 are just as melted in one when they make music as they are in Life.
>
> He talked not so little with me about my chorus, and I told him that I had just heard it performed up in Lincolnshire and he said 'they sounded lovely, didn't they; they must sound lovely'.

And then I played 3 of the Slåtter for him and 'He took a kindly attitude to it'; was very pleased, and said that I was quite the 1st who played it, as no one else 'dared to'. . . . He played me one of 'Møllarguttens gangar' (in the Slåtter) and it was certainly not a boring evening.[12]

Nansen dispatched an invitation to Grainger from the Norwegian Legation's temporary home at the Royal Palace Hotel, Kensington. The lunch would take place on the agreed date at the Bachelors' Club in Hamilton Place — the guests being adjured to use the Ladies' Entrance.

Percy Grainger's meeting with Nansen left a profound impression on the younger man; many years later, in a classic example of his impetuosity, he drafted an astonishing letter in Norwegian to the great Arctic explorer. The undated draft must have been written in late 1922; it refers to Nansen's work with refugees after the First World War, on the subject of which Grainger had just seen a film. Reminding him that they had met through the Griegs in 1906, Grainger offered to give up music simply in order to work for Nansen's committee and help the starving in Russia. He was, he wrote, fit and strong (having earlier served in the American army), was not afraid of the cold or of any kind of heavy work, spoke several languages, and would be able to learn Russian quickly. Having just completed in the autumn of 1922 a busy concert tour of Norway, he would ask Nina Grieg (with whom he had just stayed) to get in touch and tell Nansen about his musical activities.[13] This extraordinary draft, scrawled on the notepaper of a Utrecht hotel and surely never fair-copied and sent, must have been the product of a depressed and still bewildered state of mind following the suicide of Grainger's mother at the end of April 1922. His loneliness, he wrote elsewhere at the time, was 'overwhelming'. It was as if Grainger were looking to make a complete break from the past and from a present that no longer mattered to him — to make sense of a life that had until now so much devolved on his mother and to express the love that he had felt for her by taking on the cause of the poor, the hungry and the oppressed. In the end Nansen was to be awarded a Nobel Peace Prize for his work; Grainger returned to his music.

Grieg's second (and final) orchestra rehearsal took place on Wednesday the 16th. He was moderately satisfied with Tita Brand's rendering of Bergliot, which he found similar to that of her mother's; it was at least 'talented and energetic'. But he despaired of Antonia Dolores, who had, he wrote, 'no idea at all' of how to perform the three songs that she was billed to sing. He had, however, no criticism of the orchestra, which at the concert would play its heart out for him, as we can read in the reviews:

A short, spare figure stood bowing his acknowledgements of the enthusiastic applause which greeted his appearance at the Queen's Hall on Thursday afternoon, May 17. A high, slightly projecting forehead shading a pair of deep-set penetrating eyes; furrows of thought between the shaggy eyebrows; an expression of mingled seriousness and abstraction; a noble countenance crowned by an aureole of bushy, white hair from which one thick obstreperous lock falls forward on the wide brow beneath. Such in appearance is Dr. Edvard Grieg. His frame seems compounded of nervous strength and elasticity. He gives the impression of a highly original personality: simple and direct. The fine Queen's Hall Orchestra played as if thoroughly inspired by his guidance and the programme was well chosen to demonstrate the different characteristics of his genius.[14]

Although London's musical press remained hugely enthusiastic in respect of both the man and his music, one or two of the daily newspapers were more critical. 'Some of the press surly', was Grieg's note in his diary the following day. 'Easily understandable, I'm afraid to say, as I haven't been willing to talk with any interviewers.' He was clearly chiefly directing his remarks at *The Times*, whose critic gave only a few lines to the programme itself: Johanne Stockmarr, whose first appearance in London had been at a Saturday Popular Concert in December 1900 when she had played Grieg's *Ballade*, had given only a 'rather matter-of-fact' interpretation of the Piano Concerto, whereas Dolores had sung 'with artistic distinction and intelligence' the three songs that were allotted to her – both judgements that would have set Grieg's teeth on edge. The playing of the orchestra was praised, but not one word was pronounced on the merits or otherwise of Grieg's conducting. The main tenor of the piece was that Grieg had shown little development since the Piano Concerto, composed nearly forty years earlier, and since the songs as first introduced to London by the composer's wife in 1888.[15] *The Morning Post* also remarked on the fact that the programme had contained nothing new, but it was far more positive. The concert 'attracted an immense audience, and the fact is not surprising considering the enormous popularity of the Norwegian composer's works. The name of Grieg has indeed become a household word wherever music is cultivated, and fame has in the present instance happily not been deferred too long.' Grieg's style was described as 'one of surprising individuality and wondrous charm'; furthermore, he was 'admirable' as a conductor, and his beat was precise. 'The concert was altogether enormously successful, and Dr. Grieg must have been well pleased with his reception.'[16] *The Daily News*, too, was overwhelmingly positive. The Concerto, 'the event of the concert', had been 'rendered with the utmost beauty' by Stockmarr, who had accorded to it 'such musicianly and heart-felt expression':

> The reading of the work, particularly of the first movement, was greatly at variance with what one is used to, but as Grieg himself conducted we may take it to be correct. Grieg wants the movement to go, in parts, more slowly than we are accustomed to here; and there should be infinitely more expression.

At the same time, the reviewer's assessment of Antonia Dolores's rendering of the songs was somewhat closer to Grieg's own than that of his colleague on *The Times*. She was credited with singing them 'with much insight, though her voice scarcely seemed in the best of order'. As for the *Lyric Suite*, on first hearing it earlier in the year,

the writer then thought the music was interesting solely for the fascinating Grieg

QUEEN'S HALL, W.

Sole Lessees - Messrs. CHAPPELL & Co., Ltd.

GRIEG

ORCHESTRAL CONCERT

THURSDAY, MAY 17th, 1906, at 3 o'clock.

THE QUEEN'S HALL ORCHESTRA

Conducted by Dr. EDVARD GRIEG.

ANALYTICAL PROGRAMME, PRICE SIXPENCE.

Cover of Queen's Hall concert programme, London, 17 May 1906

scoring and harmonic freshness. Conducted by the composer, the suite seemed of considerably greater value than is here implied. Judging by the way Grieg directs his own compositions, he must be rated a wonderfully-gifted conductor. The balance of tone obtained is perfect, and the expression that of a great musical personality. There was no fuss in his method of conducting, but he made the men play as I, for one, have certainly never heard them play.[17]

The reactions of the audience and of the performer-in-chief were recorded by Grieg in a brief diary entry:

Concert in Queen's Hall at 3 o'clock. Tremendous reception, increasing warmth as the concert progressed, enormous enthusiasm at the end. The Lyric Suite and 1st Peer Gynt Suite went exceptionally well. So, as a matter of fact, did the rest of the concert. I'm happy at having got through it so well.

Messages to friends mirrored his enthusiastic response to the concert. 'Today you really should have been here. Orchestra fine and responsive. Everyone kind. Quoting from Vinje I can say: More did I receive than I deserved.'[18] This message to Sigrid Steenberg (a Danish-born piano teacher who lived in Northumberland) was followed by letters to the Röntgens and to Frants Beyer:

Yesterday's concert was colossal. Completely sold out, very lengthy applause. Both Suites went wonderfully. Piano Concerto performed splendidly and powerfully, beyond all expectation. Bergliot very good – à la B[rand] of course – only the songs with The Dolores were quite impossible. A pity! The orchestra sounded so beautiful and the singing dull and colourless. All sold out for next Thursday.[19]

The 17th went off marvellously. It was a glorious feeling to be allowed to represent Norway through my art on the first 17th May after our liberation. It put me in such a mood that I found the task easy. All the performances in the programme were excellent apart from the execution, or rather the non-execution of the songs. It was a daughter of Trebelli who was singing, she calls herself Dolores, and, dear God, it was doloroso in the worst sense of the word.[20]

Grainger had attended the concert together with his mother and Herman Sandby:

Never have I experienced anything ½ so moving and uplifting. I must say it was a happy day for me . . . Q's Hall was packed with men and women and the little man and the great jubilation were awfully moving. You must remember that of all the composers who have ever existed he and Bach are the ones I love most; and it was quite indescribable for me to see the little bit of a person and hear his music at the same time.[21]

The musical journals, as already observed, were full of praise for this, Grieg's last orchestral concert in London, although it was to be a week or two before Grieg would have been able to peruse them. 'On May 17th Edward Grieg should have been a happy man', ran the *Musical News* report. 'As he stepped upon the platform at Queen's Hall he met with a reception which must have convinced him that he was among friends. There was an enormous audience present to do honour to him.' The journal spelled out the composer's interpretative powers as shown in conducting the two orchestral suites:

> Grieg showed that, at any rate as regards his own works, he is a conductor of remarkable skill and delicacy. Singularly quiet in his gestures, he gets the effects he wants all the same, and it was interesting to compare his readings with others to which we are more accustomed. He brought out points which are sometimes overlooked, but speaking generally he does not over-emphasise. In the 'Death of Aase,' for instance, he did not give the picture of absolute despair which is conveyed by some readings; he chose instead to invest it with an air of sadness, much more poetic and beautiful.[22]

The Musical Times found the most remarkable feature of the afternoon to have been Stockmarr's performance of the Concerto, and it was not alone in its assessment of her interpretation as having been 'much more dramatic and intense in expression than is usually presented'. *The Musical Standard* devoted space in particular to Tita Brand and *Bergliot*, but if its initial review was complimentary ('fierce, tenacious, passionate'), a separate article by another writer in the same issue of the journal, whilst admiring the performance of both reciter and orchestra, found that the work had 'failed to make the impression intended':

> One cannot help feeling that if 'Bergliot' had been composed in the form of that much-abused product of modern days, the 'tone-poem,' with its present thematic material somewhat added to and more elaborately worked out, the result would be on a far higher musical plane than the decidedly unsatisfactory work which was presented to us on Thursday week.[23]

Like most of his colleagues, the reviewer in *The Monthly Musical Record* found little to criticize, and the performances of the two suites were considered by all to have been beyond criticism. Like his musical press colleagues, too, he was inclined to give Antonia Dolores the benefit of the doubt: she had interpreted the music 'with simplicity and feeling'.[24] As for Stockmarr, her 'great success' in London was reported on in Norway, as was the fact that she had been invited back to the capital 'for next winter' to take part in three orchestral concerts.[25]

More was to follow for Grieg on the day of the concert. 17 May was – and remains – a high point in the Norwegian calendar, celebrating as it does the Norwegian Constitution, settled on that very date in 1814 in the small town of Eidsvold. Then recently freed from centuries of Danish rule (another far-reaching consequence of the Napoleonic Wars), virtual autonomy for Norway was assured, even if it meant a not altogether willing alliance with Sweden and a share of a monarch resident in faraway Stockholm. But on that day Norway had nonetheless at last become a parliamentary democracy and would henceforth annually celebrate its new-found liberty. In 1906 Constitution Day had taken on an extra significance, as it was the first observance of the date since the final dissolution of the union with Sweden on 7 June the previous year. It was presumably in part to commemorate this special date in England that the election of King Haakon to the Royal Yacht Squadron was announced in *The Daily Telegraph* of 17 May. Meanwhile Grieg, of all people, was away from his homeland and was therefore obliged to celebrate Independence Day abroad. The Norwegian Club's invitation to him was further extended to any particular friends he wished to join him. Two days earlier a hurried note to Johannes Wolff is evidence that the presence of this much treasured friend and favourite virtuoso was almost a *sine qua non*, with Grieg enclosing a ticket for the event and adding that he was *fearfully* busy.[26]

He recorded the event in his diary:

> In the evening at the Norwegian Club. Close on 200 people. Nansen presiding. His speech in honour of the day was moving to the point of tears. A speech in my honour by Hagelund(?), a manufacturer, was *so* awful that Nansen gave another speech for me – and sure enough that was quite a different matter. The thing about Nansen is that he always knows how to strike the right note – or more correctly, the right *notes*, for he was the all-round man that evening. I responded with a speech for those who had worked for liberation for more than a generation, and among them first and foremost for Bjørnson, whose health I ended by proposing.

A more detailed account of the occasion is fortunately preserved in the handwritten minutes of the Norwegian Club (in Norwegian):

> The first big party that the new management had to organize was that for the 17th May. This Independence Day was undoubtedly the most successful 17th May arrangement that the Norwegian Club has ever had. The party was held, as in previous years, in the Hotel Cecil, (Victoria Hall) and there were 188 participants. This year's function offered many attractions and in particular the special fact that our own Minister Dr. Fr. Nansen attended & presided. Furthermore Dr. Edvard Grieg & his wife, who had had a concert at Queen's Hall this very day, did the Club the honour of accepting an invitation to dinner. Dr. Grieg brought, as guests of the Club, some of his artist friends. Consul General Ollesen & Consul Brækstad were also present, but Legation Secretary Irgens was unfortunately prevented from coming owing to family mourning. Otherwise those present were almost all permanent residents. In contrast to the previous 17th May there was a much more lively atmosphere, based on the successful outcome of the events of last year, everyone was pleased and happy about feeling completely free and independent & this feeling of freedom was further enhanced by the presence of our own Minister & Consul General.
>
> At dessert the speeches were opened by Minister Nansen in honour of King Edward, followed by a speech in honour of King Haakon. The speech in honour of the day was given by Minister Nansen in most striking style & was received with tremendous enthusiasm. Consul General Ollesen's speech in honour of Parliament was very successful. The Chairman of the Club then rose & gave a speech in well-chosen words in honour of the four official representatives of our country, following which Minister Nansen responded & concluded his speech with a toast to our country's great representatives like Ibsen, Bjørnson & Grieg, for no better (representatives) recommendation could a country have than such men. Hr. Fagelund then gave a speech

in honour of 'Grieg, the King of Music' which was received with much applause. Dr. Grieg responded to the toast with thanks.

The Club Chairman then rose with the information that Minister Nansen had done the Club the great honour of today accepting the invitation to become an honorary member and this was received with lively applause. At the same time 2 telegrams that had been received during the course of the evening were read out. The one was from Hr. Jørgenson from Karlsbad, the other from Hr. Rieber [?] in Southampton. During the course of the dinner the following telegram was sent to King Haakon & Queen Maud:

Norwegian women & men gathered to celebrate the day send to Norway's King and Queen their homage

(signed) Nansen

There followed a brief mention of the singing, after the speeches, of two songs of Grieg by the gifted Norwegian mezzo Theodora Salicath. The festivities only came

Fridtjof Nansen, caricatured by Olaf Gulbransson

to an end at two in the morning. Grieg added a further detail or two in a letter to Frants Beyer:

> You should have heard Nansen's speech in honour of Independence Day that evening. I had tears in my eyes. I was offered a toast, by someone who I think was a timber merchant (typical clumsy Norwegian!), which was just too bad for words, with the result that Nansen stood up and made another speech to me – and again tears came into my eyes. Then I spoke about what had happened in 1905 and how it had looked like a miracle, but – wasn't one. For it had all happened so very naturally. I spoke of the great men who for generations had worked towards this goal, and finally came to Bjørnson, to whom we then raised our glasses. I knew just what I wanted to talk about, and no more. And I think I succeeded. It just came out naturally. There was real jubilation among those 200 people.[27]

A quieter day followed on the 18th. The Brodskys had indeed come down to London for the concert, and they had subsequently invited the Griegs and Johannes Wolff to lunch. This was a convivial occasion among intimate friends, providing some respite from a social programme that Grieg had certainly not promised himself but that he seemed nonetheless to be enjoying. He was feeling better, after all, than he had felt for a long time; and indeed it was important that he should remain in good health, particularly with a visit to Oxford in view on 22 May, when he was to receive the second honorary doctorate that England had decided to accord him. An announcement had appeared in the 17 May edition of the *Oxford University Gazette*:

> In the CONVOCATION to be holden in the Sheldonian Theatre on Tuesday, May 22, at Two o'clock, it will be proposed to confer the Degree of D.Mus., *honoris causa*, upon EDVARD HAGERUP GRIEG.
> W. W. MERRY,
>   Vice-Chancellor

From the Norwegian Legation Nansen wrote again on the 18th. He had just received a communication from the King's Private Secretary. It would, he quoted, 'afford the King much satisfaction to receive you with Dr. Grieg on Tuesday the 28th Instant at 3-15 o clock – Plain Clothes'. Nansen took it that plain clothes meant a frock coat and concluded by congratulating Grieg on the previous day's 'glorious' concert.

The weekend proved to be a busy one. On Saturday the 19th, together with their hosts the Speyers, the Griegs were invited to lunch by Nansen, finding themselves in the company of a number of fellow Norwegians. In his diary Grieg described the occasion as 'pleasant and relaxed', and he told Beyer how kind Nansen had been to them: 'We were at lunch with him together with our hosts (who in parentheses are said to earn £70,000 sterling a year!!) and some Norwegians. It was extraordinarily enjoyable.'[28] That same evening Grieg and Nina attended a performance of *Tristan and Isolde* together with the Brodskys; 'Richter conducted brilliantly. Ternina's

Isolde consistently excellent. Van Rooy as Kurvenal ditto. But Tristan impossible both in his appearance and his singing, though he at least sang in tune.'

The Griegs' social round continued, with a day trip by rail to St Leonards on Sea on a rainy Sunday to see the Augeners – the last time Grieg was to find himself in the company of what remained of the devoted family that had done so much for him in England. Back at the Speyers' in time for dinner at eight, Grieg still found sufficient reserves of energy to accompany both Hugo Becker in the Cello Sonata and Leonora Speyer in the second Violin Sonata, the day finally coming to an end at 11.30. 'Remarkable what I'm managing here', he commented in his diary.

After a good night's sleep, there followed an even more taxing day on Monday the 21st, part of the morning being taken up with a rehearsal of the third Violin Sonata 'at Bechstein's' with Johannes Wolff, who Grieg thought played the work superbly well: 'What a joy!' Then it was off, accompanied by Nina, to lunch at the home of Henry Wood, 'who together with his wife is exceptionally kind to us'. There followed a brief interlude before the necessary preparations for what was to be an extremely busy evening:

> In the evening big reception at home at Mr. and Mrs Speyer's in honour of Mr. and Mrs Grieg! Nearly 200 people. Printed music programme. Started at almost 11! The whole programme was by Dr. Grieg, who had to play the G-major Sonata with his hostess. She has plenty of talent and spirit, but, too superficial. Nina sang 2 sets of songs and her voice took the listeners by storm. If only female vocalists would get it into their heads that *the interpretation of the poem* is everything! But – that requires a certain temperament that's allotted only to the chosen few.
>
> Lastly Percy Grainger played 2 of the Slåtter in brilliant style. Yes, he's a genius, that's for sure. I feel happy to have gained such a young friend.
>
> We got to bed at 2 o'clock. I say: Just once and never again. This was for our kind hosts as a thank-you for their hospitality. But polite society! To hell with it. Fortunately there were a few artists here. Sandby, the cellist, [and] Becker and Miss Stockmarr who played the Cello Sonata excellently. Stanford and his wife, [and] zur Mühlen.

There was inevitably a price to be paid for this hectic pace, and Grieg started to pay it on the following day. 'Very tired', he confided to his diary. He complained to Frants Beyer that he had scarcely a moment to write letters. He had received literally hundreds himself, virtually all of which lay unanswered – a fact that led some of the writers, who felt themselves insulted by the lack of a reply, to complain to Speyer. The need for rest was of course far more important for Grieg and for the success of his concerts than the business of responding to autograph hunters; but such a need was, however, not to make him many friends at Oxford, where he ought to have presented himself on the 22nd but instead stayed at home. He must have given the University authorities precious little notice, as it is perfectly clear from *The Oxford Review* of Monday 21 May that his visit the very next day was eagerly anticipated:

to-morrow we are to have a further show, when the honorary degree of Doctor of Music will be conferred upon the Norwegian composer, Greig. This is an event which has more than spectacular interest. Oxford can boast of a musical connection of considerable proportions, as the popularity of the Public Classical concerts testifies. Greig, it is true, is rarely heard at these concerts, but his music is appreciated even by the novice who struggles through his exercises. Dr. Greig, whose music is said to be enveloped with the breeze of his native pine woods, should in the natural order of events be introduced to-morrow by the Professor of Music, Sir. C. Hubert Parry, Bart., Britain's greatest living master in the use of thematic material, and the

---

PROGRAMME.

SONATA in A minor for Violoncello and Pianoforte *Grieg*
  (*a*) Allegro agitato.
  (*b*) Andante molto tranquillo.
  (*c*) Allegro marcato.
Professor HUGO BECKER and Miss JOHANNA STOCKMARR.

SONGS   ...   .   *Grieg*
  Madame and Dr. EDVARD GRIEG.

SONATA in G major for Violin and Pianoforte...   *Grieg*
  (*a*) Lento doloroso.
    Allegro vivace.
  (*b*) Allegretto tranquillo.
  (*c*) Allegro animato.
  Mrs. EDGAR SPEYER and Dr. EDVARD GRIEG.

SONGS   ...   .   *Grieg*
  Madame and Dr. EDVARD GRIEG.

TWO SLÅTTER (Norwegian Peasant Dances)...   *Grieg*
  (1) Giböens Bruremarsch.
  (2) " Rötnanesknut "; Halling.
  Mr. PERCY GRAINGER.

Programme of concert at the Speyers, London, 21 May 1906

Sheldonian will doubtless be crowded. Dr. Greig's degree will be the second of its kind conferred by this University within twelve months, Sir Edward Elgar having been the previous recipient. The Norwegian is already a Mus.Doc. of Cambridge, the honour having been conferred upon him during his third visit to this country in 1894.

However, on the day on which the ceremony was to take place, the *Review*, which carried a portrait sketch of Grieg, reported that a telegram had been received from the composer stating that he could not attend; the ceremony had therefore been postponed, with no new date yet given. Another day later a singularly unimpressed reporter, who at least now appeared to have been made aware of how to spell Grieg's name, explained (with perhaps some Oxford self-absorption) what appeared to have gone wrong:

> Genius has its privileges, but Dr. Grieg could hardly have understood the situation yesterday, or he would not have disappointed a whole bevy of Eights' visitors of one of the shows of the week. It was exasperating, to say the least, on going to the Sheldonian Theatre at two o'clock for the ladies to find nothing more novel and interesting than a notice on the doors of the Sheldonian Theatre, that the Vice-Chancellor had heard that Dr. Grieg was not coming, then to wait about to see the authorities go into the Congregation House to discuss who should have the appointing of the new Registrar. It is not as though the great man were ill; that might have been forgiven. It was simply that he thought two o'clock inconveniently early, and proposed five. Five o'clock in the Eights' Week is impossible; it could not be done for the greatest genius the world ever saw.[29]

Later in the week the *Review* carried an indignant entry under the byline 'Notes by an Oxford Lady':

> On Tuesday afternoon I hurried down to the Sheldonian to see the distinguished Norseman, and was much mystified on turning into Broad-street to see little groups of gaily-dressed ladies leaving the Sheldonian precincts and strolling aimlessly about. Could the Theatre be overflowing with sightseers, I wondered, and went straight up to an official guarding a door, who referred me to the notice on the door intimating that Dr. Grieg would not be present. When a little later I gazed upon his picture in a window in the High, I said rude things to it.[30]

Unaware of Oxford's offended reaction to his non-appearance, Grieg and Nina dined at the Café Royal with Johannes Wolff on the evening of the 22nd, with Grieg later regretting the surfeit of champagne with which Wolff had plied him, for a bad night was the consequence. He remained tired and nervous the following day, unable to catch up with an afternoon nap on his lost sleep. On this day, too, he learned of Henrik Ibsen's death. Grieg was more or less prepared for the news, as Ibsen's health had for some time been failing, but it nevertheless came as a blow. 'How much I owe him! Poor great Ibsen! He was not a happy man, for it was as though he had a lump of ice inside him that would never melt. But under that lump of ice lay a warm love of mankind.' Grieg immediately sent a telegram to Suzannah Ibsen, at the same time writing to a friend asking him to organize the dispatch of a wreath 'From Nina and Edvard Grieg':

> Ibsen's death was of course anticipated, but even so it casts an exceedingly sombre mood over my concert preparations. I would rather have been at home.
>
> Things have gone well for me beyond all expectation, so I've got through it all to date with flying colours. Tomorrow is the last concert, and no amount of persuasion will make me do more. For concert stage fright is just like sea-sickness: it gets worse and worse as the years go by.
>
> London is a terrible city for anyone with a name. Several hundred letters lie on my desk that I haven't even had the time to open. Here you have obligations left, right and centre. And then these female singers! There's the very devil in all of them. They're as stupid as they're conceited. And then these people from the press! Interviewers by the dozen – but I won't talk to a single one of them, so I have to put up with a few churlish newspapers. But you should have been at the 1st concert and seen the audience.[31]

All the major London papers carried obituaries of Ibsen – *The Times* of 24 May a particularly long one on the same day as an advertisement on its front page for the Grieg Chamber Concert announced, 'NOTICE / THE TICKETS FOR THE ABOVE CONCERT ARE ALL SOLD'. *The Daily News* went one better on the 25th, with a long article on Ibsen, then on another page a photograph of the great dramatist, and on a further page a discussion by the critic E. A. Baughan on Grieg and Ibsen, which also incorporated a review of Grieg's chamber concert.

In his diary Grieg records playing the Cello Sonata with Hugo Becker at home on the evening of 20 May, but does not make mention of any further rehearsals for his concert of the 24th – though he must certainly at some stage have rehearsed his songs with Emma Holmstrand, who was to be the soloist. He had yet another bad night before the concert, sleeping, with the help of medication, for just three hours. Feeling 'really low' throughout the morning, he took three drops of opium (shades of that very first appearance of his in London) at noon and bucked up considerably while actually on his way to the nearby Queen's Hall in mid-afternoon. He later noted with relief how 'increasingly relaxed' he had felt as the concert progressed. He had asked Grainger to turn the pages for him, and the young Australian was thrilled to be doing so. For a personal account of Grieg's last public concert in England we can best turn to the composer's diary entry for 24 May:

> The Cello Sonata with Hugo Becker went well, then Miss Emma Holmstrand sang a) 'The Enticement', b) 'The Tryst', c) 'Ragna', d) 'Ragnhild'. It was a nicely pitched voice, but otherwise absolutely nothing to speak of. The little that she got out of the songs she can mainly thank Nina for, who with her great ability to communicate her own and my intentions to others had rehearsed the songs with her when she first sang them. – Schwamm darüber [Let's forget it]. –

Then I played a) 'Myllarguten's Gangar' from the Slåtter, b) 'Folk Melody from Valders', c) 'The Mountaineer's Song' (which made quite a hit) and d) 'Wedding Day at Troldhaugen', which caused a real storm. After 3 curtain calls I had to give an encore and so chose 'Cradle Song' and after many more curtain calls the Menuetto from the Piano Sonata.

Then Miss Holmstrand sang a) 'The First Meeting', b) 'Hope' (not hopefully!), c) 'The First Primrose', d) 'Say What You Will', which she repeated. She enjoyed a success of sorts, despite a total lack of personality.

Then at last the final number: The C-minor Violin Sonata with Johannes Wolff. He played it with a more beautiful tone at the rehearsal, but what was nonetheless there was his own old élan and passion that so endear his playing to me. A storm of applause. After several curtain calls I was simply forced back to the piano. Incredibly I was still able to function and played 'To Spring'. And then came so many curtain calls that I lost count. I myself have the feeling that my piano playing was successful, though I would have achieved much finer results with a Steinway. In all it seems to me that Bechstein has seen its best days. None of the pianos I have played abroad this time have appealed to me. At any rate I can say that they do not suit *me*. For a piano virtuoso it may be another story.

When we were about to get into our carriage I was nearly smothered by young people, mostly women, who held out programmes and pencils to get my autograph. I did what I could in haste, but had to leave most of them in the lurch.

To Julius Röntgen the following day Grieg reported that the concert had seen the enthusiasm of London audiences reach its peak: 'I'm told that nothing quite like it happens in Queen's Hall.' Becker and Wolff had played superbly well, and he himself had played much better than at his recent concert in Amsterdam. The three drops of opium that he had taken had played their own part and 'normalized' his condition in a remarkable way. Both concerts had now been negotiated successfully, and Grieg was grateful that his constitution had stood up to the challenge. He had been offered a further concert for the tempting sum of £150, but his health was more important to him than the money. Furthermore, 'poor Nina' had had much to put up with over recent days owing to the 'awful' state of his nerves.[32] 'Thank God', he wrote to the Brodskys, 'that we shall soon be free birds again and can take flight from this golden nest.'

Of the concert, *The Morning Post* reported that an 'excellent performance' of the Cello Sonata had opened the programme, commending too the 'warm, impassioned playing' in the third Violin Sonata of Johannes Wolff, 'who was associated with the composer's triumph'. Grieg himself had 'delighted his audience by his delicate and refined interpretation of several of his beautiful little piano pieces . . . It is needless to add that the Norwegian master was enthusiastically received and that the concert was in every way a success.'[33] *The Times*, too, if feeling that Grieg's chief fault was to be 'too constantly charming', nonetheless found much to enthuse over in the concert and paid compliments to each of the performers, singling out Becker in particular for his playing of the Cello Sonata.[34]

As for the musical press, again there was near unanimity in praise of the afternoon's offerings, with *The Musical Standard* in the van:

This, which took place at Queen's Hall on May 24, was an altogether delightful affair. The popular composer presided at the pianoforte for the whole afternoon, playing solos, in sonatas, and accompanying, and all with that extreme refinement and subtlety that make his playing so unique a pleasure. It would seem impossible to get such delicate and fairy-like effects from a full-sized modern concert-grand. Some instrument especially imported from fairy-land one could well believe to be necessary. Grieg is a specialist in the region between *mezzo-forte* and *pianissimo*. In this apparently limited area he can find a thousand different tone-colours and he can pass from one to the other with magical effect. One moment you are in the foreground of the landscape, in the next you are far, far away, upon the distant snow-peak that is just discernible on the dim horizon. So rapidly, so magically does Grieg's marvellously romantic personality dictate these continuous and delicious kaleidoscopic effects. Physically, Grieg feels the ravage of time, and so in his playing now there are no very high lights. The picture is of necessity somewhat subdued in tone, but when, in earlier years, he had the power of truly portraying his own thunderings, the effect must have been memorable indeed. But as it is, such a delightful experience as the crowded audience had on this occasion cannot possibly be other than memorable. It was when playing the 'cello sonata with Professor Hugo Becker and the third violin sonata with M. Johannes Wolff that Grieg's loss of power was manifest. These two artists were evidently bent upon doing their utmost to honour the composer who was visiting us, and consequently both performances were simply superb. Both artists followed the lead of the composer's indications ideally, and Grieg himself was apparently delighted with their magnificent efforts. The very fine qualities of the violin sonata mentioned were never more strikingly apparent – it is surely one of the most valuable things in the violinist's portfolio. The whole thing is wrapped in romantic mystery, and when not soaring on the strains of inspired and soul-paining melody, we seem to be confronted by some dim, gigantic form which cannot be clearly distinguished, but which impresses us with all the grandeur of the ungraspable. Several exquisite songs were sung very charmingly by Mlle. Emma Holmstrand to the delicious accompaniments of the composer himself, and enjoyment reached its height in the unexampled playing by the composer of many of his most fascinating creations for the pianoforte. The concert came to an end amidst a scene of unbounded enthusiasm, and the composer's image will now remain a cherished memory in the affections of multitudes of his English admirers.[35]

Musical News, too, thought both sonatas were 'excellently played', even if the hall happened to be rather too large 'for music of this description'. The reviewer's comments on Grieg's playing of the piano pieces mirrored those of the *Standard*'s critic:

Dr. Grieg as a pianist has a delightful touch, although he does not possess leonine power, and the renderings were instinct with grace and refinement. His performance of four short pieces for pianoforte solo, selected from Op. 65, 72, and 73, roused the audience to a frenzy of delight, and he was compelled to accord a double encore . . . At the conclusion of the concert, the crowd remained applauding until the eminent composer conceded another solo.[36]

The Monthly Musical Record's review was unusually brief and matter-of-fact, but nonetheless complimentary, singling out the contribution of Emma Holmstrand, 'who has a most sympathetic voice, and sings with great artistic taste'.[37]

Grieg's earlier comments on 'churlish' reviews were also appropriate to those carried by *The Daily News* and *The Daily Telegraph* on the day following his concert. E. A. Baughan's piece in the *News* referred to 'a grey-haired elf' in whom could be imagined 'the traditional, familiar spirit of his countryside':

> The years have weakened his technique as pianist, but the intentions of the performance were clear enough. In all he aimed at a dreary restraint, which has neither passion at its heart nor ordinary sentiment, but an aloofness which suggests a naïve and simple poetry. Ordinary pianists make his music German in robustness and force; they lose the infinite variety of greys which seemed to me yesterday to be the characteristic of Grieg's music. And, strangely enough, the music aroused in one the same mood which Ibsen's plays arouse. One longed for more warmth, and, with Oswald Alving in 'Ghosts,' I could have cried aloud for the sun. It is crepuscular music; it is fresh as the dew on the grass at dawn, and limpid as streams of melted snow, but it leaves one unsatisfied and cold and even depressed.

And the *Telegraph* was distinctly uncomplimentary in its view of the solo pieces offered by Grieg:

> These were but trifles picked out from groups of kindred things, and some may have been inclined to doubt whether the dignity of the occasion was considered by the introduction of works obviously intended for drawing-room consumption. They certainly appeared too small for the place they occupied, but, on the other hand, it may have been supposed that the trifles were intended as a relief from the hearing of more serious things. Much transcending the pianoforte trifles in interest were the eight songs sung by Miss Emma Holmstrand.

What can be seen from these occasional dissenting reviews of the two 1906 concerts is of course no more than what George Bernard Shaw was fussing at in the late 1880s: an irritation felt at Grieg's enormous popularity with the concert-going public and at the relatively small scale on which he continued to work. The British press had been exceptionally kind to him until now, and for the most part it still was – in stark contrast to the situation in Germany, where many critics for whom Grieg felt considerable distaste had sniped at his work for years. However, German *audiences* were little different from the British in their admiration for his work and in their affection for his personality, and in consequence his music had no difficulty in maintaining its popularity among either country's concert-goers. Grieg's persistently worrying state of health and physical frailty had, it is generally considered, long since diverted him from such areas as the larger symphonic forms favoured by Austro-Germany or the oratorios and cantatas of Victorian England; the result was that he had early come to recognize his own strengths in adversity and to concentrate on all those shorter piano pieces of great originality and on songs which could more than hold their own in the company of music's gods. He had, after all, the priceless gift of melody in abundance and an ear for harmonies that were fresh and progressive. And who knows into what areas the late *Slåtter* might have taken him had he been granted longer and more vigorous life?

His last two public concerts in England would have been sell-outs whatever works he chose to present to his adoring public. This raises the question of why he elected to offer two such 'safe' programmes. His critics' teeth would surely have been drawn had he played a selection from the *Slåtter* alone at his final appearance. But he chose to please his audience rather than his critics, and for this he paid a critical price — even if a modest one. He was sensitive enough to regret the payment, as a letter to Julius Röntgen from London shows:

> Well, well, it is — or better, it appears — all very well and good with this popularity, but it doesn't come cheaply. My reputation as an artist suffers from it and critiques become malicious. Happier the artists who don't find so-called popularity in their lifetimes. There's nothing I can do about my music being played in third-rate hotels and by young girls.[38]

⊰ 23 ⊱

'THESE LONDON DAYS AMONGST MY MOST
HAPPY MEMORIES'

AFTER his Chamber Concert, Grieg returned to Grosvenor Street for a well-deserved rest before joining the Speyers and their guests (Hugo Becker and his wife) for an intimate dinner. He enjoyed the evening but admitted that he would have preferred it if his new and old favourites, Percy Grainger and Johannes Wolff, could have been there too. He was much taken by Grainger, who had sat at his side during the concert and turned the pages for him, and was clearly basking in the admiration and affection that the younger man had shown towards him. 'I haven't met anyone who *understands* me as he does.' They would shortly meet again.

The morning of Friday 25 May dawned, and a note of foreboding found its way into Grieg's diary: 'A touch of bronchitis. Must take care.' In spite of his complaints about the 'hundreds of letters' he had received asking for his autograph, he set to responding to as many as possible during the morning, continuing with the 'terrible job' the following day. Writing to Röntgen about his immediate plans, he commented that he would not be present at Henrik Ibsen's interment, however much he would have liked to be. The Norwegian government had decreed that Ibsen should receive a State Funeral on 1 June, but Grieg had promised the Oxford authorities that he would turn up without fail on 29 May to accept his doctoral degree.[1] The first stage of the journey home was now scheduled for the 31st. That evening was to see a special performance of Ibsen's *Ghosts* at the National Theatre in Christiania, with Grieg's 'Death of Åse' being played before the curtain rose. And King Haakon himself would be present at the funeral the following day.

Meanwhile, *The Oxford Review* was keeping a close eye on what its hero-cum-villain was up to in London, duly updating its readers on the highlights of his current visit, under the heading of 'Grieg Festival':

> When Dr. Grieg (upon whom the honorary degree of Doctor of Music is to be conferred by Convocation on Thursday) returns home next week he will take back the happiest recollections of his present visit to London. He has been 'lionised' so much

that he is now obliged to decline invitations to dinners and luncheons; his autograph has been sought for by all kinds of admirers; his two concerts at Queen's Hall have been triumphant successes; and various honours have been bestowed on him, though the greatest is still prospective. The King, who usually desires to see notable visitors to this country, has commanded Dr. Grieg and his wife to attend Buckingham Palace before they leave London. Yesterday afternoon Dr. Grieg made his last public appearance this season at Queen's Hall, and it says much for the interest taken by the public in his works, of which the programme was made up, that every seat was sold.[2]

The bout of bronchitis persisted for the next couple of days, but fortunately it did not amount to very much. It was enough, however, to worry Grieg, who was more than aware how rapidly he could succumb to chest problems. There were important engagements still to get through before his departure, and taking to his bed must not be one of them. Meanwhile, he gave an interview on the 26th to the London correspondent of the Christiania daily *Aftenposten*, and in the evening he enjoyed a visit from Grainger, Wolff and Johanne Stockmarr. Nina had written in

Sketch of Grieg in *The Oxford Review* (22 May 1906)

English to Grainger a few days earlier, making an enigmatic reference to a friend of his and Herman Sandby's, the musicologist Adela Wodehouse. 'As for Mrs. Wodehouse we are einverstanden über Samstag, nicht wahr [agreed about Saturday, aren't we]? Please do come here a little before 5 o'clock and meet me Saturday. Will you?' It is unclear what the understanding about Mrs Wodehouse might have been. There was more music-making during that relaxing Saturday evening, and Grainger played and sang a number of English folk songs that he himself had harmonized. Again, Grieg was deeply impressed: 'Here is something that suggests a new English national style.' Earlier that day, Grainger had received a telegram from Speyer: 'Will you come and dine here on Monday 28th 7.30 a little farewell dinner to the Griegs who have expressed a wish to meet you again before they go'.

The visit to Buckingham Palace had been fixed for Monday 28 May, and this meant of course a reunion with the former Prince of Wales and Princess Alexandra. Again we can turn to Grieg's diary for a detailed report of the event:

To Thomsen the court photographer in the morning. Nansen came at 1.30 and lunched with us. At 2.30 the three of us drove together to Buckingham Palace, where we had been summoned to meet the King and Queen. They were both very kind. I was so fortunate as right away to be able to tell the King that the telegram I sent him last summer on the day when Norway was within a hair's breadth of going to war, and in which I asked him for the sake of peace to intervene with the help of arbitration – that this telegram was a manifestation of the nervousness that pervaded the whole of Norway at that time, and that I hoped that he had not misunderstood it, but had perceived it for what it was. And he declared that he had indeed done so. And with that, he immediately asked if the Norwegian royal couple were popular in Norway. To this I could only say yes. Then he (who is said to be the most unmusical Englishman of all) told me that he was very fond of my music, which he often heard when it was played outside the Palace by the military band. (!)

And then something happened that I hadn't guessed: both the King and the Queen wanted to have some music. What was one to do? Into the Music Room, where I let loose on a Bechstein, and, remembering the Queen's deafness, I pounded away at the Menuetto from the Piano Sonata. And then? The King, who was sitting beside Nansen, begins quite calmly to converse aloud with him. This happened just before the Trio, and I paused at this point and looked questioningly over toward the King, who responded to my questioning look with a broad smile. Then I continued. But God help me: Once again the same story. Now I got angry and made a longer pause that, according to what Nansen said later, he understood and took to heart. It's pretty rude to request music and act like that. Then the Queen wanted to have a song: and which song? Of course: 'Min Tankes Tanke' [I Love But Thee], which sounded good in that big room.

Next we talked for a while with the Queen, who is by no means as deaf as she is said to be. She had been led to believe that we were not in Bergen when she was there 2 years ago. But next time she wanted to see us. She then asked for our signed portraits, and then we said goodbye and left. One thing one can say about the King and Queen: They were exactly the same as they were when Prince and Princess of Wales, natural and easygoing, with none of the Germanic 'von oben herab', as with the the petty nobility in das grosse Vaterland.

The Norwegian Legation Secretary Johannes Irgens and his wife were also present. Irgens recalled how the King had begun 'a whispering political discussion' with Nansen, it being 'not the kind of music that appealed' to him. When the conversation grew loud enough to disturb Grieg, as Irgens recalled, it had been Queen Alexandra who persuaded him to resume playing, the King maintaining for the rest of the recital a 'pained but absolute silence'.[3]

The Griegs' visit to the Palace was noted widely in the press, most papers simply quoting all or part of the official announcement in the *Court Circular*:

> Doctor and Mrs. Grieg had the honour of being received by Their Majesties this afternoon, being presented to the King and Queen by His Excellency Monsieur Fridtjof Nansen (Norwegian Envoy Extraordinary and Minister Plenipotentiary).
>
> The Marchioness of Lansdowne and General Sir Godfrey Clerk were in attendance.[4]

After resting for a while at home later that day, Grieg was visited by Edgar Speyer's physician, who told the composer after a chest examination that in general there seemed to be little that he need worry about. The patient himself had already noticed some improvement since the morning, 'obviously a result of the fact that I have been out in the open air a lot today and have let the warm sun shine upon me'.

The morning of Tuesday 29 May dawned, and the postponed trip to Oxford was finally undertaken:

> At 10 o'clock in the morning with the Speyers and Miss Stockmarr to Oxford, where I was created Dr. Honoris Causa with all due ceremony. Like Falstaff I have to ask: What is honour? I preferred the ceremony at Cambridge, it was somehow more festive, although here there were also speeches in Latin and gold-braided gowns and tasselled mortar-boards. In Cambridge the audience was of students; that made it more lively. Here the audience was almost entirely women. But the loud and welcoming applause at the outset and especially on leaving showed that people liked my music and that could only warm my heart.
>
> Lunch before the ceremony at the home of Mr. Strong, Dean of Christ Church College. The speech in Latin was given by the composer Hubert Parry and that raises misgivings, as English composers as a rule have the least possible regard for their foreign colleagues. We'll find out if I'm right when the speech, a copy of which I took with me, is translated.

Might Grieg have been suspicious of the 'entertaining manner', as *The Oxford Review* friskily described it, of Parry's eulogy?

> He tripped off the opening sentences in a gay allegro, then suddenly quieted down into a mild andante. After that the tempo for some sentences became exceedingly rubato, and after a few phrases prestissimo he fell into a gentle adagio patetico, finally

Grieg and Parry, Oxford University, 29 May 1906:
'a snapshot of mine – the only one that was taken of Dr Grieg and Sir Hubert Parry
about to enter the Sheldonian Theatre Oxford when the Honorary Degree of Mus.
Doc. was conferred upon your husband in 1906. The photo is not first class, but
I would deem it an honour if you would kindly accept it.'
Arthur C. Burrows to Nina Grieg, 10 June 1911; 19 St Michaels Street, Oxford.

finishing up with a cadenza molto accellerando poco a poco. Everybody who knows the Professor will understand his style perfectly.[5]

Maurice Ravel was to be similarly suspicious at Oxford in 1928, with Gordon Bryan noting 'the quizzical expression on his face while the long Latin oration was read and the anxiety with which he demanded an exact translation at the first opportunity'.[6] But Grieg need not have worried, as the substance of Parry's Latin was less facetious than its delivery:

> Dr. Edward Grieg, who can now sign himself Mus.Doc., Oxon. et Cantab., must, if he counts a knowledge of 'modern' Latin among his accomplishments, have been highly amused by the compliments heaped upon him in that tongue by Sir Hubert Parry, when, on May 29th, he was presented for the degree of Mus.Doc. at Oxford. Roughly translated the professor's speech ran thus: 'How great and how individual the beauty of his songs! The force and grace of expression, the sweetness of sound, the exquisiteness of their representation touch the innermost cords of the human heart, and by merely touching them make men stronger and better. There is no lyric bard who has to such an extent won at once the admiration of the critic and the love of the public.'[7]

Details of the ceremony were spelled out in the press. The university's Vice-Chancellor presided, senior dignitaries of various Oxford colleges were present in large numbers, and 'the semi-circle and galleries were graced with the presence of a large number of ladies.' Among those present was William Henry Hadow, formerly a lecturer on music at the University, who was also a well-known writer. Parry, who had escorted Grieg from the Divinity School to the Sheldonian Theatre, had real respect for his music. Indeed, within a few days Parry would give a lecture in the Sheldonian on the function of thematic material in musical organization, during which he would pay a 'graceful tribute' to Grieg, using as one of his illustrations Grieg's song 'The Princess', sung by Theresa Lightfoot accompanied by James Friskin.[8] Summaries of Parry's eulogy were published in the Oxford papers:

> Upon Dr. Grieg being presented for the degree by Sir C. Hubert Hastings Parry, Bart., the Professor of Music, he was greeted with hearty and prolonged applause. Sir Hubert, speaking in Latin, referred to Dr. Grieg's Scottish descent, but he was a patriotic lover of Norway, which was in every way worthy of his love. He was educated at Leipzic (to which he was sent on the advice of Ole Bull), but his German education only intensified the national character of his genius. The Professor specified, among other compositions, Dr. Grieg's incidental music to Peer Gynt, the Pianoforte Concerto, the String Quartet, and especially his songs.
>
> On leaving the Theatre, Dr. Grieg was again heartily applauded, and he acknowledged the compliment by repeatedly bowing.[9]

Grieg had appeared to some observers to be rather worried and anxious during the ceremony, and he was clearly glad when it was all over. *The Musical World* later reprinted a report that had earlier appeared in *The Manchester Guardian*:

As his eyes wandered over the tiers of young faces around him while his introducer . . . read the usual long Latin eulogy before presenting him to the Vice Chancellor, it was a sad and a strong face that we saw — one might almost have said a grim face but that there was nothing of hardness in it, a face which must have inspired both respect and affection in all who met him. Yet as the little old-looking man stood there in the red and yellow gown of a Doctor of Music there was something incongruous about his appearance — the head, encircled with long, straight white hair, appearing above the still stiffer, straighter lines of gaudy brocaded silk, which descended to the ground in the form of a regular cone. . .[10]

Just as when he had received his Cambridge degree, Grieg could see the funny side of things — the flummery, the dressing-up, the portentous speeches, the grandiose ceremony with its medieval elements. There was just time to write a letter to Brodsky before retiring for the night: 'I'm dead tired after the Oxford comedy and want to get to bed!' In an earlier letter to the Röntgens he had rephrased a promise that originally dated from Cambridge in 1894: as a doctor he would now be able to cure himself as well as all of his friends.

One promise that Grieg was extremely anxious to exact from Adolph Brodsky was that his old friend would come to Troldhaugen in the summer, a project that would have been discussed when Adolph and Anna had come down to London for the Queen's Hall orchestral concert. In what was probably the last letter that he wrote in England (one other was penned to the Belgian pianist Arthur De Greef that same evening), Grieg proposed that the visit should best take place in July — but if that should not suit, then August would do. 'I'm as gleeful as a child at the prospect of seeing you over there in our home!'[11]

For the first engagement of their last full day in England, Grieg and Nina were obliged to separate. Grieg himself had accepted an invitation to lunch with Alexander Friedrich, Margrave of Hesse, whom he had first got to know in Germany and who was in London at the time; whereas Nina stayed at home, joining the Speyers and their luncheon guest, the writer Mrs Humphry Ward. Grieg rather regretted the arrangement, as he would very much have liked to meet Mrs Ward, having always been a great admirer of her novel *Robert Elsmere*. Nevertheless, he was able to hear rather more of his own music that day than expected, in the shape of a substandard *Peer Gynt Suite* no.1 (which included an 'awful' 'Death of Åse') played by 'a minimum of instruments', and then to his surprise a rather good performance of the first movement of his Cello Sonata, followed by the second movement of his third Violin Sonata — all played while he, the Margrave, and three other 'pleasant companions' were at table.

The evening, however, was to supply far richer musical fare, and again it is to Grieg's diary that we can turn for an intimate glimpse of three even more pleasant companions:

I spent my last evening in London at home with Miss Stockmarr, Percy Grainger and

Herman Sandby. Our hosts were out and we played our part as masters of the house. First a fine dinner with 3–4 servants, then coffee and music in the Library.

Fate decreed that on this day I would get to hear the Cello Sonata for the 2nd time, as Grainger and Sandby wanted to hear my opinion of their interpretation of it. Their performance was excellent from beginning to end. There were things that Grainger got much more out of than I myself did, and on the whole I received a good lesson. It isn't often that I have an opportunity for that kind of learning.

My joy at having found and won the affection of these two young artists is great, for Sandby too is a significant talent. To be sure, the string quartet of his that I heard recently was confused and formless. But it had what is most important: ideas and a feeling for sound. I see a promising future in his talent, and as he is a cellist of real quality it is to be hoped that he will succeed in his vocation. He played the first of the 'Slåtter' on his cello. It was an excellent performance.

And how Percy Grainger played several of them on the piano! There is no Norwegian pianist at the moment who can touch him. And that is significant in more ways than one. It shows that we still do not have a Norwegian pianist who has enough understanding to tackle such challenges, and that if this understanding does not exist where it ought to, in Norway itself, then it can be found elsewhere, indeed even in Australia, where the marvellous Percy Grainger was born. In general this sermonizing about having to be a Norwegian in order to understand Norwegian music and in particular to perform it is sheer nonsense. Music that is really worthwhile, in any case, be it ever so national, rises high above the merely national level. It is cosmopolitan.

After the Cello Sonata, Miss Stockmarr played some of my 'Moods' and a couple of absolutely brilliant Preludes and Fugues by Franz Neruda in a manner that demonstrated that she is something more than just a dextrous pianist who knows how to let her fingers run about over the keys.

On Thursday 31 May, taking the 9 am boat-train from Victoria, Grieg left London for the last time. He and Nina were accompanied by Edgar and Leonora Speyer as far as Calais, where they all took lunch together before continuing on their separate ways. The Griegs travelled via Cologne and Hamburg to Copenhagen and Christiania, two familiar capitals where they would stay for a few days each before returning to Troldhaugen on 21 June.

The final word on Grieg's last visit to England goes to two items printed in *The Musical World*, a valedictory piece headed 'Good-bye, Dr. Grieg!' and a letter from the composer himself to Edgar Speyer:

Honoured by invitation from the King, hero of concerts for which tickets were unobtainable, and now Doctor of Music (*Honoris causa*) of Oxford as well as Cambridge, Dr. Edvard Grieg has returned to the land of his birth; and it is with unfeigned regret that his many friends in this country have been called upon to say 'Good-bye!' An additional element of sadness has been imparted to the fifth [*sic*] visit of Dr. Grieg by the death – within the intervening week of his public appearances – of his compatriot and erstwhile fellow-worker, Henrik Ibsen. In all the years that are yet to come, the name of Grieg will be indissolubly associated with his incidental music to Ibsen's

'Peer Gynt.' The names of both the dramatic poet and the musical composer are revered and honoured as those of patriots in the 'dark and true and tender North.' The poet, who was almost an octogenarian, has been solemnly interred with State ceremonial. Grieg goes home, we must hope, to live for many years in the peace and comfort of his well-earned retirement.[12]

Now that the London Concerts are behind me, my heart prompts me to thank you most warmly for your kind invitation to come to London, but I wish to thank you especially for having afforded me the occasion to become acquainted with the splendid Queen's Hall Orchestra and to conduct it. It is indeed an orchestra of the first rank. But, even with an orchestra of the first rank the highest achievements can only be attained with a conductor who is the orchestra's equal. Your orchestra possesses such a man in its permanent conductor, Mr. Henry Wood. What his remarkable ability, his great earnestness and art, his love for the cause has achieved, has impressed me most deeply. To my mind he stands out as one of the few truthful and self-disciplined conductors of our time. The fact that only two rehearsals were necessary for my concert and that my intentions were at once understood and felt is proof (if proof indeed were necessary) of the high standard of your orchestra. I have very rarely heard performances of my works so refined and sensitive, and equally rarely has it been my good fortune to find such sympathetic understanding and kindness from both conductor and orchestra. This has greatly facilitated my task. I beg you to convey to the whole body of artists and its great conductor my sincerest thanks for the great pleasure they have given me. I shall always treasure the remembrance of these London days amongst my most happy memories.[13]

VII

CLOSURE

⇥ 24 ⇤

'MY SUN IS ALREADY LOW IN THE WESTERN SKY'

THE Griegs' last major port of call on the way home was Christiania, where they arrived on the afternoon of 11 June 1906. Charged by Edward VII and his consort to call on their daughter and son-in-law, the Griegs presented themselves at the royal palace the following day. Edvard's diary entry for 12 June tells the story:

> Had the unpleasant duty of conveying greetings from King Edward and Alexandra to the Norwegian royal couple. We were received at 2 o'clock by both King and Queen. Both of them were very amiable and easygoing, as before, but when the conversation turns to art, to music, then there's the devil to pay. When the King maintained that King Edward loved music, I couldn't resist saying that it must be an original kind of love, as I'd nearly created a scandal at Buckingham Palace because the King sat and talked out aloud to Nansen while I played, so that I had in fact to stop twice. Then King Haakon uttered the divine and characteristic words: 'Yes, but King Edward is the kind of person who can very well listen to music and carry on a conversation at the same time!' That was more than I could take and I exclaimed, 'Well, whether he is King of England or an ordinary man, it's wrong and I do not accept it. There are some things that out of regard for my art I absolutely cannot do.' Then the King made a motion like a jumping-jack and with a smile took the conversation off on a different track. It's all very well for him to want to defend his father-in-law, but there's a limit to everything.

The conversation turned to the approaching coronation in Trondheim and – quite a new concept for Norway – to the degree of policing that it would require, not just in respect of the new king but more particularly on account of a perceived terrorist threat to visiting members of the Russian aristocracy. Grieg wrote in his diary that he had violated the rules of etiquette by himself bringing the audience to an end, the old republican standing up and – with Nina – saying good-bye to his monarch and simply 'disappearing'. 'I thought enough was enough'. It did not, however, take long for Grieg's irritability to wear off. If he was troubled by what he felt to be King Haakon's indifference to good music, he was nonetheless charmed by the

personality that lay behind the attitude, telling Henri Hinrichsen that the unpretentious King had simply shrugged his shoulders and smiled good-humouredly
on learning of Edward VII's discourtesy. 'The main thing is that he is an utterly
charming person. More's the pity that he seems to have absolutely no appreciation
for music.'[1]

The Griegs were back at Troldhaugen on 21 June, finding it newly painted and
repaired, as well as adorned for the first time with a veranda, 'all of which put me in
such a blissfully happy mood and filled me with gratitude to Frants and Marie, who
worked out all the details, and to Gabriel Smith [Marie Beyer's engineer brother],
who designed the veranda'. Two new offers from England were already waiting in
the post. The firm of Ibbs & Tillett hoped that Grieg might return in the early autumn, guaranteeing him a series of six or eight concerts at a fee of £100 per concert
and all travelling and hotel expenses; Nina would be included too.[2] And there was
an offer from Leeds for Grieg to come and conduct some of his own compositions
at the Triennial Musical Festival in October 1907.[3] A return to England in some
three months' time was clearly out of the question, but Leeds, a further year ahead,
was a different matter. Grieg drafted a reply, agreeing to the proposal and adding
that his fee would be £100. Fred Spark, Leeds Festival secretary for thirty years,
was delighted, and accepted Grieg's terms.

No sooner had Grieg settled down again at Troldhaugen than he began to be
plagued by asthma, feeling it to be a reaction to all his recent travels — travels that
had seemed to have gone so well. He had already made the decision to spend the

A salute from Grieg to Delius in June 1906 on a postcard showing a view
from Troldhaugen

autumn and winter months in Christiania, where the comparatively dry atmosphere would better accommodate his continually weak chest. After that, concerts in Prague and Berlin were to follow in the spring of 1907. He was nonetheless cheered to hear from Percy Grainger, who was enjoying the selection of songs that Grieg had given to him in London and who was also busy practising 'Wedding Day at Troldhaugen', together with two of the *Slåtter* that he had not so far tackled. 'I must say that your visit here was the loveliest time I have ever experienced. We are all longing for you to come back soon.'[4] Grieg told Hinrichsen that in his present condition the memory of Grainger's and Sandby's playing was like the sun breaking through the clouds.[5] And he wrote a fulsome letter to Grainger, extending an invitation to Troldhaugen that had almost certainly already been tendered verbally in London. 'My sun is already low in the western sky, so it had better happen soon.'[6] His correspondence with Grainger would continue until shortly before Grieg's death little more than a year later.

Grainger himself must have been involved in the decision of the Folk Song Society to offer honorary membership to Grieg. This came in the form of a letter, addressed to Doctor Edvard Grieg and dated 10 July 1906, from the Society's honorary secretary Lucy Broadwood:

> I am instructed by the Committee of the Folk Song Society, with Lord Tennyson as its President, to inform you that at their last Meeting, held on July 4th, it was proposed and unanimously agreed that you should have offered to you the Honorary Membership of the Society (in accordance with Rule X, a copy of which I enclose.)
>
> I have very great pleasure in informing you of your election, and in begging you to honour the Folk Song Society by accepting their offer, which is prompted by their knowledge of your great work for, and sympathy with Folk Music.

Grieg drafted his reply, first in Norwegian, then in English, on the back of the Society's letter:

> I have received your admirable communication of my nomination as an Honorary member of the F.S.S. and have only to say, that I feel proud and happy to have this honour, for which I beg you to express before the Committee my heartiest and respectful thanks.

Grieg's acceptance was acknowledged by Lucy Broadwood on 26 July, and she enclosed a copy of the Society's annual report, together with a list of its members. Grieg would already have noted from Broadwood's initial approach that the Society's three vice-presidents were Mackenzie, Parry and Stanford, and that J. A. Fuller-Maitland, Cecil Sharp and Ralph Vaughan Williams were numbered among the committee's members. If he found time to peruse the list of members, he would have registered names such as Elgar, Joachim and other leading musicians of the day – not forgetting Grainger, of whom it was noted in the report that he had been collecting songs in Lincolnshire. And there was Gavin Greig, MA, FEIS, of Aberdeenshire, who might just have been able to claim distant kinship. Six months later,

Grieg was able to tell Grainger that he had been receiving informative brochures from the Society. 'I admire the way in which the enterprise is organized and regret that nothing on similar lines can be organized in my homeland. But here we lack the taste for *anything* except politics and — sport!'[7] Grainger was, to his delight, elected to the Folk Song Society's committee early in 1907; he duly took Grieg's letter to a meeting in order to show to his colleagues Grieg's laudatory words.

A memorable event in the summer was another encounter for Grieg with Kaiser Wilhelm, who, cruising again in Norwegian waters, had called on the German Consul in Bergen. Conrad Mohr invited Grieg to breakfast on 6 July. Apart from the Kaiser and his guests, the Norwegian Prime Minister and his wife were also present. 'It was great to talk to Michelsen again', Grieg confided to his diary. Over coffee Grieg had a long chat with the Kaiser, partly about music, partly about the new Norwegian king and queen, and then more specifically about *Sigurd Jorsalfar*, which the Kaiser was determined to have performed in Berlin in the following season. Earlier they had also talked about the events of 1905, the Kaiser having in the mean time met King Oscar and found him 'completely disoriented' about the Norwegian question.

The other highlight of the Norwegian summer was the visit, at long last, of Adolph and Anna Brodsky. Grieg was still awaiting definite news at the end of June, telling his old friends that they simply *had* to come and that the only remaining question for him was when. A secondary question was whether the Brodskys preferred to sleep on a hard or soft mattress: 'Everything must be well orchestrated. And what diet does the violin require? Send a reply presto!'[8] There was some disappointment that the Brodskys were unable to get away immediately, but the consolation was that they would be coming early in August. Because they proposed to bring with them a niece and two of Brodsky's young violin students, the decision was made for them to put up at the Hotel Norge in the middle of Bergen (where, Grieg told them, he himself always stayed) and to spend most of their time with the Griegs, either at Troldhaugen or in and around the city itself. Another visitor to Norway this summer was Henry Wood, who holidayed in the country in July but did not meet Grieg. Delius too hoped to see Grieg again, perhaps in the mountains; but Bergen was not on his itinerary during his summer visit to Norway, and Grieg did not feel fit enough to travel elsewhere:

> I have, it is true, always had frail health. But now, with old age as well, life has become more and more of a burden to me. Through physical suffering I am unable to work, although I feel that I still have it in me. That is what makes existence so unbearable for me.[9]

This was yet another painful period for Grieg, boding ill for Brodsky's visit. The last two weeks of July were characterized by depression, breathing difficulties and an attack of rheumatism, in spite of the gloriously hot weather. As so often before, and as once more to come (with the visits in the summer of 1907 of Julius Röntgen and Percy Grainger) it was the presence of adored friends that would change things. Grieg's diary of Brodsky's visit shows how this was so.

6 August

I had the great joy of welcoming at the Hotel Norge my dear friends Adolph and Anna Brodsky, who have come over from England by steamship just to visit us. They had with them 2 boys aged 13 and 15, Toni Maaskoff and Alfred Barker, who are pupils of Brodsky's and also are boarding with him, as well as his niece, Miss Antonnia Schadowski. In clearing weather we drove in landau and gig to Troldhaugen, where a good lunch was waiting for us. What wonderful people! They seem to me to have reached a point where the heart can be refined no further.

In the aft. Brodsky wanted absolutely to have the C-minor Sonata, which he played as beautifully as ever. Nina sang, we strolled around for a while, then we went up to the tower for a moment, and our cosy time together was over. I accompanied them with Tonny and Nina to the station.

7 August

A glorious, refreshing sleep after what for me was a somewhat strenuous day. At 1 o'clock we picked up the Brodskys, and drove in 2 landaus across Mt. Fløyen and on to the end of the road, from there climbed Mt. Blåmand, where beer, port wine and cakes gave a lot of pleasure and elevated the mood, which was already high, to

The Brodskys visit Troldhaugen, August 1906
Back row: Brodsky's niece Antonia Schadowsky, Tonny Hagerup, Adolph Brodsky.
Middle row: Nina Grieg, Edvard Grieg, Anna Brodsky.
Front row: Anton ('Toni') Maaskoff, Alfred Barker.

an even higher level. Great enthusiasm about the view. Back to Fløyen, where we had dinner. After that to Hotel Norge, where the Brodskys improvised a lovely evening. Everything went as well as it possibly could. We were accompanied to the station and got home at night-time in a state of blissful exhaustion.

8 August

At 2 o'clock met the Brodskys at Hop Station. Weather still glorious. Magnificent lunch at Troldhaugen. Then a nap, and then it was Brodsky again who organized a programme of music. Both of my Violin Sonatas (G-major and F-major) had to be performed, it awakened many old memories. Then both of his pupils played. It was extremely interesting. Both of them are gifted, and both show what a great teacher Brodsky is. The 15-year-old (formerly a circus clown!) played two movements of Mendelssohn's Concerto very valiantly, but then came the 13-year-old, a mixture of Hungarian and American, who played a solo sonata by Bach. It was such an outstanding performance that one dares to expect the greatest from the lad. How moving it was to see the respect and love that these two boys have for their teacher! And how they enjoyed the situation!

Then we had supper, then Nina sang, concluding with an absolutely superb 'Ragna' and 'Hope', which she sang more beautifully than ever, so there were not many dry eyes. Then all off to the station and then the train steamed off. We strolled slowly homeward in the beautiful night, this time as far as I was concerned more tired than is permissible.

9 August

I had a hard time getting to sleep. Today I need peace and quiet. But I'm not going to get it yet. Now off to town to celebrate the Brodskys' departure with them.

10 August

It was a cheerful and delightful occasion. A jolly lunch in the Grand Café, after which we accompanied them to the railway station and with a wistful twinkle in our eyes watched them depart. Ten minutes later we ourselves left and with that I treasure yet another beautiful memory. This meeting has strengthened me, as only true understanding is capable of doing.

11 August

Today a feeling of emptiness. The stretched nerves need to relax again. What a damned business.

A year later, Anna Brodsky confided to *The Manchester Guardian* her own account of this visit, invaluable in offering an intimate picture of the Griegs' home life.[10]

If Brodsky's visit had meant reconnecting with an old and much-loved friend, it had also meant for Grieg a reconnection with Manchester. First there had been Hallé and Neruda in 1889 – just a couple of nights in the city, but a sold-out hall and huge enthusiasm from the Manchester public. Grieg had little real closeness to Hallé himself, finding him a cool and rather remote figure. On the other hand Hallé's wife (as Neruda had become) enjoyed a performing relationship with Grieg that went back many years, and their relationship of warmth and mutual esteem would stretch well into the future. Then there had been the three days spent in November 1897 at the home of Hallé's successor at the College – the first time the Brodskys and the Griegs had been able to come together in England. And of course there had again been the time the two couples spent together in London in 1906.

This time, Grieg saw Brodsky's visit as having represented for him 'medicine for body and soul', as he himself expressed it in a letter from Troldhaugen on 20 August. Brodsky had sent Grieg, as a souvenir of the occasion, photographs taken at Troldhaugen that Nina and Edvard had found 'wonderful' – as indeed they were. 'If only I could at least, as a gesture of thanks, have finished the string quartet for you!' Grieg alludes to the second Quartet (a work that had never progressed beyond two movements) and to a promise, of which Brodsky had reminded him at Troldhaugen, he had once made to write this work.

Brodsky, Manchester and the College would stay in Grieg's mind for the rest of the year. 'We continue to cherish the memory', he wrote in December, 'of those beautiful summer days that you gave us! I am so grateful to you. How much I enjoyed you! . . . P.S. What are the boys doing? Give them our warmest greetings!'[11] The boys, practising industriously, had continued for a while to accompany the Brodskys on their summer travels, which for Adolph took in a cure at Marienbad where he lost weight and in consequence felt that he would return refreshed to fiddle-playing. With renewed hopes for a completion of the Quartet, he worried that Grieg was being too severe on himself – too self-critical in other words – which could only hinder him in his work. 'Just sing, as you have always sung', was his advice.[12] Anna Brodsky and Nina continued a busy correspondence throughout the autumn, too. 'Now that several weeks have already passed I think back on Troldhaugen and ask myself if it wasn't just a happy dream. I've seldom been happier than I was in your dear, beautiful home.' She sent greetings from her niece and the two boys. 'Tony calls Grieg "The Angel".'[13] Little wonder then that Grieg's New Year's greeting to Adolph continued to extend best wishes to 'the children', at the same time recalling how so much that had been fine and good in 1906 for Nina and himself was owed to the Brodskys. 'Old age comes and I feel that your friendship means more to me than ever. May we meet again in 1907!'[14]

Darker thoughts had, however, prevailed just three months earlier, shortly after the Griegs had arrived in Christiania, where they were to overwinter at the Hotel Westminster. In a year's time, he told Henri Hinrichsen, he and Nina would be going to the Leeds Musical Festival, to which was added a gloomily prophetic note – 'so long as I do not have to make a much longer journey before then!'[15] Nonetheless, the wider world was now about to be alerted to Grieg's next visit to England in the pages of *The Musical World*, with the journal reporting that preparations for the Leeds Festival were 'advancing apace . . . Sir Charles V. Stanford was unanimously appointed as conductor of the Festival. The Executive Committee were able to report that arrangements had been made with Dr. Edvard Grieg, the Norwegian composer, to come and conduct some of his works'.[16]

Once in the Norwegian capital, Grieg happily took advantage of some of the opportunities it offered, taking in within three days at the beginning of October plays by Shakespeare and Wilde — *The Merchant of Venice* and *An Ideal Husband*, both of course in Norwegian translation — as well as a piano recital by his gifted compatriot Karl Nissen. The latter's playing of two of the *Slåtter*, however, caused some grief, expressed in the diary entry for 3 October. 'Why in all the world does Percy Grainger, the Australian, play these things perfectly where rhythm and modulation are concerned, while Karl Nissen, the Norwegian, can't get the hang of either? That's altogether the wrong way round.' Thoughts of Grainger — and then of the possibility of perhaps performing together with this pianist who understood and interpreted his music so well — recurred when Grainger told him of having heard through Stanford that Grieg would be at the Leeds Festival in the autumn of the following year. Grainger intended absolutely to be there. Grieg decided to try to get Leeds to include the Piano Concerto in the festival programme, with Grainger as soloist and himself as conductor. Informing Grainger of his decision, he added 'Next year you *must* come to Norway!'[17] Grainger's reply lacked none of his customary effusiveness and enthusiasm:

> All this about the Leeds Festival is enchanting. Even if your kind thought about letting me play your piano concerto doesn't come to anything, it would always be the most lovely thought for me to remember that you once wanted it. I really can't tell you what this means to me . . .
>
> I am sure that if you were only to express a wish regarding your piano concerto and your kind thought about me in that connection, they (in Leeds) would be only too happy to do what you wanted.
>
> It would be infinitely significant for me *if* it came to anything; but all that could obviously never be so *really* and deeply important to me as to know that you yourself have really thought out this happiness and help for me! . . .
>
> Do you mean that I could possibly come to you up in 'Troldhaugen' next summer? If you could have me, it would be glorious indeed.[18]

Although Grieg evidently felt some confidence in Grainger's ability to take on for the first time his Piano Concerto, it was a little too early to recommend him for a Munich performance of the work that he was due to conduct in the spring. He recommended instead to his Viennese publisher, Albert Gutmann, who was arranging the concert, five possible soloists (all of them 'first class'), among whom he included Leonard Borwick. In the event the choice was to fall not on Borwick but on another of his recommendations, Arthur De Greef.

Among other performances in England of Grieg's works in the latter half of 1906, those of Dan Godfrey, conductor of the Bournemouth Municipal Orchestra, must be singled out, who during the month of August programmed one of the *Norwegian Dances*, both *Peer Gynt* suites, and the overture *In Autumn*. Godfrey would remain committed to Grieg's music during the whole of his distinguished career. In October Manchester offered an unusual combination, with Olga Wood singing

'From Monte Pincio' under Richter – presumably in her husband's arrangement. It may have been 'exquisitely sung', as one reviewer had it, 'but the superabundance of the orchestral accompaniment prevented the whole effect reaching the audience'.[19] And at another concert in Manchester just a fortnight later, Theodora Salicath, 'a singer of exceptional temperament under exceptional control' (who had of course sung before Grieg in London a few months earlier), interpreted 'beautifully' three songs by Grieg, Eyvind Alnæs and Christian Sinding, with R. J. Forbes at the piano.[20] Finally, a distant voice from the village of Grez-sur-Loing in France told Grieg in October that an opera (*A Village Romeo and Juliet*) was to be performed in Berlin; knowing that Grieg expected to be in the city in the spring, Delius hoped his old friend might be able to see it. Delius's larger works were only just beginning to be published in piano score, such as the one that he was sending that same day to Grieg, *Sea Drift*.[21]

Delius was still virtually unknown in England, his London concert in 1899 having appeared to be little more than a flash in the pan. But all that was to change in just a year's time with the performance of his *Appalachia* at Queen's Hall – a performance that the conductor Thomas Beecham would have the foresight to attend. Nonetheless, some of his larger works had already made an impact in Germany, including the Piano Concerto, in which Grieg's influence is omnipresent, and Grieg must surely have been aware of the steady inroads into continental Europe's concert halls being made by the music of his closest English friend.

⊰ 25 ⊱

'WE SHALL HAVE PIANO REHEARSALS FOR LEEDS AT TROLDHAUGEN!'

Dear Sir,

We shall be pleased to perform the two works you name – if, on further consideration, you prefer them. But as we give only about an hour to your compositions, the
two you name will occupy that time. The musical public would like, I know, to have
some of your popular pieces – I mean the shorter ones. Your choral work would be
a great 'draw'.

Yrs very truly

Fred. R. Spark

THUS the sparely expressed letter addressed to Grieg from the Secretary of
the Leeds Triennial Musical Festival on 23 January 1907. Grieg had been
waiting to receive the precise dates of the festival. The letterhead told him
that it was to run from 9–12 October, dates that he underlined and further high-
lighted with two large crosses. Ever more worried as to whether his health would
stand up to yet another visit to England, he had written a few days earlier to Percy
Grainger to express the hope of seeing him both at Troldhaugen and in Leeds. 'But
I have learnt from bitter experience that I dare not make a firm commitment. My
health is much too fragile for that.' Grieg was attempting to shoehorn Grainger into
the Leeds event, and seemingly against Spark's wishes. The full programme, which
became available early in March, carried no mention of Grainger or of the Concerto; *The Musical World* commented simply that it would contain 'possibly an
orchestral work by Dr. Grieg, not yet decided upon'. The (no doubt Leeds-based)
writer enthusiastically welcomed the prospect of Grieg's participation but – quite
strikingly – seemed completely unaware of Grieg's reputation as a conductor of
his own music:

The Committee are justly proud that they have induced Dr. Grieg to visit the Festival
to conduct some of his compositions; he will, no doubt, receive one of those hearty
welcomes for which Yorkshire people are noted all the world over. Nothing is more
valuable or conducive to the understanding of modern music than the coming into

contact in this manner with a composer whose works are before the public. He may not be a great conductor – Dr. Grieg has not earned any special distinction in this department – but there is a subtle charm that a composer can often give to his work in conducting it that a more expert wielder of the bâton will fail to realise. A Festival that will give us a great work under a composer who is already great as a conductor – like Dr. Richard Strauss – will do the music-loving community a signal service. We commend the idea to progressive Sheffield![1]

Grainger played six pieces from Op. 66 and Op. 72 in Copenhagen on 26 February, the first time any of the *Slåtter* had been heard in that city, but he had to leave for London only a few days before the Griegs were due to arrive in the Danish capital, a fact that irked and saddened both men. Grieg was, however, convinced that Grainger would not fail him and that they would meet again in Norway in the summer. Where he was genuinely puzzled was that his plea for Grainger to play in Leeds had not elicited any response from Spark. He assured Grainger that he would not let the matter drop. 'He will write sometime to Leeds about me',

Frederick Spark, from a portrait by Sir George Reid

Grainger told Karen Holten, suggesting that she go to the concert which Grieg would be conducting on 21 March in Copenhagen: 'Do it, if you'd at all like to. He is such a darling & will soon die.'[2] Grieg had made no secret to Grainger of his ill health or of his expectation that death was not far away, and Grainger himself could be brutally frank and open about others no less than about himself. He was also a supreme self-publicist, taking steps to ensure that the London musical press very soon knew of his artistic feats in Denmark:

> That most virile and artistic of pianists, Mr. Percy Grainger, has been rousing Copenhagen audiences to great heights of enthusiasm by his playing. The Danish press has hailed him as being 'in the forefront of the world's pianists of to-day,' and he has been assured of 'being welcomed and honoured as a genius' whenever he cares to visit Copenhagen. At the express wish of Dr. Grieg, Mr. Grainger played (for the first time in the Danish capital) some new peasant dances (op. 72) by the Norwegian composer; they were received with much enthusiasm.[3]

Ibbs & Tillett, the London agents, had meanwhile got wind of the Leeds Festival and wrote to ask Grieg if he would be willing to play some of his piano compositions at Queen's Hall on the afternoon of Saturday 12 October after the festival had ended, enquiring as to what his terms might be.[4] Baring Bros., agents based in Cheltenham, enquired (on the understanding that the composer would be back in England in October) if Grieg might be 'disposed to give a number of Pianoforte Recitals in the principal towns' of England, enclosing a letter of introduction from Nansen, 'whom we had the opportunity of touring on his return from the Arctic Regions'.[5] Nansen's letter, while assuming that Grieg would in all likelihood not be interested, nonetheless commended the firm and its proprietor – 'an agreeable and honorable man'.[6] Grieg's decision to leave his and Nina's books, music and autographs to the public library at Bergen was also noted in London, reported in the March issue of *The Monthly Musical Record*.[7] This had followed a news item in *The Musical Standard* a little earlier: 'It is stated that Grieg and his wife both intend to leave their fortune to the "Edvard Grieg Fund" for promoting the higher musical life of Bergen.'[8]

Stanford, since 1901 chief conductor of the Leeds Festival, sent a friendly letter to Grieg outlining plans for October:

> My dear Dr. Grieg! You will soon receive an invitation for yourself and Madame Grieg to stay with Mrs. Currer Briggs at Glasgow Grange Leeds for the Festival. She is a great friend of ours, & I am sure that you will much enjoy staying there. It is a lovely house, out of the town with a beautiful garden, and they will take the greatest possible care of you. Her husband died last year to our great loss, for he was one of the chief supporters of the Festival and had been the first to support your being asked to come.
>
> I am sure you will enjoy the Festival & the splendid chorus and orchestra.
>
> Your orchestral rehearsal in London will be on Thursday October 3 at 2 o'clock at the Royal College of Music, Kensington.

We are much looking forward to seeing you and your wife, & send our warmest greetings to you both.[9]

Mrs Briggs in due course wrote to the Griegs, promising them peace and quiet in her home – no unwelcome company would be allowed to intrude upon them. Nina asked Anna Brodsky about her and discovered that she was the mother of Christopher Rawdon Briggs, second violin in the Brodsky Quartet.[10]

Quite possibly arriving in the same post as Stanford's letter was a rather touching line from Ireland. Sir Charles Villiers Stanford had been born in Ireland, where he had begun his musical studies in Dublin with Arthur O'Leary, and had by now reached the musical heights; no greater contrast could have been found than with young Vivian Lee of Woodbine Cottage, Clonminch. He had already written a little earlier to Grieg, who, one guesses, was at this stage of his life little disposed to respond to fan letters from persons unknown and far away. At all events Grieg did not keep the first letter. Might it have been the frank and youthful enthusiasm of the sender of a photograph that led him to keep the second? And might he then actually have replied to the naïve youngster who was so passionately keen to visit and even more to help him?

> I suppose you have received my letter, I will not be wanting any wages I will work hard for you if you would give me some lessons, I dont mind what kind of work I do, I do love music so very much, I can only play the Piano a little, but if you think I would not be worth teaching I would work for nothing, as it is only for music I live.
>
> I am awfully fond of your music and it is the beauty of it which makes me write to ask you if you could help me
>
> Please write soon[11]

Grieg's interest in the welfare of the dispossessed was to be in evidence a month later, when he received a begging letter from John (Johnny) Gasmann Bloom, a Norwegian musician who had been working in England for some ten years. Grieg, it seems, had known his deceased brother. Bloom had held a range of musical posts in his adopted country, among them as conductor of an orchestra in Norwood, as a singing teacher and choral instructor who had sung in the cathedral choir in York, and (his most recent post) as organist and orchestra conductor at the Royal Grand Aquarium in Brighton. Ill and down on his luck, Bloom asked if Grieg could lend him some money. Grieg immediately sent him £17, for which the recipient was pathetically grateful, promising to repay the donor as quickly as possible.[12]

The proposed visit to Leeds and England in October soon brought invitations in its wake, one of the first coming from Anna Brodsky. A delighted Nina responded by saying how much they looked forward to a second stay with the old friends in Bowdon. The Brodskys also kept the Griegs in touch with the musical progress of those two youngsters who had accompanied them to Troldhaugen, 'Toni' Maaskoff and 'Alfy' Barker, the former of whom was 'setting a good example' to the latter (who was in due course to become leader of the Hallé Orchestra). Nina's interest

in them was continually in evidence during the course of her summer correspondence with the Brodskys. Adolph Brodsky continued, justifiably, to take an almost
proprietorial pride in Grieg's Quartet, but neither would have been pleased earlier
in the year to read an issue of *The Musical World* that disparaged the composition:
'The concert opened with Grieg's tepid G minor Quartet, but the genius of the
Brodsky Quartet was insufficient to arouse anything beyond a lukewarm interest in
the string of obvious, not to say cheap, melodies of which the work is composed.'[13]
Again in Manchester, later in the spring, Hamilton Harty made an early appearance
as a Grieg executant, accompanying the Russian violinist Michael Zacharewitsch
in the final Gentlemen's Concert of the season. They 'essayed' the first Violin Sonata, 'but the pianist alone had grasped the lyrical quality of the music, so the result
was not entirely satisfactory'.[14]

Grieg conducted two concerts in Copenhagen in March. From there it was on
to Berlin for a rehearsal of *Bergliot* at the end of the month for a later concert, before resuming his travels to conduct in Munich. Still troubled about his punishing
schedule and continuingly worried about his health, he wrote to Beyer. 'No, I tell
myself, you're too old and ailing for this kind of thing. No more of it. But then
there's this Music Festival in Leeds in the autumn.'[15] Back in Berlin, one of the
first people he met was Stanford, who saw both Grieg and Joachim 'within half an
hour of each other' on 9 April, the date of the first orchestral rehearsal for Grieg's
concerts on 12 and 14 April. Stanford confessed himself 'frightened' about Grieg,
whose exhaustion was very much in evidence. Nonetheless, there was another
meeting for the composer with the Kaiser just a few hours before the first of these
two concerts, in the company of Saint-Saëns and Massenet among others. With the
Monte Carlo Opera being in town, Xavier Leroux, the composer of *Dorothea*, and
the company's director Raoul Gunsbourg were also present. If the lunch party at
the palace was distinguished by its French character, Grieg was disappointed that
so many of these 'great men', as he described them, could only converse in their
own language, since his own French was poor. Fortunately, Prince Albert of Mo-
naco spoke fluent English, and Grieg felt much more comfortable talking with him
– a measure, perhaps, of how far his command of English had progressed since
those first hesitant days in London in 1888. Five days later the Griegs set off once
again for concerts in Leipzig and Kiel, finally returning to Copenhagen at the end
of April.

'Just heard from the Leeds Festival people; so that's going to come off, I think;
dear old darling Grieg.' Grainger's confirmation to Karen Holten on 6 April that all
had finally fallen into place for the autumn engagement was followed a month later
by a notification that he sent to Johan Svendsen:

> I have just been engaged to play Grieg's concerto (under his own conducting) at the
> big music festival in Leeds next October. He has been *so* kind to me, and even asked
> the Committee to have me play his piano concerto. It is an enormous pleasure and
> honour for me![16]

The Brodsky Quartet:
Adolph Brodsky, Carl Fuchs, Simon Speelman, Christopher Rawdon Briggs

Grainger could now see an added justification for a trip to Norway in the summer —
the heaven-sent opportunity to study the Concerto with Grieg himself. Still unsure
as to whether Grieg's health would allow of a visit, he made a hesitant enquiry:

> Do you think that you and dear Fru Grieg can have me at 'Troldhaugen' this summer
> for a short time! Or would I be in the way this time?
>
> It would be so glorious to be with you sometime, but only if it didn't intrude.
>
> If it *should* be possible that you could have me this summer, what time do you think
> it could be? I ask as I will arrange my other plans according to what suits you …
>
> Obviously I expect to hear 'no' to my question about the visit to you, if it *in any
> way* would inconvenience or disturb you.[17]

The reply from Grieg was, perhaps necessarily, uncertain in character. He and
Nina were staying in a sanatorium near Copenhagen — the inevitable consequence
of yet another alarming downturn in his health — and things unfortunately seemed
to be getting worse:

> I had to tell you all this so that you can understand that I am in no condition to make
> the beautiful summer plans that I had hoped to make. Still, I am counting on the
> peace and quiet of our home so that I might have the joy of seeing you with us at
> Troldhaugen in July. It is likely that my friend Julius Röntgen from Amsterdam will be

coming between the 15th and 25th of July, and I would be happy if you two could get to know one another. I will therefore recommend that you plan to come to us on the 15th of July. But I must warn you that at our house everything is simple and modest ... We shall have piano rehearsals for Leeds at Troldhaugen![18]

During the early summer, preparations continued apace for the Leeds Festival. Spark had engaged Olga Wood to sing a selection of Grieg's songs, and therefore asked the composer if he would be prepared to accompany her. A few days later the singer wrote to Grieg, with a slightly different slant on the subject:

I have been engaged to sing at the Leeds Festival and I am proud to say, your songs with orchestra, so I hope very much Madame Grieg will hear me first when she will be in London, and that I shall be able to please you – I have sung them last winter in Manchester with Dr Richter – I hope you will conduct the songs yourself, as they come next to the Piano Concerto. My husband joins me in very kind regards to you and Madame Grieg.[19]

It was left to Nina to reply:

My husband is not well for the moment and he therefore begs me to write to you and assure you that he is very much delighted to hear that you are singing his songs in Leeds. Of course he will conduct them himself with pleasure. If you will sing them for me in London I shall be very glad to have the chance of hearing you. It seems as if you should prefer to sing them in German? You may do that of course, if you find them badly translated in English and if you like it better.[20]

Other soloists engaged by Spark to sing under Grieg's baton in Leeds were Plunket Greene, Kirkby-Lunn and, finally, Marie Brema (as the Vølva in *Scenes from 'Olav Trygvason'*).

Still more arrangements needed to be made. A further approach from Leeds had come from Edgar Haddock, joint director of the Leeds College of Music, who had written suggesting that he play the violin sonatas together with the composer whilst Grieg was in the city. He expressed himself disappointed at Grieg's necessarily negative response: 'Permit me to say that my regret is the greater when I learn that the cause of your decision is bad health.'[21] Nevertheless, Grieg allowed London arrangements after the festival to go ahead, and Robert Newman duly confirmed two Queen's Hall engagements. There was to be an orchestral concert on 15 October (preceded by orchestral rehearsals on the 14th and 15th), in which Anton Sistermans was to sing a selection of Grieg's songs and Johanne Stockmarr would play the Piano Concerto, with orchestral works by Grieg making up the rest of the programme. This would be followed a week later by another all-Grieg programme – this time a chamber concert – in which the composer would be at the piano to play a number of solo pieces and would accompany first Ellen Beck in a further selection of his songs and then Adolph Brodsky in the second Violin Sonata; and the Brodsky Quartet would play the String Quartet.[22] Stockmarr had only just played the Grieg Concerto in London at the final concert on 30 May of the Philharmonic

Society's season. *The Musical Standard* felt that it had been 'beautifully performed' by the soloist. 'The orchestra, however, lacked the romance necessary to a perfect performance of this highly-imaginative work.'[23]

The prospectus for Leeds was now out. The event had had its origins in the opening of the Town Hall by Queen Victoria in 1858, when the first Musical Festival formed part of the ceremony connected with the building's inauguration. Sterndale Bennett had conducted this festival, which had included the first performance of *The May Queen*. Although intended as a triennial event, it was slow to get off the ground, and the citizens of Leeds had to wait until 1874 for their second festival, from which year onwards its triennial character was assured. Costa was the conductor of this and the following festival, and he was succeeded from 1880 by Sullivan. *The Martyr of Antioch* was written for Sullivan's first festival, as was John Francis Barnett's *The Building of the Ship*. Among festival commissions over subsequent years were works by composers as varied as Dvořák, Macfarren, Parry, Barnby, Corder, Stanford, Coleridge-Taylor and Mackenzie. For the 1907 festival there were also to be several first performances, and composers who were coming to conduct their own works included Elgar, Vaughan Williams, Boughton, Bantock, Parry, Brewer, Somervell and Stanford. It had been hoped that Glazunov would come to conduct the first performance in England of his 8th Symphony, but he expressed regret that his duties at the Conservatoire in St Petersburg would not allow him to leave the city in October. Grieg's participation, as *the* foreign celebrity, was noted in the prospectus. 'The musical public will welcome the special visit of Dr. Edvard Grieg, the Norwegian Composer, who will conduct a first performance in this country of three scenes from his uncompleted Opera, *Olav Trygvason*. He will also conduct his Pianoforte Concerto.' The press had a little earlier taken up the refrain:

> The selection of works by Dr. Edvard Grieg, who has promised to visit Leeds and conduct some of his compositions, has not been settled, but Dr. Grieg had, said Mr. Spark, expressed a wish to have included the choral work 'Olav Trygvason', for chorus, solo voices, and orchestra, which would occupy about forty minutes. Not much is known of the choral writings of Dr. Grieg in this country, though his instrumental pieces are numerous and popular, but great interest will certainly be taken in the production of this work by so great a composer.[24]

About this same time there had also come a letter from the Royal Manchester College of Music Club, signed by the club's honorary secretary Webster Millar, a distinguished singer in his own right. Edvard and Nina Grieg had been invited jointly to become patrons of the club, and Nina had already told Anna Brodsky that she and her husband were delighted for their names to be used for a good purpose. Millar in his turn was delighted:

> It is my pleasant duty to convey to you the heartfelt thanks of the Committee and Members of the R.M.C.M. Club, for the very great honour you have done us by

becoming our Patrons . . . We hope to do good work amongst students who like ourselves have left their College Days behind them, by enabling them to remain in the College atmosphere, and continue to be mutually helpful, as in Student days.[25]

Percy Grainger sent Grieg a greeting for his 64th birthday on 15 June, proposing dates for his visit. Grieg was grateful for the birthday wishes, but confessed that he had recently been so poorly that he himself had not wished for 'many happy returns of the day':

> Until a few days ago I was quite sure that I would have to renounce the pleasure of seeing you here. But during the few days I have spent here in peace and quiet, I have got my sleep back – and with it a strengthening of the nerves. . . . That you can arrive here around 21st July will suit me perfectly. I hope that by then my health will have improved even more. I shall write to Julius Röntgen immediately urging him to be here at the same time as you. If only the weather could get better. It's constantly cold, rainy and windy.[26]

Earlier in the month Grainger had given a recital in the Aeolian Hall in London, with *The Musical Standard*'s reviewer finding his programme adventurous and his playing exciting. 'To be able to play Debussy, Grieg, Bach and Brahms, so that each composer has a separate pinnacle, an individual and distinct atmosphere, is quite as much as any piano virtuoso ought to expect to accomplish.' Grainger had achieved this standard 'admirably', and the Grieg folk dances and songs had been 'so exhilarating and gladdening, so full of an out-of-doors vigour' – a perfect summation of the young pianist's approach to performance.[27]

A LAST VISITOR

'THE orchestra in Leeds is large, 20 fiddles on each side etc. In response to your suggestion I shall write to the management right away with regard to ordering the material.' So wrote Grieg to Henri Hinrichsen on 21 July 1907, expecting Julius Röntgen to arrive that same evening, and expecting Grainger, this 'young genius of an Australian pianist and composer', to come just two days later. 'It's going to be lively at Troldhaugen.' In fact Grainger would not arrive at the Griegs' until the 25th. Grieg had emerged from his latest bout of illness and depression, and his sense of elation was almost palpable. His first major engagement of the autumn was to be at Leeds, and together with Grainger, a youngster whom he could call his newest friend, he would be able to concentrate on revisiting the nearly forty-year-old Concerto. Added to this, one of his oldest and dearest friends would also be at Troldhaugen. All this would prove to be an extraordinary blessing in the darkening evening of his life.

The welcoming party at Troldhaugen on the morning of 25 July was larger than Grainger had expected, for he records in his diary that 'the Griegs, Miss Grieg, Miss Hagerup, Frants Beyer, & Julius Röntgen' were all there to meet him.[1] He was delighted to make the acquaintance of Beyer – the original collector, after all, of the Op. 66 folk-tunes and 'a good, stout soul, steeped in folklore & f-music' – and he was disappointed to hear that Röntgen was going to be leaving for Denmark so soon as the following day. After breakfast and then 'a few hours practice' in Grieg's composing hut down near the waterside, Grainger returned to the house to find that two German admirers of Grieg had called and wanted to take a photograph. Grieg was 'refreshingly short worded' with them but consented to a snapshot being taken of himself and Nina together with Grainger and Röntgen, and a promise was made by the visitors that copies would be sent. 'Grieg says it's a historic moment, us 4 together', Grainger noted in his diary. It had been arranged that all would have lunch at the Beyers', where there was more music-making: 'Grieg rows us both ways across the wee bit of fjord, asthma and all.' Grieg asked Grainger to play some of the folk-song settings that he remembered from their encounters in

London, and then Grainger played some of the *Slåtter* that he had practised that same morning.

There was more music-making on the following day, but Julius Röntgen's departure was now imminent, and after breaking away for a swim Grainger returned to the house to urge him to take out membership of the English Folk Song Society. Then the friends all accompanied Röntgen to Bergen to see him off on the evening boat to Copenhagen. Röntgen remembered touchingly how Grieg slowly led the way towards the boat:

> I let him go on for a while. When I subsequently overtook him, he said to me: 'I feel and know it for sure that we shall not see each other again. My powers are at an end and it cannot last much longer. We must say goodbye for good.' I was deeply affected and told him how difficult he made my leaving with those words. Then the others joined us and Grieg immediately suppressed his sombre tone. We reached the boat and said 'farvel'. I saw Grieg step into his carriage, and went on up, deeply moved, to my cabin.[2]

Röntgen was subsequently to play an important part in the development of Grainger's international career as a pianist, and Grainger himself later noted, 'It was he who later (1910), by his kindliness and generosity, started my concert career in Holland. Thus through Grieg I was freed from the misery of being a "society pianist" in London and started to earn my way by serving the broad public rather

Grieg, Percy Grainger, Nina Grieg, and Julius Röntgen at Troldhaugen, 25 July 1907

than a narrow class.'[3] The passport to this international career, as opposed to the solo and shared recitals in smaller halls and in the homes of London society hostesses that had largely characterized Grainger's progress to date, was to be the Grieg Concerto.

Grainger spent much of the 27th in starting to make for his host a new translation of *The Mountain Thrall*. He had for some time been concerned about the quality of the English versions of many of Grieg's vocal works:

> I explained to him in our conversations in Norwegian (Grieg spoke English and German, but preferred to speak in his native tongue) that many of the translations of his songs were very inferior. He accepted my services in trying to better these translations. He would often spend one or two hours of intense thought over the proper meaning and significance of just a few words. Indeed his concentration and persistence were such that they would wear out the average person. His application to detail was limitless. Nothing was too small to merit his closest attention.[4]

On the 29th the morning started with Grainger practising alone the solo part of the Concerto. He was then joined by Grieg and they rehearsed together for an hour or so. In the afternoon there was a walk in the nearby countryside, with Grieg unburdening himself to Grainger on his treatment at the hands of the German press:

> Ja; for anything to be approved of by Germans, it must fit comfortably into a little box that they choose for it. They tried me in the Wagner box, & I wouldn't fit. And they tried me in the Brahms box & that also didn't do. They say: 'he wont fit anywhere; therefor he cant exist.' They couldn't guess that I might fit a little box of my own. So they have to do with overlooking me. The press is rasende [enraged] over my success with the Berlin public. The tone of their notices made me feel that I had grossly neglected my obvious duty of dying some years ago.

The pattern of music-making – sometimes in the company of Frants Beyer – and excursions continued over the following days. On one occasion Beyer showed to Grainger some of the folk-songs – words and tunes – that he had noted down in the Jotunheim region, and this provoked Grainger to urge both him and Grieg to work towards the setting up, more or less on the English lines, of a Norwegian Folk Song Society. He was, however, preaching with all the enthusiasm of youth to the relatively elderly. 'They like the idea', he noted, adding with perhaps a tinge of disappointment: 'But it'd be tough work to bring them to actual practical energy.'

Grainger rightly sensed that Grieg's real appreciation of him was largely based on his unique qualities as a pianist. On the whole Grieg appeared happy to tolerate minor excursions on Grainger's part into composition and folk-song collecting, but anxious that a far greater – as he saw it – executional talent should not be traduced, or at least diluted, by such excursions. Grieg saw him, Grainger felt, as a 'flawless' propagandist for Op. 66 and Op. 72, and by extension for the Concerto, and clearly considered that it was as a performing artist that the true path to greatness lay for Grainger. 'Note the name', Grieg wrote to the Russian pianist and conductor Alexander Siloti two weeks later. 'You will without any doubt get to hear of him. Incidentally, he has the same absurd idea as you: he doesn't want to be a pianist, but – something else! In other words: "Dort wo Du nicht bist, dort ist das Glück!" ['There where you are not, there is happiness!', a line from Schubert's lied 'Der Wanderer', ᴅ489, words by Georg Philipp Schmidt von Lübeck]'

Grainger's last complete day spent with the Griegs (part of the morning again being spent on the Concerto) was marked by an afternoon excursion into Bergen and then on up Blåmanden, one of the hills above the city. It was very much a family trip – 'the Gs, Miss Hagerup, Miss G, & I' – and Grieg, initially reluctant to undertake the climb, decided nonetheless to make the effort:

> As he mounts higher Gr gets more & more puffed, & weaker, but also pluckier. He wont speak but keeps on mounting & stopping for breath, each after t'other. One sees he is using much spirit for the effort. At the top at last he feels boyishly glorious. The view *is* heartlifting.

On 4 August Grainger left Troldhaugen by carriage for Bergen. Grieg, Nina, and her sister Tonny accompanied him all the way to the quayside, with Grieg pointing out en route the old family home and reminiscing about his childhood:

> G has had a nice cabin booked for me on the 'Dronningen'. All is tenderness & lovingness as ever, & when after the last bell they (both Griegs, & Frøken Hagerup) stand (crowd-crushed) on quay to wave farewell, Grieg's affectionate little face looms so baby-sweet, world-untouched, blue-eyed, spiritual, amongst the crowd.

⁂ 27 ⁂

'THE TRIP TO ENGLAND SEEMS TO ME
MORE THAN DOUBTFUL'

A FEW letters that Grieg devoted to friends and colleagues during August contain eulogies of Grainger, together with references to the forthcoming Leeds Festival. 'What an artist and what a human being!' he told the young Danish composer Hakon Børresen. 'In October he is to play my Concerto in Leeds, a place where I too am "supposed" to appear.'[1] To Peters in Leipzig went instructions:

> Kindly send the material ordered for Leeds (through Augener?) *NB, the new editions of op. 16 and 46*, to Herr Percy Grainger, c/o E. L. Robinson, 7 Wigmore St, W. London. He is the pianist of genius who is to play the Concerto in Leeds and who has promised to take with him both works to the London rehearsal that is to take place on the 3rd October. I repeat: the *new* editions. Should I receive the old one, I shall be unhappy. In the Olav Trygvason orchestral parts a few bowing and fingering indications are missing; I shall send these in a few days and beg you to correct them before their dispatch to England.[2]

Just five days later another note to Peters went off; it accompanied a score of the *Scenes from Olav Trygvason*, which contained the promised corrections to the parts. Once fully corrected in Leipzig, they then needed to be sent to England. Grieg closed on a dispirited note: 'Here it's simply dreadfully cold, rainy and windy.' And in a postscript to another letter Grieg instructed Percy Grainger, 'Please, don't write to Mr. Plunket Greene. Mr. Sistermans *will sing*. In his last letter he says that the songs suit him very well! Oh, these singers!'[3] Harry Plunket Greene, the distinguished Irish bass-baritone, was indeed to sing at the festival, but Anton Sistermans, his equally fine Dutch counterpart and by some considered unsurpassed as a singer of lieder, was engaged for Grieg's songs at the Queen's Hall concert on 16 October.

Grainger had written to thank Grieg for his stay at Troldhaugen and had suggested that the Folk Song Society would appreciate a statement from the Norwegian master. Grieg, describing Grainger as having 'enriched the evening of my life', readily complied:

> I have once again immersed myself in your folk-song arrangements and it is becoming ever more clear to me how brilliant they are. You have given here a very important indication of the way in which the English folk song (in my opinion so very different from both the Scotch and the Irish) has the requisite qualities to be elevated to the level of art, thereby creating an English music that stands on its own. It could without doubt constitute the material foundation of a national style, as has happened in other countries. Including the culturally most developed countries. It has impressed me to observe the seriousness and the energy with which the English 'Folksong Society' is pursuing its work. May it receive ever new infusions of strength and enthusiasm to continue its work! And may you, too, in the midst of your diverse – and for you and your art most important – activities, be able to find the time and strength to give to this cause the benefit of your own personality![4]

That the talking at Troldhaugen about the work of the Folk Song Society had not fallen on stony ground is clear from this endorsement from Grieg and also from the fact that Julius Röntgen took the step of joining as an ordinary member later in the year.[5]

The forthcoming concerts in Leeds, London and now planned for in Berlin were going to be a challenge, so much so that Grieg had to decline an invitation from Alexander Siloti to come to Russia later in the year. It was, he said, 'just out of the question' – he would be exhausted after the London and Berlin concerts. 'It's likely that I will have to cancel everything, for my health is worse than it has ever been.' The tone of his remarks to Siloti was gloomy in the extreme. 'Unfortunately, I can no longer count on any future. I am a sickly 64-year-old, and after this winter I shall withdraw from all public appearances.'[6] Another letter dispatched that same day went to his Danish organist friend Gottfred Matthison-Hansen, with Grieg lamenting the quite awfully wintry weather that then prevailed in Bergen – it was, as he wrily admitted, unfortunately 'the dish of the day'. 'If I'm not beforehand obliged to send my regrets, then I leave in a fortnight's time for England, where I shall conduct "Olav Trygvason" at the Leeds Festival with a chorus of 400 and an orchestra of 120. How marvellous it *could* be!'[7] He was down in his hut practising when Nina wrote to Grainger on 15 August on the subject of arrangements for Leeds, informing him that she and her husband would be staying with Mrs Briggs. She wrote again on the 24th, including a further reference to their prospective hostess, to point out that they would be leaving Bergen at the end of the following week. The plan was first to travel to Christiania and then to go on to Copenhagen in order to give Grieg the benefit of a few days' stay at Skodsborg sanatorium, a little outside the Danish capital. They would then continue their journey and cross over to England.

Grieg and Nina had for a short while already sought the benefit of a better climate for Edvard's condition, spending a few days inland at Voss where the mountain air might have helped his breathing and enabled him to sleep. But no, the sleepless nights had continued. Skodsborg had gained a reputation for success in this area of therapy and it would represent one last throw of the dice. 'Things absolutely can't continue as they are at the present. Because gradually my strength is ever more disappearing.' It was not at all unlikely, Grieg told Röntgen, that he would have to give up the England trip. The major current item of musical news – the death of Joseph Joachim – had given him further pause for thought, if in another direction. He had never been particularly close to the great violinist and saw himself as having taken other paths from those taken by Joachim. Nonetheless he confessed himself to be an admirer of Joachim's 'noble objectivity and mastery as a violinist' – a slightly cool assessment, perhaps, of one of the greatest instrumentalists of his age.[8] The somewhat earlier death in June of Agathe Backer Grøndahl, that true champion of his music, had given him far greater cause for grief.

On 25 August, Grieg penned his first diary entry for nearly three weeks:

> The 6th–25th has been continuous suffering. Breathing difficulties and insomnia increasing. We spent the 20th, and 21st and 22nd with the Beyers, Tonny and Elisabeth at Voss. I hoped that the inland climate would allow me to sleep. But no. All I can say is that my general condition has improved. We had one calm, warm, sunny day, I think the *only* such day in the whole summer and I felt that that was what I needed. But the next day it poured down again and so it has continued.
>
> Yesterday evening (the 24th) Klaus Hanssen [Grieg's doctor] and his wife came to see us, and oddly enough they arrived at exactly the same time as my new masseur, Hr. Olsen, who was going to give me massage and 'compresses' à la Skodsborg. Klaus examined me with the greatest care and stayed during the entire treatment. The upshot is that the massage therapy is to be discarded, as it is hard on the nerves, but the compresses are to be continued, as they did me some good and made it possible for me to get a little night-time sleep, at least for the first part of the night.
>
> Today the 25th wretched after breakfast, I just don't know why, it must be the strain of the massage yesterday evening.

The following day found Grieg still troubled over preparations for England. Peters had already sent uncorrected orchestral parts of the *Scenes from Olav Trygvason* to Leeds, with the understandable result that the composer was ill pleased:

> The complete material of op. 50 has been delivered to Leeds already at the *beginning of July* and in consequence *uncorrected*! It cannot be left at that and I ask you urgently to arrange that at least newly revised *orchestral parts* be sent. I have to hold the only preparatory orchestral rehearsal *myself* in London and everything there must go smoothly, with not a single minute to be lost.

Augener would see to it, he wrote, that the corrected parts would be ready for Thursday 3 October at three o'clock, when the festival's London rehearsal, in the Concert Hall of the Royal College of Music, was to take place. 'Since I also have to go through the Piano Concerto and the 1st Peer Gynt Suite at this rehearsal, kindly send, as agreed, the material for both of these works to Herr Percy Grainger in

London.' Grieg closed by apologising for his poor handwriting: he was simply too unwell to do any better.[9]

So often in the past a glut of articles had appeared in the English press shortly before Grieg's visits. In respect of his impending visit, a forerunner had just appeared in *The Musical Standard* of 24 August in the form of a piece written by Charles W. Wilkinson, giving 'practical hints as to performance' of 'Wedding Day at Troldhaugen'.[10] And a week later the same journal pointed out to its readers a number of forthcoming 'items of importance':

> The directors of the Queen's Hall Orchestra, Limited, announce that Dr. Edvard Grieg, M. Eugene Ysaye, and Herr Fritz Kreisler have accepted their invitations to give Special Concerts at Queen's Hall on the following dates: Wednesday, October 16, at 3 p.m., Grieg Orchestral Concert . . . Wednesday, October 23, at 3 p.m., Grieg Chamber Concert.[11]

More soberly, and under the same heading, it was reported that Fred Spark, secretary of the Leeds Musical Festival, had fallen between the train and the platform at a small station a few miles out of Leeds. All that was reported was the 'shock' that he had sustained and the fact that he might easily have lost his life. Grieg was not to hear of this, for a postcard from the Festival Office, signed by Assistant Secretary W. A. Allsop and dealing with a query of the composer's in relation to chorus parts, was addressed care of Peters in Leipzig and reached Troldhaugen too late for him to see it. 'Mr. Spark', wrote Allsop, 'has been quite unable to attend to anything for some days, in consequence of a serious railway accident.' Spark had nonetheless charged him to say that 'everything will be right' and that he would be writing to Grieg shortly.[12] But the accident had been serious indeed, and Spark, a major figure in the story of music-making in Leeds, died a little later.

Herbert Austin Fricker, the organist and chorus-master of the Festival, who was in charge of preparations for the performance of *Olav Trygvason*, also wrote a letter that Grieg was never to see:

> I hope that you will forgive the rudeness in not acknowledging the receipt of your letter to me before, but I was away on my holidays when your letter arrived. I at once posted it on to Mr Spark the Hon: Sec: of the Festival for him to see to arrange for alterations in the Chorus parts as indicated in your letter.
>
> I have only just returned from my holidays & have seen Mr Spark this morning who has returned your letter to me.
>
> I will personally see that your wishes are attended to & I sincerely trust that the performance of Olav Trygvason at the coming Leeds Festival will be a great success & that you will be pleased with the efforts of our Chorus.
>
> We consider it a great honour for Leeds that you should visit us for your delightful music has won for itself a very warm place in our hearts.[13]

The latest therapies at home had not had the hoped-for effect, and it was finally deemed prudent for Grieg to be admitted to hospital in Bergen on 27 August. He spent four nights there as an in-patient, recording only briefly in a diary entry on the 30th that the period had been 'Spent at the hospital in Bergen under Klaus Hanssen's observation. Also under a worsening of the illness, unfortunately. The 1st night was without sleep, the 2nd and 3rd I slept on chloral.' On the 28th, while in hospital, he wrote one last letter. It was to Louis Monastier-Schroeder, a Swiss theologian with whom he had been in contact for some years. Among other matters Monastier-Schroeder had recently written and asked for Grieg's views on the subject of religion. 'Nothing would please me more than to tell you', Grieg replied;

> But to do that I need better health than I have at present. And yet – this does not require many words: During a visit to England in 1888 I was impressed by the 'Unitarian' views, and in the nineteen years that have passed since then I have held to them.[14]

As with this final letter, so too with the final diary entry, where there would be just one more reference to England. Grieg returned to Troldhaugen on Saturday 31 August, the date on which he penned this last entry:

> Today, the 31st, no good for anything, as *Isopral* didn't help at all, so I lay awake virtually the entire time. The whole thing is most depressing, Nevertheless we ought to prepare for the trip overland on the 3rd. What matters is getting away from this climate even if this time around the trip to England seems to me more than doubtful.

On the following day, Klaus Hanssen and Frants and Marie Beyer came to dinner. They did their best to convince Grieg to abandon the tour to Leeds and to London, but he stubbornly maintained that he would stick to his plans. 'These concerts give me strength', he insisted, even drawing from some last reserve sufficient energy to practise a few of the piano pieces he was to perform in England. On Monday 2 September, the Griegs packed their bags and were driven in the company of the Beyers into Bergen, where the intention was that they should stay at the Hotel Norge until they were ready to leave on the first leg of their circuitous journey to England. Grieg even visited his tailor to order a new suit to take with him. He looked terribly ill. The next day Dr Hanssen forbade all plans for further travel and had him admitted for a second time to hospital. Frants Beyer visited him in the evening and knew that this was the end. After lapsing briefly into a coma, Grieg died in the early hours of Wednesday 4 September.

⁂

One of the earliest notifications of Grieg's death came in the form of a telegram handed in at Bergen at 10.20 that morning. It was addressed to Professor Brodsky, Musical College, Manchester, and read: 'After few days illness Edvard died quietly this night. Nina.' It was received at the Manchester post office at 10.34. Brodsky immediately resolved to travel to Bergen for Grieg's funeral. Similar telegrams also went to other friends and musical associates. By mid-day, newspaper placards on

London's streets were announcing that a 'famous composer' had died. And Cho-pin's Funeral March was added to the evening's Promenade Concert programme at Queen's Hall, with the sorrowful note that the piece was 'played in memory of Edvard Grieg'. It followed a performance of the *Peer Gynt Suite* no. 1, and while it was played the entire audience remained standing.[15] *The Tribune* carried a news item from its Christiania correspondent with a dateline of 4 September, which gave a clear indication of how seriously Grieg's death was taken in the Norwegian capital:

> Tonight a special mourning performance took place at the National Theatre here, the Director delivering an oration in memory of the deceased, and the orchestra playing the first part of the suite 'Peer Gynt,' ending with the death of Aase. Queen Maud, who had already telegraphed early this morning her condolences to Mme. Nina Grieg, was present, together with Queen Alexandra, the Empress Dowager of Russia, and Princess Victoria.[16]

Of Grieg's final days, *The Tribune* told its readers,

> The event was wholly unexpected, although the great composer had of late been in a very delicate state of health, and carefully avoided bad weather. He had counter-acted a growing physical weakness by incessant intellectual activity, but yesterday, feeling his strength failing, he remarked to some of his friends, 'All will soon be over with me.' Of late he also suffered from insomnia, which increased his weakness still more. Notwithstanding this he had just prepared two Concertos [*sic*] for London.... His luggage had already been brought to the steamer, and rooms were engaged for him at the Grand Hotel here. He felt exhausted, however, and having consulted his physician, he was advised to move to a hospital, in order that he might be examined more closely. Accordingly, he drove last night to a hospital, where his general condition became rapidly worse. Soon after midnight his heart began to show signs of failing, and at 3.30 a.m. he peacefully expired in the presence of his wife, the cause of death being dyspnœa of the lungs.[17]

A week later Nina followed up her telegram to Henri Hinrichsen with the first letter she had written since the death of her husband, although she confessed that she found it difficult to express herself in German:

> Things went badly for him all summer, ever more badly, he was always freezing and had less and less breath. Energetic as he was up to the end, he still hoped to fulfil his engagements in England, practised the piano and studied his scores in spite of ever increasing weakness. Finally the doctor (his loyal friend) wanted to have him in hos-pital, he went, but came back again after a few days and wanted to leave for Kristiania. I saw that this was impossible, but still packed everything up and got Troldhaugen in proper order for the winter. When we arrived at the hotel, Grieg was so weak that I sent for the doctor, and he then forbade the trip.
>
> The next day Grieg went into the hospital again, and that night he passed away. He suffered dreadfully from breathlessness, but, thank God, fell asleep as peacefully as a child. On that last night in my unutterable grief the doctor sent me away and when

I was fetched life had been extinguished. I was with him in the hospital room until half past ten in the evening.[18]

On the day before the funeral, Adolph Brodsky wrote home to Manchester to tell his wife of his final encounter with his old friend:

This morning, my dearest, Halvorsen came and fetched me, carrying my violin, and we went for a rehearsal. We worked on two small pieces, both of them by Grieg: Funeral March and Våren (In Spring) for string orchestra. Afterwards we went for a walk. On the way I ordered a wreath from the Brodsky Quartet. After our walk we went to the Museum to see Grieg. Today it wasn't open to the public, and we found Nina, Tony and a whole array of Grieg's relatives there. I can't tell you the impression the deceased made on me. There was such a calm expression on his face, such a spiritual beauty (in spite of the fact that his eyes were closed). It was impossible to tear oneself away.

And so it was that dear Nina stood and looked at him with wide, wondering eyes, then kissed him with tears in her eyes, and then, sobbing, she embraced her sister, who was also crying. An impression which will always be with me. More than 45 wreaths from various deputations, among which I shall lay a wreath from the Quartet, are to be placed on his coffin; but I have also been asked to lay a wreath from the Concertgebouw Orchestra in Amsterdam, as they haven't any representative here. I have said that I was happy to do this. All this will be official tomorrow.

I have got to know the closest of his friends, Mr. and Mrs. Frants Beyer, who was his neighbour and friend of many years. A very nice man. He told me that he had been a witness to Grieg's sufferings during those final days – it was terrible, and we have to be glad that he has been released from this pain (he was constantly fighting for breath and couldn't sleep). When he was admitted to the hospital, he had a premonition of his death, but hadn't expected it so soon – nor indeed had anyone. At all events he died in his sleep and he himself wasn't aware that he was dying, there being nothing to betray this in the peaceful expression on his face. Today, i.e. very shortly, we shall gather at one of his relatives, Nina will be there too, and we shall lunch together. To-morrow Frants Beyer has invited us to his home after the burial – it's just over the way from Troldhaugen, so I shall also be sure to see the spot where we had such a happy time at Troldhaugen last year.

It's time to close, Halvorsen will be here shortly to fetch me. He is very able, quite simply achieving wonders with an orchestra brought together from every possible quarter, among them amateurs too.

The weather stays fine. I'm sitting in my room with the window open looking out over the balcony. My room, no. 28, is very close to our rooms last year, do you remember? Nos. 30, 31, 32. So many memories here! How wonderful Bergen is! But he who graced it now lies dead . . .[19]

The funeral took place on Monday 9 September after a weekend during which Grieg's body had lain in state in Bergen, and it seemed as if the whole of Bergen had turned out in silent tribute to Norway's most celebrated musical son. The crowd watching the procession, estimated at some 40–50,000, included, it was reported, representatives of many nations and of many musical activities. *The Musical Standard* carried a brief report of the event, from which it is clear that in terms of foreign representation England ceded clear pride of place to Germany:

> The funeral of Edvard Grieg took place at noon on Monday, in the presence of a large assemblage. The first part of the funeral service was held in the Museum of Art and Industry. Among those following the coffin, besides the members of the deceased's family, were General Nissen, who represented King Haakon, and representatives of the German Emperor, the Norwegian Government and the Storthing. On the arrival of the funeral procession at the crematorium the Rev. Mr. Konow delivered an impressive address, and, after a hymn had been sung, the body was placed in the furnace. In depositing a wreath on the coffin, the representative of the Emperor William gave expression to the deep sorrow of the Emperor and the German people at Grieg's death and dwelt on Grieg's influence on German music.[20]

For a more detailed description of the funeral we can turn to Adolph Brodsky, who wrote of the occasion for the readers of *The Manchester Guardian*:

> The most imposing and the most impressive feature of Grieg's funeral was the crowd. In my estimate there must have been between 40,000 and 50,000 people. There was no cold curiosity, no fighting for places, no stretching of necks to see better; from old man to urchin, all had the same grave expression of face which showed that they felt their loss.
>
> The programme of the ceremony, which was to begin at noon, was as follows:– (1) 'Varen' ('In Spring'), by Grieg, played by the string orchestra; (2) Folk-song, by Grieg, sung by the male choir; (3) the laying down of the wreaths; (4) song for male voices, sung by the same choir, also composed by Grieg; and (5) 'Funeral March' for orchestra, by Grieg. The orchestra was a scratch orchestra gathered from the theatre, music-halls, and amateurs; I offered my services as a violinist, and they were accepted. Halvorsen, conductor of the National Theatre, Christiania, conducted. He is the husband of one of Grieg's nieces and a former pupil of mine from the Leipzig Conservatoire. The Funeral March was composed by Grieg about 40 years ago, on the death of his friend Nordraak (who had such a great influence on Grieg as a composer), and is written for a military band only. But the only available military band in Bergen is so miserable that Halvorsen at the eleventh hour orchestrated it for an ordinary orchestra. And he did it so well, and the instrumentation was so completely in Grieg's manner, that it sounded as if it had been done by Grieg himself. It is a beautiful piece, a genuine 'Grieg,' and ought to become in its present form a standing piece on the repertory of the leading orchestras. It could also be used as a welcome variety for the Dead March of 'Saul.' There were 57 wreaths, which had to be 'laid down' by nearly as many delegates; and the Kaiser's delegate, Legationsrat S[c]heller Steinwarts (himself a good musician and personal friend of Grieg), made the only long oration – and a beautiful one. The German Emperor's wreath came next after the wreath of the King and Queen of Norway, which was 'laid down' by General Nissen. Then came wreaths from the Storthing, from the Norwegian Government, from the municipalities of Bergen and Christiania, from the Imperial Chancellor, von Bülow;

from the Royal Academy, Berlin; from the Queen's Hall Orchestra, London; from the Concert Gebouw Orchestra, Amsterdam; and from the Brodsky Quartet, Manchester. As I brought a wreath from the Brodsky Quartet, the Committee asked me to take charge of the wreath of the Concert Gebouw Orchestra, which I did. In German, I bade our dear friend farewell, and said that his works would remain to give him immortality so long as true and noble art endured. I and the other bearers then lifted the coffin and carried it outside to the hearse – a beautifully decorated cart drawn by four black horses. So it stood visible to everybody. As we passed throught the streets, the houses draped with flags, all the people uncovered their heads. The procession consisted of hundreds of deputations with standards inscribed with the names of the societies to which the deputations belonged. There were about 10,000 people in the procession. We who followed directly after the hearse were quite out of town when the end of the procession was still passing through the streets of Bergen. No rain fell, although it looked very threatening during the morning. All the schools, all the shops, and all the mills were closed. Outside the town we passed through an alley of trees surrounded by the fjords and mountains; the view was overpowering. At a certain spot the hearse stopped, and the procession, with their standards, passed before the hearse, and every deputation lowered their standard before the coffin and passed on. It was nearly an hour before the last standard was lowered. Afterwards we drove to the cemetery, on a hill a few miles ouside the town. Kaiser, King, Government, towns, professional musicians, students, workmen, peasants – they all were united and led by one idea – to do homage to the remains of Grieg. Perhaps music is, after all, the real 'peacemaker'; it reminds us that, in spite of difference in birth, social position, religious opinion, we are brethren and must must try to love each other.[21]

Also in the paper was a paragraph noting that the two forthcoming concerts at Queen's Hall were now to take place as *In Memoriam* concerts and moreover quoting extracts from Grieg's letter to Grainger dated 11 August. And there was a further note:

> Reuter's Agency is requested by Madame Grieg to publish the following:–
>
> CHRISTIANIA, WEDNESDAY.
>
> My most heartfelt thanks to all who honoured the memory of my husband and bestowed their sympathy on me.
>
> (Signed) NINA GRIEG

The Musical Standard, in common with other papers, also announced (in its issue of 14 September) that the two Grieg concerts scheduled for October in London would now be given 'In Memoriam'. A week later the journal noted that the Kaiser's telegram of condolence to Nina, in which he had spoken of Grieg's influence on modern German music, had proved 'far from pleasing' to German musicians, such influence – the *Standard* tending to agree – being in fact difficult to discern.[22]

Grieg's death was widely reported in the British press, as was to be expected, and the musical press carried long reports, often as a lead article in their September issues. The general tone was an admixture of respect and affection. *The Musical World* captured that tone in its opening paragraph:

The news of the sudden death of the Norwegian composer, Dr. Edvard Grieg, which took place at Bergen on the 4th inst., was received with something akin to dismay in numberless homes in this country, where he, in company with Mendelssohn, has been most cherished and loved of all the composers of this or any age. No other composer, since Mendelssohn, has commanded, by the impelling force of his music, such love and affection.[23]

Almost inevitably, there was some regret in the various obituaries and appreciations that Grieg had on the whole not commanded the larger musical forms, but more often than not there was an acceptance that this had probably been due to the ill health he had suffered throughout his adult life. The mastery he had continued to show in music of a smaller scale was generally warmly and gratefully acknowledged. *The Musical Standard*, in 'A Second Appreciation', written by Herbert Antcliffe, felt that with Grieg's death,

> the world has lost the last of the great lyrical composers of the nineteenth century. He possessed in the highest degree all the qualities which go to make the ideal lyricist – simplicity, grace and strength, combined with the rare gift of conciseness, and an idiom both original and striking . . . his music rarely demands a knowledge of its programme for the appreciation of its highest qualities. Without reference to the source of its inspiration it overflows with all that makes for loveliness and beauty . . . His visits to this country have been too few and far between, and the one which he was just about to make – for which he was actually at the time of his death preparing – was being looked forward to very keenly by many of his admirers both in London and the Northern Counties.[24]

In *Musical Opinion* it was Antcliffe again who was given the responsibility for a joint summation of the contributions that Grieg and Joachim had made to the world of music; he closed by expressing the view that both were 'absolutely united in their high aims, in their intense love of the past and in their certain hope of the future; and both by their works have done much to infuse in the younger generations the same characteristics'.[25] And *The Monthly Musical Record* gave an overview of Grieg's life and composing career, adding a small personal touch:

> The last evening he said to his nurse, 'I am not able to sleep; I shall have another restless night.' Later on, feeling that he was dying, he said to his wife, who for thirty years had been his faithful and sympathetic companion, 'So this is the end.'[26]

As might have been expected, the major newspapers in London and the provinces also contributed with obituary notices and summaries of the composer's life. The friends in England reacted too. Stanford noted on 9 September:

> I hope the tale of tragedies is over for the present. We have had enough and to spare. I always was frightened about Grieg since I saw him in Berlin and am only thankful that there was no catastrophe (later on) at Leeds itself. I saw both him and Jo for the last time on the same day (April 9) within half an hour of each other.

To Grainger he wrote: 'We have certainly had a share of losses this summer. You

QUEEN'S HALL.

Sole Lessees · Messrs. CHAPPELL & Co., LTD.

GRIEG

(IN MEMORIAM)
CONCERTS.

Orchestral Concert,
WEDNESDAY, OCTOBER 16th, 1907,
AT 3 O'CLOCK.

PROGRAMME.

TRAUERMARSCH - - - -	-	Grieg
(First performance in England.)		
OVERTURE - In Autumn -	-	Grieg
SONGS { (a) Henrik Wergeland / (b) Der Einsame / (c) Ein Schwan	}	- Grieg
CONCERTO in A minor for Pianoforte and Orchestra - - - -	-	Grieg
ROMANCE with Variations for Orchestra	-	Grieg
SONGS { (a) Die Prinzessin / (b) Mit einer Wasserlilie / (c) "Am schönsten Sommerabend war's" / (d) Die Odaliske / (e) Im Kahne	}	Grieg
SUITE No. 1 - - Peer Gynt -	-	Grieg

Vocalist—
Herr ANTON SISTERMANS.

Solo Pianoforte—
Miss JOHANNE STOCKMARR.

THE QUEEN'S HALL ORCHESTRA.
CONDUCTOR—
Mr. HENRY J. WOOD.

Chamber Concert,
WEDNESDAY, OCTOBER 23rd, 1907,
AT 3 O'CLOCK.

PROGRAMME.

STRING QUARTET in G minor	-	- Grieg
SONGS { (a) "Voer hilset, I Damer" / (b) Zur Rosenzeit / (c) Ein Traum	}	Grieg
PIANOFORTE SOLOS { (a) Resignation (from Op. 73) / (b) She Dances ,, ,, 57 / (c) Home-sickness ,, ,, 57 / (d) Gangar (D major),, ,, 72	}	Grieg
SONGS · { (a) From Monte Pincio / (b) At the Bier of a Young Woman / (c) On the Way Home / (d) "Thy warning is good"	}	Grieg
SONATA No. 2, in G, for Violin and Pianoforte		Grieg

Vocalist—
Miss ELLEN BECK.
(Chamber Singer to the King of Denmark.)

Solo Violin—
Dr. ADOLPH BRODSKY.

THE BRODSKY QUARTET.
Dr. ADOLPH BRODSKY.   Mr. SIMON SPEELMAN.
Mr. C. RAWDON BRIGGS.   Mr. CARL FUCHS.

Solo Pianoforte—
Mr. PERCY GRAINGER.

TICKETS—7/6, 5/- (Reserved); **2/6, 1/-** (Unreserved).
At usual Agents' Chappell's Box Office, Queen's Hall; and of
The Queen's Hall Orchestra, Ltd., 320 Regent Street, W.

ROBERT NEWMAN, Manager.

Handbill for the Grieg *In Memoriam* Concerts, London, 16 and 23 October 1907

will feel this greatly: and it is sad for Leeds too, when they hoped to welcome him so warmly.'[27]

'Until the day before his death', Nina wrote to Delius in answer to his own letter of condolence, 'he still hoped to go to England, to fulfil his obligations. He rallied so marvellously and gathered together what remained of his energy just so as to be able to live long enough for this.'[28] Later that month Percy Grainger sent her a copy of Whitman's *Leaves of Grass*, inscribed 'Fondly & thankfully from Percy. 29.9.07.'

At the Leeds Festival Stanford took charge of the works that Grieg had been expected to conduct. *The Monthly Musical Record* duly reported,

> The unexpected death of Grieg naturally threw a shade over that part of the festival connected with his music. The Scenes from 'Olav Trigvason,' though well rendered, needed perhaps the hand of the departed master fully to bring out their point and meaning. The performance, however, of the 'Peer Gynt' Suite, No. 1, under Sir Charles Stanford's direction, was altogether admirable; that he managed to get such delicate tones from the larger body of strings was quite surprising.
>
> The pianoforte concerto in A minor was also played by Mr. Percy Grainger at the Saturday evening concert, and in a letter written shortly before his death the composer spoke in high terms of the pianist's rendering of his work.[29]

The Musical Standard commended the soloists in *Olav Trygvason*, finding the work's last scene to be 'by far the most pleasing'. As for the Suite, it was 'played as the London Symphony Orchestra have played it many times before: that is, to perfection'. Two days later came the festival's final concert. Four of Grieg's songs were sung by Mrs Henry Wood and accompanied by Grainger: they received 'full justice' at the hands of their interpreters. Grainger then played the Concerto, 'a work which we felt that we heard as Grieg intended it to be played'. The reviewer, 'A.M.R.', thought 'this young pianist should have a future before him. His touch is deliciously crisp, and his technique is never allowed to obscure the feeling of the music'.[30]

The two *In Memoriam* concerts in London then followed on 16 and 23 October, in the programmes that had been agreed with Grieg. An addition was the Funeral March originally composed to commemorate the death of Nordraak, opening the first concert, with both orchestra and audience standing throughout. This was the first time that the work had been heard in England in its orchestral setting. Reviews of both concerts were admiring and acknowledged the high quality of the artists, even if in one quarter Anton Sistermans was thought to be 'out of voice'. The overall quality brought *The Musical Times* to the conclusion that they were 'the most memorable concerts of the last month'.[31] Poignantly, Wood had included in his Promenade Concert of 22 October Delius's as yet unknown Piano Concerto. Nothing of Delius's had been heard in London's major concert halls since 1899, but the performance of the Concerto (followed just a month later by *Appalachia*) was to institute a vogue for Delius's music – music that was already well established in Germany. Had Grieg lived and had he conducted these London concerts, he would at last have been able to hear a work composed in maturity by his oldest English friend and a work that would be taken up by Grainger with the same enthusiasm as he dedicated to the A-minor Concerto.

There were other memorial concerts featuring Grieg's music in towns and cities throughout England. Johanne Stockmarr and Ellen Beck gave an all-Grieg chamber concert in London on 28 October. 'The popularity of the artists and their well chosen programme can be gauged by the fact that the audience overflowed the limited confines of the Steinway Hall.'[32] Manchester, Leeds and Bradford, among others, celebrated Grieg in their concert programmes. In Birmingham, Hermann Georg Fiedler, outgoing chairman of the University Musical Society, wrote and told Elgar that he understood the Society would be giving their first concert of the new season on 30 October 'In memory of Grieg'. Grainger, meanwhile, carried the flag to Copenhagen, playing the Concerto at a Grieg Memorial concert at which Queen Alexandra was present together with the King and Queen of Denmark, King George of Greece, and various other royals. Nina was there, too, and in a letter to the Brodskys remarked how 'wonderfully' Grainger had played the Concerto and the *Slåtter*.

Then, at the first concert of its 96th season on 29 January 1908, the Philharmonic Society paid its own tribute by opening its programme ('In Memory of Dr. Grieg and Dr. Joachim') with Grieg's 'Funeral March'. In April, at an all-Grieg Lamoureux Concert in Paris conducted by Johan Halvorsen (and in the presence of Minister Wedel Jarlsberg), the young British virtuoso Mark Hambourg played the Concerto. And at the end of that same month there was a notable concert at the Royal Palace in Christiania, again conducted by Halvorsen, in connection with a visit to Norway of Edward VII and Queen Alexandra. Grieg's music only took up a part of the programme, being represented by two movements from the first *Peer Gynt Suite* and by *Last Spring*, but it had an indelible effect on the royal audience, hosted by King Haakon and Queen Maud. King Edward congratulated Halvorsen warmly: 'Very well done. You have a splendid orchestra, played well together. I enjoyed your compositions very much.'[33]

Later, in 1909, Nina finally succumbed to the blandishments of her friends and came to England, again accompanied by her sister. They stayed in Bowdon with the Brodskys and in London with Grainger, renewing contact with Henry Wood and his wife. (Grainger had earlier played the A-minor Concerto under Wood at a Promenade Concert on 17 August.) Nina recalled her visit with pleasure:

> Well, wasn't it strange that I came to enjoy myself so much in England? I hadn't at all thought that I would, quite the contrary I was dreadfully worried about going out into the world again without Edvard. At the beginning it was terribly hard ... and had I been on my own I think I would have turned back again already in Berlin. But then we settled into the quiet life at the Brodskys in rural calm, wandered over the open fields where cows and sheep gently grazed, from where you could see the mountains of Wales on the far horizon and where the bells rang out from the old ivy-covered church. In all this peace and quiet, with these two wonderful people, in their cosy, harmonious home, where his talented and mostly Russian pupils came in and out and played ravishingly, I came to myself again and we both thought, Tonny and I, that it

was so good to be there. We often visited the famous Bayreuth conductor Hans Richter, who was indescribably kind to us, (he and his family) and finally he played the 'Peer Gynt Suite' at his first Manchester concert of the season, so preventing me from hearing the Piano Concerto, which was being played the same evening in London by Frk. Stockmarr, but there was nothing to be done about that. We were down there at Bowdon for 4 weeks, 20 min. by train from Manchester and then went on to London, where we stayed with Percy Grainger and his mother and had the loveliest music days since [my husband's] death. Percy played for me masses of things both by Edvard and others, he taught me much about modern music, Fauré, Debussy and also some English things. Both he and his mother couldn't do enough for me.[34]

This was the first of several visits to the Brodskys that Nina would make over the years. Even without Grieg himself, the ties were to remain strong, and in October and November 1912 Nina acted as accompanist in several Grieg recitals in London and Brighton, spending some time too at Bowdon again. She was exceptionally

The widowed Nina Grieg and her sister Tonny visit the Brodskys at Bowdon

warmly received and had offers to tour widely the following year. All these she declined, perhaps aware that really it would have been her name rather than her pianistic talents that had the drawing power. Nonetheless her attraction for audiences remained, and we find her, for example, accompanying recitals in Copenhagen and Christiania in 1914. She lived on until 1935, with Copenhagen becoming her preferred home.

England had always had its attractions for Edvard Grieg. Quite apart from the fact that his music was greatly loved here, there was always the promise for him of a useful supplementary income, something much desired by the time of his first professional visit to these shores. The building of Troldhaugen had been costly, and London, of all cities, offered — as his friend Delius was able to remind him — opportunities to recoup some of his outlay. Each time Grieg came to England, sales of his music would increase, and his concerts would almost always be sold out. For the most part he would be the guest of such dedicated friends as the Augeners, the Hardings and the Brodskys, whilst it would fall to the Speyers to supply a palatial home for his last visit. If the friendship with Delius had begun in Leipzig, there were many other musicians actually living and working in England who came to know and admire Grieg personally through his visits: Stanford, Parry, Grove, Prout, Wood, Grainger, and so many more. Previous generations of Griegs had come to London in pursuance of the family business or on official matters relating to the Bergen Consulate, with London a fixed point in their lives from a fairly early age. Edvard Grieg, coming to England as a pianist and conductor in the performance and promotion of his own works, finally arrived relatively late in his life on the London scene. Having found his calling, he had freed himself from the ties that Bergen and business together represented and had stepped onto the world's stage. Norway, 'this splendid land of which my art is but a poor reflection',[35] would always provide the spectacular backdrop to his career and to the core and character of his music, but for appreciable periods of his life England took centre stage.

Delius was not alone among British composers of subsequent generations who have acknowledged the influence of Grieg on their own music: Arnold Bax, Havergal Brian, Balfour Gardiner, Gustav Holst, E. J. Moeran, C. W. Orr, Cyril Scott, Ronald Stevenson, Peter Warlock — all have sung Grieg's praises. 'As a schoolboy,' wrote Imogen Holst, 'Gustav preferred playing Grieg to any other composer.' Furthermore, musicologists have discerned Grieg's influence in the works of composers as diverse as Butterworth, Elgar, Holbrooke, Hurlstone, Vaughan Williams, and no doubt others still. All had found in Grieg a voice that was refreshing: cool and limpid at times, ravishing and robust at others. What can surely be asserted with confidence is that Grieg's music still retains the ability to enchant and enthral not only English audiences but music lovers the world over.

NOTES

Full bibliographical references are given in the Bibliography below. All originals of letters to Grieg are in GA, unless otherwise indicated. Grieg's letters to Frants Beyer are in the Royal Archives, Oslo, and NB. Grieg's letters to Johan Halvorsen are in GA and NB. Grieg's letters to Oscar Meyer are published in 'Briefe Edvard Grieg's an Oscar Meyer' (see Bibliography). Grieg's letter to Narciso Vert is in a private collection. Nina Grieg's letters to Hanchen Alme are in a private collection and published in *Din hengivne Nina* (see Bibliography).

Abbreviations

BL	British Library	RNCM	Royal Northern College of Music, Manchester
DTA	Delius Trust Archive		
EG	Edvard Grieg	SB	Staatsbibliothek zu Berlin
GA	Grieg Archives, Bergen Public Library	SMF	Stiftelsen Musikkulturens Främjande, Stockholm
GM	Grainger Museum, University of Melbourne		
		TM	Tchaikovsky Museum, Klin
HG	Haags Gemeentemuseum, The Hague	TR	Grieg Museum, Troldhaugen
KBK	Det kgl. Bibliotek (Royal Library), Copenhagen	ULC	University Library, Cambridge
NA	National Archive, Kew	*LMC*	*The London Musical Courier*
NB	Nasjonalbiblioteket (National Library), Oslo	*MN*	*Musical News*
		MO	*Musical Opinion*
NG	Nina Grieg	*MMR*	*The Monthly Musical Record*
NYPL	New York Public Library	*MS*	*The Musical Standard*
PML	Pierpont Morgan Library, New York	*MT*	*The Musical Times*
RCM	Royal College of Music	*MW*	*The Musical World*
RIHA	Russian Institute of History of the Arts, St Petersburg	*NM-R*	*Nordisk Musik-Revue*
		NM-T	*Nordisk Musik-Tidende*

Chapter 1: A British Inheritance

1. NA, Foreign Office Correspondence Books 22 and 73 are the principal source of information relating to the Grieg family's consular activities in Bergen.

2. Finck, *Edvard Grieg*, 5.

3. Born Alexander Greig in Aberdeenshire, he eventually changed the spelling of his surname to Grieg, the more accurately to reflect in the Bergen dialect its original Scottish pronunciation.

Chapter 2: The Leipzig Student and Some English Contemporaries

1. Bridge, *A Westminster Pilgrim*, 307.
2. Grieg, *Artikler og taler*, ed. Gaukstad, 27.
3. Jacobs, *Arthur Sullivan*, 21.
4. *MN* (8 Dec. 1900): 506.
5. Grieg, *Artikler og taler*, ed. Gaukstad, 21–2.
6. Barnett, *Musical Reminiscences*, 41.
7. 'In memoriam: Arthur Sullivan, 1842–1900', *MT* (Dec. 1900). It is elsewhere stated that it was Edward Dannreuther who lent his Shakespeare to Sullivan.
8. Constance Bache, *Brother Musicians*, 132.
9. Ibid., 138–9.
10. Ibid., 142.
11. Ibid., 140.
12. Grieg, *Artikler og taler*, ed. Gaukstad, 26–7.
13. Ibid., 26.
14. Ibid., 27.
15. *MS* (24 Aug. 1901): 119. Finn Benestad comments that this early quartet was performed in Bergen on 21 May 1862.
16. Grieg, *Dagbøker*, ed. Benestad; *Diaries, Articles, Speeches*, trans. Benestad and Halverson.

Chapter 3: 'Wieniawski has urged me to go to London'

1. *MMR* (March 1871): 31.
2. *MMR* (July 1873): 94.
3. *MMR* (Sept. 1873): 120–21.
4. *MMR* (Nov. 1873): 149.
5. *MMR* (April 1871): 51.
6. *MMR* (Feb. 1872): 27.
7. *MMR* (April 1873): 51.
8. *MMR* (July 1871): 94.
9. *MMR* (Nov. 1872): 166.
10. *MMR* (March 1871): 31; (May 1871): 94.
11. Gosse, *Two Visits to Denmark*, 221–2.
12. *MMR* (Jan. 1873): 7.
13. Anton Hartvigson to EG, 2 March 1874; 66 St Mary's Terrace, Maida Hill, London W.
14. *MMR* (May 1874): 74.
15. *MT* (May 1874): 479.
16. *MMR* (Aug. 1874): 117.
17. *MMR* (Jan. 1875): 1–2.
18. *MMR* (March 1874): 44.
19. *MMR* (March 1875): 41.
20. *MMR* (May 1875): 70.
21. *MMR* (Sept. 1875): 131–2.
22. *MMR* (Jan. 1876): 10.
23. *MMR* (Jan. 1876): 11–12.
24. *MMR* (July 1876): 112.
25. Grieg, *Artikler og taler*, ed. Gaukstad, 81.
26. *MMR* (Feb. 1876): 24.
27. *MMR* (Dec. 1877): 195.
28. *MMR* (Jan. 1877): 12.
29. *MMR* (Feb. 1877): 28.
30. Kennedy, *The Hallé Tradition*, 48.
31. *MMR* (March 1877): 48.
32. *MT* (March 1877): 120.
33. EG to Gottfred Matthison-Hansen, 13 Aug. 1877; Børve, Hardanger [KBK].
34. *MMR* (March 1878): 43.
35. *MMR* (Dec. 1878): 186–7.
36. Smyth, *Impressions that Remained*, I: 271.
37. EG to Ethel Smyth, 17 April 1879; Copenhagen; quoted ibid., II: 50.

Chapter 4: 'It is my intention to visit England'

1. Niecks, 'Edvard Grieg, the Norwegian Composer'.
2. Max Abraham to EG, 10 Nov. 1879; Leipzig.
3. Abraham to EG, 29 Nov. 1879; Leipzig.
4. EG to August Manns, 2 Dec. 1879; Hotel König von Dänemark, Copenhagen [RCM].
5. EG to Clara Schumann, 2 Dec. 1879; Copenhagen [SB].
6. Clara Schumann to EG, 4 Jan. 1880; Frankfurt.
7. Edward Dannreuther to EG, 10 Dec. 1879; 12 Orme Square, London W.
8. EG to Johan Andreas Budtz Christie, 10 Dec. 1879; Copenhagen.
9. S. Arthur Chappell to EG, 29 Dec. 1879; 50 New Bond Street, London.

10. Dannreuther to EG, n.d.; 12 Orme Square, London.

11. EG to the Philharmonic Society, 4 Jan. 1880; Copenhagen [BL].

12. EG to Abraham, 21 June 1880.

13. Dibble, 'Edward Dannreuther', 292.

14. *MMR* (Feb. 1880): 24.

15. *MT* (Aug. 1880): 115, 412.

16. *MMR* (Nov. 1884): 260.

17. *MMR* (Feb. 1887): 45.

18. Andreas Pettersson to EG, 8 Nov. 1880; 17 Warwick Place, Rugby (in Swedish).

19. Pettersson to EG, 15 Jan. 1883; 17 Warwick Place, Rugby (in Swedish).

20. Pettersson to EG, 28 May / 17 June 1883; 19 Warwick Street, Rugby (in Swedish).

21. *MT* (July 1880): 355 = *MMR* (July 1880): 100.

22. *MMR* (April 1883): 97.

23. *MMR* (Jan. 1881): 17. The reviewer describes her wrongly as Norwegian.

24. *MMR* (Feb. 1881): 36.

25. Henry W. Carte to EG, 13 July 1882.

26. Monttie & Son to EG, 30 Oct. 1882.

27. *MMR* (July 1883): 166–7.

28. *MS* (2 Dec. 1899): 351.

29. Percy Grainger papers [GM].

30. EG to Johan Andreas Budtz Christie, 28 Dec. 1883.

31. EG to Carl Warmuth, 10 Jan. 1884 [NB].

32. EG to August Winding, 4 May 1884; Rome [KBK].

33. *MMR* (April 1884): 92.

34. EG to Charles Harding, 26 Aug. 1884; Lofthus; in English [PML].

35. Emma Mundella to EG, 21 Oct. 1884; 2 Grenville Street, Brunswick Square, London W.C.

36. *MMR* (Dec. 1885): 276.

37. *MMR* (Jan. 1886): 17.

38. Ibid., 20.

39. *MT* (Jan. 1886): 20.

40. *NM-T* 7/3 (March 1886): 46.

41. Julius Röntgen to EG, 10 June 1886; Amsterdam.

42. Abraham to EG, 3 Aug. 1886; Leipzig.

43. EG to Abraham, 18 Aug. 1886.

44. *MMR* (Nov. 1884): 260. One can only assume that the reviewer considered the work the equal of Grieg's other 'descriptive' pieces.

45. *MMR* (Dec. 1886): 281, 282.

46. *MT* (March 1887): 153.

47. *MMR* (March 1887): 66.

48. Charles Harding to EG, 31 Oct. 1887; Edgbaston.

49. EG to Didrik Grønvold, 21 Nov. 1887; Leipzig [NB].

50. Berger, *Reminiscences*, 102. The original date of publication of this book is problematic. Its first printing bore no date, but a copy in my possession has a presentation inscription (not by Berger himself) dated 'Christmas 1912'. The publishers evidently soon corrected the omission: another copy in my possession, inscribed by Berger, has the date 1913 printed on the title page.

51. Ehrlich, *First Philharmonic*, 138.

52. *MMR* (Dec. 1887): 283.

53. *MT* (Dec. 1887): 725.

54. Eaton Faning to EG, 15 Oct. 1887; Meadowside, Harrow on the Hill. Cf. G. F. Ogilvie, 'Harrow School Music Society and Its Director', *The Strand Musical Magazine*, 1 (Jan.–June 1895): 13–16; and 'Eaton Faning', *MT* (Aug. 1901): 513–26.

55. Smyth, *Impressions That Remained*, II: 166–7.

56. Sinding to EG, 1 June 1888; Leipzig.

57. Halvorsen, 'Hvad jeg husker fra mit liv'.

58. *The Musician* [Philadelphia], 2 (1897): 185.

59. MS in GM.

60. *NM-T* 9/1 (Jan. 1888): 12.

61. Birch, *Vikings in London*, 31.

62. Clara Rotter to Nina Grieg, 2 May 1888; Ivy House, The Burroughs, Hendon, N.W.

63. Remo, *La Musique au pays des brouillards*, 20.

64. EG to Frants Beyer, 19 Jan. 1888.

65. Hurum, *Vennskap*, 105.

66. Ibid., 119.

67. *NM-T* 9/2 (Feb. 1888): 28.

68. *MT* (Feb. 1888): 73–6.

69. Ibid., 87.

70. *MMR* (Feb. 1888): 44.

71. *MMR* (March 1888): 68.

72. *MT* (Feb. 1888): 91.

73. *MMR* (April 1888): 90.

74. EG to Beyer, 13 Feb. 1888; Leipzig.

75. EG to Beyer, 20 Feb. 1888.

76. EG to Beyer, 21 March 1888; Leipzig.

77. EG to Beyer, 24 March 1888; Leipzig.

78. Carrie Faning to EG, 6 March 1888; Harrow on the Hill.

79. W. J. Leaver to EG, 31 March 1888; Blackheath.

80. *MT* (April 1888): 229.

81. *MT* (May 1888): 294.

82. Strutte, *Tchaikovsky*, 113.

83. Tchaikovsky to EG, 24 April / 6 May 1888; Klin, near Moscow.

84. EG to Beyer, 12 April 1888; Leipzig.

85. Delius to EG, 12 April 1888; Claremont, Bradford.

86. T. T. Rowe to EG, 13 April 1888; Nottingham.

87. Cf. *MT* (May 1888): 281–2; (June 1888): 356, 367; (July 1888): 421; (Nov. 1888): 678.

Chapter 5: 'A Hearty Welcome to These Shores to Edvard Grieg'

1. *Clapham Antiquarian Society Newsletter*, 28 (Jan. 1950), §2, 'Victorian Clapham'.

2. Svendsen to EG, 27 April 1888; Copenhagen.

3. Pettersson to EG, 24 April 1888; 19 Warwick Street, Rugby.

4. Anton Hartvigson to EG, [24 April 1888]; 18 Fulham Place, Maida Hill.

5. Anton Hartvigson to EG, [April 1888]; on the headed notepaper of the German Athenaeum, 93 Mortimer Street. For further information on Campbell and the Royal Normal College, see J. E. Woolacott, 'The Royal Normal College and Academy of Music for the Blind', *The Strand Musical Magazine*, 5 (Jan.–June 1897): 72–7.

6. NG to Delius, 26 April 1888; 5 The Cedars, Clapham Common, London [DTA].

7. Svendsen to EG, 6 May 1888; Copenhagen.

8. Coates, *Suite in Four Movements*, 129–30.

9. I am particularly grateful to Bridget Palmer, Assistant Librarian, RAM, for her kind help in the quest for this phantom performance.

10. Stanley Hawley to EG, 25, 28 April 1888; Winchmore Hill, N.

11. Cowen, *My Art and My Friends*, 93.

12. Frederic Cowen to EG, 24 April [1888]; Amity House, 73 Hamilton Terrace, London N.W.

13. *The Queen: The Lady's Newspaper* (5 May 1888).

14. *MT* (June 1888): 356.

15. *MMR* (May 1888): 97–8.

16. Ibid., 118.

17. Ibid., 113.

18. Dannreuther to EG, 29 April / 4 May 1888; 12 Orme Square, W.

19. Cowen, *My Art and My Friends*, 150.

20. *The Daily News* (4 May 1888).

21. *The Standard* (4 May 1888).

22. *The Queen* (12 May 1888).

23. *MT* (June 1888): 345–6.

24. *MO* (June 1888): 415.

25. *MMR* (June 1888): 136.

26. *Lady's Pictorial: A Newspaper for the Home* (12 May 1888): 519.

27. Cowen, *My Art and My Friends*, 95–6.

28. Fifield, *True Artist and True Friend*, 160.

29. *MN* (1 April 1899): 330.

30. Cf. *NM-T* 9/5 (May 1888): 74–6; *Musikbladet* 5/9–10 (30 May 1888): 153–4.

31. *NM-T* 9/6 (June 1888): 82–5.

32. Elkin, *Royal Philharmonic*, 84.

33. Sinding to EG, 7 May 1888; Leipzig. For more on Braun, see pp. 149–50.

34. Svendsen to EG, 14 May 1888; Copenhagen.

35. Moir Clark to EG, 11 April 1888; 29 Montague Street, Russell Square, London.

36. Moir Clark to EG, 11 July 1888; Holdt's Hotel, Bergen.

37. Clotilde Kleeberg to EG, 4 May 1888; 6 Chandos Street, Cavendish Square, W.

38. EG to Dannreuther, 5 May 1888; Clapham Common [NB].

39. Pettersson to EG, n.d. [May 1888]; 19 Warwick Street, Rugby.

40. M. Saunders, Chappell & Co., to EG, 8 May 1888; 50 New Bond Street.

41. EG to Adolph Brodsky, 10 May 1888; London [RNCM].

42. Fuller-Maitland, *A Door-Keeper of Music*, 112.
43. *MMR* (June 1888): 136.
44. Bridge, *A Westminster Pilgrim*, 307.
45. *The Standard* (17 May 1888).
46. *The Daily News* (17 May 1888).
47. *NM-T* 9/5–6 (May–June 1888).
48. NG to Hanchen Alme, 20 May 1888; London [private collection]. *Din hengivne Nina*, ed. Simonsen and Mydske, 72–3.
49. EG to Martin Henriques, 19 May 1888; Queen's Hotel, Ventnor, Isle of Wight [NB].
50. *MS* (1 Aug. 1903): 74.
51. *MMR* (July 1888): 161 = *MO* (July 1888): 453–4. The same reviewer was serving both journals.
52. EG to Tchaikovsky, 26 May 1888; Brobyværk, Fyn [TM].
53. *MW* (15 May 1906): 124.
54. Sinding to EG, 1 June 1888; Leipzig.
55. Quoted in Hurum, *I Edvard Grieg's verden*, 269.
56. *MT* (Aug. 1888): 458.
57. *MMR* (Jan. 1889): 1.

Chapter 6: The Birmingham Musical Festival

1. *MMR* (July 1888): 159.
2. Edgar Haddock to EG, 25 May 1888; Leeds.
3. George Augener to EG, 12 June / 29 July 1888; Clapham.
4. Röntgen to EG, 16 July 1888; Badenweiler.
5. Berger to EG, 31 July 1888; London.
6. Charles Harding to EG, 13 May 1888; 16 Augustus Rd., Edgbaston.
7. Ada J. Harding to NG, 13 May [1888]; 16 Augustus Road, Edgbaston.
8. Didrik Grønvold to EG, 28 July 1888; Bergen. Grønvold left Bergen by steamer that same evening, bound for St Ives. He expected to arrive in Birmingham around 25 Aug., when he hoped to meet Grieg at the Hardings' home.
9. Quoted in Smith, *The Story of Music in Birmingham*, 39.
10. Quoted in Fifield, *True Artist and True Friend*, 220.
11. W. T. Edgley, quoted in Smith, *The Story of Music in Birmingham*, 48.
12. Charles Harding to EG, 23 July 1888; 16 Augustus Rd, Edgbaston, Birmingham.
13. *MO* (Nov. 1897): 95.
14. EG to Johan Halvorsen, 31 Dec. 1888; Bergen.
15. Halvorsen to EG, 9 April 1888; 4 Langstane Place, Aberdeen.
16. *MT* (Sept. 1888): 540.
17. Martin, *Norwegian Life and Landscape*, 21.
18. Monroe, *In Viking Land*, 91–2.
19. EG to Röntgen, 19 June 1892; Troldhaugen [HG].
20. *The Birmingham Daily Gazette* (22 Aug. 1888).
21. *The Birmingham Daily Post* (22 Aug. 1888).
22. *The Birmingham Daily Post* (23 Aug. 1888).
23. Graves, *The Life & Letters of Sir George Grove*, 337.
24. *The Birmingham Daily Post* (24 Aug. 1888).
25. Bridge, *A Westminster Pilgrim*, 123.
26. Jacks, *Life and Letters of Stopford Brooke*, II: 633.
27. Quoted in Norris, *Stanford, the Cambridge Jubilee and Tchaikovsky*, 390.
28. *The Birmingham Daily Post* (27 Aug. 1888).
29. *The Birmingham Daily Post* (30/31 Aug. 1888).
30. *MMR* (Aug. 1888): 177.
31. *MT* (Oct. 1888): 601.
32. *The Birmingham Daily Mail* (30 Aug. 1888).
33. *MMR* (Oct. 1888): 220.
34. *MO* (Oct. 1888): 14.
35. *The Birmingham Weekly Post* (1 Sept. 1888).
36. Grønvold, *Diktere og Musikere*, 46–9; repr. from articles orig. pubd in *Dagbladet* (Sept. 1888).
37. *NM-T* 9/9 (Sept. 1888): 138.
38. *The Birmingham Daily Gazette* (31 Aug. 1888).
39. *The Midland Counties Herald* (6 Sept. 1888).
40. *MMR* (Oct. 1888): 221, 223.

41. *The Birmingham Daily Post* (31 Aug. 1888).

42. Graves, *The Life and Letters of Sir George Grove*, 337.

43. Graves, *Hubert Parry*, I: 219.

44. Ibid., 291

45. Barnett, *Musical Reminiscences and Impressions*, 305.

46. Ibid., 330.

47. Edvard Grieg, 'Antonín Dvořák', in *Diaries, Articles, Speeches*, trans. Benestad and Halverson, 199–202; orig. pubd in *Verdens Gang* [Christiania] (13 May 1904).

48. *The Birmingham Daily Post* (3 Sept. 1888).

49. EG to Delius, 23 Sept. 1888; Troldhaugen [DTA].

50. EG to Charles Harding, 23 Oct. 1888; Bergen [SMF].

51. *The Birmingham Daily Post* (3 Sept. 1888).

52. Lara, *Finale*, 65.

53. EG to Louis Monastier-Schroeder, 28 Aug. 1907; Bergen.

54. EG to Thomas Ball Barratt, 17 May 1905;

Copenhagen [NB]. There are further Unitarian links with Norway in the fiction of Harriet Martineau (1802–1876) and Edna Lyall (1857–1903), who both came from Unitarian backgrounds and both of whom travelled in Norway and used Norwegian locales in one or another of their novels.

55. Henry Edward Rensburg to EG, 11 Nov. 1888; Liverpool.

56. EG to Rensburg, 20 Nov. 1888; Bergen [BL, Mus. 309, Rensburg MSS, III, fol. 110ʳ].

57. EG to Charles Harding, 18 Jan. 1893; Leipzig [private collection].

58. EG to Charles Harding, 28 Aug. 1903; Troldhaugen.

59. Charles Harding to EG, 14 Dec. 1888; Edgbaston.

60. Ada J. Harding to EG, 19 Sept. [1888]; Edgbaston.

61. Lara, *Finale*, 62–3.

62. *The Birmingham Daily Post* (1 Sept. 1888).

Chapter 7: A Musical Lion in London and Manchester

1. EG to Delius, 23 Sept. 1888; Troldhaugen [DTA].

2. *The Athenaeum*, undated clipping [1888].

3. *MT* (Dec. 1888): 724–5.

4. *MMR* (Dec. 1888): 281.

5. *NM-T* 9/12 (Dec. 1888): 188.

6. *MMR* (Dec. 1888): 282.

7. *MO* (Jan. 1889): 173.

8. *MT* (Dec. 1888): 726. It should be added that this suite was not 'first written for the pianoforte'; the reviewer may have confused it with the *Holberg Suite*.

9. Nina Grieg to Hanchen Alme, 19 Dec. 1888; Bergen [private collection].

10. EG to Delius, 6 Nov. 1888; Troldhaugen [DTA].

11. Delius to EG, [mid Nov.] 1888; Ville d'Avray.

12. EG to Abraham, 28 Dec. 1888; Bergen; 'Sorry, impossible' in English.

13. *NM-T* 10/1 (Jan. 1889): 10.

14. *MS* (19 Jan. 1889): 48.

15. Ibid., 44; (2 March 1889): 170.

16. W. C. Stockley to EG, 2 Jan. 1889; 123 Colemore Row, Birmingham.

17. Charles Harding to EG (addressed to London), 22 Jan. 1889; Edgbaston.

18. Charles Harding to EG (addressed to Leipzig), 22 Jan. 1889; Edgbaston.

19. Berger to EG, 3 Feb. 1889 London.

20. EG to Berger, 5 Feb. 1889; Leipzig [BL].

21. EG to Delius, 4 Feb. 1889; Leipzig [DTA].

22. EG to Beyer, 4 Feb. 1889; Leipzig.

23. EG to Charles Hallé, 13 Feb. 1889; Leipzig.

24. EG to Abraham, 20 Feb. 1889; Clapham.

25. Frederick Corder to EG, 14 March 1889; 59 Tisbury Road, W. Brighton.

26. *MMR* (March 1889): 66, 70; *simile*, (April–July).

27. *MS* (17 Nov. 1894): 380–1.

28. A German-born violinist who came to England in 1880 and taught at Cambridge, where he formed a string quartet.

29. *MMR* (March 1889): 66.

30. *MMR* (April 1889): 88–9 = *MO* (April 1889): 327.

31. *The Illustrated London News* (2 March 1889): 262.
32. *The Globe and Traveller* (25 Feb. 1889).
33. *MS* (2 March 1889): 167.
34. *MT* (March 1889): 152–3.
35. *The Queen* (2 March 1889): 272.
36. *The Star* (1 March 1889).
37. *Pall Mall Gazette* (25 March 1889).
38. EG to Delius, 24 Feb. 1889; Clapham [DTA].
39. Cf. *NM-T* 10/4 (April 1889): 52.
40. *MT* (April 1889): 216.
41. *The Court Circular and Court News* (2 March 1889): 195.
42. *The Queen* (2 March 1889): 272.
43. *MO* (April 1889): 327.
44. *MS* (2 March 1889): 167.
45. *The Graphic* (2 March 1889). The journal also included the portrait wood-engraving of the composer reproduced on p. 157 above, after the photograph by Elliott & Fry reproduced as the frontispiece to this book.
46. *The Saturday Review* (2 March 1889): 252.
47. *Lady's Pictorial* (2 March 1889).
48. EG to Berger, 26 Feb. 1889 [BL].
49. EG to Berger, 1 March 1889; Clapham [BL].
50. *The Queen* (23 Feb. 1889): 242.
51. Fuchs, *Musical and Other Recollections*, 75.
52. *MT* (April 1889): 228.
53. *Manchester Evening News* (1 March 1889).
54. *Pall Mall Gazette* (1 March 1889).
55. *The Manchester Examiner and Times* (1 March 1889).
56. *MT* (April 1889): 228.
57. Sinding to EG, 20 Nov. 1888; Leipzig.
58. *MT* (Jan. 1898): 34.

Chapter 8: The Man on the Clapham Omnibus

1. *Dagbladet* [Christiania] (18 March 1889).
2. Quoted in Charteris, *The Life and Letters of Sir Edmund Gosse*, 223–4. Gosse mistakenly remembered the year in which the incident took place as 1870.
3. Conradi, *Den Norske Klub i London*, 20–21.
4. Lasson, *Livet og lykken*, 36–7.
5. EG to Hans Lien Brækstad, 2 March 1889; Clapham [NB].
6. The *Pall Mall Gazette* (13 March 1889) informs us that whenever Joachim comes to England 'he makes his domicile in the house of his brother, Mr. H. Joachim, on the pleasant heights of Camden-Hill'. Grieg himself enters the exact address in his notebook as 13 Airlie Gardens, indicating the nearest station as Addison Road.
7. EG to Sigurd Hals, 8 March 1889; Clapham.
8. *Pall Mall Gazette* (11 March 1889).
9. *The Queen* (16 March 1889).
10. *Lady's Pictorial* (16 March 1889).
11. *MT* (April 1889): 216.
12. *Lady's Pictorial* (16 March 1889).
13. *The Saturday Review* (23 March 1889): 347.
14. *The Times* (11 March 1889).
15. *The Globe and Traveller* (11 March 1889).
16. *The Graphic* (16 March 1889).
17. *The Saturday Review* (23 March 1889): 347.
18. *MS* (16 March 1889): 206.
19. *NM-T* 10/4 (April 1889): 52.
20. EG to Abraham, 9 March 1889; Clapham.
21. *The Globe and Traveller* (11 March 1889).
22. 'Mary Wakefield (1853–1910) and the Competition Festival Movement', in Hyde, *New-Found Voices*, 143.
23. *MMR* (April 1889): 90.
24. EG to Berger, 11 March 1889; Clapham [BL].
25. Mackenzie, *A Musician's Narrative*, 191, 193.
26. *Pall Mall Gazette* (15 March 1889).
27. *Lady's Pictorial* (23 March 1889).
28. *The Times* (15 March 1889).
29. *Lady's Pictorial* (23 March 1889).
30. *The Globe and Traveller* (15 March 1889).
31. *MO* (April 1889): 328–9 = *MMR* (April 1889): 90.
32. *MN* (2 Sept. 1899): 200.
33. *MT* (April 1889): 214.
34. *The Graphic* (23 March 1889).
35. *The Queen* (23 March 1889).
36. *The Saturday Review* (23 March 1889): 347.
37. *MS* (23 March 1889): 226.

38. *The Star* (16 March 1889).
39. *NM-T* 10/4 (April 1889): 49–50.
40. EG to Beyer, 16 March 1889; Clapham.
41. 'Mr. Johannes Wolff', *The Strand Musical Magazine*, 6 (July–Dec. 1897): 144.
42. Honor Brooke to EG, 30 Dec. 1888; 1 Manchester Square, London, W.
43. EG to Beyer, 16 March 1889; Clapham. Grieg reports in English the conversational exchange with the Brooke daughters. In a postscript he sends a greeting from Honor Brooke to Beyer.
44. Jacks, *Life and Letters of Stopford Brooke*, II: 450. I have relied in part on this source for the resumé of Brooke's life and works; a useful further source is Fred L. Standley, *Stopford Brooke* (New York: Twayne, 1972).

Chapter 9: 'The Grieg fever is still raging'

1. *The Court Circular* (23 March 1889).
2. Reported in *NM-T* 10/4 (April 1889): 52.
3. *MMR* (April 1889): 91.
4. *MT* (April 1889): 217.
5. *The Star* (21 March 1889).
6. EG to Abraham, 20 March 1889; Clapham.
7. EG to Röntgen, 23 Aug. 1907; Troldhaugen [HG].
8. EG to Brækstad, 22 March 1889; Clapham [NB].
9. *The Illustrated London News* (6 April 1889).
10. *Clapham Observer* (6 April 1889).
11. *Pall Mall Gazette* (26 March 1889).
12. *The Court Journal* (30 March 1889): 448 = *The Court Circular* (30 March 1889): 302.
13. EG to Abraham, 19 March 1889; Clapham.
14. *NM-T* 10/4 (April 1889): 53–4.
15. *MS* (27 June 1903): 410.
16. Wedel Jarlsberg, *Reisen gjennem livet*, 47.
17. Fredrik Wedel Jarlsberg to EG, 21 April 1893; Légation de Suède et de Norvège en Espagne, Madrid.
18. *The Court Journal* (30 March 1889): 448 = *The Court Circular* (30 March 1889): 302.
19. EG to Abraham, 29 March 1889; Clapham.
20. *Punch* (30 March 1889): 145. Cowen must long since have given up any effort to have his Christian name spelt correctly in the journals of the day.
21. *The Times* (29 March 1889).
22. Fuller-Maitland: *A Door-Keeper of Music*, 112–13.
23. *The Globe and Traveller* (28 March 1889).
24. *MO* (May 1889): 379 = *MMR* (May 1889): 112.
25. *MT* (May 1889): 278.
26. *The Queen* (6 April 1889): 444.
27. *The Saturday Review* (6 April 1889): 412.
28. *MS* (6 April 1889): 270.
29. *Pall Mall Gazette* (29 March 1889).
30. *NM-T* 10/4 (April 1889): 54.
31. EG to Abraham, Clapham, 29 March 1889.
32. *The Queen* (6 April 1889): 444.
33. *MS* (6 April 1889): 271.
34. *MT* (May 1889): 279.
35. *MMR* (May 1889): 112 = *MO* (May 1889): 379.
36. *The Graphic* (6 April 1889): 359.
37. Myles Birket Foster, 'Edvard Grieg', *The Leisure Hour* [London] (Jan.–Oct. 1889): 336–7. Thomas B. Willson incidentally contributes 'A Walk through Jötunheim [*sic*]' on pp. 491–4.
38. EG to Sigurd Hals, 3 April 1889; Clapham.
39. *MMR* (May 1889): 112.

Chapter 10: Staying in Touch with England

1. S. Arthur Chappell to EG, 1 June 1889; London.
2. EG to Brækstad, 17 April 1889; Leipzig [NB].
3. EG to Sigurd Hals, 12 April 1889; Paris.
4. George Augener to EG, 12 April 1889; Clapham.
5. EG to Sigurd Hals, 17 April 1889; Leipzig.

6. See Carley, *Grieg and Delius*, 86–90, for Delius's description of this tour by the three composers.

7. EG to Abraham, 12 June 1889; Troldhaugen. Abraham to EG, 18 June 1889; Leipzig.

8. *MS* (20 April 1889): 312; (4 May 1889): 354.

9. *The Star* (13 July 1889).

10. *NM-T* 10/6 (June 1889): 91.

11. *MS* (29 June 1889): 519.

12. *MS* (18 May 1889): 398.

13. *MT* (Dec. 1889): 726.

14. *MO* (Jan. 1890): 179.

15. *MMR* (Oct. 1889): 233.

16. EG to Brækstad, 31 Oct. 1889; Christiania; 'never mind' in English [NB].

17. Berger, *Reminiscences*, 103.

18. EG to Abraham, 11 Nov. 1889; Copenhagen.

19. *MT* (Nov. 1889): 654.

20. EG to Brækstad, 16 Dec. 1889; Paris [NB].

21. EG to Brækstad, 20 Dec. 1889; Paris [NB].

22. *MT* (Dec. 1889): 723.

23. *MT* (June 1890): 365.

24. EG to Abraham, 5 Jan. 1890; Paris.

25. *MMR* (March 1890): 63. The inclusion in this concert of the Intermezzo in F major from Svendsen's Symphony no. 2 reminds us that Svendsen and his work remained a feature of London's musical scene.

26. *The Star* (14 Feb. 1890).

27. *MMR* (April 1890): 88 = *MO* (April 1890): 301.

28. *MT* (April 1890): 213.

29. *The Star* (3 March 1890).

30. *MMR* (April 1890) = *MO* (April 1890).

31. *MT* (April 1890): 216.

32. Ibid.

33. *The Star* (7 March 1890).

34. Chappell to EG, 11 April 1890; London.

35. *MO* (July 1890): 426 = *MMR* (July 1890): 160.

36. *MT* (May 1890): 278–9.

37. R. Roy Paterson to EG, 16 May 1890; Edinburgh.

38. Paterson to EG, 3 June 1890; Edinburgh.

39. *MN* (10 Nov. 1900): 404.

40. Ebenezer Prout to EG, 28 Aug. 1890; Smebys Hotel, Bergen.

41. See Fjågesund and Symes, *The Northern Utopia*, 70.

42. Ibid., 74.

43. Geo. Wynne to EG, 20 May 1889; Plymouth.

44. G. H. Johnstone, 27 Aug. 1890; 37 & 38 Northampton Street, Birmingham.

45. *MMR* (Aug. 1890): 183.

46. *MMR* (Nov. 1890): 255.

47. *MT* (Sept. 1890): 540.

48. *MO* (Dec., 1890): 97.

49. *MMR* (Jan. 1891): 17.

50. EG to Delius, 1 May 1891; Christiania [DTA].

51. *MT* (Feb. 1892): 89–90.

52. Quoted in *MS* (23 Feb. 1907): 127.

53. Pearson, *Beerbohm Tree*, 63.

54. *MS* (3 June 1899): 341–2.

55. See Whitebrook, *William Archer*, 112.

56. Information kindly supplied by Lewis Foreman (pers. comm.).

57. Alderman Fred R. Spark to EG, 3 March 1892; Leeds.

58. *MS* (8 Nov. 1900): 352.

59. EG to Brækstad, 14 May 1892; Bergen [NB].

60. George Bainton to EG, 18 March 1892; Coventry.

61. See Jones, 'Edgar Bainton'.

62. *MT* (July 1892): 400.

63. *MT* (Aug. 1892): 497.

64. EG to Abraham, 10 Aug. 1892; Troldhaugen.

65. NG to Delius, 26 Oct. 1892; Christiania [DTA].

66. EG to Dr John Peile, 22 Dec. 1892; Leipzig [ULC]. Peile (1838–1910) was Master of Christ's College and was Vice-Chancellor of the University from 1891–3. Grieg's reply was further delayed in reaching Peile: although despatched from Leipzig on the 23rd and arriving in Cambridge the following day, his letter had then to be readdressed to Bournemouth, where Peile was evidently spending the Christmas holiday.

67. EG to Stanford, 20 Jan. 1893; Leipzig.

68. EG to Berger, 23 Jan. 1893; Leipzig [BL].

69. Hans Richter to EG, 16 Jan. 1893; Vienna.

70. EG to Richter, 20 Jan. 1893; Leipzig [NB].

71. NG to Delius, 21 Jan. 1893; Leipzig [DTA].

72. EG to Harding, 18 Jan. 1893; Leipzig [private collection].

73. Arthur De Greef to Berger, 3 Feb. 1893; Brussels.

74. NG to Delius, 8 April 1893; Menton [DTA].

75. EG to Abraham, 16 April 1893; Menton.

76. *MMR* (Feb. 1893): 40.

77. *MMR* (May 1893): 111.

78. *MT* (June 1893): 349.

79. Charles Sayle to EG, 17 May 1893; Cambridge.

80. A. Austen Leigh to EG, 23/31 May 1893; The Lodge, King's College, Cambridge.

81. Quoted in Leigh, *Augustus Austen Leigh*, 210–11.

82. George Augener to EG, 30 May 1893; Wiesbaden. About this time the Augener home was accorded a nominal change of address: 47 North Side, Clapham Common.

83. Stanford to EG, 6 June 1893; Cambridge.

84. Dibble, *Charles Villiers Stanford*, 430–31.

85. Norris, *Stanford, the Cambridge Jubilee and Tchaikovsky*, 395. Norris's book treats all aspects of the Jubilee expertly and exhaustively.

86. NG to Delius, 14 June 1893; Grefsen Bad [DTA].

87. *Orkestertidende* 2/4 (Dec. 1893): 22.

88. *MMR* (Oct. 1893): 232.

89. NG to Anna Brodsky, 18 Feb. 1893; Leipzig [RNCM].

90. Arthur De Greef to Berger, 3 Sept. 1893; Brussels.

91. Elkin, *Royal Philharmonic*, 90.

92. EG to Anna Brodsky, 7 Nov. 1893; Copenhagen [RNCM]. Anna Brodsky to EG, 27 Nov. 1893; New York.

93. *MMR* (Jan. 1894): 1.

Chapter 11: 'I shall be acting in a comedy in Cambridge'

1. EG to Beyer, 19 Jan. 1894; Copenhagen.

2. EG to Sedley Taylor, 12 Feb. 1894; Leipzig [ULC].

3. *MS* (3 March 1894): 191. A more specific announcement appeared in *MS* (28 April 1894): 358.

4. George Augener to EG, 24 Jan. 1894; Clapham.

5. EG to Iver Holter, 16 March 1894; Geneva [NB].

6. EG to Beyer, 7 March 1894; Menton.

7. *MT* (March 1894): 195.

8. *MMR* (Feb. 1894): 39.

9. Reviews in *Dagens Nyheter*, quoted in *MN* (18 Nov. 1899): 448.

10. Speyer, *My Life and Friends*, 117–18.

11. *MS* (28 April 1894): 60. The 24 Feb. issue had announced the date of the performance as 25 April.

12. 'Grieg on Schumann', *MS* (3 Feb. 1894): 93–4.

13. *MN* (10, 17 March 1894): 219–20, 243. *Musical Notes* (Aug. 1894), 253, picked up the same item in briefer form.

14. Jones, 'How Composers Work', 210–11.

15. EG to Brækstad, 2 April 1894; Menton [NB].

16. Goubault, 'Grieg et la critique musicale française', 141.

17. EG to Beyer, 6 May 1894; London.

18. *MO* (July 1889): 473.

19. Edmund Gosse to Max Beerbohm, 14 June 1920; London. Quoted in Charteris, *The Life and Letters of Sir Edmund Gosse*, 464–5.

20. EG to Beyer, 6 May 1894; Clapham.

21. *Cambridge Daily News* (9 May 1894). Also quoted in the weekly *The Cambridge Independent Press* (11 May 1894).

22. *MT* (June 1894): 386.

23. *Cambridge University Reporter* (15 May 1894): 760. Translation from the Latin by Lesley Scott, 2004. The quotations at the end are from Horace's *Odes* 1.4, lines 1, 4, 6–7; trans. John Conington (London: George Bell & Sons, 1882).

24. *MN* (26 May 1894): 487.

25. Leigh, *Augustus Austen Leigh*, 263.

26. EG to Abraham, 22 Aug. 1895; Troldhaugen / 8 Oct. 1895; Christiania.

27. EG to Delius, [12 May 1894]; Clapham [DTA].

28. EG to Abraham, 19 May 1894.

29. EG to Delius, 25 May 1894; London [DTA].

30. Shaw, *Diaries*, entry for 13 March 1889.
31. 'Musicians of the Day: Edvard Hagerup Grieg' [with portrait], *MS* (12 May 1894): 393 and Supplement.
32. Mackenzie, *A Musician's Narrative*, 191.
33. *The Times* (26 May 1894).
34. *MO* (July 1894): 621.

35. *MS* (2 June 1894): 459.
36. *MN* (2 June 1894): 508.
37. *MMR* (June 1894): 136.
38. *MT* (June 1894): 389.
39. EG to Delius, 25 May 1894; London [DTA].
40. *MN* (2 June 1894): 511.

Chapter 12: 'Your music is so universal a favourite in England'

1. William Augener to EG, 29 June / 21 Aug. 1894; 86 Newgate Street, London.
2. *MMR* (Oct. 1894): 226; *MS* (27 Oct. 1894): 324–5.
3. *MMR* (Sept. 1894): 209.
4. EG to Albert Gutmann, 28 Nov. 1894; Copenhagen [NB].
5. EG to Oscar Meyer, 9 Nov. 1894; Copenhagen.
6. EG to Iver Holter, 1 Jan. 1895; Copenhagen [NB].
7. Daniel J. Wood to EG, 8 Jan. 1895; Exeter.
8. Revd Walter M. Watkins-Pitchford to EG, 6 Feb. 1895; to NG, 16 May 1895; Solihull, Birmingham.
9. Thomas White, Pharmaceutical Chemist, to EG, 29 May 1895; Queenstown.
10. John Edmund Barkworth to EG, 7 March 1895; Paris.
11. *MS* (2 Feb. 1895): 94.
12. *MMR* (April 1895): 89.
13. *MS* (9 March 1895): 216.
14. *MMR* (July 1895): 162.
15. *MS* (7 Sept. 1895): 153–4, 161.
16. *MMR* (March 1895): 63.
17. *The Morning Post* (5 Aug. 1895).
18. *MT* (Jan. 1896): 30.
19. *MS* (23 March 1895): 238.
20. Ebenezer Prout to EG, 9 June 1895; 12 Greenwood Road, Dalston, London, N.E.
21. O. A. Mansfield, 'Musical Discrepancies', *The Musical Quarterly*, 5 (1919): 479–93 at 482, quoted in Firman, 'Ebenezer Prout in Theory and Practice'.
22. EG to Brodsky, 6 Nov. 1895; Leipzig [RNCM].
23. Brodsky to EG, 10 Nov. 1895; 96 Acomb Street, Manchester.

24. EG to Brodsky, 16 Nov. 1895; Leipzig [RNCM].
25. Brodsky to EG, 2 Dec. 1895; 96 Acomb Street, Manchester.
26. EG to Brodsky, 9 Dec. 1895; Leipzig [RNCM].
27. Brodsky to EG, 13 / 20 Dec. 1895; 96 Acomb Street, Manchester.
28. EG to Brodsky, 25 Dec. 1895; Leipzig [RNCM].
29. EG to Halvorsen, 12 Jan. 1896; Leipzig.
30. EG to Holter, 12 Jan. 1896; Leipzig [NB]. I was unaware of the existence of this letter when my *Grieg and Delius* went to press in 1993 and was consequently unable to record this further meeting of the two composers.
31. EG to Gerhard Armauer Hansen, 19 Jan. 1896 Leipzig [NB].
32. Elizabeth Robins to EG, 25 Jan. 1896; 28 Manchester Square Mansions, Dorset Street, London W.
33. Brækstad to EG, 24 Jan. 1896; National Liberal Club, Whitehall Place, London S.W.
34. William Archer to EG, 25 Jan. 1896; 40 Queen Square, London W.C.
35. George Grove to EG, 21 Jan. 1896; Lower Sydenham, London S.E.
36. EG to Oscar Meyer, 4 Feb. 1896; Leipzig.
37. J.H.G., 'Grieg and our Pianists', *MS* (1 Feb. 1896): 69.
38. *MS* (15 Feb. 1896): 109.
39. Ibid.
40. Waldemar Norman-Neruda, W. Norman-Neruda & Co., Concert Agents, to EG, 23 Jan. 1896; 10 Vigo Street, London W.
41. EG to Anna Brodsky, 16 March 1896; Leipzig [RNCM].
42. *MMR* (April 1896): 88.

43. *MMR* (May 1896): 111.
44. *MS* (28 March 1896): 206.
45. EG to Delius, 18 June 1896; Troldhaugen [DTA].
46. *MS* (18 July 1903): 36.
47. EG to Gutmann, 8 Oct. 1896; Bergen [NB].
48. *MMR* (Dec. 1896): 272, 275–8.

Chapter 13: 'One who has exhausted the joys of fame and being adored'

1. EG to Edvard Neovius, 30 Jan. 1897; Leipzig.
2. Berger to EG, 21 March 1897; 6 York Street, Portman Square, London.
3. Berger to EG, 14 April 1897; ibid.
4. EG to Berger, 22 April 1897; Hotel King of Denmark, Copenhagen; in English [BL].
5. *MMR* (April 1897): 91.
6. EG to Abraham, 18 May 1897; Troldhaugen.
7. *MMR* (May 1897): 104.
8. EG to Berger, 26 May 1897; Bergen [BL].
9. EG to Abraham, 19 June 1897; Troldhaugen.
10. *The Musician* [London] (12 May 1897): 2.
11. *The Musician* (28 July 1897): 236.
12. EG to Berger, 5 July 1897; Bergen; in English [BL].
13. Berger to EG, 8 July 1897; 6 York Street, Portman Square, London.
14. EG to Berger, 13 July 1897; Bergen [BL].
15. Berger to EG, 30 July 1897; 6 York Street, Portman Square, London.
16. EG to August Winding, 12 July 1897; Troldhaugen [KBK].
17. EG to Berger, 12 Aug. 1897; Bergen [BL].
18. *MS* (21 Aug. 1897): 125.
19. Quoted in C. Fred Kenyon, 'A Chat with Mr. Frederick Dawson', *MS* (6 Nov. 1897): 293–5.
20. Frederic Cowen to EG, 12 Aug. [1897]; 73 Hamilton Terrace, London N.W.
21. *LMC* (2 Sept. 1897): 117.
22. *Musical Answers* [London] (Oct. 1897): 76.
23. EG to Brodsky, 3 Sept. 1897; Troldhaugen [RNCM].
24. *MMR* (Oct. 1897): 233. 'Gnome Dance' = 'In the Hall of the Mountain King'.
25. EG to Abraham, 4 Sept. 1897; Troldhaugen.
26. Abraham to EG, 9 Sept. 1897; Wiesbaden; 'latest composition' and 'noveltie' [*sic*] in English.
27. George Augener to EG, 24 Sept. 1897; 47 North Side, Clapham Common, London, S.W.; 'comfortable' and 'at home' in English.
28. EG to Röntgen, 17 Oct. 1897; Copenhagen [HG].
29. EG to Anna Brodsky, 47 North Side, Clapham Common, London, S.W., 22 Oct. 1897 [RNCM].
30. *The Musician* [London] (27 Oct. 1897): 462.
31. EG to Abraham, 26 Oct. 1897; Clapham Common; 'Afternoon' and 'Evening' (in the concert list) in English.
32. Quoted in *The Musician* (13 Oct. 1897): 428.
33. EG to Berger, 26 / 27 October 1897; Clapham [BL].
34. EG to Oscar Meyer, 28 Oct. 1897; Clapham.
35. *MMR* (Nov. 1897): 260, 249, 261.
36. *Lady's Pictorial* (13 Nov. 1897). The journal also carried a review of the Philharmonic concert.
37. NG to Hanchen Alme, 3 Dec. 1897; 47 North Side, Clapham Common, London S.W. [private collection].
38. *LMC* (4 Nov. 1897): 265.
39. *MT* (Dec. 1897): 816. Works by Handel, Beethoven and Mendelssohn had made up the rest of the programme.
40. *MMR* (Dec. 1897): 288.
41. *MS* (13 Nov. 1897): 317.
42. *MN* (13 Nov. 1897): 431.
43. *MN* (20 Nov. 1897): 456.
44. *MN* (27 Nov. 1897): 477.
45. *LMC* (25 Nov. 1897): 315.
46. EG to Johan Selmer, 11 Nov. 1897; Clapham [NB].
47. EG to Brodsky, 15 Nov. 1897; St. Leonards on the Sea [*sic*], 68 Marina [RNCM].
48. EG to Röntgen, 19 Nov. 1897; Clapham [HG].

49. *The Liverpool Courier* (22 Nov. 1897).
50. *The Liverpool Mercury* (22 Nov. 1897).
51. *MN* (27 Nov. 1897): 483.
52. *The Liverpool Courier* (22 Nov. 1897).
53. *The Liverpool Daily Post* (22 Nov. 1897).
54. *The Liverpool Mercury* (22 Nov. 1897).
55. *LMC* (25 Nov. 1897): 328.
56. *MS* (11 Dec., 1897): 379–80.
57. Ibid., 380.
58. R. T. Bodey to EG, 26 Nov. 1897; 103 Hartington Road, Liverpool.
59. *MW* (12 Aug. 1905): 113.
60. *LMC* (25 Nov. 1897): 315.
61. *The Times* (23 Nov. 1897).
62. *MS* (27 Nov. 1897): 345–6.
63. *LMC* (25 Nov. 1897): 315.
64. Bennett, *Journals*, 61–2.
65. EG to Brodsky, 21 Nov. 1897 [RNCM].
66. *The Sunday Chronicle* [Manchester] (28 Nov. 1897).
67. *Manchester Evening News* (25 Nov. 1897).
68. Cumberland, *Set Down in Malice*, 226–7.
69. Fuchs, *Musical and Other Recollections*, 75.
70. EG to Brækstad, 25 Nov. 1897; Manchester [NB].
71. *MT* (Jan. 1898): 39.
72. *The Birmingham Daily Mail* (27 Nov. 1897).
73. *The Birmingham Daily Gazette* (27 Nov. 1897).
74. *LMC* (2 Dec. 1897): 344.

Chapter 14: A First – and Last – Appearance in Scotland

1. J. M. Morries Stirling to EG, 20 Sept. 1890; Gogar House, Stirling.
2. See the second extended quotation on p. 273.
3. W. A. Gray to EG, 16 Jan. 1894; Elgin, Scotland.
4. Gray, 'Among the Fjords with Edvard Grieg', 264, 267.
5. *MO* (Dec. 1897): 182.
6. *Edinburgh Evening News* (1 Dec. 1897); *The Weekly Scotsman* (4 Dec. 1897).
7. *MS* (4 Dec. 1897): 358.
8. *MT* (Jan. 1898): 41.
9. *The Evening Dispatch* [Edinburgh] (1 Dec. 1897).
10. Information kindly supplied by Thom Dibdin, Edinburgh, 16 June 2003. James C. Dibdin was the author of *The Annals of the Edinburgh Stage, with an Account of the Rise and Progress of Dramatic Writing in Scotland* (Edinburgh: R. Cameron, 1888) and other books.

Chapter 15: 'The Queen is sweet'

1. EG to Brækstad, 1 Dec. 1897; Clapham [NB].
2. *MS* (11 Dec. 1897): 378; *MT* (1 Jan. 1898): 27.
3. *MN* (11 Dec. 1897): 526.
4. *The Year's Music* (1896), 7–8.
5. *The Times* (8 Dec. 1897). 'Intermezzo' was an unusual designation for the 'Gavotte', which Grieg composed in 1867 and in 1872 incorporated as the second number, 'At the Matching Game', in the incidental music for Bjørnson's play *Sigurd Jorsalfar*, Op. 22. It was also one of the *Three Orchestral Pieces from 'Sigurd Jorsalfar'*, Op. 56, no. 1.
6. EG to Beyer, 10 Dec. 1897; Clapham.
7. EG to Abraham, 10 Dec. 1897.
8. EG to Röntgen, 10 Dec. 1897; Clapham [HG].
9. *Lady's Pictorial* (18 Dec. 1897): 923.
10. *MS* (11 Dec. 1897): 381.
11. *The Stroud Journal* (26 Jan. 1856).
12. EG to Abraham, 10 Dec. 1897; Clapham.
13. Max O'Rell, *John Bull og hans Ø: Engelske Nutidssæder og Skikke*, trans. Donald Lobedanz from the French original's 42nd edn (Copenhagen: Gyldendalske Boghandels Forlag, 1884), 174–5.
14. *LMC* (9 Dec. 1897): 361.
15. Kuhe, *My Musical Recollections*, 241, 257.
16. *Brighton Society* (11 Dec. 1897).

17. *Brighton Society* (4 Dec. 1897).
18. *Brighton Society* (18 Dec. 1897).
19. *The Brighton Standard and Fashionable Visitors' List* (16 Dec. 1897).

20. *LMC* (16 Dec. 1897): 380, 375.
21. EG to Beyer, 14 Dec. 1897; Clapham.
22. EG to Joachim Grieg, 16 Dec. 1897; Clapham.

Chapter 16: 'Tomorrow: Finish! Hurrah!'

1. EG to Narciso Vert, 12 Dec. 1897; London [coll. Tore Severeide Johansen].
2. EG to Vert, 14 Dec. 1897; Clapham. Grieg's own English spelling.
3. *The Times* (14 Dec. 1897).
4. *MT* (Jan. 1898): 27; on Grieg's favourite work, see pp. 218–19 above.
5. *MMR* (Jan. 1898): 17.
6. *MS* (18 Dec. 1897): 394.
7. *Lady's Pictorial* (18 Dec. 1897): 923.
8. All these performances were noted in *MN* (18 Dec. 1897): 551.

9. *MT* (Jan. 1898): 27.
10. *Harold Bauer: His Book*, 143–4.
11. *Lady's Pictorial* (25 Dec. 1897): 967.
12. EG to Röntgen, 16 Dec. 1897; Clapham [HG].
13. Fifield, *Ibbs and Tillett*, 27–8.
14. EG to Joachim Grieg, 16 Dec. 1897; Clapham.
15. *MS* (8 Dec. 1900): 354–5.
16. EG to Abraham, 21 Dec. 1897; Clapham.

Chapter 17: 'All these people so much want to see you over here and among them again!'

1. Quoted in Gaukstad, 'Christian Sinding og Adolf Brodsky', 137–8.
2. Sinding to Brodsky, Thursday afternoon, [April?] 1898; London [RNCM].
3. *MT* (Feb. 1898): 118.
4. EG to Brækstad, 6 Feb. 1898; Leipzig [NB].
5. Brækstad to EG, 21 Feb. 1898; 33 Hailsham Avenue, Streatham Hill, London S.W. (on the headed notepaper of the National Liberal Club, Whitehall Place, S.W.).
6. *MN* (29 Jan. 1898): 111–13.
7. *The Daily Chronicle* (17 Jan. 1898).
8. EG to Halvorsen, 19 March 1898; Leipzig.
9. EG to Signe Lund-Skabo, 15 March 1898; Leipzig [NB].
10. John Parr, 'Bassoon-ist', to EG, 1 June 1898; 25 Catherine Road, Sheffield.
11. Edmund Gosse to EG, 22 June 1898; 29 Delamere Terrace, Westbourne Square, W.
12. Brækstad to EG, 8 July 1898; Streatham Hill, S.W.
13. *MMR* (Aug. 1898): 169–71.
14. *MS* (30 July 1898): 73–4.
15. EG to Henri Hinrichsen, 9 Aug. 1898; Troldhaugen.

16. EG to Oscar Meyer, 18 August 1898; Troldhaugen.
17. *MMR* (Nov. 1898): 258, 248.
18. *MN* (4 Feb. 1899): 118.
19. *MS* (4 Feb. 1900): 72–3.
20. *MN* (14 May 1898): 475; (8 Jan. 1898): 31; (11 Oct. 1902): 303.
21. William Augener to EG, 22 Aug. 1898; Zermatt.
22. Edgar Haddock and G. Percy Haddock to EG, 4 Aug. 1898; Leeds College of Music, Cookridge Street, Leeds.
23. Brækstad to EG, 19 Sept. 1898; Streatham Hill, S.W.
24. *MS* (24 Sept. 1898): 203.
25. *MS* (22 Oct. 1898): 265.
26. *MN* (22 Oct. 1898): 360.
27. *MN* (26 Nov. 1898): 484.
28. *MS* (15 April 1899): 237.
29. EG to John and Marie Grieg, 28 Oct. 1898; Odnæs.
30. *Charles Darwins liv og breve, med et kapitel selvbiografi*, 3 vols., ed. Francis Darwin, trans. M. Søraas (Christiania: Det norske aktieforl., 1888–9); orig., *The Life and Letters*

of Charles Darwin, including an Autobiographical Chapter (London: John Murray,
1887). Mrs Humphry Ward, *Robert Elsmere*,
3 vols. (London: Smith, Elder, 1888), was
available in Norwegian, trans. Carl Keilhau
(Christiania, 1890–91).

31. *MN* (12 Nov. 1898): 435.

32. *MS* (19 Nov. 1898): 331.

33. Roger Ascham, 'The Late Andreas Pettersson', letter to the editor, *MS* (7 Jan. 1899):
15.

34. 'Scandinavian Musical Intelligence', *MN* (4
March 1899): 229.

35. EG to Sigurd Hals, 26 Nov. / 13 Dec. 1898;
Copenhagen.

36. *The Manchester Guardian* (10 Feb. 1899),
repr. in Arthur Johnstone, *Musical Criticisms* (Manchester: University Press, 1905),
162–3.

37. EG to Johan Selmer, 11 Nov. 1897; Clapham
[NB].

38. *MMR* (Jan. 1900): 2.

39. *The Times* (9 Aug. 1899) = *MN* (12 Aug.
1899): 145.

40. Berger to EG, 5 Aug. 1899; 6 York Street,
Portman Square, London.

41. *MMR* (Oct. 1899): 233.

42. *MN* (14 Oct. 1899): 321.

43. *MN* (21 Oct. 1899): 353.

44. *MMR* (Nov. 1899): 258.

45. *MS* (23 Sept. 1899): 207 = *MN* (16 Sept.
1899).

46. *MMR* (Dec. 1899): 276.

47. *MMR* (Feb. 1900): 42.

48. Brækstad to EG, 4 Jan. 1900; Streatham
Hill.

49. EG to Abraham, 13 June 1900; Troldhaugen.

50. Chappell to EG, 28 June 1900; 50 New
Bond Street, London.

51. *MMR* (Aug. 1900): 173.

52. NG to Anna Brodsky, 25 July 1900; Troldhaugen [RNCM].

53. George Augener to EG, 26 July 1900; Clapham.

54. Wm Cecil Slingsby to EG, 20 Aug. 1900;
Beech Hill, Carleton, Skipton-in-Craven
[Yorkshire].

55. Slingsby, *Norway: The Northern Playground*, 215, 13.

56. Brækstad to EG, 4 Oct. 1900; Christiania.

57. Wood, *My Life of Music*, 196.

58. *MS* (8 Nov. 1900): 352.

59. EG to Olav Anton Thommessen, 18 Dec.
1900; Voksenkollen Sanatorium [NB].

60. Peter Rosenkrantz Johnsen to EG, 19 Dec.
1900; Eugenie gade 12, [?Christiania].

61. EG to Beyer, 24 Dec. 1900; Voksenkollen
Sanatorium.

62. EG to Henri Hinrichsen, 23 June 1900;
Troldhaugen.

63. Benestad and Schjelderup-Ebbe, *Edvard
Grieg: The Man and the Artist*, 362.

64. *MMR* (Jan. 1901): 8, contained two paragraphs on Abraham.

Chapter 18: 'My health says no, and that must, after all, take precedence'

1. EG to Beyer, 21 Jan. 1901; Copenhagen.

2. EG to Berger, 1 Feb. 1901; Copenhagen
[BL].

3. Robert Newman to EG, 5 Feb. 1901; Queen's
Hall, Langham Place, London W.

4. EG to Berger, 8 Feb. 1901; Copenhagen
[BL].

5. Shelley Fisher, Secretary, Trinity College,
London, to EG, 9 Feb. 1901.

6. Berger to EG, draft letter, 11 Feb. 1901 [BL].

7. EG to Beyer, 11 Feb. 1901; Copenhagen.

8. Berger to EG, draft letter, 22 Feb. 1901 [BL].

9. EG to Berger, 24 Feb. 1901; Copenhagen
[BL].

10. EG to Olav Anton Thommessen, 22 Feb.
1901; Copenhagen [NB].

11. *MS* (16 March 1901): 101.

12. EG to Edward MacDowell, 8 April 1901;
Copenhagen [NYPL].

13. *MS* (23 March 1901): 184.

14. *MMR* (March 1901): 58.

15. *MN* (23 March 1901): 273.

16. NG to Anna Brodsky, 4 April 1901; Copenhagen [RNCM].

17. EG to Hinrichsen, 18 April 1901; Copenhagen.
18. *MN* (8 June 1901): 549.
19. H. L. Brækstad, *Ole Bull: Biografisk skitse; Sælges til indtægt for Ole-Bull Monumentet i Bergen* (Bergen: B. Giertsen, 1885).
20. EG to Hinrichsen, 24 Sept. 1901; Troldhaugen.
21. *MN* (15 June 1901): 561.
22. Berger to EG, 14 Oct. 1901; London.
23. EG to Berger, 18 Oct. 1901; Bergen [BL].
24. EG to George Augener, undated draft.
25. *MMR* (June 1903): 118.
26. EG to Louis Monastier-Schroeder, 3 July 1906; Troldhaugen. Grieg, *Brev i utvalg*, ed. Benestad, II: 411.
27. For an account of the impetus that Riseley gave to music-making in Bristol, see Bowen, *Rejoice Greatly*.
28. EG to George Riseley, draft letter, 20 Feb. 1902; Copenhagen.
29. EG to George Riseley, draft letter, 12 March 1902; Copenhagen.
30. *MS* (19 April 1902): 252.
31. Brækstad to EG, 18 May 1902; 33 Hailsham Avenue, Streatham Hill, London, S.W. [NB].
32. EG to Brækstad, 28 May 1902; Troldhaugen [NB].
33. Stepán Esipoff to EG, 24 June 1902; c/o Messrs. Augener & Co., 199 Regent Str., London.

34. A. Maude to EG, 25 June 1902; 102 Banbury Rd, Oxford.
35. *MS* (19 April 1902): 254.
36. *MS* (31 March 1906): 200.
37. W. Gray Tisdale to EG, 31 July 1902; Chapel Hill, Barham, nr Canterbury.
38. James Watt jnr to EG, n.d.; Home Lodge, Palace Road, Streatham, S.W.
39. Annie E. Keeton to EG, 15 May [no year]; Delganny, Egham, Surrey.
40. A. E. Keeton, 'Edvard Hagerup Grieg: The Scandinavian Tone Poet', *Temple Bar: A London Magazine*, 113 (Jan.–April 1898): 275–8.
41. See *MS* (27 Oct. 1900): 260.
42. EG to Beyer, 3 Aug. 1902; Troldhaugen.
43. EG to Hinrichsen, 25 May 1903; Hotel Westminster, Christiania.
44. J. H. S. Jackson to EG, 11 June / 26 July 1904; Broadway, West Croydon, Surrey.
45. *MS* (5 July 1902): 13.
46. EG to Albert Langen, 28 Aug. 1902; Troldhaugen [NB].
47. EG to Beyer, 2 Sept. 1902; Troldhaugen.
48. EG to Sigurd Hals, 3 Sept. 1902; Troldhaugen.
49. EG to Hals, 16 Sept. 1902; Troldhaugen.
50. EG to George Riseley, draft letter in English, n.d.
51. *MS* (4 Oct. 1902): 214.
52. *MN* (18 Oct. 1902): 324.
53. *The Manchester Guardian* (5 Nov. 1902).

Chapter 19: 'How grateful I am that you remembered my 60th birthday'

1. *MS* (21 Feb. 1903):117.
2. EG to Hals, 6 March 1903; Hotel Fønix, Copenhagen.
3. *MS* (23 May 1903): 325.
4. *MMR* (June 1903): 105.
5. EG to Alexander Siloti, 26 Aug. 1902; Troldhaugen [RIHA].
6. Edvard Grieg, 'Tale for Bjørnson', in *Artikler og taler*, ed. Gaukstad, 198.
7. Delius to EG, n.d.; Grez sur Loing.
8. EG to Delius, 1 Sept. 1903; Troldhaugen [DTA]; 'allright' in English.

9. EG to Charles Harding, 28 Aug. 1903; Troldhaugen.
10. *MS* (18 July 1903): 36.
11. *MS* (15 Aug. 1903): 99.
12. Ibid., 98.
13. *MMR* (Dec. 1903): 229.
14. *MMR* (Jan. 1904): 16.
15. NG to Anna Brodsky, 23 Jan. 1904; Hotel Westminster, Christiania [RNCM].
16. *MMR* (July 1905): 137.
17. EG to Hinrichsen, 21 July 1904; Troldhaugen.

18. EG to Hals, 15 July 1904; Troldhaugen.
19. Quoted in Matthew-Walker, *The Recordings of Edvard Grieg*, 28.
20. George Augener to EG, 10 Dec. 1904; 47 Clapham Common, North Side, London, S.W.
21. *In Memoriam: Charles Harding; A Sermon Preached at the Old Meeting Church, Birmingham, on Sunday Morning, January 8th, 1905, by the Rev. Joseph Wood*. 10pp.

Chapter 20: 'I implore Your Majesty . . . to prevent the shame and disaster'

1. *MW* (21 Jan. 1905): 47.
2. M. C. Golding Bright to EG, 30 March 1905; 20 Green Street, Leicester Square, W.C.
3. EG to Brodsky, 19 April 1905 Hotel Fønix, Copenhagen [RNCM].
4. EG to Brodsky, 29 May 1905; Hotel Westend, Christiania [RNCM].
5. *MMR* (March 1905): 57.
6. EG to Edgar Speyer, 22 May 1905; Copenhagen.
7. Robert Newman to EG, 19 June 1905; Queen's Hall Orchestra, Ltd., 320 Regent Street, W.
8. 'Confessions of Grieg', *MW* (15 July 1905): 39.
9. *MS* (22 July 1905): 52–3.
10. *MMR* (Sept. 1905): 161–2.
11. EG to Dagny Bjørnson Langen, 7 / 18 Aug. 1905; Troldhaugen [NB].
12. *MW* (12 Aug. 1905): 109.
13. *MMR* (Feb. 1906): 41.
14. EG to Louis Monastier-Schroeder, 15 Oct. 1905; Christiania.
15. Rosa Newmarch to EG, 14 Oct. / 5 Nov. 1905; 52, Campden Hill Square, London, W.
16. EG to Beyer, 20 Dec. 1905; Hotel Westminster, Christiania.
17. *MS* (27 Jan. 1906): 57.
18. *LMC* (5 May 1906): 217.
19. *MW* (15 Feb. 1906): 49.
20. *MMR* (Dec. 1905): 231.
21. EG to Beyer, 6 Jan. 1906; Christiania.

Chapter 21: 'Grieg is to pay us a visit'

1. *MS* (16 Dec. 1905): 394.
2. Brodsky to EG, 6 Jan. 1906; 3 Laurel Mount, Bowdon, Cheshire.
3. EG to Brodsky, 25 Jan. 1906; [Christiania] [RNCM].
4. EG to Beyer, 6 Jan. 1906; Christiania.
5. EG to Hinrichsen, 19 Feb. 1906; Hotel Westminster, Christiania.
6. F. S. Hess to EG, 26 Feb. 1906; Raymead, 176 Belsize Road, Abbey Road, N.W.
7. McKenna, *Myra Hess*, 26.
8. EG to Hinrichsen, 4 March 1906; Christiania.
9. *NM-R* 6/6 (March 1906): 46.
10. Robert Newman to EG, 9 March 1906; Queen's Hall Orchestra, Ltd., 320 Regent Street, W.
11. Newman to EG, 20 March 1906; ibid.
12. EG to John Lane, 12 March 1906; Christiania.
13. *MS* (28 April 1906): 267.
14. *MW* (15 Sept. 1905): 179.
15. *MS* (5 May 1906): 281; repr. from 'A Composer's Geniality', *Daily Mail* (1 May 1906).
16. Archief Julius Röntgen, Nederlands Muziekinstituut, The Hague: 'Erinnerungen und Briefe', 443–5. Transcribed from the original German by Jurjen Vis, Amsterdam.

Chapter 22: 'So many curtain calls that I lost count'

1. *MW* (15 May 1906): 124.
2. *The Strad* (March 1893): 207.
3. *MMR* (April 1906): 89.
4. EG to Hinrichsen, 10 May 1906; Claridge's Hotel, London.
5. Röntgen, 'Erinnerungen und Briefe', 443–5.
6. EG to Hinrichsen, 10 May 1906.
7. *MN* (12 May 1906): 478.
8. *The Daily News* (14 May 1906).
9. Wood, *My Life of Music*, 259.
10. NG to Hanchen Alme, 15 May 1906; London [private collection].
11. EG to Nansen, 16 May 1906; 46 Grosvenor Street [NB].
12. Percy Grainger to Karen Holten, 18 May 1906; London [GM].
13. Grainger to Fridtjof Nansen, undated draft letter; copy kindly supplied by Grainger's publisher Barry Peter Ould.
14. L.L., 'Grieg in London', *MS* (26 May 1906): 320.
15. *The Times* (18 May 1906).
16. *The Morning Post* (18 May 1906).
17. J.H.G.B., 'Grieg at Queen's Hall – Novel Reading of Concerto', *The Daily News* (18 May 1906).
18. EG to Sigrid Steenberg, 17 May 1906; 46 Grosvenor Street, London. Grieg quotes from Aa. O. Vinje's poem 'Spring', which he had set as Op. 33, no. 2.
19. EG to Julius and Mien Röntgen, 18 May 1906; 46 Grosvenor Street, London [HG].
20. EG to Beyer, 22 May 1906; London.
21. Grainger to Karen Holten, 18 May 1906; London [GM].
22. *MN* (26 May 1906): 526.
23. A.M.W., 'Accompanied Recitation', *MS* (26 May 1906): 321.
24. *MMR* (June 1906): 122–3.
25. *NM-R* 6/10 (July 1906): 111.
26. EG to Johannes Wolff, 15 May 1906; [London] [PSU].
27. EG to Beyer, 22 May 1906; London.
28. Ibid.
29. *The Oxford Review* (23 May 1906).
30. Ibid. (26 May 1906).
31. EG to Hals, 23 May 1906; 46 Grosvenor Street, London W.
32. EG to Röntgen, 25 May 1906; 46 Grosvenor Street, London W. [HG].
33. *The Morning Post* (25 May 1906).
34. *The Times* (25 May 1906).
35. P.S., 'The Second Grieg Concert', *MS* (2 June 1906): 341–2.
36. *MN* (26 May 1906): 526.
37. *MMR* (June 1906): 123.
38. EG to Röntgen, 25 May 1906; 46 Grosvenor Street, London W. [HG].

Chapter 23: 'These London days amongst my most happy memories'

1. EG to Röntgen, 25 May 1906; 46 Grosvenor Street, London W. [HG].
2. *The Oxford Review* (25 May 1906).
3. Irgens, *En norsk diplomats liv*, 56.
4. *The Times* (29 May 1906).
5. *The Oxford Review* (30 May 1906).
6. Quoted in Demuth, *Ravel*, 41.
7. Quoted from *The Daily Telegraph* by *MN* (9 June 1906): 585.
8. *The Oxford Times* (9 June 1906).
9. *The Oxford Review* (29 May 1906). Substantially = *The Oxford Chronicle* (1 June 1906) and *The Oxford Times* (2 June 1906).
10. *MW* (16 Sept. 1907).
11. EG to Brodsky, 29 May 1906; 46 Grosvenor Street, London W. [RNCM].
12. *MW* (16 June 1906): 154.
13. *MS* (23 June 1906): 394 = *MW* (16 July 1906): 6 (with slight variations). Translated from a letter of thanks that Grieg had sent to Edgar Speyer, part of which was also reproduced in *MO*. A lead article in *MMR* (July 1906): 427, was entitled 'Norwegian Music'; it was occasioned not only by Grieg's recent visit but also by the recent coronation in Norway and the death of Ibsen.

Chapter 24: 'My sun is already low in the western sky'

1. EG to Hinrichsen, 29 June 1906; Troldhaugen.
2. Ibbs & Tillett to EG, 11 June 1906; 19 Hanover Square, London W.
3. Fred R. Spark, Leeds Triennial Musical Festival, to EG, 18 June 1906.
4. Grainger to EG, 22 June 1906; 14 Upper Cheyne Row, Chelsea, London S.W.
5. EG to Hinrichsen, 29 June 1906; Troldhaugen.
6. EG to Grainger, 30 June 1906; Troldhaugen [GM].
7. EG to Grainger, 17 Jan. 1907; Christiania [GM].
8. EG to Adolph and Anna Brodsky, 30 June 1906; Troldhaugen [RNCM].
9. EG to Delius, 21 July 1906; Troldhaugen [DTA].
10. Brodsky, 'A Visit to Edvard Grieg'. A much abbreviated version was published in *MW* (16 Oct. 1916): 88–9.
11. EG to Brodsky, 14 Dec. 1906; Christiania [RNCM].
12. Brodsky to EG, 30 Aug. 1906; Marienbad.
13. Anna Brodsky to NG, [early Sept. 1906]; Marienbad.
14. EG to Brodsky, 31 Dec. 1906; Christiania [RNCM].
15. EG to Hinrichsen, 28 Sept. 1906; Christiania.
16. *MW* (16 Oct. 1906): 108.
17. EG to Grainger, 27 Nov. 1906; Christiania [GM].
18. Grainger to EG, 8 Dec. 1906; 14 Upper Cheyne Row, Chelsea, S.W.
19. *MW* (15 Nov. 1906): 144.
20. Ibid.
21. Delius to EG, 11 Oct. 1906; Grez-sur-Loing.

Chapter 25: 'We shall have piano rehearsals for Leeds at Troldhaugen!'

1. *MW* (16 March 1907): 62.
2. Grainger to Karen Holten, 13 March 1907; London [GM].
3. *MW* (16 March 1907): 57.
4. Ibbs & Tillett to EG, 9 March 1907; 19 Hanover Square, London W.
5. Baring Bros. to EG, 22 March 1907; Montpellier Chambers, Cheltenham.
6. Fridtjof Nansen to EG, 11 March 1907; 36 Victoria Street, Légation de Norvège, Londres.
7. *MMR* (March 1907): 66.
8. *MS* (9 Feb. 1907): 94.
9. Stanford to EG, 26 March 1907; 50 Holland Street, Kensington, London.
10. NG to Anna Brodsky, 10 June 1907; Skodsborg Sanatorium [RNCM].
11. Vivian Lee to EG, 25 March 1907; Woodbine Cottage, Clonminch, Tullamore, Queens County, Ireland.
12. John G. Bloom to EG, 23 April / 6 May 1907; Edgware Road, London, N.
13. *MW* (15 Feb. 1907): 50.
14. *MW* (16 May 1907): 127.
15. EG to Beyer, 3 April 1907; Munich.
16. Grainger to Svendsen, 3 May 1907; 5 Harrington Road, South Kensington, S.W., London [GM].
17. Grainger to EG, 14 May 1907; 5 Harrington Road, South Kensington, S.W., London.
18. EG to Grainger, 28 May 1907; Skodsborg Sanatorium [GM].
19. Olga Wood to EG, 5 June 1907; 4 Elsworthy Road, London N.W.
20. NG to Olga Wood, undated draft in English.
21. Edgar Haddock to EG, 17 May 1907; Leeds College of Music, Cookridge Street, Leeds.
22. Robert Newman to EG, 5 June 1907; Queen's Hall Orchestra, Ltd., 320 Regent Street.
23. *MS* (8 June 1907): 365.
24. Undated and unattributed clipping in GA.
25. Webster Millar to Edvard and Nina Grieg, 4 June 1907; 12 Scarsdale Road, Victoria Park, Manchester.

26. EG to Grainger, 30 June 1907; Troldhaugen [GM].

27. *MS* (22 June 1907): 388.

Chapter 26: A Last Visitor

1. Grainger's 12-page diary/memoir of his visit to Grieg, the source of unannotated quotations in this chapter, is held in GM. A detailed account of the visit is given in Carley, 'The Last Visitor'.
2. Röntgen, *Grieg*, 118.
3. Quoted in Wrobel, *The Nordic Inspiration*, 3.
4. 'Glimpses of Genius: An Interview Secured Expressly for The Etude, with the Distinguished Pianist-Composer Percy Grainger', *The Etude* [Philadelphia] (Oct. 1921): 631.

Chapter 27: 'The trip to England seems to me more than doubtful'

1. EG to Hakon Børresen, 5 Aug. 1907; Troldhaugen [KBK].
2. EG to Paul Ollendorff (Head Clerk, C. F. Peters), 8 Aug. 1907; Troldhaugen.
3. EG to Grainger, 11 Aug. 1907; Troldhaugen [GM]; postscript in English.
4. Ibid.
5. See Dean-Smith (ed.), 'Letters to Lucy Broadwood', 254–7.
6. EG to Siloti, 16 Aug. 1907; Troldhaugen [RIHA].
7. EG to Matthison-Hansen, 16 Aug. 1907; Troldhaugen [KBK].
8. EG to Röntgen, 23 Aug. 1907; Troldhaugen [HG].
9. EG to Paul Ollendorff, 26 Aug. 1907; Troldhaugen.
10. *MS* (24 Aug. 1907): 122–3.
11. *MS* (31 Aug. 1907): 142.
12. W. A. Allsop to EG, 31 Aug. 1907; Leeds Musical Festival Office, Great George Street, Leeds.
13. H. A. Fricker to EG, 3 Sept. 1907; Leeds.
14. EG to Louis Monastier-Schroeder, 28 Aug. 1907; Bergen Hospital [NB].
15. *MMR* (Oct. 1907): 232 = *MW* (16 Sept. 1907): 74.
16. Unattributed clipping in the autograph letter-book of August Manns [RCM].
17. Ibid.
18. NG to Hinrichsen, 11 Sept. 1907; Troldhaugen.
19. Adolph Brodsky to Anna Brodsky, 8 Sept. 1907; Bergen [RNCM]; in Russian. Norwegian trans. in Gaukstad, 'Adolf Brodsky om Griegs begravelse'.
20. *MS* (14 Sept. 1907): 160.
21. Dr. Adolph Brodsky, 'Grieg's Funeral', *The Manchester Guardian* (12 Sept. 1907).
22. *MS* (21 Sept. 1907): 186.
23. *MW* (16 Sept. 1907): 65.
24. *MS* (21 Sept. 1907): 185.
25. *MO* (Dec. 1907): 177. The journal had initially marked Grieg's death in its October issue by reprinting the obituary from *The Times*.
26. *MMR* (Oct. 1907): 217–18.
27. Stanford to Grainger, 6 Sept. 1907 [GM].
28. NG to Delius, 16 Sept. 1907; Troldhaugen [DTA].
29. *MMR* (Nov. 1907): 243.
30. *MS* (19 Oct. 1907): 241–3.
31. *MT* (Nov. 1907): 739.
32. *MS* (2 Nov. 1907): 278.
33. *Aftenposten* (1 May 1908).
34. NG to Hanchen Alme, 2 Dec. 1909; Hotel Bristol, Copenhagen [private collection].
35. Quoted in Hurum, *Vennskap*, 118.

BIBLIOGRAPHY

ANDERSEN, Rune J. *Edvard Grieg: Et kjempende menneske*. [Oslo]: J. S. Cappelens Forlag, 1993.

BACHE, Constance. *Brother Musicians: Reminiscences of Edward and Walter Bache*. London: Methuen, 1901.

BAILIE, Eleanor. *The Pianist's Repertoire: Grieg; A Graded Practical Guide*. London: Valhalla Publications, 1993.

BARNETT, John Francis. *Musical Reminiscences and Impressions*. London: Hodder & Stoughton, 1906.

BAUER, Harold. *Harold Bauer: His Book*. New York: Norton, 1948.

BENESTAD, Finn, and BROCK, Hella. *Edvard Grieg: Briefwechsel mit dem Musikverlag C. F. Peters, 1863–1907*. Frankfurt: C. F. Peters, 1997.

BENESTAD, Finn, and SCHJELDERUP-EBBE, Dag. *Edvard Grieg: Mennesket og kunstneren*. Oslo: H. Aschehoug, 1980.

—— and ——. *Edvard Grieg: The Man and the Artist*. Trans. William H. Halverson and Leland B. Sateren. Lincoln, NE, and London: University of Nebraska Press, 1988.

—— and ——. *Johan Svendsen: The Man, the Maestro, the Music*. Trans. William H. Halverson. Columbus, OH: Peer Gynt Press, 2000.

BENESTAD, Finn, and STAVLAND, Hanna de Vries. *Edvard Grieg und Julius Röntgen: Briefwechsel 1883–1907*. Amsterdam: Koninklijke Verenigung voor Nederlandse Muziekgeschiedenis, 1997.

BENNETT, Arnold. *The Journals of Arnold Bennett: 1896–1910*. Ed. Newman Flower. London: Cassell, 1932.

BERGER, Francesco. *Reminiscences, Impressions & Anecdotes*. London: Sampson Low, Marston, [1912].

BIRCH, John. *Vikings in London: 100 Years, Den Norske Klub*. London: Den Norske Klub, 1987.

BOWEN, George S. *Rejoice Greatly: Bristol Choral Society, 1889-1989*. Bristol: White Tree Books, 1988.

BRÆKSTAD, H. L. *The Constitution of the Kingdom of Norway: An Historical and Political Survey*. London: David Nutt, 1905.

BRIDGE, Frederick. *A Westminster Pilgrim: Being a Record of Service in Church, Cathedral, and Abbey, College, University and Concert-Room, with a Few Notes on Sport*. London: Novello; Hutchinson, [1919].

BRODSKY, Anna. 'A Visit to Edvard Grieg'. 2 parts. *The Manchester Guardian* (17/19 Sept. 1907).

CARLEY, Lionel. *Delius: A Life in Letters*, I: *1862–1908*. London: Scolar Press; Cambridge, MA: Harvard University Press, 1983.

——. *Delius: A Life in Letters*, II: *1909–1934*. Aldershot and Brookfield, VT: Scolar Press, 1988.

——. *Grieg and Delius: A Chronicle of their Friendship in Letters*. London and New York: Marion Boyars, 1993.

——. 'Grieg and Musical Life in England'. *Musik & Forskning*, 20 (1994): 73–92.

——. 'Landscapes: Grieg and Delius'. *The Grieg Companion*, 1 (1996): 12–24.

——. 'The Last Visitor: Percy Grainger at Troldhaugen'. *Studia musicologica norvegica*, 25 (1999), 189–208.

——. 'Granger's Promotion of Grieg'. *Troldhaugens skriftserie* [Bergen] (2000): 173–6.

——. 'Grieg and Grainger: Background to a Friendship'. *The Grieg Companion*, 5 (2000): 12–20.

——. 'Percy Grainger's Memories of the Griegs'. *In a Nutshell* [University of Melbourne], 10/1 (March 2002): 11–14; 10/2 (June 2002): 9–12; 10/4 (Dec. 2002): 22 (Errata).

——. 'From British Consular Representatives in Bergen to a Norwegian Composer in London: The Griegs'. *Anglo-Norse Review* [London] (Winter 2004): 9–12.

——. 'In Praise of Hans Lien Brækstad'. *Anglo-Norse Review* (Summer 2005): 4–10.

CHARTERIS, Evan. *The Life and Letters of Sir Edmund Gosse*. London: William Heinemann, 1931.

COATES, Eric. *Suite in Four Movements: An Autobiography*. London: Heinemann, 1953.

CONRADI, G. *Den Norske Klub i London*. London: Den Norske Klub, 1937.

COWEN, Frederic H. *My Art and My Friends*. London: Edward Arnold, 1913.

CUMBERLAND, Gerald. *Set Down in Malice: A Book of Reminiscences*. London: Grant Richards, 1919.

DAHL, Erling, jr. *Edvard Grieg: His Life and Music*. Troldhaugen: Edvard Grieg Museum, 2002.

——. *Troldhaugen*. Troldhaugen: Edvard Grieg Museum, 2002.

DEAN-SMITH, Margaret (ed.). 'Letters to Lucy Broadwood: A Selection from the Broadwood Papers at Cecil Sharp House'. *Journal of the English Folk Dance and Song Society*, 9 (1964 [issued in June 1965]): 233–68.

DEMUTH, Norman. *Ravel*. The Master Musicians. London: J. M. Dent & Sons, 1947.

DIBBLE, Jeremy. 'Edward Dannreuther and the Orme Square Phenomenon'. In *Music and British Culture, 1785-1914: Essays in Honour of Cyril Ehrlich*, ed. Christina Bashford and Leanne Langley, 275–98. Oxford: Oxford University Press, 2000.

——. *Charles Villiers Stanford: Man and Musician*. Oxford: Oxford University Press, 2002.

DREYFUS, Kay. *The Farthest North of Humanness: Letters of Percy Granger, 1901–14*. Melbourne: Macmillan, 1985.

DYBSAND, Øyvin. *Johan Halvorsen (1864–1935): En undersøkelse av hans kunstneriske virke og en stilistik gjennomgang av han komposisjoner*. Forthcoming.

EHRLICH, Cyril. *First Philharmonic: A History of the Royal Philharmonic Society*. Oxford: Clarendon Press, 1995.

EIKENES, Eivind A. C. *Edvard Grieg fra dag til dag.* Stavanger: E. A. C. Eikenes, 1993.

ELKIN, Robert. *Royal Philharmonic: The Annals of the Royal Philharmonic Society.* London: Rider, [1946].

FIFIELD, Christopher. *True Artist and True Friend: A Biography of Hans Richter.* Oxford: Clarendon Press, 1993.

——. *Ibbs and Tillett: The Rise and Fall of a Musical Empire.* Aldershot and Burlington, VT: Ashgate, 2005.

FINCK, Henry T. *Edvard Grieg.* London and New York: John Lane, 1906. Rev. and enl. as *Grieg and His Music.* London and New York: John Lane, 1909.

FIRMAN, Rosemary. 'Ebenezer Prout in Theory and Practice', *Brio*, 41/2 (Autumn 2004): 15–34.

FJÅGESUND, Peter, and SYMES, Ruth A. *The Northern Utopia: British Perceptions of Norway in the Nineteenth Century.* Amsterdam: Rodopi, 2003.

FOREMAN, Lewis. *Music in England, 1885–1920, as Recounted in Hazell's Annual.* London: Thames Publishing, 1994.

——, and FOREMAN, Susan. *London: A Musical Gazetteer.* New Haven and London: Yale University Press, 2005.

FOSTER, Beryl. *The Songs of Edvard Grieg.* Aldershot and Brookfield, VT: Scolar Press, 1990.

——. *Edvard Grieg: The Choral Music.* Aldershot and Brookfield, VT: Ashgate, 1999.

FUCHS, Carl. *Musical and Other Recollections of Carl Fuchs, 'Cellist.* Manchester: Sherratt & Hughes, 1937.

FULLER-MAITLAND, J. A. *A Door-Keeper of Music.* London: John Murray, 1929.

GAUKSTAD, Øystein. 'Edvard Grieg og Adolf Brodsky'. *Norsk Musikktidsskrift*, 4 (1967): 1–12, 41–50.

——. 'Christian Sinding og Adolf Brodsky'. *Norsk Musikktidsskrift*, 4 (1967): 131–7.

——. 'Adolf Brodsky om Griegs begravelse'. *Norsk Musikktidsskrift*, 4 (1967): 139.

GOSSE, Edmund. *Two Visits to Denmark: 1872, 1874.* London: Smith, Elder, 1911.

GOUBAULT, Christian. 'Grieg et la critique musicale française'. In *Grieg et Paris: Romantisme, symbolisme et modernisme franco-norvégiens*, ed. Harald Herresthal and Danièle Pistone, 139–49. Caen: Presses Universitaires de Caen, 1996.

GRAVES, Charles L. *The Life & Letters of Sir George Grove, C.B.* London: Macmillan, 1903.

——. *Hubert Parry: His Life and Works.* London: Macmillan, 1926.

GRAY, W. A. 'Among the Fjords with Edvard Grieg'. *The Woman at Home: Annie S. Swan's Magazine*, 1 (1884): 263–70.

GRIEG, Edvard. 'Briefe Edvard Grieg's an Oscar Meyer'. *Die Musik*, 8 (1908/9): 330–41.

——. *Artikler og taler.* Ed. Øystein Gaukstad. Oslo: Gyldendal Norsk Forlag, 1957.

——. *Brev til Frants Beyer, 1872–1907.* Ed. Finn Benestad and Bjarne Kortsen. Oslo: Universitetsforlaget, 1993.

——. *Dagbøker: 1865, 1866, 1905, 1906 og 1907.* Ed. Finn Benestad. Bergen: Bergen Offentlige Bibliotek, 1993.

——. *Brev i utvalg, 1862–1907.* 2 vols. Ed. Finn Benestad. Oslo: Aschehoug, 1998.

——. *Letters to Colleagues and Friends.* Selected and edited by Finn Benestad; trans. William H. Halverson. Columbus, OH: Peer Gynt Press, 2000.

——. *Diaries, Articles, Speeches.* Ed. and trans. Finn Benestad and William H. Halverson. Columbus, OH: Peer Gynt Press, 2001.

GRIEG, Nina. *Din hengivne Nina: Nina Griegs brev til Hanchen Alme, 1864–1935*. Ed. Lisbeth Tornberg Simonsen and Maj-Liss Grynning Mydske. Oslo: Emilia, 1995.

The Grieg Companion: Journal of The Grieg Society of Great Britain. Ed. Robert Matthew-Walker. London: The Grieg Society, 1996– .

GRINDE, Kirsti. *Répertoire de la presse musicale: Nordisk musik-tidende, 1880–1892; Orkestertidende, 1892–1894*. Ann Arbor, MI: UMI, 1996.

GRINDE, Nils. *Norsk Musikkhistorie: Hovedlinjer i norsk musikkliv gjennom 1000 år*. Oslo, Bergen, and Tromsø: Universitetsforlaget, 1971; 3rd edn, 1981.

——. *A History of Norwegian Music*. Trans. William H. Halverson and Leland B. Sateren. Lincoln, NE, and London: University of Nebraska Press, 1991.

——. *Halfdan Kjerulf, Nordmann og Europeer: En komponist og hans tid*. Oslo: Musikk-Husets Forlag, 2003.

GRØNVOLD, Didrik. *Diktere og Musikere: Personlige erindringer om noen av dem*. Oslo: Cammermeyers Boghandel, 1945.

HAAVET, Inger Elisabeth. *Nina Grieg: Kunstner og kunstnerhustru*. Oslo: Aschehoug, 1998.

HALVORSEN, Johan. 'Hvad jeg husker fra mit liv (til mine barn)'. Unpublished typescript, transcribed and edited by Rolf Grieg Halvorsen, 1936, supplemented by posthumous papers (newspaper clippings, articles, letters). Collection of Stein Grieg Halvorsen.

HANDFORD, Margaret. *Sounds Unlikely: Six Hundred Years of Music in Birmingham*. Birmingham: Birmingham and Midland Institute, 1992.

HAWEIS, H. R. 'The Chopin of the North: An Interview with Mr. E. Grieg'. *Pall Mall Gazette* (20 March 1889).

HORTON, John. *Grieg*. The Master Musicians. London: J. M. Dent & Sons, 1974.

HURUM, Hans Jørgen. *I Edvard Grieg's verden*. Oslo: Gyldendal Norsk Forlag, 1959.

——. *Vennskap: Edvard Grieg og Frants Beyer i lys av glemte brev*. Oslo: Grøndahl & Søn, 1989.

HYDE, Derek. *New-Found Voices: Women in Nineteenth-Century English Music*. 3rd edn. Aldershot: Ashgate, 1998.

IRGENS, Francis. *En norsk diplomats liv*. Oslo: Dreyer, 1952.

JACKS, Lawrence Pearsall. *Life and Letters of Stopford Brooke*. 2 vols. London: John Murray, 1917.

JACOBS, Arthur. *Arthur Sullivan: A Victorian Musician*. Oxford: Oxford University Press, 1984.

JONES, Francis Arthur. 'How Composers Work'. *The Strand Magazine*, 7 (Jan.–June 1894): 206–11, 428–34.

JONES, Michael. 'Edgar Bainton: Musical and Spiritual Traveller'. *British Music*, 12 (1990): 19–40.

JORDAN, Sverre. *Edvard Grieg: En oversikt over hans liv og verker*. Bergen: Edvard Griegs Fond, [1954]; Supplement I: *Rettelser og senere tilkomne Opplysninger*, 1959.

KENNEDY, Michael. *The Hallé Tradition: A Century of Music*. Manchester: Manchester University Press, 1960.

——. *The History of the Royal Manchester College of Music, 1893–1972*. Manchester: Manchester University Press, 1971.

KLEIN, Hermann. *Thirty Years of Musical Life in London, 1870–1900*. New York: The Century Co., 1903.

KUHE, Wilhelm. *My Musical Recollections*. London: Richard Bentley & Son, 1896.

LARA, Adelina de. *Finale*. In collaboration with Clare H. Abrahall. London: Burke, 1955.

LARSEN, Karen. *A History of Norway*. Princeton: Princeton University Press, 1950.

LASSON, Bokken. *Livet og Lykken*. Oslo: Gyldendal Norsk Forlag, 1940.

LAWFORD-HINRICHSEN, Irene. *Music Publishing and Patronage: C. F. Peters, 1800 to the Holocaust*. Kenton, Middlesex: Edition Press, 2000.

LAYTON, Robert. 'Grieg and England'. *Studia musicologica norvegica*, 19 (1993): 103–9.

——. *Grieg*. London, New York, and Sydney: Omnibus Press, 1998.

LEIGH, William Austen. *Augustus Austen Leigh, Provost of King's College, Cambridge: A Record of College Reform*. London: Smith, Elder, 1906.

MCKENNA, Marian C. *Myra Hess: A Portrait*. London: Hamish Hamilton, 1976.

MACKENZIE, Sir Alexander Campbell. *A Musician's Narrative*. London: Cassell, 1927.

MARTIN, Anthony. *Norwegian Life and Landscape*. London: Elek Books, 1952.

MARTIN, A. J., and WULFSBERG, F. (eds). *Across the North Sea*. Oslo: Aschehoug, 1955.

MATTHEW-WALKER, Robert. *The Recordings of Edvard Grieg: A Tradition Captured*. St Austell: DGR, [1993].

MONRAD-JOHANSEN, David. *Edvard Grieg*. Trans. Madge Robertson. New York: American Scandinavian Foundation, 1938; repr. Tudor Publishing Company, 1945.

MONROE, W. S. *In Viking Land: Norway; Its Peoples, Its Fjords and Its Fjelds*. London: G. Bell & Sons, 1908.

MUSGRAVE, Michael. *The Musical Life of the Crystal Palace*. Cambridge: Cambridge University Press, 1995.

NIECKS, Frederick. 'Edvard Grieg, The Norwegian Composer: A Critical Study, Preceded by a Short Chapter on Folk-Music and Nationality Considered in Their Relations to Art-Music.' *The Monthly Musical Record*, (July 1879): 98–101, (Aug. 1879): 113–14, (Sept. 1879): 129–30.

NORRIS, Gerald. *Stanford, the Cambridge Jubilee and Tchaikovsky*. Newton Abbot, London, and North Pomfret, VT: David & Charles, 1980.

PEARSON, Hesketh. *Beerbohm Tree: His Life and Laughter*. London: Methuen, 1956.

REMO, Félix. *La Musique au pays des brouillards, suivi de quelques biographies inédites d'artists contemporains: Étude humoristique et anecdotique de l'état actuel de la musique en Angleterre*. Paris: L'Auteur, 1885.

RÖNTGEN, Julius. *Grieg*. The Hague: J. Philip Kruseman, 1930.

RUGSTAD, Gunnar. *Christian Sinding, 1856–1941: En biografisk og stilistik studie*. Oslo: Cappelen, 1979.

SHAW, George Bernard. *The Diaries, 1885–1897*. Ed. and annotated by Stanley Weintraub. University Park, PA, and London: Pennsylvania State University Press, 1986.

——. *Shaw's Music: The Complete Musical Criticism*. 3 vols. Ed. Dan H. Laurence. London: Max Reinhardt, The Bodley Head, 1981.

SLINGSBY, Wm Cecil. *Norway: The Northern Playground; Sketches of Climbing and Mountain Exploration in Norway between 1872 and 1903*. Edinburgh: David Douglas, 1904. Repr. with notes, introd., and appendices by Tony Howard, David Durkan, and Ian Robertson. Findon: Ripping Yarns.com, 2003.

SMITH, Eric F. *Clapham: An Historical Tour*. Clapham: Battley Brothers, 1982.

SMITH, J. Sutcliffe. *The Story of Music in Birmingham*. Birmingham: Cornish Brothers, 1945.

SMYTH, Ethel. *Impressions that Remained: Memoirs.* 2 vols. London: Longmans Green, 1919.

SPEYER, Edward. *My Life and Friends.* London: Cobden-Sanderson, 1937.

STAVLAND, Hanna de Vries. *Julius Röntgen og Edvard Grieg: Et musikalsk vennskap.* Bergen: Alma Mater, 1994.

STOCKLEY, W. C. *Fifty Years of Music in Birmingham, being the Reminiscences of W. C. Stockley from 1850 to 1900.* Birmingham: Hudson & Son, 1913.

STREIT, Wilhelm. *Celebrated Musicians of All Nations: A Collection of Portraits, with Short Biographical Notices.* Translated from the German with an Appendix for England by M. F. S. Hervey. Dresden: W. Streit; London: Sampson Low, Marston; New York: E. Schuberth, [1883].

STRUTTE, Wilson. *Tchaikovsky: His Life and Times.* Tunbridge Wells: The Baton Press, 1979.

THOMASON, Geoff. 'Grieg in Manchester'. Unpublished paper, delivered to the IAML/IASA Congress, Oslo, Aug. 2004.

TORSTEINSON, Sigmund. *Troldhaugen: Nina og Edvard Griegs hjem.* Oslo: Gyldendal Norsk Forlag, 1959

VIS, Jurjen. *Gaudeamus! Biografie van Julius Röntgen.* Forthcoming.

VOLLESTAD, Per. *Jeg bærer min hatt som jeg vil: Christian Sinding, en komponist og hans sanger.* Oslo: Norges Musikkhøgskole, 2002.

WARRINER, John (ed.). *National Portrait Gallery of British Musicians.* Introd. Joseph Bennett. London: Sampson Low, Marston, [1896].

WEDEL JARLSBERG, F. *Reisen gjennem livet.* Oslo: Gyldendal, 1932.

WHITEBROOK, Peter. *William Archer: A Biography.* London: Methuen, 1993.

WOOD, Henry J. *My Life of Music.* London: Gollancz, 1938.

WROBEL, Elinor. *The Nordic Inspiration: Percy Grainger, 1882–1961, and Edvard Grieg, 1843–1907; An Exhibition to Commemorate the 150th Anniversary of Grieg.* Exhibition catalogue. Melbourne: Grainger Museum, University of Melbourne, 1993.

WYNDHAM, H. Saxe. *August Manns and the Saturday Concerts: A Memoir and a Retrospect.* London, Felling-on-Tyne and New York: Walter Scott, 1909.

Also consulted: *The London Musical Courier, Musical News, Musical Opinion, The Monthly Musical Record, The Musical Standard, The Musical Times, The Musical World, The Strand Musical Magazine, Nordisk Musik-Revue, Nordisk Musik-Tidende* and other daily, weekly and monthly journals published in Britain and in Norway.

INDEX OF GRIEG'S WORKS

The indexes cover the Preface and the main text only. Variant spellings or misspellings in the text are given in parentheses after the main entry.

GENERAL INDEX

———•◦•———